PERSISTENT QUESTIONS
IN PUBLIC DISCUSSION

PERSISTENT QUESTIONS IN PUBLIC DISCUSSION

ADDRESSES AND ESSAYS

EDITED BY

ALEXANDER M. DRUMMOND
PROFESSOR OF PUBLIC SPEAKING IN CORNELL UNIVERSITY

AND

EVERETT LEE HUNT
ASSISTANT PROFESSOR OF PUBLIC SPEAKING IN CORNELL UNIVERSITY

THE CENTURY CO.
New York & London
1924

Printed in U. S. A.

PREFACE

"Public opinion," says James Bryce, "is a better ruler, when its will can be ascertained, than the ballot." The will of the public must be formed and made known through unceasing discussion. A public-minded interest in the problems that affect the beliefs and conduct of all citizens is necessary if public discussion is to result in enlightened public opinion. A relatively small number of men, who, as legislators, administrators, and publicists, find their professional career in public affairs, give constant attention to significant events and opinions. But the interest and judgment of the much larger class primarily occupied with private pursuits must correct and modify the views of public leaders and statesmen. This larger class, if it does not originate, must constantly mold public opinion.

The purpose of this collection is to provide stimulating material dealing with questions that are constantly before the public.

These addresses and essays discuss some persistent problems which are always current; problems which are, as Aristotle says in his analysis of the subjects with which an Athenian counselor should be familiar, "the chief subjects, about which all men debate, and on which those who offer counsel speak." The subjects here treated are not the only basic questions of public discussion, nor are these addresses necessarily superior to others that might have been chosen. Judgments would differ, even if no material were rendered unavailable by terms of copyright. No attempt has been made to present all the problems in their latest aspects. Questions which have long been old, and which will long be new, may often best be viewed with some perspective of time. But it has not been forgotten that new occasions teach new duties, and much of the material included has been written by men who have had opportunities to see the developments of some of these problems since 1914. Selections have been sought which, whatever their date, will provoke further thought concerning fundamental issues on which an educated citizen should have enlightened opinions, and which he should be able to discuss intelligently. It is also believed that these addresses are worthy of study as representative public discussions.

As an aid to further investigation of fact and opinion, lists of supplementary readings have been placed in the appendix. Suggestions are also offered for the use of the material in college courses and in discussion groups.

For judgments upon the effectiveness of these addresses and essays, and for coöperation in developing a method of procedure in the classroom, the editors are indebted to their colleagues, past and present members of the Department of Public Speaking in Cornell University,—Messrs. G. B. Muchmore, Harry Caplan, H. A. Wichelns, H. H. Hudson, Robert Hannah, W. M. Parrish, C. K. Thomas, Marvin Bauer, and L. S. Hultzen.

The generosity of authors and publishers in permitting the use of copyrighted addresses and essays is gratefully acknowledged. Detailed statements will be found in connection with the separate articles.

CONTENTS

vii

CONTENTS

AMERICAN CHARACTER AND IDEALS

FIVE AMERICAN CONTRIBUTIONS TO CIVILIZATION [1]

Charles W. Eliot

[Charles William Eliot (1834-   ) was President of Harvard University for forty years, retiring from office in 1909. In this period he accomplished the evolution of Harvard from what James Bryce termed ''a struggling college with uncertain relations to learning and research,'' into a genuine university in the European sense. President Eliot looked upon the university as a great center for the best intellectual and moral forces in our national life; hence he regarded its presidency as a public office. ''For half a century,'' says John Jay Chapman, ''President Eliot was one of the great personal figures in American life. He was known to every man in America and to many people in Europe. He was not a political figure, not an artist, nor a thinker; he was the embodiment of a mood of the American people. . . . Before his day no one used to ask who was President of Harvard University. At the close of his day the President of Harvard was a national figure, and the Presidents of all other colleges in the country were persons to be reckoned with.'' Elihu Root, in 1923, speaking at the presentation of a medal to Dr. Eliot for distinguished public service, characterized him as the greatest molder of public opinion America had produced in half a century. Dr. Eugen Kuehnemann, in an essay written for the *Deutsche Rundschau* when President Eliot retired, says:

> The creator of this new American university has always made it a point to explain and urge his ideas and convictions publicly. It is very characteristic that by far the larger part of Eliot's writings consist of public addresses afterwards printed. In a democracy the spoken word is the normal means of disseminating ideas aiming to influence the whole community. In this, then, Eliot's practice is typical of republican institutions. Taken as a whole his speeches not only give us his peculiar confession of faith as an educator; they discuss the problems of education in their intimate relation to American ideals.

President Eliot's most notable addresses, and they cover almost all the great subjects of public discussion in his time, have been collected in *Educational Reform, American Contributions to Civilization,* and *The Durable Satisfactions of Life.*

Of President Eliot as a speaker, John Jay Chapman, who had little sympathy with Eliot's policies at Harvard, says:

> His voice was remarkable,—a low vibrant controlled melodious voice that seemed to have much reverence in it, the voice, you would say, of a cultivated man. And yet President Eliot had not the point of view of a cultivated man, nor had he reverence for cultivation *per se.*

[1] Reprinted by permission of the Century Co., from *American Contributions to Civilization and Other Essays and Addresses.*

Questions and topics for the discussion of this address, and of other phases of the general subject with which it deals, will be found on pages 488 and 492.

(See Eliot's address, *A New Definition of the Cultivated Man.*—Ed.)
He regarded cultivation somewhat as Michael Angelo regarded the
painting of the Venetian school,—as a thing fit for women. Life was
greater than culture. . . . If there was about Dr. Eliot an absence
of cultivation, there was the presence of force. The voice was force;
its vibrations were the vibrations of force. The modulations of it
were modulations of force. Behind it there was a two-handed engine
of human pertinacity, an intellect very accurately limited and a
genius for the understanding of men.

Professor Irvah Winter, of Harvard, dedicated his text-book, *Public Speaking*, to "Charles William Eliot, who for many years has taught by example
the power and beauty of perfected speech."

Five American Contributions to Civilization was delivered at Chautauqua,
New York, in August, 1896.]

Looking back over forty centuries of history, we observe that
many nations have made characteristic contributions to the progress of civilization, the beneficent effects of which have been permanent, although the races that made them may have lost their
national form and organization, or their relative standing among
the nations of the earth. Thus, the Hebrew race, during many
centuries, made supreme contributions to religious thought; and
the Greek, during the brief climax of the race, to speculative
philosophy, architecture, sculpture, and the drama. The Roman
people developed military colonization, aqueducts, roads and
bridges, and a great body of public law, large parts of which still
survive; and the Italians of the middle ages and the Renaissance
developed ecclesiastical organization and the fine arts, as tributary
to the splendor of the church and to municipal luxury. England, for several centuries, has contributed to the institutional
development of representative government and public justice; the
Dutch, in the sixteenth century, made a superb struggle for free
thought and free government; France, in the eighteenth century,
taught the doctrine of individual freedom and the theory of human rights; and Germany, at two periods within the nineteenth
century, fifty years apart, proved the vital force of the sentiment
of nationality. I ask you to consider with me what characteristic
and durable contributions the American people have been making
to the progress of civilization.

(1) The first and principal contribution to which I shall ask your
attention is the advance made in the United States, not in theory
only, but in practice, toward the abandonment of war as the
means of settling disputes between nations, the substitution of
discussion and arbitration, and the avoidance of armaments. If
the intermittent Indian fighting and the brief contest with the

Barbary corsairs be disregarded, the United States have had only four years and a quarter of international war in the one hundred and seven years since the adoption of the Constitution. Within the same period the United States have been a party to forty-seven arbitrations—being more than half of all that have taken place in the modern world. The questions settled by these arbitrations have been just such as have commonly caused wars, namely, questions of boundary, fisheries, damage caused by war or civil disturbances, and injuries to commerce. Some of them were of great magnitude, the four made under the treaty of Washington (May 8, 1871) being the most important that have ever taken place. Confident in their strength, and relying on their ability to adjust international differences, the United States have habitually maintained, by voluntary enlistment for short terms, a standing army and a fleet which, in proportion to the population, are insignificant.

The beneficent effects of this American contribution to civilization are of two sorts: in the first place, the direct evils of war and of preparations for war have been diminished; and secondly, the influence of the war spirit on the perennial conflict between the rights of the single personal unit and the powers of the multitude that constitute organized society—or, in other words, between individual freedom and collective authority—has been reduced to the lowest terms. War has been, and still is, the school of collectivism, the warrant of tyranny. Century after century, tribes, clans, and nations have sacrificed the liberty of the individual to the fundamental necessity of being strong for combined defense or attack in war. Individual freedom is crushed in war, for the nature of war is inevitably despotic. It says to the private person: "Obey without a question, even unto death; die in this ditch, without knowing why; walk into that deadly thicket; mount this embankment, behind which are men who will try to kill you, lest you should kill them; make part of an immense machine for blind destruction, cruelty, rapine, and killing." At this moment every young man in Continental Europe learns the lesson of absolute military obedience, and feels himself subject to this crushing power of militant society, against which no rights of the individual to life, liberty, and the pursuit of happiness avail anything. This pernicious influence, inherent in the social organization of all Continental Europe during many centuries, the American people have for generations escaped, and they show other nations how to escape it. I ask your attention to the favorable conditions under which this contribution of the United States to civilization has been made.

There has been a deal of fighting on the American continent during the past three centuries; but it has not been of the sort which most imperils liberty. The first European colonists who occupied portions of the coast of North America encountered in the Indians men of the Stone Age, who ultimately had to be resisted and quelled by force. The Indian races were at a stage of development thousands of years behind that of the Europeans. They could not be assimilated; for the most part they could not be taught or even reasoned with; with a few exceptions they had to be driven away by prolonged fighting, or subdued by force so that they would live peaceably with the whites. This warfare, however, always had in it for the whites a large element of self-defense—the homes and families of the settlers were to be defended against a stealthy and pitiless foe. Constant exposure to the attacks of savages was only one of the formidable dangers and difficulties which for a hundred years the early settlers had to meet, and which developed in them courage, hardiness, and persistence. The French and English wars on the North American continent, always more or less mixed with Indian warfare, were characterized by race hatred and religious animosity—two of the commonest causes of war in all ages; but they did not tend to fasten upon the English colonists any objectionable public authority, or to contract the limits of individual liberty. They furnished a school of martial qualities at small cost to liberty. In the War of Independence there was a distinct hope and purpose to enlarge individual liberty. It made possible a confederation of the colonies, and, ultimately, the adoption of the Constitution of the United States. It gave to the thirteen colonies a lesson in collectivism, but it was a needed lesson on the necessity of combining their forces to resist an oppressive external authority. The war of 1812 is properly called the Second War of Independence, for it was truly a fight for liberty and for the rights of neutrals, in resistance to the impressment of seamen and other oppressions growing out of European conflicts. The civil war of 1861-65 was waged, on the side of the North, primarily, to prevent the dismemberment of the country, and, secondarily and incidentally, to destroy the institution of slavery. On the Northern side it therefore called forth a generous element of popular ardor in defense of free institutions; and though it temporarily caused centralization of great powers in the government, it did as much to promote individual freedom as it did to strengthen public authority.

In all this series of fightings the main motives were self-defense, resistance to oppression, the enlargement of liberty, and the conservation of national acquisitions. The war with Mexico, it is true, was of a wholly different type. That was a war of conquest, and of conquest chiefly in the interest of African slavery. It was also an unjust attack made by a powerful people on a feeble one; but it lasted less than two years, and the number of men engaged in it was at no time large. Moreover, by the treaty which ended the war, the conquering nation agreed to pay the conquered eighteen million dollars in partial compensation for some of the territory wrested from it, instead of demanding a huge war-indemnity, as the European way is. Its results contradicted the anticipations both of those who advocated and of those who opposed it. It was one of the wrongs which prepared the way for the great rebellion; but its direct evils were of moderate extent, and it had no effect on the perennial conflict between individual liberty and public power.

In the meantime, partly as the results of Indian fighting and the Mexican war, but chiefly through purchases and arbitrations, the American people had acquired a territory so extensive, so defended by oceans, gulfs, and great lakes, and so intersected by those great natural highways, navigable rivers, that it would obviously be impossible for any enemy to overrun or subdue it. The civilized nations of Europe, western Asia, and northern Africa have always been liable to hostile incursions from without. Over and over again barbarous hordes have overthrown established civilizations; and at this moment there is not a nation of Europe which does not feel obliged to maintain monstrous armaments for defense against its neighbors. The American people have long been exempt from such terrors, and are now absolutely free from this necessity of keeping in readiness to meet heavy assaults. The absence of a great standing army and of a large fleet has been a main characteristic of the United States, in contrast with the other civilized nations; this has been a great inducement to immigration, and a prime cause of the country's rapid increase in wealth. The United States have no formidable neighbor, except Great Britain in Canada. In April, 1817, by a convention made between Great Britain and the United States, without much public discussion or observation, these two powerful nations agreed that each should keep on the Great Lakes only a few police vessels of insignificant size and armament. This agreement was made but four years after Perry's naval victory on Lake Erie, and only three years after the burning of Washington by a British force. It was one of the first acts of Monroe's first administration, and it would be difficult to find in all history a more judicious or effectual agreement between two powerful neighbors. For eighty years this beneficent convention has helped to keep the peace. The European way would have been to build competitive fleets, dockyards, and fortresses, all of which would have helped to bring on war during the periods of mutual exasperation which have occurred since 1817. Monroe's second administration was signalized, six years later, by the declaration that the United States would consider any attempt on the part of the Holy Alliance to extend their system to any portion of this hemisphere as dangerous to the peace and safety of the United States. This announcement was designed to prevent the introduction on the American continent of the horrible European system—with its balance of power, its alliances offensive and defensive in opposing groups, and its perpetual armaments on an enormous scale. That a declaration expressly intended to promote peace and prevent armaments should now be perverted into an argument for arming and for a belligerent public policy is an extraordinary perversion of the true American doctrine.

The ordinary causes of war between nation and nation have been lacking in America for the last century and a quarter. How many wars in the world's history have been due to contending dynasties; how many of the most cruel and protracted wars have been due to religious strife; how many to race hatred! No one of these causes of war has been efficacious in America since the French were overcome in Canada by the English in 1759. Looking forward into the future, we find it impossible to imagine circumstances under which any of these common causes of war can take effect on the North American continent. Therefore, the ordinary motives for maintaining armaments in time of peace, and concentrating the powers of government in such a way as to interfere with individual liberty, have not been in play in the United States as among the nations of Europe, and are not likely to be.

Such have been the favorable conditions under which America has made its best contribution to the progress of our race.

There are some people of a perverted sentimentality who occasionally lament the absence in our country of the ordinary inducements to war, on the ground that war develops certain noble qualities in some of the combatants, and gives opportunity for the practice of heroic virtues, such as courage, loyalty, and self-sacrifice. It is further said that prolonged peace makes nations effeminate, luxurious, and materialistic, and substitutes for the high ideals of the patriot soldier the low ideals of the farmer, manufacturer, tradesman, and pleasure-seeker. This view seems to me to err in two opposite ways. In the first place, it forgets that war, in spite of the fact that it develops some splendid virtues, is the most horrible occupation that human beings can possibly engage in. It is cruel, treacherous, and murderous. Defensive warfare, particularly on the part of a weak nation against powerful invaders or oppressors, excites a generous sympathy; but for every heroic defense there must be an attack by a preponderating force, and war, being the conflict of the two, must be judged by its moral effects not on one party, but on both parties. Moreover, the weaker party may have the worse cause. The immediate ill effects of war are bad enough, but its after effects are generally worse, because indefinitely prolonged and indefinitely wasting and damaging. At this moment, thirty-one years after the end of our civil war, there are two great evils afflicting our country which took their rise in that war, namely, (1) the belief of a large proportion of our people in money without intrinsic value, or worth less than its face, and made current solely by act of Congress, and (2) the payment of immense annual sums in pensions. It is the paper-money delusion born of the civil war which generated and supports the silver-money delusion of to-day. As a consequence of the war, the nation has paid $2,000,000,000 in pensions within thirty-three years. So far as pensions are paid to disabled persons, they are a just and inevitable, but unproductive expenditure; so far as they are paid to persons who are not disabled,— men or women,—they are in the main not only unproductive but demoralizing; so far as they promote the marriage of young women to old men, as a pecuniary speculation, they create a grave social evil. It is impossible to compute or even imagine the losses and injuries already inflicted by the fiat-money delusion; and we know that some of the worst evils of the pension system will go on for a hundred years to come, unless the laws about widows' pensions are changed for the better. It is a significant fact that of the existing pensioners of the war of 1812 only twenty-one are surviving soldiers or sailors, while 3826 are widows.[1]

War gratifies, or used to gratify, the combative instinct of mankind, but it gratifies also the love of plunder, destruction, cruel discipline, and arbitrary power. It is doubtful whether fighting with modern appliances will continue to gratify the savage instinct of combat; for it is not likely that in the future two opposing lines of men can ever meet, or any line or column reach an enemy's intrenchments. The machine-gun can only be compared to the scythe, which cuts off every blade of grass within its sweep. It has made cavalry charges impossible, just as the modern ironclad has made impossible the manœuvers of one of Nelson's fleets. On land, the only mode of approach of one line to another must hereafter be by concealment, crawling, or surprise. Naval actions will henceforth be conflicts between opposing machines, guided, to be sure, by men; but it will be the best machine that wins, and not necessarily the most enduring men. War will become a contest between treasuries or war-chests; for now that 10,000 men can fire away a million dollars' worth of ammunition in an hour, no poor nation can long resist a rich one, unless there be some extraordinary difference between the two in mental and moral strength.

The view that war is desirable omits also the consideration that modern social and industrial life affords ample opportunities for the courageous and loyal discharge of duty, apart from the barbarities of warfare. There are many serviceable occupations in civil life which call for all the courage and fidelity of the best soldier, and for more than his independent responsibility, because not pursued in masses or under the immediate command of superiors. Such occupations are those of the locomotive engineer, the electric lineman, the railroad brakeman, the city fireman, and the policeman. The occupation of the locomotive engineer requires constantly a high degree of skill, alertness, fidelity, and resolution, and at any moment may call for heroic self-forgetfulness. The occupation of a lineman requires all the courage and endurance of a soldier, whose lurking foe is mysterious and invisible. In the two years, 1893, and 1894, there were 34,000 trainmen killed and wounded on the railroads of the United States, and 25,000 other railroad employes besides. I need not enlarge on the dangers of the fireman's occupation, or on the disciplined

[1] June 30, 1895.

gallantry with which its risks are habitually incurred. The policeman in large cities needs every virtue of the best soldier, for in the discharge of many of his most important duties he is alone. Even the feminine occupation of the trained nurse illustrates every heroic quality which can possibly be exhibited in war; for she, simply in the way of duty, without the stimulus of excitement or companionship, runs risks from which many a soldier in hot blood would shrink. No one need be anxious about the lack of opportunities in civilized life for the display of heroic qualities. New industries demand new forms of fidelity and self-sacrificing devotion. Every generation develops some new kind of hero. Did it ever occur to you that the "scab" is a creditable type of nineteenth century hero? In defense of his rights as an individual, he deliberately incurs the reprobation of many of his fellows, and runs the immediate risk of bodily injury, or even of death. He also risks his livelihood for the future, and thereby the well-being of his family. He steadily asserts in action his right to work on such conditions as he sees fit to make, and, in so doing, he exhibits remarkable courage, and renders a great service to his fellow-men. He is generally a quiet, unpretending, silent person, who values his personal freedom more than the society and approbation of his mates. Often he is impelled to work by family affection, but this fact does not diminish his heroism. There are file-closers behind the line of battle of the bravest regiment. Another modern personage who needs heroic endurance, and often exhibits it, is the public servant who steadily does his duty against the outcry of a party press bent on perverting his every word and act. Through the telegram, cheap postage, and the daily newspaper, the forces of hasty public opinion can now be concentrated and expressed with a rapidity and intensity unknown to preceding generations. In consequence, the independent thinker or actor,, or the public servant, when his thoughts or acts run counter to prevailing popular or party opinions, encounters sudden and intense obloquy, which, to many temperaments, is very formidable. That habit of submitting to the opinion of the majority which democracy fosters renders the storm of detraction and calumny all the more difficult to endure—makes it, indeed, so intolerable to many citizens, that they will conceal or modify their opinions rather than endure it. Yet the very breath of life for a democracy is free discussion, and the taking account of all opinions honestly held and reasonably expressed. The unreality of the vilification of public men in the modern press is often revealed by the sudden change when an eminent public servant retires or dies. A man for whom no words of derision or condemnation were strong enough yesterday is recognized to-morrow as an honorable and serviceable person, and a credit to his country. Nevertheless, this habit of partizan ridicule and denunciation in the daily reading-matter of millions of people calls for a new kind of courage and toughness in public men, and calls for it, not in brief moments of excitement only, but steadily, year in and year out. Clearly, there is no need of bringing on wars in order to breed heroes. Civilized life affords 'plenty of opportunities for heroes, and for a better kind than war or any other savagery has ever produced. Moreover, none but lunatics would set a city on fire in order to give opportunities for heroism to firemen, or introduce the cholera or yellow fever to give physicians and nurses opportunity for practising disinterested devotion, or condemn thousands of people to extreme poverty in order that some well-to-do persons might practise a beautiful charity. It is equally crazy to advocate war on the ground that it is a school for heroes.

Another misleading argument for war needs brief notice. It is said that war is a school of national development—that a nation, when conducting a great war, puts forth prodigious exertions to raise money, supply munitions, enlist troops, and keep them in the field, and often gets a clearer conception and a better control of its own material and moral forces while making these unusual exertions. The nation which means to live in peace necessarily foregoes, it is said, these valuable opportunities of abnormal activity. Naturally, such a nation's abnormal activities devoted to destruction would be diminished; but its normal and abnormal activities devoted to construction and improvement ought to increase.

One great reason for the rapid development of the United States since the adoption of the Constitution is the comparative exemption of the whole people from war, dread of war, and preparations for war. The energies of the people have been directed into other channels. The progress of applied science during the present century, and the new ideals concerning the well-being of human multitudes, have opened great fields for the useful application of national energy. This immense territory of ours, stretching from ocean to ocean, and for the most part but imperfectly developed and sparsely settled, affords a broad field for the beneficent application of the richest national forces during an indefinite period. There is no department of national activity in which we could not advantageously put forth much more force than we now expend; and there are great fields which we have never cultivated at all. As examples, I may mention the post-office, national sanitation, public works, and education. Although great improvements have been made during the past fifty years in the collection and delivery of mail matter, much still remains to be done both in city and country, and particularly in the country. In the mail facilities secured to our people, we are far behind several European governments, whereas we ought to be far in advance of every European government except Switzerland, since the rapid interchange of ideas, and the promotion of family, friendly, and commercial intercourse, are of more importance to a democracy than to any other form of political society. Our national government takes very little pains about the sanitation of the country, or its deliverance from injurious insects and parasites; yet these are matters of gravest interest, with which only the general government can deal, because action by separate States or cities is necessarily ineffectual. To fight pestilence needs quite as much energy, skill, and courage as to carry on war; indeed, the foes are more insidious and awful, and the means of resistance less obvious. On the average and the large scale, the professions which heal and prevent disease, and mitigate suffering, call for much more ability, constancy, and devotion than the professions which inflict wounds and death and all sorts of human misery. Our government has never touched the important subject of national roads, by which I mean not railroads, but common highways; yet here is a great subject for beneficent action through government, in which we need only go for our lessons to little republican Switzerland. Inundations and droughts are great enemies of the human race, against which government ought to create defenses, because private enterprise cannot cope with such wide-spreading evils. Popular education is another great field in which public activity should be indefinitely enlarged, not so much through the action of the Federal government,—though even there a much more effective supervision should be provided than now exists,—but through the action of States, cities, and towns. We have hardly begun to apprehend the fundamental necessity and infinite value of public education, or to appreciate the immense advantages to be derived from additional expenditure for it. What prodigious possibilities of improvement are suggested by the single statement that the average annual expenditure for the schooling of a child in the United States is only about eighteen dollars! Here is a cause which requires from hundreds of thousands of men and women keen intelligence, hearty devotion to duty, and a steady uplifting and advancement of all its standards and ideals. The system of public instruction should embody for coming generations all the virtues of the medieval church. It should stand for the brotherhood and unity of all classes and conditions; it should exalt the joys of the intellectual life above all material delights; and it should produce the best constituted and most wisely directed intellectual and moral host that the world has seen. In view of such unutilized opportunities as these for the beneficent application of great public forces, does it not seem monstrous that war should be advocated on the ground that it gives occasion for rallying and using the national energies?

(2) The second eminent contribution which the United States have made to civilization is their thorough acceptance, in theory and practice, of the widest religious toleration. As a means of suppressing individual liberty, the collective authority of the Church, when elaborately organized in a hierarchy directed by one head and absolutely devoted in every rank to its service, comes next in proved efficiency to that concentration of powers in government which enables it to carry on war effectively. The Western Christian Church, organized under the Bishop of Rome, acquired, during the middle ages, a centralized authority which quite overrode both the temporal ruler and the rising spirit of nationality. For a time Christian Church and Christian State acted together, just as in Egypt, during many earlier centuries, the great powers of civil and religious rule had been united. The Crusades marked the climax of the power of the Church. Thereafter, Church and State were often in conflict; and during this prolonged conflict the seeds of liberty were planted, took root, and made some sturdy growth. We can see now, as we look back on the history of Europe, how fortunate it was that the colonization of North America by Europeans was deferred until after the period of the Reformation, and especially until after the Elizabethan period in England, the Luther period in Germany, and the splendid struggle of the Dutch for liberty in Holland. The founders of New England and New York were men who had imbibed the principles of resistance both to arbitrary civil power and to universal ecclesiastical

authority. Hence it came about that within the territory now covered by the United States no single ecclesiastical organization ever obtained a wide and oppressive control, and that in different parts of this great region churches very unlike in doctrine and organization were almost simultaneously established. It has been an inevitable consequence of this condition of things that the Church, as a whole, in the United States has not been an effective opponent of any form of human rights. For generations it has been divided into numerous sects and denominations, no one of which has been able to claim more than a tenth of the population as its adherents; and the practices of these numerous denominations have been profoundly modified by political theories and practices, and by social customs natural to new communities formed under the prevailing conditions of free intercourse and rapid growth. The constitutional prohibition of religious tests as qualifications for office gave the United States the leadership among the nations in dissociating theological opinions and political rights. No one denomination or ecclesiastical organization in the United States has held great properties, or has had the means of conducting its ritual with costly pomp or its charitable works with imposing liberality. No splendid architectural exhibitions of Church power have interested or overawed the population. On the contrary, there has prevailed in general a great simplicity in public worship, until very recent years. Some splendors have been lately developed by religious bodies in the great cities; but these splendors and luxuries have been almost simultaneously exhibited by religious bodies of very different, not to say opposite, kinds. Thus, in New York city, the Jews, the Greek Church, the Catholics, and the Episcopalians have all erected, or undertaken to erect, magnificent edifices. But these recent demonstrations of wealth and zeal are so distributed among differing religious organizations that they cannot be imagined to indicate a coming centralization of ecclesiastical influence adverse to individual liberty.

In the United States, the great principle of religious toleration is better understood and more firmly established than in any other nation of the earth. It is not only embodied in legislation, but also completely recognized in the habits and customs of good society. Elsewhere it may be a long road from legal to social recognition of religious liberty, as the example of England shows. This recognition alone would mean, to any competent student of history, that the United States had made an unexampled contribution to the reconciliation of just governmental power with just freedom for the individual, inasmuch as the partial establishment of religious toleration has been the main work of civilization during the past four centuries. In view of this characteristic and infinitely beneficent contribution to human happiness and progress, how pitiable seem the temporary outbursts of bigotry and fanaticism which have occasionally marred the fair record of our country in regard to religious toleration! If any one imagines that this American contribution to civilization is no longer important,—that the victory for toleration has been already won,—let him recall the fact that the last years of the nineteenth century have witnessed two horrible religious persecutions, one by a Christian nation, the other by a Moslem,—one, of the Jews by Russia, and the other, of the Armenians by Turkey.

(3) The third characteristic contribution which the United States have made to civilization has been the safe development of a manhood suffrage nearly universal. The experience of the United States has brought out several principles with regard to the suffrage which have not been clearly apprehended by some eminent political philosophers. In the first place, American experience has demonstrated the advantages of a gradual approach to universal suffrage, over a sudden leap. Universal suffrage is not the first and only means of attaining democratic government; rather, it is the ultimate goal of successful democracy. It is not a specific for the cure of all political ills; on the contrary, it may itself easily be the source of great political evils. The people of the United States feel its dangers to-day. When constituencies are large, it aggravates the well-known difficulties of party government; so that many of the ills which threaten democratic communities at this moment, whether in Europe or America, proceed from the breakdown of party government rather than from failures of universal suffrage. The methods of party government were elaborated where suffrage was limited and constituencies were small. Manhood suffrage has not worked perfectly well in the United States, or in any other nation where it has been adopted, and it is not likely very soon to work perfectly anywhere. It is like freedom of the will for the individual—the only atmosphere in which virtue can grow, but an atmosphere in which sin can also grow. Like freedom of the will, it needs to be surrounded with checks and safeguards, particularly in the childhood of the nation;

but, like freedom of the will, it is the supreme good, the goal of perfected democracy. Secondly, like freedom of the will, universal suffrage has an educational effect, which has been mentioned by many writers, but has seldom been clearly apprehended or adequately described. This educational effect is produced in two ways. In the first place, the combination of individual freedom with social mobility, which a wide suffrage tends to produce, permits the capable to rise through all grades of society, even within a single generation; and this freedom to rise is intensely stimulating to personal ambition. Thus every capable American, from youth to age, is bent on bettering himself and his condition. Nothing can be more striking than the contrast between the mental condition of an average American belonging to the laborious classes, but conscious that he can rise to the top of the social scale, and that of a European mechanic, peasant, or tradesman, who knows that he cannot rise out of his class, and is content with his hereditary classification. The state of mind of the American prompts to constant struggle for self-improvement and the acquisition of all sorts of property and power. In the second place, it is a direct effect of a broad suffrage that the voters become periodically interested in the discussion of grave public problems, which carry their minds away from the routine of their daily labor and household experience out into larger fields. The instrumentalities of this prolonged education have been multiplied and improved enormously within the last fifty years. In no field of human endeavor have the fruits of the introduction of steam and electrical power been more striking than in the methods of reaching multitudes of people with instructive narratives, expositions, and arguments. The multiplication of newspapers, magazines, and books is only one of the immense developments of the means of reaching the people. The advocates of any public cause now have it in their power to provide hundreds of newspapers with the same copy, or the same plates, for simultaneous issue. The mails provide the means of circulating millions of leaflets and pamphlets. The interest in the minds of the people which prompts to the reading of these multiplied communications comes from the frequently recurring elections. The more difficult the intellectual problem presented in any given election, the more educative the effect of the discussion. Many modern industrial and financial problems are extremely difficult, even for highly-educated men. As subjects of earnest thought and discussion on the farm, and in the work-shop, factory, rolling-mill, and mine, they supply a mental training for millions of adults, the like of which has never before been seen in the world.

In these discussions, it is not only the receptive masses that are benefited; the classes that supply the appeals to the masses are also benefited in a high degree. There is no better mental exercise for the most highly trained man than the effort to expound a difficult subject in so clear a way that the untrained man can understand it. In a republic in which the final appeal is to manhood suffrage, the educated minority of the people is constantly stimulated to exertion, by the instinct of self-preservation as well as by love of country. They see dangers in proposals made to universal suffrage, and they must exert themselves to ward off those dangers. The position of the educated and well-to-do classes is a thoroughly wholesome one in this respect: they cannot depend for the preservation of their advantages on land-owning, hereditary privilege, or any legislation not equally applicable to the poorest and humblest citizen. They must maintain their superiority by being superior. They cannot live in a too safe corner.

I touch here on a misconception which underlies much of the criticism of universal suffrage. It is commonly said that the rule of the majority must be the rule of the most ignorant and incapable, the multitude being necessarily uninstructed as to taxation, public finance, and foreign relations, and untrained to active thought on such difficult subjects. Now, universal suffrage is merely a convention as to where the last appeal shall lie for the decision of public questions; and it is the rule of the majority only in this sense. The educated classes are undoubtedly a minority; but it is not safe to assume that they monopolize the good sense of the community. On the contrary, it is very clear that native good judgment and good feeling are not proportional to education, and that among a multitude of men who have only an elementary education, a large proportion will possess both good judgment and good feeling. Indeed, persons who can neither read nor write may possess a large share of both, as is constantly seen in regions where the opportunities for education in childhood have been scanty or inaccessible. It is not to be supposed that the cultivated classes, under a régime of universal suffrage, are not going to try to make their cultivation felt in the discussion and disposal of public questions. Any result under universal suffrage is a complex effect of the discussion of the public question in hand by the educated classes in the presence of the comparatively uneducated, when a majority of both classes taken together is ultimately to settle the question. In practice, both classes divide on almost every issue. But, in any case, if the educated classes cannot hold their own with the uneducated, by means of their superior physical, mental, and moral qualities, they are obviously unfit to lead society. With education should come better powers of argument and persuasion, a stricter sense of honor, and a greater general effectiveness. With these advantages, the educated classes must undoubtedly appeal to the less educated, and try to convert them to their way of thinking; but this is a process which is good for both sets of people. Indeed, it is the best possible process for the training of freemen, educated or uneducated, rich or poor. *powerless*

It is often assumed that the educated classes become impotent in a democracy, because the representatives of those classes are not exclusively chosen to public office. This argument is a very fallacious one. It assumes that the public offices are the places of greatest influence; whereas, in the United States, at least, that is conspicuously not the case. In a democracy, it is important to discriminate influence from authority. Rulers and magistrates may or may not be persons of influence; but many persons of influence never become rulers, magistrates, or representatives in parliaments or legislatures. The complex industries of a modern state, and its innumerable corporation services, offer great fields for administrative talent which were entirely unknown to preceding generations; and these new activities attract many ambitious and capable men more strongly than the public service. These men are not on that account lost to their country or to society. The present generation has wholly escaped from the conditions of earlier centuries, when able men who were not great land-owners had but three outlets for their ambition—the army, the church, or the national civil service. The national service, whether in an empire, a limited monarchy, or a republic, is now only one of many fields which offer to able and patriotic men an honorable and successful career. Indeed, legislation and public administration necessarily have a very secondhand quality; and more and more legislators and administrators become dependent on the researches of scholars, men of science, and historians, and follow in the footsteps of inventors, economists, and political philosophers. Political leaders are very seldom leaders of thought; they are generally trying to induce masses of men to act on principles thought out long before. Their skill is in the selection of practicable approximations to the ideal; their arts are arts of exposition and persuasion; their honor comes from fidelity under trying circumstances to familiar principles of public duty. The real leaders of American thought in this century have been preachers, teachers, jurists, seers, and poets. While it is of the highest importance, under any form of government, that the public servants should be men of intelligence, education, and honor, it is no objection to any given form, that under it large numbers of educated and honorable citizens have no connection with the public service.

Well-to-do Europeans, when reasoning about the working of democracy, often assume that under any government the property-holders are synonymous with the intelligent and educated class. That is not the case in the American democracy. Anyone who has been connected with a large American university can testify that democratic institutions produce plenty of rich people who are not educated and plenty of educated people who are not rich, just as medieval society produced illiterate nobles and cultivated monks.

Persons who object to manhood suffrage as the last resort for the settlement of public questions are bound to show where, in all the world, a juster or more practicable regulation or convention has been arrived at. The objectors ought at least to indicate where the ultimate decision should, in their judgment, rest—as, for example, with the land owners, or the property-holders, or the graduates of secondary schools, or the professional classes. He would be a bold political philosopher who, in these days, should propose that the ultimate tribunal should be constituted in any of these ways. All the experience of the civilized world fails to indicate a safe personage, a safe class, or a safe minority, with which to deposit this power of ultimate decision. On the contrary, the experience of civilization indicates that no select person or class can be trusted with that power, no matter what the principle of selection. The convention that the majority of males shall decide public questions has obviously great recommendations. It is apparently fairer than the rule of any minority, and it is sure to be supported by an adequate physical force. Moreover, its decisions are likely to enforce themselves. Even in matters of doubtful prognostication, the fact that a majority of the males do the prophesying tends to the fulfilment of the prophecy. At any rate, the adoption or partial adoption of universal male suffrage by several civilized nations is coincident with unexampled ameliorations in the condition of the least fortunate and most numerous classes of the population. To this general amelioration many causes have doubtless contributed; but it is reasonable to suppose that the acquisition of the power which comes with votes has had something to do with it.

Timid or conservative people often stand aghast at the possible directions of democratic desire, or at some of the predicted results of democratic rule; but meantime the actual experience of the American democracy proves: 1, that property has never been safer under any form of government; 2, that no people have ever welcomed so ardently new machinery, and new inventions generally; 3, that religious toleration was never carried so far, and never so universally accepted; 4, that nowhere have the power and disposition to read been so general; 5, that nowhere has governmental power been more adequate, or more freely exercised, to levy and collect taxes, to raise armies and to disband them, to maintain public order, and to pay off great public debts—national, State, and town; 6, that nowhere have property and well-being been so widely diffused; and 7, that no form of government ever inspired greater affection and loyalty, or prompted to greater personal sacrifices in supreme moments. In view of these solid facts, speculations as to what universal suffrage would have done in the seventeenth and eighteenth centuries, or may do in the twentieth, seem futile indeed. The most civilized nations of the world have all either adopted this final appeal to manhood suffrage, or they are approaching that adoption by rapid stages. The United States, having no customs or traditions of an opposite sort to overcome, have led the nations in this direction, and have had the honor of devising, as a result of practical experience, the best safeguards for universal suffrage, safeguards which, in the main, are intended to prevent hasty public action, or action based on sudden discontents or temporary spasms of public feeling. These checks are intended to give time for discussion and deliberation, or, in other words, to secure the enlightenment of the voters before the vote. If, under new conditions, existing safeguards prove insufficient, the only wise course is to devise new safeguards.

The United States have made to civilization a fourth contribution of a very hopeful sort, to which public attention needs to be directed, lest temporary evils connected therewith should prevent the continuation of this beneficent action. The United States have furnished a demonstration that people belonging to a great variety of races or nations are, under favorable circumstances, fit for political freedom. It is the fashion to attribute to the enormous immigration of the last fifty years some of the failures of the American political system, and particularly the American failure in municipal government, and the introduction in a few States of the rule of the irresponsible party foremen known as "bosses." Impatient of these evils, and hastily accepting this improbable explanation of them, some people wish to depart from the American policy of welcoming immigrants. In two respects the absorption of large numbers of immigrants from many nations into the American commonwealth has been of great service to mankind. In the first place, it has demonstrated that people who at home have been subject to every sort of aristocratic or despotic or military oppression become within less than a generation serviceable citizens of a republic; and, in the second place, the United States have thus educated to freedom many millions of men. Furthermore, the comparatively high degree of happiness and prosperity enjoyed by the people of the United States has been brought home to multitudes in Europe by friends and relatives who have emigrated to this country, and has commended free institutions to them in the best possible way. This is a legitimate propaganda vastly more effective than any annexation or conquest of unwilling people, or of people unprepared for liberty.

It is a great mistake to suppose that the process of assimilating foreigners began in this century. The eighteenth century provided the colonies with a great mixture of peoples, although the English race predominated then, as now. When the Revolution broke out, there were already English, Irish, Scotch, Dutch, Germans, French, Portuguese, and Swedes in the colonies. The French were, to be sure, in small proportion, and were almost exclusively Huguenot refugees, but they were a valuable element in the population. The Germans were well diffused, having established themselves in New York, Pennsylvania, Virginia, and Georgia. The Scotch were scattered through all the colonies. Pennsylvania, especially, was inhabited by an extraordinary mixture of nationalities and religions. Since steam-navigation on the Atlantic and railroad transportation on the North American continent became cheap and easy, the tide of immigration has greatly increased; but it is very doubtful if the amount of assimilation going on in the nineteenth century has been any larger, in proportion to the population and wealth of the country, than it was in the eighteenth. The main difference in the assimilation going on in the two centuries is this, that in the eighteenth century the newcomers were almost all Protestants, while in the nineteenth century a considerable proportion have been Catholics. One result, however, of the importation of large numbers of Catholics into the United States has been a profound modification of the Roman Catholic Church in regard to the manners and customs of both the clergy and the laity, the scope of the authority of the priests, and the attitude of the Catholic Church toward public education. This American modification of the Roman Church has reacted strongly on the Church in Europe.

Another great contribution to civilization made by the United States is the diffusion of material well-being among the population. No country in the world approaches the United States in this respect. It is seen in that diffused elementary education which implants for life a habit of reading, and in the habitual optimism which characterizes the common people. It is seen in the housing of the people and of their domestic animals, in the comparative costliness of their food, clothing, and household furniture, in their implements, vehicles, and means of transportation, and in the substitution, on a prodigious scale, of the work of machinery for the work of men's hands. This last item in American well-being is quite as striking in agriculture, mining, and fishing, as it is in manufactures. The social effects of the manufacture of power, and of the discovery of means of putting that power just where it is wanted, have been more striking in the United States than anywhere else. Manufactured and distributed power needs intelligence to direct it: the bicycle is a blind horse, and must be steered at every instant; somebody must show a steam-drill where to strike and how deep to go. So far as men and women can substitute for the direct expenditure of muscular strength the more intelligent effort of designing, tending, and guiding machines, they win promotion in the scale of being, and make their lives more interesting as well as more productive. It is in the invention of machinery for producing and distributing power, and at once economizing and elevating human labor, that American ingenuity has been most conspicuously manifested. The high price of labor in a sparsely-settled country has had something to do with this striking result; but the genius of the people and of their government has had much more to do with it. As proof of the general proposition, it suffices merely to mention the telegraph and telephone, the sewing-machine, the cotton-gin, the mower, reaper, and threshing-machine, the dish-washing machine, the river steamboat, the sleeping-car, the boot and shoe machinery, and the watch machinery. The ultimate effects of these and kindred inventions are quite as much intellectual as physical, and they are developing and increasing with a portentous rapidity which sometimes suggests a doubt whether the bodily forces of men and women are adequate to resist the new mental strains brought upon them. However this may prove to be in the future, the clear result in the present is an unexampled diffusion of well-being in the United States.

These five contributions to civilization—peace-keeping, religious toleration, the development of manhood suffrage, the welcoming of newcomers, and the diffusion of well-being—I hold to have been eminently characteristic of our country, and so important that, in spite of the qualifications and deductions which every candid citizen would admit with regard to every one of them, they will ever be held in the grateful remembrance of mankind. They are reasonable grounds for a steady, glowing patriotism. They have had much to do, both as causes and as effects, with the material prosperity of the United States; but they are all five essentially moral contributions, being triumphs of reason, enterprise, courage, faith, and justice, over passion, selfishness, inertness, timidity, and distrust. Beneath each one of these developments there lies a strong ethical sentiment, a strenuous moral and social purpose. It is for such work that multitudinous democracies are fit.

In regard to all five of these contributions, the characteristic policy of our country has been from time to time threatened with reversal—is even now so threatened. It is for true patriots to insist on the maintenance of these historic purposes and policies of the people of the United States. Our country's future perils, whether already visible or still unimagined, are to be met with courage and constancy founded firmly on these popular achievements in the past.

The American people have made 5 characteristic and durable contributions to civilization, namely: an advance toward the abandonment of war; a broad acceptance of the widest religious toleration; the safe development of nearly universal manhood suffrage; (4) successful assimilation of immigrants; (5) the diffusion of material wellbeing among the population.

AMERICAN CHARACTER [1]

Brander Matthews

[James Brander Matthews (1852-   ), Professor of Dramatic Literature in Columbia University, and Member of the American Academy of Arts and Letters, says in his autobiography, *These Many Years,* that he was educated for the profession of millionaire. ''To be a millionaire as my father conceived it for me was to practice one of the learned professions, as necessary to the state as any one of its older brethren, medicine or the law or the church.'' The family fortune was greatly reduced before it came into the younger Matthews's hands, but these reverses did not occur until his formal education had been completed. His early travels gave him familiarity with European culture, and his autobiography tells of contacts with the most notable literary figures of his time. He is the author of many volumes,— plays, biographies, essays and criticisms. His volume, *The American of the Future and Other Essays,* in which *American Character* appeared, contains a number of essays of interest to the student of American character. *American Character* was delivered before Phi Beta Kappa of Columbia University in March, 1905.]

I

In a volume recording a series of talks with Tolstoi, published by a French writer in the final months of 1904, we are told that the Russian novelist thought the Dukhobors had attained to a perfected life, in that they were simple, free from envy, wrath, and ambition, detesting violence, refraining from theft and murder, and seeking ever to do good. Then the Parisian interviewer asked which of the peoples of the world seemed most remote from the perfection to which the Dukhobors had elevated themselves; and when Tolstoi returned that he had given no thought to this question, the French correspondent suggested that we Americans deserved to be held up to scorn as the least worthy of nations.

The tolerant Tolstoi asked his visitor why he thought so ill of us, and the journalist of Paris then put forth the opinion that we Americans are ''a people terribly practical, avid of pleasure, sys-

[1] From *The American of the Future and Other Essays.* (Copyright, 1909, Charles Scribner's Sons.) Reprinted by permission.
Questions and topics for the discussion of this address and of other phases of the general subject with which it deals, will be found on pages 489 and 492.

tematically hostile to all idealism. The ambition of the American's heart, the passion of his life, is money; and it is rather a delight in the conquest and possession of money than in the use of it. The Americans ignore the arts; they despise disinterested beauty. And, now, moreover, they are imperialists. They could have remained peaceful without danger to their national existence; but they had to have a fleet and an army. They set out after Spain and attacked her; and now they begin to defy Europe. Is there not something scandalous in this revelation of the conquering appetite in a new people with no hereditary predisposition toward war?''

It is to the credit of the French correspondent that, after setting down this fervid arraignment, he was honest enough to record Tolstoi's dissent. But although he dissented, the great Russian expressed little surprise at the virulence of this diatribe. No doubt it voiced an opinion familiarized to him of late by many a newspaper of France and of Germany. Fortunately for us, the assertion that foreign nations are a contemporaneous posterity is not quite true. Yet the opinion of foreigners, even when most at fault, must have its value for us as a useful corrective of conceit. We ought to be proud of our country; but we need not be vain about it. Indeed, it would be difficult for the most patriotic of us to find any satisfaction in the figure of the typical American which apparently exists in the mind of most Europeans, and which seems to be a composite photograph of the backwoodsman of Cooper, the negro of Mrs. Stowe, and the Mississippi river-folk of Mark Twain, modified, perhaps, by more vivid memories of Buffalo Bill's Wild West. Surely this is a strange monster; and we need not wonder that foreigners feel toward it as Voltaire felt toward the prophet Habakkuk, whom he declared to be ''capable of anything.''

It has seemed advisable to quote here what the Parisian journalist said of us, not because he himself is a person of consequence, indeed, he is so obscure that there is no need even to mention his name, but because he has had the courage to attempt what Burke declared to be impossible—to draw an indictment against a whole nation. It would be easy to retort on him in kind, for unfortunately,—and to the grief of all her friends,—France has laid herself open to accusations as sweeping and as violent. It would be easy to dismiss the man himself as one whose outlook on the world is so narrow that it seems to be little more than what he can get through a chance slit in the wall of his own self-sufficiency. It would be easy to answer him in either of these fashions, but what is easy is rarely worth while; and it is wiser to weigh what he said and to see if we cannot find our profit in it.

Sifting the essential charges from out the mass of his malevolent accusation, we find this Frenchman alleging, first, that we Americans care chiefly for making money; second, that we are hostile to art and to all forms of beauty; and thirdly, that we are devoid of ideals. These three allegations may well be considered, one by one, beginning with the assertion that we are mere money-makers.

II

Now, in so far as this Frenchman's belief is but an exaggeration of the saying of Napoleon's that the English were a nation of shopkeepers, we need not wince, for the Emperor of the French found to his cost that those same English shopkeepers had a stout stomach for fighting. Nor need we regret that we can keep shop profitably, in these days when the doors of the bankers' vaults are the real gates of the Temple of Janus, war being impossible until they open. There is no reason for alarm or for apology so long as our shopkeeping does not cramp our muscle or curb our spirit, for, as Bacon declared three centuries ago, "walled towns, stored arsenals and armories, goodly races of horse, chariots of war, elephants, ordnance, artillery and the like, all this is but a sheep in a lion's skin, except the breed and disposition of the people be stout and warlike."

Even the hostile French traveler did not accuse us of any flabbiness of fiber; indeed, he declaimed especially against our "conquering appetite," which seemed to him scandalous "in a new people with no hereditary predisposition toward war." But here he fell into a common blunder; the United States may be a new nation—although, as a fact, the stars-and-stripes is now older than the tricolor of France, the union-jack of Great Britain, and the standards of those newcomers among the nations, Italy and Germany—the United States may be a new nation, but the people here have had as many ancestors as the population of any other country. The people here, moreover, have "a hereditary predisposition toward war," or at least toward adventure, since they are, every man of them, descended from some European more venturesome than his fellows, readier to risk the perils of the western ocean and bolder to front the unknown dangers of an unknown land. The warlike temper, the aggressiveness, the imperialistic sentiment—these are in us no new development of unexpected ambition; and they ought not to surprise anyone familiar with the way in which our forefathers grasped this Atlantic coast first, then thrust themselves across the Alleghanies, spread abroad to the Mississippi, and reached out at last to the Rockies and to the Pacific. The lust of adventure may be dangerous, but it is no new thing; it is in our blood, and we must reckon with it.

Perhaps it is because "the breed and disposition of the people" is "stout and warlike" that our shopkeeping has been successful enough to awaken envious admiration among other races whose energy may have been relaxed of late. After all, the arts of war and the arts of peace are not so unlike; and in either a triumph can be won only by an imagination strong enough to foresee and to divine what is hidden from the weakling. We are a trading community, after all and above all, even if we come of fighting stock. We are a trading community, just as Athens was, and Venice and Florence. And like the men of these earlier commonwealths, the men of the United States are trying to make money. They are striving to make money, not solely to amass riches, but partly because having money is the outward and visible sign of success—because it is the most obvious measure of accomplishment.

In his talk with Tolstoi, our French critic revealed an unexpected insight when he asserted that the passion of American life was not so much the use of money as a delight in the conquest of it. Many an American man of affairs would admit without hesitation that he would rather make half a million dollars than inherit a million. It is the process he enjoys, rather than the result; it is the tough tussle in the open market which gives him the keenest pleasure, and not the idle contemplation of wealth safely stored away. He girds himself for battle and fights for his own hand; he is the son and the grandson of the stalwart adventurers who came from the Old World to face the chances of the new. This is why he is unwilling to retire as men are wont to do in Europe when their fortunes are made. Merely to have money does not greatly delight him—although he would regret not having it; but what does delight him unceasingly is the fun of making it.

The money itself often he does not know what to do with; and he can find no more selfish use for it than to give it away. He seems to recognize that his making it was in some measure due to the unconscious assistance of the community as a whole; and he feels it his duty to do something for the people among whom he lives. It must be noted that the people themselves also expect this from him; they expect him sooner or later to pay his footing. As a result of this pressure of public opinion and of his own lack of interest in money itself, he gives freely. In time he comes to find pleasure in this as well; and he applies his business sagacity to his benefactions. Nothing is more characteristic of modern American life than this pouring out of private wealth for public service. Nothing remotely resembling it is to be seen now in any country of the Old World; and not even in Athens in its noblest days was there a larger-handed lavishness of the individual for the benefit of the community.

Again, in no country of the Old World is the prestige of wealth less powerful than it is here. This, of course, the foreigner fails to perceive; he does not discover that it is not the man who happens to possess money that we regard with admiration but the man who is making money, and thereby proving his efficiency and indirectly benefiting the community. To many it may sound like an insufferable paradox to assert that nowhere in this civilized world today is money itself of less weight than here in the United States; but the broader his opportunity the more likely is an honest observer to come to this unexpected conclusion. Fortunes are made in a day almost, and they may fade away in a night; as the Yankee proverb put it pithily, "It's only three generations from shirt-sleeves to shirt-sleeves." Wealth is likely to lack something of its glamor in a land where well-being is widely diffused and where a large proportion of the population have either had a fortune and lost it or else expect to gain one in the immediate future.

Probably also there is no country which now contains more men who do not greatly care for large gains and who have gladly given up money-making for some other occupation they found more profitable for themselves. These are the men like Thoreau—in whose *Walden*, now half a century old, we can find an emphatic declaration of all the latest doctrines of the simple life. We have all heard of Agassiz,—best of Americans, even though he was born in another republic,—how he repelled the proffer of large terms for a series of lectures with the answer that he had no time to make money. Closely akin was the reply of a famous machinist in response to any inquiry as to what he had been doing—to the effect that he had accomplished nothing of late,—"we have just been

building engines and making money, and I'm about tired of it."
There are not a few men today in these toiling United States who
hold with Ben Jonson that "money never made any man rich,
—but his mind."

But while this is true, while there are some men among us who
care little for money, and while there are many who care chiefly
for the making of it, ready to share it when made with their fellow-citizens, candor compels the admission that there are also not
a few who are greedy and grasping, selfish and shameless, and
who stand forward, conspicuous and unscrupulous, as if to justify
to the full the aspersions which foreigners cast upon us. Although
these men manage for the most part to keep within the letter of
the law, their morality is that of the wrecker and of the pirate. It
is a symptom of health in the body politic that the proposal has
been made to inflict social ostracism upon the criminal rich. We
need to stiffen our conscience and to set up a loftier standard of
social intercourse, refusing to fellowship with the men who make
their money by overriding the law or by undermining it—just as
we should have declined the friendship of Captain Kidd laden
down with stolen treasure.

In the immediate future these men will be made to feel that
they are under the ban of public opinion. One sign of an acuter
sensitiveness is the recent outcry against the acceptance of
"tainted money" for the support of good works. Although it is
wise always to give a good deed the credit of a good motive, yet
it is impossible sometimes not to suspect that certain large gifts
have an aspect of "conscience money." Some of them seem to
be the result of a desire to divert public attention from the evil
way in which the money was made to the nobler manner in which
it is spent. They appear to be the attempt of a social outlaw
to buy his peace with the community. Apparently there are rich
men among us, who, having sold their honor for a price, would
now gladly give up the half of their fortunes to get it back.

Candor compels the admission also that by the side of the criminal rich there exists the less noxious but more offensive class of
the idle rich, who lead lives of wasteful luxury and of empty excitement. When the French reporter who talked with Tolstoi
called us Americans "avid of pleasure" it was this little group
he had in mind, as he may have seen the members of it splurging
about in Paris, squandering and self-advertising. Although these
idle rich now exhibit themselves most openly and to least advan-

tage in Paris and in London, their foolish doings are recorded superabundantly in our own newspapers; and their demoralizing influence is spread abroad. The snobbish report of their misguided attempts at amusement may even be a source of danger in that it seems to recognize a false standard of social success or in that it may excite a miserable ambition to emulate these pitiful frivolities. But there is no need of delaying longer over the idle rich; they are only a few, and they have doomed themselves to destruction, since it is an inexorable fact that those who break the laws of nature can have no hope of executive clemency.

"Patience a little; learn to wait,
Years are long on the clock of fate."

III

The second charge which the wandering Parisian journalist brought against us was that we ignore the arts and that we despise disinterested beauty. Here again the answer that is easiest is not altogether satisfactory. There is no difficulty in declaring that there are American artists, both painters and sculptors, who have gained the most cordial appreciation in Paris itself, or in drawing attention to the fact that certain of the minor arts—that of the silversmith, for one, and for another, that of the glass-blower and the glass-cutter—flourish in the United States at least as freely as they do anywhere else, while the art of designing in stained glass has had a new birth here, which has given it a vigorous vitality lacking in Europe since the Middle Ages. It would not be hard to show that our American architects are now undertaking to solve new problems wholly unknown to the builders of Europe, and that they are often succeeding in this grapple with unprecedented difficulty. Nor would it take long to draw up a list of the concerted efforts of certain of our cities to make themselves more worthy and more sightly with parks well planned and with public buildings well proportioned and appropriately decorated. We might even invoke the memory of the evanescent loveliness of the White City that graced the shores of Lake Michigan a few years ago; and we might draw attention again to the Library of Congress, a later effort of the allied arts of the architect, the sculptor, and the painter.

But however full of high hope for the future we may esteem these several instances of our reaching out for beauty, we must

admit—if we are honest with ourselves—that they are all more
or less exceptional, and that to offset this list of artistic achievements the Devil's Advocate could bring forward a damning catalogue of crimes against good taste which would go far to prove
that the feeling for beauty is dead here in America and also the
desire for it. The Devil's Advocate would bid us consider the
flaring and often vulgar advertisements that disfigure our highways, the barbaric ineptness of many of our public buildings,
the squalor of the outskirts of our towns and villages, the hideousness and horror of the slums in most of our cities, the negligent
toleration of dirt and disorder in our public conveyances, and
many another pitiable deficiency of our civilization present in the
minds of all of us.

The sole retort possible is a plea of confession and avoidance,
coupled with a promise of reformation. These evils are evident
and they cannot be denied. But they are less evident today than
they were yesterday; and we may honestly hope that they will
be less evident tomorrow. The bare fact that they have been observed warrants the belief that unceasing effort will be made to
do away with them. Once aroused, public opinion will work its
will in due season. And here occasion serves to deny boldly the
justice of a part of the accusation which the French reporter
brought against us. It may be true that we "ignore the arts"—
although this is an obvious overstatement of the case; but it is not
true that we "despise beauty." However ignorant the American
people may be as a whole, they are in no sense hostile toward art
—as certain other peoples seem to be. On the contrary, they
welcome it; with all their ignorance, they are anxious to understand it; they are pathetically eager for it. They are so desirous
of it that they want it in a hurry, only too often to find themselves
put off with an empty imitation. But the desire itself is indis-
putable; and its accomplishment is likely to be helped along by
the constant commingling here of peoples from various other
stocks than the Anglo-Saxon, since the mixture of races tends
always to a swifter artistic development.

It is well to probe deeper into the question and to face the fact
that not only in the arts but also in the sciences we are not doing
all that may fairly be expected of us. Athens was a trading city
as New York is, but New York has had no Sophocles and no
Phidias. Florence and Venice were towns whose merchants were
princes, but no American city has yet brought forth a Giotto, a

Dante, a Titian. It is now nearly threescore years and ten since Emerson delivered his address on the "American Scholar," which has well been styled our intellectual Declaration of Independence, and in which he expressed the hope that "perhaps the time is already come . . . when the sluggard intellect of this continent will look from under its iron lids and fulfil the postponed expectation of the world with something better than the exertions of a mechanical skill." Nearly seventy years ago was this prophecy uttered which still echoes unaccomplished.

In the nineteenth century, in which we came to maturity as a nation, no one of the chief leaders of art, even including literature in its broadest aspects, and no one of the chief leaders in science, was native to our country. Perhaps we might claim that Webster was one of the world's greatest orators and that Parkman was one of the world's greatest historians; but probably the experts outside of the United States would be found unprepared and unwilling to admit either claim, however likely it may be to win acceptance in the future. Lincoln is indisputably one of the world's greatest statesmen; and his fame is now firmly established throughout the whole of civilization. But this is all we can assert; and we cannot deny that we have given birth to very few indeed of the foremost poets, dramatists, novelists, painters, sculptors, architects or scientific discoverers of the last hundred years.

Alfred Russel Wallace, whose renown is linked with Darwin's and whose competence as a critic of scientific advance is beyond dispute, has declared that the nineteenth century was the most wonderful of all since the world began. He asserts that the scientific achievements of the last hundred years, both in the discovery of general principles and in their practical application, exceed in number the sum total of the scientific achievements to be credited to all the centuries that went before. He considers, first of all, the practical applications, which made the aspect of civilization in 1900 differ in a thousand ways from what it had been in 1801. He names a dozen of these practical applications: railways, steam navigation, the electric telegraph, the telephone, frictionmatches, gas-lighting, electric-lighting, the phonograph, the Roentgen rays, spectrum analysis, anesthetics, and antiseptics. It is with pride that an American can check off not a few of these utilities as being due wholly or in large part to the ingenuity of one or another of his countrymen.

But his pride has a fall when Wallace draws up a second list, not of mere inventions but of those fundamental discoveries, of those fecundating theories underlying all practical applications and making them possible, of those principles "which have extended our knowledge or widened our conceptions of the universe." Of these he catalogues twelve; and we are pained to find that no American has had an important share in the establishment of any of these broad generalizations. He may have added a little here and there, but no single one of all the twelve discoveries is mainly to be credited to any American. It seems as if our French critic was not so far out when he asserted that we were "terribly practical." In the application of principles, in the devising of new methods, our share was larger than that of any other nation. In the working out of the stimulating principles themselves, our share was less than "a younger brother's portion."

It is only fair to say, however, that even though we may not have brought forth a chief leader of art or of science to adorn the wonderful century, there are other evidences of our practical sagacity than those set down by Wallace, evidences more favorable and of better augury for our future. We derived our language and our laws, our public justice and our representative government from our English ancestors, as we derived from the Dutch our religious toleration and perhaps also our large freedom of educational opportunity. In our time we have set an example to others and helped along the progress of the world. President Eliot holds that we have made five important contributions to the advancement of civilization. First of all, we have done more than any other people to further peace-keeping and to substitute legal arbitration for the brute conflict of war. Second, we have set a splendid example of the broadest religious toleration—even though Holland had first shown us how. Thirdly, we have made evident the wisdom of universal manhood suffrage. Fourthly, by our welcoming of newcomers from all parts of the earth, we have proved that men belonging to a great variety of races are fit for political freedom. Finally, we have succeeded in diffusing material well-being among the whole population to an extent without parallel in any other country in the world.

These five American contributions to civilization are all of them the result of the practical side of the American character. They may even seem commonplace as compared with the conquering exploits of some other races. But they are more than merely

practical; they are all essentially moral. As President Eliot insists, they are "triumphs of reason, enterprise, courage, faith and
justice over passion, selfishness, inertness, timidity, and distrust.
Beneath each of these developments there lies a strong ethical sentiment, a strenuous moral and social purpose. It is for such
work that multitudinous democracies are fit."

IV

A "strong ethical sentiment," and a "strenuous moral purpose" cannot flourish unless they are deeply rooted to idealism.
And here we find an adequate answer to the third assertion of
Tolstoi's visitor, who maintained that we are "hostile to all idealism." Our idealism may be of a practical sort, but it is idealism
none the less. Emerson was an idealist, although he was also a
thrifty Yankee. Lincoln was an idealist, even if he was also a
practical politician, an opportunist, knowing where he wanted to
go, but never crossing a bridge before he came to it. Emerson
and Lincoln had ever a firm grip on the facts of life; each of
them kept his gaze fixed on the stars—and he also kept his feet
firm on the soil.

There is a sham idealism, boastful and shabby, which stares at
the moon and stumbles in the mud, as Shelley and Poe stumbled.
But the basis of the highest genius is always a broad common
sense. Shakspere and Molière were held in esteem by their comrades for their understanding of affairs; and they each of them
had money out at interest. Sophocles was entrusted with command in battle; and Goethe was the shrewdest of the Grand
Duke's counselors. The idealism of Shakspere and of Molière, of
Sophocles and of Goethe, is like that of Emerson and of Lincoln;
it is unfailingly practical. And thereby it is sharply set apart
from the aristocratic idealism of Plato and of Renan, of Ruskin
and of Nietzsche, which is founded on obvious self-esteem and
which is sustained by arrogant and inexhaustible egotism. True
idealism is not only practical, it is also liberal and tolerant.

Perhaps it might seem to be claiming too much to insist on
certain points of similarity between us and the Greeks of old.
The points of dissimilarity are only too evident to most of us;
and yet there is a likeness as well as an unlikeness. Professor
Butcher has recently asserted that "no people was ever less detached from the practical affairs of life" than the Greeks, "less

insensible to outward utility; yet they regarded prosperity as a means, never as an end. The unquiet spirit of gain did not take possession of their souls. Shrewd traders and merchants, they were yet idealists. They did not lose sight of the higher and distinctively human aims which give life its significance." It will be well for us if this can be said of our civilization two thousand years after its day is done; and it is for us to make sure that "the unquiet spirit of gain" shall not take possession of our souls. It is for us also to rise to the attitude of the Greeks, among whom, as Professor Butcher points out, "money lavished on personal enjoyment was counted vulgar, oriental, inhuman."

There is comfort in the memory of Lincoln and of those whose death on the field of Gettysburg he commemorated. The men who there gave up their lives that the country might live, had answered to the call of patriotism, which is one of the sublimest images of idealism. There is comfort also in the recollection of Emerson, and in the fact that for many of the middle years of the nineteenth century he was the most popular of lecturers, with an unfading attractiveness to the plain people, perhaps because, in Lowell's fine phrase, he "kept constantly burning the beacon of an ideal life above the lower region of turmoil." There is comfort again in the knowledge that idealism is one manifestation of imagination, and that imagination itself is but an intenser form of energy. That we have energy and to spare, no one denies; and we may reckon him a nearsighted observer who does not see also that we have our full share of imagination even though it has not yet expressed itself in the loftiest regions of art and of science. The outlook is hopeful, and it is not true that

"We, like sentries are obliged to stand
In starless nights and wait the appointed hour."

The foundations of our commonwealth were laid by the sturdy Elizabethans who bore across the ocean with them their portion of that imagination which in England flamed up in rugged prose and in superb and soaring verse. In two centuries and a half the sons of these stalwart Englishmen have lost nothing of their ability to see visions and to dream dreams, and to put solid foundations under their castles in the air. The flame may seem to die down for a season, but it springs again from the embers most unexpectedly, as it broke forth furiously in 1861. There was imagination at the core of the little war for the freeing of Cuba—

the very attack on Spain which the Parisian journalist cited to Tolstoi as the proof of our predatory aggressiveness. We said that we were going to war for the sake of the ill-used people in the suffering island close to our shores; we said that we would not annex Cuba;; we did the fighting that was needful—and we kept our word. It is hard to see how even the most bitter of critics can discover in this anything selfish.

There was imagination also in the sudden stopping of all the steam-craft, of all the railroads, of all the street-cars, of all the incessant traffic of the whole nation, at the moment when the body of a murdered chief magistrate was lowered into the grave. This pause in the work of the world was not only touching, it had a large significance to anyone seeking to understand the people of these United States. It was a testimony that the Greeks would have appreciated; it had the bold simplicity of an Attic inscription. And we would thrill again in sympathetic response if it was in the pages of Plutarch that we read the record of another instance: When the time arrived for Admiral Sampson to surrender the command of the fleet he had brought back to Hampton Roads, he came on deck to meet there only those officers whose prescribed duty required them to take part in the farewell ceremonies as set forth in the regulations. But when he went over the side of the flagship he found that the boat which was to bear him ashore was manned by the rest of the officers, ready to row him themselves and eager to render this last personal service; and then from every other ship of the fleet there put out a boat, also manned by officers, to escort for the last time the commander whom they loved and honored.

V

As another illustration of our regard for the finer and loftier aspects of life, consider our parks, set apart for the use of the people by the city, the state, and the nation. In the cities of this new country the public playgrounds have had to be made, the most of them, and at high cost—whereas the towns of the Old World have come into possession of theirs for nothing, more often than not inheriting the private recreation-grounds of their rulers. And Europe has little or nothing to show similar either to the reservations of certain states, like the steadily enlarging preserves in the Catskills and the Adirondacks, or to the ampler national parks,

the Yellowstone, the Yosemite and the Grand Canyon of the Colorado, some of them far larger in area than one at least of the
original thirteen states. Overcoming the pressure of private greed,
the people have ordained the preservation of this natural beauty
and its protection for all time under the safe guardianship of the
nation and with free access to all who may claim admission to
enjoy it.

In like manner many of the battlefields, whereon the nation
spent its blood that it might be what it is and what it hopes to be
—these have been taken over by the nation itself and set apart
and kept as holy places of pilgrimage. They are free from the
despoiling hand of any individual owner. They are adorned with
monuments recording the brave deeds of the men who fought there.
They serve as constant reminders of the duty we owe to our
country and of the debt we owe to those who made it, and who
saved it for us. And the loyal veneration with which these fields
of blood have been cherished here in the United States finds no
counterpart in any country in Europe, no matter how glorious
may be its annals of military prowess. Even Waterloo is in private hands; and its broad acres, enriched by the bones of thousands, are tilled every year by the industrious Belgian farmers.
Yet it was a Frenchman, Renan, who told us that what welds men
into a nation, is "the memory of great deeds done in common and
the will to accomplish yet more."

According to the theory of the conservation of energy, there
ought to be about as much virtue in the world at one time as at
another. According to the theory of the survival of the fittest,
there ought to be a little more now than there was a century ago.
We Americans today have our faults, and they are abundant
enough and blatant enough, and foreigners take care that we shall
not overlook them; but our ethical standard—however imperfectly
we may attain to it—is higher than that of the Greeks under Pericles, of the Romans under Cæsar, of the English under Elizabeth.
It is higher even than that of our forefathers who established our
freedom, as those know best who have most carefully inquired into
the inner history of the American Revolution. In nothing was
our advance more striking than in the different treatment meted
out to the vanquished after the Revolution and after the Civil
War. When we made our peace with the British the native Tories
were proscribed, and thousands of loyalists left the United States
to carry into Canada the indurated hatred of the exiled. But

after Lee's surrender at Appomattox, no body of men, no single man indeed, was driven forth to live an alien for the rest of his days; even though a few might choose to go, none were compelled.

This change of conduct on the part od those who were victors in the struggle was evidence of an increasing sympathy. Not only is sectionalism disappearing, but with it is departing the feeling that really underlies it—the distrust of those who dwell elsewhere than where we do. This distrust is common all over Europe to-day. Here in America it has yielded to a friendly neighborliness which makes the family from Portland, Maine, soon find itself at home in Portland, Oregon. It is getting hard for us to hate anybody—especially since we have disestablished the devil. We are good-natured and easy-going. Herbert Spencer even denounced this as our immediate danger, maintaining that we were too good-natured, too easy-going, too tolerant of evil; and he insisted that we needed to strengthen our wills to protest against wrong, to wrestle with it resolutely, and to overcome it before it is firmly rooted.

VI

We are kindly and we are helpful; and we are fixed in the belief that somehow everything will work out all right in the long run. But nothing will work out all right unless we so make it work; and excessive optimism may be as corrupting to the fiber of the people as "the Sabbathless pursuit of fortune," as Bacon termed it. When Mr. John Morley was last in this country he seized swiftly upon a chance allusion of mine to this ingrained hopefulness of ours. "Ah, what you call optimism," he cried, "I call fatalism." But an optimism which is solidly based on a survey of the facts cannot fairly be termed fatalism; and another British student of political science, Mr. James Bryce, has recently pointed out that the intelligent native American has—and by experience is justified in having—a firm conviction that the majority of qualified voters are pretty sure to be right.

Then he suggested a reason for the faith that is in us, when he declared that no such feeling exists in Europe, since in Germany the governing class dreads the spread of socialism, in France the republicans know that it is not impossible that Monarchism and Clericalism may succeed in upsetting the republic, while in Great

Britain each party believes that the other party, when it succeeds, succeeds by misleading the people, and neither party supposes that the majority are any more likely to be right than to
be wrong.

Mr. Morley and Mr. Bryce were both here in the United States
in the fall of 1904, when we were in the midst of a presidential
election, one of those prolonged national debates, creating incessant commotion, but invaluable agents of our political education
in so far as they force us all to take thought about the underlying
principles of policy by which we wish to see the government
guided. It was while this political campaign was at its height
that the French visitor to the Russian novelist was setting his
notes in order and copying out his assertion that we Americans
were mere money-grubbers, "systematically hostile to all idealism." If this unthinking Parisian journalist had only taken the
trouble to consider the addresses which the chief speakers of the
two parties here in the United States were then making to their
fellow-citizens in the hope of winning votes, he would have discovered that these practical politicians, trained to perceive the subtler
shades of popular feeling, were founding all their arguments on
the assumption that the American people as a whole wanted to
do right. He would have seen that the appeal of these stalwart
partizans was rarely to prejudice or to race-hatred—evil spirits
that various orators have sought to arouse and to intensify in the
more recent political discussions of the French themselves.

An examination of the platforms, of the letters of the candidates, and of the speeches of the more important leaders on both
sides revealed to an American observer the significant fact that
"each party tried to demonstrate that it was more peaceable,
more equitable, more sincerely devoted to lawful and righteous
behavior than the other"; and "the voter was instinctively credited with loving peace and righteousness, and with being stirred
by sentiments of good-will toward men." This seems to show
that the heart of the people is sound, and that it does not throb
in response to ignoble appeals. It seems to show that there is here
the desire ever to do right and to see right done, even if the will
is weakened a little by easy-going good-nature, and even if the will
fails at times to stiffen itself resolutely to make sure that the right
shall prevail.

"Liberty hath a sharp and double edge fit only to be handled
by just and virtuous men," so Milton asserted long ago, adding

that "to the bad and dissolute, it becomes a mischief unwieldy in their own hands." Even if we Americans can clear ourselves of being "bad and dissolute," we have much to do before we may claim to be "just and virtuous." Justice and virtue are not to be had for the asking; they are the rewards of a manful contest with selfishness and with sloth. They are the results of an honest effort to think straight, and to apply eternal principles to present needs. Merely to feel is only the beginning; what remains is to think and to act.

A British historian, Mr. Frederic Harrison, who came here to spy out the land three or four years before Mr. Morley and Mr. Bryce last visited us, was struck by the fact—and by the many consequences of the fact—that "America is the only land on earth where caste has never had a footing, nor has left a trace." It seemed to him that "vast numbers and the passion of equality tend to low averages in thought, in manners, and in public opinion, which the zeal of the devoted minority tends gradually to raise to higher planes of thought and conduct." He believed that we should solve our problems one by one because "the zeal for learning, justice and humanity" lies deep in the American heart. Mr. Harrison did not say it in so many words, but it is implied in what he did say, that the absence of caste and the presence of low averages in thought, in manners, and in public opinion, impose a heavier task on the devoted minority, whose duty it is to keep alive the zeal for learning, justice and humanity.

Which of us, if haply the spirit moves him, may not elect himself to this devoted minority? Why should not we also, each in our own way, without pretense, without boastfulness, without bullying, do whatsoever in us lies for the attainment of justice and of virtue? It is well to be a gentleman and a scholar; but after all it is best to be a man, ready to do a man's work in the world. And indeed there is no reason why a gentleman and a scholar should not also be a man. He will need to cherish what Huxley called "that enthusiasm for truth, that fanaticism for veracity, which is a greater possession than much learning, a nobler gift than the power of increasing knowledge." He will need also to remember that

"Kings have their dynasties—but not the mind;
Cæsar leaves other Cæsars to succeed,
But Wisdom, dying, leaves no heir behind."

American character is not
on the whole unworthy, in spite of criticism to the contrary for the average
American are not out for money alone, are
rather practical than imaginative,
and they are not altogether lacking in
idealism.

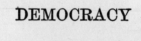

DEMOCRACY

DEMOCRACY [1]

John Stuart Blackie

[John Stuart Blackie (1809-1895), Scottish professor and man of letters, was in 1839 appointed to the Chair of Humanity (by which was meant Latin) at Marischal College, Aberdeen. In 1851 he was elected to the Chair of Greek at the University of Edinburgh. In Edinburgh he was a public figure, his genial eccentricities being the subject of many stories. As a lecturer he made his personality felt in all parts of Scotland. Among his numerous works may be mentioned *A Translation of Faust into English Verse*, *A Metrical Translation of the Lyrical Dramas of Æschylus*, and *What Does History Teach?* An account of the debate with Ernest Jones upon Democracy, is given in the biography of Blackie by his sister, Anna M. Stoddart:

It was early in November, 1866, that, presiding at a meeting of the Working Men's Club, at its institute in the High Street of Edinburgh, Professor Blackie launched forth into an invective against the Reform Bill, which at that time was in process of incubation, and charging somewhat unadvisedly down the vistas of "manhood suffrage" and "the ballot," flung a challenge in the faces of their champions. This was reported in the *Scotsman* of November 12 as follows:

"If you will appoint a night for a lecture, and set Blackie on the one side, and Bright, or Beales, or Jones, or M'Laren, or the honorable member, the Lord Advocate, for whom I have the greatest respect, on the other side,—then with Aristotle in the one pocket and Plato in the other, and a great deal of Scotch rummlegumption in the front battery, I think they will find me a sharp customer."

There is little doubt that the gauntlet was a mere rhetorical flourish, and that he expected no knight of reform to pick it up. He did not account himself a politician, and was seldom acquainted with the *pros* and *cons* of party questions. His opinions on these were evolved in the manner which he indicated himself—from classic precedent and his own consciousness. But reckless rhetoric in print is apt to rouse a Nemesis. The Scottish National Reform League played the part of the goddess, and inspired Mr. Ernest Jones, then known as an able advocate of Manhood Suffrage, to respond to the challenge. The Professor, astounded to find himself the representative of a party, backed by the *optimi*, at whom he was as wont to fling his spear as at their political opponents, wriggled restlessly at first; but the ranks both of supporters and of foes closed around him, and he buckled on his armor in the face of the inevitable. Mr. Ernest Jones accepted all the terms of the original challenge, genially asking to be enlightened as to the value of

[1] Reprinted from *Democracy: An Address by Professor Blackie of Edinburgh; and a Reply by the late Ernest Jones of Manchester.* Second Edition. Manchester: Abel Heywood and Son. London: Simpkin, Marshall and Co., 1885.
Questions and topics for the discussion of this address, and of other phases of the general subject with which it deals, will be found on pages 493 and 500.

"rummlegumption." The Reform League instructed the secretary of the Working Men's Club to make the necessary arrangements, and it was finally settled to engage the Music Hall in George Street for the evenings of the third and fourth of January, 1867, when Democracy should on the first night be handled by the challenger, and on the second be supported by Mr. Jones on precisely the same terms of ancient precedent as those used in the attack. Of course this gave an advantage to the first speaker, who could carefully prepare and execute his indictment, while the defence was perforce almost extempore; but Professor Blackie forwarded a copy of his address some days beforehand to Mr. Jones, who proved to be a man of fine classical attainments, and to whom the subject was fully familiar. . . .

His lecture lasted nearly three hours, and was heard with close attention, marked by vivacious cheering and hissing on the part of the audience. He bore the counter-demonstration with perfect good humor, retorting at times on his opponents with the gibe that his wisest remarks were best hissed. On the next evening Mr. Jones proved easily enough that at all events Greece and Venice reached their culmination under republican rule. The lances clashed briskly, but neither was shivered. The fight closed where it began.

The progress of democracy since 1867 may seem to leave to this debate only an historical significance. But the fundamental issues raised by Blackie— liberty, equality, self-government, majority rule,—have occupied the minds of men since the days of Plato's *Republic* and Aristotle's *Politics*. Blackie's fears, as those of Plato and Aristotle, still find expression among us. The general tone of political thought since the war that was to make the world safe for democracy, has not been optimistic. "The question, whether men will rise toward the higher standard which the prophets of democracy deemed possible," says James Bryce in concluding his *Modern Democracies,* "has been exercising every thoughtful mind since August, 1914, and it will be answered less hopefully now than it would have been at any time in the hundred years preceding."

This debate is also of interest as an example of an older type of public address, with its background of classical allusion and precedent, and its historical analogies. It also exhibits the fears and hopes with which Europe has watched America, and shows how our institutions have furnished arguments to conservatives, liberals and radicals. James Russell Lowell's address on *Democracy,* delivered at Birmingham in 1884, when he was ambassador to England, was intended to allay the fears of European conservatives. It should be read in connection with this debate. It was inevitable that Lowell should discuss the issues raised by Blackie, for the year of Lowell's speech marked the passage of the Third Reform Bill, which extended to agricultural laborers the franchise granted to householders in the boroughs in 1867, thus carrying still further a principle which had seemed dangerously democratic to Blackie at the time of the Second Reform Bill. The agitation of 1884 led to a renewed interest in the debate between Blackie and Jones, and in 1885 it was reprinted, with a preface stating that "earnest politicians will find a careful study of these pages suggestive" at a time "when for practical purposes England starts in a career of democratic government." In 1924 it seems worth while to call attention yet again to this discussion.]

"The best of all animals, when governed by law and justice, is man; when without them, the most terrible."[1] This is the sentence

---

[1] Aristotle's *Pol.*, 1, 2—Bekker.

of Aristotle, the most sagacious and most far-sighted of political writers, and, of all speculative men, certainly the most practical. And to this undeniable dictum we may, without fear of question, add, that of all animals man is the most difficult to govern, and of all arts, the art of government is that one which at once demands the greatest talents for success, and entails the most terrible penalties by failure.[1] Nevertheless, and in spite of the terrible lessons of history written everywhere in characters of blood, there has always been a class of persons of hasty wit and superficial conclusions, who have been of opinion that the government of human beings is one of the simplest of all arts—as simple, in fact, as any sum in addition,—and that the one infallible way to find the wisdom by which a community of reasonable beings shall be governed, is to gather them into indiscriminate masses, portion them off like sheep into separate pens, take the votes of the several pens by the poll, add the votes together, and the sum will give a verdict which, by a cunning machinery of social wire-pulling (well understood in America), will give good government. The maintainers of this opinion are known in history as democrats, and universal suffrage is the watchword of their doctrine. The social system of which they are the advocates is so flattering to human pride, and opens up so patent a road to the ignorant and the conceited, the presumptuous and the unscrupulous, that, notwithstanding its essential unreasonableness, it has always commanded a large amount of popular sympathy. Even in Great Britain, a country the most naturally averse to the practical assertion of one-sided political ideas, it has occasionally showed face; and at the present moment the country is being perambulated and agitated by popular orators, who, though in words they sometimes express a certain vague admiration for the mixed constitution under which this country has grown and prospered, do in fact maintain the most unqualified principles of democracy, and appeal to the verdict of the masses as the only standard of political rectitude. That any large influential class of this practical-minded community should have faith in a delusive conceit which every memorable fact of history contradicts, I cannot believe; but that there are thousands and tens of thousands in this island, especially among those who are called the "working classes," ignorant

---

[1] "When one measures the whole circle of the Social Sciences, one is frightened at all that they require,—study, talent, genius, and elevation of character."—Sismondi, *Essays*, London, 1847, p. 289.

enough to allow themselves to be juggled out of reason and common sense by general assertions about the transcendental virtues of democracy, that is, about the transcendental wisdom of themselves, made by men of talent and eloquence, only an amiable and voluntary blindness could deny. Besides, in politics, there are always half a dozen reasonably sensible men—men who, from their education, ought to know better,—who will allow themselves to be borne along by a popular current of unreason, and even indulge in a little flirtation with principles, from the serious assertion of which they would be the first to recoil.

It has occurred to me, therefore, that I may be doing a little, public service at the present juncture, by stating, not in the style of a political declamation from the hustings, but of a large philosophical survey, the fundamental fallacies which lie at the bottom of this idol-worship of the multitude which is now attempted to be imposed upon us; and, in doing so, I shall certainly not follow the example of great popular orators, by indulging in extravagant laudations of one party, and equally extravagant denunciations of the other; but I will endeavour to state the case as fairly as possible for both parties, and to paint out the fair democratic delusion in the first place with colours as roseate as the most fervid apostle might desire. And I will do this with the greater confidence of being able to sketch a faithful portraiture, because I am by birth and habit a man of the people, in nowise connected with what is popularly called the Aristocracy, and earnestly desirous that all classes of the people should possess that weight in the government of this country which a fair consideration of their relative positions, and a just estimate of the quality and the quantity of their social contributions, might recommend. I start, therefore, with stating the case for democracy thus:—

I. All men are naturally free. God has given to his creatures certain functions and capacities, which require room and scope for their exercise; and the more room the better. No limits or bounds to free activity ought to be allowed in society beyond what God has constituted. Especially, no laws ought to be made by one class of men to give enlargement to their own sphere of action by the process of compulsory circumscription of the natural sphere of their neighbours. As the greatest happiness of the greatest number is the measure of legislative wisdom, so the greatest liberty of the greatest number is the measure of national greatness. To be free is to be strong; not to be free is to be weak. To be free is to exercise lordship; not to be free is to endure slavery. To be free is to be a man; to be a slave is to be a chattel. The watchword of humanity, the war-cry of heroism, the stamp of moral dignity, is FREEDOM.

II. All men are naturally equal. By this is not meant, of course, that all men are equal in talents, in character, in excellence of any kind, any more than they are in physical confirmation or in stature. Inequality is one of the most prominent facts of nature and of life, though we must never forget how large a share convention, and institution, and usurped force may have had in producing inequality where God meant equality. But what the enlightened advocates of democracy mean, when they assert the natural equality of all men, is that in reference to matters of social organism one man is as good as another. Every man has life and rights, and in fact stakes his all in the society to which he belongs; the poorest man as much, and generally perhaps much more, than the richest. Therefore socially each man is on a level. Absolute equality is the law of all free institutions. If it were not so, a few might combine by force and fraud to deprive the many of the common birthright of humanity, as, indeed, the few powerful have in all ages combined to over-ride, oppress, and keep in thralled servitude the feeble many. The only remedy for this is political equality.

III. As in the individual, so in the body social, self-government is the word which expresses the healthy state of perfect manhood. Nations, like individuals, go through their successive stages of infancy, boyhood, and pupilage; but a full grown man requires no tutors or curators, and a full-grown nation no governors. The people by natural right is its own sovereign; and any persons holding situations of command in a well-constituted republic are merely put forth for the sake of convenience as the obedient organs of the public will. The real king is always the people, asserting itself fully and without restraint in free congregations of equal units.

IV. The preceding proposition expresses the true principle on which representative government proceeds. A House of Representatives represents the interests, the wishes, and the wisdom of the free, equal, and independent people; and such a body becomes necessary in large communities only from the practical difficulty of the whole people occupying themselves at one time and place, for considerable spaces of time, with the discussion and conduct of public business. Representative bodies, therefore, are not, properly speaking, deliberative bodies; for, if they were entitled to deliberate and decide on independent grounds, they would be assuming for a few the prerogative which, according to the principle of a consistent democracy, can belong only to the whole. A people who should elect representatives with the right of free deliberation, might readily find their own dearest interests disowned by the very men whom they had elected to be their champions. A House of Representatives, therefore, is only a committee of the people, and exists only for the sake of carrying their decisions into execution.

V. The legitimate method by which the people declare their will, and pronounce their decisions, is by the vote of the majority. Any other method denies the natural equality of mankind, and establishes an oligarchy more or less insidious and oppressive. That the majority is always right in all cases no man will assert. In scientific questions, and in matters remote from public view, the decision of a skilled minority will of course justly prevail. But in the affairs of daily life, in matters of common interest and concern, a common man will generally have a shrewd guess what ought to be done, though he cannot always marshal his reasons scientifically. It is the greatest of all delusions to suppose that profound study is necessary for the first steps of political action. Every man knows his own interest, and the people know what is practically for their benefit in matters before their nose better than the most subtle speculator. A sensible tradesman who reads the newspapers, will, in nine cases out of ten, give a more just decision in political matters than a learned professor who quotes Thucydides, Machiavelli, and Aristotle. The general agreement of the mass of the people in practical matters, is, in fact, the only safeguard to society against the cunning devices of oligarchs, the crotchets of ideal speculators, and the bookish pedantry of the learned.

These, so far as I have been able to make the analysis, are the leading propositions which express the principles and the purposes of the democratic party. I have stated them as fairly, and with as much decision, as I could; and, did space allow, I should be quite willing further to exhibit a large array of facts from history, which would seem to lend them the most ample justification. The glories of Salamis and Marathon; the intellectual triumphs of ancient Athens, and the political ascendency of ancient Rome;

the patriotic achievements of the Swiss and the Belgians; the triumph of Luther over Pope Leo, and of the Covenanters over Charles II.; the downfall of feudalism in France by the Revolution of 1789; the creation of a Prussian people by the Baron Stein in 1808; the overthrow of Napoleon by the great national uprising in 1813;—these are but a few of the greatest and most glorious events of history, from which a popular orator could lightly garnish forth the great epos of Liberty, Equality, and Fraternity. But I will leave panoramic pictures of this kind to those to whom it more properly belongs. For my argument they are not necessary, as I fully admit everything they contain, and yield to no man in the fervour with which I read the records of those struggles by which the liberty and independence of the great nations of the world have been established. But in moral questions neither panoramic pictures nor closely-marshalled propositions are of any practical value, so long as they are one-sided. Every moral proposition has its counter proposition, without which the truth can no more be eliminated than an equation can be worked without the values on both sides. I shall therefore proceed to analyse the above five propositions, and by meeting each assertion with its contrary, prepare the way for that full statement of political truth, with which no extreme doctrine, whether of democarcy or aristocracy, can ever be made to harmonize.

First, as to FREEDOM. It is certainly true that birds were not made for cages, and that to be a natural, normal, proper bird, a winged creature ought to be allowed to fly. So man, in order to be man, and no chattel, must be free. A civil society of slaves is nonsense in the statement. Only free-men, as Aristotle teaches, can constitute a State. But freedom does not mean absolute freedom; on the contrary, it rather means only the equal acknowledgement of just and fair restraints. Mere liberty, though a very great thing to a bird, is the first and lowest and smallest condition of human society. Freedom, however much belauded, is, in fact, that quality or function which man shares in common with children, savages, madmen, and wild beasts. All these naturally rejoice only in freedom, and disown all restraint. The imposition of restraints upon liberty is the first great act of civilisation; and to increase restrictions is, in the general case, to make progress in legislation. No doubt, unwise restrictions have sometimes been made by intermeddling rulers, which required to be removed; but law, nevertheless, means restraint; and to be lawless is to be free.

It is with the power of human liberty as with the force of steam in a steam-engine; it is only by being confined and regulated and controlled that it becomes anything more than an idle puff or an inorganic blast. We must say, therefore, that, always supposing the existence of native social forces, not freedom but order is the grand distinctive principle of civil society. God made the world, by freedom certainly, in one sense, that is, by His own free will, but not less by restraint, by subjecting His own free thought to that law of self-consistent energy, by which a chaos becomes a cosmos. Order is the grand regulating principle of all things. The stars are not free to move otherwise than in their appointed courses; the flowers divide themselves into finely calculated sections, by laws than which no mathematics are more ingenious; even the storms and the winds have their laws, to which only the imperfection of our calculating machines, and the narrowness of our survey, give an appearance of instability. Let us say, therefore, as the counterpart of the first proposition, that the whole universe is subjected to law, and perishes and falls into chaos the moment it attempts to live by mere freedom. In this respect, the moral world, as we should anticipate, is the exact image of the physical. A congregation of the masses of people, blown up with the idea of liberty, can only produce confusion and anarchy, unless these masses are willing to submit themselves to the constraints of reason and law. History has shown this both on the large and small scale, a thousand times. Unreined liberty leads to violence and passion; violence leads to strife and civil war; civil war ends in confusion and exhaustion; and the necessary conclusion is dissolution, destruction, and mutual extermination; unless the cure be sought, where, after such a process, it has alone been found, in military despotism. The class of men, therefore, who inflame the passions of the masses by vague harangues about liberty, are to be accounted among the greatest enemies of the people, specially of the working man. Personally, there are no doubt great differences among such men. I am willing to think that many of them are honourable and high-principled; self-contained crotchet-mongers, sentimental idealists, fantastic philanthropists, meagre theorizers whom all facts have not taught, may form a large proportion; but the selfish, the ambitious, the conceited, the envious, and the proud, certainly contribute their quota; while to some the terrible description of the apostle Jude may be literally applicable: "Raging waves of the sea, foaming out their own shame; wandering stars, to whom is reserved the blackness of darkness for ever." And again: "These are murmurers, complainers, walking after their own lusts; and their mouth speaketh great swelling words, having men's persons in admiration because of advantage." On the contrary, the happy results of order, under the constraining power of reason, in society, are love, harmony, moderation, and toleration; right and justice in the administration of the laws; stability in social institutions; peace, prosperity, and permanence. Liberty is a wild horse, which can only be made serviceable to the commonwealth by being saddled and bridled by the great master, Order; it is a wine which, unless carefully used under the prescription of a wise physician, lifts a man for a moment into an imaginary heaven, only that it may plunge him into a real hell.

The next favourite watchword of the democrat is EQUALITY. It expresses a fundamental point essentially necessary in his system, but which is, unfortunately, also his weakest point. It is no doubt perfectly true that all men have two eyes and two legs. All men can look and walk, and eat and drink and sleep, and do everything which a pig can do as well as a man. In these low matters we find a general sort of equality amongst all men; but precisely as we mount in the scale of excellence, the equality vanishes, and the most glaring inequality everywhere meets our eye. All men see, but few men observe accurately; and fewer still have moral and intellectual insight. We are all naturally ignorant, stupid, obstinate, conceited, passionate, and require to be trained by a long process to any high degree of intelligence and virtue. The difference between one man and another in respect of natural capacity is immeasurable; in respect of acquired worth even greater; and it is this acquired worth, much more than native talent, which renders a man fit to take any share beneficially in the conduct of public business. In every view, however, the striking fact is that eminent talent, and accurate knowledge, and high principle, are rare; and the points in which all men are equal are precisely those from which the highest human excellence is excluded. It is a sound observation of Williams, the Polynesian missionary, that "in the lowest stages of civilization democracy prevails, all heads being of an equal height." If, therefore, we are to rise in the scale of being, we must accustom ourselves habitually to recog-

nise the great counter truth of the democratic equality, viz., the
aristocratic principle of subordination and superiority.

"We live by admiration, hope, and love,"

as Wordsworth sings, and Plato teaches;[1] and we advance in moral
and spiritual dignity just in proportion as we acquire the habit
of acknowledging superiority, instead of assuming equality, with
our fellow-men. In this view, the democratic temper, which
teaches every man to say to his neighbour, "I am as good as you,
and perhaps a little better," must be regarded as one of the greatest antagonist powers to all popular improvement. Self-respect
is no doubt a virtue; but it is very closely allied to self-importance
and self-conceit, and is in any view a very cheap virtue compared
with the aristocratic and Christian one of "honouring all men."
Instead of being blown up with a false idea of equality, men ought
to be taught to know their true position, and willingly to subject
themselves to their natural superiors. The feeble ought readily
to submit themselves to the firm, the ignorant to the well-informed,
the bad to the good. But of this healthy feeling of respect and
reverence for what is superior, democracy knows nothing. The
result is that wherever that system of government flourishes, there
we find the rank hotbed of conceit, insolence, vain confidence, irreverence, and hollow pretension of all kinds. The thorough democrat is the sworn enemy of all eminence; he hates to hear any man
praised as in any way superior to the crowd; he banishes Aristides,
because he is sick of hearing him called the Just; his whole instincts and striving lead him to reduce everything to the dead
level of his pet equality. He is thus in a state of open rebellion
against the laws of nature and the institution of God. For everywhere in Nature, in every organic body, as well as in all societies,
there is a high and a low, a controlling and a ministrant power,
a dominant and a subordinate, a part formed to govern, and a
part formed to obey.[2] Whoso does not know this has not learned
the first lesson of social science; and if he has not learned it from
the prophets, philosophers, and apostles of antiquity, he will certainly not learn it from the demagogues and popular orators of

---

[1] Μάλα γὰρ φιλόσοφον τοῦτο τὸ πάθος τὸ θαυμάζειν. Reverence is the special gift
of a philosopher.—*Theœtet.* 155 D.

[2] Τὸ μὲν γὰρ ἄρχειν καὶ ἄρχεσθαι οὐ μόνον τῶν ἀναγκαίων ἀλλὰ καὶ τῶν συμφερόντων
ἐστί. The power of governing and of obedience are not only necessary but
beneficial.—Aristotle, *Pol.* I, 5.

these days, who preach political equality, despise dominion, speak evil of dignities, and earn cheap applause from an immaculate populace by haranguing against the vices of a bloated aristocracy. The third point of democracy is SELF-GOVERNMENT. The proposition expressive of this contains the greatest of all the fallacies in the democratic logic. The real fact is the exact contrary. A multitude of human beings indiscriminately congregated, that is, acting only as a quantitative force without any regard to quality, never did, and in its very nature never can, perform the functions of governing. Where thousands and tens of thousands of persons, the most variously constituted, individually perhaps sensible and reasonable enough, are brought together, on a sudden notice, to deliberate on the most perplexed and difficult subjects, and this not under the guidance of cool reason, but, as generally happens in political assemblies, lashed into a temporary madness by the spur of ambition, and confounded by the jugglery of faction; under such circumstances, nothing short of a miracle could lead to cool deliberation; and cool deliberation is the necessary condition of all that rational leading of reasonable beings which is called government. Left to its natural tendencies, every multitude resolves into confusion, or rushes on to perdition. Of this the great poet who sang his grand minstrel notes, not for ancient Greece only, but for all times and all places, has left us a striking picture in the well-known popular assembly in the Second Book of the Iliad, to which Agamemnon, deluded by a lying dream, had appealed for final decision at a critical moment of the war. With characteristic fickleness and faint-heartedness, the common people of the camp, after nine years' expenditure of life and resources, were willing to give up their greatest national expedition, and lay Europe a slave at the foot of Asia, merely that they might go home a year sooner and see their wives. But this inglorious resolution, hastily taken and hastily attempted to be put into execution, was at once checked by the interference of that national aristocracy, which in ancient Greece, as in modern Britain, has so often proved itself the stoutest champion of popular rights, and the most clear-sighted discerner of popular interests. The wise Ulysses makes the round of the camp, and happily finds the ear of the people not yet altogether deaf to the appeal of reason, and their heart yet pervious to the sting of virtuous reproach. He tells them plainly, what infatuated democrats yet require to be told——

Οὐκ ἀγαθὸν πολυκοιρανίη
"Ill fares the States where the many rule!"

recalls them to their natural subjection to their superiors, and at
the same time takes occasion, in a few masterly lines, to give a
portrait of the demagogic man, ill-formed, ill-favoured, envious,
spiteful, and slanderous, whose vocation it is to flatter the lowest
class of society, and to malign the highest. Hear how he has it:—

> "The ugliest man was he who came to Troy,
> With squinting eyes, and one distorted foot,
> His shoulders broad, and buried in his breast,
> His narrow head, with scanty growth of hair." [1]

But it is not in profane poetry alone that we find the portraiture
of the true nature of all popular assemblies. The sacred history
of the New Testament, rich in many texts which the most orthodox
preachers never think of applying, supplies an illustration of the
true character of a Greek ecclesia, not inferior to that given by
Homer. In the nineteenth chapter of the Acts of the Apostles,
we are informed that when St. Paul was at Ephesus, then a sort
of Liverpool or Glasgow to the western coast of Asia, there arose
no small stir about the new doctrine which the apostle preached.
The people, who in all countries are generally opposed to reforms
in religion, and ready to cry heresy against reasonable preachers
and apostles of all kinds, found on this occasion, as is found also
in the most recent times, their piety powerfully aided by their
pocket, and brought the prejudices of superstition and the interests of the craft to bear in a combined battery against the strange
gospeller. A meeting of the working men of Ephesus, especially
the silversmiths, who made shrines to Diana, was accordingly held;
and this meeting, after the usual number of eloquent addresses by
the chief men of the craft, seconded no doubt by some of the most
popular clergy of the city, framed resolutions to the effect that
the preaching of the apostles ought to be put down, as derogatory
to the dignity of the goddess, and hostile to the interests of the
craft. Immediately thereupon, while yet their livers were hot
with sacred wrath, they had a great public meeting in the theatre
attended not merely by the silversmiths, but by the whole body
of the working classes and other citizens, of whom, on account of
the haste of the proceedings, the greater part knew not wherefore

[1] *The Iliad of Homer.* By Edward Earl of Derby. Vol. i. p. 45.

they were come together. However, on being informed that Jews were at the bottom of the commotion—a race whom they heartily hated, just as orthodox Scotchmen hate Papists and Unitarians— they set up a bawling and a braying, and a hissing and a bellow- ing, like a congregation of asses, serpents, and geese; and for the space of two hours caused the air to resound—for the theatre in Ephesus was open—with the cry of "GREAT IS DIANA OF THE EPHESIANS!" By this prodigious amount of breath, the pulmonary force of the working classes had exhausted itself; and the town-clerk, standing up quietly, informed the assembly that there was really no cause for disturbance, that at all events noth- ing could be done in this way of universal roaring, and that their only plan was to get a lawyer to draw out an indictment against the strange preachers, and bring the matter before the lawcourts; and with these words he dismissed the assembly. Such was a democratic meeting eighteen hundred years ago in one of the richest and most influential cities of ancient Greece; and no person who has had any experience of political life in this country, can doubt that the same chaotic element exists still among in- discriminate tumultuous assemblies, of men called reasonable— an element which bursts out occasionally with volcanic violence, even when the most approved engines are applied to keep it under restraint. How, indeed, can it be otherwise? "Pure democracy," as a great Scotch thinker and statesman said, "is the absurdest of all forms of government, because in it the directing and the re- straining powers are one, which is impossible."[1] Exactly so; but democratic speakers always declare that the masses of the people need no restraint; they restrain themselves; they are at once horse and rider; they have only to open their mouth, and then—VOX POPULI VOX DEI! This is the theory; but universal experience has taught that popular assemblies which pretend to govern, must in fact be governed,—governed either by their natural heads, as in the example of the Iliad, or by those occasional captains of popular movements whom their admirers call friends of the peo- ple, but whom I, marking an old Greek thing by an old Greek name, prefer to call demagogues. This observation leads us to the next two propositions of the democratic creed, containing the machinery by means of which organized popular assemblies hope to escape the danger of hasty counsels and tumultuous pro- ceedings.

[1] Sir James Mackintosh, in Life by his Son, vol. i. p. 92.

The grand modern device for making democracy innocuous is supposed to be REPRESENTATIVE GOVERNMENT. The great majority of democrats in these times, I presume, have acquired so much wisdom from the experience of centuries, as to be willing to allow that the convocation of large masses of men for purposes of government leads only to confusion. They feel that the swelling sea of human passions which rages contagiously in popular assemblies requires a breakwater,—and this breakwater they find in representation. That representative assemblies, in which the people act indirectly through their deputies, are a capital improvement on the old Greek ecclesia and the Roman *comitia*, where the most important functions of government were performed directly by an indiscriminate mass voting on the principle of universal suffrage, no one, however superficially acquainted with the history of the ancient republics, will deny; but to imagine that this device alone is sufficient to preserve the mixed constitutions of Great Britain from being swamped by a rush of democratic forces, is a great delusion. Let us consider what a House of Representatives really means, or rather, if reason is to have anything to say in the matter, ought to mean. In our House of Commons we wish to represent the intelligence, virtue, and substance of the people. We wish to bring together a certain number of wise and good men, selected on account of their wisdom and goodness, of all varieties and grades of opinion, to deliberate with a calm, cool, and reasonable survey on the difficult problems of public policy. How are we to get hold of such men? In many ways, but certainly not exclusively in the way imagined by democrats. For, according to their system, the House of Commons cannot have the four qualities which it is absolutely necessary that a deliberative assembly should possess—variety, coolness, wisdom, and independence. In fact, your democrat still practically believes in the old fallacy, that an indiscriminate multitude can deliberate; and accordingly he sends up, instead of counsellors, mere delegates, to spout forth on a larger stage the concluded deliberations of the sovereign people. Accordingly, if at any time his favourite schemes are thwarted by the caution and moderation of the aristocratic party in the House of Commons, he goes forth into the green fields, and the crowded squares, and appeals to that great court of supreme wisdom in political matters, which with him is final—the acclamation of the millions. The man who does this, however unselfish he may be in his purpose, and pure in his intent, is the declared enemy to the constitution of this country. He excites the people to turn the national senate of free and independent counselors into a congregation of mere mechanical organs, and slavish echoes of the popular voice. This, no doubt, is the most consistent of all courses on his part; but to thinking men it merely exhibits the great roaring sea of popular unreason, acting as in classical times, and not a whit the better for the patent breakwater. The fact is, that if by the representative system we are to represent only the hasty conclusions and the one-sided violent views of great masses of men indiscriminately called together at the call of ambitious demagogues and the spur of venomous faction, our imagined advantage above the ancients falls to the ground. The House of Commons becomes only a standing deputation of the mere numerical majorities of the people. Two essential qualities of such an assembly are one-sidedness and dependence. Now, two sides of a case stated with coolness and comprehensiveness are, as every court of justice knows, the indispensable condition of a sound deliberation. But in a democratic House of Commons, constituted by universal suffrage, two sides of a great public question could seldom be heard. The kind of men who can look quietly round and round a subject would never be returned. Such a man for instance, as the late George Cornwall Lewis, according to a recent wise remark of the *Times*,[1] could not possibly be chosen by purely democratic electors. They elect the man who represents most decidedly their prejudices and their passions—for no man, as Sismondi well expresses it, can delegate the wisdom which he does not possess,—and if he, on any occasion, should take a fancy to have an independent opinion, they will soon let him know that he does not understand his duty, and must be dismissed. Thus deliberation in the great council of the nation becomes a farce, democracy rides rampant in a senate of servile sworn delegates, and modest reason, baffled by the intemperance of faction, and gagged by the intolerance of the popular will, shrinks into her private shell and retires.

A few words remain to be said on the democratic method of dealing with public questions by the vote of the MAJORITY. When reasonable beings meet together for the sake of deciding any matter, they mean to decide it not by the greatest show of hands, but by the greatest show of reason. What people ought to desire is, to be governed by the wisest and best of the community, how-

[1] Leading Article, December 3, 1866.

ever few, not by the mere arithmetical majority of men having, or imagined to have, an opinion. And yet, if some thousands of men parade the streets in monster processions five miles long, declaring that they wish some change in the constitution of this country, some people are apt to think that a potent reason in favour of such a change has been produced. It may be so; but in this view politics is a matter with which reason has little to do, and a company of men becomes influential by mere physical demonstration of swarming units, like an invasion of Norway rats. But the fact is that, as Goethe has it, men are governed at bottom by three things,—by wisdom, by authority, and by appearance; and that no government which appeals finally to mere numbers can stand. This were possible only if popular assemblies generally consisted of wise men, and if, being wise, they were able to continue wise, under the exacerbations, irritations, and excesses of a popular election. But neither of these conditions squares with the fact. We must say, therefore, that an appeal to the decision of the majority is always the resource of despair; and, if there be any other method of attaining a more reasonable result in matters of social action, these methods ought first to be exhausted. Now, here the obvious method occurs of sifting the masses, so as to eliminate the worst elements and retain the best, before the arithmetical process of counting polls commences. A majority of a select or sifted mass will produce a very different result from a majority of an indiscriminate and tumultuous mass, as the conduct of all kinds of business sufficiently shows. No doubt the select body may sometimes indulge in jobbery or downright swindle; and this malversation of a clique may often be rectified by the calling in of a large and loose multitude with effect; but these are exceptional cases, and the rule is, that no business can be conducted rationally by any other than a select minority of the select. A set of cool officials, sitting round a green table and taking the vote by a majority in a matter of professional business, which all of them understand, is a very different thing from a promiscuous assembly, voting on a matter which they either have not studied at all, or contemplate only through the false medium of party glamour and the fumes of a feverish self-importance. Even in select bodies, men have often the sense to allow the business to fall into the hands of the one man who knows what he is about; and under this intelligent despotism the society prospers. But in politics, so soon as you rouse the passions of an indiscriminate multitude, such a voluntary submission to a reasonable lordship is not to be looked for. No wild beast elects the man who is to tame it. The majority, in the most perilous and critical matters, as I read history, is pretty sure to be either wrong altogether, or wrong in the excess of what it passionately feels to be right. If no method can be devised by which the fatal decisions of excited multitudes may be reversed, the doom of the commonwealth is sealed. Precisely when the storm rages loudest the pilot will be most wanted; but he will not be found. The mutinous crew in the hour of peace had cast the wise captain overboard, and in the hour of imminent shipwreck nothing remains for them but to choose for their master the most energetic of the mutineers. This has been the experience of all democracies. The natural lord was banished, who used whips occasionally; and an artificial lord is created who lashes with scorpions for a perpetuity.[1]

So much for the folly of committing the control of public affairs to the decision of a mere majority. But the injustice of it is no less flagrant. One of the great objects of all government, perhaps the principal object, is to protect the weak against the strong, that is, in many cases, to protect minorities against majorities. Now if, according to the theory of democratic politicians,

[1] "Certainly the direction of a State is more difficult than that of a ship; nevertheless, if a ship on an unknown sea had on board with a thousand ignorant persons one skilful pilot, these ignorant persons would be mad if they did not give up the helm to him, or if they pretended to regulate his navigation by the majority of suffrages. It is not the pilot who has the right to direct the ship; it is the right of all those who are running a common risk, to profit by the skill of the most skilful for the safety of the lives and property of all. The object of association is, in fact, to bring forward the greatest talent and the greatest virtue, in order to employ them for the greatest good of all. In a time of great danger, of deep feeling, the instinct by which to discover greatness is not wanting to the masses, and genius often takes its true place without trouble. But it is rare that political questions inspire the people with the sentiment of danger and the necessity of confidence at the same time. Most frequently, if we asked each individual for his opinion, we should be far from obtaining in reply the expression of the national opinion. The ignorant populace, given up almost everywhere to retrograde prejudices, will refuse to favour its own progress. The more ignorant the people are, the more are they opposed to all kinds of development; the more they are deprived of all enjoyment, and the more are they obstinately, angrily attached to their habits, as to the only possession they have left; like horses, which in a fire it is impossible to force out of a stable in flames. Count the voices in Spain and Portugal, they will be for the maintenance of the Inquisition. Count them in Russia, they will be for the despotism of the Czar. Count them everywhere, they will be for those laws, for those local customs which most require to be corrected, they will be for prejudices; it would seem that this word, appropriated to opinions adopted by vulgar minds without discussion, says enough; it suffices to teach us that the masses hold to opinions ready made, that only the small number of thinkers rise above them to consider them anew."—Sismondi, *Essays*, pp. 289, 290.

we override the whole country with a uniform system of governing by majorities, the necessary effect of this, as society is at
present constituted, is to put the middle and higher classes everywhere at the disposal of the lower and lowest classes, wherever
those classes are inspired by a common passion, and choose to
combine for political purposes. And what is this but virtually
to disfranchise the upper classes, to disfranchise, in fact, everything but workmen, and to create a despotism of one class of society, that is, of those who work mainly by their hands, over
every other class,—to prostrate quality before quantity, to annihilate all virtue, excellence, and dignity in the commonwealth before what I do not hesitate to call the brute demonstration of superior numbers? But the working classes, perhaps, are so wise,
so virtuous, and so moderate, that they will never abuse the
enormous power with which democracy is prepared to intrust them.
The man who utters one word to encourage this very natural conceit on the part of the multitude is either a flatterer or a fool.[1]
It is the most undisputed of all maxims in political science, that,
whosoever is intrusted with political power is disposed to abuse
it, and will certainly abuse it, unless a sharp-eyed precaution be
kept constantly awake. The working classes in congregation assembled, merely because they can outvote the rest of the community by seven to three, have no immunity from the common
frailties of human nature. If the oligarchy of mediæval Venice
perpetrated dark deeds at which humanity even now shudders,
the democracy of Edinburgh or London will be prepared to do
the same, when the real or imagined necessity arises. Nay more,
there is a contagious power in a multitude which naturally leads
to excesses, from which the wise caution of an oligarchy would
shrink. I believe all men have naturally a tyrannical seed in them,

[1] The Trades'-Unions have asserted in the strongest terms, and in fact their
whole organization implies, the right of every mere majority to control a
minority by the physical force. I extract from the *Pall Mall Gazette* the following utterance of one of the ringleaders of the Trades'-Union at Sheffield:—
"I maintain that all those who get their living by a trade are bound to
obey the laws of the union of the trade. After entering a trade it is not a
voluntary act of theirs to become members of that trade's union. The rebel
States wanted to secede, to be expelled from the Union, but the United States
thrashed them into obedience. So with trades' unions. It is their duty to
thrash all into submission who get their living by the trade, and who will
not obey the laws of the union without thrashing. If in so doing they
become obnoxious to Parliament law, they take the consequences. Never in
the history of the world have any men allowed a smaller number of men to
do as they liked. No man can do so unless with the consent of those around
him. There is either an eye to convey determined indignation, or a hand to
strike down the offender."

which passion, and ambition, and the exercise of power can at any time call forth into ripeness; but political and ecclesiastical majorities have been in the constant habit of cheering themselves on to deeds of injustice, thinking that they were doing God service.[1]

But we shall be told now, I presume, that all the above objections to democratic rule apply only to rude and uncultivated nations, and have no force in reference to the educated and Christianized masses of this Protestant country. To a man with his eyes open, who sees how elections are conducted, and on what grounds candidates are rejected or returned, this assertion must stand out as only one among the many commonplaces of flattery with which popular orators feed the ears of hearers whose willingness to be deluded is always much greater than their readiness to learn. As for Christianity, I have yet to learn that it has ever leavened the public morality to such an extent as to have had any appreciable effect on political affairs. We have only the other day witnessed a small act of a modern politico-military drama, in which kings, and cabinet-ministers, and people cheered themselves on to the commission of one of the most flagrant breaches of international law that history has to record. And as to internal politics, if there is a scene in the public life of this country in which the old Adam, as our theologians phrase it, revels as in a Saturnalia, it is a hotly contested election. In many cases it is hopeless to be returned without a preparation of intrigue, a machinery of corruption, and a battery of lies, with which a gentleman of high character and lofty Christian principle could have nothing to do. But let that pass. Are we not an educated people, being under a process of education at least, talking even of compulsory education: is there not great hope here? On this point, again, I have the misfortune to think that a great amount of popular delusion is abroad. People talk as if the human brain were a collection of empty boxes, which merely required to be filled with the due amount of cognitional wares in order to be well furnished. But this is not the case. The acquisition of knowledge is a slow growth, not a hasty manufacture, to be turned out in

[1] The best example of the tyrannous tendencies of all majorities is to be found in the democratic, or at least republican, constitution of the Scottish General Assembly. In that body, any independent thinker is sure to be overborne and ejected, though learning, philosophy, and piety may all plead loudly in his favour; whereas, within the pale of the aristocratic Church of England, every variety of opinion has hitherto found a generous and a considerate toleration.

measurable quantities by schoolmasters, professors, and education boards. The element of education no doubt has its value, and, in an indirect way, as I will afterwards attempt to show, may easily be made to exercise a certain political weight; but a direct knowledge-qualification for the masses would result in a portentous system of artificial cramming which would be no genuine test of real knowledge. But mere knowledge is a very small element in the qualifications of a good elector. What we want is wisdom, clear-headedness, discretion, moderation, coolness, independence, moral courage, experience of life, and position in society. Of these qualities a property qualification may afford a certain rough guarantee; a knowledge qualification will afford none. Such knowledge as might be brought up by any young man of one-and-twenty before an education board, would be a test of conceit rather than of wisdom. Young men are naturally conceited, and no amount of scholastic or academical outfit can shake the conceit out of them. A little knowledge is sometimes a useful thing, but only in the hands of a wise man; in the hands of a fool it is dangerous; and in the difficult and perplexed problems of politics, most of us are foolish enough till we are taught to reef the sails of our conceit by the severe lessons of experience. No young man, however well educated, should have anything to do with politics (for genius like that of Pitt is always exceptional), and he seldom intermeddles with it, indeed, as daily experience shows, without hurting both himself and the community to which he belongs.

In these remarks I speak from observation, but principally, also, from what I know best,—my own experience. I have devoted a great deal of time to the study of history and politics, and I have found it one of the most difficult of all practical sciences. I cannot, therefore, but feel surprised exceedingly at the readiness with which some people are prepared to blurt out the dogma that a little superficial schoolmaster's work is to be a sufficient safeguard against the obvious danger of intrusting the control of public affairs to majorities of the least thoughtful, the least instructed, and the least experienced part of the community. But in case my views on this point may be thought singular, I shall set down here the opinion of one of the best and wisest men who in modern times have given their ripe conclusions on political matters to the public, I mean M. de Sismondi:—

"Others refer us to the progress of knowledge and to the care that will be taken of the education of the people. We eagerly accept the augury; we hope that really free governments will feel that their first duty is to give to all citizens, not the power of leading and governing others, but the power of conducting and governing themselves; that they will not relax their efforts to put knowledge within the reach of all, virtue within the reach of all; that they will fix their attention on increasing the comforts of the poor, on one side to keep them from temptation, on the other to give them more leisure, and more means of exercising their intellectual faculties as well as their hands. But whatever may be their efforts, as long as there are rich and poor there will be men who cannot devote all their time to meditation and study; there will be others who can only give up to them some moments every day, and that with a body fatigued by manual labor, and a mind distracted by the cares of life.

Would it be expedient to level all conditions, to divide equally all possessions, and afterwards to maintain the equality of these divisions? But supposing that this order of things were possible, it would not do away with the necessity of manual labor, which even then must fill the greatest part of the existence of all; it would only be to forbid a life of study and meditation to every one; the nation would only be so much the less elevated, when every one was forbidden to raise himself; and yet it would not be possible to level native talent. Even in a nation equal in wealth, universal suffrage would always leave virtue, talent, and genius in the minority. Shall a more reasonable plan be followed? Shall the developement and the progress of all be favoured without disturbing the differences of rank? Then every rank of intelligence will be more advanced than it is now, but the distance between them will be always the same. It cannot be, it never will be, that a majority can be composed of superior men."—*Essays*, pp. 299, 300.

Our array of democratic propositions and aristocratic counterpropositions is now complete. What is the inference? Not, I beg you to observe, that the democratic propositions are altogether false, or the aristocratic ones altogether true; but that whatever truth, or fragment of truth, each one of the former class may contain, is liable to be met by a counter truth of the other class, which both from abstract reasoning and concrete experience possesses at least an equal guarantee. If any man supposes from any of the above statements that I appear here as an advocate either of unlimited monarchies, as in that of Prussia before 1815, or of unlimited oligarchies, as in mediæval Venice, he never was more mistaken. I have stated the case on both sides, because I believe both sides taken together contain the whole truth, either side taken by itself only half the truth, and consequently, when set up for the whole, a lie. And this is only a particular instance of one of the most deeply seated and widely acting laws of this universe of God, that the healthy condition of any organic thing only then exists when there is a well calculated balance of the opposite forces of which it is composed. All excellence is a combination of apparent incompatibles. One-sidedness, though manifesting itself generally with outward signs of force, is always fundamentally weakness, and a mistake. And this, again, is only another form of Aristotle's grand practical maxim, that virtue consists in the mean between two extremes. All extremes are wrong, and can only become right by being neutralized, as in the common case of chemical action, with their contraries. Oligarchy is wrong; democracy is wrong. They are both extremes, and both despotisms. Oligarchy is the cold, cunning, secret despotism of the few over the many; democracy is the hot, violent, overbearing despotism of the many over the few. Now with neither of these can a sound political philosophy have anything to do. The last thing, however, that parties are inclined to listen to is moderation. Whether in Church or State party-men are possessed by the notion that if their ideas had full swing evils would speedily cease, and the millennium forthwith commence. But from these popular delusions it is the very business of science to keep the mind free; it is the function of the great statesman to step in between the contending parties and teach them to accept a healthy compromise. But how difficult this just balance of power is to achieve in the political world, the history of great nations and the fate of famous constitutions sufficiently shows. It has been achieved, to my knowledge, only once on a great and successful scale, and that is in the glorious British Constitution. In this Constitution the adverse elements of monarchy, aristocracy, and democracy have, by the special favour of Divine Providence, been combined in such cunning proportions as to make it stand for a political model by the general consent of thinkers. And yet this is the Constitution which popular orators are doing all they can to persuade the working classes of this country to vilipend and to misprise! Our checks and our balances have been all a mistake. We are to look to America for a model. Political perfection consists only in the unqualified sovereignty of the numerical masses. Democracy, or the sovereignty of that largest and lowest class of people who work by their hands, over those who work with their heads, is the panacea for all political evils!

With men who at this time of day have been led so far astray, as, in the full exercise of adult intelligence, to proclaim such principles, it is not to be imagined that authorities or facts will have any greater weight than reasons. Nevertheless, for the complete statement of the question, and for the consideration of those who have not yet sold their souls to a one-eyed, unhistorical view of political science, we shall now proceed to state the opinions which the greatest political thinkers have expressed on democracy; and thereafter take a bird's-eye view of the experience of democratic government in ancient and modern times, as it has been exhibited in the public life of some of the most famous States. Of political philosophers Plato is one of the first, as well as one of the most notable; and though he was naturally of Absolutist, or, as we would phrase it, ultra-Tory principles, and with all his wisdom not free from crotchets, yet he had the sense to see that the mixed constitution of Sparta, in which, to an Athenian eye at least, the opposite elements of aristocracy, monarchy, and democracy seemed to balance each other, contained an element of safety which to the one-sided democratic organism of his own country was denied.[1] And, in fact, the political wisdom of Solon, which was afterwards overborne by democracy, consisted in establishing, or endeavouring to establish, in Athens, that just mixture of aristocratic and democratic forces, of which our present democratic agitators are so eager to rob the favoured inhabitants of this island.[2] Of a more utilitarian character than Plato, and dealing rather in hard facts than in high speculations, Aristotle, in his great political work, maintains strongly that the best constitution, at least the best which there is hope of realizing, is a mixture of oligarchy and democracy; and he insists strongly, throughout the whole fourth book, on the safety of keeping political power in the hands of the middle classes, and not allowing it to get into the hands of the lowest.[3] But the most important witness from among the Greeks, in my opinion, is Polybius, who, having lived both

---

[1] ἡ βασιλεία παρ᾽ ὑμῖν ἐξ ὧν ἔδει σύμμικτος γενομένη καὶ μέτρον ἔχουσα σωθεῖσα αὐτὴ σωτηρίας τοῖς ἄλλοις γέγονεν αἰτία. —Laws, III. 692 A. Your kingship having of necessity become compressed and limited, has itself been saved, and has become a source of safety to the rest of the community.

[2] Σόλωνα μίξαντα καλῶς τὴν πολιτείαν.—Ar. Pol. 11. 12. Solon, who wisely formed the state by combining. By the demagogic measures of Clisthenes and Pericles, the republic, however wisely constituted by Solon, declined into an abominable democracy, conducted not by the laws, but by the headstrong will of the people.—Schoemann On the Popular Assemblies of the Athenians. Cambridge, 1838, p. 17.

[3] πολιτεία μῖξις ὀλιγαρχίας καὶ δημοκρατίας.—Pol. IV. 8. The State is a mixture of oligarchy and democracy.

among Greeks and Romans, had a larger field of political induction before him than even Aristotle, and whose authority in such matters is esteemed by the best political writers as second only to that of Thucydides. Like all Greeks he carried in his heart a harshly-graven outline of the hideousness of democracy, and had arrived at the conclusion, which all sensible men now believe, that the best form of government is neither monarchy, nor aristocracy, nor democracy, but a composite form, embracing the virtues and neutralizing the evils of all the three.[1] And with profound insight he remarks that every social organism contains in its own essence the connate seeds of its own destruction, just as iron begets rust, and wood is subject to the dry-rot, which there is no possibility of preventing, except by the inoculation of a counteracting principle from within. Among the Romans, Cicero, who had ample experience of aristocracy and democracy, and of that death-struggle between them both which ended in the establishment of a military despotism, though he saw deeper into the flaws of the Roman political organism than the Greek historian, agrees with him in the general principle that a mixed government is the only safe one. He repeats the great and the terrible truth, to which a certain infatuation makes impassioned democrats and despots equally deaf, that there is no simple and unmixed form of government: *"quod non habeat iter ad finitimum quoddam malum praeceps ac lubricum,"* that is to say, the more unmixed any form of government is, the more patent and slippery does the road lie, down to the evil which ever loves to lodge next door to what is best. And to avoid this hasty descent from the pinnacle of triumph to the pit of perdition, the only safeguard is, instead of democracy, or any other simple form of government, *"illud quod conflatum fuerit ex omnibus."* So much for the ancients. Among modern writers the agreement on this point has been no less striking. The late Cornwall Lewis, whose learning was equal to his judgment, refers to Machiavel, Paruta, Blackstone, Burlamaqui, Paley, Zaccaria, Bellarmine, Filangieri, and Bentiveglio;[3] and he might have referred to a witness even stronger—the homage of admiration and envy which the British Constitution has commanded from all the peoples of modern Europe.

---

[1] δῆλον γὰρ ὡς ἄριστον μὲν ἡγητέον πολιτείαν τὴν ἐκ πάντων συνεστῶσαν.—*Polyb.* VI. 3. For it is plain that we must regard as the best constitution that which partakes of all the (these three) elements.

[2] *Republ.* I. 27. 28. That which will have been forged of all.

[3] *Methods of Observation and Reasoning in Politics*, vol. ii, p. 76.

Such is the weight of authority in this matter. Let us now look at facts. First, and most famous of course, we have Athens. Here, if anywhere, democracy, it should seem, may congratulate itself of having achieved a splendid triumph. But the case is just the reverse. As compared with Oriental slavery, indeed, such liberty was a great thing—the greatest thing, perhaps, next to Hebrew prophecy, in the ancient world; but as an experiment in constitution-making, compared with the present constitution of Great Britain, or even with the old classical constitutions of Rome and Sparta, the democracy of Athens was a splendid failure. Liberty and unfettered individualism are necessary to literature; creative genius acknowledges no fetters but those which it shapes for itself. In the enjoyment of this liberty, and with a fine physical and intellectual endowment from God, poetry, philosophy, and science, in ancient Athens, shot forth an efflorescence and fruitage of power such has been seldom equalled, and perhaps never surpassed. But this rich exhibition of intellectual force might have taken place under a limited monarchy as well as in the midst of a licentious democracy, as the names of Shakspeare and Bacon, Jeremy Taylor and Isaac Newton, loudly proclaim. The fall of Attic political liberty, in truth, dates, we may almost say, from the epoch of its greatest literary triumphs. The popular power evoked by the great struggle at Marathon and Salamis, as is wont to be the case with weak mortality in the hour of success, forthwith became rampant, and refused to acknowledge the last of those salutary checks which the aristocratic wisdom of the past had retained. The jurisdiction of the Court of the Areopagus was curtailed; and the prophetic spirit of the wise tragedian saw already in vision the brilliant dissolution of a State where cleverness without reverence, and impetuosity without restraint, could at any moment plunge the people into an ill-considered and perilous war:—

> "From Anarchy
> And slavish masterdom alike my ordinances
> Preserve my people. Cast not from your walls
> All high authority; for where no fear
> Awful remains, what mortal will be just!" [1]

But the warning was vain. The cautious counsel of Pericles was forgotten; the dazzling blackguardism of Alcibiades prevailed; the expedition to Syracuse was undertaken; and in a few years

[1] *The Furies*, by Æschylus.

Sparta trod on the neck of Athens, and the way was prepared for the golden keys and the iron hand of Philip of Macedon. The splendour of unfettered Athenian democracy conveys thus a less valuable lesson to political science than its brevity. Aristocratic Sparta prevailed, not in intellectual vivacity indeed, but in permanency of political influence. For her one hundred years of unfettered democracy Athens paid dearly with more than two thousand years of political servitude. And now that by the glorious popular uprising of 1821, the Greek people have again won for themselves an acknowledged standing-room among the nations, they have risen only to make a series of governmental blunders, of which the inherent vice of democracy is perhaps the most powerful cause. They have, indeed, had sense enough to follow the example of Sparta rather than of Athens, in preferring to be governed by one hereditary king rather than by five hundred elected counsellors; but they have failed to perceive the great truth that a hereditary monarchy can never actually prove an effective engine of good government, unless when supported by a strong aristocracy, as in England, or by a well-marshalled bureaucracy, as in Prussia. The long political history of Athens, therefore, from the unfortunate abolition of the kingship to the present hour, is only a protracted lecture on the vanity of all attempts at self-government on the part of unchecked multitudes. In the good old plan of balancing one force by another, lies the great secret of political as of dynamical equilibrium. The history of ancient Rome teaches exactly the same lesson. All the soundest social life of the Eternal City, as well as its proudest political triumphs, belong to the period when the aristocratic element was so strong as to justify Polybius in saying, that in power, though not in form, the constitution of Rome contained within itself that mixed balance of monarchic, aristocratic, and democratic forces which he admired.[1] I do not stand here as the apologist of the Roman aristocracy; a close examination might show, perhaps, that they contributed as much to the ultimate ruin of their country as the democracy; but one thing is quite certain,—democracy increased as Rome rushed to its degradation; and Julius Cæsar, according to a well-known law noticed by Plato,[2] mounted to absolute power, having commenced life in the capacity of what, in the Italian Re-

---

[1] *Hist.*, VI, 12.

[2] ὅταν περ φύηται τύραννος ἐκ προστατικῆς ῥίζης καὶ οὐκ ἄλλοθεν ἐκβλαστάνει. Then obviously whenever a despot grows up, his origin may be traced wholly to this championship, which is the stem from which he shoots. *Republic*, VIII, 565 D.

publics of the middle ages, was called a *Capitano del Popolo*.[1]
And what political lessons do these Italian Republics themselves
teach, of which, after an existence equally brief as brilliant, every
trace has long since disappeared from the map of Europe? The
great virtue of a popular government is energy; and when this
form of government conspires with happy circumstances and a
finely constituted people, an epoch of highly potentiated democracy will generally be marked by the most splendid outburst of
intellectual and artistic talent. Such was the case with mediæval
Italy, and specially with the great republic of Florence; but whosoever looks beyond the surface into that region, where the names of
Dante, Petrarch, and Boccaccio usher in the brightness of modern
literature, will find little in annals scarred with faction and soaked
in blood, to warrant any high-flown eulogium on the virtues of
democratic institutions.[2] Of more recent European republics,
Holland in the same manner has ceased to exist. With the heroic
struggle for the rights of conscience maintained by the Dutch
States against Spanish bigotry and tyranny, every man with a
heart in his bosom will warmly sympathize; but in arguing from
wars of national independence, we ought never to forget that they
really prove nothing in favour of the form of government out of
which they may have arisen or in which they may terminate.
The Prussian people, under the unlimited despotism of the great
Frederick, fought as heroically and as successfully against the
triple coalition of Russia, Austria, and France, as ever democratic
Attica did against Darius and Xerxes. When people are fighting
for their existence, it is a great man that is necessary more than

[1] "What good could come of a community in which peace and war, the
appointment and deposition of the general and officers of the army, and the
management of the public money and property, depended on the humours of
the multitude, and their leaders, elected as whim or circumstance might
determine?"—Mommsen, *History of Rome*, vol. i, p. 803—German.

[2] Of Padua, Lord Brougham says, "The government of Padua was at different times almost purely democratic, when the people so far prevailed over the
nobles as to vest the whole administration in the companies of artisans.
Nothing could exceed the levity and uncertainty of the Paduan councils so
long as this democratic influence prevailed; but it was always remarked,
that when the errors, inconsistencies, and incapacity of the popular government had brought the state within a hair's-breadth of destruction, the nobles
were looked on as the only resource, and generally interfered with effect."
—*Political Philosophy*, ch. xxiii. And to the same effect Professor Spalding:
"Within those Italian cities that had been most decidedly free, the dissensions
which had preceded their overthrow, *removing all partial privileges and all
real distinctions of rank, and in most places laying the nobles at the foot of
the third estate*, did by this very means weaken all orders of the community,
and generated that spiritless apathy with which the subjects of the Italian
principalities submitted to the rule of their despotic masters."—*Italy*, vol. ii.
p. 133.

a good constitution; and in such cases, as an ancient soldier well
remarked, an army of stags with a lion at their head, is better
than an army of lions with a stag for their general. On the internal management of the Dutch States during the period when
the name of a republic lasted, I have not made any special studies;
but if we are to trust to Sir William Temple, who had ample
means of being well informed, the government of Amsterdam,
the capital of the ruling province, in the hands of a body of a hundred senators, elected first by the people for life, and then, to
avoid popular brawls, by themselves, was a civic oligarchy rather
than a democracy.[1] But a better claim than that of Holland to be
considered as the representative of republican institutions in modern Europe may be advanced by Switzerland. In regard to this
country, the remark of Montesquieu holds good, that it is the
nature of a republic to possess only a small territory, without
which condition, indeed, it cannot exist.[2] But besides this, any
person who has political insight must see that the continuance of
this republican federation in the midst of a surrounding system
of monarchies, is owing more to its strong mountain barriers,
and the constant jealousy of France and Austria, than to any
special virtue for self-defence which its free constitutions present.
Had Switzerland stood in the same geographical relation to one
great power as it now does to two, it would long ago have been
absorbed by that power, just as Circassia has been by Russia, and
Denmark will be by Prussia. In respect of internal government,
the great Swiss writer whom we have several times quoted, while
he rejoices with a just pride in the fact that his mother country
has "sought her liberty with more or less success in *balanced
constitutions,*" does not fail to point out the warning fact that "in
Switzerland there are many republics, where the democratic principle has prevailed in all its rigour, where each intellect as well as
each will is reckoned equal, and *where universal suffrage has
stifled public opinion.*"[3] And whereas some might imagine

[1] Sir William Temple's Works, London, 1740, vol. i, p. 31.
[2] *Spirit of Laws*, VIII. 16. De Tocqueville, while he is too wise positively
to assert the impracticability of anything but a small republic, nevertheless
says:—"It may be advanced with confidence that the existence of a great
republic will always be exposed to far greater perils than that of a small
one."—Vol. i. p. 189.
[3] *Political Essays*, p. 297, where he goes on to give the details: "In the
centre of Switzerland the three little cantons of Uri, Schwitz, and Unterwalden are pure democracies; among shepherds, almost equal in fortune, as
well as in intelligence, it was not thought necessary to preserve greater
influence for opinions resulting from mere deliberation; the elections as well
as the laws, as well as all public resolutions, are carried by the votes of

that it is only among the lumpish and dull peasantry that such exhibitions take place, he tells us that "it is precisely in those republics where the constitution appears most liberal that the sovereign citizenship has most oppressed the peasants, and excited the most bitter resentment, as at Zurich, Schaffhausen, and Basle." "And everywhere in Switzerland," he adds, "the friends of progress are opposed and resisted by the democratic spirit, or the supremacy which universal suffrage gives to those who know nothing, over those who wish for the advance of true liberty." So much for Switzerland. Of the ghastly phantoms, and blood-gouted spectres of the various forms of French democracy, as they have been exhibited across the Channel, for the disturbance, and it might be hoped the instruction, of the rest of the world, during the last seventy years, one who reprobates democracy, as I do, might easily work up a panorama that might be more effective than many arguments. But I shall suppose all this done, and even leave the democratic champion, part of whose creed it is to suppose that the people never can do wrong, in the possession of the field, when he maintains that had it not been for the abuses of monarchical and aristocratical government for centuries, and the suppression of parliamentary government in France, these revolutionary excesses never could have been committed. This is all very true; though it is certainly by no means the most complimentary apology for popular atrocities to say that because the king behaved like a fool, and the noblemen like brutes, the people were pardonable in behaving like fiends. But France is no longer the favourite arsenal whence our British democrats filch their weapons. They have sense enough to see that the despotism by universal suffrage, which is the existing form of government in that country, has been as much the effect of popular excess as of aristocratic mis-

universal suffrage, by all the male inhabitants above the age of eighteen assembled in the Landsgemeine; it is really a will of their own, which the citizens of these little cantons express in these assemblies of all the people; but this will is constantly retrograde. In spite of their confederates, in spite of the clamour of Europe, they have continued the use of torture in their tribunals; they have kept up the custom of contracts to enter into the service of foreign powers; and these men, so proud and so jealous of their liberty, are the most eager to sell themselves to despots, to enable them to keep other nations in chains; every year, in short, and at every diet, they solicit their confederates to proscribe the liberty of the press. We must not suppose, however, that there are not in Uri, Schwitz, and Unterwalden, men whose more enlightened intellect, whose more elevated character, recoils from torture, trading in men, and the censorship of the press; no doubt they would form public opinion, if time were given them; but before every discussion, universal suffrage decides, by a majority, in favour of the gross ignorance of the great number, against the virtuous intelligence of some few."

government. They therefore, ever eager to juggle themselves with some new delusion, point to America as to the promised Utopia of political perfection. Here there is no king to waste the public money in a superfluous civil list, no aristocracy to goad the people by pride and oppression into periodical fits of mutiny and madness. Beyond the Atlantic, therefore, in a land remote from the hereditary encumbrances and the servile decrepitude of European States—there we must accept the pure issue. Let it be so. Nothing could give a benevolent mind greater pleasure than to learn that in any quarter of the globe, under new and favourable circumstances, swarming millions of energetic human beings had at last succeeded in governing themselves by their collective wisdom alone, without the necessity of any of those checks and bulwarks which in other civil societies had hitherto been found necessary. No man should despair of his kind; and if it should have pleased God to create a superior race of reasonable beings beyond the Atlantic, capable of solving easily social problems which have puzzled all the rest of the world, it will be our business to look on with admiration and gratitude, not with envy and detraction. But if there be any truth at all in the principles above advanced, if men, acting in political masses, are not less, but certainly more, exposed to the common weaknesses of humanity, than when acting as individuals, one thing is certain, that in order that an unchecked democracy may succeed in America, or elsewhere, it will require much more than the average amount of virtue in the mass of the people; or, in the words of Chancellor Kent, "to counteract the dangerous tendency of such combined forces as universal suffrage, frequent elections, all offices for short periods, all officers elective, and an unchecked press, and to prevent them from racking and destroying our political machines, the people must have a larger share than usual of that wisdom which is first pure, then peaceable, gentle, and easy to be entreated."[1] And if they do not possess this evangelic wisdom, then it requires no peculiar political sagacity to be able to predict that even those most cunning political machines, put together with consummate science by such men as Washington, Madison, and Hamilton, will, like so many other made constitutions, prove, in some violent crisis, only a very curious tissue of packthread and silk-twist to bind an infuriated tiger. Let us inquire, therefore, where the evidences of this peculiarly evangelic wisdom are found, and how they display themselves

[1] *The American Union.* By James Spence. London, 1861. Page 41.

in counteracting the evils which all agree are part of the dowry of a purely democratic constitution.

On entering on this part of the argument I will make two confessions: *first,* that I have never been in America; *second,* that I am most anxious to believe the best of my fellow-beings, and that one of the greatest practical errors of my life has been in thinking too well of persons who have turned out to be either knaves or fools. I have, accordingly, sought in all quarters for witnesses on which I might found the belief that the Americans are a superior type of human beings; but I have failed to find them. I was directed by Mr. Bright to study De Tocqueville, which I did with the utmost care, but found there chiefly the most damning evidence against the system which the eloquent Manchester Gracchus so potently admires. By the much-vaunted American prosperity I am nothing moved. It is only material prosperity at the best; and this sort of advancement, in all stages of society, is as often connected with debasing as with elevating influences. That a young and vigorous offshoot of Great Britain, in a new country, with plenty of room, no dangerous neighbours,[1] a great demand for labour, and a constant importation of fresh labourers, should increase marvellously in those good things which political economists tabulate with pride, but which Plato, Aristotle, and the Apostle Paul estimate at their true value, is only natural, and need cause no particular outcry. "Let none admire," says Milton, "that riches grow in hell." Instead of boasting about this amazing material prosperity, it would be well if both they and we bore habitually in mind the great truth which Channing told them, that noble growths are slow, and that the timbers of a stout man-of-war are made of oak, not of poplar.[2] But they have more than material advantages, we are told; they are a better educated people; the intelligence of the masses in that part of the world is something wonderful. I am glad to believe that the machinery of popular education in many of the States is far superior to what yet exists in our island, and might furnish a model after which even the best-educated parts of Scotland might be improved. But I have already stated the grave consideration that schools can furnish only the smallest part of the education necessary to make an intelligent citizen; and we must loudly proclaim, moreover, that

---

[1] "In the New World man has no other enemy than himself."—De Tocqueville. Yes; but that is the most dangerous of all. The old Adam is a terrible monster, made up of a tiger, a fox, a viper, and an ass.
[2] Spence, *The American Union,* p. 24.

a clever fellow is by no means synonymous with a good character.[1]
An American writer observes: "Never had country better laws
than ours; *but the true trouble is that THE PEOPLE ARE COR-
RUPT.* The maxim of 'ALL'S FAIR IN POLITICS,' operating
on a *population relaxed by an overwhelming prosperity, and
cursed with a preternatural sharpness, has debauched the morality
of the whole population. So long as the rulers only of a people
are dishonest, liberty is safe; but what is to become of a nation, the
people of which are corrupt?"* [2] It would appear, therefore, that,
in spite of their smartness and cleverness, the people are not
morally superior to the democracy which has ruled in other countries. It does not appear that the American people, in their
political capacity, are free from a single vice which stained the
most corrupt democracy of ancient Rome, or of mediæval Florence.
The great original sin of all democracy, the assumed right of the
majority to dictate to the minority, has developed itself there in
the most gigantic form; and not always, we must add, a despotism
of the real majority, but, as frequently happens, a despotism and
terrorism of the violent, the passionate, and the unscrupulous,
though a minority, over the majority of the moderate, cool, and
reasonable part of the community. This is so notorious that it is
hardly necessary to adduce proofs. De Tocqueville mentions particularly the case of the drinking habits of Philadelphia:—

"Some one observed to me one day, in Philadelphia, that almost all
crimes in America are caused by the abuse of intoxicating liquors, which
the lower classes can procure in great abundance, from their excessive
cheapness. 'How comes it,' said I, 'that you do not put a duty upon
brandy?' 'Our legislators,' rejoined my informant, 'have frequently
thought of this expedient; but the task of putting it in operation is a
difficult one; a revolt might be apprehended; and *the members who should
vote for a law of this kind would be sure of losing their seats.'* 'Whence
I am to infer,' replied I, 'that the drinking population constitutes the
majority in your country, and that temperance is somewhat unpopular.'" [3]

Even more instructive is the following demonstration on the
part of the tyrannical majority at Baltimore in 1812, occasioned

[1] The thorough-going advocates of all sorts of moral and intellectual skepticism, and unblushing advocates of the theory that all right is convention,
and all might is right, the well-known sophists, whom, in spite of Mr. Grote,
I cannot force myself to admire, were all very clever fellows—δεινοί as
Plato has it.
[2] Quoted by Spence, p. 71.
[3] *Democracy in America.* By Alexis de Tocqueville. London, 1838. Vol. ii.
p. 46.

by the circumstance that a newspaper editor had had the misfortune to entertain opinions contrary to those of the masses, and had also the moral courage to express them:—

"A striking instance of the excesses which may be occasioned by the despotism of the majority occurred at Baltimore in the year 1812. At that time the war was very popular in Baltimore. A journal which had taken the other side of the question excited the indignation of the inhabitants by its opposition. The populace assembled, broke the printing-presses, and attacked the houses of the newspaper editors. The militia was called out, but no one obeyed the call; and the only means of saving the poor wretches who were threatened by the frenzy of the mob, was to throw them into prison as common malefactors. But even this precaution was ineffectual; the mob collected again during the night; the magistrates again made a vain attempt to call out the militia; the prison was forced, one of the newspaper editors was killed upon the spot, and the others were left for dead; the guilty parties were acquitted by the jury when they were brought to trial.

I said one day to an inhabitant of Pennsylvania, 'Be so good as to explain to me how it happens, that in a State founded by Quakers, and celebrated for its toleration, freed blacks are not allowed to exercise civil rights. They pay the taxes; is it not fair that they should have a vote?'

'You insult us,' replied my informant, 'if you imagine that our legislators could have committed so gross an act of injustice and intolerance.'

'What, then, the blacks possess the right of voting in this country?'

'Without the smallest doubt.'

'How comes it, then, that at the polling-booth this morning I did not perceive a single negro in the whole meeting?'

'This is not the fault of the law: the negroes have an undisputed right of voting; but they voluntarily abstain from making their appearance.'

'A very pretty piece of modesty on their parts;' rejoined I.

'Why, the truth is that they are not disinclined to vote, but they are afraid of being maltreated; in this country the law is sometimes unable to maintain its authority, without the support of the majority. But in this case the majority entertains very strong prejudices against the blacks, and the magistrates are unable to protect them in the exercise of their legal privileges.'

'What, then, the majority claims the right not only of making the laws, but of breaking the laws it has made?' " [1]

Then he sums up these and other instances with the emphatic sentence, "Despotism enslaves the body; democracy enslaves the soul." [2] It is plain, therefore, that the brute principle of governing by a majority, in America as elsewhere, by the simple law of dynamical forces, has produced its necessary result—the pros-

[1] De Tocqueville, vol. ii. p. 87.
[2] *Ibid.*, p. 91.

tration of all real liberty, and the establishment of a moral, sometimes a purely physical, despotism.

Closely connected with the despotic character of the popular will in America, is the crude delight with which the people swallow the grossest flattery, and their puerile sensibility to blame; and in this respect the many-headed blatant beast in the extreme West, whom we are now called on to fall down and worship, is not a whit inferior to the one-headed monsters of whom we read in the annals of Oriental despotism. In ancient Greece, also, so glaring was the servility to which democracy had reduced the individual mind, that Socrates, in one of the most effective Dialogues of Plato, does not hesitate to define public speaking as a principal branch of the great art of flattery, of which gastronomy and confectionery are well-known subsidiary branches.[1]   On this subject the impartial De Tocqueville is no less distinct :—

"Works have been published in the proudest nations of the Old World, expressly intended to censure the vices and deride the follies of the times: Labruyere inhabited the palace of Louis XIV when he composed his chapter upon the Great, and Molière criticised the courtiers in the very pieces which were acted before the Court.   But the ruling power in the United States is not to be made game of; the smallest reproach irritates its sensibility, and the slightest joke which has any foundation in truth renders it indignant; from the style of its language to the more solid virtues of its character, everything must be made the subject of encomium.   No writer, whatever be his eminence, can escape from this tribute of adulation to his fellow citizens.   The majority lives in the perpetual practice of self-applause."[2]

And what kind of government, let me ask, is actually produced by this many-headed despot, living in the constant exercise of insolent coercion, and fed on the dainty diet of self-applause? Is it free from intrigue and cabal, from bribery and corruption, from parliamentary juggle and swindle of all sorts? Quite the contrary. One cannot look even superficially into the foul atmosphere of political life in that country, without becoming painfully aware of a degree of gross corruption and shameless unscrupulousness, to which the worst revelations of our bribery-committees cannot afford a parallel. That faction, intrigue, and corruption are the natural defects of elective government is one of the most elementary truths in political science; but "when the head of the

---

[1] τέχνη κολακική.   "Art of flattery."   Plato, *Gorgias*, 463 A.
[2] De Tocqueville, vol. ii. p. 92.

State can be re-elected, these evils rise to a great height, and compromise the very existence of a country.''[1] Whoever denies that such intrigue and corruption are rife in America, must be struck with a blindness which scarcely a miracle could cure. The Americans are fond of slang; and so they have added not a few phrases to the English language, as used in that part of the world, by which various species of political iniquity are expressed. One of these slang words is ''log-rolling,'' the meaning of which is thus explained by Mr. Spence:—

"The title of the Morrill Tariff commences, 'An Act, to provide for the payment of outstanding treasury notes, to authorize a loan,' etc., etc. How come matters, so entirely distinct, to be mixed with the details of a tariff, of necessity complex enough when alone? Because the bill is a specimen of that original species of American legislation known as 'log-rolling.' The meaning of the phrase is this,—'You help to roll my log and I'll help to roll yours.' When two logs are put into one bill, there are, at once, two classes interested in its success. Each may, and frequently does, exceedingly dislike his friend's log; but this is a tame feeling, as compared with interest in his own. The one is a question of his own private advantage, whilst the other concerns nothing beyond the mere public. There is, however, a difficulty in the way of this contrivance, if too much time be afforded. Some one who is not of the compact, may be officious enough to separate the logs; or their united strength may be doubtful against a strong opposition, if there be time for thorough investigation. It follows that a 'log-rolling' bill has many more chances of getting through, by 'rushing' it. This means, to keep it back till the last few days of the session, and then, amidst a crowd of other measures, by dint of vehemence, under cover of confusion, and with the powerful aid of the 'lobby,' to rush it through. This bill was rushed. Its fate was very doubtful; there was a very strong opposition. But there was the other log in it. If rejected, it was now too late to bring in a fresh measure, to provide for the treasury notes, and the loan, and thus many were driven to support it, in order to avert the injury of stopping the wheels of government."[2]

Then as to bribery. The worst kind of pecuniary corruption prevails in America. In this country, election agents bribe the lowest classes of the populace; in America honorable members are paid openly for their votes, and their price is known.

"A very able lobby agent, who has been in the business many years, has given us an inkling of the mode of procedure. 'When we get to Albany,' said he, 'we make out our lists, and, after studying them and comparing notes, we *classify* members, and make an estimate of what it is going to

[1] De Tocqueville, vol. i. p. 155.
[2] *The American Union*, p. 187.

cost to get our bills through. We find out about how much each man expects, and who is running him. Then we arrange the thing in New York
with certain people, whose consent is necessary. The price for a vote
ranges from fifty dollars to five hundred, unless it is that of a chairman of
a committee. *He* wants more, because he has to appear on the record as
originating the measure.'

It was probably one of these originating gentlemen who could explain
the testimony given recently in an Albany corruption case by a lady who
proved herself a true helpmeet to her husband. She testified that a lobby
agent called at her house one Sunday afternoon, when there was 'some conversation' respecting the accused Senator, which the court 'ruled out.' She
continued thus: 'The next morning I put 2500 dols. in greenbacks into a
yellow envelope, and gave it to my only son, eleven years old. The boy
got into the wagon with his father. *I never saw the money again.*'

If there is in this world a man who can be truly said to *know* anything,
Mr. Thurlow Weed knows the Legislature of the State of New York. His
testimony respecting the corruption in that Legislature, as given in the
Daily Times, a few months ago, is as follows:—

'Formerly the *suspicion* of corruption in a member would have put
him "into Coventry," while *knowledge* of such an offence would have
insured the expulsion of the offender. Now "bribery and corruption"
prevail to an extent greater than existed in the worst days of the Parliament of England, where, happily for England, the practice has been re-
formed, as it must be here, or corruption will undermine the government.
No measure, however meritorious, escapes the attention of "strikers."
Venal members openly solicit appointment on paying committees. In the
better days of legislation, when no unlawful motive existed, it was considered *indelicate* in a member to indicate to the Speaker any preference
about committees. The evil has been growing, each year being worse than
the preceding, until reform is sternly demanded. Could the secret history
of the present Legislature be exposed to the public gaze, popular indignation would be awakened to a degree heretofore unknown. In the Assembly
everything was struck at. Not even a religious charity found exemption.
The sources of rapacious corruption were the Assembly Railroad Committee, and the Committee on Cities and Villages. I say this upon reliable
authority, to correct the *Tribune* and *Times,* in both of which journals
this Legislature is commended for its integrity. That there were honest
and honorable members in both houses, by whose integrity and firmness
much bad legislation was arrested, is true. The Senate, fortunately, presents an inflexible majority of upright members; while in the House, the
Ring was formidable enough to put through whatever paid or promised
to pay liberally, in defiance and derision of the efforts of an honest
minority.' " [1]

If, after revelations of this kind, men who certainly possess
eloquence, and who ought to possess intelligence, shall still continue to perambulate the country, exciting discontent against our

[1] *North American Review* for October 1866, p. 457.

noble Constitution, and holding up this base and blushless transatlantic democracy as a model for our imitation, I can only believe
that both they and their listeners are already become the living
proofs of the grim old adage—*Quos Deus vult perdere,* etc.:
WHOM GOD MEANS TO DESTROY HE FIRST MAKES MAD.

A volume would not exhaust the foul catalogue of social vices
and corruptions which have sprung from the American democracy
as from their natural hotbed. To me the degradation of the moral
character of the individuals who are the instruments of a democratic system is a much more sad consideration than the system
itself. But where every man is a politician, and politics is made
up of violence, intrigue, and venality, the only way to escape the
taint is to retire from the contagious atmosphere altogether. And
this is exactly what the best men, by a natural instinct of self-
conservation, do in modern America, so they did also in ancient
Attica.[1] Politics, we are told, beyond the Atlantic, are neglected
by men of high talent and character. They cease to be matter of
independent and manly opinion; they degenerate into a trade. Men
of wealth, and literary taste, and commercial standing, are outrun
by the large class of office-holders who make a trade of Politics.
The whole power of election practically passes into the hands of a
knot of professional politicians, composed of briefless barristers,
physicians without patients, of schemers and place-hunters, who
devote themselves to the service of the party in order to be elected
to some little salaried place.[2] Even when left free from the spur
of the ambitious demagogue, the magic oil of the flatterer, and the
glamour of the political dreamer, the people have, for the most
part, neither the will nor the power to find out the best men to
lead them. I do not say that, individually, they might not be able
to put their finger on the men of whose character and talents they
are most proud; but when acting in masses under the boiling fever

[1] De Tocqueville (ii. 2-10), stating it is a general rule that in the United
States the most talented individuals are rarely placed at the head of affairs,
notes an exception to this in the following remarkable words:—"In dangerous times, genius no longer abstains from presenting itself in the arena;
and the people, alarmed by the perils of their situation, *bury their envious
passions in a short oblivion.*" Plato says that wise men will seek public
life, not as a good thing, but as a necessary duty (*Rep.* 450 D); but in a
field where power, and place, and influence are the reward, the most ambitious,
the most unscrupulous, and the most selfish men will generally be more eager
in the race. These are the men who are not so apt to inquire whether an
occupation be noble or necessary, as whether it be profitable. And even their
wives and daughters sometimes may have more to say in the matter than
their own ambition or their itch for Parliamentary manipulation.
[2] Spence, *The American Union,* p. 35.

of political or ecclesiastical excitement, there is a great chance
that they will elect the most violent or the most cunning, rather
than the most wise and virtuous man.[1] Besides, we must bear in
mind that there is a seed of evil in the human heart, apt to shoot
up into diabolical vices at all times, but specially worked and
manured into rankness by the machinery of democracy. One of
the ugliest and most truly diabolical feelings in the breast of man
—ENVY—grows up in America, as in all democracies, as naturally
and necessarily as goose-foot on a dunghill. Hear on this point
the great French thinker :—

"Moreover, the democracy is not only deficient in that soundness of
judgment which is necessary to select men really deserving of its confidence, but it has neither the desire nor the inclination to find them out.
It cannot be denied that democratic institutions have a very strong tendency to promote the feeling of *envy* in the human heart; not so much
because they afford to every one the means of rising to the level of any
of his fellow-citizens, as because those means perpetually disappoint the
persons who employ them. Democratic institutions awaken and foster a
passion for equality which they can never entirely satisfy. This complete
equality eludes the grasp of the people at the very moment at which it
thinks to hold it fast, and 'flies,' as Pascal says, 'with eternal flight;' the
people is excited in the pursuit of an advantage, which is the more precious
because it is not sufficiently remote to be unknown, or sufficiently near
to be enjoyed. The lower orders are agitated by the chance of success,
they are irritated by its uncertainty; and they pass from the enthusiasm
of pursuit to the exhaustion of ill-success, and lastly to the acrimony of
disappointment. Whatever transcends their own limits appears to be an
obstacle to their desires, and there is no kind of superiority, however
legitimate it may be, which is not irksome in their sight."[2]

These facts might be sufficient to brush the paint from the fair
transatlantic harlot who has been set up for us to worship—after
an old French model—as the goddess of political reason. But the
damning exposure of the system of government in the city of New
York, which appeared in a number of the influential American
Quarterly above quoted, can scarcely be passed over in silence.
It appears, from that article—an article based on the most indis-

---

[1] This is just the doctrine of moral philosophy which the advocates of
democracy constantly forget. How is it that the morality and the reason of
all masses of men often produce results of which the individuals comprising
the mass would be ashamed? There are three virtues which the people,
acting in masses, never have practised—justice, gratitude, and mercy ; and
yet the persons constituting the masses may often be in nowise destitute of
these virtues. How is this?

[2] De Tocqueville, vol. ii, pp. 4, 5.

putable public documents, and which no American durst have published had it not been desperately true—that the management of the affairs of that great and prosperous city has fallen into the hands literally of a gang of thieves, and that the State Government in Albany is not much better. The twenty-four councillors, who are handsomely paid for the privilege of stealing from the public purse, are composed principally of men under thirty, belonging to what in New York is called the "ruling class," consisting of "butchers' boys who have got into politics, bar-keepers who have taken a leading part in primary ward-meetings, and young fellows who hang about engine-houses and billiard-rooms." By these four-and-twenty choice senators of a democratic constituency, elected by universal suffrage, the municipal business of New York is conducted on the principle of, in the first place, devising measures the passing of which will gratify large bodies of voters, and create the greatest expenditure of public money, and then "rushing it" through by the votes of the gang, who not only form a constant majority of three-fourths, but are dexterous masters of various ingenious and effective methods of preventing the attendance of the half-dozen honest men who may happen to be in the council, and who might sometimes be able to stop the progress of some unblushing job. Even the vile obscenities recorded in the pages of Suetonius and Petronius, are to an uncorrupted mind less revolting than the brazen rascality and staring selfishness which is the soul of the municipal administration of New York. The article must be read and studied by all who would have any adequate conception of the gross profligacy and stony heartlessness which universal suffrage has elevated into the seat of magisterial authority in that city. But for the sake of those who do not possess the book, one or two extracts will vividly explain the manner of conducting civic business in the municipal pandemonium:—

"The most usual manner of stealing is to receive money for awarding or procuring contracts, appointments, donations, or increase of salaries, which money, of course, the favoured person gets back, if he can, from the public treasury; and he usually can. The President of the Board of Health, last spring, when New York was threatened with the cholera, had occasion to remonstrate with a person who held the contract for removing dead animals from the streets, and threatened him with the breaking of the contract if its conditions were not better complied with. 'That would be rather hard, Mr. Schultz,' replied the man, 'for that contract cost me 60,000 dols.' And well it might; for the city pays 25,000 dols. a year for getting rid of a commodity every pound of which ought to yield the city a revenue. A dead horse, worth twenty dollars, the city pays for having carted off to where it can be conveniently converted into twenty dollars. Another contractor receives 21,000 dollars a year for removing night soil, which could be sold for enough to pay the cost of its removal. By various extra charges, the holders of this contract have continued to swell their gains incredibly. Mr. Jackson Schultz, the energetic and capable President of the Board of Health, has recently published his conviction, that the 'total swindle under this contract is 111,000 dols.,' and we have had the advantage of hearing him demonstrate the fact. The story, however, is too long for our very limited space.

Does any one need evidence that the men who award such contracts, in the teeth of opposition and elucidation, receive a large share of the plunder? The fact is as certain as though ten witnesses swore to having seen the money to them in hand paid. Three years ago a contract was awarded for sweeping the streets for ten years, at 495,000 dols. a year. Since the accession to power of the New Board of Health, responsible men have handed in a written offer to buy the remainder of the contract for a quarter of a million dollars, i.e., to clean the city for seven years at 495,000 dols. a year, and give the city a quarter of a million dollars for the privilege. There are those about the city offices who know, or think they know, how the plunder of this contract is divided. We believe we are not violating any confidence, expressed or implied, when we say, that it is the conviction of the Board of Health that 100,000 dols. per annum of the proceeds of this contract are divided among certain politicians; that a certain lawyer, who engineered the project, and stands ready to defend it, receives a salary of 25,000 dols. per annum as 'counsel to the contract;' and that the men in whose name the contract is held are 'dummies,' who get 6,000 dols. a year for the use of their names and for their labor in superintending the work. The contract is further burdened with the support of several hundred cripples, old men, and idle men, all of whom are voters, who are put in the street cleaning force by Aldermen and Councilmen who want their votes and the votes of their relatives, thus kindly relieved of maintaining aged grandfathers, lame uncles, and lazy good-for-nothings. These statements, we are aware, cannot be proved. Such compacts are not trusted to paper; and a witness driven to bay can always balk his assailant by refusing to criminate himself. The reader therefore may decline to believe these details. One thing remains, and is certain, that the working men of New York are annually plundered of two hundred thousand dollars per annum by this single contract." [1]

Of the iniquitous system of selling public offices, reminding us of well-known facts of the worst days of the Roman Empire, the following contains a specimen:—

"It was recently proved, in the presence of the Governor of the State, that the appointment to the office of Corporation Attorney was sold to one incumbent for the round sum of 10,000 dollars. This is bad enough,

[1] *North American Review*, pp. 433-435.

but worse remains to be told. Sworn testimony (from thirty-six witnesses) taken by a committee of investigation, establishes the appalling fact, that appointments to places in the public schools are systematically sold in some of the wards,—the wards where the public schools are almost the sole civilizing power, and where it is of unspeakable importance that the schools should be in the hands of the best men and women. One young lady, who had just buried her father and had a helpless mother to support, applied for a situation as teacher, and was told, as usual, that she must pay for it. She replied that she could not raise the sum demanded, the funeral expenses having exhausted the family store. She was then informed that she could pay 'the tax' in instalments. Another poor girl came on the witness-stand on crutches, and testified that she had paid 75 dollars for a situation of 300 dollars a year. Another lady went to a member of the Ring, and told him, with tears, that she saw no way of procuring the sum required, nor even of saving it from the slender salary of the place. The man was moved by her anguish, took compassion upon her, and said he would remit *his share* of 'the tax.' It was shown, too, that the agent of all this foul iniquity was no other than the principal of one of the schools. It was he who received and paid over the money wrung from the terror and necessities of underpaid and overworked teachers. We learn from the report of the committee that the Ring in this ward was originally formed for the express purpose of giving the situation in a new and handsome school 'to the highest bidder'; and, as the opening of the new school involved the discharge of a small number of teachers employed in the old schools, the Ring had both the fear and the ambition of the teachers to work upon. 'There was a perfect reign of terror in the ward," says the report of the investigating committee. 'The agent performed his duty with alacrity, and with a heartlessness worthy of the employers. It appears that he not only summoned the teachers to come to him, but that he called on their parents and friends as to the amount they should pay for their appointments—the sums varying from 50 to 600 dollars, according to the position sought.'

And who were the Ring that perpetrated this infamy? They were a majority of the trustees elected by the people, and the School Commissioner elected by the people,—six poor creatures, selected from the grog-shop and the wharf, and intrusted with the most sacred interest of a republic, the education of its children. It was known before that in some of the wards the school trustees were drunkards; it was known before that little children were piled up, like flower-pots in a greenhouse, in small, ill-ventilated rooms; but no one supposed, before this investigation in 1864, that men could be elected to office who were capable of such revolting meanness as this."

Then to show how little the ballot-box and other cunning inventions of democratic machinery are able to keep out the devil, in the shape of the omnipotent dollar, take the following statement:—

---

[1] *North American Review*, pp. 437, 438.

"At the present time, as we are informed, by one whose opportunities of knowledge are unequalled, all the political concerns of the city are controlled by about seven men,—heads of city departments and others. In most of the wards, a nomination to office by the party which is ludicrously styled Democratic insures an election by the people: and it is these seven men who work the machinery by which Democratic nominations are ground out. They are the power behind the ballot-box, greater than the ballot-box itself. Candidates for Congress, for the State Legislature, for the numerous boards of city legislators, must pass the ordeal of their inspection, and pay their price, before their names can go upon the 'slate;' and such is the absoluteness of their power over ignorant voters, that they have caused to be elected to Congress by Irish votes a man who, as editor of a 'Know-Nothing' newspaper, had been employed for seven years in vilifying Irishmen and their religion. They have taken up a man who commanded one of the companies of artillery that marched from the field of Bull Run because their 'time was up,' and, while the whole civilized world was pointing at him the finger of scorn, elected him to one of the most lucrative offices in the United States. Of late years, these lords of the town have had the deep cunning to give a few of their best appointments and several minor offices to Republicans, as part of their system of preventing investigation. This was a master stroke. Most of the publishers of newspapers were already bribed to silence by the Corporation advertising, and all the reporters were hired not to report anything disagreeable by the annual gift of two hundred dollars." [1]

Let us not suppose that I state these facts as all the truth about America. No man admires more than I do the enterprise, vigour, and active talent which that people have displayed on many fields. But what I am now talking of is their political system, and the moral debasement which it entails on a naturally noble people. I have no pleasure in exposing their faults, but rather great pain. What I say I say in defence of our mixed constitution, and to expose the mischievous error of those who delude the ignorant and ill-informed masses in this country, by exhibiting universal suffrage as the grand panacea for all political evils. I am willing to allow as much excellence and efficiency in American democracy as can be proved. But the shield is not all gold. I have turned round the copper side. Let those who are capable of judging judge.

The subject of this lecture does not absolutely require me to say anything about the schemes of Parliamentary reform at pres-

---

[1] *North American Review*, p. 449. In reference to the case of New York, to those who say that it is an exceptional case, my answer is *1st*, That in many of our large cities there is a large amount of the same class of people which constitutes the lowest class in that city; and *2nd*, that the case of New York is a fair instance of what universal suffrage on American ground and under American influence can do for good government.

ent being agitated in this country. Nevertheless, it would be affectation to pretend that what I have brought forward in reference to the vices of democratic government has no reference to the present movement. On the contrary, nothing could have induced me to expose these hideous details of social corruption, had I not seen with open eyes that not a few of my countrymen are on the point of rushing into a course, which, unless wisely checked, must infallibly end in a similar ruin. I do not say that the majority of the working classes, any more than the learned and eloquent gentleman, the late Lord Advocate of the Whig Government, are democrats in principle, and mean seriously to do anything that will seriously disturb the fine social balance of our mixed constitution; but from my position as a thinking man, uninfluenced by the movements of parties, I can distinctly discern that they are being borne along by a current which they will not long be able to control, that they have been submitting to a dictation which they ought to have scorned, and that they are using levers with which they will shake the foundations of the house in which they dwell. It is because the proposed Reform Bills of the most recent epoch of our legislation are democratic, and purely democratic, in their tendency, that as a student of history and a friend of reason, I have from the beginning decidedly opposed them. Let no man imagine, however, that I am opposed to the recent Reform Bills, because they propose to give a large increase of electoral power to the working classes. I have not the slightest objection to the working classes. Many of them are doubtless more intelligent, and more trustworthy, in a political capacity, than some classes of those immediately above them in the social scale. But what I object to is the principle on which it is proposed to give these classes additional votes; the principle of representing numbers alone, and determining all public questions in the last resort by the votes of the majority. This is the soul of the democratic despotism, and the rule of unreason, the iniquity of which it has been the object of the present lecture to establish. Rather than make a single movement towards disturbing the balance of our mixed constitution, proceeding on a principle so utterly false, and of which it is impossible to limit the operation within any bounds short of manhood suffrage, I am content that we should have no Reform Bill at all. To a person, indeed, like myself, looking on the whole matter merely as a man and a citizen, it showed like a madness from the beginning to talk of another Reform Bill at all, so closely on the back of the sweeping measure of 1832. To some people, indeed, that Reform Bill, of which the consequences have in the main been salutary, forms the principal argument in favour of another dose of the same Whig medicine. Never was popular logic more at fault. I have heard of a patient who, having benefited by a prescription to take six drops of a strong medicine per day, took a bottle, and killed himself. We constantly see people in Scotland who, having made themselves comfortable by taking a tumbler of toddy, make fools of themselves by taking three, and beasts of themselves by taking six. The men who brought in the great Reform Bill of 1832 declared that it was to be a final measure; and they were wise. A final measure it certainly ought to have been *in that direction*. Any other reform for the same purpose as that, viz., for the curtailment of aristocratic influence, would certainly not be wanted; and in point of fact, is not wanted. The whole history of this country shows that the power of the monarchic and aristocratic elements in our constitution has been step by step diminishing. According to all rational calculation, what we require now is not an increase of democratic force, but rather some regulative and counteracting principle to prevent its abuse. The whole course of our legislation since the Reform Bill, whether in the hands of Whigs or Tories, has been by the people, and for the people; and among the people, no class at the present moment receives a larger amount of parliamentary and public consideration than the working classes. No class, by the change in the value of money, and other causes, has been rising more rapidly into social weight and significance. If I were to judge by what I see and read, they are in much greater danger of being spoiled by those who flatter them, than of being oppressed by those who don't represent them. In point of number and talent they have as many representatives in the House of Commons as any other class. Our House of Commons is already as democratic as it can be made, without destroying the just influence of the middle and upper classes. Our system of election is already too democratic in many respects to afford any rational guarantee for the return of members to the great National Council who possess the essential requisites of large views and independent character. I see manifest signs in various places, of the democratic habit of degrading a national councillor into a local deputy, of sending up a partisan instead of a thinker, or preferring the spokesman of a faction to the advocate of a people. I see men of high character and intelligence rudely called to account, re-

proached, slandered, and dismissed, merely because they did their
duty in the House of Parliamentary deliberation with more than
common intelligence, independence, and courage. And, what is
worse, I see men afraid to speak the truth, and willing to set their
names to measures of which they do not approve, merely to tide
over the moment, to "settle the question," and to stop the mouth of
dangerous declaimers. Is this not democracy? And we are to have
more of it, forsooth! If a Reform Bill, on American principles,
be carried in this country, one result of it I can predict with
perfect certainty, that it will not improve the character of our
national councillors. We shall have fewer of the rare and useful
class of cool thinkers, more of the speaking trumpets of local faction, the standard-bearers of popular passion, and the vendors of
speculative crotchets. I say therefore, again, much rather no
Reform Bill at all than one that shall acknowledge no principle
other than that which has produced the greatest of all social tyran-
nies in America. But was not the Reform Bill of 1832 founded
on that very principle of government by a majority, which is now
denounced as democratic? Unquestionably it was, to a certain extent; but it was not therefore a good principle for all Bills, because it did no harm—(if indeed it did no harm)—in that Bill.
That Bill placed power in the hands of the middle classes,—the
body which, as the medium between the upper and lower social
extremes, Aristotle declared to be safest.[1] The majority constituted by it was a majority of the select, if not of the best, at least of
those who, as large experience has proved, can be most safely intrusted with political power. The majority now proposed to be
established may form a majority of the lower and sub-middle
classes against the middle and upper classes; and there lies the
fault. The first care of a wise Reform Bill at the present crisis,
should be not to disfranchise the natural civic aristocracy of the
country in favor of the democracy. It is a law of God which cannot be contravened, that the high should rule the low; and that
civil government should not be thrown into the hands of those
who, by nature and the unchangeable constitution of things, are
least capable of governing. Do I then mean to treat the working
classes as serfs,—to give them no voice in what concerns their own
life and liberty, to declare them for ever incapable of social man-

[1] ὅπου δὲ τὸ τῶν μέσων ὑπερτείνει πλῆθος, ἐνταῦθ' ἐνδέχεται πολιτείαν εἶναι μόνιμον.—
Pol. IV, 12. "Then only can the government be stable, when the middle class
exceeds one or both the others."

hood? Not at all. I do not grudge them representation; I only refuse them domination. If a Reform Bill must be brought in to
"settle the question," to allay some real and much imaginary discontent, and to stifle the demagogues (though this will never be
possible), let us have a Reform Bill which, instead of crouching to
John Bright, and borrowing stale formulas of French liberty-
mongers, shall distinctly and decidedly denounce the insufficiency
of the democratic principle, and give us some reasonable guarantee for the preservation both of our civic and of our family aristocracy. Let us show the world that our British brain is capable
of containing more than one idea at a time, and that we are not
to be clamoured out of our common sense or cheated of our historic memories by the silly admiration of an ambitious theory.
Let us give the working classes votes, that is to say, more votes
than they have now,—for their actual influence is already considerable; but let us represent other things besides hands and labour.
Every wise politician will agree with Aristotle's doctrine, that it
is politic to give as many persons as possible some share in the
government of the country, because there are always some persons
who will imagine that, being excluded from political influence, they
are oppressed, and there will always be another class of persons
eager to rise into importance by fanning this feeling into a flame.
It may be true, moreover, that there is a certain virtue of moral
and intellectual training in the exercise of the franchise that ought
not to be overlooked. Perhaps, also, as Dr. Paley said, the discussion of political questions over a mug of beer in a village pot-
house may save from worse recreations. This is a view of the
matter, indeed, to which individually I attach little or no weight,
because my observation seems to teach me that politics is a trade
which, generally speaking, does more to debase than to elevate
those who have much to do with it; and I cannot see how entering
with keen interest into all the selfish details of political partisan-
ship should contribute anything towards making a man more
intelligent, more virtuous, or more happy. I could point out to
the working classes many more rational ways of spending their
idle hours than in blowing storms in some civic or ecclesiastical
tea-kettle. But if they will have it otherwise, let it be; only let
me have a vote as well as you; let learning be represented as well
as labour; do not, while you claim political influence for yourselves, insist on having it in such a way as will virtually disfranchise all other classes of the community, and give us a House of

Commons dictated by mere numbers. In one word, save us from America!

In accordance with all that has been above argued, the three points to be kept before the eye of the statesman in the preparation of a British Reform Bill for the year 1867 should be—(1) The securing of an adequate representation to the working classes; (2) A special representation for the civic, moral, and intellectual aristocracy of the people; (3) The provision of such a variety of entrances to the House of Commons as shall rescue the country from the danger of a one-sided and one-idea'd assembly of councillors elected under the swamping influence of an impassioned majority.[1] But before stating specially by what arrangements these objects could be attained, I will take the liberty of quoting a scheme of Sismondi, prepared with a view to a Reform Bill in France, at once popular and aristocratic. This scheme will at least show that the conclusions to which the present discourse has arrived are not peculiar to the writer, but have been reached independently by one of the greatest political thinkers of the age.

"Certainly, we have not the penetration to propose an electoral law, and if we allow ourselves here to make some calculations, it is only to make it understood how, by adopting the complicated system of the English, instead

[1] The importance of this point was recognized by Alexander Hamilton, one of the great framers of the American constitution. I quote his opinion from De Tocqueville:—

"There are some who would be inclined to regard the servile pliancy of the Executive to a prevailing current, either in the community or the legislature, as its best recommendation. But such men entertain very crude notions, as well of the purposes for which government was instituted, as of the true means by which the public happiness may be promoted. The republican principle demands that the deliberative sense of the community should govern the conduct of those to whom they intrust the management of their affairs; but it does not require an unqualified complaisance to every sudden breeze of passion, or to every transient impulse which the people may receive from the arts of men who flatter their prejudices to betray their interests. It is a just observation that the people commonly *intend* the *public good.* This often applies to their very errors. But their good sense would despise the adulator who should pretend that they always *reason right* about the *means* of promoting it. They know from experience that they sometimes err; and the wonder is that they so seldom err as they do, beset, as they continually are, by the wiles of parasites and sycophants; by the snares of the ambitious, the avaricious, the desperate; by the artifices of men who possess their confidence more than they deserve it; and of those who seek to possess, rather than to deserve it. When occasions present themselves in which the interests of the people are at variance with their inclinations, it is the duty of persons whom they have appointed to be the guardians of those interests, to withstand the temporary delusion, in order to give them time and opportunity for more cool and sedate reflection. Instances might be cited in which a conduct of this kind has saved the people from very fatal consequences of their own mistakes, and has procured lasting monuments of their gratitude to the men who had the courage and magnanimity enough to serve them at the peril of their displeasure."—P. 179.

of the simple but deceptive system of the French, a much greater part of the nation might be associated in the elections, and still that share preserved to the national intelligence which it ought to have. We will propose, for example, to give two-fifths of the national representation to the democracy, two-fifths to the most enlightened and intelligent part of the nation, who inhabit towns, and there develop material prosperity; a fifth to that part occupied in intellectual interests. We will lower the census to 100 fr. in obedience to the present clamour; and giving to 84 departments (Paris not included) two deputies for each department, to be elected in the chief place, we shall have 168 deputies, representing particularly the democracy of the country, perhaps, more probably, the nobility, who will seize on it. We will add 42 deputies elected by the 21 greater cities in France, in purely democratic assemblies, such as those of Westminster and Preston in England, giving a vote to whoever can read and write. We would give an equal number of deputies, 210, to the burgesses of towns, requiring for their admission to the freedom a complete education in the secondary schools, and a degree of fortune which places them above manual labour. We would reserve at least 105 deputies for learned professions, in which all those who had received a superior education and taken degrees, should have the honour of being inscribed, and we would allow these last elections to be made by letters, that they might point out the most eminent persons, not in the provinces only, but in France. We should thus have a representation of 525 members, to the election of whom a very considerable part of the nation would have contributed, but in which, however, the share of intelligence and real will, would have been preserved." [1]

Let us now see how the conditions of the problem might be dealt with, having a due regard to the present political condition of this country. In the first place, I would start from the last great Reform Bill as an accomplished fact. It is; therefore let it be. In the second place, I would provide for the more extended representation of the working classes, either by lowering the present general franchise, as was proposed by the late Whig Government, to £7, or by creating for them a special franchise, analogous to that possessed by the English and Irish Universities. This might be done by dividing the country into districts, and enacting that all the working classes within each district, who paid certain taxes and a certain low house-rent, should elect their own member, over and above the present representation of counties and burghs. In the third place, I would balance this democratic force by the creation of a special representation, for what I have called the natural, moral, and intellectual aristocracy of the community; and I would take these just as I find them in publicly recognised corporations, such as the Universities, the Faculty of Advocates and Writers to the Signet, the Colleges of Physicians and Surgeons, the Royal

[1] *Essays*, p. 313.

Academy of Painting, Sculpture, and Architecture, the Royal Society, and such like. The giving of a special suffrage to these bodies would secure the triple advantage of directly representing intelligent minorities, of favouring education indirectly, and of opening a door of entrance to the House of Commons, to gentlemen of culture and intelligence who might not be disposed, in Alexander Hamilton's phrase, to submit "with unqualified complaisance to every sudden breeze of popular passion." By such a scheme as this, and in many other ways, a just and reasonable Reform Bill might be passed, which would maintain the balance of the constitution, and not expose us to the shame of following, as a herd of slavish imitators, in the wake of vulgar French and American precedents. I do not make these suggestions with any crotchety preference. I should be content with any Bill that in some shape or other would acknowledge the principle of social aristocracy, and make a manly protest against the degrading doctrines of American democracy. The public is well acquainted with the sentiments of not a few intelligent persons, who have published their thoughts on this subject, with the view of doing something to prevent us steering right into the Maelstrom of democratic unreason. But whether it be the blind power of precedent, or whether it be laziness, or whether it be that those who should be our leaders are under some fatal necessity of being led, I do not see that public men in this country have ever bestowed on any of these proposals the attention which they deserve. To turn a reasonable proposal into a laugh is one of the most common artifices of the public oratory which pleases the multitude. The principle, for instance, advocated by Professor Lorimer of this city, and Mr. Macfie of Liverpool, of giving to certain persons a plurality of votes, is in the highest degree just and reasonable;[1] it is only when curiously carried out in certain details that it becomes exposed to the light missiles of those who delight in any superficial semblance of incongruity. A similar remark may be made on the various proposals which have been brought forward for enfranchising the, at present, disfranchised minorities. To none of these has any reasonable objection been made; only the strength of the popular will, already strongly set in for democ-

[1] See *Constitutionalism of the Future*, by James Lorimer, Esq., 1867, 2nd edition; and *Speech delivered at a Meeting of the Liverpool Reform League* on Dec. 19, 1866, including extracts from Archbishop Whately and John Stuart Mill, on Plurality of Votes as a needful element in any Final scheme of Parliamentary Reform. London: Longman, 1867.

racy, must prevail, and the incapacity of the popular brain to entertain more than one idea at a time! From politicians under the influence of such unreasoning forces, of course no reasonable product can be expected. If the little child will kick and roar and spit out the medicine, and the doctor is not firm, the disease must run its course. But one thing is certain; a Reform Bill in the direction of American democracy, in this country at the present moment, will lead, by an inevitable tendency, to the overthrow of the British Constitution. Where the ground is slippery and the atmosphere turbid as in politics, great blunders are the most natural thing in the world; but the consequences which follow on a one-eyed policy will not be retarded because the counsels of public men have been amiably hasty, perhaps, and their motives chivalrously pure. One false step, made in the direction in which we are now moving, never can be retraced. The same complexity of parties, the same compliance with clamour, the same cowardly compromise with absurdity which may lead to the triumph of the present movement, will, in the course of another thirty years, lead to another instalment of American liberty; and then comes, according to Mr. Bright—Paradise, according to New York precedents—Pandemonium. Before a House of Commons nominated by trade's unions and over-awed by fervid demagogues, the constitution of this country would not last a year. The House of Lords, that wonderful incarnation of all that is stable, graceful, and chivalrous in society, would be voted an encumbrance; the Crown denounced as an expensive toy; and the Multitude and Mammon—the mechanical forces and the material interests— would enter into the undisputed heirship of the world-renowned British Constitution. May God long preserve us from such a consummation!

DEMOCRACY VINDICATED [1]

Ernest Jones

[Ernest Charles Jones (1819-1868), Welsh poet, novelist, orator and politician, was associated with the Chartist movement, which took its name from "The People's Charter," drawn up in 1838. It demanded universal manhood suffrage, annual parliaments, voting by ballot, no property qualifications for suffrage, payment of members of parliament, and equal voting districts. This does not now seem to be a dangerously radical platform, but Ernest Jones, as an advocate of physical force in carrying out his program, served two years in gaol for seditious speeches. He was for a time editor of the *People's Paper*. His novels and stories are of small value, but some of his poems show considerable lyrical power. R. R. Gammage, in his *History of the Chartist Movement*, gives an account of Jones's political activities, but his relations with Jones were such that his opinions cannot be accepted without reserve. Gammage says:

> From some cause or other, Jones, in 1846, became a politician as well as a poet. Unknown previously to the working class, he came into their ranks under the patronage of Feargus O'Connor. An aristocrat is always most acceptable to the working class, even to Democrats, and the young sprig of Aristocracy, promoted, as O'Connor would have said, to the ranks of Democracy, was received with enthusiasm. He possessed exactly the qualities for captivating the crowd, with the single exception that, unlike his patron O'Connor, he was small in stature; but his voice was stentorian, his language brilliant, his delivery good, his action heroic—and, above all, he had a concealed cunning, which had the advantage of bearing every appearance of the most extreme candour. In the art of flattery, no demagogue ever excelled him.

Jones's political opponents regarded him as a very attractive and honorable, if mistaken, person.]

We are met in consequence of a challenge given by Professor Blackie at the Annual Soiree of the Edinburgh Working Men's Club and Institute. It is not I who sought this controversy; it is not I who ventured to intrude upon your time; but when a challenge was given to principles in which I believe, and which, with the best of my humble powers, I am determined to defend, and when my name was coupled with that challenge, I felt it

[1] Reprinted from *Democracy: An Address by Professor Blackie of Edinburgh; and a Reply by the late Ernest Jones of Manchester*. Second Edition. Manchester: Abel Heywood and Son. London: Simpkin, Marshall & Co., 1885. Questions and topics for the discussion of this address, and of other phases of the general subject with which it deals, will be found on pages 495 and 500.

to be my duty as a citizen, and my duty to myself, not to shrink from the encounter, but to trust to the candour of a Scottish audience, however varying in opinion, as no doubt we are to-night, and not basely to desert my colours when battle had been offered.

Before, however, proceeding to address you in answer to the observations made with so much ability last night, I must take exception to one line of argument pursued by the learned Professor. He assumed throughout that democracy meant the rule of the working classes, to the exclusion of all others; and then he reasoned as though the working classes were a mob, the ὄχλος, and not the δῆμος.[1] He denounces license, and calls it "liberty"; he advocates tyranny, and names it "order." Democracy means not the rule of a class, but of a nation—it embraces all, it tempers one class with another—it does not exclude the peer or the prince; on the contrary, it embraces them, it harmonises them—a peerage may flourish in its midst, and a throne is but the representative of one of its highest and noblest forms. There may be democracy under a king as well as under a president; and that system of checks and counter-checks, that tempering influence to which allusion has been made, is perhaps more perfectly realised under a democracy than under any form.

We have been invited to condemn democratic institutions upon several grounds. First, because they are asserted to have failed in various countries and ages. I join issue with the conclusions drawn from those precedents. Before it is permissible to argue from a former failure, that democracy would be injurious in the present day, it is requisite to show that the conditions in both cases are the same. I believe in the progressive development of the human mind. I believe that the human race possesses one great collective life, having its infancy, and ripening to its manhood; and I protest against demanding from the infancy of nations that which their maturity can alone achieve. I protest against measuring the child by the standard of the man.

Before my learned opponent is entitled to say that because, as he alleges, democracy failed in ancient Greece and Italy, it must fail with us as well, he is bound to show that there is no difference between heathen Athens or pagan Rome, and Christian Britain in the nineteenth century.

Before he is entitled to say that, as he alleges, democracy failed in modern France, therefore it must fail in modern England too,

---

[1] The mob, and not the people.

he is bound to show that there is no difference between a country bowed for seven centuries beneath oppression terrible to contemplate, and our own, where

"Freedom broadens slowly down
From precedent to precedent";

between France, where bigotry and atheism divided the public mind, and Britain, where, with all her faults, religion still sits throned upon the people's hearts; between France, where licentious tyranny mocked at every virtue and trampled on every right, and Britain, where the virtues of the throne are but an emblem of the virtues of the nation; between the land of Charles the Ninth and Louis Quinze, and the empire of Elizabeth and Queen Victoria.

Before he has a right to say that democracy fails in Australia, and therefore must fail in Scotland too, he must show us that there is no difference between this glorious country and this noble people, and the colonies to which the gold diggings lured the adventurous avarice of the world, and the undisciplined swarms of coolie immigrants, to mingle with the convict population of the Motherland.

Before he can be permitted to say that because, under a supposed democracy, licentiousness and corruption reign in New York, they would reign in Edinburgh also, he must prove that the sea-side midden, which receives and retains the refuse of the world, is on an equality with the Athens of the North.

But I will meet him on the ground he himself has chosen. I will go with him to ancient Greece; I will follow him to classic Rome; I will accompany him to revolutionary France; I will walk by his side through our Australian colonies, and attend his footsteps to republican America; and I undertake to show that, in them all, democracy has been the founder and saviour of the people's greatness.

I ask him to come with me to the ancient world. No doubt he has lingered long within its confines.

πολλῶν δ'ἀνθρώπων ἴδεν ἄστεα καὶ νόον ἔγνω,[1] though, perhaps, the whole line scarcely applies to him—ἄστεα ἴδεν no doubt; whether νόον ἔγνω, we shall presently perceive.[2]

---

[1] "And many were the men whose towns he saw and whose spirit he learned."
[2] "He saw their towns," no doubt; "whether he learned their spirits," we shall presently perceive.

Come with me to Athens.—The reforms of Kleisthenes gave birth to Athenian democracy. Before them, it cannot be said to have existed. Before them, the four Ionic tribes, to which admission could be gained only by the phratriæ and gentes, ruled Athens as an aristocratic and moneyed oligarchy. Kleisthenes sought to destroy their power, and give the vote even to resident aliens and emancipated slaves. How did your aristocracy and moneyed class now act. They, Athenian citizens,—they, the guardians of the State,—called in the hereditary enemies of the country, the royalist armies of Sparta, betrayed Athens and all its strongholds to the foe, and instituted a reign of terror, in which Kleisthenes and seven hundred patriot families were banished out of that little community. But the people rose in their might, after all seemed lost forever; they rose, and fought, and conquered; the foul tyrants were displaced; the cruel invader was expelled; the exiles returned in triumph; the reforms of Kleisthenes were enacted, and democracy reigned in Athens. Now, mark what was its effect. Herodotus, the Greek historian, tells us:—

"The Athenians accordingly increased in power; and equality of rights shows, not in one instance only, but in every way, what an excellent thing it is. For the Athenians, when governed by tyrants, were superior in war to none of their neighbours; but, when freed from tyrants, became by far the first." [1]

Grote, our own great historian of Greece, says, alluding to that very passage of Herodotus:—

"Stronger expressions cannot be found to depict the rapid improvement wrought in the Athenian people by their new democracy. Of course, this did not arise merely from suspension of previous cruelties, or better laws, or better administration. These, indeed, were essential conditions; but the active transforming cause here was, the principle and system of which such amendments formed the detail, the grand new idea of a sovereign people composed of free and equal citizens, or liberty and equality—to use words which so profoundly moved the French nation half a century ago. It was this comprehensive political idea which acted with electric effect upon the Athenians, creating within them a host of sentiments, motives, sympathies, and capacities, to which they had before been strangers.

Among the Athenian citizens, certainly, it (democracy) produced a strength and unanimity of the positive political sentiment, such as has rarely been seen in the history of mankind, which excites our surprise and admiration all the more when we compare it with the apathy which had preceded.

[1] Herodotus, *Terpsichore*, 5, 78.

The democracy was the first creative cause of that astonishing, personal, and many-sided energy which marked the Athenian character for a century downwards from Kleisthenes; that the same ultra-Hellenic activity did not longer continue is referable to other causes, which will be hereafter explained."

Yes! note the contrast. Democracy repelled the mighty armaments of Persia; aristocracy had surrendered their country to the tyranny of Sparta!

But mark, once more. From some of those "other causes" to which Grote alludes, aristocracy and plutocracy resumed sway in Athens when Pericles, a descendant from Kleisthenes on the female side, destroyed the tyrannical power of the Areopagus, and established the dicasteries or jury courts, which restored democracy.

Now mark: here you have, in one dramatic picture, the relative merits of democracy, aristocracy, and monarchy placed side by side. How did aristocracy, which comprised the moneyed class of Athens, behave? It opposed the building of the long walls connecting Athens with its ports, and essential for the very independence of the State, because, if those walls were built, they could no longer maintain their own supremacy by rendering their country a slave of Sparta. Again, they call those very Spartans in; a bloody and undecided battle was fought within sight of the capital; and even, when this infamy did not avail them, they resorted to assassination, and a Bœotian, hired by them, murdered Ephialtes, the great friend and ally of Pericles in his reforms. When my learned opponent alluded to the bowl of Socrates, why did he forget the dagger of Ephialtes?

Now look at monarchy. The joint kings of Sparta, who came at the beck of the rich and high-born in Athens to drown her liberties in blood, were Pausanias and Leotychides. Pausanias was carried dying from the sanctuary, whither he had flown to escape the consequences of his crimes—for he had agreed to betray, for money, his country and Greece to the Persians; and Leotychides was tried and convicted of having received bribes from the satraps of the great king, and sold for money the cause of Sparta, Greece, and civilisation, to the barbarians of Asia.

So much for monarchy and aristocracy in ancient Greece. Now for democracy.

Under democracy, Athens rapidly rose to her greatest prosperity and power; and, to quote the words of history, "no state has ever exhibited so much intellectual activity, and so great a progress in art, as was displayed by Athens in the period which elapsed between the twenty years' truce and the breaking out of the Peloponnesian war.''

But judge of it in the words of Pericles—that Pericles who, with the generosity democracy so nobly displays, himself proposed the recall of Cimon, the leader of the aristocratic party:—

"We enjoy a form of government which does not copy the laws of our neighbours; but we are ourselves rather a pattern to others than imitators of them. In name, from its not being administered for the benefit of the few, but of the many, it is called a democracy; but, with regard to its laws, all enjoy equality as regards their private differences; while, with regard to public rank, according as each man has reputation for anything, he is preferred for public honours, not so much from consideration of party, as of merit; nor again, on the ground of poverty, while he is able to do the State any good service, is he prevented by the obscurity of his position." [1]

Such was democracy in ancient Greece. Under it, the human race achieved the most exalted greatness it ever attained, until Christianity brought elements more lofty still to sanctify the mind and purify the heart of man.

Come now to Rome.—There royalty, and there a patrician moneyed caste, had divided the people into two nations—the one a sort of pariah-race, the other a haughty oligarchy, which passed a law declaring it pollution for the high-born to intermarry with the honest plebeian classes.

I will describe to you, in the words of our great historian, Macaulay, what this governing class had brought Rome to:—

The plebeians "were excluded from the higher magistracies; they were excluded from all share in the public lands; and they were ground down to the dust by partial and barbarous legislation touching pecuniary contracts. *The ruling class in Rome was a moneyed class,* and it made and administered the laws with a view solely to its own interest. The great men held a large portion of the community in dependence by means of advances at enormous usury. The law of debt, framed by creditors, and for the protection of creditors, was the most horrible that has ever been known among men. The liberty, and even the life of the insolvent were at the mercy of the patrician money-lenders. Children often became slaves in consequence of the misfortunes of their parents. The debtor was imprisoned, not in a public gaol, under the care of impartial public functionaries, but in a private workhouse belonging to the creditor. Frightful stories were told respecting these dungeons. It is said that torture and

[1] Thucydides, b. 37.

brutal violation were common; that tight stocks, heavy chains, scanty measures of food, were used to punish wretches guilty of nothing but poverty; and that brave soldiers, whose breasts were covered with honourable scars, were often marked still more deeply on the back by the scourges of high-born usurers." [1]

Add to this a monopoly of the land, that has its parallel in England and Scotland only. The free yeomanry were destroyed, and hired labour and slave labour alone cultivated the soil.

What, think you, would have been the end of this, had it been permitted to continue? Rome would never have left her mark upon the page of history: her arts and arms, her patriotism and her literature, would never have been the teachers and ensamples of the world, but some of History's noblest and fullest pages would have been a dreary blank.

Against this the Roman people struggled, and the Licinian Rogations were proposed. Now mark; for ten years the mighty contest lasted, and yet during all that time, so noble was the conduct of democracy in Rome, no act of bloodshed, not even a riot, appears to have occurred, though the people, the plebeians, had the physical force upon their side.

Macaulay says: "The struggle appears to have been the fiercest that ever in any community terminated without an appeal to arms. If such a contest had raged in any Greek city, the streets would have run with blood. But, even in the paroxysms of faction, the Roman retained his gravity, his respect for law, and his tenderness for the lives of his fellow-citizens." [2]

At length the good cause triumphed. And what was the result? Listen to the words of Macaulay:—"The Licinian laws were carried. The results of this great change were singularly happy and glorious. Two centuries of prosperity, harmony, and victory followed the reconciliation of the orders. Men who remembered Rome engaged in waging petty wars almost within sight of the capitol, lived to see her the mistress of Italy. While the disabilities of the plebeians continued, she was scarcely able to maintain her ground against the Volscians and Hernicans; when those disabilities were removed, she rapidly became more than a match for Carthage and Macedon." [3]

Such was democracy in ancient Rome. Nay! follow the dark

[1] Macaulay, *Historical Note to Lays*, pp. 110, 111.
[2] Macaulay, *ibid.*, pp. 112, 113.
[3] Macaulay, *ibid.*, pp. 113, 114.

current of the years down to later Rome. Even with Rienzi, the
last flame of its long sunset, democracy was the agent that made
the parting glory linger for a few brief hours. And now, what
ushers in returning greatness to that classic land? Democratic
Italy, the Italy of Garibaldi, the foremost democrat of Europe;
and its foremost democrat is also its greatest man! The Italy of
manhood suffrage is purging bigotry and brigandage from its
South; and under circumstances of colossal difficulty, under trials
that have few parallels, showing an example of self-denial and
moderation, of peace, order, and forbearance, such as democracy
alone has ever given to the world, and such as must extort even
from my opponent the meed of admiration.

Do you challenge me with France? I accept the challenge, and
I ask—Is democracy alone to be measured by the standard of the
gods? Do you demand of us perfection, while you concede to yourselves the right to every frailty? Must we be more than men,
while you are permitted to be less? If you would test French
democracy, do not look alone at its excesses. Ask: *What did it
find France?* Answer: *What has it made of it?* It found France
trodden down beneath a feudal aristocracy, which not only robbed
the working man of every right, but even by law violated the
inmost sanctities of home. It found the revenues in the hands of
financial farmers, who ruined every trade, destroyed every industry, and made the country helplessly, hopelessly, irretrievably
bankrupt. Rapine and usury reigned from end to end, and famine stalked over all the confines of the land. Bigotry and ignorance upheld immorality and vice, and terror alone kept in
subjection the festering mass of misery to which the people had
been reduced. Then the Genius of democracy took this poor benighted people by the hand, and led it from the valley of the
shadow of death to the upper lights of liberty and life. True,
by the paths of terror. True, the guillotine smote as sharply as
the sword of battle. True, fantastic and horrible excesses were
committed, like the enthronement of the Goddess of Reason. No
doubt the recoil was terrible, but so had been the repression. The
one was the offspring of the other. Put your seven centuries of
atheism in practice against their few weeks of atheism in theory.
Put the dungeons of your Bastile against their scaffolds of the
Place de Grève, and record this difference between them: that
in those dungeons seven centuries heard your victims groan, while
seven months cleared off the anger of the people. And add to it

this: that our victims were plotting with the foreigner against the State; yours were murdered for private cruelty, and greed, and lust. Instead of tracing thence a reason for not granting their rights to the people, see what comes of keeping them back, and be wise in time. But if you would test democracy, look to *the results*. What did it make of France? It found the land held by a few nobles and the people starving; it turned it into six million freehold farms, and gave plenty to the people. In the land of aristocracy, one lost battle decided the fate of the country. Under democracy the deluge of banded Europe swept over it in vain, and the occupying armies passed away as trackless as shadows from its sunny plains. The results:—In the land of St. Bartholomew it made religion free. In the land of the Bastile it made a jury the arbiter of the individual's liberty. In the land of Louis Quatorze it established Parliamentary representation. True, a Napoleon now reigns; true the press is trammelled; true, Parliament has been coerced, though it is slowly but surely recovering its lost ascendancy; but I tell you a people cannot leap at one bound from seven centuries of serfdom to the calm heights of perfected liberty. You are the very man who tells us progression must go slowly; and yet, when the French people leaped to liberty by the only pathway tyranny had left for them, you reproach them because they have not done that which you yourself declare to be impossible! Yes, Liberty marches by progressive steps; calm and gentle as a child if you treat her fairly, terrible as an angry giant if you try to chain her down. The first step was in '79, the second in '30, the third in '48—each time more merciful and more mild; and Napoleon is but one of the outward forms of this transition period—the cloud between one sunrise and another; and even he is obliged to disguise his imperial mantle with the colours of the morning, to reign in the name of liberty and truth, and to bow before the virtues of the people.

Do you taunt me with Australia? Do you quote against me some unknown clergyman, whose book is not yet published? Against him I call in aid the authority of Mr. Hutton, Minister of Public Works in South Australia, and for fourteen years a member of the Legislature, who tells us that he had, in Australia, the fullest experience of both systems—that of a restricted franchise, and that of democracy. Under the old system, he says, expense, riot, tumult, disorder, and violence were the rule; under the latter, peace and order are ennobling the country. But here, too, I say, test democracy by the results. Is it true or not that our Australian colonies are becoming more prosperous every day? Is it true or not that they are becoming more peaceable and more orderly every day? Is it true or not, that they are becoming more intellectual every day? Are they going downward or growing up? Let the answer to that question decide the issue there.

But I am invited to America—the country that spent £600,000,-000, and a quarter of a million of its best blood, to preserve the Union and liberate the slave! the country that, having succeeded in both, pays off its debts at the rate of £30,000,000 per annum! the country where the Sanitary and Christian Commission raised for its soldiers £2,000,000! the country whose grand system of free schools is the admiration of the world! the country where, within five years, seven million dollars were given by private individuals to literary institutions! the country of which "wise" men have said it was rushing to bankruptcy and ruin, yet in which, during the war, £5,000,000 were contributed to the establishment of universities! the country where education stands higher than in any other country in the world, and of which the Professor coolly tells us that it cares only for its material prosperity! What has the learned Professor to say of this great country? That "there is rowdyism and immorality in New York, and bribery in Albany!" and, very appropriately, he quotes Mr. Spence, the apologist of the South, the champion of rebellion, the defender of one of the blackest crimes that man ever committed on men—the slavery of four million human beings. "In New York!" But why not tell us of Philadelphia and Cincinnati; of Baltimore and Pittsburg; of Boston, with its public library, planned only in 1852, yet containing 120,000 volumes, lent entirely free to every inhabitant over sixteen years of age, who merely gives his name and address, with a population so noble that not a book is lost or stolen in a twelve-month; of Chicago, numbering 200,000 inhabitants, founded only thirty-two years ago, yet already possessing two theological colleges, some of the finest upper schools in the world, and a flourishing university; of that great constellation of order-loving, moral, and prosperous municipalities, that shines along the surface of the land? Why talk of New York alone, and pick out the one black spot upon the face of the sun? Why select as your authority a partisan article from a partisan Review, for whose truth there is no single voucher? Why not ascertain whether you are correct before you make a statement such as that about the Government not daring to levy a tax on spirits because the drunken nation would not permit it, when the fact is that at this very moment brandy is one of the most heavily taxed things in all America? Why, quoting De Tocqueville, assert that, at Philadelphia, the populace would not allow the negro electors to go to the polling-booths, when the fact is, that when De Tocqueville wrote, there was not a negro who had a vote at all! It was reserved for democracy to give it to them. But New York does not represent democracy—it represents that which you created with your system; the Romish-Irish, the refuse of your monarchies and aristocracies—the men whom you have degraded by your class rules in Britain, Germany, and France—swarm there and make it what it is, that it may stand as a foil to the great democracy, and enable us to say—"Look on this picture, and on this." Such men the rule of the few creates—*they are your handiwork,* they come fresh from *your* hands. And *now behold the children of democracy.* And they stand side by side. There, in the *State* of New York, they are. "God made the country, and man made the town." Old England peopled the *City* of New York, but New England fashioned the population of the *State!*

Listen to what Dr. M'Cosh says of the two:—"English travellers have given us a picture of the state of things in that city (New York); of its disgraceful saloons with their female waiters, and its drunkenness on the Lord's Day. No steps were taken to suppress this by the municipal authorities, who owe their election to the Romish-Irish, and a degraded population—the refuse of all countries. But the State of New York, with its high-toned country population, interfered, and passed a law to *stamp out* these places of wickedness and temptation. During the two months—May and June—of the execution of the law, the arrests diminished from 1078 to 502—that is, one-half." Yes! and since then the State has taken from the City the management of its police, its fire-brigade, and its central park; and is substituting morality and order for licentiousness and license. And mark! in the *States,* manhood suffrage is the law as well as in the *City.* Democracy is correcting the offspring of class rule.

You say—*look at New York.* I say—*look at America.* Turn from a New York row to that noble spectacle, the re-election of President Lincoln; when, after years of civil war, the bitterest ever waged,—when every passion would be stirred to its profoundest depths, and faction did its uttermost to inflame the partisan,—

two hostile parties went to the ballot-urn of democracy, and not a riot disgraced the wide circle of the Northern States, but in majestic peace and order that unequaled people registered the fiat of its will. You have seen in New York the creation of European class rule; again, I say, behold the creation of democracy!

Listen to the same authority I have already quoted:—

"The laws favour education, in some states make it compulsory; but in fact it is mainly promoted by the spirit of the people. The young people remain longer at school than they do in this country, and, as a rule, the common people are all well educated. The artisan class there, male and female, like the middle class here, can talk with you on the topics of the day, and they know the history of their own country and of ours, and the elements of science, mental and physical."

Behold the country democracy, according to the same witness:—

"I wish I could convey you all to a New England village of the better sort, such as I lived in once and again. I reckon it the finest sight in America, one of the finest sights in the world, to a philanthropist. The houses are not in close streets like ours, but are separate from one another, and embosomed with trees in a garden, and each with four, five, or six apartments. There is sure to be a school, or church, or churches, in the village, but possibly no public-house within five or six miles. Nearly every man there reads his daily newspaper, and many of them see a monthly religious or literary magazine. I was in villages with several hundreds of a population, in which there was not a family to whom you could offer a piece of cast-off clothing, or of bread, without giving offence. To my unspeakable gratification, I found like communities springing up all over the West—in Ohio, Illinois, Wisconsin, and away beyond the Mississippi, in Minnesota and Iowa." "A New England village of the better class is a perfect picture of peace on the Lord's-day."

Now behold the town democracy; and I quote from the same source:—

"I found much the same state of things in the large cities, so far as they are not flooded with strangers."

Hear what Dr. M'Cosh says of the factory population:—

"At the Pacific Mills, Lawrence, Massachusetts, there are 4000 work-people, and it is a beautiful sight to see them so neatly dressed as they go into and issue from the mills. The females in one department receive a dollar and fifteen cents a day, and in another a dollar and forty-five cents. The unmarried girls live in boarding-houses, which I visited. They have a common sitting-room, comfortably furnished; and they have a separate dining-hall, where I saw them seated at as comfortable a meal as the middle-classes have in this country; while every two persons have a neatly-furnished bedroom. The skilled workers get towards 1000 dollars a year, and the foremen (section men) towards 1500 dollars. These foremen have houses provided for them, for which they pay 175 dollars a year, and their houses are each three stories high, with a front door and eleven apartments. Connected with the mills are a reading-room and a large library, for which each worker has to pay a small sum. It is proper to add, that I found the workpeople in a like condition of comfort in Baltimore, Philadelphia, and in other places South and West."

Such are the effects of democratic government on the mental culture and the material well-being of the people. It takes those whom your system has corrupted, and degraded, and debased, and turns them into the worthy citizens of the happiest country in the world. Do you doubt that the same causes would produce the same effects here? Are we not the same race? Are they not of our flesh and blood—our brothers and our sisters—immortal souls—those coins of Heaven's treasury, from whom, by your base handling, you have effaced the effigy of the King of kings, but whom the mint of freedom has re-stamped with the image of their God?

We have made the circuit of the nations and the ages: although the learned Professor has not thought right to allude more than in a passing word to those other instances of successful and beneficent democracy—Switzerland, or the Dutch Republic, which owed its rise to democracy, even though oligarchy ruled in after-days; and although he forgot the great Flemish cities, whose democracies resisted the Burgundians and the French; or some of the commonwealths of mediæval Italy, forgetting that the noblest hours of Florence were those when democracy ruled, and Savonarola led the people; and although, in mentioning South America, he has overlooked Chile, that prosperous and noble democracy, whose public debt, at this very moment, stands at a higher quotation than that of Great Britain; and although he has omitted altogether Denmark, and the Spanish States till Ferdinand and Charles the Fifth; and Italy, which at this very moment is standing so gloriously the great transition test.

Strange that, wherever democracy has reigned, there has society reached its highest development, moral, social, and intellectual. Nay, the nearer approach to democratic institutions, the greater the happiness and goodness of the people. Britain herself bears witness. She has been called the Ark of Freedom—(is

America its Ararat?)—and has she not been the foremost of the
nations of the modern world, until now ceding the palm to a nation
more democratic than her own?

And has not this great people, this British people, given the
pledges of its fitness to enjoy its right of freedom? True, you
pick out all the dark spots you can. True, amid the broad sunshine of the summer day, you hunt out the little caves where
shadows lie. Let's have them all! Where are they? Oh, you
think you have found one: *Trades Unions.* But they originated
when little children were working sixty hours at a stretch in the
factories of England. They originated when the discharge-note
system doomed the independent operative to utter starvation or the
workhouse. They originated when the workhouses sold pauper
children to distant factory masters. They are strict, no doubt;
but do you not flog and brand, and even shoot, the deserter from
your army? They merely ostracise the renegades from theirs.
And have the masters not their combinations, almost irresistible,
because they monopolise nearly all the adits to employment? Do
they not now meet and regulate the prices of coal and iron? Do
they not now combine and lock out a little nation at a time? Why
blame the men for measures, even tyrannical, in self-defence?
What were the Corn Laws but a gigantic kind of trades union of
the aristocracy, to keep bread dear and starve the working classes?
But have not those trades unions carried the Ten Hours Bill?
Have they not succeeded in wresting from your friends the concession of the factory schools? Read the history of those unions.
in the returning bloom on labour's cheek, and the light of intelligence rekindling in its eyes.

I ask my learned opponent to show me any great measure which
the working classes have not either originated or at least supported. Who supported Catholic emancipation, the admission of
the Jews to Parliament, the repeal of the Test and Corporation
Acts, the liberation of the West Indian slaves, the abolition of
the Taxes on Knowledge, Free-trade, and Reform? The men
whom you would deprive of power. Who opposed all these? The
class who kept the power from them.

You tell us that our demonstrations are brute force. Why,
where have we been for the last twelve or fourteen years? Have
we not been utterly quiet, passive, merely sending up our memo-
rials and petitions, laying our arguments before the supreme wisdom of the governing classes? And they treated those arguments

with contempt. We are ready now to give up our demonstrations to-morrow if you will admit a deputation representing the people to the bar of the House of Commons, respectfully to urge their rights. We are ready to give up our demonstrations if you will treat the people with respect. We are not "cattle." We have a better argument than brute force; but when you spurn our deputations, when you ridicule our arguments, and when you refuse to listen to our prayers—nay, when you invite us to "come out"—when you refuse to give us Reform because you state, "You are apathetic, you do not ask for it: show yourselves; where are you?"—then we come and say, "Here we are!"

But now look at the sunshine. It covers the whole picture. What has been the voice of the masses—that nation within a nation, our working men—whom you would place outside the brotherhood of man? Show me any great measure, religious, social, political, which they did not either originate or support. Look at Catholic emancipation; look at the admission of Jews to Parliament; look at the repeal of the Test and Corporation Acts; look at the abolition of Taxes on Knowledge; look at the extinction of West Indian slavery; look at Free-trade; look at Reform! Who were *for* these? *The men you would exclude.* Who were *against* these? *The classes who exclude them.* Who sided with the North and liberty? Who demanded justice for Jamaica? Who carried out Co-operation against adverse laws? Who met the charge of drunkenness with a temperance movement, that for its magnitude and excellence has no parallel in any other country? Go back and tell me who swelled the ranks of the Lollards? Who followed in the path of Wycliffe? Who rallied at the voice of Knox? Who resisted the aggression of Laud? In his own words, "A lot of mean and inconsiderable people." Yes! *The* people,—the very class of whom you say they are not fit to take their rightful share in the government of themselves, yet they were obliged to put right the men by whom you say it is fit they should be governed.

And how do you treat this noble people? Is there one spark of generous confidence, one ember of brotherly love, in your breast? The working men who are electors are scarcely one in eight of the constituencies; indeed, one in nine would be nearer the truth. The working men who are electors are but one in forty-eight of the male adults of the United Kingdom.

And on what ground do you exclude them? Is it education?

I have answered that already, for an education is not the lore of schools alone—it is to think rightly and to act honestly in the position God has allotted to you in life. Education! Instead of wanting education to fit them for the franchise, they need the franchise to enable them to obtain education. Look at America, where manhood suffrage has created the best-educated people in the world. Look at the co-operative societies, where, from their, profits, the working men unanimously vote large sums to establish schools and libraries for working men. Education! give them manhood suffrage, and, in six months, education would be made compulsory throughout the country.

Again, I ask, on what ground do you exclude them? Is it property? The annual income of the working classes is £418,000,000. The *acknowledged* income of all the other classes combined is but £326,000,000, though some think that £100,000,000 more is dishonestly evaded. And yet you assume to base your franchise on property. You concede a special virtue to a £10 franchise; a franchise that says—John Milton, in a lodging, is not fit to vote, and Jack Sheppard, in a £10 house, is a respectable elector. But see where your £10 theory will land you. You say a £10 rental argues superior mental and moral qualifications, and therefore you give it a vote and exclude £5 because they who pay it cannot be so good and virtuous as the others, and, being more numerous, would swamp all those above them. But if £10 is so much better than £5, then £20 must be proportionally better than the £10. Surely we ought to have the wisest and the best to govern us, and preserve them from being swamped by inferior beings! Then give us twenty-pounders, and away with all below! But in London and elsewhere there are a few thousand-pounders. Fancy the virtue of a thousand-pounder! But these are the least numerous of all. Why let their superior wisdom and virtue be swamped by the ignorance and vice below? Why adulterate the superior article? Winnow the chaff from this imperial corn, and let us be governed by a score or so of most immaculate Dean Pauls!

And what is this great enigma of choosing a representative? You admit that working men can learn to make a watch or a steam engine, to fulfil every other function of life—can manage a benefit society, govern a building club, or create and control the colossal commercial undertakings which the Co-operative movement has called into existence. They can do all this—they can do, and do well, every other thing in life—they can comprehend the doctrines of salvation, and fit themselves for heaven when they die—but they cannot choose between my Lord Tomnoddy and a sensible fellow-citizen as their representative in the House of Commons.

But when all this is answered—when fitness is achieved—when education is won—all is not enough—nothing has been gained; we are still great criminals, for the Professor has invented a new crime—*the crime of numbers.* We are too many; therefore some of us are to go without our rights. But who are to be the victims? Who is to be *depontanus?* Who is to decide? What sin have *I* committed? Why am just I to suffer, because I happen to have too many brothers? That is my father's fault, not mine; punish him, not me. In some countries, we read, population is kept down by the destruction of a certain number of new-born children. The Professor wants to introduce a sort of political infanticide. But I rebel against it. I have a right to my life, and if so, I have a right to all the rights of life; and the power of looking after my own interests is one of the most important of those rights. We know that, by a compensating law in nature, where the population exceeds the means of support, the deficiency corrects the surplus. But, so long as the Almighty gives human life to an immortal soul, and the means of bodily sustenance on earth, are you to step before the prerogative of God, and say to the Deity: "You have created too many; it is not good that these are here; and to punish them for having been created, we will deprive them of their rights, and rectify the error of Providence by the injustice of man?"

But your whole argument of numbers proceeds on a succession of fallacies. The interests of the working classes must be either identical with those of other classes, or hostile to them. If identical, where is the danger? For, rest assured, men will look after their own interests in the long run. If hostile, you will agree with me that good government is the greatest possible good to the greatest possible number; and that it is a reason why "the greatest possible number" should have it in their power to look after their own interests. Again, you presuppose that all the working classes, on all questions, at all times, like one vast machine, would all vote one way at all elections; and, that being done, that their representatives would all, with the same regularity, vote one way in Parliament. There never was a greater delusion. Sir, there are as many diversities of opinion, as many conflicting interests, among the working classes, as exist in any other class of the community. And beneath such chimerical fears as these, the rights and happiness of twenty million men, women, and children are trampled in the dust!

But I maintain that manhood suffrage meets your very objection. It is the only means for obtaining the rule of a safe majority—the government of the better class; the only means of putting an end to corruption and intimidation. Show me any other mode for winnowing the chaff from the corn. How will you secure the good and exclude the bad from your constituencies? Your property qualification does not. Witness Yarmouth and Totness, St. Albans and Nottingham, Lancaster and Reigate—the discovered criminals: we say nothing of the undiscovered. Your education test cannot. I presume all your present electors can read, and write, and cipher or where's the use of your £10 test?—and you see what they are worth. Indeed, sir, our criminal calendars show that nearly all the more serious crimes, excepting those of highway robbery, are committed by persons who can read and write, and that well. Show me, then, how you will divide the good from the bad. Show me your Ebal and your Gerizim. Ascend your electoral Nebo, and, with your limited vision, look into the hearts of men, and tell me who are fit, and who are unfit, to cross your political Jordan into the promised land of liberty. Now, manhood suffrage, though it may admit the bad (we exclude, of course, every convicted criminal—all Reformers do), is certain to catch the good within its net. It is the only plan that makes sure of them. And I believe that the good are the majority of the human race in every Christian land. Were it otherwise, society could not go on. I see the proof of it in America, where all are tried. My opponent says that Christianity has had little influence on politics. It is high time, then, that it had some influence. I believe that Christianity has not been sent on earth in vain. Wherever evil predominates, States perish. Turkey dies, though you have tried to save it. Persia perishes, though it is almost unassailed.

But democracy is not only the securer of the good, it is the purifier of the bad as well. Show me how you will stop corruption and intimidation without manhood suffrage and the ballot. Not by adding a few scores of voters to a depraved constituency. Instead of cleansing the latter you corrupt the former. You clear not the fetid pool by pouring in a few drops of crystal water; instead of thus purifying the polluted, you pollute the pure. You

must send the full tide of the stainless river in, before you can
wash the corruption away. Test it by the present. Where are
electors intimidated? Wherever they are few. Where are they
corrupted? Where they are not too numerous to be bribed. Do
you hear of venality or coercion in Birmingham or the Tower
Hamlets, in Edinburgh or in Glasgow? Even an approach to manhood suffrage, you see, reduces the evil. Add to it the ballot,
and bribery and corruption are at an end. Where are the purses
that could bribe the majority of seven million electors? and
where is the fool to attempt it, when he could never tell how the
man he bribed had voted after all?

But because I assert and believe in the truth and desirability of
complete democracy, do not suppose I stand here to resist any sensible, or large, or even moderate measure of Reform that is sound
in principle. I defend that which you attack; but because I do
so, and avow my belief in the excellence of manhood suffrage, and
because I am determined, in my humble way, to struggle for that
manhood suffrage to the last hour of my life, do not suppose I
would throw an impediment in the way of any measure that was
sound or wise, or that conceded a fair proportion, or rather a fair
instalment, of justice to the working classes.

And is it needed, this great Reform—is it needed? Are we not
walking in the downward path of Rome and mediæval France?
Is not aristocracy doing here exactly what it did there? In Rome
and in France wealth accumulated and the land was monopolised.

*Reform saved Rome from Revolution. Revolution saved France
from ruin.* Which are we to have here—

REVOLUTION OR REFORM?

Here, too, wealth accumulates in few hands. Here, too, the earth
is monopolised by a few families. Here, too, as in Rome, our public lands, our commons, have been annexed to the possessions of
those who had too much before. Already the English labourer has
to walk eight miles to and from his daily toil. Here, too, the evil
grows. At the close of the last century we had still 250,000 landed
proprietors; now we have less than 30,000. Here, too, the people
shrink and dwindle beneath this system: four times since the great
French war has the standard for the army been lowered. Where
is this to end?

"Ill fares the land, to hastening ills a prey,
Where wealth accumulates and men decay,
Princes and lords may flourish and may fade;
A breath can make them, as a breath has made;
But a bold peasantry, their country's pride,
When once destroyed, can never be supplied."

There is a party in the country that has called or calls itself Liberal—I call it Whig. It professes to be in favour of Reform, but it does nothing for it. It keeps the question open, because keeping it open keeps political capital in its pocket. I am an utter opponent of the Tories; but I must say this, "Give me a Tory sooner than a Whig." The Whigs are the political adventurers; they are the place-hunters; they are the men who dip their hands into the pocket of the people. They are the men who are the tried politicians; and on each side of them stand two classes— the thief is in the middle this time—the one is the Tory and the other is the Radical. Let us have a fight, the Tory and the Radical; but the way to enable us to get at each other is to knock down the Whig from between us.

I admire the ability of my learned opponent; I respect his straight-forwardness. I am sorry to lose him from the ranks of real Liberals; I am anxious to regain him. But I confess I am surprised at such politics in him. Strange that a man who has revelled in the regions of classic democracy should be the upholder of restricted representation! Strange that *he* should fight for a brick-and-mortar franchise, in whose ears the words of Nicias have rung:—

ἄνδρες γὰρ πόλις καὶ οὐ τείχη οὐδὲ νῆες ἀνδρῶν κεναί.[1]

Strange that he should be the champion of a lath-and-plaster suffrage, before whose eyes the lines of Sophocles have flashed:—

ὡς οὐδέν ἔστιν οὔτε πύργος οὔτε ναῦς
ἔρημος ἀνδρῶν μὴ ξυνοικούντων ἔσω.[2]

But he is a philosopher, and has quoted Aristotle and Plato. I adopt Aristotle's words:—

[1] "For men, and not walls or ships in which are no men, constitute a state." Thucydides VII, 77.
[2] "Since walled town, or ship, neither is anything if it is void and no men dwell with thee therein." Sophocles, *Œdipus Rex*, 56, 57.

"The best of all animals, when governed by law and justice, is man; when without them, the most terrible."

Just so. Then carry out the maxim you yourself have quoted, and be true to Aristotle by withholding justice from us no longer. You bid us "learn to know the wisest and the best." Just so; but pray do give us the chance of electing them when we have found them out. You mention Plato, who lived and wrote when democracy had sunk beneath foreign swords, and corruption was brought into a virtually enslaved and degraded country; that was democracy no more of which Plato spoke, as witness his own words:—

"This, in my opinion, is a democracy: when the poor, getting the upper hand in the State, kill some and banish others, sharing equally and with the remaining citizens the magistracies and high offices."[1]

You know, and history proves, that was no picture of democracy in Athens.

But I, too, will quote from a philosopher, and the authority I quote from is greater far than Plato's. He spoke in Athens, too; he taught in the same city where Plato lived; he exhorted the same people at whom Plato sneered. That man was Paul, the ambassador of God, before whom the wisdom of the wise is but as the babbling of children, and the teaching of your schools but as the lisping of babes. You are at issue with his law.

He told the countrymen of Plato, "God hath made of one blood all nations of men;" but your doctrine would divide one people into many nations.

He was the minister of One who taught the great law of human liberty—"Brethren, ye have been called unto *liberty!*" "We are the children, not of the bondman, but of the free."

He taught the doctrine of equality—"I mean not that other men be eased and ye burdened, but by an equality . . . that there be equality." "Be ye not the servants of men." "If ye have respect for persons ye commit sin, and are convinced of the law as transgressors;" but you tell us we must reverence an aristocracy of men!

"Neither be ye called master. But he that is greatest among you shall be your servant;" but you tell us we must pay homage to a House of Lords!

[1] *Rep.* viii, 10.

"Be thou not called Rabbi;" but you wish to have a Right Reverend Father in God, my Lord the Bishop, introduced among the republican Churches of your own country!

You tell us that the curse of God rests on the rule of the majority; but the very first meeting of the Christian Church, called to elect a successor to Judas, elected that successor in the presence of the Apostles, by an appeal to the majority. God said, the voice of a majority was to elect an *apostle:* you say it must not even elect the pettiest borough member!

Again: at the second meeting of the Church, the Apostles called the multitude together to elect deacons, and they were elected by the majority. The Apostles did that: the men who would carry out the plan they gave, you call adventurers, demagogues, and enemies!

Do not say, these teachings apply to spiritual things alone; they were the gospel of liberty on *earth* as well as in *heaven.* There is but one truth, and it is universal; for the Almighty is its source. There is no contradiction, as you assert, in the world-plan of the Creator; what is a truth for the highest archangel is the same truth for the lowest worm that crawls upon the earth.

Do you deny the application to our earthly affairs? Then listen:—

"What mean ye that ye beat my people to pieces, and grind the faces of the poor?" "Do not rich men oppress ye, and drag ye before the judgment seats?" In one year alone, 1864,—the last return given under the Master and Servants Act,—10,246 working men were imprisoned at the suit of their masters—not one master at the suit of the men!

"Woe be to them that join house to house, that lay field to field." Twelve men own about the half of Scotland, one hundred and fifty divide the half of England between them.

"Woe unto you, for ye lade men with burdens grievous to be borne, and ye yourselves touch not the burden with one of your fingers." The cattle-plague legislation will supply you with the most modern illustration.

"Behold, the hire of your labourers, who have reaped your fields, which is of you kept back by fraud, crieth, and the cries have entered the ears of the Lord." The wages of labourers in your aristocratic English counties are 12s. and 10s. and 9s. and 8s.—even 7s. per week.

You tell us that God made the aristocracy. Listen whether He did:—

"Jesus called them to Him, and saith unto them: Ye know that they which are accounted to rule over the Gentiles exercise lordship over them; and their great men exercise authority upon them. But so shall it not be among you: but whosoever will be great among you shall be your minister; and whosoever will be chiefest shall be the least. For even the Son of Man came not to be ministered unto, but to minister."

That, Sir, is democracy—its fountainhead and source, its seal and sanction from the King of kings. Tell me of your Platos and Aristotles after this!

And the poor were our Lord's special care. Has He not said, when asked for a sign of his divinity—

"The blind receive sight and the lame walk, the lepers are cleansed and the deaf hear, the dead are raised up, *and the poor have the gospel preached to them.*" Yes! last but greatest evidence of all—greater even than the raising of the dead was the raising of the poor!—"The poor have the gospel preached to them."

The poor can come to the communion of the Lord. Do you exclude them there because of their numbers or their poverty? Do you believe that God, who gave them the franchise of heaven, would with-hold from them the franchises of earth?

Oh! let us have more of the Divine Spirit of the gospel in our dealings one with another. It is the great want of the age. Instead of severing class from class, we need drawing man to man. Perish your class distinctions, and mend your Christianity! "Thou shalt love the Lord with all thy heart, and with all thy soul, *and thy neighbour as thyself.* On these two commandments hang all the law and the prophets." *Sir! we are your neighbours.* We say to you, "Whatsoever ye would that men should do to you, do you even so unto them." When you realise this you have democracy, for democracy is but Christianity applied to the politics of our worldly life.

And now, if one brain has been touched with a nobler thought, if one heart has been warmed by a kindlier feeling, our two nights' labour has not been in vain. But, whatever the result, we poor soldiers of democracy will still struggle on with will unfaltering, and with undiminished faith:

καλὸν γὰρ τὸ ἄθλον, καὶ ἡ ἐλπὶς μεγάλη.[1]

---

[1] "Noble is the prize, and our hope great."

LIBERTY OF THOUGHT AND DISCUSSION

THE BASIS OF TOLERATION [1]

Walter Bagehot

[Walter Bagehot (1826-1877) has been characterized by Woodrow Wilson as a wit and a seer, a literary politician who had "the genius to see deep into affairs, and the discretion to keep out of them." To many, Bagehot is chiefly known as an original political economist and a lucid political thinker. Others care most for the brilliance and wisdom of his literary studies, and wonder why he is so little read.

Receiving his bachelor's degree from the University of London in 1846, Bagehot read law for a time, hesitating between the bar and his father's bank. During a stay in Paris he addressed to the editor of the *Inquirer* a brilliant and somewhat cynical series of letters on the French *coup d'etat* of 1851, developing the thesis that "the most essential mental quality for a free people, whose liberty is to be progressive, permanent, and on a large scale, is much *stupidity.*" Upon his return to England he joined his father in the Somersetshire Bank and in his other business as a merchant and ship owner. He became editor of the *Economist;* and by his essays, *The Postulates of Political Economy,* and his book *Lombard Street,* he made a reputation as an original thinker in the field of economics. His work, *The English Constitution,* showed him to be a realistic and imaginative observer of the actual world of politics. He was the first to point out the error of the makers of the Constitution of the United States in supposing that they were following English precedents in their doctrine of checks and balances. His *Physics and Politics* is an application of the scientific contributions of Darwin, Wallace and Huxley to political philosophy. In this, his chapter *The Age of Discussion,* is of special interest to students of toleration. Among his literary studies, especial attention might be called to his essays on Shakespeare, Milton, Shelley, Hartley Coleridge, and Tennyson, Browning and Wordsworth.

Bagehot made two or three efforts to get into Parliament, but after an illness abandoned the attempt, and believed that his political judgment was sounder as a detached observer. "As a speaker," says his intimate friend, R. H. Hutton, "he did not often succeed. His voice had no great compass, and his manner was somewhat odd to ordinary hearers." But his talk was his chief charm for his friends. One of them, T. S. Osler, said,

As an instrument for arriving at truth, I never knew anything like a talk with Bagehot. Foremost was his power of getting at the heart of a subject, taking you miles beyond your starting point in a sentence, generally by dint of sinking to a deeper stratum. The next was his instantaneous appreciation of the bearing of everything you yourself said, making talk with him, as Roscoe once remarked, 'like riding a horse with a perfect mouth.' But most unique of all was his

[1] Reprinted by permission of Longmans, Green and Co., from *The Works and Life of Walter Bagehot,* where it appears as the *Metaphysical Basis of Toleration.*

Questions and topics for the discussion of this essay, and of other phases of the general subject with which it deals, will be found on pages 501 and 505.

power of keeping up animation without combat. I never knew a power
of discussion, of co-operative investigation of truth, to approach it.
It was all stimulus, and yet no contest.

Those who conceive of public speaking as discussion may learn much from
Bagehot. The essay on toleration here printed first appeared in the *Contemporary Review*, April, 1874.]

One of the most marked peculiarities of recent times in England
is the increased liberty in the expression of opinion. Things are
now said constantly and without remark, which even ten years
ago would have caused a hubbub, and have drawn upon those who
said them much obloquy. But already I think there are signs of
a reaction. In many quarters of orthodox opinion I observe a
disposition to say, "Surely this is going too far; really we cannot
allow such things to be said." And what is more curious, some
writers, whose pens are just set at liberty, and who would, not at
all long ago, have been turned out of society for the things that
they say, are setting themselves to explain the "weakness" of
liberty, and to extol the advantages of persecution. As it appears
to me that the new practice of this country is a great improvement
on its old one, and as I conceive that the doctrine of Toleration
rests on what may be called a metaphysical basis, I wish shortly
to describe what that basis is.

I should say that, except where it is explained to the contrary,
I use the word "Toleration" to mean toleration by law. Toleration by Society of matters not subject to legal penalty is a kindred
subject on which, if I have room, I will add a few words, but in
the main I propose to deal with the simpler subject,—toleration by
law. And by toleration, too, I mean, when it is not otherwise said,
toleration in the public expression of opinions. Toleration of
acts and practices is another allied subject on which I can, in
a paper like this, but barely hope to indicate what seems to me
to be the truth. And I should add, that I deal only with the discussion of impersonal doctrines. The law of libel, which deals
with accusations of living persons, is a topic requiring consideration by itself.

Meaning this by "toleration," I do not think we ought to be
surprised at a reaction against it. What was said long ago of
slavery seems to be equally true of persecution,—it "exists by
the law of nature." It is so congenial to human nature, that it
has arisen everywhere in past times, as history shows; that the
cessation of it is a matter of recent times in England; that even

now, taking the world as a whole, the practice and the theory of it
are in a triumphant majority. Most men have always much preferred persecution, and do so still; and it is therefore only natural
that it should continually reappear in discussion and argument.

One mode in which it tempts human nature is very obvious.
Persons of strong opinions wish, above all things, to propagate
those opinions. They find close at hand what seems an immense
engine for that propagation; they find the *State*, which has often
in history interfered for and against opinions,—which has had a
great and undeniable influence in helping some and hindering
others,—and in their eagerness they can hardly understand why
they should not make use of this great engine to crush the errors
which they hate, and to replace them with the tenets they approve.
So long as there are earnest believers in the world they will always
wish to punish opinions, even if their judgment tells them it is
unwise, and their conscience that it is wrong. They may not
gratify their inclination, but the inclination will not be the less
real.

Since the time of Carlyle, "earnestness" has been a favourite
virtue in literature, and it is customary to treat this wish to twist
other people's belief into ours as if it were a part of the love of
truth. And in the highest minds so it may be. But the mass of
mankind have, as I hold, no such fine motive. Independently of
truth or falsehood, the spectacle of a different belief from ours
is disagreeable to us, in the same way that the spectacle of a different form of dress and manners is disagreeable. A set of school-
boys will persecute a new boy with a new sort of jacket; they will
hardly let him have a new-shaped penknife. Grown-up people
are just as bad, except when culture has softened them. A mob
will hoot a foreigner who looks very unlike themselves. Much
of the feeling of "earnest believers" is, I believe, altogether the
same. They wish others to think as they do, not only because they
wish to diffuse doctrinal truth, but also and much more because
they cannot bear to hear the words of a creed different from their
own. At any rate, without further analysing the origin of the
persecuting impulse, its deep root in human nature, and its great
power over most men, are evident.

But this natural impulse was not the only motive—perhaps was
not the principal one—of historical persecutions. The main one,
or a main one, was a most ancient political idea which once ruled
the world, and of which deep vestiges are still to be traced on

many sides. The most ancient conception of a State is that of a "religious partnership," in which any member may by his acts bring down the wrath of the gods on the other members, and so to speak, on the whole company. This danger was, in the general conception of the time, at once unlimited and inherited; in any generation, partners A, C, D, etc., might suffer loss of life, or health, or goods—the whole association even might perish, because in a past generation the ancestors of Z had somehow offended the gods. Thus the historian of Athens tells us that after a particular act of sacrilege—a breach of the local privileges of sanctuary—the perpetrators were compelled "to retire into banishment"; and that those who had died before the date he is speaking of were "disinterred and cast beyond the borders." "Yet," he adds, "their exile continuing, as it did; only for a time, was not held sufficient to expiate the impiety for which they have been condemned. The Alkmoönids, one of the most powerful families in Attica, long continued to be looked upon as a tainted race, and in cases of public calamity were liable to be singled out as having by their sacrilege drawn the judgment of the gods upon their countrymen." [1] And as false opinions about the gods have almost always been thought to be peculiarly odious to them, the misbeliever, the "miscreant," has been almost always thought to be likely not only to impair hereafter the salvation of himself and others in a future world, but also to bring on his neighbours and his nation grievous calamities immediately in this. He has been persecuted to stop political danger more than to arrest intellectual error.

But it will be said: Put history aside, and come to things now. Why should not those who are convinced that certain doctrines are errors, that they are most dangerous, that they may ruin man's welfare here and his salvation hereafter, use the power of the State to extirpate those errors? Experience seems to show that the power of the State can be put forth in that way effectually. Why, then, should it not be put forth? If I had room, I should like for a moment to criticise the word "effectually." I should say that the State, in the cases where it is most wanted, is not of the use which is thought. I admit that it extirpates error, but I doubt if it creates belief—at least, if it does so in cases where the persecuted error is suitable to the place and time. In such cases,

[1] Grote's *History of Greece*, part 2, chap. 10.

I think the effect has often been to eradicate a heresy among the few, at the cost of creating a scepticism among the many; to kill the error no doubt, but also to ruin the general belief. And this is the cardinal point, for the propagation of the "truth" is the end of persecution; all else is only a means. But I have not space to discuss this, and will come to the main point.

I say that the State power should not be used to arrest discussion, because the State power may be used equally for truth or error, for Mohammedanism or Christianity, for belief or no-belief, but in discussion truth has an advantage. Arguments always tell for truth as such, and against error as such; if you let the human mind alone, it has a preference for good argument over bad; it oftener takes truth than not. But if you do not let it alone, you give truth no advantage at all; you substitute a game of force, where all doctrines are equal, for a game of logic, where the truer have the better chance.

The process by which truth wins in discussion is this,—certain strong and eager minds embrace original opinions, seldom all wrong, never quite true, but of a mixed sort, part truth, part error. These they inculcate on all occasions, and on every side, and gradually bring the cooler sort of men to a hearing of them. These cooler people serve as quasi-judges, while the more eager ones are a sort of advocates; a Court of Inquisition is sitting perpetually, investigating, informally and silently, but not ineffectually, what on all great subjects of human interest, is truth and error. There is no sort of infallibility about the court; often it makes great mistakes, most of its decisions are incomplete in thought and imperfect in expression. Still, on the whole, the force of evidence keeps it right. The truth has the best of the proof, and therefore wins most of the judgments. The process is slow, far more tedious than the worst Chancery suit. Time in it is reckoned not by days, but by years, or rather by centuries. Yet on the whole, it creeps along, if you do not stop it. But all is arrested, if persecution begins— if you have a *coup d'état*, and let loose soldiers on the court; for it is perfect chance which litigant turns them in, or what creed they are used to compel men to believe.

This argument, however, assumes two things. In the first place, it presupposes that we are speaking of a state of society in which discussion is possible. And such societies are not very common. Uncivilised man is not capable of discussion: savages have been justly described as having "the intellect of children with the passions and strength of men."[1] Before anything like speculative argument can be used with them, their intellect must be strengthened and their passions restrained. There was, as it seems to me, a long preliminary period before human nature, as we now see it, existed, and while it was being formed. During that preliminary period, persecution, like slavery, played a most considerable part. Nations mostly became nations by having a common religion. It was a necessary condition of the passage from a loose aggregate of savages to a united polity, that they should believe in the same gods and worship these gods in the same way. What was necessary was, that they should for a long period—for centuries, perhaps—lead the same life and conform to the same usages. They believed that the "gods of their fathers" had commanded these usages. Early law is hardly to be separated from religious ritual: it is more like the tradition of a Church than the enactments of a statute-book. It is a thing essentially immemorial and sacred. It is not conceived of as capable either of addition or diminution; it is a body of holy customs which no one is allowed either to break or to impugn. The use of these is to aid in creating a common national character, which in after-times may be tame enough to bear discussion, and which may suggest common axioms upon which discussion can be founded. Till that common character has been formed, discussion is impossible; it cannot be used to find out truth, for it cannot exist; it is not that we have to forego its efficacy on purpose, we have not the choice of it, for its prerequisites cannot be found. The case of civil liberty is, as I conceive, much the same. Early ages need a coercive despotism more than they need anything else. The age of debate comes later. An omnipotent power to enforce the sacred law is that which is then most required. A constitutional opposition would be born before its time. It would be dragging the wheel before the horses were harnessed. The strongest advocates both of Liberty and Toleration may consistently hold that there were unhappy ages before either became possible, and when attempts at either would have been pernicious.

The case is analogous to that of education. Every parent wisely teaches his child his own creed, and till the child has attained a certain age, it is better that he should not hear too much of any other. His mind will in the end be better able to weigh argu-

[1] Sir John Lubbock's *Prehistoric Times*, p. 465. Vol. 3.

ments, because it does not begin to weigh them so early. He will hardly comprehend any creed unless he has been taught some creed. But the restrictions of childhood must be relaxed in youth, and abandoned in manhood. One object of education is to train us for discussion, and as that training gradually approaches to completeness, we should gradually begin to enter into and to take part in discussion. The restrictions that are useful at nine years old are pernicious at nineteen.

This analogy would have seemed to me obvious, but there are many most able persons who turn the matter just the other way. They regard the discipline of education as a precedent for persecution. They say, "I would no sooner let the nation at large read that bad book than I would let my children read it." They refuse to admit that the age of the children makes any difference. At heart they think that they are wiser than the mass of mankind, just as they are wiser than their children, and would regulate the studies of both unhesitatingly. But experience shows that no man is on all points so wise as the mass of men are after a good discussion, and that if the ideas of the very wisest were by miracle to be fixed on the race, the certain result would be to stereotype monstrous error. If we fixed the belief of Bacon, we should believe that the earth went round the sun; if we fixed that of Newton, we should believe "that the Argonautic expedition was a real event, and occurred B. C., 937; that Hercules was a real person, and delivered Theseus, another real person, B. C., 936; that in the year 1036 Ceres, a woman of Sicily, in seeking her daughter who was stolen, came into Attica, and there taught the Greeks to sow corn." And the worst is, that the minds of most would-be persecutors are themselves unfixed: their opinions are in a perpetual flux; they would persecute all others for tenets which yesterday they had not heard of and which they will not believe to-morrow.

But it will be said, the theory of Toleration is not so easy as that of education. We know by a certain fact when a young man is grown up and can bear discussion. We judge by his age, as to which every one is agreed. But we cannot tell by any similar patent fact when a State is mature enough to bear discussion. There may be two opinions about it. And I quite agree that the matter of fact is more difficult to discover in one case than in the other; still it is a matter of fact which the rulers of the State must decide upon their responsibility, and as best they can. And the highest sort of rulers will decide it like the English in India—with no reference to their own belief. For years the English prohibited the preaching of Christianity in India, though it was their own religion, because they thought that it could not be tranquilly listened to. They now permit it, because they find that the population can bear the discussion. Of course, most Governments are wholly unequal to so high a morality and so severe a self-command. The Governments of most countries are composed of persons who wish everybody to believe as they do, merely because they do. Some here and there, from a higher motive, so eagerly wish to propagate their opinions, that they are unequal to consider the problem of toleration impartially. They persecute till the persecuted become strong enough to make them desist. But the delicacy of a rule and the unwillingness of Governments to adopt it, do not prove that it is not the best and the right one. There are already in inevitable jurisprudence many lines of vital importance just as difficult to draw. The line between sanity and insanity has necessarily to be drawn, and it is as nice as anything can be. The competency of people to bear discussion is not intrinsically more difficult than their competency to manage their own affairs, though perhaps a Government is less likely to be impartial and more likely to be biased in questions of discussion than in pecuniary ones.

Secondly, the doctrine that rulers are to permit discussion, assumes not only, as we have seen, that discussion is possible, but also that discussion will not destroy the Government. No Government is bound to permit a controversy which will annihilate itself. It is a trustee for many duties, and if possible, it must retain the power to perform those duties. The controversies which may ruin it are very different in different countries. The Government of the day must determine in each case what those questions are. If the Roman Emperors who persecuted Christianity really did so because they imagined that Christianity would destroy the Roman Empire, I think they are to be blamed not for their misconception of duty, but for their mistake of fact. The existence of Christianity was not really more inconsistent with the existence of the Empire in the time of Diocletian than in that of Constantine; but if Diocletian thought that it was inconsistent, it was his duty to preserve the Empire.

It will be asked, "What do you mean by preserving a society? All societies are in a state of incipient change; the best of them are often the most changing; what is meant, then, by saying you will 'preserve' any? You admit that you cannot keep them unaltered, what then do you propose to do?" I answer that, in this respect, the life of societies is like the life of the individuals composing them. You cannot interfere so as to keep a man's body unaltered; you can interfere so as to keep him alive. What changes in such cases will be fatal, is a question of fact. The Government must determine what will, so to say, "break up the whole thing" and what will not. No doubt it may decide wrong. In France, the country of experiments, General Cavaignac said, "A Government which allows its principle to be discussed, is a lost Government," and therefore he persecuted on behalf of the Republic, thinking it was essential to society. Louis Napoleon similarly persecuted on behalf of the Second Empire; M. Thiers on behalf of the Republic again; the Duc de Broglie now persecutes on behalf of the existing nondescript. All these may be mistakes, or some of them, or none. Here, as before, the practical difficulties in the application of a rule do not disprove its being the true and the only one.

It will be objected that this principle is applicable only to truths which are gained by discussion. "We admit," such objectors say, "that where discussion is the best or the only means of proving truth, it is unadvisable to prohibit that discussion, but there are other means besides discussion of arriving at truth, which are sometimes better than discussion even where discussion is applicable, and sometimes go beyond it and attain regions in which it is inapplicable; and where those more efficient means are applicable, it may be wise to prohibit discussion, for in these instances discussion may confuse the human mind and impede it in the use of those higher means. The case is analogous to that of the eyes. For the most part it is a sound rule to tell persons who want to see things, that they must necessarily use *both* their eyes, and rely on them. But there are cases in which that rule is wrong. If a man wants to see things too distant for the eyes, as the satellites of Jupiter and the ring of Saturn, you must tell him, on the contrary, to shut one eye and look through a telescope with the other. The ordinary mode of using the common instruments may, in exceptional cases, interfere with the right use of the supplementary instruments." And I quite admit that there are such exceptional cases and such additional means; but I say that their existence introduces no new difficulty into the subject, and that it is no reason for prohibiting discussion except in the cases in which we have seen already that it was advisable to prohibit it.

Putting the matter in the most favourable way for these objectors, and making all possible concessions to them, I believe the exceptions which they contend for must come at last to three.

First, there are certain necessary propositions which the human mind *will* think, must think, and cannot help thinking. For example, we must believe that things which are equal to the same thing are equal to each other,—that a thing cannot *both* be and not be,—that it must *either* be or not be. These truths are not not gained by discussion; on the contrary, discussion presupposes at least some of them, for you cannot argue without first principles any more than you can use a lever without a fulcrum. The prerequisites of reasoning must somehow be recognized by the human mind before we begin to reason. So much is obvious, but then it is obvious also that in such cases attempts at discussion cannot do any harm. If the human mind has in it certain first principles which it cannot help seeing, and which it accepts of itself, there is no harm in arguing against those first principles. You may contend as long as you like, that things which are equal to the same thing are *not* equal to each other, or that a thing *can* both exist and not exist at the same time, but you will not convince any one. If you could convince anyone you would do him irreparable harm, for you would hurt the basis of his mind and destroy the use of his reason. But happily you cannot convince him. That which the human mind cannot help thinking it cannot help thinking, and discussion can no more remove the primary perceptions than it can produce them. The multiplication table will remain the multiplication table, neither more nor less, however much we may argue either for it or against it.

But, though the denial of the real necessary perceptions of the human mind cannot possibly do any harm, the denial of alleged necessary perceptions is often essential to the discovery of truth. The human mind, as experience shows, is apt to manufacture sham self-evidences. The most obvious case is, that men perpetually "do sums" wrong. If we dwell long enough and intently enough on the truths of arithmetic they are in each case self-evident; but, if we are too quick, or let our minds get dull, we may make any number of mistakes. A certain deliberation and a certain intensity are both essential to correctness in the matter. Fictitious necessities of thought will be imposed on us without end unless we are careful. The greatest minds are not exempt from the risk of such mistakes even in matters most familiar to them. On the contrary, the history of science is full of cases in which the ablest men and the most experienced assumed that it was impossible to think things which are in matter of fact true, and which it has since been found possible to think quite easily. The mode in which these sham self-evidences are distinguished from the real ones is by setting as many minds as possible to try as often as possible whether they can help thinking the thing or not. But such trials will never exist without discussion. So far, therefore, the existence of self-evidences in the human mind is not a reason for discouraging discussion, but a reason for encouraging it.

Next, it is certainly true that many conclusions which are by no means self-evident and which are gradually obtained, nevertheless, are not the result of discussion. For example, the opinion of a man as to the characters of his friends and acquaintances is not the result of distinct argument, but the aggregate of distinct impressions: it is not the result of an investigation consciously pursued, but the effect of a multiplicity of facts involuntarily presented; it is a definite thing and has a most definite influence on the mind, but its origin is indefinite and not to be traced; it is like a great fund raised in very small subscriptions and of which the subscribers' names are lost. But here, again, though these opinions too were not gained by discussion, their existence is a reason for promoting discussion, not for preventing it. Everyday experience shows that these opinions as to character are often mistaken in the last degree. Human character is a most complex thing, and the impressions which different people form of it are as various as the impressions which the inhabitants of an impassable mountain have of its shape and size. Each observer has an aggregate idea derived from certain actions and certain sayings, but the real man has always or almost always said a thousand sayings of a kind quite different and in a connection quite different; he has done a vast variety of actions among "other men" and "other minds"; a mobile person will often seem hardly the same if you meet him in very different societies. And how, except by discussion, is the true character of such a person to be decided? Each observer must bring his contingent to the list of *data;* those data must be arranged and made use of. The certain and positive facts as to which every one is agreed must have their due weight; they must be combined and compared with the various impressions as

to which no two people exactly coincide. A rough summary must
be made of the whole. In no other way is it possible to arrive
at the truth of the matter. Without discussion each mind is dependent on its own partial observation. A great man is one image
—one thing, so to speak—to his valet, another to his son, another
to his wife, another to his greatest friend. None of these must
be stereotyped; all must be compared. To prohibit discussion is
to prohibit the corrective process.

Lastly, I hold that there are first principles or first perceptions
which are neither the result of constant though forgotten trials
like those last spoken of, nor common to all the race like the first.
The most obvious seem to me to be the principles of taste. The
primary perceptions of beauty vary much in different persons,
and for different persons at different times, but no one can say
that they are not most real and most influential parts of human
nature. There is hardly a thing made by human hands which is
not affected more or less by the conceptions of beauty felt by the
maker; and there is hardly a human life which would not have
been different if the idea of beauty in the mind of the man who
lived it had been different.

But certainly it would not answer to exclude subjects of taste
from discussion, and to allow one school of taste-teachers to reign
alone, and to prohibit the teaching of all rival schools. The effect
would be to fix on all ages the particular ideas of one age on a
matter which is beyond most others obscure and difficult to reduce
to a satisfactory theory. The human mind evidently differs at
various times immensely in its conclusions upon it, and there is
nothing to show that the era of the persecutor is wiser than any
other era, or that his opinion is better than any one else's.

The case of these variable first principles is much like that of
the "personal equation," as it is called in the theory of observations. Some observers, it is found, habitually see a given phenomenon, say the star coming to the meridian, a little sooner than
most others; some later; no two persons exactly coincide. The first
thing done when a new man comes into an observatory for practical work is to determine whether he sees quick or slow; and this
is called the "personal equation." But, according to the theory of
persecution, the national astronomer in each country would set up
his own mind as the standard; in one country he would be a quick
man, and would not let the slow people contest what he said; in
another he would be a slow man, and would not tolerate the quick

people, or let men speak their minds; and so the astronomical observations—the astronomical *creeds* if I may say so—of different countries would radically differ. But as toleration and discussion are allowed, no such absurd result follows. The observations of different minds are compared with those of others, and truth is assumed to lie in the mean between the errors of the quick people and the errors of the slow ones.

No such accurate result can be expected in more complex matters. The phenomena of astronomical observation relate only to very simple events, and to a very simple fact about these events. But perceptions of beauty have an infinite complexity: they are all subtle aggregates of countless details, and about each of these details probably every mind in some degree differs from every other one. But in a rough way the same sort of agreement is possible. Discussion is only an organised mode by which various minds compare their conclusions with those of various others. Bold and strong minds describe graphic and definite impressions: at first sight these impressions seem wholly different. Writers of the last century thought classical architecture altogether superior to Gothic; many writers now put it just the other way, and maintain a mediæval cathedral to be a thing altogether superior in kind and nature to anything classical. For years the world thought Claude's landscapes perfect. Then came Mr. Ruskin, and by his ability and eloquence he has made a whole generation depreciate them, and think Turner's altogether superior. The extrication of truth by such discussions is very slow; it is often retarded; it is often thrown back; it often seems to pause for ages. But upon the whole it makes progress, and the principle of that progress is this: Each mind which is true to itself, and which draws its own impressions carefully, and which compares those impressions with the impressions of others, arrives at certain conclusions, which as far as that mind is concerned are ultimate, and are its highest conclusions. These it sets down as expressively as it can on paper, or communicates by word of mouth, and these again form data which other minds can contrast with their own. In this incessant comparison eccentric minds fall off on every side; some like Milton, some Wordsworth, some can see nothing in Dryden, some find Racine intolerably dull, some think Shakespeare barbarous, others consider the contents of the *Iliad* "battles and schoolboy stuff." With history it is the same; some despise one great epoch, some another. Each epoch has its violent partisans, who will listen to nothing else, and who think every other epoch in comparison mean and wretched. These violent minds are always faulty and sometimes absurd, but they are almost always useful to mankind. They compel men to hear neglected truth. They uniformly exaggerate their gospel; but it generally is a gospel. Carlyle said many years since of the old Poor-law in England: "It being admitted then that outdoor relief should at once cease, what means did great Nature take to make it cease? She created various men who thought the cessation of outdoor relief the one thing needful." In the same way, it being desirable that the taste of men should be improved on some point, Nature's instrument on that point is some man of genius, of attractive voice and limited mind, who declaims and insists, not only that the special improvement is a good thing in itself, but the best of all things, and the root of all other good things. Most useful, too, are others less apparent; shrinking, sensitive, testing minds, of whom often the world knows nothing, but each of whom is in the circle just near him an authority on taste, and communicates by personal influence the opinions he has formed. The human mind of a certain maturity, if left alone, prefers real beauty to sham beauty, and prefers it the sooner if original men suggest new charms, and quiet men criticise and judge of them.

But an æsthetical persecution would derange all this, for generally the compulsive power would be in the hands of the believers in some tradition. The State represents "the rough force of society," and is little likely to be amenable to new charms or new ideas; and therefore the first victim of the persecution would be the original man who was proposing that which in the end would most improve mankind; and the next would be the testing and discerning critic who was examining these ideas and separating the chaff from the wheat in them. Neither would conform to the old tradition. The inventor would be too eager; the critic too scrupulous; and so a heavy code of ancient errors would be chained upon mankind. Nor would the case be at all the better if by some freak of events the propounder of the new doctrine were to gain full control, and were to prohibit all he did not like. He would try, and try in vain, to make the inert mass of men accept or care for his new theory, and his particular enemy would be the careful critic who went with him a little way and then refused to go any further. If you allow persecution, the partisans of the new sort of beauty will, if they can, attack those of the old sort; and the partisans of the old sort will attack those of the new sort; while both will turn on the quiet and discriminating person who is trying to select what is good from each. Some chance taste will be fixed for ages.

But it will be said, "Whoever heard of such nonsense as an æsthetical persecution? Everybody knows such matters of taste must be left to take care of themselves; as far as they are concerned, nobody wants to persecute or prohibit." But I have spoken of matters of taste because it is sometimes best to speak in parables. The case of morals and religion, in which people have always persecuted and still wish to persecute, is the very same. If there are (as I myself think there are) ultimate truths of morals and religion which more or less vary for each mind, some sort of standard and some kind of agreement can only be arrived at about it in the very same way. The same comparison of one mind with another is necessary; the same discussion; the same use of criticising minds; the same use of original ones. The mode of arriving at truth is the same, and also the mode of stopping it.

We now see the reason why, as I said before, religious persecution often extirpates new doctrines, but commonly fails to maintain the belief in old tenets. You can prevent whole classes of men from hearing of the religion which is congenial to them, but you cannot make men believe a religion which is uncongenial. You can prevent the natural admirers of Gothic architecture from hearing anything of it, or from seeing it; but you cannot make them admire classical architecture. You may prevent the admirers of Claude from seeing his pictures, or from praising them; but you cannot make them admirers of Turner. Just so, you may by persecution prevent minds prone to be Protestant from being Protestant; but you will not make men real Catholics; you may prevent naturally Catholic minds from being Catholic; but you will not make them genuine Protestants. You will not make those believe your religion who are predisposed by nature in favor of a different kind of religion; you will make of them, instead, more or less conscious sceptics. Being denied the sort of religion of which the roots are in their minds and which they could believe, they will forever be conscious of an indefinite want. They will constantly feel after something which they are never able to attain; they will never be able to settle upon anything; they will feel an instinctive repulsion from everything; they will be sceptics at heart, because they were denied the creed for which their heart craves;

they will live as indifferentists, because they were withheld by force from the only creed to which they would not be indifferent. Persecution in intellectual countries produces a superficial conformity, but also underneath an intense, incessant, implacable doubt.

Upon examination, therefore, the admission that certain truths are not gained by discussion introduces no new element into the subject. The discussion of such truths is as necessary as of all other truths. The only limitations are that men's minds shall in the particular society be mature enough to bear the discussion, and that the discussion shall not destroy the society.

I acknowledge these two limitations to the doctrine that discussion should be free, but I do not admit another which is often urged. It is said that those who write against toleration should not be tolerated; that discussion should not aid the enemies of discussion. But why not? If there is a strong Government and a people fit for discussion, why should not the cause be heard? We must not assume that the liberty of discussion has no case of exception. We have just seen that there are, in fact, several such. In each instance, let the people decide whether the particular discussion shall go on or not. Very likely, in some cases, they may decide wrong; but it is better that they should so decide, than that we should venture to anticipate all experience, and to make sure that they cannot possibly be right.

It is plain, too, that the argument here applied to the toleration of opinion has no application to that of actions. The human mind in the cases supposed, learns by freely hearing all arguments, but in no case does it learn by trying freely all practices. Society, as we now have it, cannot exist at all unless certain acts are prohibited. It goes on much better because many other acts are prohibited also. The Government must take the responsibility of saying what actions it will allow; that is its first business, and the allowance of all would be the end of civilization. But it must, under the conditions specified, hear all opinions, for the tranquil discussion of all more than anything else promotes the progressive knowledge of truth, which is the mainspring of civilization.

Nor does the argument that the law should not impose a penalty on the expression of any opinion equally prove that society should not in many cases apply a penalty to that expression. Society can deal much more severely than the law with many kinds of acts, because it need be far less strict in the evidence it requires. It can take cognisance of matters of common repute and of things of which every one is sure, but which nobody can prove. Particularly, it can fairly well compare the character of the doctrine with the character of the agent, which law can do but imperfectly, if at all. And it is certain that opinions are evidence of the character of those who hold them—not conclusive evidence, but still presumptive. Experience shows that every opinion is compatible with what every one would admit to be a life fairly approvable, a life far higher than that of the mass of men. Great scepticism and great belief have both been found in characters whom both sceptics and believers must admire. Still, on the whole, there is a certain kinship between belief and character; those who disagree with a man's fundamental creed will generally disapprove of his habitual character. If, therefore, society sees a man maintaining opinions which by experience it has been led to connect with actions such as it discountenances, it is justified in provisionally discountenancing the man who holds those opinions. Such a man should be put to the proof to show by his life that the opinions which he holds are not connected with really pernicious actions, as society thinks they are. If he is visibly leading a high life, society should discountenance him no longer; it is then clear that he did not lead a bad life, and the idea that he did or might lead such a life was the only reason for so doing. A doubt was suggested, but it also has been removed. This habit of suspicion does not, on the whole, impair free discussion; perhaps even it improves it. It keeps out the worst disputants, men of really bad character, whose opinions are the results of that character, and who refrain from publishing them, because they fear what society may say. If the law could similarly distinguish between good disputants and bad, it might usefully impose penalties on the bad. But, of course, this is impossible. Law cannot distinguish between the niceties of character; it must punish the publication of an opinion, if it punishes at all, no matter whether the publisher is a good man or whether he is a bad one. In such a matter, society is a discriminating agent: the law is but a blind one.

To most people I may seem to be slaying the slain, and proving what no one doubts. People, it will be said, no longer wish to persecute. But I say, they do wish to persecute. In fact, from their writings, and still better from their conversation, it is easy to see that very many believers would persecute sceptics, and that very many sceptics would persecute believers. Society may be wiser; but most earnest believers and most earnest unbelievers are not at all wiser.

WHAT MODERN LIBERTY MEANS [1]

Walter Lippmann

[Walter Lippmann (1889-   ) was graduated from Harvard in 1909. He has served as an associate editor of the *New Republic* and on the staff of the New York *World*. In 1917 he was appointed Assistant to the Secretary of War. He was secretary of the organization directed by Colonel House to prepare data for the Peace Conference at Versailles. Among his books are, *A Preface to Politics, Drift and Mastery, The Stakes of Diplomacy,* and *Public Opinion. What Modern Liberty Means* first appeared in the *Atlantic Monthly* for November, 1919. It has since been included in a volume by Mr. Lippmann entitled *Liberty and the News.*

Mr. Lippmann regards persuasion as "a self-conscious art and a regular organ of popular government." The chapter entitled "The Making of a Common Will," in his *Public Opinion,* is an excellent study of persuasive discourse; it examines acutely a typical campaign speech, the speaker, and the audience as factors in a persuasive effort to produce a desired vote. Mr. Lippmann's analytical study is of interest to any one who would mold public opinion; and what is equally important, it is useful to one who would resist the force of a public opinion which has been too readily shaped.]

From our recent experience it is clear that the traditional liberties of speech and opinion rest on no solid foundation. At a time when the world needs above all other things the activity of generous imaginations and the creative leadership of planning and inventive minds, our thinking is shriveled with panic. Time and energy that should go to building and restoring are instead consumed in warding off the pin-pricks of prejudice and fighting a guerrilla war against misunderstanding and intolerance. For suppression is felt, not simply by the scattered individuals who are actually suppressed. It reaches back into the steadiest minds, creating tension everywhere; and the tension of fear produces sterility. Men cease to say what they think; and when they cease to say it, they soon cease to think it. They think in reference to their critics and not in reference to the facts. For when thought

[1] Reprinted from *Liberty and the News,* by permission of and special arrangement with Harcourt, Brace and Co.

Questions and topics for the discussion of this essay, and of other phases of the general subject with which it deals, will be found on pages 502 and 505.

becomes socially hazardous, men spend more time wondering about the hazard than they do in cultivating their thought. Yet nothing is more certain than that mere bold resistance will not permanently liberate men's minds. The problem is not only greater than that, but different, and the time is ripe for reconsideration. We have learned that many of the hard-won rights of man are utterly insecure. It may be that we cannot make them secure simply by imitating the earlier champions of liberty.

Something important about the human character was exposed by Plato when, with the spectacle of Socrates's death before him, he founded Utopia on a censorship stricter than any which exists on this heavily censored planet. His intolerance seems strange. But it is really the logical expression of an impulse that most of us have not the candor to recognize. It was the service of Plato to formulate the dispositions of men in the shape of ideals, and the surest things we can learn from him are not what we ought to do, but what we are inclined to do. We are peculiarly inclined to suppress whatever impugns the security of that to which we have given our allegiance. If our loyalty is turned to what exists, intolerance begins at its frontiers; if it is turned, as Plato's was, to Utopia, we shall find Utopia defended with intolerance.

There are, so far as I can discover, no absolutists of liberty; I can recall no doctrine of liberty, which, under the acid test, does not become contingent upon some other ideal. The goal is never liberty, but liberty for something or other. For liberty is a condition under which activity takes place, and men's interests attach themselves primarily to their activities and what is necessary to fulfil them, not to the abstract requirements of any activity that might be conceived.

And yet controversialists rarely take this into account. The battle is fought with banners on which are inscribed absolute and universal ideals. They are not absolute and universal in fact. No man has ever thought out an absolute or a universal ideal in politics, for the simple reason that nobody knows enough, or can know enough, to do it. We all use absolutes, because an ideal which seems to exist apart from time, space, and circumstance has a prestige that no candid avowal of special purpose can ever have. Looked at from one point of view universals are part of the fighting apparatus in men. What they desire enormously they easily come to call God's will, or their nation's purpose. Looked at genetically, these idealizations are probably born in that spiritual reverie where all men live most of the time. In reverie there is neither time, space, nor particular reference, and hope is omnipotent. This omnipotence, which is denied to them in action, nevertheless illuminates activity with a sense of utter and irresistible value.

The classic doctrine of liberty consists of absolutes. It consists of them except at the critical points where the author has come into contact with objective difficulties. Then he introduces into the argument, somewhat furtively, a reservation which liquidates its universal meaning and reduces the exalted plea for liberty in general to a special argument for the success of a special purpose.

There are at the present time, for instance, no more fervent champions of liberty than the western sympathizers with the Russian Soviet government. Why is it that they are indignant when Mr. Burleson suppresses a newspaper and complacent when Lenin does? And, *vice versa*, why is it that the anti-Bolshevist forces in the world are in favor of restricting constitutional liberty as a preliminary to establishing genuine liberty in Russia? Clearly the argument about liberty has little actual relation to the existence of it. It is the purpose of the social conflict, not the freedom of opinion, that lies close to the heart of the partisans. The word liberty is a weapon and an advertisement, but certainly not an ideal which transcends all special aims.

If there were any man who believed in liberty apart from particular purposes, that man would be a hermit contemplating all existence with a hopeful and neutral eye. For him, in the last analysis, there could be nothing worth resisting, nothing particularly worth attaining, nothing particularly worth defending, not even the right of hermits to contemplate existence with a cold and neutral eye. He would be loyal simply to the possibilities of the human spirit, even to those possibilities which most seriously impair its variety and its health. No such man has yet counted much in the history of politics. For what every theorist of liberty has meant is that certain types of behavior and classes of opinion hitherto regulated should be somewhat differently regulated in the future. What each seems to say is that opinion and action should be free; that liberty is the highest and most sacred interest of life. But somewhere each of them inserts a weasel clause to the effect that "of course" the freedom granted shall not be employed too destructively. It is this clause which checks exuberance and re-

There is no absolutist in liberty.

minds us that, in spite of appearances, we are listening to finite men pleading a special cause.

Among the English classics none are more representative than Milton's *Areopagitica* and the essay *On Liberty* by John Stuart Mill. Of living men Mr. Bertrand Russell is perhaps the most outstanding advocate of "liberty." The three together are a formidable set of witnesses. Yet nothing is easier than to draw texts from each which can be cited either as an argument for absolute liberty or as an excuse for as much repression as seems desirable at the moment. Says Milton :

Yet if all cannot be of one mind, as who looks they should be? this doubtles is more wholesome, more prudent, and more Christian that many be tolerated, rather than all compell'd.

So much for the generalization. Now for the qualification which follows immediately upon it.

I mean not tolerated Popery, and open superstition, which as it extirpats all religions and civill supremacies, so itself should be extirpat, provided first that all charitable and compassionat means be used to win and regain the weak and misled: that also which is impious or evil absolutely either against faith or maners no law can possibly permit, that intends not to unlaw itself: but those neighboring differences, or rather *indifferences,* are what I speak of, whether in some point of doctrine or of discipline, which though they may be many, yet need not interrupt the unity of spirit, if we could but find among us the bond of peace.

With this as a text one could set up an inquisition. Yet it occurs in the noblest plea for liberty that exists in the English language. The critical point in Milton's thought is revealed by the word "indifferences." The area of opinion which he wished to free comprised the "neighboring differences" of certain Protestant sects, and only these where they were truly ineffective in manners and morals. Milton, in short, had come to the conclusion that certain conflicts of doctrine were sufficiently insignificant to be tolerated. The conclusion depended far less upon his notion of the value of liberty than upon his conception of God and human nature and the England of his time. He urged indifference to things that were becoming indifferent.

If we substitute the word indifference for the word liberty we shall come much closer to the real intention that lies behind the

classic argument. Liberty is to be permitted where differences
are of no great moment. It is this definition which has generally
guided practice. In times when men feel themselves secure, heresy
is cultivated as the spice of life. During a war liberty disappears
as the community feels itself menaced.

When revolution seems to be contagious, heresy-hunting is a
respectable occupation. In other words, when men are not afraid,
they are not afraid of ideas; when they are much afraid, they are
afraid of anything that seems, or can even be made to appear,
seditious. That is why nine tenths of the effort to live and let
live consists in proving that the thing we wish to have tolerated is
really a matter of indifference.

In Mill this truth reveals itself still more clearly. Though his
argument is surer and completer than Milton's, the qualification is
also surer and completer.

Such being the reasons which make it imperative that human beings
should be free to form opinions, and to express their opinions without
reserve; and such the baneful consequences to the intellectual and through
that to the moral nature of man, unless this liberty is either conceded or
asserted in spite of prohibition, let us next examine whether the same
reasons do not require that men should be free to act upon their opinions,
to carry these out in their lives, without hindrance, either moral or
physical, from their fellow men, so long as it is at their own risk and
peril. *This last proviso is of course indispensable.* No one pretends
that actions should be as free as opinions. On the contrary, *even opinions lose their immunity* when the circumstances in which they are expressed are such as to constitute their expression a positive instigation
to some mischievous act.

"At their own risk and peril." In other words at the risk of
eternal damnation. The premise from which Mill argued was that
many opinions then under the ban of society were of no interest
to society, and ought therefore not to be interfered with. The
orthodoxy with which he was at war was chiefly theocratic. It assumed that a man's opinions on cosmic affairs might endanger his
personal salvation and make him a dangerous member of society.
Mill did not believe in the theological view, did not fear damnation,
and was convinced that morality did not depend upon the religious
sanction. In fact, he was convinced that a more reasoned morality
could be formed by laying aside theological assumptions. "But no
one pretends that actions should be as free as opinions." The
plain truth is that Mill did not believe that much action would re-

sult from the toleration of those opinions in which he was most interested.

Political heresy occupied the fringe of his attention, and he uttered only the most casual comments. So incidental are they, so little do they impinge on his mind, that the arguments of this staunch apostle of liberty can be used honestly, and in fact are used, to justify the bulk of the suppressions which have recently occurred. "Even opinions lose their immunity, *when the circumstances* in which they are expressed are such as to constitute their expression a positive instigation to some mischievous act." Clearly there is no escape here for Debs or Haywood or obstructors of Liberty Loans. The argument used is exactly the one employed in sustaining the conviction of Debs.

In corroboration Mill's single concrete instance may be cited: "An opinion that corn dealers are starvers of the poor, or that private property is robbery, ought to be unmolested when simply circulated through the press, but may justly incur punishment when delivered orally to an excited mob assembled before the house of a corn dealer, or when handed about among the same mob in the form of a placard."

Clearly Mill's theory of liberty wore a different complexion when he considered opinions which might directly affect social order. Where the stimulus of opinion upon action was effective he could say with entire complacency, "The liberty of the individual must be thus far limited; he must not make himself a nuisance to other people." Because Mill believed this, it is entirely just to infer that the distinction drawn between a speech or placard and publication in the press would soon have broken down for Mill had he lived at a time when the press really circulated and the art of type-display had made a newspaper strangely like a placard.

On first acquaintance no man would seem to go further than Mr. Bertrand Russell in loyalty to what he calls "the unfettered development of all the instincts that build up life and fill it with mental delights." He calls these instincts "creative"; and against them he sets off the "possessive impulses." These, he says, should be restricted by "a public authority, a repository of practically irresistible force whose function should be primarily to repress the private use of force." Where Milton said no "tolerated Popery," Mr. Russell says, no tolerated "possessive impulses." Surely he is open to the criticism that, like every authoritarian who has preceded him, he is interested in the unfettered development of only that which seems good to him. Those who think that ''enlightened selfishness'' produces social harmony will tolerate more of the possessive impulses, and will be inclined to put certain of Mr. Russell's creative impulses under lock and key.

The moral is, not that Milton, Mill, and Bertrand Russell are inconsistent, or that liberty is to be obtained by arguing for it without qualifications. The impulse to what we call liberty is as strong in these three men as it is ever likely to be in our society. The moral is of another kind. It is that the traditional core of liberty, namely, the notion of indifference, is too feeble and unreal a doctrine to protect the purpose of liberty, which is the furnishing of a healthy environment in which human judgment and inquiry can most successfully organize human life. Too feeble, because in time of stress nothing is easier than to insist, and by insistence to convince, that tolerated indifference is no longer tolerable because it has ceased to be indifferent.

It is clear that in a society where public opinion has become decisive, nothing that counts in the formation of it can really be a matter of indifference. When I say ''can be,'' I am speaking literally. What men believed about the constitution of heaven became a matter of indifference when heaven disappeared in metaphysics; but what they believe about property, government, conscription, taxation, the origins of the late war, or the origins of the Franco-Prussian War, or the distribution of Latin culture in the vicinity of copper mines, constitutes the difference between life and death, prosperity and misfortune, and it will never on this earth be tolerated as indifferent, or not interfered with, no matter how many noble arguments are made for liberty, or how many martyrs give their lives for it. If widespread tolerance of opposing views is to be achieved in modern society, it will not be simply by fighting the Debs' cases through the courts, and certainly not by threatening to upset those courts if they do not yield to the agitation. The task is fundamentally of another order, requiring other methods and other theories.

The world about which each man is supposed to have opinions has become so complicated as to defy his powers of understanding. What he knows of events that matter enormously to him, the purposes of governments, the aspirations of peoples, the struggle of classes, he knows at second, third, or fourth hand. He cannot go and see for himself. Even the things that are near to him have become too involved for his judgment. I know of no man, even among those who devote all of their time to watching public affairs, who can even pretend to keep track, at the same time, of his city government, his state government, Congress, the departments, the industrial situation, and the rest of the world. What men who make the study of politics a vocation cannot do, the man who has an hour a day for newspapers and talk cannot possibly hope to do. He must seize catchwords and headlines or nothing.

This vast elaboration of the subject-matter of politics is the root of the whole problem. News comes from a distance; it comes helter-skelter, in inconceivable confusion; it deals with matters that are not easily understood; it arrives and is assimilated by busy and tired people who must take what is given to them. Any lawyer with a sense of evidence knows how unreliable such information must necessarily be.

The taking of testimony in a trial is hedged about with a thousand precautions derived from long experience of the fallibility of the witness and the prejudices of the jury. We call this, and rightly, a fundamental phase of human liberty. But in public affairs the stake is infinitely greater. It involves the lives of millions, and the fortune of everybody. The jury is the whole community, not even the qualified voters alone. The jury is everybody who creates public sentiment—chattering gossips, unscrupulous liars, congenital liars, feeble-minded people, prostitute minds, corrupting agents. To this jury any testimony is submitted, is submitted in any form, by any anonymous person, with no test of reliability, no test of credibility, and no penalty for perjury. If I lie in a lawsuit involving the fate of my neighbor's cow, I can go to jail. But if I lie to a million readers in a matter involving war and peace, I can lie my head off, and, if I choose the right series of lies, be entirely irresponsible. Nobody will punish me if I lie about Japan, for example. I can announce that every Japanese valet is a reservist, and every Japanese art store a mobilization center. I am immune. And if there should be hostilities with Japan, the more I lied the more popular I should be. If I asserted that the Japanese secretly drank the blood of children, that Japanese women were unchaste, that the Japanese were really not a branch of the human race after all, I guarantee that most of the newspapers would print it eagerly, and that I could get a hearing in churches all over the country. And all this for the simple reason that the public, when it is dependent on testimony and protected by no rules of evidence, can act only on the excitement of its pugnacities and its hopes.

The mechanism of the news-supply has developed without plan, and there is no one point in it at which one can fix the responsibility for truth. The fact is that the subdivision of labor is now accompanied by the subdivision of the news-organization. At one end of it is the eye-witness, at the other, the reader. Between the two is a vast, expensive transmitting and editing apparatus. This machine works marvelously well at times, particularly in the rapidity with which it can report the score of a game or a transatlantic flight, or the death of a monarch, or the result of an election. But where the issue is complex, as for example in the matter of the success of a policy, or the social conditions among a foreign people, —that is to say, where the real answer is neither yes or no, but subtle and a matter of balanced evidence,—the subdivision of the labor involved in the report causes no end of derangement, misunderstanding, and even misrepresentation.

Thus the number of eye-witnesses capable of honest statement is inadequate and accidental. Yet the reporter making up his news is dependent upon the eye-witnesses. They may be actors in the event. Then they can hardly be expected to have perspective. Who, for example, if he put aside his own likes and dislikes would trust a Bolshevik's account of what exists in Soviet Russia or an exiled Russian prince's story of what exists in Siberia? Sitting just across the frontier, say in Stockholm, how is a reporter to write dependable news when his witnesses consist of *emigrés* or Bolshevist agents?

At the Peace Conference, news was given out by the agents of the conferees and the rest leaked through those who were clamoring at the doors of the Conference. Now the reporter, if he is to earn his living, must nurse his personal contacts with the eye-witnesses and privileged informants. If he is openly hostile to those in authority, he will cease to be a reporter unless there is an opposition party in the inner circle who can feed him news. Failing that, he will know precious little of what is going on.

Most people seem to believe that, when they meet a war correspondent or a special writer from the Peace Conference, they have seen a man who has seen the things he wrote about. Far from it. Nobody, for example, saw this war. Neither the men in the trenches nor the commanding general. The men saw their trenches, their billets, sometimes they saw an enemy trench, but nobody, unless it be the aviators, saw a battle. What the correspondent saw, occasionally, was the terrain over which a battle had been fought; but what they reported day by day was what they were told at press headquarters, and of that only what they were allowed to tell.

At the Peace Conference the reporters were allowed to meet periodically the four least important members of the Commission, men who themselves had considerable difficulty in keeping track of things, as any reporter who was present will testify. This was supplemented by spasmodic personal interviews with the commissioners, their secretaries, their secretaries' secretaries, other newspaper men, and confidential representatives of the President, who stood between him and the impertinences of curiosity. This and the French press, than which there is nothing more censored and inspired, a local English trade-journal of the expatriates, the gossip of the Crillon lobby, the Majestic, and the other official hotels, constituted the source of the news upon which American editors and the American people have had to base one of the most difficult judgments of their history. I should perhaps add that there were a few correspondents occupying privileged positions with foreign governments. They wore ribbons in their buttonholes to prove it. They were in many ways the most useful correspondents because they always revealed to the trained reader just what it was that their governments wished America to believe.

The news accumulated by the reporter from his witnesses has to be selected, if for no other reason than that the cable facilities are limited. At the cable office several varieties of censorship intervene. The legal censorship in Europe is political as well as military, and both words are elastic. It has been applied, not only to the substance of the news, but to the mode of presentation, and even to the character of the type and the position on the page. But the real censorship on the wires is the cost of transmission. This in itself is enough to limit any expensive competition or any significant independence. The big Continental news agencies are subsidized. Censorship operates also through congestion and the resultant need of a system of priority. Congestion makes possible good and bad service, and undesirable messages are not infrequently served badly.

When the report does reach the editor, another series of interventions occurs. The editor is a man who may know all about something, but he can hardly be expected to know all about every-

thing. Yet he has to decide the question which is of more importance than any other in the formation of opinions, the question
where attention is to be directed. In a newspaper the heads are
the foci of attention, the odd corners the fringe; and whether one
aspect of the news or another appears in the center or at the
periphery makes all the difference in the world. The news of the
day as it reaches the newspaper office is an incredible medley of
fact, propaganda, rumor, suspicion, clues, hopes, and fears, and
the task of selecting and ordering that news is one of the truly
sacred and priestly offices in a democracy. For the newspaper is
in all literalness the bible of democracy, the book out of which a
people determines its conduct. It is the only serious book most
people read. It is the only book they read every day. Now the
power to determine each day what shall seem important and what
shall be neglected is a power unlike any that has been exercised
since the Pope lost his hold on the secular mind.

The ordering is not done by one man, but by a host of men, who
are on the whole curiously unanimous in their selection and in
their emphasis. Once you know the party and social affiliations of
a newspaper, you can predict with considerable certainty the perspective in which the news will be displayed. This perspective is
by no means altogether deliberate. Though the editor is ever so
much more sophisticated than all but a minority of his readers,
his own sense of relative importance is determined by rather stand-
ardized constellations of ideas. He very soon comes to believe
that his habitual emphasis is the only possible one.

Why the editor is possessed by a particular set of ideas is a
difficult question of social psychology, of which no adequate analysis has been made. But we shall not be far wrong if we say that
he deals with the news in reference to the prevailing *mores* of his
social group. These *mores* are of course in a large measure the
product of what previous newspapers have said; and experience
shows that, in order to break out of this circle, it has been necessary
at various times to create new forms of journalism, such as the
national monthly, the critical weekly, the circular, the paid advertisement of ideas, in order to change the emphasis which had become obsolete and habit-ridden.

Into this extremely refractory, and I think increasingly dis-
serviceable mechanism, there has been thrown, especially since the
outbreak of war, another monkey-wrench—propaganda. The word,
of course, covers a multitude of sins and a few virtues. The virtues

can be easily separated out, and given another name, either advertisement or advocacy. Thus, if the National Council of Belgravia wishes to publish a magazine out of its own funds, under its own imprint, advocating the annexation of Thrums, no one will object. But if, in support of that advocacy, it gives to the press stories that are lies about the atrocities committed in Thrums; or, worse still, if those stories seem to come from Geneva, or Amsterdam, not from the press-service of the National Council of Belgravia, then Belgravia is conducting propaganda. If, after arousing a certain amount of interest in itself, Belgravia then invites a carefully selected correspondent, or perhaps a labor leader, to its capital, puts him up at the best hotel, rides him around in limousines, fawns on him at banquets, lunches with him very confidentially, and then puts him through a conducted tour so that he shall see just what will create the desired impression, then again Belgravia is conducting propaganda. Or if Belgravia happens to possess the greatest trombone-player in the world, and if she sends him over to charm the wives of influential husbands, Belgravia is, in a less objectionable way, perhaps, committing propaganda, and making fools of the husbands.

Now, the plain fact is that out of the troubled areas of the world the public receives practically nothing that is not propaganda. Lenin and his enemies control all the news there is of Russia, and no court of law would accept any of the testimony as valid in a suit to determine the possession of a donkey. I am writing many months after the Armistice. The Senate is at this moment beginning to consider the question whether it will guarantee the frontiers of Poland; but what we learn of Poland we learn from the Polish Government and the Jewish Committee. Judgment on the vexed issues of Europe is simply out of the question for the average American; and the more cocksure he is, the more certainly is he the victim of some propaganda.

These instances are drawn from foreign affairs, but the difficulty at home, although less flagrant, is nevertheless real. Theodore Roosevelt, and Leonard Wood after him, have told us to think nationally. It is not easy. It is easy to parrot what those people say who live in a few big cities and who have constituted themselves the only true and authentic voice of America. But beyond that it is difficult. I live in New York and I have not the vaguest idea what Brooklyn is interested in. It is possible, with effort, much more effort than most people can afford to give, for me to know what a few organized bodies like the Non-Partisan League, the National Security League, the American Federation of Labor, and the Republican National Committee are up to; but what the unorganized workers, and the unorganized farmers, the shop-keepers, the local bankers and boards of trade are thinking and feeling, no one has any means of knowing, except perhaps in a vague way at election time. To think nationally means, at least, to take into account the major interests and needs and desires of this continental population; and for that each man would need a staff of secretaries, traveling agents, and a very expensive press-clipping bureau.

We do not think nationally because the facts that count are not systematically reported and presented in a form we can digest. Our most abysmal ignorance occurs where we deal with the immigrant. If we read his press at all, it is to discover "Bolshevism" in it and to blacken all immigrants with suspicion. For his culture and his aspirations, for his high gifts of hope and variety, we have neither eyes nor ears. The immigrant colonies are like holes in the road which we never notice until we trip over them. Then, because we have no current information and no background of facts, we are, of course, the undiscriminating objects of any agitator who chooses to rant against "foreigners."

Now, men who have lost their grip upon the relevant facts of their environment are the inevitable victims of agitation and propaganda. The quack, the charlatan, the jingo, and the terrorist, can flourish only where the audience is deprived of independent access to information. But where all news comes at second-hand, where all the testimony is uncertain, men cease to respond to truths, and respond simply to opinions. The environment in which they act is not the realities themselves, but the pseudo-environment of reports, rumors, and guesses. The whole reference of thought comes to be what somebody asserts, not what actually is. Men ask, not whether such and such a thing occurred in Russia, but whether Mr. Raymond Robins is at heart more friendly to the Bolsheviki than Mr. Jerome Landfield. And so, since they are deprived of any trustworthy means of knowing what is really going on, since everything is on the plane of assertion and propaganda, they believe whatever fits most comfortably with their prepossessions.

That this breakdown of the means of public knowledge should occur at a time of immense change is a compounding of the difficulty. From bewilderment to panic is a short step, as everyone knows who has watched a crowd when danger threatens. At the present time a nation easily acts like a crowd. Under the influence of headlines and panicky print, the contagion of unreason can easily spread through a settled community. For when the comparatively recent and unstable nervous organization which makes us capable of responding to reality as it is, and not as we should wish it, is baffled over a continuing period of time, the more primitive but much stronger instincts are let loose.

War and Revolution, both of them founded on censorship and propaganda, are the supreme destroyers of realistic thinking, because the excess of danger and the fearful overstimulation of passion unsettle disciplined behavior. Both breed fanatics of all kinds, men who, in the words of Mr. Santayana, have redoubled their effort when they have forgotten their aim. The effort itself has become the aim. Men live in their effort, and for a time find great exaltation. They seek stimulation of their effort rather than direction of it. That is why both in war and revolution there seems to operate a kind of Gresham's Law of the emotions, in which leadership passes by a swift degradation from a Mirabeau to a Robespierre; and in war, from a high-minded statesmanship to the depths of virulent, hating jingoism.

The cardinal fact always is the loss of contact with objective information. Public as well as private reason depends upon it. Not what somebody says, not what somebody wishes were true, but what is so beyond all our opining, constitutes the touchstone of our sanity. And a society which lives at second-hand will commit incredible follies and countenance inconceivable brutalities if that contact is intermittent and untrustworthy. Demagoguery is a parasite that flourishes where discrimination fails, and only those who are at grips with things themselves are impervious to it. For, in the last analysis, the demagogue, whether of the Right or the Left, is, consciously or unconsciously, an undetected liar.

Many students of politics have concluded that, because public opinion was unstable, the remedy lay in making government as independent of it as possible. The theorists of representative government have argued persistently from this premise against the believers in direct legislation. But it appears now that, while they have been making their case against direct legislation, rather successfully it seems to me, they have failed sufficiently to notice the increasing malady of representative government.

Parliamentary action is becoming notoriously ineffective. In

America certainly the concentration of power in the Executive is
out of all proportion either to the intentions of the Fathers or to
the orthodox theory of representative government. The cause is
fairly clear. Congress is an assemblage of men selected for local
reasons from districts. It brings to Washington a more or less
accurate sense of the superficial desires of its constituency. In
Washington it is supposed to think nationally and internationally.
But for that task its equipment and its sources of information are
hardly better than that of any other reader of the newspaper.
Except for its spasmodic investigating committees, Congress has
no particular way of informing itself. But the Executive has.
The Executive is an elaborate hierarchy reaching to every part of
the nation and to all parts of the world. It has an independent
machinery, fallible and not too trustworthy, of course, but nevertheless a machinery of intelligence. It can be informed and it can
act, whereas Congress is not informed and cannot act.

Now the popular theory of representative government is that the
representatives have the information and therefore create the
policy which the executive administers. The more subtle theory is
that the executive initiates the policy which the legislature corrects
in accordance with popular wisdom. But when the legislature is
haphazardly informed, this amounts to very little, and the people
themselves prefer to trust the executive which knows, rather than
the Congress which is vainly trying to know. The result has been
the development of a kind of government which has been harshly
described as plebiscite autocracy, or government by newspapers.
Decisions in the modern state tend to be made by the interaction,
not of Congress and the executive, but of public opinion and the
executive.

Public opinion for this purpose finds itself collected about special groups which act as extra-legal organs of government. There
is a labor nucleus, a farmers' nucleus, a prohibition nucleus, a
National Security League nucleus, and so on. These groups conduct a continual electioneering campaign upon the unformed,
exploitable mass of public opinion. Being special groups, they
have special sources of information, and what they lack in the
way of information is often manufactured. These conflicting pressures beat upon the executive departments and upon Congress, and
formulate the conduct of the government. The government itself
acts in reference to these groups far more than in reference to the
district congressman. So politics as it is now played consists in

coercing and seducing the representative by the threat and the appeal of these unofficial groups. Sometimes they are the allies, sometimes the enemies, of the party in power, but more and more they are the energy of public affairs. Government tends to operate by the impact of controlled opinion upon administration. This shift in the locus of sovereignty has placed a premium upon the manufacture of what is usually called consent. No wonder that the most powerful newspaper proprietor in the English-speaking world declined a mere government post.

No wonder, too, that the protection of the source of its opinion is the basic problem of democracy. Everything else depends upon it. Without protection against propaganda, without standards of evidence, without criteria of emphasis, the living substance of all popular decision is exposed to every prejudice and to infinite exploitation. That is why I have argued that the older doctrine of liberty was misleading. It did not assume a public opinion that governs. Essentially it demanded toleration of opinions that were, as Milton said, indifferent. It can guide us little in a world where opinion is sensitive and decisive.

The axis of the controversy needs to be shifted. The attempt to draw fine distinctions between "liberty" and "license" is no doubt part of the day's work, but it is fundamentally a negative part. It consists in trying to make opinion responsible to prevailing social standards, whereas the really important thing is to try and make opinion increasingly responsible to the facts. There can be no liberty for a community which lacks the information by which to detect lies. Trite as the conclusion may at first seem, it has, I believe, immense practical consequences, and may perhaps offer an escape from the logomachy into which the contests of liberty so easily degenerate.

It may be bad to suppress a particular opinion, but the really deadly thing is to suppress the news. In time of great insecurity, certain opinions acting on unstable minds may cause infinite disaster. Knowing that such opinions necessarily originate in slender evidence, that they are propelled more by prejudice from the rear than by reference to realities, it seems to me that to build the case for liberty upon the dogma of their unlimited prerogatives is to build it upon the poorest foundation. For, even though we grant that the world is best served by the liberty of all opinion, the plain fact is that men are too busy and too much concerned to fight more than spasmodically for such liberty. When freedom of opinion is revealed as freedom of error, illusion, and misinterpretation, it is virtually impossible to stir up much interest in its behalf. It is the thinnest of all abstractions and an over-refinement of mere intellectualism. But people, wide circles of people, are aroused when their curiosity is balked. The desire to know, the dislike of being deceived and made game of, is a really powerful motive, and it is that motive that can best be enlisted in the cause of freedom.

What, for example, was the one most general criticism of the work of the Peace Conference? It was that the covenants were not openly arrived at. This fact stirred Republican Senators, the British Labor Party, the whole gamut of parties from the Right to the Left. And in the last analysis lack of information about the Conference *was* the origin of its difficulties. Because of the secrecy endless suspicion was aroused; because of it the world seemed to be presented with a series of accomplished facts which it could not reject and did not wish altogether to accept. It was lack of information which kept public opinion from affecting the negotiations at the time when intervention would have counted most and cost least. Publicity occurred when the covenants were arrived at, with all the emphasis on the *at*. This is what the Senate objected to, and this is what alienated much more liberal opinion than the Senate represents.

In a passage quoted previously in this essay, Milton said that differences of opinion, "which though they may be many, yet need not interrupt the unity of spirit, if we could but find among us the bond of peace." There is but one kind of unity possible in a world as diverse as ours. It is unity of method, rather than of aim; the unity of the disciplined experiment. There is but one bond of peace that is both permanent and enriching: the increasing knowledge of the world in which experiment occurs. With a common intellectual method and a common area of valid fact, differences may become a form of coöperation and cease to be an irreconcilable antagonism.

That, I think, constitutes the meaning of freedom for us. We cannot successfully define liberty, or accomplish it, by a series of permissions and prohibitions. For that is to ignore the content of opinion in favor of its form. Above all, it is an attempt to define liberty of opinion in terms of opinion. It is a circular and sterile logic. A useful definition of liberty is obtainable only by seeking the principle of liberty in the main business of human life, that is to say, in the process by which men educate their response and learn to control their environment. In this view liberty is the name we give to measures by which we protect and increase the veracity of the information upon which we act.

Modern liberty means not the toleration of indifferences, but the protection and increase of the veracity of the information upon which we act.

ECONOMIC SOCIETY

THE SOCIAL PLAINT [1]

Elisha Benjamin Andrews

[Elisha Benjamin Andrews (1844-1917) was appointed Professor of History and Political Economy at Brown University in 1882. Six years later he went to Cornell University, to the Chair of Political Economy and Public Finance, and a year later he returned to Brown as President. In 1898 he became Superintendent of Schools in Chicago. Two years later he accepted the Chancellorship of the University of Nebraska, retiring in 1908.

Among his books are a *History of the United States,* and *Institutes of Economics.* *The Social Plaint* was delivered before the New York Alumni of Phi Beta Kappa, May 23, 1892.]

Is the social body, economically speaking, well or ill? It is certainly complaining, and suffers painful attacks. Some tell us that these are purely superficial, and that the subject is, after all, in the best of health. Others will have it that the case is truly serious, so that naught but blood-letting will restore normal tone and strength. Still others declare the patient hopelessly gone. Not taking sides, at least with this or that extreme, and not presuming to suggest either diagnosis or treatment, we will in this paper attempt an examination and registry of symptoms.

Let it be distinctly understood that the criticism to follow is not of this or that man, or of particular men at all. Individuals are only in the rarest instances to blame for any ills from which society may suffer. They, the good as well as the bad, are the creatures of the system in which they are bound up; and in general, so long as this is unchanged, they cannot be censured for proceeding as they do. Wrongs that individual action might conceivably cure are often due to ignorance, which, in economic matters is still terribly dense. To represent employers as so many heartless Shylocks, each bent upon getting from the poor his pound of flesh, betrays slight preparation for discussing the relations of labor and capital. What is commonly said against the existing economic order needs sifting, of course. The fact of poverty is

[1] Reprinted from the *New World,* June, 1892.

Questions and topics for the discussion of this address, and of other phases of the general subject with which it deals, will be found on pages 506 and 510.

not necessarily a just impeachment of this order. Many of the poor are poor because of indolence or thriftlessness, for which they deserve to suffer. Even if laziness is sometimes constitutional, unless it can be shown that the constitution has derived its perverse bent from social maladjustments, suffering through such laziness may be, sociologically considered, not an evil at all, but of remedial tendency, and therefore a good instead.

Nor is it a proper complaint that some are better off than others. They may have wrought or economized better. We feel as by a sort of intuition that gain gotten by the honest, open use of one's own powers, without artificial or accidental advantage of any kind, is earned,—that it belongs to the possessor, so that no other has any right to view his possession as a hardship. That the gain has arisen through superior native endowment no unprejudiced mind would regard as impairing the title, unless this has worked its victory through craft and cunning. It is only accidental or artificial advantages to which our moral sense objects.

We should, however, not abate sharp criticism of our economic doings, if the evil attaching to them seem inevitable. Though it seem so, it may not really be so, and in troubles thus perilous to humanity's advance, we have no right to remit efforts at reform so long as a ray of hope remains. Conveyance of one's thought across this continent in an hour, and of one's body in a week, was formerly deemed impossible. Poverty may yet disappear.

Nor does one at all bar out or weaken an indictment of society's ways by inquiring for the complainant's theory of remedy. He may state grievances truly, though neither a theorist nor a practitioner. Perhaps no help whatever is in store. Very many have hope on this point rather than confidence. Shall we, therefore, call evil good? Nay, not even were an oracle from heaven to declare all hope vain. That unrighteousness can never be banished from the earth does not turn it into righteousness. If the exploiting of the weak by the strong, and of the honest by the cunning, the unwilling beggar, the starving babe, the gaunt woman sewing twenty continuous hours at the machine for the wage of a shilling, and the agricultural laborer, who just manages, by agonizing toil, year in and year out, to keep death's clutch soft upon his throat,— if these are perpetual phenomena, so surely are they perpetual wrongs and with our living and our dying breath they ought to be proclaimed as such.

Evaporating, then, the agitator's plaint, we find solid matter about as follows: In the first place, many men are rich, either altogether without economic merit, or wholly out of proportion to their economic merit. This will have to be admitted, however loosely and largely one interprets economic merit; or however great allowance we make for intellectual labor in its various kinds. By economic merit is meant the quality which attaches to any human action, or line of action, in virtue of its advantageousness, on the whole, and in the long run, to the material weal of the community. It assumes three forms. A man may claim economic merit, when and so far as he is a wage-earner in any useful calling; when and so far as he earns economic profits, that is, secures profits by effort and agency of a genuinely economic kind, without trick, theft, monopoly, or any artificial advantage; and when and so far as he owns capital as distinguished from unproductive wealth. Capital is productive wealth. Hence a holder of capital must be, indirectly at any rate, a wealth-user. Such a functionary is called economically meritorious at this point, not as a final judgment, or to beg the question against Socialists, but provisionally, for the sake of argument. One could doubtless grant that this is a lower form of merit than would be realized were the holder also a worker; yet in society as at present organized, the mere holder of capital must be regarded as deserving well. We see this instantly if we suppose owners of capital to consume it instead of retaining it. We waive for the moment the question whether private capital is, on the whole, administered as well, as truly for society's good, as if society owned and administered it all, although the difference is certainly smaller than Socialists contend.

These, then,—wages-earning, profits-earning, and interest-earning,—are the three forms of economic merit; but it goes almost without saying that wealth comes to many who are not meritorious in any one of these ways, and to many others out of all proportion to their merit. Some flourish by gambling; whether this takes place at the faro table or on the stock exchange makes no difference. The gambler produces nothing, yet he lives, and often thrives. This means that he is a leech, the rest of us having to share our blood with him. The immeasurable evils which have fastened upon stock operations all honest people bewail, and with justice. It is, of course, difficult to lay down a fair and tenable definition of legitimate speculation. The best one, perhaps, tests legitimacy by genuine intention to transfer the goods. It is pleasing to know that a professed intention to transfer is insisted upon in all the regular exchanges, whenever "futures" are trafficked in, and is implied in the printed forms of contract provided for such transactions. The precise difference between an exchange and a "bucket-shop" is usually declared to be, that in the latter the "puts," "calls," "straddles," and the rest, are nothing but bets on the market prices. Bucket-shops are doubtless the more exclusively given up to this practice, but, in spite of rules, it is dreadfully prevalent in the exchanges as well.[1]

We can see that proper speculation is advantageous. It acts like a governor to a steam-engine, preventing prices from rising so high or falling so low as they otherwise must. Shocks in the market that but for it would be terrible, are so distributed by it as to render them least harmful. The effect of absolutely wise speculation would be to annihilate speculation. Honest speculation is, therefore, negatively productive, like the work of judges, army, and police; it is not creative of wealth, but preventive of loss. Gambling manifestly lacks this saving character. It does not steady prices, but the reverse. At best it but transfers property from pocket to pocket.

Other economic parasites fatten on the produce of cheating, stealing, and robbery. Such, of course, earn nothing: as little when they proceed by "freezing out" small stock holders, or by forming sub-corporations to secure all the profits of main corporations under forms of law, or by creating artificial "corners" or artificial fluctuations in prices, as when they deftly pick your pockets or bravely throttle you upon the road. Individuals often secure great fortunes by mere chance, happening to be so circumstanced at some felicitous phase of business meteorology as to fill their buckets from the golden shower. Such beneficiaries are, of course, not thieves; on the other hand, they are not creators, but only receivers of social wealth.

Multitudes more prey upon society through monopoly. This may be created consciously and artificially, as in some of the great trusts now so numerous, or it may arise *bona fide*, in a natural way, without self-seeking on the part of any one, through well-meant but unwise legislation. The mere existence of monopoly in any quarter is no sign of wrong. Many monopoly concerns actually earn a large part of their profits, and some earn all. So far, they are not to be condemned. But the gains of others are clearly inequitable; they are not, like genuine wages or profits, a blessing

---

[1] Compare, on this general subject, More's *Utopia*, Chap. XII.

to all society, but are simply so much subtracted from the social store, impoverishing society for the monopolists' behoof. Many mistakenly suppose monopoly to exist only where every sort of competition is absent. It is not necessary, in order that an establishment, or a banded group of establishments, may put an undue price upon its goods, that it should directly control the entire production. Immediately mastery of a majority is practically the mastery of all. This is demonstrable at once *a priori* and from experience. One can maintain a monopoly until his competitors, offering at a lower price, produce enough to supply the market. Up to that limit their competition is formal only; they in fact participate in the extraordinary gains. Albert Schaeffle,[1] with many others, has pointed out that Ricardo's law of rent applies in a sense, under established industrial habits, to all business. The goods of any given kind, sold at a given hour, in any given market, bring not the cost of their production plus a fair profit, but the cost of the part of them, be it never so small, which cost the most. On all the cheaper portions some one has a bonanza. If such cheapness was begotten of skill, careful oversight, or any other form of strictly economic activity, the abnormal profit was earned. In any event we must regard it as legitimate, existing conditions being presupposed; but in ninety-nine per cent of such cases the bonanza can be traced more or less completely to mere luck.

The case is nearly the same if riches are acquired by simple shrewdness, even though this falls short of criminality, provided the shrewdness is not an element in economic merit. During our war, for instance, telegraph lines being then not extensive in the East, a certain sharp cotton speculator used to cause every steamer approaching Calcutta from Europe to be boarded far out, and the tendency of cotton ascertained and signalled to him long before the ship touched. A fleet vessel of his own, with steam up, would be waiting at the outer anchorage, which, on receiving word from the proprietor by another signal to "buy" or "sell," sped to carry this command to all his agents in the Pacific cotton ports, where its execution swelled his gold pile by millions every time. Such gains may be technically legitimate, and in international trade perhaps unavoidable; but, so far as the internal economic system of any country offers facilities for such gold-winning extraordinary, as in great land speculations, all will feel that it is still imperfect.

If he who is unduly enriched by a monopoly has himself created

[1] *Bau und Leben des socialen Körpers*, III, 431, 435.

the monopoly, we are quite sure to condemn the man; but we often do this without observing that just such evils as he has effected befall us each day, in ways for which not men but the economic system is at fault. The unfair gain which accrues to multitudes from protective and other laws, hurts society only in the same way as the unearned increment of land values does. In a vast majority of cases the taker of pure economic rent earns nothing, however honestly or truly he may have earned the capital with which he bought the privilege of rent-taking. The main difference is, that protective laws, so-called, are young, while land laws are so old that most people, and, with regret be it added, some economists, take them as ordinances of nature or of God.

One of the worst evils of the sort now under survey, making some men rich at others' expense, and wholly apart from economic merit, is fluctuation in the purchasing power of money. It is peculiarly bad, because it is sweeping in its operation, and also because it works so silently and subtly that only the trained mind can see what is doing. If general prices fall, holders of money and of titles calling for money grow rich by cutting coupons, taking to themselves so much of society's pile for no equivalent whatever, of course making the rest in like degree poorer. If general prices rise, the reverse infelicity occurs. Special attention is called to the fact that it is quite immaterial whether the fatal change in the value of money arises from new plenty or new scarcity of money itself, or because of extra dearness or cheapness on the part of general commodities. It is as truly a source of robbery in the one case as in the other. In addition to the cheat which all general price fluctuations entail, falling prices have the additional baneful effect of painfully discouraging industry and production,—an effect which has had as much to do as any one thing with the hard times of recent years. Through rise and fall in money values, then, as well as through mere luck, through monopoly, through theft, and through gambling, it actually does come to pass that, under our present economic practice, one section of society eats, drinks, and is merry, in whole or in part, at the expense of the rest, very much as if the latter were slaves.

On the other hand,—the counterpart of this proposition,—a great many men are poor without the slightest economic demerit. They are people who do the best they can, and always have done so; they are not dissipated, indolent, thriftless, or prodigal of children, but quite free from these vices, being in every way exemplary

citizens and worthy members of the community. Yet they are
poor, often very poor, never free from fear of want, doomed for
life to the alternative of hard labor or starvation, and as thoroughly cut off from all means of culture proper, as completely
precluded from the rational living of life, as were the Helots of old
Sparta. Such human beings are to be found in every city of the
world. They are less numerous in America than in Europe, but
America has them, too. Let him who doubts read Mrs. Helen
Campbell's *Prisoners of Poverty,* or better, go among these poor
people, converse with them, and judge for himself.[1]

It has been carefully computed that in representative districts of
East London, no less than 55 per cent of the very poor, and fully
68 per cent of the other poor, are so because of deficiency of employment, while only 4 per cent of the very poor, and none of the
other poor, are loafers. It is estimated that 53 per cent of the
needy in New York City suffer for work instead of aid and the
willing idlers among those are certainly no more numerous proportionally than in London. According to the "Massachusetts Labor Statistics" for 1887, almost a third of the people in that State
returned as usually engaged in remunerative toil were unemployed
during nearly a third of the census year, 1885; the working people
of the state, as a whole, average to the employed at their main
occupations less than eleven months of the year. These results are
not far from normal for this country, while for most others they
are much too good to be normal. It must be admitted that the
extreme division of labor has wrought its curse as well as its
blessing. According to the Massachusetts statistics only about one
in eighteen of those deprived of their usual employments turned to
another.

Most well-to-do people, whether millionaires or ordinary *bourgeois,* know, in effect, absolutely nothing about the truly poor.
Mr. H. M. Hyndman does: "I have watched friends of mine who
have had to go round week after week, month after month, maybe,
seeking for a job. Such men do not parade their griefs; never, or
very rarely, ask a middle-class man for help, and would utterly
scorn to beg. Yet, as a highly skilled artisan said to me only a few
days ago, "I would almost as soon go begging bread as begging
work; they treat you as if it were a favor you asked." I have
watched such men, I say, skilled and unskilled, too, and the mental

---

[1] For the poverty of East London, see Mr. Charles Booth's *Labour and
Life of the People,* Vol. I. G. P. Putnam's Sons, 1889.

effect upon them of these long periods or short periods of workless-
ness is more depressing than I can describe. Let a man have been
never so thrifty, if he has a wife and children, a few weeks of idleness sweep away his savings; then he begins to pawn what little
things he has; later he gets behind with his rent. His more fortunate comrades help him,—this is invariable, so far as I have seen,
among all classes of laborers; and then, if he is lucky, he gets into
work again; if not, his furniture goes, and he falls into dire poverty. All the time not only has the man himself been suffering and
losing heart, but his wife has been fretting herself to death and
the children have been half-fed. In the winter time, when the
uncertainty of getting work becomes, in most of our great industrial cities, the certainty of not getting it for a large percentage
of the laboring men and women, things are, of course, at their
worst. After having vainly trudged from workshop to workshop,
from factory to factory, from wharf to wharf, after having, perhaps, fought fiercely, but unsuccessfully, for a few hours' work
at the dock gates, the man returns home, weary, hungry, half dead
and ashamed of his growing raggedness, to see his home without
firing or food, perhaps to go to bed, in order to try and forget the
misery around him.

But is not the condition of the poor continually improving?
Yes, and no. Undoubtedly the average wage-worker can earn more
pounds of wheat, meat, and coal, and more yards of cloth, by
twelve hours' work to-day than fifty years ago, and probably
enough more to make up for the greater unsteadiness of labor now.
Mr. Giffen's statistics for England are well known. In the industries figured upon by him, wages have advanced since 1820-25
between 10 and 160 per cent. The average may be about 50 per
cent. The English income-tax, *per capita*, has increased as follows:
in 1865-69 it was £14; in 1870-74, £15 6s.; in 1875-79, £17 4s.; and
in 1880-84, £17 2s. There are endless figures of the same tenor,
which we need not cite. Mr. Giffen says that the wealth of Great
Britain advances at the rate of three per cent yearly; population,
only 1.3 per cent. How speedily, at this pace, may we not expect
poverty to be extinguished! For this country the improvement is
at least no less; we doubt if it is greater. Mr. Edward Atkinson's
roseate pictures of laborers' progress are familiar to all. The
French *savant*, M. Chevallier, has surveyed, as best he could, the
whole industrial world, and is very sure that the laborer has advanced everywhere.

In all probability the figures usually presented upon this subject, taken literally and for the time to which they relate, are not false. Materially, the workingman is gaining a little. Well may we rejoice that his wage is no longer the scanty four shillings a week, fixed for Warwickshire hands in 1588, under Queen Elizabeth's Statute of Labourers. His very discontent, by a well-known law of human nature, proves that he is profiting. Yet many representations, as commonly pressed and understood, mislead. Thus when Mr. Goschen, a few years ago, following Mr. Giffen's line of argument,[1] showed that the number of small fortunes and incomes in England was increasing faster than large, faster than fortunes in general, faster than population, he did not touch the really poor at all. He dealt with incomes from $750 a year upwards, estates under $5000 in value, house rents of $100 and on, small shareholdings, small insurance policies, and the like. But what is all this to the caravans of poor fellows with starvation incomes, or none at all? Is it not almost mockery to argue hope from a more felicitous distribution of "estates," "rents," "policies," and "shares," in Britain, when English villages, unable to give employment, are emptying their impoverished sons and daughters into the cities at the rate of sixty thousand or seventy thousand yearly, only to make their situation, if possible, worse yet; when, as a report of Mr. Burnett, labor correspondent of the Board of Trade, assures us, the sweating system is forcing men and women to work sometimes for thirty-three, and even thirty-six, consecutive hours to avoid starvation, and when the hungry hordes of East London poor, but for the Christian work done among them, or for fear of the police, would speedily march to the sack of the West End![2]

In our own country one hears equally inclusive utterances regarding the masses' welfare. On reading them, we sometimes really pity the mill-owners, and wonder why they do not take work as hands in the mills. The common statement about wages as increasing faster than income from invested wealth, neither has, nor can have, statistical proof, because we have no public or even private registry of profits.[3] So, too, the apparent fact that a greater and greater proportion of the nation's product goes year by year as wages, does not necessarily imply a rising rate of wages, but may

[1] London *Times*, weekly, October 9, 1887.
[2] The Earl of Meath, *Nineteenth Century*, January, 1889.
[3] The recent statistics of the Massachusetts Bureau, 1891, appear to be excellent, so far as they go.

accompany falling wages, and it will do so if population increases faster than wages fund. And when wages statistics are adduced to show improvement, nothing can exceed the recklessness with which they are sometimes made and handled. Wages of superintendence frequently swell the apparent average. Account is rarely taken of shut-downs and slack work, or of those unable to find work at all. The system of fines, often as vicious as it is common, is also ignored.[1]

In many respects, indeed, the toiling masses are no whit better off to-day than in England four centuries ago. The late Thorold Rogers, describing the Plantagenet and Tudor age, declares that then "there were none of those extremes of poverty and wealth which have excited the astonishment of philanthropists, and are now exciting the indignation of the workmen. . . . Of poverty which perishes unheeded, of a willingness to do honest work and a lack of opportunity, there was little or none. The essence of life was that every one knew his neighbor, and that every one was his brother's keeper." The fact is, that while the poor man has been getting on, he has not retained his old-time closeness to the average weal. Let us take a rubber strap, fasten one end, and extend the other till the length is doubled. If, now, we note the changes in the relative positions of points between the middle and the fixed extremity, we shall find that each, though farther from the end than before, is also farther from the middle; that besides, the points nearest the end have moved least, those nearest the middle, most. Of those between the middle and the free end, all are now further beyond the middle than before, while each has gained the more the remoter it was at first. Much in this way has society stretched out in the matter of economic welfare. There, at the fixed point of dire poverty, stand the mighty masses, as they have always stood. Our heaping up of wealth, Pelion upon Ossa, elevates them no iota. Their neighbors have removed from the dead point a little, but the center has gone away from them still more. Those nearer the average at first, and yet beneath it, have drifted further from the fixed extreme, but not one among them is so close to the middle as he began. Only when you pass beyond the average do you come to men who have gained upon the average, and these

[1] These errors, which of course, he could not correct, must be allowed for in M. E. Chevallier's *Les Salaires au XIXe Siècle*, a very instructive work on the whole; the author is, however, too hostile to coöperation and profit-sharing.

have accomplished this in proportion to the advantage which they
had at the start.[1]

While the poor man should be very glad that his toil brings him
more and better food, raiment, and shelter than once, the fact that
it does so is no sign that his condition is "improved" in the sense
in which this expression is usually understood. Richer supply for
one's mere bodily wants does not signify that one is getting forward or even holding one's own, in humanity's general advance.
Let man, as a race, remove further and further from the condition of brutes, and let me, in the mean time, keep as near to the
average of human weal as ever,—that is what I want. So long as
I am falling behind the average comfort, welfare, culture, intelligence, and power, it insults my manhood to remind me that my
sweat commands per drop a little more bread. "It is written, man
shall not live by bread alone." And in this higher life, the only
one in respect to which it is really worth while to discuss the question at length, hosts of men in civilized countries are making no
progress whatever, but are relatively losing ground.

To be sure, "the workman is now a freeman, and, compared with
his progenitors, an educated man. If not taught in the schools,
he has learned from the increasing progress which he beholds
everywhere around him. In the railway carriage he visits the
great towns; the newspaper gives him intelligence of all that is
going on from day to day in the most distant portions of the
earth; he hears discussed, with more or less accuracy and information, the leading topics of the age. So, life itself for him is a great
public school. But when he beholds the vast accumulation of
wealth in the hands of the higher class, which affords to them
luxury, the ease, the social distinction, and the means of enjoyment denied to him, and when he reflects that this wealth is mainly
created by the toil of himself and his fellow-laborers, he is naturally filled with discontent and envy, wherein may yet, perhaps,
be found the seeds of anarchy. Amid such circumstances he is
exposed, on the one hand, to the teachings of socialistic advocates;

[1] We do not forget the difficulty of laying a solid basis for this analysis.
The *personnel* of "the rich" and of "the poor" of course changes incessantly.
A penniless fellow strikes "pay gravel," and is a millionaire; another man
just as suddenly falls from opulence to rags. Still a basis is attainable. The
economic fortune of many an identical man, family, or community, which for
the last fifty years shows no break, paroxysm, or absolute change of any
kind, can be seen to have altered greatly in relation to the material welfare
of the country as a whole.

and, on the other hand, to the inculcation of the doctrine of passive obedience, and to that blasphemous as well as puerile philosophy which would enjoin him to submit meekly, in the name of reason or religion, to a condition of things which is abhorrent to every sentiment of justice and to every feeling of humanity."[1]

From this point of view, the wages-system itself, inevitable as it after all seems to be, is yet an evil, at least in comparison with the older one of masters, associates, and apprentices. It has become the order of things for human beings to work on a gigantic scale for other human beings as servants, menials, serfs, being granted access to the means of production not in their own right as men, but by the gracious favor of their more lordly fellows. The effect is to put a stain upon toil as dishonorable. If you are verdant enough still to speak of the "dignity of labor," people smile at you. That old aphorism has gone to the rubbish pile. Witness the pride of many *bourgeois* aristocrats, who boast of it as a special claim to consideration, that neither they nor their ancestors ever got a living by work. Equally significant is the assumption, both haughty and common, of capitalists, that they are the "guardians" of labor. But every one notices that wage-workership is widely regarded less humbling in proportion as it ceases to involve subjection to individuals. As a rule, work for a private corporation even, is more desired than work for A or B; work for a great public corporation, responsible to society, is still more desired; work for churches and educational institutions is yet more sought after; while work for the state is so enticing that even at the most moderate wages, and in spite of an all too insecure tenure, a hundred applicants scramble for every post.

How slight is even the economic betterment usually alleged, compared with what, from foreknowledge of the character of the age, one would have been justified in anticipating. Such progress in all the industrial arts, such cheapening of wares, such opening of new continents in North and South America and in Africa and Australia, the richest in bread-yield and beef-yield of any beneath the sun, should, it would seem, have annihilated poverty. Yet the amelioration is only well perceptible for wage-workers as a class, and for the unskilled it is hardly this. Still less can any general law of economic progress, covering the centuries, be established. On the contrary, the passing of this age of industrial advance and

[1] Rees, *From Poverty to Plenty*, pp. 65 *seq.* London, Wyman & Sons, 1888.

of world-wide land utilization with so slight gain in the ordinary comforts of life on the part of the laboring man, goes far to preclude all hope of great improvement for him under present economic conditions.

Thorold Rogers noticed that the trades correctly cited by Mr. Giffen as showing an advance of wages since 1833 have each had the advantage of a trade-union, and Rogers apparently cherished strong hope that unions were to introduce the laborers' millennium. I am unable to share this pleasing view. Each trade-union will benefit its own members, not unmixedly, indeed, because it always levels downward more or less in quality of work and in wages; but trade-unions often operate against one another, and they continually keep down instead of elevating the unskilled masses. Even an industrial trust, like the Knights of Labor, cannot exert its central power without forcing the abler and better workmen to make common cause with the poorer, so as greatly to impede production; nor will such an organization ever be in condition to enforce a general strike, because of the "scab" laborers constantly ready and competent for so many kinds of work. To exclude foreigners, which, so long as our protective laws continue, would be just, would not rid us of "scab" help. The increase of home population would soon furnish this. It is hard to see any likelihood under the present economic system, unless a good deal modified, of any such continence on the part of the laboring masses in our cities, as will deliver them for any length of time from the grip of Ricardo's iron law. Self-interest will never do it. This is a point where the *laissez-faire* theory of society most visibly breaks down. Morality and higher intelligence would do it, but we fear that these can never be engendered in sufficient degree amidst the existing poverty and strife of classes.

One has a right to complain touching the idle wealth which the present order of things heaps up, and the still greater quantities of wealth which are wasted out and out. If any one of our numberless millionaires wishes to turn some millions of capital into non-capital wealth in the form of needlessly large houses and grounds, gorgeous equipage and clothing, fancy wines and viands, or works of art never to be seen but in his own house, there is nothing to hinder him and much in the way of example to tempt him. Yet his act abstracts these millions from the wage-fund as permanently and effectually as if they were sunk in the mid-Atlantic, leaving many a work-seeker to hunger or starvation, who, had the

man built factories or railways with his pelf, might have been well
off.

It is amazing in view of this process, continually going on, to
hear some of our brightest thinkers arguing as if poverty were
always due to the fault of the people who suffer from it, as if there
were some providence or natural law which would make it impossible for one man ever to smart for the misdeeds of another. Not
seldom the exact reverse occurs. This, in fact, is one of the very
worst vices of present industry, that it not seldom visits curses
upon men for results which they had not the slightest hand in
originating. It is said that profits are justifiable because the employer takes risks,—a position entirely just so long as the present
system prevails. But it is not the profitmaker alone who is involved in the risks he takes. His help are bound up with him, and
if he is proved to be rash, while he himself will only have to surrender this or that luxury, they may starve or freeze. When
over-production, again, either alone or aided by over-speculation or
by those changes in the value of money already referred to, has
evoked a commercial crisis, the poor, who have had nothing whatever to do with causing it, are its most pitiable and helpless
victims.

Socialists have said none too much about the cross purposes
which, of necessity, prevail in our unregulated production. Let
the business man be as careful as he may, under the prevalent
business methods he cannot but take most dangerous risks. There
are now only the roughest means for ascertaining what the next
season's demand for this or that line of goods is to be, and still
poorer chance for learning what the output by competitors is to
be. Notwithstanding all that trusts have so excellently done to
forecast and regulate output,[1] every year's operation of many a
manufactory is to a great extent a game of hazard. Lines of business are over-wrought, begetting glut and necessitating sales below
cost; needless plant is set out, which must decay or burn. Losses
in these ways are crushing, and are so much the more sad in that
they are intrinsically needless. Through such waste of capital, interest rises, and wage-yielding businesses which might have flourished are prevented from starting. Prices fluctuate abnormally,
deranging and discouraging industry. Mills that were in opera-

---

[1] A merit of the trust-system usually not recognized. Compare the author's
article on "Economic Reform Short of Socialism," in *The International
Journal of Ethics*, April, 1892.

tion close, the operatives, who had absolutely no part in the errors which brought the crisis, being the chief sufferers. One earnest writer refers to such dislocations of industry all the economic troubles of the time.[1] We see here, again, that poverty does not always befall men by their own fault, but very often through the crime or stupidity of others.

We have space merely to name a few unfortunate features not so strictly of an economic nature, which attach to the prevalent industrial course of things. Wealth is for man, not man for wealth. It is conceivable that a given line of production should favor the amassing of wealth in a most eminent degree, and yet be so baneful ethically, for instance, as not to deserve toleration. To be laid to the account of the existing economic dispensation is most of the fraud and villainy in industrial life. If you are a grocer, and other grocers sand their sugar, you must, or, unless you have immense capital, leave the business. If you manufacture clothing, and the fashion in that line of production is to beat sewing-women down to starvation wages, you must do thus, or you are lost. You may wince or protest, but your position is such that you cannot obey conscience without becoming a martyr. This is why the best men in a trade do not fix its maxims and practices, but the worst.

It is a fact that our present plan of industry presses men with indescribably strong motives to gamble, to depress wages to the utmost, and to cheat in the quality of wares. Many resist nobly. Many others yield, but with a stout inward protest which would do honor to them were it known. People dislike to do wrong; but in hundreds of cases, if not as a rule, they must do wrong or fail in business. The meanest man undersells the noblest and, either financially or morally, drives him to the wall.[2] Honesty is often as uneconomical in face of the customer as in face of the tax-assessor. Out of this murderous competition there is a survival not of the fittest but of the unfittest, the sharpest, the basest.

When great wealth has been amassed, even honestly, another fearful pressure is brought to bear upon its possessor to regard it too much as an end, and to bend all his energy to the further swelling of the pile, how inordinate soever it may be. He overworks himself; he takes colossal risks; he frets; he passes sleep-

---

[1] W. Smart, *The Contemporary Review*, 1888.
[2] Read, in Mrs. Helen Campbell's *Prisoners of Poverty*, the chapter entitled "Two Hospital Beds."

less nights. He forgets his obligations to family, society, and God. He reads naught but market-reports. Think, he does not; he only reckons. Such a life is not rational, and its general prevalence through generations cannot but make us more a race of Babbage calculators than of moral beings.

Lastly, much of the wealth itself, invested in idle or positively harmful luxuries, is lost to society as truly as if sunk in the Pacific Ocean. Any one who will reflect can easily make himself heart-sick by computing what a large proportion of existing wealth has been put into forms that not only do not afford wages to labor, but are a moral if not an economic disadvantage to the owners themselves. This is not condemning luxury, but only useless and damaging luxury, which, of course, no economist can approve; nor can any one else do so, without repudiating altruism and going to the baldest egoism in ethics.

I do not believe that socialism is coming; but I expect a moral growth of society which will bring with it many changes, some of them radical, in the economic structure and methods of society. Workingmen's complaints are not all wanton and they cannot be dismissed with a puff. That pleasing optimism which views all increase of wealth as inevitably, under natural law, a blessing to wage-workers, is very shallow. Both the socialist on the one hand and the *laissez-faire* theorist on the other, are in too great haste to generalize. At present our business is the analysis of social conditions,—deep, patient and undogmatic.

EDUCATION AND THE SOCIALIST MOVEMENT [1]

John Bates Clark

[John Bates Clark (1847-   ) was graduated from Amherst College in 1872. Since 1895 he has been Professor of Political Economy in Columbia University. He is recognized as one of the clearest thinkers of the present day in the field of economic philosophy. Among his notable contributions to economic thought are, *The Philosophy of Wealth, The Distribution of Wealth, The Control of Trusts,* and *The Problem of Monopoly.*

Education and the Socialist Movement appeared in the *Atlantic Monthly* for October, 1906. It was originally delivered as a Phi Beta Kappa address at Columbia University.]

In a noteworthy address delivered at Princeton University, President Cleveland expressed the hope that our higher institutions of learning would range themselves like a wall barring the progress of revolutionary doctrines. If one may judge by appearances, this hope has not been realized. There may be a smaller percentage of educated persons than of uneducated ones in the ranks of radical socialism. Those ranks are most readily recruited from the body of ill-paid workingmen; but there are enough highly educated persons in them to prove that socialism and the higher culture are not incompatible; and a question that is well worth asking and, if possible, answering, is, What is likely to be the permanent attitude of a scientific mind toward the claims of thoroughgoing socialism? Will it be generally conservative or the opposite? Will there be an alliance between intelligence and discontented labor—the kind of union that was once cynically called a "coalition of universities and slums"? If so, it will make a formidable party.

It is clear, in the first place, that the scientific habit of thought makes one hospitable to new ideas. A man who cultivates that habit is open to conviction where an ignorant person is not so. He is accustomed to pursue the truth and let the quest lead him where it will. He examines evidence which appears to have force, even

[1] Reprinted by permission of the author, from the *Atlantic Monthly*, October 1906.

Questions and topics for the discussion of this address, and of other phases of the general subject with which it deals, will be found on pages 507 and 510.

although the conclusion to which it leads may be new and un-
pleasant.

Now, at the very outset of any inquiry about socialism, there
appear certain undisputed facts which create a *prima facie* case
in its favor; and the first of them is the beauty of the ideal which
it presents: humanity as one family; men working together as
brethren, and enjoying, share and share alike, the fruits of their
labor—what could be more attractive? There will be an abundance for every one, and as much for the weak as for the strong;
and there will be no cause for envy and repining. There will be
fraternity insured by the absence of subjects of contention. We
shall love our brethren because we shall have no great cause to
hate them; such is the picture. We raise just here no question
as to the possibility of realizing it. It is a *promised* land and not
a real one that we are talking about, and for the moment we
have given to the socialists *carte blanche* to do the promising.
The picture that they hold up before us certainly has traits of
beauty. It is good and pleasant for brethren to dwell together in
unity *and in abundance*.

Again, there is no denying the imperfections of the present system both on its ethical and on its economic side. There is enormous
inequality of conditions—want at one extreme and inordinate
wealth at another. Many a workingman and his family are a
prey to irregular employment and continual anxiety. For such
persons what would not a leveling out of inequalities do? To a
single capitalist personally a billion dollars would mean palaces,
yachts, and a regiment of retainers. It would mean a redoubling
of his present profusion of costly decorations, clothing and furnishings, and it would mean the exhausting of ingenuity in inventing pleasures, all of which, by a law of human nature, would
pall on the man from mere abundance. What would the billion-
aire lose by parting with ninety-nine one-hundredths of his
wealth? With the modest ten millions that would be left he
could have every pleasure and advantage that money ought to
purchase. What would not the sum he would surrender do for a
hundred thousand laborers and their families? It would provide
comfort for something like half a million persons. It would give
them means of culture and of health, banish the hunger specter,
and cause them to live in mental security and peace. In short,
at the cost of practically nothing for one man, the redistribution

we have imagined would translate half a million persons to a comfortable and hopeful level of life.

Again, the growth of those corporations to which we give the name of "trusts" has lessened the force of one stock argument against socialism, and added a wholly new argument in its favor. The difficulty of managing colossal enterprises formerly stood in many minds as the chief consideration against nationalization of capital and industry. What man, or what body of men, can possibly be wise and skilful enough to handle such operations? They are now, in some instances, in process of handling them, and those who wish to change the present order tell us that all we have to do is to transfer the ownership of them to the state, and let them continue working as they do at present. We have found men wise enough to manage the trusts, and probably, in most cases, they were honest enough to do so in the interest of the stockholders. On the question of honesty the socialist has the advantage in the argument, for he will tell us that with the private ownership of capital made impossible by law, the temptation to dishonesty is removed. If the socialistic state could be warranted free from "graft," this would constitute the largest single argument in its favor.

It is, indeed, not the same thing to manage a myriad of industries as to manage a single one, because certain nice adjustments have to be made between the several industries, and we shall see what this difficulty signifies; but as we are looking only at *prima facie* claims, we will give to the argument from the existence of trusts all the force that belongs to it.

As the difficulty of nationalizing production has been reduced, the need of it has been increased, for the trusts are becoming partial monopolies, able to raise prices, reduce wages, cheapen raw materials, and make themselves, if they shall go much farther in this line, altogether intolerable. Indeed, the single fact of the presence of private monopoly, and the lack of any obvious and sure plan of successfully dealing with it, has been enough to convert a multitude of intelligent men to the socialistic view.

Here, then, is a list of arguments making an effective case for socialism: the beauty of its ideal, the glaring inequalities of the present system, the reduction of the difficulty of managing great industries through public officials, the growing evils of private monopoly, and the preference for public monopoly as a mode of escape. They captivate a multitude of persons, and it is time carefully to weigh them. It is necessary to decide whether the promises of the socialistic state are to be trusted. Would the ideal materialize? Is it a substantial thing, within reachable distance, or is it a city in the clouds? If it is not wholly away from the earth, is it on the delectable mountains of a remote millennium? Is it as wholly desirable as it at first appears?

There are some considerations which any educated mind should be able to grasp, which reduce the attractiveness of the socialistic ideal itself. Shall we transform humanity into a great band of brethren by abolishing private property? Differences of wealth which now excite envy would, of course, be removed. The temptation to covetousness would be reduced, since there would not be much to covet. There would be nothing a man could do with plunder—unless he could emigrate with it. Would "hatred and all uncharitableness" be therefore completely absent, or would they be present in a form that would still make trouble?

Even though there would be no differences of possessions between man and man, there would be great differences in the desirability of different kinds of labor. Some work is safe and some is dangerous. Some is agreeable and some is disagreeable. The artist, the author, the scientist, the explorer, and the inventor take pleasure in their work; and that is not often to be said of the stoker, the grinder of tools, the coal miner, or the worker in factories where explosives or poisons are made. It is not to be said of any one who has to undergo exhausting labor for long hours. In industries managed by the state there would be no practicable way of avoiding the necessity of assigning men to disagreeable, arduous, unhealthful, or dangerous employments. Selections of men for such fields of labor would in some way have to be made, and those selected for the undesirable tasks would have to be held to them by public authority. Well would it be if the men so consigned, looking upon the more fortunate workers, were not good material for an army of discontent. Well would it be if their discontent were not turned into suspicion of their rulers and charges of favoritism in personal treatment. There would not be, as now, an abstraction called a "system," on which, as upon the camel's back, it would be possible to load the prevalent evils. Strong in the affections of the people must be the *personnel* of a government that could survive the discontent which necessary inequalities of treatment would excite. Would the government be likely to be thus strong in popular affection? We may judge as to this if we look at one further peculiarity of it.

The pursuit of wealth now furnishes the outlet for the overmastering ambition of many persons. In the new state, the desire to rise in the world would have only one main outlet, namely politics. The work of governing the country, and that of managing its industries, would be merged in one great official body. The contrast between rulers and ruled would be enormously heightened by this concentration of power in the hands of the rulers, and by the further fact that the ruled would never be able, by means of wealth, to acquire an offset for the advantages of officeholding. The desire for public position must therefore be intensified.

There would be some prizes to be gained, in a worthy way, by other kinds of service, such as authorship, inventions and discovery; but the prizes which would appeal to most men would be those of officialdom. Is it in reason to suppose that the method of securing the offices would then be better than it is at present? Would a man, under the new *régime,* work quietly at his task in the shoe shop, the bakery, or the mine, waiting for the office to which he aspired to seek him out, or would he try to make terms with other men for mutual assistance in the quest of office? Would rings be less general than they are now? Could there fail to be bosses and political machines? Would the Tammanys of the new order, then, be an improvement on the Tammanys of the old order? To the sober second thought which mental training ought to favor, it appears that the claim of the socialistic state to a peculiar moral excellence brought about by its equality of possessions needs a very thorough sifting.

Without making any dogmatic assertions, we may say that there would certainly have to be machines of some sort for pushing men into public offices, and that these would have very sinister possibilities. They would be opposed by counter machines, made up of men out of office and anxious to get in. "I am able to see," said Marshal MacMahon, when nearing the end of his brief presidency of the French Republic, "that there are two classes of men —those who command and those who must obey." If the demarcation were as sharp as that in actual society, and if the great prizes in life were political, brief indeed might be the tenure of place by any one party, and revolutions of more than South American frequency might be the normal state of society. One may look at the ideal which collectivism presents, with no thought of such dangers; but it is the part of intelligence at least to take account of them.

Besides the fact that some would be in office and others out, and that some would be in easy and desirable trades and others in undesirable ones, there would be the further fact that some would live in the city and some in the country, and that the mere localizing of occupations would afford difficulty for the ruling class and be a further cause of possible discontent. But a much more serious test of the capacity of the government would have to be made in another way. Very nice adjustments would have to be made between agriculture on one hand, and manufactures and commerce on the other; and further adjustments would have to be made between the different branches of each generic division. All this would be done, not automatically as at present, by the action of demand and supply in a market, but by the voluntary acts of officials. Here is the field in which the wisdom of officials would be overtaxed. They might manage the mills of the steel trust, but it would trouble them to say how many men should be employed in that business and how many in every other, and of the men in that generic branch, how many should work in Pittsburgh and how many in the mines of Michigan and Minnesota.

A fine economic classic is the passage in which Bishop Whately describes the difficulty of provisioning the City of London by the action of an official commissariat, and contrasts it with the perfection with which this is now done without such official control. Individuals, each of whom seeks only to promote his own interest, work in harmony, prevent waste, and secure the city against a lack of any needed element. Far greater would be the contrast between satisfying by public action every want of a nation, and doing this by the present automatic process; and yet crude thought even calls competition ''chaotic,'' and calls on the state to substitute an orderly process. Into that particular error discriminating thought will not readily fall.

Difficulties which a discerning eye perceives, and an undiscerning one neglects, thus affect the conclusion that is reached as to whether a socialistic plan of industry could or could not be made to work. Ignorance does not so much as encounter the real difficulties in the case, but lightly assumes that the plan would work, and is eager to try it. I am not, here and now, claiming that the difficulties cited positively prove that the scheme would not work. Granting now, for the sake of further argument, that it could be made to work—that on the political side it would proceed smoothly and peaceably, and that on the economic side it would run on no fatal rocks—would it give a material result worth having?

Here is a chance for a wider range of difference between the conclusions of different minds. There are three specific consequences of the socialistic plan of industry, each of which is at least possible; and a prospect that all of them would occur together would suffice to deter practically every one from adhering to this plan. Estimates of the probability of these evils will vary, but that each one of the three is possible, is not to be denied. Of these results, the first is, on the whole, the gravest. It is the check that socialism might impose on technical progress. At present we see a bewildering succession of inventions transforming the industries of the world. Machine after machine appears in rapid succession, each displacing its predecessor, working for a time and giving way to still better devices. The power of man over nature increases with amazing rapidity. Even in the relatively simple operations of agriculture, the reaper, the thresher, the seeder, and the gang plow enable a man today to do as much work as could a score of men in the colonial period of American history. In manufacturing, the gain is greater; and in transportation, it is indefinitely greater. The progress goes on without cessation, since the thing which guarantees it is the impulse of self-preservation. An employer *must* improve his mechanism if his rivals do. He must now and then get ahead of his rivals if he is to make any profit. Conservatism which adheres to the old is self-destruction, and a certain audacity affords the nearest approach to safety. From this it comes about, first, that forward movements are made daily and hourly in some part of the field; and, secondly, that with every forward movement the whole procession must move on to catch up with its new leader.

Now, it is possible to suppose that under socialism an altruistic motive may lead men to make inventions and discoveries. They may work for the good of humanity. The desire for distinction may also impel them to such labors, and non-pecuniary rewards offered by the state may second this desire. The inventive impulse may act even where no reward is in view. Men will differ greatly in their estimates of the amount of progress that can be gained in this way; but the thing that may be affirmed without danger of denial is, that the competitive race absolutely compels progress at a rate that is inspiringly rapid, and that there is much uncertainty as to the amount of progress that would be secured where other motives are relied on. Officialdom is generally unfavorable to the adoption of improved devices, even when they are presented; its boards have frequently been the graveyards of inventions, and there is no blinking the uncertainty as to whether a satisfactory rate of improvement could be obtained where the methods of production should be at the mercy of such boards. The keener the intelligence, the more clearly it will perceive the importance of progress, and the immeasurable evil that would follow any check upon it; the more also it will dread every cause of uncertainty as to the maintenance of the present rate of improvement.

An important fact concerning competitive industry is the ease with which new technical methods translate themselves, first into temporary profits for employers, and then into abiding returns for other classes. The man who introduces an efficient machine makes money by that means until his competitors get a similar appliance, after which the profit vanishes. The product of the machine still enriches society, by diffusing itself among the people in the shape of lower prices of goods. The profit from any one such device is bound to be temporary, while the gain that comes from cheap goods is permanent. If we watch some one industry, like shoemaking or cotton spinning, we find profits appearing and vanishing, and appearing again and vanishing again. If we include in our vision the system as a whole, we find them appearing now in one branch of industry, now in another, and now in still another, shifting forever their places in the system, but always present somewhere. Steel, cotton, wool, machinery, or flour, takes its turn in affording gains to its producer, and these gains constitute the largest source of additions to capital. These natural profits in themselves burden nobody. Not only is there in them no trace of exploitation of labor, but from the very start the influence that yields the profit improves the condition of labor, and in the end labor, as the greatest of all consumers, gets the major benefit.[1]

Now, an important fact is that such profits based on improved

---

[1] A fuller treatment of this subject would take account of the incidental evils which inventions often cause, by forcing some persons to change their employments, and would show that these evils were once great but are now smaller and destined to diminish.

technical processes naturally, and almost necessarily, add themselves to capital. The employer wishes to enlarge his business while the profits last—"to make hay while the sun shines." He has no disposition to spend the income which he knows will be transient, but has every disposition to enlarge the scale of his operations and provide a permanent income for the future. Easily, naturally, painlessly, the great accretions of capital come; mainly by advances in technical operations of production.

In the socialistic state all the incomes of the year would be pooled. They would make a composite sum out of which every one's stipend would have to be taken. There would be no special and personal profit for any one. The gains that come from improved technique would not be distinguishable from those that come from other sources. Every one would be a laborer, and every one would get his daily or weekly stipend; and if capital had to be increased,—if the needs of an enlarging business had to be provided for at all,—it could only be done by withholding some part of that stipend. It would be an unwelcome way of making accumulations. It would mean the conscious acceptance by the entire working class of a smaller income than might otherwise be had. If one has heroic confidence in the far-seeing quality and in the generous purpose of the working class, he may perhaps think that it will reconcile itself to this painful self-denial for the benefit of the future; but it is clear that there are large probabilities in the other direction. There is danger that capital would not be thus saved in sufficient quantity, and that if it were not so, no power on earth could prevent the earning capacity of labor from suffering in consequence. From mere dearth of capital the socialistic state, though it were more progressive than we think, would be in danger of becoming poorer and poorer.

There is another fact concerning the present system which a brief study of economics brings to every one's attention and which has a very close connection with the outlook for the future of laborers. It is the growth of population. The Malthusian doctrine of population maintains that increased wages are followed by a quick increase in the number of working people, and that this brings the wages down to their former level. On its face it appears to say that there is not much hope of permanent gains for labor, and it was this teaching which was chiefly responsible for giving to political economy the nickname of the "dismal science." It is true that the teachings of Malthus contain a proviso whereby it is not impossible under a certain condition that the wages of labor may permanently increase. Something may raise the standard of living more or less permanently, and this fact may nullify the tendency of population to increase unduly. Modern teachings make the utmost of this saving proviso, and show that standards have in fact risen, that families of the well-to-do are smaller than those of the empty-handed laborers, and that, with advancing wages based on enlarged producing power, the workers may not see their gains slipping from their hands in the old Malthusian fashion, but may hold them more and more firmly. Progress may cause further progress.

Now, socialism proposes to place families in a condition resembling that in which, in American history, the natural growth has been most rapid, the condition, namely, in which children are maintained without cost to parents, as they were when they lived on farms and were set working at an early age. If this should mean that the old Malthusian law would operate in the socialistic state, the experiment would be hopelessly wrecked. If the state provides for children from their birth to the end of their lives, the particular influence that puts a check on the size of families will be absent. One may not affirm with positiveness that the worst form of Malthusianism would actually operate under socialism; nothing but experiment will give certain knowledge in this particular; but what a little discernment makes perfectly certain is, that there would be danger of this.

Quite apart, then, from political uncertainties, three coördinate influences on the purely economic side must be taken full account of by anybody who would intelligently advocate the nationalizing of production. There are: first, the probable check on technical progress; secondly, the difficulty encountered in enlarging capital; and, thirdly, the possible impetus to the growth of population. If the first two influences were to work without the other, socialism would mean that we should all slowly grow poor together; and if the third influence were also to operate, we should grow poor very rapidly.

We have not proved, as if by incontestable mathematics, that socialism is not practicable and not desirable. We have cited facts which lead a majority of persons to believe this. The unfavorable possibilities of socialism bulk large in an intelligent view, but positive proof as to what would happen in such a state can come only through actual experience. Some country must turn itself into an experimental laboratory for testing the collective mode of production and distribution, before the world can definitely know what that process would involve. In advance of this test, there is a line of inquiry which yields a more assured conclusion than can any estimate of a state which, as yet, is imaginary. It is the study of the present industrial system and its tendencies. When we guess that the collective management of all production by the state would fail to work, and would lead to poverty even if it succeeded in working, we are met by those who guess it would succeed and lead to general abundance; and they will certainly claim that their guesses are worth as much as ours. As to the tendencies of the present state, and the outlook they afford, it is possible to know much more. The testimony of facts is positive as to some things, and very convincing as to others.

No one is disposed to deny the dazzling series of technical improvements which the rivalries of the present day insure. There is not only progress, but a law of progress; not only the productive power that we are gaining, but the force that, if allowed to work, will forever compel us to gain it. There is no assignable limit to the power that man will hereafter acquire over nature. Again and again, in the coming years and centuries, will the wand of inventive genius smite the rock and cause new streams of wealth to gush forth; and, as already said, much of this new wealth will take naturally and easily the form of capital. It will multiply and improve the tools that labor works with; and a fact which science proves is that the laborer, quite apart from the capitalist, thrives by the operation. He gets higher and higher pay as his method of laboring becomes more fruitful. It is as though he were personally bringing for his own use new streams from the rock; and even though this worker were striking a landlord's rock with a capitalist's hammer, the new stream could not fail to come largely to himself.

Mere labor will have increasing power to create wealth, *and to get wealth,* as its methods improve and its tools more and more abound. This will not transform the workingman's whole life in a day—it will not instantly place him where the rubbing of a lamp will make genii his servants, but it will give him to-morrow more than he gets to-day, and the day after to-morrow still more. It will enable his own efforts to raise him surely, steadily, inspiringly, toward the condition of which he dreams. It will throw sunshine on the future hills—substantial and reachable hills, though less brilliant than pictured mountains of cloudland.

Well within the possibilities of a generation or two is the gain that will make the worker comfortable and carefree. Like the village blacksmith, he may "look the whole world in the face" with independence, but with no latent enmity. Manly self-assertion there may be, with no sense of injury. The well-paid laborer may stand before the rich without envy, as the rich will stand before him without pity or condescension. It may be that the condition, described by Edward Atkinson, in which it "will not pay to be rich" because of the cares which wealth must bring, may never arrive. It will always be better to have something than to have nothing; but it may, at some time, be better to have relatively little than to have inordinately much; and the worker may be able to come nearer and nearer to the state in which, for him, comforts are plentiful and anxieties are scarce. Amid a vast inequality of possessions, there may be less and less of inequality of genuine welfare. Many a man with a modest store may have no wish to change lots with the multimillionaire. For comfortable living, for high thinking, and for the finer traits of humanity, the odds may be in his favor.

In such a state there might easily be realized a stronger democracy than any which a leveling of fortunes would bring. Pulling others down that we may pull ourselves up is not a good initial step in a *régime* of brotherhood; but raising ourselves and others together is the very best step from the first and throughout. And the fraternity which comes in this way is by far the finer, because of inequality of possessions. If we can love no man truly unless we have as much money as he has, our brotherly spirit is of a very peculiar kind, and the fraternity that would depend on such a leveling would have no virility. It would have the pulpy fiber of a rank weed, while the manlier brotherhood that grows in the midst of inequality has the oaken fiber that endures. The relatively poor we shall have with us, and the inordinately rich as well; but it is in the power of humanity to project its fraternal bonds across the chasms which such conditions create. Though there be thrones and principalities in our earthly paradise, they will not mar its perfection, but will develop the finer traits of its inhabitants.

This state is the better because it is not cheaply attained. There are difficulties to be surmounted, which we have barely time to mention and no time to discuss. One of the greatest of these is the vanishing of much competition. The eager rivalry in perfecting methods and multiplying products, which is at the basis of our confidence in the future, seems to have here and there given place to monopoly, which always means apathy and stagnation. We have before us a struggle—a successful one, if we rise to the occasion—to keep alive the essential force of competition; and this fact reveals the very practical relation which intelligence sustains to the different proposals for social improvement. It must put us in the way of keeping effective the mainspring of progress—of surmounting those evils which mar the present prospect. Trained intelligence here has its task marked out for it; it must show that monopoly can be effectively attacked, and must point out the way to do it—a far different way from any yet adopted. Our people have the fortunes of themselves, their children, and their children's children, in their own hands. Surely, and even somewhat rapidly, may the gains we have outlined be made to come by united effort guided by intelligent thought.

It requires discernment to estimate progress itself at its true value. John Stuart Mill made the remark that no system could be worse than the present one, if that system did not admit of improvement. This remark could be made of any system. However fair a social state might at the outset appear, it would be essentially bad if it could never change for the better. The society in which efficient methods supplant inefficient ones, and in which able directors come naturally into control of production, insures a perpetual survival of excellence, and however low might be the state from which such a course of progress took its start, the society would ultimately excel any stationary one that could be imagined. A Purgatory actuated by the principle which guarantees improvement will surpass, in the end, a Paradise which has not this dynamic quality. For a limited class in our own land—chiefly in the slums of cities—life has too much of the purgatorial quality; for the great body of its inhabitants the condition it affords, though by no means a paradise, is one that would have seemed so to many a civilization of the past and to many a foreign society of to-day. On its future course it is starting from a high level, and is moved by a powerful force toward an ideal which will some day be a reality, and which is therefore inspiring to look upon, even in the distance.

Like Webster, we may hail the advancing generations and bid them welcome to a land that is fairer than our own, and promises to grow fairer and fairer forever. That this prospect be not imperiled—that the forces that make it a reality be enabled to do their work—is what the men of the future ask of the intelligence of to-day.

EDUCATION

EDUCATION FOR EFFICIENCY[1]

Eugene Davenport

[Eugene Davenport (1856-   ) was Dean of the College of Agriculture at the University of Illinois from 1895 to 1922. By his writing and speaking he has been influential in bringing public opinion to the support of state universities and to a program of universal education. His conception of the principles which should control public educational policy is set forth in the address *Education for Efficiency*, which forms a chapter in a volume of that title which he published in 1909. The chapter as printed, Professor Davenport states, covers the general line of thought developed in an address at the dedication of a new agricultural building at the University of Tennessee in 1909.]

It is dangerous to attempt to educate a live boy
with no reference to the vocational.

The first general principle to be recognized is this: That industrial education cannot be considered by itself alone any more than industrial people can live alone. It is at best but part of a general scheme of education that aims at a higher efficiency of all classes of people, and it is in this light that industrial education should be studied and its problems solved.

The most significant educational fact to-day is that men of all classes have come to look upon education as a thing that will better their condition; and they mean by that, first of all, something to make their labor more effective and more profitable; and second, they mean something that will enable them to live fuller lives. They have no very clear idea of the methods for bringing it all about, nor have they any very good means of impressing their views and desires upon us at educational conventions; but to better their condition through education is the abiding faith and purpose of all men everywhere, and they will persist until it is realized.

The ruling passion of the race to-day is for education; and colleges and schools of all sorts, both public and private, day classes

[1] Reprinted from Davenport's *Education for Efficiency* by special permission of D. C. Heath and Company. All rights reserved.
Questions and topics for the discussion of this address, and of other phases of the general subject with which it deals, will be found on pages 511 and 516.

and night classes, winter and summer, are filled to overflowing. The only educational institution that is being deserted is the old-time district school, and that is failing only where it is unable to satisfy the new demands, and where this occurs its lineal successor is the public high school, which is everywhere becoming the favorite agency of modern education of the masses in America.

The training of the young for the duties of life is no longer left to the charity of the church nor to private endowment, however munificent.

We do not ask a man to pay the expense of his own education, and we no longer require the parent to pay for the school of his child. We have come to recognize that in the last analysis the child belongs to the community, and public welfare requires that he be educated. So we have the policy of universal education well established among us and the largest item of public as well as of private expense is for schools.

Now this is not sentiment, it is business; it is not charity, it is statesmanship. We propose to maintain all sorts of education for all sorts of people, and to keep them in school as long as we can— so far have we gone already in this worship of the idol of our day and time.

Yes, truly the ruling passion of the race is for education. Individuals would amass wealth; individuals would exert influence and power; individuals would live lives of luxury and ease, but the common purpose of the masses of men from all the walks of life is a set determination to acquire knowledge. Daughters of washerwomen graduate from the high school, and ditchers' sons go to college—not by ones and twos, but literally by hundreds and thousands, and if the ruling passion fails in individual cases, we have a law that puts the child into school, willy-nilly, on the ground that to this extent, at least, he is public property.

Now what is to be the consequence of all this? What will the daughter of the washerwoman do after she has graduated from the high school? Will she take her mother's place at the tub? What think you? If not, how will the washing be done? and was her schooling a blessing or a curse to the community?—because the tub must stay; and if she does take her place at the tub, was her schooling a blessing or a curse to her? Will the ditcher's son inherit the father's spade? and if not, how will ditches be dug if all men are to be educated? How will the world's work get done if education takes men and women out of useful and needful occupations and makes them over into pseudo ladies and gentlemen of leisure? How, too, will their own bills be paid except they labor as men have always labored? It is idle to say that a portion of the race should be left ignorant that they may perform the undesirable though necessary labor. The "portion" objects, and what are we going to do about it? Now these are disagreeable questions, and we would rather not be forced to answer them; but they are fundamental, and will soon begin to answer themselves in some fashion under our system of education, which is rapidly becoming universal.

We are now engaged in the most stupendous educational, social, and economic experiment the world has ever undertaken—the experiment of universal education; and whether in the end universal education shall prove a blessing or a curse to us will depend entirely upon our skill in handling the issues it has raised for our solution. We have entered too far upon this experiment over to retire from it, even if we desired to do so, which we do not; and if the outcome is to be safety and not anarchy, and if it is all to result in further development of the race and not in retrogression, then a few fundamentals must soon be clearly recognized and brought into and made a part of our educational ideals, policies, and methods.

First, if we are to have universal education, it must contain a large element of the vocational, because all the needful activities must be maintained in the educated state as heretofore. The race cannot progress any more in the future than in the past except by the expenditure of large amounts of human energy. This being so, education cannot be looked upon as an avenue to a life of ease, or as a means of giving one man an advantage over another, whereby he may exist upon the fruit of that other's labor and the sweat of that other's brow. It might do for a few; it cannot do for the mass, whose efficiency must be increased and not decreased by education; because in the last analysis education is a public as well as a personal matter, and the interests of the state require that the ratio of individual efficiency in all lines shall be constantly increased.

Second, within the limits of needful activities one occupation is as important as another, and a system of universal education must enrich them all, or the end will be disastrous. We need to change our views concerning what have been regarded as menial employments. In the millennium no woman will make her living over the

washtub, nor will she sing the song of the shirt day and night forever; but neither will education and elevation free her, or any
one else, from a fair share of the drudgery of life, because the
needful things must still be done. Nor must we fail to remind ourselves that not all the labor of the world is at the washtub, or at
the bottom of the ditch, because the price of success in any calling is
unremitting and exhausting toil, against which education is no
insurance whatever. It can only promise that faithful labor shall
have its adequate and sure reward. And that is enough, for no
man has a right to ask that he be freed from labor on this earth;
he can only pray to be relieved from the burden of aimless and
fruitless drudgery—which is the blessed assurance of education.

While education is no relief from labor, or even drudgery, it
ought, however, to lesson the totality of drudgery by the further
utilization of mechanical energy and the more economic and intelligent direction of human effort. Education will never fully
justify itself until this shall have been accomplished and the human
machine be liberated from the last form of slavery—the drudgery
that is born of ignorance.

No man, then, educated or uneducated, has a right to be useless. Most men will continue to earn and ought to earn, in one way
or another, the funds to pay their bills, and in this natural way
will the world's work get done in the future as in the past. The
education of all men, therefore, is, or should be, in a broad sense
vocational, and the so-called learned professions are but other
names for developed industries. In this broad sense every useful
activity is included, from farming to music and painting, poetry
and sculpture; from engineering to medicine and law, philosophy
and theology; as wide and as varied as the activities and capacities
of the human race—so wide and so varied must our education be
if it is to be universal and be safe.

Measured by this standard, farming has the same claims upon
education as have language and literature, but no more; for both
are useful, or may be, though in different ways. Which is more
useful we cannot tell any more than we can tell whether food
or religion is the more essential to human life; or whether art or
industry contributes most to its fullest development. We only
know that all things within the range of human capacity are useful, and that education may, if it will, enrich them all.

Now this demand is right, for, unless universal education can be
so administered as not greatly to disturb the relations of needful

activities, it will prove in the end a curse instead of a blessing, and it is the business of educators now soberly to consider the consequences of headlong policies, however promising in direct results, if they do not reckon with the inevitable outcome.

Third, in the working out of these plans such policies and methods must be observed as shall prevent social cleavage along vocational lines. Unless we can do this, democracy will, in the end, fail. We cannot go on with one half of the people educated and the other half ignorant, any more than we could live with one half free and the other half slave. No more can we live with one half educated to one set of ideals and the other half to another. If we attempt it, we shall have, in due time, not civilization—but a tug of war between highly educated but mutually destructive human energies. The only safety for us now is in the education of all classes to common ideals of individual efficiency and public service along needful lines and with common standards of citizenship. To this end the individual must have training, both vocational and humanistic, and it is better if he does not know just when or how he is getting either the one or the other.

Fourth, remembering that what is one man's vocation is another's avocation, and that what is technical and professional to one is humanistic to another; remembering that all study is educational and that utility does not lessen its value; remembering, too, that much of our education comes from association and that the best of it comes in no other way—remembering all these and many other considerations well known to the thinking man, we must agree that *in a system of universal education the best results will always follow when as many subjects as possible and as many vocations as may be are taught together in the same school, under the same management and to the same body of men.* In no other way can a perfectly homogeneous population be secured. In no other way can universal efficiency be so closely combined with good citizenship. In no other way can activity and learning be so intimately united. In no other way can morals and good government be so safely intrusted to a free people.

As I see it, the greatest hindrance to the natural evolution of a single system of schools adapted to the education of all classes of our people is academic tradition which needs substantial modification in a number of important particulars.

The truth is, there is no such thing as a "general education," except one that fits for nothing in particular, leaving the possessor stranded without occupation or other field for the exercise of his trained activities. In so far as this type of general education exists among us, the quicker we abolish it the better. For example, it has been fashionable to speak of the courses in the arts and sciences as "general," "non-technical," or "liberal," using the terms synonymously and as opposed to the technical or professional.

Now this is inaccurate and leads to much confusion of mind. Courses in the arts and sciences are not by nature general and non-technical, because an examination of the facts will discover that most of the students taking those courses in colleges are taking them for professional purposes in preparation for definite careers, generally teaching; possibly banking, railroad administration, or the business of an analytical or manufacturing chemist or some other gainful occupation. That is to say, the courses in the arts and sciences are mostly taken as professional or vocational courses the same as are those in engineering and agriculture.

The best evidence of this erroneous use of terms is that those who make most of the distinction between the technical and the non-technical courses; those who talk most about the latter being liberal as distinct from the former; those who outcry loudest against commercializing education are teachers themselves, who are earning money like farmers. Now by what rule do we adjudge that farming is a calling and teaching a profession? that engineering is industrial and journalism liberal? that courses fitting for farming are technical and narrow, and those fitting for teaching or making chemical determinations are general and liberal? The truth is they are all alike vocational; they are all professional; they all open avenues whereby men and women earn money to pay their bills, and ninety-nine out of a hundred of those who are good for anything in any and all these courses are taking them for the same purpose, viz., to afford a congenial field of activity whereby the individual may become a worthy and self-sustaining member of society.

The truth is that the distinction between the technical and the non-technical, the professional and the non-professional, the narrow and the liberal, does not inhere in courses of study leading to graduation, for the same subject may be either the one or the other, according to the point of view of the student and the purpose for which it is taken. For example, chemistry *per se* is neither technical nor non-technical, narrow nor liberal. It is a great field of science. As explored and studied by an agricultural student, or by one who proposes to make his living as an analytical or a manufacturing chemist—to them it is a technical subject, while to the student of literature it becomes a non-technical and therefore a liberal subject, because it liberalizes him and broadens his outlook upon the world and helps to connect him with the farmer and manufacturing chemist. To the prospective teacher it becomes technical or non-technical; vocational or non-vocational, according as he proposes or does not propose to teach it. To the farmer, chemistry is a technical subject, and literature and history non-technical, and therefore liberal. To the teacher of history, conditions would be reversed.

Another academic reform is to get over our horror of the vocational. The old-line courses were as distinctly vocational to the learned professions as are the newer courses to the industrial occupations. The services of education to the industries of life and the ordinary occupations of men have been so recent that final adjustments are not yet made. We are only gradually beginning to learn that every useful man, educated or uneducated, has a calling and that the line between the technical and the non-technical, between the narrow and the liberal, runs across individuals, not between them. *Every properly educated man is trained both vocationally and liberally,* but one vocation is not necessarily more liberal than another except as the practitioner makes it so. To succeed in any calling requires the possession of a body of specific knowledge relating directly to that calling, mostly useless professionally to one of another calling, but far from useless as a liberalizer.

Every man, to be efficient, needs the vocational; to be happy and safe he needs the other. John Bessmer was a barber and made his living by his scissors, but meteorology was his avocation. He was the best barber I ever knew, but he talked most about meteorology. The ditcher will not ditch all his waking hours. What will he think about when he is awake and not in the ditch? Then is when his avocation, the liberal part of his education, is his comfort and our safety, for the mind is an unruly member, and if the man has no training beyond his vocation, his intellect is at sea, without chart, compass, or rudder, and the human mind adrift is a dangerous engine of destruction.

It is well that we who are bent most upon industrial training and development do not forget these considerations, and in our enthusiasm for technical instruction we see to it also that every individual has a fair share of the liberal as well, for the chief distinction of the educated man is, after all, his ability to view the world from a standpoint broader than his own surroundings.

Another relic of academic ancient history that ought to be eliminated is that habit of thought which runs in the form of set courses of study four years long. This habit of thought has stood in the way of the proper and adequate development of agriculture in our colleges, and is now standing in the way of high-school differentiation and the development of industrial courses therein.

For example, it has been assumed without discussion that a student desiring instruction in agriculture must enter upon a set course for four years, and that unless he graduated he had somehow failed, or the course was too long. It never seemed to occur to our educational fathers and grandfathers that perhaps the course was not adapted to his needs any more than it seems to occur to some of our contemporaries that men go to school to study *subjects, not set courses,* and that the benefits of our instruction are by no means confined to those who graduate.

There is nothing sacred about four years, or about a particular association of subjects. We must get over our fetish worship of what we call a "course of study" and bestow our attention upon "courses of instruction." Our somewhat uniform failure to do this has been responsible for much special and unnecessary limitation in the subject of agriculture. Let me illustrate: A good friend some months ago asked me this question: "Why do you not have a two-years course in agriculture in the University of Illinois?" I replied by asking, "Tell me first why do you have one in your university?" He replied, "Because many young men cannot, or will not, stay for a four-years course." And I said, "Then of course you have also two-year courses in the arts and sciences, and in engineering." And he said with an elevation of the eyebrows, very significant, "No, of course not." Then I said, "Why not? Do all or most of your students in the other colleges remain and complete four-year courses?" He had to answer, "No, not a third of them." I think I had answered his question, but to make sure I said, "When the other colleges of the University of Illinois find it necessary or desirable to put in two-year courses because not more than one student in three or four stays to graduate, then I suppose we shall do the same; but until then I think we shall continue to teach subjects to those who come, and bestow honors on those who have earned the usual amount of credit.'' Here is a good illustration of our futile efforts to hammer a new subject into line with ancient academic custom, as if graduation from something, even a two-years course, were the chief end of the schooling process.

This same old habit of thought is the bane of the high schools to-day in their effort to serve the people. Many of them consider the limit reached when a four-years course is offered, made up largely out of old-line subjects with little or no reference to local needs, and when we talk about instruction in vocational subjects they remind us that the ''course is full.'' This mistaken attitude on the part of too many high school men will do more than all other causes combined to force upon us a multitude of separate technical schools and destroy the opportunity of the high schools forever, because men are as firmly bent on vocational education of a secondary grade to-day as their fathers were bent on industrial education of collegiate grade half a century ago. The same forces are at work in high schools now as were at work among colleges then, and the issue will be the same. Either the high schools will expand and teach the vocational, or other schools will be established that will do it.

One good friend whom I greatly honor, because he is many years my senior, and many degrees my superior in every sense, writing me on this point, said in substance: ''Your idea that all subjects needful to the life of the community should be taught in the same school is fine in theory, but how are you going to get it all into the course, and what shall be *left out?*'' How this instinctive attitude of mind clings to us academic people! It is not much found except among professional educators, and with them it is one of the relics of academic ancient history, dating back to the time when the college provided a set course for all students and which, when full, was *full* in the same sense that the jug is full.

Recently the colleges have learned the lesson of the tremendous complexity of modern demands, and they are beginning to realize something of the depth and breadth of the meaning of universal education; at least that it means the education of many men for many things and by means of various materials and methods. This involves many courses in one school. It requires that colleges teach subjects rather than set courses; and nothing is full so long as any branch of knowledge and activity remains undeveloped and men and money hold out. The colleges have learned this; it is also the lesson for the secondary schools; indeed, in a very large sense the land-grant university is the model for the public high school.

Our children look to the schools to fit them for the many duties of life. Let them not be disappointed. To this end we must construct such educational policies and employ such materials and methods as shall make the school a true picture of life outside in all its essential activities. To accomplish this we must introduce vocational studies freely, not for their pedagogic influence, but for their own sake and for the professional skill and creative energy they will give the learner. We must do this, too, without excluding the non-professional either from the school or from the individual.

Take a specific instance outside of agriculture, but one which is typical of thousands of cases. There are many good families whose daughters feel the need of earning some little money during years of young womanhood between the school age and matrimony. They are good typical American girls, worthy the love and the service of any man, and sometime the hero will come. In the meantime, what?

We will suppose that the girl in question looks with favor upon stenography and typewriting as a congenial employment. Now I put the question flatly, remembering there are many like her in the same community,—shall the high school put in courses of typewriting and stenography which she may take in connection with her humanistic studies and her domestic science which she will one day need?—for this typical girl is, or should be, a prospective wife and mother. Will the school do this? or will it force her to leave her high school in order to get elsewhere this vocational training which she thinks she must have, because of temporary needs, and which the high school will not give her lest it should be suspected of commercializing education.

I am thankful that many high schools are already putting in vocational courses. May their numbers increase. It is far better to hold this girl in the high school and teach her also the things she will one day need much more than she will then need her stenography and typewriting,—it is better for her and it is better for the community than it is to force her, in early years and under the exigency of immediate needs, to abandon the greater for the less. Yes, it is better to take stenography and typewriting, telegraphy and bookkeeping into the high school than it is to drive our girls out of it even into the night schools. A proper policy at this point will save to American wifehood and American homes thousands of bachelor maids and factory girls, and do more to reduce the ratio of divorce than any other civilizing force with which we hold acquaintance.

What is true of many girls is doubly true of most boys. If they are good for anything, the impulse to be doing something definite takes hold of them early, and the only way to keep a live boy in school or to make him good for anything after he leaves it is to be certain that some portion of his curriculum relates directly to some form of business activity outside. *It is dangerous to attempt to educate a live boy with no reference to the vocational.*

The trouble has been in the past, and is yet, that our courses of instruction have been too few. We have not sufficiently distinguished between what a single individual could take and what the community as a whole ought to know. Accordingly, men seeking education have found much of the subject-matter and of the method grossly unsuited to the uses they hoped to make of it, and have either left the school, sacrificing their broader opportunity, or have stayed to the sacrifice of their efficiency.

The universities have been first to recognize this fact and to meet it. With the best of them there is no thought of a set course which every individual must take, but rather the aim is to offer instruction in as many as possible of the branches of knowledge that interest and profit men. The result is that in these institutions few men are taking courses with a fixed sequence, but each is after the instruction which will best fit his needs, and often two men take the same subject side by side with a very different purpose and from a very different point of view.

Now the efficiency of modern university education, especially along new lines, is becoming notable, and institutions conducted upon this plan are overrun with students seeking definite instruction for definite purposes, all of which indicates the educational policy that best meets the needs of the people. Here is the cue to the general plan that should characterize the high schools, upon which educators ought to bestow some degree of special attention, because it is in the secondary schools and not in the colleges that the American people will mostly be educated.

A third particular in which we need academic reformation is this: Not only college courses, but high school courses, as well, are planned and conducted almost solely in the interest of the few who graduate, with but little reference to the masses who drop by the wayside. If our system of education is to achieve the highest results, it must recognize the natural difference in men, both qualitatively and quantitatively, and while it trains the brightest and best for the positions of most responsibility and therefore of honor, it must so shape its policy that those who for any reason cannot, or do not, remain to the limit of time, or whose academic ability is mediocre shall drop naturally into useful places for which their little schooling has somewhat definitely prepared them. Thus will our human flotsam and jetsam be lessened, and thus shall we become more homogeneous as a people. Thus too shall we be consistent, for does not our education aim to be universal?

Our high schools, or rather their constituency, are suffering cruelly at this point to-day. The chief object in too many ambitious schools is to get on the accredited list of as many universities as possible, graduate as many students as may be, and get them into college. So intense is this purpose that in too many instances the course of study and the methods of work are inadvertently but largely shaped in the interest of those who are to graduate, though we know only too well that their ratio is small, and that of those who go to college it is still smaller.

It is time the high schools served the interests of their community first of all; and if they will do that thoroughly, the colleges will manage to connect with them on some terms mutually satisfactory. If that is impossible, then let the high school faithfully discharge its natural functions to the community that gives it life and support, and leave adjustments to the universities. The few who go beyond the high school will be abundantly able to take care of themselves *if only their training has been thorough*, and they have learned habits of efficiency. I protest against the reduction of the American high school to the basis of a college preparatory school, unless it is first built upon what is a rational education for the masses of men. We have no right to reduce, impoverish, or distort the educational opportunity of the great mass of people who depend upon the high school for their only education, in the interest of the few who go to college.

We are nearing the time when for various reasons we shall revolutionize our secondary education as we have already revolutionized our college standards. We shall offer many courses of instruction in many subjects, some vocational, others not; some vocational to certain students, not so to others, and all in the same school. We shall not be on sound ground in this matter until things are so fixed that when a boy or girl comes into contact with our school system at any point, even for a short time, he or she will at once and of necessity strike something *vocational* and also something *not vocational;* to the end that, however soon the student leaves the system, he will carry out into life at least something which will make him more efficient at some point, and also more cultivated, because the schools have taught him something of actual life, not only in the abstract but in its application.

The greatest trouble with our educational system to-day is that it is laid out too much on the plan of a trunk line railroad without side switches or way stations, but with splendid terminal facilities, so that we send the educational trains thundering over the country, quite oblivious of the population except to take on passengers, and these we take on much as the fast train takes mail bags from the hood. We do our utmost to keep them aboard, to the end, and we work so exclusively for this purpose that those who leave us are fitted for no special calling, and drop out for no special purpose, but roll off like chunks of coal by the wayside— largely a matter of luck as to what becomes of them. I would reconstruct the policy of the system by making all trains local, both to take on and *leave off passengers;* and I would pay much attention to the sidings, and the depots, and their surroundings at the way stations, to the end that those who do not complete the journey may find congenial surroundings and useful employment in some calling along the line. I mean by this that while vocation should be neither the end nor the means of the educational process, yet it should be its inseparable concomitant. This is education for efficiency and service, whether it ever earns an academic degree or not.

We need not fear real education for real efficiency, but we may well tremble when we see a whole people gorging themselves with a mass of knowledge that has no application to the lives they are to live, for this will breed in the end dissatisfaction and anarchy. The best illustration of this educational short-sightedness is the fondness of many a classically educated colored brother for Latin, Greek, and Hebrew, not so much for what they can do for him, or help to do for himself or others, as because the acquisition of language is a pleasant exercise and its possession is a satisfying novelty. Fortunately Booker T. Washington and Tuskegee are in the land, but unfortunately our educational blunders are not limited to the colored race. It is a notable and perhaps significant fact that a very large proportion of the tramps of the country have had the advantages of our schools.

Another point at which our minds are in danger of wandering far afield is in regard to the natural function of the secondary school. The American high school is a new institution, and like all new institutions it lacks ideals and methods. It has displaced, in the West at least, the old-time academy whose function it was to fit for college. The high school, lacking models, has followed very largely and quite naturally the plan of the academy whose mantle it has inherited. In this it has erred. *The modern high school is not the lineal descendant of the old-time academy, and its primary function is not to fit for college. It is a new institution, and its function is to educate its natural and local constituency for the duties of life. ,It is as thoroughly a public institution as is the state university and it should serve its community in the same way and with the same spirit that the university serves the larger and more complex unit.*

It is the first business of the high schools to serve the public needs directly through the masses of men and women who constitute their natural constituency, not indirectly through the colleges. Their service to education and to civilization is primary, fundamental, and direct, not secondary and preparatory. Nor in saying this do I reflect upon the great work of our institutions of highest learning; far from it. No man can exceed me in admiration of the supreme service of the colleges and the universities of the country, but that supreme service must be rendered without overshadowing, distorting, or injuring that other service, which, after all, is more direct, reaches a larger number, and without which the influence of the colleges and universities will be largely dissipated and lost.

If the existing high schools will earnestly address themselves to this great duty, they will become, next to the church, the most powerful educating and elevating agencies of our civilization; but if they do not, then as sure as time passes, another system of schools will arise that will do it, and the time will not be long hence until they will divide the field with technical schools and play a losing game of chance with them. The first independent schools will be trade schools in the cities and agricultural schools in the country, and this lead will be followed by others until we shall have a whole system of vocational schools of all conceivable sorts; and the high schools will be stripped, first of one opportunity to serve their constituency and then of another, until their usefulness will be lessened, if not entirely destroyed in the eyes of the people, who alone can support them, and they will be relegated to girls' schools and training schools for college admission.

This is no fanciful picture, and I am convinced that unless we are quick to read and heed the handwriting on the wall to-day the next decade or two will witness the permanent decline of the high school under the onslaught of the multitude of independent vocational schools that will spring up everywhere and which will seem to serve well because the service is direct and plainly useful. The only great future for the high school is to add vocational work, making the separate technical school unnecessary, if not impossible. If they will do this, their future and their service are assured; but if the people find it necessary to establish another system of secondary education as they did a new system of collegiate grade, then they will do it; but if they do, they will certainly insist upon a fair division of the revenues, because modern high schools are not private institutions as were the old-time colleges; they are in every sense of the term public institutions.

Experience in university circles has shown that the separate professional college was necessary in the past only because of the indifference to new demands of the institutions then existing. As soon, however, as the universities seriously set about studying the new problem from their own standpoint it was found that there was really nothing incompatible between the old and the new ideals, but rather that it took the two together to make a complete system of education, and where the two have been already joined, —the professional and the cultural, the industrial and the humanistic,—there has education flourished best in the last decade; there is the educational impulse strongest to-day, and there, if wise counsels prevail, will develop in good time the greatest educational strength and creative power of this most virile of people; not only along industrial lines, but along artistic and humanistic lines as well.

If the high schools make the most of their opportunity they will develop into a great system capable of training the masses of our people not only industrially but for all the duties of life, and in a way that can never be equaled by any multiple system of separate vocational schools, however well established and conducted. One school with many courses, not many schools with different courses—that is the plan for American secondary education. Such a school would be large enough and strong enough to afford an excellent education within walking or driving distance of every young person—an ideal not attainable by any system of separate schools that can ever be established. I have unlimited faith in the final development of the high school, and cannot condemn in terms too strong a pessimistic or a carping spirit toward this new and remarkable system of education at the very doors of the people; and I cannot oppose too strongly any and all influences that tend to make its proper evolution either impossible or more difficult.

We must not underrate the importance of the average citizen. either to himself or to the community, for the common man with an opportunity is a common man no longer. If we would know what a community of common people can do when it addresses itself seriously and *en masse* to a single purpose, consider the success of that little German village in breeding canaries, marvel upon the achievements in the Passion Play at Oberammergau, or even the singing of the Messiah in that little Swedish village of Kansas, as described in a recent *Outlook*.

Remembering what the common man may do, with proper ideals and advantages, there is no higher duty now resting upon all of us, and especially upon educators, than to unite education and activity by the closest possible bonds, to prevent on the one hand the acquirement of knowledge to no purpose, and on the other the development of operative skill with little knowledge of the true relations of things; to see to it that no individual shall be compelled to choose betwen an education without a vocation, and a vocation without an education. This supreme responsibility rests heavily upon every American community just now, and in our enthusiasm for education that is useful it is well if we temper our enthusiasm with judgment and keep always in mind the fundamentals on which all real education must rest. If this be true, it is imperative that the high school as an educational institution should take hold of and care for all the essential activities of its community; and if the clay working or some other interest develop into a separate organization with a separate plant, that it still be under the control of the high school, as the different colleges of a university are under one control, and their policies and aims, though different, are yet harmonized into a common purpose of training for actual, not apparent, efficiency.

To teach all subjects to all men in the same school—this is the great educational, social, and economic opportunity of America, where both collegiate and secondary education are in the hands of the general public and not of any sect, class, or faction. If we throw away this natural advantage, bought with blood and treasure, or if we neglect to make the most of it, we are guilty before the nation and the race of a breach of trust second only to the sin of treason.

If we follow precedent blindly and transport that alien institution, the European trade school, and transplant it into the free soil of America simply because it is temporarily easier than to complete the system we have so splendidly begun, then shall we commit an educational blunder that is inexcusable, and we shall richly deserve the anathemas that will be ours from generations yet unborn when they come to see the handicap we have laid upon them and the natural advantages we have sacrificed.

I would have it so that the occupation of an American citizen may not be known by his dress, his manner, his speech, or his prejudices. If we can realize this ideal, it will be to our perpetual advantage, for it will insure not only our economic independence but our social comfort, our racial progress, and our national safety. If all this is to come about, we have some thinking to do now, for, as I have remarked elsewhere, more depends on what *we do now,* than can depend upon what we or others think and say and try to do twenty-five or fifty years from now.

When the materials for American educational history are all gathered, and when time enough has elapsed for its various elements to assume their true proportions and perspective, it will be found that the most significant fact in the educational movement of our day and time was the agitation that led up to the establishment of the state university.

In a very large sense the founding of that unique institution of learning introduced two new and distinctive elements into our philosophy of education, both of which bid fair to be permanent, and to control even to the extent of revolutionizing our educational ideals.

The first of these fundamental doctrines was this—that no single class of men and no single class of subjects should dominate the educational policies of this people; and the second was that in the last analysis higher education is a public and not a personal matter.

The state universities were established primarily to teach the branches of knowledge especially related to the industries of life; but their field has broadened in the doing, and their success has shown not only that learning may be useful without losing its educative value, but that all branches of learning are both useful and educative, and thereby worthy of being taught to somebody; that in the interest of the public it is the business of a school as of a university to teach more things than any single man may desire to know, and that it is the business of our institutions of learning to reflect in their laboratories and in their classrooms the life and essential activities of our civilization, at least in all its major aspects.

The other new idea introduced through the state university is that education is first of all a public rather than a personal matter. Colleges had long been maintained for the convenience of those who desired and were able to pay for an education, and those who took these courses did so with a view to bettering their condition personally. While the campaign for industrial education savored largely of personal needs and class equality in educational opportunity, yet in its working out we have discovered the deeper principle; viz., that the public is not well served until we educate freely for all useful activities, to the end that these activities shall be in the hands of educated men, under whom only will they develop and by which development only will our civilization as a whole prosper and progress. The ultimate purpose of a great system of education is and must be the development of human activities, both industrial and non-industrial, and our great demand upon the individuals that have enjoyed its advantages is service—service in something, somewhere; anything, anywhere.

The great mass of human happiness will always arise out of doing well the common things of life, and the happiness of the individual will lie in that creative genius which does to-day the same thing it did yesterday, but does it better. All else is spice and seasoning to life, and as we cannot live on cakes and spices, so the enduring things will always be the useful things. There will be no educated aristocracy, for education will have a higher purpose than to give one man an advantage over another.

Every man's life is a comedy, a tragedy, or a symphony, according as he is educated. It was a great thing when the common man first lifted up his head, looked about him and said, "I, too, will be educated." It is our business to see to it that that high resolve shall not destroy the race, but shall still further bless it.

THE THEORY OF THE LIBERAL COLLEGE [1]

Alexander Meiklejohn

[Alexander Meiklejohn (1872-   ) came from England to America in 1880. He was graduated from Brown University in 1893 and received the Ph.D. from Cornell University in 1897. He was Professor of Logic and Metaphysics, and Dean at Brown University from 1906 until 1912, when he accepted the Presidency of Amherst College. He resigned this office in 1923. His conception of liberal education has been set forth in many addresses before various audiences, and it has exercised great influence in American education. His views concerning college training are stated in his volume, *The Liberal College*. The address here printed was delivered at his inauguration as President of Amherst College.]

In the discussions concerning college education there is one voice which is all too seldom raised and all too often disregarded. It is the voice of the teacher and the scholar, of the member of the college faculty. It is my purpose to devote this address to a consideration of the ideals of the teacher, of the problems of instruction as they present themselves to the men who are giving the instruction. And I do this not because I believe that just now the teachers are wiser than others who are dealing with the same questions, but rather as an expression of a definite conviction with regard to the place of the teacher in our educational scheme. It is, I believe, the function of the teacher to stand before his pupils and before the community at large as the intellectual leader of his time. If he is not able to take this leadership, he is not worthy of his calling. If the leadership is taken from him and given to others, then the very foundations of the scheme of instruction are shaken. He who in matters of teaching must be led by others is not the one to lead the imitative undergraduate, not the one to inspire the confidence and loyalty and discipleship on which all true teaching depends. If there are others who can do these things better than the college teacher of to-day, then we must bring them within the college walls. But if the teacher is to be deemed worthy of his task, then he must be recognized as the teacher of

[1] Reprinted by permission of the Century Co., from *Freedom and the College*. Questions and topics for the discussion of this address, and of other phases of the general subject with which it deals, will be found on pages 513 and 516.

us all, and we must listen to his words as he speaks of the matters entrusted to his charge.

In the consideration of the educational creed of the teacher I will try to give, first, a brief statement of his belief; second, a defense of it against other views of the function of the college; third, an interpretation of its meaning and significance; fourth, a criticism of what seem to me misunderstandings of their own meaning prevalent among the teachers of our day; and, finally, a suggestion of certain changes in policy which must follow if the belief of the teacher is clearly understood and applied in our educational procedure.

I

First, then, What do our teachers believe to be the aim of college instruction? Wherever their opinions and convictions find expression, there is one contention which is always in the foreground, namely, that to be liberal, a college must be essentially intellectual. It is a place, the teachers tell us, in which a boy forgetting all things else, may set forth on the enterprise of learning. It is a time when a young man may come to awareness of the thinking of his people, may perceive what knowledge is and has been and is to be. Whatever light-hearted undergraduates may say, whatever the opinions of solicitous parents, of ambitious friends, of employers in search of workmen, of leaders in church or state or business,—whatever may be the beliefs and desires and demands of outsiders,—the teacher within the college, knowing his mission as no one else can know it, proclaims that mission to be the leading of his pupil into the life intellectual. The college is primarily not a place of the body, nor the feelings, nor even of the will; it is, first of all, a place of the mind.

II

Against this intellectual interpretation of the college our teachers find two sets of hostile forces constantly at work. Outside the walls there are the practical demands of a busy commercial and social scheme; within the college there are the trivial and sentimental and irrational misunderstandings of its own friends. Upon each of these our college teachers are wont to descend as Samson upon the Philistines, and when they have had their will, there is little left for another to accomplish.

As against the immediate practical demands from without, the issue is clear and decisive. College teachers know that the world must have trained workmen, skilled operatives, clever buyers and sellers, efficient directors, resourceful manufacturers, able lawyers, ministers, physicians, and teachers. But it is equally true that in order to do its own work, the liberal college must leave the special and technical training for these trades and professions to be done in other schools and by other methods. In a word, the liberal college does not pretend to give all the kinds of teaching which a young man of college age may profitably receive; it does not even claim to give all the kinds of intellectual training which are worth giving. It is committed to intellectual training of the liberal type, whatever that may mean, and to that mission it must be faithful. One may safely say, then, on behalf of our college teachers, that their instruction is intended to be radically different from that given in the technical school or even in the professional school. Both these institutions are practical in a sense which the college, as an intellectual institution, is not. In the technical school the pupil is taught how to do some of the mechanical operations which contribute to human welfare. He is trained to print, to weave, to farm, to build; and for the most part he is trained to do these things by practice rather than by theory. His possession when he leaves the school is not a stock of ideas, of scientific principles, but a measure of skill, a collection of rules of thumb. His primary function as a tradesman is not to understand but to do, and in doing what is needed he is following directions which have first been thought out by others and are now practised by him. The technical school intends to furnish training which, in the sense in which we use the term, is not intellectual but practical.

In the corresponding way the work of the professional school differs from that of the liberal college. In the teaching of engineering, medicine, or law we are or may be beyond the realm of mere skill and within the realm of ideas and principles. But the selection and the relating of these ideas is dominated by an immediate practical interest which cuts them off from the intellectual point of view of the scholar. If an undergraduate should take away from his studies of chemistry, biology and psychology only those parts which have immediate practical application in the field of medicine, the college teachers would feel that they had failed to give to the boy the kind of instruction demanded of a college. It is not their purpose to furnish applied knowledge in this sense. They are not willing to cut up their sciences into segments and to allow the student to select those segments which may be of service in the practice of an art or a profession. In one way or another the teacher feels a kinship with the scientist and the scholar which forbids him to submit to this domination of his instruction by the demands of an immediate practical interest. Whatever it may mean, he intends to hold the intellectual point of view and to keep his students with him if he can. In response, then, to demands for technical and professional training our college teachers tell us that such training may be obtained in other schools; it is not to be had in a college of liberal culture.

In the conflict with the forces within the college our teachers find themselves fighting essentially the same battle as against the foes without. In a hundred different ways the friends of the college, students, graduates, trustees, and even colleagues seem to them so to misunderstand its mission as to minimize or to falsify its intellectual ideals. The college is a good place for making friends; it gives excellent experience in getting on with men; it has exceptional advantages as an athletic club; it is a relatively safe place for a boy when he first leaves home; on the whole it may improve a student's manners; it gives acquaintance with lofty ideals of character, preaches the doctrine of social service, exalts the virtues and duties of citizenship. All these conceptions seem to the teacher to hide or to obscure the fact that the college is fundamentally a place of the mind, a time for thinking, an opportunity for knowing. And perhaps in proportion to their own loftiness of purpose and motive they are the more dangerous as tending all the more powerfully to replace or to nullify the underlying principle upon which they all depend. Here again when misconception clears away, one can have no doubt that the battle of the teacher is a righteous one. It is well that a boy should have four good years of athletic sport, playing his own game and watching the games of his fellows; it is well that his manners should be improved; it is worth while to make good friends; it is very desirable to develop the power of understanding and working with other men; it is surely good to grow in strength and purity of character, in devotion to the interests of society, in readiness to meet the obligations and opportunities of citizenship. If any one of these be lacking from the fruits of a college course we may well complain of the harvest. And yet is it not true that by sheer pressure of these, by the driving and pulling of the social forces within and

without the college, the mind of the student is constantly torn
from its chief concern? Do not our social and practical interests
distract our boys from the intellectual achievements which should
dominate their imagination and command their zeal? I believe
that one may take it as the deliberate judgment of the teachers
of our colleges to-day that the function of the college is constantly misunderstood, and that it is subjected to demands which,
however friendly in intent, are yet destructive of its intellectual
efficiency and success.

III

But now that the contention of the teacher has been stated and
reaffirmed against objections, it is time to ask, What does it mean?
And how can it be justified? By what right does a company of
scholars invite young men to spend with them four years of discipleship? Do they, in their insistence upon the intellectual quality
of their ideal, intend to give an education which is avowedly unpractical? If so, how shall they justify their invitation, which
may perhaps divert young men from other interests and other
companionships which are valuable to themselves and to their
fellows? In a word, what is the underlying motive of the teacher,
what is there in the intellectual interests and activities which seems
to him to warrant their domination over the training and instruction of young men during the college years?

It is no fair answer to this question to summon us to faith in
intellectual ideals, to demand of us that we live the life of the
mind with confidence in the virtues of intelligence, that we love
knowledge and because of our passion follow after it. Most of us
are already eager to accept intellectual ideals, but our very devotion to them forbids that we accept them blindly. I have often
been struck by the inner contradictoriness of the demand that we
have faith in intelligence. It seems to mean, as it is so commonly
made to mean, that we must unintelligently follow intelligence,
that we must ignorantly pursue knowledge, that we must question
everything except the business of asking questions, that we think
about everything except the use of thinking itself. As Mr. F. H.
Bradley would say, the dictum, ''Have faith in intelligence,'' is so
true that it constantly threatens to become false. Our very conviction of its truth compels us to scrutinize and test it to the end.

How then shall we justify the faith of the teacher? What

reason can we give for our exaltation of intellectual training and activity? To this question two answers are possible. First, knowledge and thinking are good in themselves. Secondly, they help us in the attainment of other values in life which without them would be impossible. Both these answers may be given and are given by college teachers. Within them must be found whatever can be said by way of explanation and justification of the work of the liberal college.

The first answer receives just now far less of recognition than it can rightly claim. When the man of the world is told that a boy is to be trained in thinking just because of the joys and satisfactions of thinking itself, just in order that he may go on thinking as long as he lives, the man of the world has been heard to scoff and to ridicule the idle dreaming of scholarly men. But if thinking is not a good thing in itself, if intellectual activity is not worth while for its own sake, will the man of the world tell us what is? There are those among us who find so much satisfaction in the countless trivial and vulgar amusements of a crude people that they have no time for the joys of the mind. There are those who are so closely shut up within a little round of petty pleasures that they have never dreamed of the fun of reading and conversing and investigating and reflecting. And of these one can only say that the difference is one of taste, and that their tastes seem to be relatively dull and stupid. Surely it is one function of the liberal college to save boys from that stupidity, to give them an appetite for the pleasures of thinking, to make them sensitive to the joys of appreciation and understanding, to show them how sweet and captivating and wholesome are the games of the mind. At the time when the play element is still dominant it is worth while to acquaint boys with the sport of facing and solving problems. Apart from some of the experiences of friendship and sympathy I doubt if there are any human interests so permanently satisfying, so fine and splendid in themselves, as are those of intellectual activity. To give our boys that zest, that delight in things intellectual, to give them an appreciation of a kind of life which is well worth living, to make them men of intellectual culture —that certainly is one part of the work of any liberal college.

On the other hand, the creation of culture as so defined can never constitute the full achievement of the college. It is essential to awaken the impulses of inquiry, of experiment, of investigation, of reflection, the instinctive cravings of the mind. But no liberal

college can be content with this. The impulse to thinking must be
questioned and rationalized as must every other instinctive response. It is well to think, but what shall we think about? Are
there any lines of investigation and reflection more valuable than
others, and if so, how is their value to be tested? Or again, if the
impulse for thinking comes into conflict with other desires and
cravings, how is the opposition to be solved? It has sometimes
been suggested that our man of intellectual culture may be found
like Nero fiddling with words while all the world about him is
aflame. And the point of the suggestion is not that fiddling is a
bad and worthless pastime, but rather that it is inopportune on
such an occasion, that the man who does it is out of touch with
his situation, that his fiddling does not fit his facts. In a word,
men know with regard to thinking, as with regard to every other
content of human experience, that it cannot be valued merely in
terms of itself. It must be measured in terms of its relation to
other contents and to human experience as a whole. Thinking is
good in itself,—but what does it cost of other things, what does it
bring of other values? Place it amid all the varied contents of
our individual and social experience, measure it in terms of what
it implies, fix it by means of its relations, and then you will know
its worth not simply in itself but in that deeper sense which comes
when human desires are rationalized and human lives are known
in their entirety, as well as they can be known by those who are
engaged in living them.

In this consideration we find the second answer of the teacher
to the demand for justification of the work of the college. Knowledge is good, he tells us, not only in itself, but in its enrichment
and enhancement of the other values of our experience. In the
deepest and fullest sense of the words, knowledge pays. This
statement rests upon the classification of human actions into two
groups, those of the instinctive type and those of the intellectual
type. By far the greater part of our human acts are carried on
without any clear idea of what we are going to do or how we are
going to do it. For the most part our responses to our situations
are the immediate responses of feeling, of preception, of custom,
of tradition. But slowly and painfully, as the mind has developed,
action after action has been translated from the feeling to the idea-
tional type; in wider and wider fields men have become aware of
their own modes of action, more and more they have come to understanding, to knowledge of themselves and of their needs. And the

principle underlying all our educational procedure is that, on the whole, actions become more successful as they pass from the sphere of feeling to that of understanding. Our educational belief is that in the long run if men know what they are going to do and how they are going to do it, and what is the nature of the situation with which they are dealing, their response to that situation will be better adjusted and more beneficial than are the responses of the feeling type in like situations.

It is all too obvious that there are limits to the validity of this principle. If men are to investigate, to consider, to decide, then action must be delayed and we must pay the penalty of waiting. If men are to endeavor to understand and know their situations, then we must be prepared to see them make mistakes in their thinking, lose their certainty of touch, wander off into pitfalls and illusions and fallacies of thought, and in consequence secure for the time results far lower in value than those of the instinctive response which they seek to replace. The delays and mistakes and uncertainties of our thinking are a heavy price to pay, but it is the conviction of the teacher that the price is as nothing when compared with the goods which it buys. You may point out to him the loss when old methods of procedure give way before the criticism of understanding, you may remind him of the pain and suffering when old habits of thought and action are replaced, you may reprove him for all the blunders of the past; but in spite of it all he knows and you know that in human lives taken separately and in human life as a whole men's greatest lack is the lack of understanding, their greatest hope to know themselves and the world in which they live.

Within the limits of this general educational principle the place of the liberal college may easily be fixed. In the technical school pupils are prepared for a specific work and are kept for the most part on the plane of perpetual action, doing work which others understand. In the professional school, students are properly within the realm of ideas and principles, but they are still limited to a specific human interest with which alone their understanding is concerned. But the college is called liberal as against both of these because the instruction is dominated by no special interest, is limited to no single task, but is intended to take human activity as a whole, to understand human endeavors not in their isolation but in their relations to one another and to the total experience which we call the life of our people. And just as we believe that the building of ships has become more successful as men have come to a knowledge of the principles involved in their construction; just as the practice of medicine has become more successful as we have come to a knowledge of the human body, of the conditions within it and the influences without;—just so the teacher in the liberal college believes that life as a total enterprise, life as it presents itself to each one of us in his career as an individual,—human living,—will be more sucessful in so far as men come to understand it and to know it as they attempt to carry it on. To give boys an intellectual grasp on human experience—this it seems to me is the teacher's conception of the chief function of the liberal college.

May I call attention to the fact that this second answer of the teacher defines the aim of the college as avowedly and frankly practical. Knowledge is to be sought chiefly for the sake of its contribution to the other activities of human living. But on the other hand, it is as definitely declared that in method the college is fully and unreservedly intellectual. If we can see that these two demands are not in conflict but that they stand together in the harmonious relation of means and ends of instrument and achievement, of method and result, we may escape many a needless conflict and keep our educational policy in singleness of aim and action. To do this we must show that the college is intellectual, not as opposed to practical interests and purposes, but as opposed to unpractical and unwise methods of work. The issue is not between practical and intellectual aims but between the immediate and the remote aim, between the hasty and the measured procedure, between the demand for results at once and the willingness to wait for the best results. The intellectual road to success is longer and more roundabout than any other, but they who are strong and willing for the climbing are brought to higher levels of achievement than they could possibly have attained had they gone straight forward in the pathway of quick returns. If this were not true the liberal college would have no proper place in our life at all. In so far as it is true, the college has a right to claim the best of our young men to give them its preparation for the living they are to do.

IV

But now that we have attempted to interpret the intellectual mission of the college, it may be fair to ask, ''Are the teachers and scholars of our day always faithful to that mission? Do their statements and their practice always ring in accord with the principle which has been stated?'' It seems to me that at two points they are constantly off the key, constantly at variance with the reasons by which alone their teaching can be justified.

In the first place, it often appears as if our teachers and scholars were deliberately in league to mystify and befog the popular mind regarding this practical value of intellectual work. They seem not to wish too much said about the results and benefits. Their desire is to keep aloft the intellectual banner, to proclaim the intellectual gospel, to demand of student and public alike adherence to the faith. And in general when they are questioned as to results they give little satisfaction except to those who are already pledged to unwavering confidence in their *ipse dixits*. And largely as a result of this attitude the American people seem to me to have little understanding of the intellectual work of the college. Our citizens and patrons can see the value of games and physical exercises; they readily perceive the importance of the social give and take of a college democracy; they can appreciate the value of studies which prepare a young man for his profession and so anticipate or replace the professional school; they can even believe that if a boy is kept at some sort of thinking for four years his mind may become more acute, more systematic, more accurate, and hence more useful than it was before. But as for the content of a college course, as for the value of knowledge, what a boy gains by knowing Greek or economics, philosophy or literature, history or biology, except as they are regarded as having professional usefulness, I think our friends are in the dark and are likely to remain so until we turn on the light. When our teachers say, as they sometimes do say, that the effect of knowledge upon the character and life of the student must always be for the college an accident, a circumstance which has no essential connection with its real aim or function, then it seems to me that our educational policy is wholly out of joint. If there be no essential connection between instruction and life, then there is no reason for giving instruction except in so far as it is pleasant in itself, and we have no educational policy at all. As against this hesitancy, this absence of a conviction, we men of the college should declare in clear and unmistakable terms our creed—the creed that knowledge is justified by its results. We should say to our people so plainly that they cannot misunderstand, ''Give us your boys, give us the means we need, and we will so train and inform the minds of those boys that their own lives and the lives of the men about them shall be more successful than they could be without our training. Give us our chance and we will show your boys what human living is, for we are convinced that they can live better in knowledge than they can in ignorance.''

There is a second wandering from the faith which is so common among investigators that it may fairly be called the ''fallacy of the scholar.'' It is the belief that all knowledge is so good that all parts of knowledge are equally good. Ask many of our scholars and teachers what subjects a boy should study in order that he may gain insight for human living, and they will say, ''It makes no difference in what department of knowledge he studies; let him go into Sanscrit or bacteriology, into mathematics or history; if only he goes where men are actually dealing with intellectual problems, and if only he learns how to deal with problems himself, the aim of education is achieved, he has entered into intellectual activity.'' This point of view, running through all the varieties of the elective system, seems to me hopelessly at variance with any sound educational doctrine. It represents the scholar of the day at his worst both as a thinker and as a teacher. In so far as it dominates a group of college teachers it seems to me to render them unfit to determine and to administer a college curriculum. It is an announcement that they have no guiding principles in their educational practice, no principles of selection in their arrangement of studies, no genuine grasp on the relationship between knowledge and life. It is the concerted statement of a group of men each of whom is lost within the limits of his own special studies, and who as a group seem not to realize the organic relationships between them nor the common task which should bind them together.

In bringing this second criticism against our scholars I am not urging that the principle of election of college studies should be entirely discontinued. But I should like to inquire by what right and within what limits it is justified. The most familiar argument in its favor is that if a student is allowed to choose along the lines of his own intellectual or professional interest he will have enthusiasm, the eagerness which comes with the following of one's own bent. Now just so far as this result is achieved, just so far as the quality of scholarship is improved, the procedure is good and we may follow it if we do not thereby lose other results more valuable than our gain. But if the special interest comes into conflict with more fundamental ones, if what the student prefers is opposed to what he ought to prefer, then we of the college cannot leave the choice with him. We must say to him frankly, "If you do not care for liberal training you had better go elsewhere; we have a special and definite task assigned us which demands that we keep free from the domination of special or professional pursuits. So long as we are faithful to that task we cannot give you what you ask."

In my opinion, however, the fundamental motive of the elective system is not the one which has been mentioned. In the last resort our teachers allow students to choose their own studies not in order to appeal to intellectual or to professional interest, but because they themselves have no choice of their own in which they believe with sufficient intensity to impose it upon their pupils. And this lack of a dominating educational policy is in turn an expression of an intellectual attitude, a point of view, which marks the scholars of our time. In a word, it seems to me that our willingness to allow students to wander about in the college curriculum is one of the most characteristic expressions of a certain intellectual agnosticism, a kind of intellectual bankruptcy, into which, in spite of all our wealth of information, the spirit of the time has fallen. Let me explain my meaning.

The old classical curriculum was founded by men who had a theory of the world and of human life. They had taken all the available content of human knowledge and had wrought it together into a coherent whole. What they knew was, as judged by our standards, very little in amount. But upon that little content they had expended all the infinite pains of understanding and interpretation. They had taken the separate judgments of science, philosophy, history, and the arts, and had so welded them together, so established their relationships with one another, so freed them from contradictions and ambiguities that, so far as might be in their day and generation, human life as a whole and the world about us were known, were understood, were rationalized. They had a knowledge of human experience by which they could live and which they could teach to others engaged in the activities of living.

But with the invention of methods of scientific investigation and discovery there came pouring into the mind of Europe great masses of intellectual material,—astronomy, physics, chemistry. This content for a time it could not understand, could not relate to what it already knew. The old boundary lines did not enclose the new fields, the old explanations and interpretations would not fit the new facts. Knowledge had not grown, it had simply been enlarged, and the two masses of content, the old and the new, stood facing each other with no common ground of understanding. Here was the intellectual task of the great leaders of the early modern thought of Europe: to re-establish the unity of knowledge, to discover the relationships between these apparently hostile bodies of judgments, to know the world again, but with all the added richness of the new insights and the new information. This was the work of Leibnitz and Spinoza, of Kant and Hegel, and those who labored with them. And in a very considerable measure the task had been accomplished, order had been restored. But again with the inrush of the newer discoveries, first in the field of biology and then later in the world of human relationships, the difficulties have returned, multiplied a thousand fold. Every day sees a new field of facts opened up, a new method of investigation invented, a new department of knowledge established. And in the rush of it all these new sciences come merely as additions, not to be understood but simply numbered, not to be interpreted but simply listed in the great collection of separate fields of knowledge. If you will examine the work of any scientist within one of these fields you will find him ordering, systematizing, reducing to principles, in a word, knowing every fact in terms of its relation to every other fact and to the whole field within which it falls. But at the same time these separate sciences, these separate groups of judgment, are left standing side by side with no intelligible connections, no establishment of relationships, no interpretation in the sense in which we insist upon it with each of the fields taken by itself. Is it not the characteristic statement of a scholar of our time to say, "I do not know what may be the ultimate significance of these facts and these principles; all that I know is that if you will follow my methods within my field you will find the facts coming into order, the principles coming into simple and coherent arrangement. With any problems apart from this order and this arrangement I have intellectually no concern."

It has become an axiom with us that the genuine student labors within his own field. And if the student ventures forth to examine the relations of his field to the surrounding country he very easily becomes a popularizer, a *litterateur*, a speculator, and worst of all unscientific. Now I do not object to a man's minding his own intellectual business if he chooses to do so, but when a man minds his own business because he does not know any other business, because he has no knowledge whatever of the relationships which justify his business and make it worth while, then I think one may say that though such a man minds his own affairs he does not know them, he does not understand them. Such a man, from the point of view of the demands of a liberal education, differs in no essential respect from the tradesman who does not understand his trade or the professional man who merely practices his profession. Just as truly as they, he is shut up within a special interest; just as truly as they, he is making no intellectual attempt to understand his experience in its unity. And the pity of it is that more and more the chairs in our colleges are occupied by men who have only this special interest, this specialized information, and it is through them that we attempt to give our boys a liberal education, which the teachers themselves have not achieved.

I should not like to be misunderstood in making this railing accusation against our teachers and our time. If I say that our knowledge is at present a collection of scattered observations about the world rather than an understanding of it, fairness compels the admission that the failure is due to the inherent difficulties of the situation and to the novelty of the problems presented. If I cry out against the agnosticism of our people it is not as one who has escaped from it, nor as one who would point the way back to the older synthesis, but simply as one who believes that the time has come for a reconstruction, for a new synthesis. We have had time enough now to get some notion of our bearings, shocks enough to get over our nervousness and discomfiture when a new one comes along. It is the opportunity and the obligation of this generation to think through the content of our knowing once again, to understand it, so far as we can. And in such a battle as this, surely it is the part of the college to take the lead. Here is the mission of the college teacher as of no other member of our common life. Surely he should stand before his pupils and before all of us as a man who has achieved some understanding of this human situation of ours, but more than that, as one who is eager for the conflict with the powers of darkness and who can lead his pupils in enthusiastic devotion to the common cause of enlightenment.

V

And now, finally, after these attacks upon the policies which other men have derived from their love of knowledge, may I suggest two matters of policy which seem to me to follow from the definition of education which we have taken. The first concerns the content of the college course; the second has to do with the method of its presentation to the undergraduate.

We have said that the system of free election is natural for those to whom knowledge is simply a number of separate departments. It is equally true that just in so far as knowledge attains unity, just so far as the relations of the various departments are perceived, freedom of election by the student must be limited. For it at once appears that on the one side there are vast ranges of information which have virtually no significance for the purposes of a liberal education, while on the other hand there are certain elements so fundamental and vital that without any one of them a liberal education is impossible.

I should like to indicate certain parts of human knowledge which seem to me so essential that no principle of election should ever be allowed to drive them out of the course of any college student.

First, a student should become acquainted with the fundamental motives and purposes and beliefs which, clearly, or unclearly recognized, underlie all human experience and bind it together. He must perceive the moral strivings, the intellectual endeavors, the esthetic experiences of his race, and closely linked with these, determining and determined by them, the beliefs about the world which have appeared in our systems of religion. To investigate this field, to bring it to such clearness of formulation as may be possible, is the task of philosophy—an essential element in any liberal education. Secondly, as in human living, our motives, purposes, and beliefs have found expression in institutions,—those concerted modes of procedure by which we work together,—a student should be made acquainted with these. He should see and appreciate what is intended, what accomplished, and what left undone by such institutions as property, the courts, the family, the church, the mill. To know these as contributing and failing to contribute to human welfare is the work of our social or humanistic sciences, into which a boy must go on his way through the liberal college. Thirdly, in order to understand the motives and the institutions of human life one must know the conditions which surround it, the stage on which the game is played. To give this information is the business of astronomy, geology, physics, chemistry, biology and the other descriptive sciences. These a boy must know, so far as they are significant and relevant to his purpose. Fourthly, as all three of these factors, the motives, the institutions, the natural processes have sprung from the past and have come to be what they are by change upon change in the process of time, the student of human life must try to learn the sequence of events from which the present has come. The development of human thought and attitude, the development of human institutions, the development of the world and of the beings about us—all these must be known, as throwing light upon present problems, present instrumentalities, present opportunities in the life of human endeavor. And in addition to these four studies which render human experience in terms of abstract ideas, a liberal education must take account of those concrete representations of life which are given in the arts, and especially in the art of literature. It is well that a boy should be acquainted with his world not simply as expressed by the principles of knowledge but also as depicted by the artist with all the vividness and definiteness which are possible in the portrayal of individual beings in individual relationships. These five elements, then, a young man must take from a college of liberal training, the contributions of philosophy, of humanistic science, of natural science, of history, and of literature. So far as knowledge is concerned, these at least he should have, welded together in some kind of interpretation of his own experience and of the world in which he lives.

My second suggestion is that our college curriculum should be so arranged and our instruction so devised that its vital connection with the living of men should be obvious even to an undergraduate. A little while ago I heard one of the most prominent citizens of this country speaking of his college days, and he said, "I remember so vividly those few occasions on which the professor would put aside the books and talk like a real man about real things." Oh, the bitterness of those words to the teacher! Our books are not dealing with the real things, and for the most part we are not real men either, but just old fogies and bookworms. And to be perfectly frank about the whole matter, I believe that in large measure our pupils are indifferent to their studies simply because they do not see that these are important.

Now if we really have a vital course of study to present I believe that this difficulty can in large measure be overcome. It is possible to make a freshman realize the need of translating his experience from the forms of feeling to those of ideas. He can and he ought to be shown that now, his days of mere tutelage being over, it is time for him to face the problems of his people, to begin to think about those problems for himself, to learn what other men have learned and thought before him; in a word, to get himself ready to take his place among those who are responsible for the guidance of our common life by ideas and principles and purposes. If this could be done, I think we should get from the reality-loving American boy something like an intellectual enthusiasm, something of the spirit that comes when he plays a game that seems to him really worth playing. But I do not believe that this result can be achieved without a radical reversal of the arrangement of the college curriculum. I should like to see every freshman at once plunged into the problems of philosophy, into the difficulties and perplexities about our institutions, into the scientific accounts of the world especially as they bear on human life, into the portrayals of human experience which are given by the masters of literature. If this were done by proper teaching, it seems to me the boy's college course would at once take on significance for him; he would understand what he is about; and though he would be a sadly puzzled boy at the end of the first year, he would still have before him three good years of study, of investigation, of reflection, and of discipleship, in which to achieve, so far as may be, the task to which he has been set. Let him once feel the problems of the present, and his historical studies will become significant; let him know what other men have discovered and thought about his problems, and he will be ready to deal with them himself. But in any case, the whole college course will be unified and dominated by a single interest, a single purpose,—that of so understanding human life as to be ready and equipped for the practice of it. And this would mean for the college, not another seeking of the way of quick returns, but rather an escape from aimless wanderings in the mere by-paths of knowledge, a resolute climbing on the high road to a unified grasp upon human experience.

I have taken so much of your time this morning that an apology seems due for the things I have omitted to mention. I have said nothing of the organization of the college, nothing of the social life of the students, nothing of the relations with the alumni, nothing of the needs and qualifications of the teachers, and even within the consideration of the course of study, nothing of the value of specialization or of the disciplinary subjects or of the training in language and expression. And I have put these aside deliberately, for the sake of a cause which is greater than any of them—a cause which lies at the very heart of the liberal college. It is the cause of making clear to the American people the mission of the teacher, of convincing them of the value of knowledge: not the specialized knowledge which contributes to immediate practical aims, but the unified understanding which is Insight.

RELIGION

RELIGION

THE RELIGION OF THE FUTURE [1]

Charles W. Eliot

[A note concerning Charles W. Eliot appears elsewhere in this volume with his address, *Five American Contributions to Civilization*. *The Religion of the Future* is a lecture that was delivered at the close of the eleventh session of the Harvard Summer School of Theology, July 22, 1909, two months after Dr. Eliot had retired from the Presidency of Harvard University at the age of seventy-five.]

As students in this summer's School of Theology you have attended a series of lectures on fluctuations in religious interest, on the frequent occurrence of religious declines followed soon by recoveries or regenerations both within and without the churches, on the frequent attempts to bring the prevalent religious doctrines into harmony with new tendencies in the intellectual world, on the constant struggle between conservatism and liberalism in existing churches and between idealism and materialism in society at large, on the effects of popular education and the modern spirit of inquiry on religious doctrines and organizations, on the changed views of thinking people concerning the nature of the world and of man, on the increase of knowledge as affecting religion, and on the new ideas of God. You have also listened to lectures on Psychotherapy, a new development of an ancient tendency to mix religion with medicine, and on the theory of evolution, a modern scientific doctrine which within fifty years has profoundly modified the religious conceptions and expectations of many thinking people. You have heard, too, how the new ideas of democracy and social progress have modified and ought to modify not only the actual work done by the churches, but the whole conception of the function of churches. Again, you have heard how many and how profound are the religious implications in contemporary philosophy. Your attention has been called to the most recent views concerning the conservation of energy in the universe, to the wonderful phenomena of radio-activity, and to the most recent defini-

[1] Reprinted from *The Durable Satisfactions of Life* by permission of the author and of the T. Y. Crowell Company.
Questions and topics for the discussion of this address, and of other phases of the general subject with which it deals, will be found on pages 517 and 524.

tions of atom, molecule, ion, and electron—human imaginings which have much to do with the modern conceptions of matter and spirit. The influence on popular religion of modern scholarship applied to the New Testament has also engaged your attention; and, finally, you have heard an exposition of religious conditions and practices in the United States which assumed an intimate connection between the advance of civilization and the contemporaneous aspects of religions, and illustrated from history the service of religion—and particularly of Christianity—to the progress of civilization through its contributions to individual freedom, intellectual culture, and social co-operation.

The general impression you have received from this comprehensive survey must surely be that religion is not a fixed, but a fluent thing. It is, therefore, wholly natural and to be expected that the conceptions of religion prevalent among educated people should change from century to century. Modern studies in comparative religion and in the history of religions demonstrate that such has been the case in times past. Now the nineteenth century immeasurably surpassed all preceding centuries in the increase of knowledge, and in the spread of the spirit of scientific inquiry and of the passion for truth-seeking. Hence the changes in religious beliefs and practices, and in the relation of churches to human society as a whole, were much deeper and more extensive in that century than ever before in the history of the world; and the approach made to the embodiment in the actual practices of mankind of the doctrines of the greatest religious teachers was more significant and more rapid than ever before. The religion of a multitude of humane persons in the twentieth century may, therefore, be called without inexcusable exaggeration a "new religion," —not that a single one of its doctrines and practices is really new in essence, but only that the wider acceptance and better actual application of truths familiar in the past at many times and places, but never taken to heart by the multitude or put in force on a large scale, are new. I shall attempt to state without reserve and in simplest terms free from technicalities, first, what the religion of the future seems likely not to be, and, secondly, what it may reasonably be expected to be. My point of view is that of an American layman, whose observing and thinking life has covered the extraordinary period since the *Voyage of the Beagle* was published, anæsthesia and the telegraph came into use, Herbert Spencer issued his first series of papers on evolution, Kuenen, Robertson

Smith, and Wellhausen developed and vindicated Biblical criticism, J. S. Mill's *Principles of Political Economy* appeared, and the United States by going to war with Mexico set in operation the forces which abolished slavery on the American continent—the period within which mechanical power came to be widely distributed through the explosive engine and the applications of electricity, and all the great fundamental industries of civilized mankind were reconstructed.

1. The religion of the future will not be based on authority, either spiritual or temporal. The decline of the reliance upon absolute authority is one of the most significant phenomena of the modern world. This decline is to be seen everywhere,—in government, in education, in the church, in business, and in the family. The present generation is willing, and indeed often eager, to be led; but it is averse to being driven, and it wants to understand the grounds and sanctions of authoritative decision. As a rule, the Christian churches, Roman, Greek, and Protestant, have heretofore relied mainly upon the principle of authority, the Reformation having substituted for an authoritative church an authoritative book; but it is evident that the authority both of the most authoritative churches and of the Bible as a verbally inspired guide is already greatly impaired, and that the tendency towards liberty is progressive, and among educated men irresistible.

2. It is hardly necessary to say that in the religion of the future there will be no personifications of the primitive forces of nature, such as light, fire, frost, wind, storm, and earthquake, although primitive religions and the actual religions of barbarous or semi-civilized peoples abound in such personifications. The mountains, groves, volcanoes, and oceans will no longer be inhabited by either kindly or malevolent deities; although man will still look to the hills for rest, still find in the ocean a symbol of infinity, and refreshment and delight in the forests and the streams. The love of nature mounts and spreads, while faith in fairies, imps, nymphs, demons, and angels declines and fades away.

3. There will be in the religion of the future no worship, express or implied, of dead ancestors, teachers, or rulers; no more tribal, racial, or tutelary gods; no identification of any human being, however majestic in character, with the Eternal Deity. In these respects the religion of the future will not be essentially new, for nineteen centuries ago Jesus said, "Neither in this moun-

tain, nor in Jerusalem, shall ye worship the Father. . . . God is a Spirit; and they that worship Him must worship in spirit and truth." It should be recognized, however, first, that Christianity was soon deeply affected by the surrounding paganism, and that some of these pagan intrusions have survived to this day; and, secondly, that the Hebrew religion, the influence of which on the Christian has been and is, very potent, was in the highest degree a racial religion, and its Holy of Holies was local. In war-times, that is, in times when the brutal or savage instincts remaining in humanity become temporarily dominant, and good-will is limited to people of the same nation, the survival of a tribal or national quality in institutional Christianity comes out very plainly. The aid of the Lord of Hosts is still invoked by both parties to international warfare, and each side praises and thanks Him for its successes. Indeed, the same spirit has often been exhibited in civil wars caused by religious differences.

> "Now glory to the Lord of Hosts, from whom all glories are!
> And glory to our sovereign liege, King Henry of Navarre!"

It is not many years since an Archbishop of Canterbury caused thanks to be given in all Anglican churches that the Lord of Hosts had been in the English camp over against the Egyptians. Heretofore the great religions of the world have held out hopes of direct interventions of the deity, or some special deity, in favor of his faithful worshippers. It was the greatest of Jewish prophets who told King Hezekiah that the King of Assyria, who had approached Jerusalem with a great army, should not come into the city nor shoot an arrow there, and reported the Lord as saying, "I will defend this city to save it, for my own sake, and for my servant David's sake." "And it came to pass that night, that the angel of the Lord went forth, and smote in the camp of the Assyrians an hundred fourscore and five thousand: and when they arose early in the morning, behold, they were all dead corpses." The new religion cannot promise that sort of aid to either nations or individuals in peril.

4. In the religious life of the future the primary object will not be the personal welfare or safety of the individual in this world or any other. That safety, that welfare or salvation, may be incidentally secured, but it will not be the prime object in view. The religious person will not think of his own welfare or security, but of service to others, and of contributions to the common good.

The new religion will not teach that character is likely to be suddenly changed, either in this world or in any other,—although in any world a sudden opportunity for improvement may present itself, and the date of that opportunity may be a precious remembrance. The new religion will not rely on either a sudden conversion in this world or a sudden paradise in the next, from out a sensual, selfish, or dishonest life. It will teach that repentance wipes out nothing in the past, and is only the first step towards reformation, and a sign of a better future.

5. The religion of the future will not be propitiatory, sacrificial, or expiatory. In primitive society fear of the supernal powers, as represented in the awful forces of nature, was the root of religion. These dreadful powers must be propitiated or placated, and they must be propitiated by sacrifices in the most literal sense, and the supposed offences of man must be expiated by sufferings which were apt to be vicarious. Even the Hebrews offered human sacrifices for generations; and always a great part of their religious rites consisted in sacrifices of animals. The Christian church made a great step forward when it substituted the burning of incense for the burning of bullocks and doves; but to this day there survives not only in the doctrines but in the practices of the Christian church the principle of expiatory sacrifice. It will be an immense advance if twentieth-century Christianity can be purified from all these survivals of barbarous, or semi-barbarous, religious conceptions; because they imply such an unworthy idea of God.

6. The religion of the future will not perpetuate the Hebrew anthropomorphic representations of God, conceptions which were carried in large measure into institutional Christianity. It will not think of God as an enlarged and glorified man, who walks "in the garden in the cool of the day," or as a judge deciding between human litigants, or as a king, Pharaoh, or emperor, ruling arbitrarily his subjects, or as the patriarch who, in the early history of the race, ruled his family absolutely. These human functions will cease to represent adequately the attributes of God. The nineteenth century has made all these conceptions of deity look archaic and crude.

7. The religion of the future will not be gloomy, ascetic, or maledictory. It will not deal chiefly with sorrow and death, but with joy and life. It will not care so much to account for the evil and the ugly in the world as to interpret the good and the beauti-

ful. It will believe in no malignant powers—neither in Satan nor in witches, neither in the evil eye nor in the malign suggestion. When its disciple encounters a wrong or evil in the world, his impulse will be to search out its origin, source, or cause, that he may attack it at its starting-point. He may not speculate on the origin of evil in general, but will surely try to discover the best way to eradicate the particular evil or wrong he has recognized.

Having thus considered what the religion of the future will not be, let us now consider what its positive elements will be.

The new thought of God will be its most characteristic element. This ideal will comprehend the Jewish Jehovah, the Christian Universal Father, the modern physicist's omnipresent and exhaustless Energy, and the biological conception of a Vital Force. The Infinite Spirit pervades the universe, just as the spirit of a man pervades his body, and acts, consciously or unconsciously, in every atom of it. The twentieth century will accept literally and implicitly St. Paul's statement, "In Him we live, and move, and have our being," and God is that vital atmosphere, or incessant inspiration. The new religion is therefore thoroughly monotheistic, its God being the one infinite force, but this one God is not withdrawn or removed, but indwelling, and especially dwelling in every living creature. God is so absolutely immanent in all things, animate and inanimate, that no mediation is needed between him and the least particle of his creation. In his moral attributes, he is for every man the multiplication to infinity of all the noblest, tenderest, and most potent qualities which that man has ever seen or imagined in a human being. In this sense every man makes his own picture of God. Every age, barbarous or civilized, happy or unhappy, improving or degenerating, frames its own conception of God within the limits of its own experiences and imaginings. In this sense, too, a humane religion has to wait for a humane generation. The central thought of the new religion will therefore be a humane and worthy idea of God, thoroughly consistent with the nineteenth-century revelations concerning man and nature, and with all the tenderest and loveliest teachings which have come down to us from the past.

The scientific doctrine of one omnipresent, eternal Energy, informing and inspiring the whole creation at every instant of time and throughout the infinite spaces, is fundamentally and completely inconsistent with the dualistic conception which sets spirit over against matter, good over against evil, man's wickedness against God's righteousness, and Satan against Christ. The doctrine of God's immanence is also inconsistent with the conception that he once set the universe a-going, and then withdrew, leaving the universe to be operated under physical laws, which were his vicegerents or substitutes. If God is thoroughly immanent in the entire creation, there can be no "secondary causes," in either the material or the spiritual universe. The new religion rejects absolutely the conception that man is an alien in the world, or that God is alienated from the world. It rejects also the entire conception of man as a fallen being, hopelessly wicked, and tending downward by nature; and it makes this emphatic rejection of long-accepted beliefs because it finds them all inconsistent with a humane, civilized, or worthy idea of God.

If, now, man discovers God through self-consciousness, or, in other words, if it is the human soul through which God is revealed, the race has come to the knowledge of God through knowledge of itself; and the best knowledge of God comes through knowledge of the best of the race. Men have always attributed to man a spirit distinct from his body, though immanent in it. No one of us is willing to identify himself with his body; but on the contrary every one now believes, and all men have believed, that there is in a man an animating, ruling, characteristic essence, or spirit, which is himself. This spirit, dull or bright, petty or grand, pure or foul, looks out of the eyes, sounds in the voice, and appears in the bearing and manners of each individual. It is something just as real as the body, and more characteristic. To every influential person it gives far the greater part of his power. It is what we call the personality. This spirit, or soul, is the most effective part of every human being, and is recognized as such, and always has been. It can use a fine body more effectively than it can a poor body, but it can do wonders through an inadequate body. In the crisis of a losing battle it is a human soul that rallies the flying troops. It looks out of flashing eyes, and speaks in ringing tones, but its appeal is to other souls, and not to other bodies. In the midst of terrible natural catastrophes,—earthquakes, storms, conflagrations, volcanic eruptions,—when men's best works are being destroyed and thousands of lives are ceasing suddenly and horribly, it is not a few especially good human bodies which steady the survivors, maintain order, and organize the forces of rescue and relief. It is a few superior souls. The leading men and women in any society, savage or civilized, are the strongest personalities,—the personality being primarily spiritual, and only secondarily bodily. Recognizing to the full these simple and obvious facts, the future religion will pay homage to all righteous and loving persons who in the past have exemplified, and made intelligible to their contemporaries, intrinsic goodness and effluent good-will. It will be an all-saints religion. It will treasure up all tales of human excellence and virtue. It will reverence the discoverers, teachers, martyrs, and apostles of liberty, purity, and righteousness. It will respect and honor all strong and lovely human beings,—seeing in them in finite measure qualities similar to those which they adore in God. Recognizing in every great and lovely human person individual will-power which is the essence of the personality, it will naturally and inevitably attribute to God a similar individual will-power, the essence of his infinite personality. In this simple and natural faith there will be no place for metaphysical complexities or magical rites, much less for obscure dogmas, the result of compromises in turbulent conventions. It is anthropomorphic; but what else can a human view of God's personality be? The finite can study and describe the infinite only through analogy, parallelism, and simile; but that is a good way. The new religion will animate and guide ordinary men and women who are putting into practice religious conceptions which result directly from their own observation and precious experience of tenderness, sympathy, trust, and solemn joy. It will be most welcome to the men and women who cherish and exhibit incessant, all-comprehending good-will. These are the "good" people. These are the only genuinely civilized persons.

To the wretched, sick, and downtrodden of the earth, religion has in the past held out hopes of future compensation. When precious ties of affection have been broken, religion has held out prospects of immediate and eternal blessings for the departed, and has promised happy reunions in another and a better world. To a human soul, lodged in an imperfect, feeble, or suffering body, some of the older religions have held out the expectation of deliverance by death, and of entrance upon a rich, competent, and happy life,—in short, for present human ills, however crushing, the widely accepted religions have offered either a second life, presumably immortal, under the happiest conditions, or at least peace, rest, and a happy oblivion. Can the future religion promise that sort of compensation for the ills of this world any more than it can promise miraculous aid against threatened disaster? A candid reply to this inquiry involves the statement that in the future religion there will be nothing "supernatural." This does not mean that life will be stripped of mystery or wonder, or that the range of natural law has been finally determined; but that religion, like all else, must conform to natural law so far as the range of law has been determined. In this sense the religion of the future will be a natural religion. In all its theory and all its practice it will be completely natural. It will place no reliance on any sort of magic, or miracle, or other violation of, or exception to, the laws of nature. It will perform no magical rites, use no occult processes, count on no abnormal interventions of supernal powers, and admit no possession of supernatural gifts, whether transmitted or conferred, by any tribe, class, or family of men. Its sacraments will be, not invasions of law by miracle, but the visible signs of a natural spiritual grace, or of a natural hallowed custom. It may preserve historical rites and ceremonies, which, in times past, have represented the expectation of magical or miraculous effects; but it will be content with natural interpretations of such rites and ceremonies. Its priests will be men especially interested in religious thought, possessing unusual gifts of speech on devotional subjects, and trained in the best methods of improving the social and industrial conditions of human life. There will always be need of such public teachers and spiritual leaders, heralds, and prophets. It should be observed, however, that many happenings and processes which were formerly regarded as supernatural have, with the increase of knowledge, come to be regarded as completely natural. The line between the supposed natural and the supposed supernatural is, therefore, not fixed but changeable.

It is obvious, therefore, that the completely natural quality of the future religion excludes from it many of the religious compensations and consolations of the past. Twentieth-century soldiers, going into battle, will not be able to say to each other, as Moslem soldiers did in the tenth century, "If we are killed to-day, we shall meet again to-night in Paradise." Even now, the mother, who loses her babe, or the husband his wife, by a preventable disease, is seldom able to say simply, "It is the will of God! The babe—or the woman—is better off in heaven than on earth. I resign this dear object of love and devotion, who has gone to a happier world." The ordinary consolations of institutional Christianity no longer satisfy intelligent people whose lives are broken by the sickness or premature death of those they love. The new religion will not attempt to reconcile men and women to present ill by promises of future blessedness, either for themselves or for others. Such promises have done infinite mischief in the world, by inducing men to be patient under sufferings or deprivations against which they should have incessantly struggled. The advent of a just freedom for the mass of mankind has been delayed for centuries by just this effect of compensatory promises issued by churches.

The religion of the future will approach the whole subject of evil from another side, that of resistance and prevention. The Breton sailor, who had had his arm poisoned by a dirty fish-hook which had entered his finger, made a votive offering at the shrine of the Virgin Mary and prayed for a cure. The workman to-day, who gets cut or bruised by a rough or dirty instrument, goes to a surgeon, who applies an antiseptic dressing to the wound, and prevents the poisoning. That surgeon is one of the ministers of the new religion. When dwellers in a slum suffer the familiar evils caused by overcrowding, impure food, and cheerless labor, the modern true believers contend against the sources of such misery by providing public baths, playgrounds, wider and cleaner streets, better dwellings, and more effective schools,—that is, they attack the sources of physical and moral evil. The new religion cannot supply the old sort of consolation; but it can diminish the need of consolation, or reduce the number of occasions for consolation.

A further change in religious thinking has already occurred on the subject of human pain. Pain was generally regarded as a punishment for sin, or as a means of moral training, or as an expiation, vicarious or direct. Twentieth-century religion, gradually perfected in this respect during the last half of the nineteenth century, regards human pain as an evil to be relieved and prevented by the promptest means possible, and by any sort of available means, physical, mental, or moral; and, thanks to the progress of biological and chemical science, there is comparatively little physical pain nowadays which cannot be prevented or relieved. The invention of anæsthetics has brought into contempt the expiatory, or penal, view of human pain in this world. The younger generations listen with incredulous smiles to the objection made only a little more than sixty years ago by some divines of the Scottish Presbyterian church to the employment of chloroform in childbirth, namely, that the physicians were interfering with the execution of a curse pronounced by the Almighty. Dr. Weir Mitchell, a physician who has seen much of mental pain as well as of bodily, in his poem read at the fiftieth anniversary of the first public demonstration of surgical anæsthesia, said of pain:

"What purpose hath it? Nay, thy quest is vain:
Earth hath no answer: If the baffled brain
Cries, 'Tis to warn, to punish, Ah, refrain!
When writhes the child, beneath the surgeon's hand,
What soul shall hope that pain to understand?
Lo! Science falters o'er the hopeless task,
And Love and Faith in vain an answer ask. . . ."

A similar change is occurring in regard to the conception of divine justice. The evils in this world have been regarded as penalties inflicted by a just God on human beings who had violated his laws; and the justice of God played a great part in his imagined dealings with the human race. A young graduate of Andover Theological Seminary once told me that when he had preached two or three times in summer in a small Congregational church on Cape Cod, one of the deacons of the church said to him at the close of the service, "What sort of sentimental mush is this that they are teaching you at Andover? You talk every Sunday about the love of God; we want to hear about his justice." The future religion will not undertake to describe, or even imagine, the justice of God. We are to-day so profoundly dissatisfied with human justice, although it is the result of centuries of experience of social good and ill in this world, that we may well distrust human capacity to conceive of the justice of a morally perfect, infinite being. The civilized nations now recognize the fact that legal punishments usually fail of their objects, or cause wrongs and evils greater than those for which the punishments were inflicted; so that penology, or the science of penalties, has still to be created. It is only very lately that the most civilized communities began to learn how to deal with criminal tendencies in the young. In the eyes of God human beings must all seem very young. Since our ideas of God's modes of thinking and acting are necessarily based on the best human attainments in similar directions, the new religion cannot pretend to understand God's justice, inasmuch as there is no human experience of public justice fit to serve as the foundation for a true conception of God's. The new religion will magnify and laud God's love and compassion, and will not venture to state what the justice of God may, or may not, require of himself, or of any of his finite creatures. This will be one of the great differences between the future religion and the past. Institutional Christianity as a rule condemned the mass of mankind to eternal torment; partly because the leaders of the churches thought they understood completely the justice of God, and partly because the exclusive possession of means of deliverance gave the churches some restraining influence over even the boldest sinners, and much over the timid. The new religion will make no such pretensions, and will teach no such horrible and perverse doctrines.

Do you ask what consolation for human ills the new religion will offer? I answer, the consolation which often comes to the sufferer from being more serviceable to others than he was before the loss or the suffering for which consolation is needed; the consolation of being one's self wiser and tenderer than before, and therefore more able to be serviceable to human kind in the best ways; the consolation through the memory, which preserves the sweet fragrance of characters and lives no longer in presence, recalls the joys and achievements of those lives while still within mortal view, and treasures up and multiplies the good influences they exerted. Moreover, such a religion has no tendency to diminish the force in this world, or any other, of the best human imaginings concerning the nature of the infinite Spirit immanent in the universe. It urges its disciples to believe that as the best and happiest man is he who best loves and serves, so the soul of the universe finds its perfect bliss and efficiency in supreme and universal love and service. It sees evidence in the moral history of the human race that a loving God rules the universe. Trust in this supreme rule is genuine consolation and support under many human trials and sufferings. Nevertheless, although brave and patient endurance of evils is always admirable, and generally happier than timid or impatient conduct under suffering or wrong, it must be admitted that endurance or constancy is not consolation, and that there are many physical and mental disabilities and injuries for which there is no consolation in a literal sense. Human skill may mitigate or palliate some of them, human sympathy and kindness may make them more bearable, but neither religion nor philosophy offers any complete consolation for them, or ever has.

In thus describing the consolations for human woes and evils which such a religion can offer, its chief motives have been depicted. They are just those which Jesus said summed up all the commandments, love toward God and brotherliness to man. It will teach a universal good-will, under the influence of which men, will do their duty, and at the same time, promote their own happiness. The devotees of a religion of service will always be asking what they can contribute to the common good; but their greatest service must always be to increase the stock of good-will among men. One of the worst of chronic human evils is working for daily bread without any interest in the work, and with ill-will toward the institution or person that provides the work. The work of the world must be done; and the great question is, shall it be done happily or unhappily? Much of it is to-day done unhappily. The new religion will contribute powerfully toward the reduction of this mass of unnecessary misery, and will do so chiefly by promoting good-will among men.

A paganized Hebrew-Christianity has unquestionably made much of personal sacrifice as a religious duty. The new religion will greatly qualify the supposed duty of sacrifice, and will regard all sacrifices as unnecessary and injurious, except those which love dictates and justifies. "Greater *love* hath no man than this, that a man lay down his life for his friends." Self-sacrifice is not a good or a merit in itself; it must be intelligent and loving to be meritorious, and the object in view must be worth its price. Giving up attractive pleasures or labors in favor of some higher satisfaction, or some engrossing work, is not self-sacrifice. It is a renunciation of inferior or irrelevant objects in favor of one superior object; it is only the intelligent inhibition of whatever distracts from the main pursuit, or the worthiest task. Here, again, the new religion will teach that happiness goes with dutifulness even in this world.

All the religions have been, to a greater or less extent, uplifting and inspiring, in the sense that they raised men's thoughts to some power above them, to some being or beings, which had more power and more duration than the worshippers had. When kings or emperors were deified, they were idealized, and so lifted men's thoughts out of the daily round of their ordinary lives. As the objects of worship became nobler, purer, and kinder with the progress of civilization, the prevailing religion became more stimulating to magnanimity and righteousness. Will the future religion be as helpful to the spirit of man? Will it touch his imagination as the anthropomorphism of Judaism, polytheism, Islam, and paganized Christianity have done? Can it be as moving to the human soul as the deified powers of nature, the various gods and goddesses that inhabited sky, ocean, mountains, groves, and streams, or the numerous deities revered in the various Christian communions,—God the Father, the Son of God, the Mother of God, the Holy Ghost, and the host of tutelary saints? All these objects of worship have greatly moved the human soul, and have inspired men to thoughts and deeds of beauty, love, and duty. Will the new religion do as much? It is reasonable to expect that it will. The sentiments of awe and reverence, and the love of beauty and goodness, will remain, and will increase in strength and influence. All the natural human affections will remain in full force. The new religion will foster powerfully a virtue which is comparatively new in the world—the love of truth and the passion for seeking it, and the truth will progressively make men free; so that the coming generations will be freer, and therefore more productive and stronger than the preceding. The new religionists will not worship their ancestors; but they will have a stronger sense of the descent of the present from the past than men have ever had before, and each generation will feel more strongly than ever before its indebtedness to the preceding.

The two sentiments which most inspire men to good deeds are love and hope. Religion should give freer and more rational play to these two sentiments than the world has heretofore witnessed; and the love and hope will be thoroughly grounded in and on efficient, serviceable, visible, actual, and concrete deeds and conduct. When a man works out a successful treatment for cerebrospinal meningitis—a disease before which medicine was absolutely helpless a dozen years ago—by applying to the discovery of a remedy ideas and processes invented or developed by other men studying other diseases, he does a great work of love, prevents for the future the breaking of innumerable ties of love, and establishes good grounds for hope of many like benefits for human generations to come. The men who do such things in the present world are ministers of the religion of the future. The future religion will prove, has proved, as effective as any of the older ones in inspiring men to love and serve their fellow-beings,—and that is the true object and end of all philosophies and all religions; for that is the way to make men better and happier, alike the servants and the served.

The future religion will have the attribute of universality and of adaptability to the rapidly increasing stores of knowledge and power over nature acquired by the human race. As the religion of a child is inevitably very different from that of an adult, and must grow up with the child, so the religion of a race whose capacities are rapidly enlarging must be capable of a corresponding development. The religion of any single individual ought to grow up with him all the way from infancy to age; and the same is true of the religion of a race. It is bad for any people to stand still in their governmental conceptions and practices, or in the organization of their industries, or in any of their arts or trades, even the oldest; but it is much worse for a people to stand still in their religious conceptions and practices. Now, the new religion affords an indefinite scope, or range, for progress and development. It rejects all the limitations of family, tribal, of national religion. It is not bound to any dogma, creed, book, or institution. It has the whole world for the field of the loving labors of its disciples; and its fundamental precept of serviceableness admits an infinite variety and range in both time and space. It is very simple, and therefore possesses an important element of durability. It is the complicated things that get out of order. Its symbols will not relate to sacrifice or dogma; but it will doubtless have symbols, which will represent its love of liberty, truth, and beauty. It will also have social rites and reverent observances; for it will wish to commemorate the good thoughts and deeds which have come down from former generations. It will have its saints; but its canonizations will be based on grounds somewhat new. It will have its heroes; but they must have shown a loving, disinterested, or protective courage. It will have its communions, with the Great Spirit, with the spirits of the departed, and with living fellow-men of like minds. Working together will be one of its fundamental ideas,—of men with God, of men with prophets, leaders, and teachers, of men with one another, of men's intelligence with the forces of nature. It will teach only such uses of authority as are necessary to secure the coöperation of several or many people to one end; and the discipline it will advocate will be training in the development of coöperative good-will.

Will such a religion as this make progress in the twentieth-century world? You have heard in this Summer School of Theology much about the conflict between materialism and religious idealism, the revolt against long-accepted dogmas, the frequent occurrence of waves of reform, sweeping through and sometimes over the churches, the effect of modern philosophy, ethical theories, social hopes, and democratic principles on the established churches,

and the abandonment of churches altogether by a large proportion
of the population in countries mainly Protestant. You know, too,
how other social organizations have, in some considerable measure,
taken the place of churches. Millions of Americans find in
Masonic organizations, lodges of Odd Fellows, benevolent and fraternal societies, granges, and trades-unions, at once their practical
religion, and the satisfaction of their social needs. So far as
these multifarious organizations carry men and women out of
their individual selves, and teach them mutual regard and social
and industrial coöperation, they approach the field and functions
of the religion of the future. The Spiritualists, Christian Scientists, and mental healers of all sorts manifest a good deal of ability
to draw people away from the traditional churches, and to dis-
credit traditional dogmas and formal creeds. Nevertheless, the
great mass of the people remain attached to the traditional
churches, and are likely to remain so,—partly because of their
tender associations with churches in the grave crises of life, and
partly because their actual mental condition still permits them to
accept the beliefs they have inherited or been taught while young.
The new religion will therefore make but slow progress, so far
as outward organization goes. It will, however, progressively
modify the creeds and religious practices of all the existing
churches, and change their symbolism and their teachings concerning the conduct of life. Since its chief doctrine is the doctrine of a sublime unity of substance, force, and spirit, and its
chief precept is, Be serviceable, it will exert a strong uniting influence among men.

Christian unity has always been longed for by devout believers,
but has been sought in impossible ways. Authoritative churches
have tried to force everybody within their range to hold the same
opinions and unite in the same observances, but they have won
only temporary and local successes. As freedom has increased in
the world, it has become more and more difficult to enforce even
outward conformity; and in countries where church and state have
been separated, a great diversity of religious opinions and practices has been expressed in different religious organizations, each
of which commands the effective devotion of a fraction of the population. Since it is certain that men are steadily gaining more and
more freedom in thought, speech and action, civilized society might
as well assume that it will be quite impossible to unite all religiously minded people through any dogma, creed, ceremony, ob-

servance, or ritual. All these are divisive, not uniting, wherever a reasonable freedom exists. The new religion proposes as a basis of unity, first, its doctrine of an immanent and loving God, and, secondly, its precept, Be serviceable to fellow-men. Already there are many signs in the free countries of the world that different religious denominations can unite in good work to promote human welfare. The support of hospitals, dispensaries, and asylums by persons connected with all sorts of religious denominations, the union of all denominations in carrying on Associated Charities in large cities, the success of the Young Men's Christian Associations, and the numerous efforts to form federations of kindred churches for practical purposes, all testify to the feasibility of extensive coöperation in good works. Again, the new religion cannot create any caste, ecclesiastical class, or exclusive sect founded on a rite. On these grounds it is not unreasonable to imagine that the new religion will prove a unifying influence and a strong reinforcement of democracy.

Whether it will prove as efficient to deter men from doing wrong and to encourage them to do right as the prevailing religions have been, is a question which only experience can answer. In these two respects neither the threats nor the promises of the older religions have been remarkably successful in society at large. The fear of hell has not proved effective to deter men from wrongdoing, and heaven has never yet been described in terms very attractive to the average man or woman. Both are indeed unimaginable. The great geniuses, like Dante and Swedenborg, have produced only fantastic and incredible pictures of either state. The modern man would hardly feel any appreciable loss of motive-power toward good or away from evil if heaven were burnt and hell quenched. The prevailing Christian conceptions of heaven and hell have hardly any more influence with educated people in these days than Olympus and Hades have. The modern mind craves an immediate motive or leading, good for to-day on this earth. The new religion builds on the actual experience of men and women and of human society as a whole. The motive powers it relies on have been, and are, at work in innumerable human lives; and its beatific visions and its hopes are better grounded than those of traditional religion, and finer,—because free from all selfishness, and from the imagery of governments, courts, social distinctions, and war.

Finally, this twentieth-century religion is not only to be in harmony with the great secular movements of modern society—democracy, individualism, social idealism, the zeal for education, the spirit of research, the modern tendency to welcome the new, the fresh powers of preventive medicine, and the recent advances in business and industrial ethics—but also in essential agreement with the direct, personal teachings of Jesus, as they are reported in the Gospels. The revelation he gave to mankind thus becomes more wonderful than ever.

WHAT IS THE ATTITUDE OF COLLEGE STUDENTS TOWARD ORGANIZED RELIGION?[1]

Albert Parker Fitch

[Albert Parker Fitch (1877-   ) was graduated from Harvard College in 1900, and from Union Seminary in 1903. He was ordained in the Congregational ministry, and served two pastorates before becoming President of Andover Theological Seminary in 1909. In 1917 he was made Professor of the History of Religion in Amherst College. Among his books are, *Religion and the Undergraduate, Can the Church Survive in the Present Order?* and *Preaching and Paganism*.

The essay here printed appeared in the *Journal of Religion* for March, 1921.]

I

It is not easy to give any answer to this question which will be sufficiently accurate to be illuminating. It is never a simple matter to discern what youth is thinking or feeling, either on those matters which it believes to be important to itself or those which it is aware we propose or desire it should regard as such. There is always a gulf fixed between middle age and youth though for the most part age only dimly comprehends it. We who have grown up remember our childhood with sufficient and rather sentimental clearness and we have a vivid realization alike of the trials, the responsibilities, and the privileges of age. But the years of our adolescence tend to fade from our memory. Those days of swift transition, of continuous experimentation, of unrelated, irresponsible, and ephemeral expansions left no enduring marks upon the tablets of the mind. For the most part we have so far forgotten their significance that we do not even realize they have passed out of our recorded consciousness.

This largely accounts, I think, for the characteristic impatience of our self-protective prudence with the gay and careless destructiveness of newly awakened life. This is why age has more of jealousy than sympathy for youth and why it is more prone to

[1] Reprinted from the *Journal of Religion* by permission of the author and the University of Chicago Press.

Questions and topics for the discussion of this essay, and of other phases of the general subject with which it deals, will be found on pages 518 and 523.

expect adolescence to understand and pay tribute to what appear to it the self-evident standards of maturity, than to remember the need and difficulty of thinking itself back into the morning of life. Few older men can deal with youth imaginatively. Hence professor and student live side by side in outer decorum and superficial companionship, but the real springs of action and the scales of value by which youth builds its life are often carefully concealed.

This is particularly true when the discussion deals with matters of faith and conduct. The sense of the maladjustment between an older and a younger generation is strongest here. Youth does not understand its own attitude toward religion any too well. It is both self-conscious and self-exacting and these traits increase the inhibitions induced by the sense of the obtuseness and remoteness of older lives. Moreover, youth is not unaware that the reasons age brings forward in the support of established institutions are often more ostensible than real, that it is not so much the intrinsic worth of organized religion as it is its by-product of stability, comfort, and professional security which endears it to its defenders. *The Profits of Religion* is a grotesquely unfair and one-sided book but there is truth in it and just the kind of truth that youth can perceive. Youth thinks that age demands more of it in the way of intellectual and moral docility than it, itself, is prepared to give.

In short, a community of young people strives on the whole toward higher standards of thought and conduct than does the armored and respectable middle age around it. However fantastic and perverse some of its contemporary expressions may seem, nevertheless it is generally distinguished by ethical insight and moral sensitiveness. Youth sometimes fails dreadfully but it is more honest with itself regarding its failures, realizes their nature more keenly, and takes them more seriously than does the older life about it. Hence the spiritual atmosphere of a college or a parish, which offers the only medium for the exchange of real thought and emotion, is clouded by false values. The young idealists in it are tongue-tied and uncertain except when talking among themselves; the older formalists are too exacting, especially of other people, and too expressive, at least in public. Hence the initial suspicion with which youth regards both professional advocates and conventional forms of religion; hence the voluntary expression of religion among the better under-graduates is meager, reticent, not easily analyzed. Quite aside from any other reasons there is something inherent in the nature of the relationship and the different status of the lives composing it in a college community which makes a just and accurate common understanding difficult.

The first thing, then, to remember about such a discussion as this is the peril of quick answers. We are hearing a good deal at present about the godlessness of modern youth and the immorality of the present generation. But easy summations of undergraduate attitudes, either by way of censorious condemnation or sentimental praise, are all likely to go wide of the mark. We should understand youth better, if we were more confident of it, more critical of ourselves; if we approached it with a mixture of disinterested and expectant observation and some personal humility. There is something truly ironical in the apparent simplicity of academic relationships, something almost fatuous in the bland acceptance on the part of older men and women of the mere appearances in youth of virtue or vice, piety or irreligion. There is something, too, profoundly unjust in the easy generalizations, the all but absolute judgments by which an established order betrays its resentment at the critical scrutiny or frank hostility of young life.

II

Let us attempt then a dispassionate analysis, from the point of view of the churches, of the undergraduate community. We shall discern at once three conventional attitudes toward organized religion on the part of college students. They are all of them classic; they illustrate, in the realm of the religious interests, corresponding reactions having the same characteristic emphases and approaches which may be found in the economic and social and political life of the time. First: there is the natural conformist. He is the boy who is temperamentally "good," who identifies religious faith with external moral practices. He issues from average, middle-class American life, the son of a thrifty, practical, unimaginative household. He has had a sober and careful bringing up. He has been taught to read the Scriptures, to say his prayers, to attend church. There is often a frank and naïve strain of commercialism in his piety; he has been schooled to remember that social disgrace or academic failure, or material ruin, are the punishments of irreligion and immorality. He largely conceives of religion in the terms of group respectability; assumes that the content of the moral law is practically unchanging from generation to generation. Wrong and right are simple and self-evident; they are mutually exclusive territories, separated by clear boundary lines. Faith and character are achieved by remaining in the right territory.

Boys of this group often have substantial sanity, a rather shrewd and sensible scale of values. But their imaginative deficiencies, their narrow range of desires and interests, with the accompanying intolerance and complacency make them unlovable and relatively negligible figures among their peers. This group has sent many recruits into the ministry in the past. Some of them have become saints and have deepened and enriched the life of the profession. But on the whole they have not strengthened it. They have not had enough creative ability to be great preachers. They have approached the ministry with a too simple notion of its duties; it has been strangely mechanicalized in their minds. It has appeared to consist of preaching pleasantly an accepted message furnished ready to their hands, of making routine calls, of gently perpetuating existing organizations—even if with a slowly diminishing momentum! Instinctively they have expected the institution to carry them; the office to make the man, not the man the office. It was such innocuous, if complacent conformity which the late William E. Godkin had in mind, when, referring to a distinguished foreign university, he observed that it was an ideal place for those youth who were chiefly interested "in lawn tennis, gardening, and true religion."

The numbers of these men, however, are diminishing in the college just as middle-class religion, with its passion for respectability and its identification of faith with conventional conduct is, in proportion to the growth of the population, everywhere diminishing as well.

Second: there is the group of the young institutionalists. They are a more characteristic product of our present society and therefore more significant to our discussion. They come from a richer and wider environment, are more developed personalities, than their conforming comrades. They do not share in the moral naïveté of the first class; sometimes they do not share its moral scruples either. The boys of this group identify religion with a half-romantic, half-mythical allegiance to impressive and picturesque institutions. They link up this allegiance in their minds with subscription to creed, a sort of class allegiance to the formulæ promulgated by an imperial and established organization. There are certain classic statements of the Christian faith. They move the imagination, both subdue and elevate the minds of sensitive and reflective youth, partly by their aesthetic and mystical appeal, partly by the very prestige of their antiquity. They are the confessions of faith of a splendid and imperial standing order. They appeal to the best in the aristocratic impulse, its sense of the continuity of life, its perception that you must not divorce the present from the past, its understanding of the slowly refining, carefully garnered deposit which makes up all that is best in human experience.

These youth are not moved by any terrific moral struggle or by the evangelical passion for soul-saving. The prophetic note in them is absent. They are Churchmen; social and religious Conservatives. Sometimes when they grow older they, like John Neville Figgis, carry side by side with medieval forms of religion quite radical views in political economy and social science. But essentially religion is to them a perpetuation of an established and authoritative order.

When these men enter the ministry, they become not so much the shepherds of sheep as spiritual governors of parishes. The world regards with something of reluctant admiration, something more of covert hostility and distrust, their amalgam of the urbane manners and self-assurance of this world, with the offices of priest and preacher. Boys whose religious instinct expresses itself in these ways are increasing among us and they are turning naturally to the Roman and Anglican communions. The main current of our age flows steadily and relentlessly against the institutionalist and his type of religion. But there are many cross-currents in any generation and a new exaltation of institutional religion is one of them which is discernible at this moment. As the American home becomes more and more sophisticated and society becomes older, more highly developed and rigid in its customs, allegiance to all established institutions grows among us. It represents the determined effort of a relatively completed and well adjusted social order to defend itself, its achievements no less than its privileges, from the crudeness and destructiveness of the new forces now struggling upward in society. Most men who have gained anything of permanence hate and fear change. They identify the accompaniments of a new order, its bohemian living, its flippant and reckless iconoclasm, its attacks upon special privilege with the order itself. This, they think, is all there is to it. So they withdraw into the citadel of institutional orthodoxies.

A fair number of college men who are now entering the ministry are of this group. It does not matter much what learning they receive in college which seems to vitiate either the historic pretensions or the intellectual statements of their faith. They have already cast in their lot with the older order, they are not inquirers so much as they are partisans. They will by no means be a negligible force in the coming generation. By no perceivable possibility can they become the leaders of the age into which we are now advancing. But they will skilfully and resolutely oppose it; they are far more formidable opponents than their simpler brethren of the first group, and they will have considerable influence.

Third: there is the young humanitarian. He is a common and obvious type of undergraduate, more in evidence a decade ago than now, the boy who expresses his religion through its substitutes, who meets his spiritual problem by evading it. He puts effects in the place of causes; practical efficiency takes the place of spiritual insight. The ardent if superficial humanism of recent years has produced the youth who identifies religion with social reform, piety with organized benevolence, and spiritual leadership with administrative efficiency. To work is to pray, social service is character, a rarefied amiability is faith.

Such a lad is a past master at planning a missionary campaign, engineering a student conference, and "promoting" a Bible class. He knows how to "swing it right." He sees nothing incongruous in organizing a risqué undergraduate vaudeville show to raise money for the support of a settlement house. He will be found teaching at a down-town mission, or acting as scoutmaster for local gamins, or installed as a religious work director. He is a wholesome and aggressive youth, friendly, rather too approachable, amazingly able and resourceful in practical affairs. He has character, is not imaginative, is terribly at ease in Zion. It is largely from this group that the ever-to-be-replenished ranks of student Christian association secretaries, graduate secretaries, student-volunteer leaders, are recruited.

These men, for the most part, accept the essentials of the present order. They do not scrutinize the intellectual and emotional sources of our present religious and economic structure. They would rather mitigate its abuses than reform its principles. They are natural if unconscious pragmatists. Their passion is for action; they want always to be "doing things." The goal of social service, which is ever before their eyes, and their passion for "results" makes them superficial leaders. They take refuge from the difficulties of thought in the opportunities of action.

A few of these men, not many, go into the ministry. Generally speaking, it repels them by its emphasis upon religious passion and spiritual insight. Also, they are contemptuous of what seem to be the lax business methods and practical inefficiency of the average church. They are not so large a group in the college as they were before the war, for its brutal dislocations shook this type of youth out of his notion of salvation by expansion and reformation by machinery.

III

Probably all the men of these three groups which we have been discussing represent when combined decidedly less than half the undergraduate body. The remainder of it, which is a substantial majority of the whole number, forms the group which is most significant to our purpose. It can be classified under two heads. First there are the modern pagans. A large number of contemporary undergraduates are not irreligious to-day, they are non-religious. They are neither hostile nor contemptuous as regards religion; they are indifferent to it, they know nothing about it, they are relatively incapable of experiencing it. There is much truth in the neglected Calvinistic doctrines of election and predestination. Probably all men cannot be saved; some of them are antecedently incapable of salvation. Such boys as I am describing are the natural product of the materialism and commercialism which represents one-half of the American character of the moment; they are neither very much better nor worse than the homes from which they issue. But this group of obtuse and unawakened lads is one of the most significant factors in undergraduate life, more characteristic of the immediate problem which confronts the college and the nation than any one of the other groups we have as yet mentioned. The grosser forms of immorality are not common among them, they are more vulgar than vicious, hopelessly secular, but not bad. Their language is callously profane and has a sort of a-moral coarseness about it. Their literature is principally *Snappy Stories,* the *Saturday Evening Post* and the sporting pages of the daily prints. Their most natural occupations appear to be striving for some club, indulging in college gossip, or indefinite discussion of athletic events in which they themselves took no part, and alternating between the "movies" and innumerable dances.

In short, they are men in whom the æsthetic, intellectual, and spiritual interests are almost wholly undeveloped and to whom organized religion makes no contribution and for which they feel no slightest need. Religion in general would seem to have no *quid pro quo* to offer them. The number of these men has very largely increased in the American college. They are changing its habits of thought and conduct, its scale of values as regards courses, the whole æsthetic and emotional level of the group. They undertake their four years of college life mostly for social or practical reasons and they leave college nearly always for business or for law.

If organized religion wants to test out how much of a power it still is in the college, let it see if it can evangelize this group. Success or failure with them would be an actual measure of its vitality, a real snatching of brands from the burning. The other groups we have discussed are temperamentally disposed toward some sort of acceptance of the churches. This group is one of the two for whose salvation the churches specifically exist. We should never draw many leaders from its numbers; can we recruit the laity from it? It is significant that at present this group remains almost wholly untouched either by college preaching or by the Y. M. C. A. activities of the undergraduate body.

Finally, there are the intellectual and æsthetic radicals. This group probably comprehends by far the largest number of valuable men in the college community. It is composed of the boys who have both intellectual and emotional equipment and along with their brains and their heart, they have the accompanying spirit of the adventurer. Such youth are natural come-outers. They are possessed of character as well as intellect. Their moral code is often not that of their elders and they are sometimes rather brutal in their disdain of inherited prohibitions. But they have a code of their own, they govern their lives, keep their appetites within reasonable bounds, respect themselves. They have a passion for intellectual integrity and for accurate appreciations and judgments. They are unsentimental by nature, and

dislike, as they dislike few other things, the boy who is only temperamentally or emotionally religious. They have a disconcerting
habit of ignoring the considerations of expediency or the sensitiveness of their interlocutors when scrutinizing a conviction or
analyzing an institution.

Now the most significant fact we have yet touched upon is that
these men also are almost wholly outside the influence of organized religion. The first reason for this is either the lack of any
religious training in their homes or church in their earlier
youth, or, as is more often the case, their having received a training which has been both mistaken and inadequate in content.
Neither Sunday school nor minister ever pointed out to them the
difference between scientific and religious truth. Scientific truth
is the exact agreement of observation and judgment with
fact. It is an affair of the intellect, it calls for mental accuracy, is capable of precise demonstration. Ethical truth is the
harmonious adjustment of conduct to the moral and social constitution of man. Insight into the nature of this adjustment is as
much, if not more, an affair of the imagination than of the mind;
the allegiance to ethical truth might be called more of a practical
than an intellectual experience. Moral truth is not capable of
mathematical demonstration, but only of a gradual and relative
verification in experience. Religious truth again is the perception of the right relations between man and the universe as a
whole. Such truth is generally presented to mankind in the form
of personalities, it comes in the guise of personages who by their
imaginative insight, their spiritual intuitiveness, have worked
out or grasped an attitude both toward men and God which satis-
fies and interprets the lives and consciences of those who behold
it. There are speculative, mystical, and æsthetic values in religious truth which do not enter into scientific observation of fact.
The imagination plays a part here which it does not play with the
natural investigator.

Now such fundamental distinctions are primary elements in
religious growth and education. But for the most part they are
not given by churches or parents. Able youth are sent to
college believing that the truth of religion stands or falls with historical accuracy of the gospel narrative or with the correctness of
inherited systems of opinion. They have been encouraged to identify religious truth either with theological beliefs or with faith in
some inerrant writings or with the concept of an omniscient Christ.

When the church says that Jesus is the truth, it is talking of truth as a form of personality, as a system of relations, and of the Lord Jesus as being, by the common consent of human experience and observation, all that a man ought to be in these relations. He is truth in its final form, a true person. All this, these men have not been taught; they suppose that what the church asserts as "true," is some particular brand of theological or ecclesiastical orthodoxy. Thus, their teaching before ever they come to college has given them no preparation for what they will find there; it not only has been deficient but it has been positively false.

The inevitable of course happens when these boys of potential intellectual and æsthetic power are introduced to the free intellectual processes and stimulated by the sudden expansion of scientific knowledge which come to them as undergraduates. They quickly perceive how far the thought and feeling and knowledge of their day have outstripped the creed and practice of ecclesiastical, as of other contemporary, organizations. They perceive that to some real degree the churches are outmoded in conduct and reactionary in belief. They are aware how far contemporary psychological and social science has advanced beyond the consciousness of most preachers and how dreadfully it discredits their usual concepts regarding nature and human life. They have an acute and somewhat exaggerated perception of how discarded is the philosophic view of the world which lies behind classic systems of theology and they see how inconsistent with the ethics of Jesus is both the theory and the practice of our imperialistic and ruthlessly competitive society. They are aware that consciously or unconsciously the laity support the churches quite as much for social and economic as for religious reasons. In short, they perceive that their inherited ethical, theological, and ecclesiastical orthodoxies will not stand the test of scientific investigations and they think these are to be identified with religion. Hence, not understanding the nature of religious truth they soon lose any sense of the value of it. In the beginning, they look with scorn upon the minister as the official of an order of ideas which he must know is no longer defensible and they regard the church as a drag upon society.

Now these are able boys. And before they are through their Senior year they have become more or less aware of the difference between religion and theology, an art and its science, the self-verifying moral and spiritual experience of the Lord Jesus and any particular philosophic or practical implications with which men have clothed it. They have come to perceive the difference between religious and scientific truths. But it is then, for the most part, too late to reclaim them, because their active lives have already gotten substitutes for the faith which they discarded. They are absorbed in intellectual pursuits. Just as we are told of Darwin that his early and vivid delight in music became entirely atrophied through long absorption in purely scientific pursuits so the interest of these youths in the distinctively religious expression of their ethical and imaginative life has perished. They give themselves to philosophy or economics or political science; they are still devoted men but their devotion is to wisdom, they worship truth, not the God of truth. They are young men of character, but it is respect for themselves and humanity, not awe and loyalty in the presence of a holy being, which is alike the motive and the sanction of their conduct. Some of them give a genuine discipleship to the old classic ideals of beauty and justice. They prefer this to the personalized and too often the timid and obscurantist religion of the churches.

Other men in this group, not possessing as great intellectual power or as keen scientific interests, hold aloof from organized religion for æsthetic reasons. They are sensitive to the various aspects of beauty. Indeed, boys who understand the significance and value of the æsthetic world are rapidly on the increase in this group. To them the stenciled walls and carpeted floors, the anomalous furnishings and frock-coated officials, the popular romantic and quite irreligious music of the average Protestant sanctuary are both ludicrous and repellent. With all the joyous cruelty of youth they pitilessly analyze and condemn it.

More and more the college is training these abler youth to a critical appreciation of the intimate and significant relationship between sublime ideas and deep emotions and a restrained and beautiful, an austere and reverent, expression of them. The very age itself, with its immensely increased interest in the dramatic and plastic and descriptive arts, tends more and more to feed their imaginative life and to make the standards of that life more consciously exacting. But our average non-liturgical service has not much to offer their critically trained perceptions. They find little of beauty or of awe in the Sunday morning service. Indeed our church habits are pretty largely the transfer into the sanctuary of the hearty conventions of middle-class family life. The expressions and attitudes of life which are precious to such youth, the subtle and precise and mystical ones get small recognition here. They feel like uncomfortable outsiders or truculent misfits in the Sunday morning congregation. Therefore, partly for reasons of intellectual integrity and partly for reasons of a genuine æsthetic distaste and partly because organized religion has been crowded out by other interests which also feed mind and spirit they avoid the Christian church. It does not seem to move in their world. They are quite aware that it tries to stand for, and once did stand for, real values. They, too, think those values are real but that they are no longer within its custody.

It is conceded that very few of the abler men in college today, either the students of distinguished intellectual or creative capacity, are turning toward the Christian ministry. It does not seem to me difficult in the light of what we have been saying to understand why. It is not because these men are devoid of religious capacity or of ethical loyalties. Quite the contrary; they are the men who are going to be the leaders of the higher life of their generation. But modern life offers many new professions and occupations into which imaginative spirits and keen minds may enter. The new engineering professions, the opportunities of big business, give scope for the work of the constructive imagination and the analysis of the keen mind, which an earlier and simpler age denied. Political and economic reform calls for the highest moral and mental qualities. Hence it is not altogether consonant with the genius of our day that it should produce such conventionally religious spirits as medieval civilization gave birth to. Nevertheless, the general defection of this group upon the Christian ministry and the churches is gravely significant as to the probable immediate future of organized religion. For if we have lost our hold on men of this sort, then, whether or not we win the battle at any other point of the line, our real success in controlling the thought and feeling of society is problematic indeed. If we have lost these men as both laymen and leaders in the churches, all other gains are gravely diminished thereby.

It would not be true, I suppose, of this group, that they would say that the ministry is not a "man-sized" job. They began, in the first flush of intellectual activity in their Sophomore year, by saying that, but now they would be quite aware that religious and moral leadership of this generation offers a herculean task. But they have become indifferent to it and are rather of the conviction that the churches are neither able nor indeed anxious to really undertake it. There is plenty of dormant religious capacity in this group, much unexpressed spiritual ability. But it regards the only ministry possible for it in this generation, because the only one compatible with clear thinking and fine feeling, as one outside of the ecclesiastical institution. This is obviously a half-truth, by no means a perfectly just attitude. But then all human convictions are combinations of half-truths; vague hearsay, blank prejudice, fond fancy, are component parts of all our thinking and feeling. We shall never gain the men of this group by railing at them or by pitying ourselves for their unsympathetic attitude or by denying the large measure of justification that lies beneath it. If we ever do win back their allegiance it will be by a generous and frank appreciation of those very gifts of intellect and character which have turned them away. And we shall make a grave mistake if we suppose that in any age of the world keen minds and tempered spirits have been shut up to our expression of the higher life.

My general attitude must be clear from the foregoing observations. The attitude of college students toward organized religion is very far from what we should like it to be, but the trouble is not so much with these young men as with our own organizations. Able and sensitive youth are naturally religious. They are also naturally scrupulous that whatever of religion they bring themselves to openly espouse, shall be candid in spirit, intelligent in content, beautiful and dignified in expression. If there is to be again a warm and confident alliance between academic and ecclesiastical life and if the ablest youths are again to enter the ministry, the churches will have to change more than the colleges. In so far as religious institutions adapt their interpretations of religious experience to the world-view of to-day, according as they promulgate a moral code not formed to meet the problems of a vanished and simpler order of society but adapted to the new and urgent problems of an urban and industrial civilization, and in so far as they can recognize that the beautiful has as much place in life as the holy and the good, they will interest and attract undergraduate life. There is an infinite pathos in the wistfulness with which many idealistic boys regard the church to-day as an organization hostile to mental freedom, indifferent to beauty, and insistent on a procrustean morality; there is something deeper than pathos in the indifference and almost contempt which exists between so many youth in the coming generation and the Christian church. In their heart of hearts these boys would like to worship, to believe, to openly espouse a holy and a sacrificial life. If that be true, what is the reason the church can do so little with them?

The religion of college students is
not what it should be because of
(1) the conformists, (2) industrialists
(3) humanitarians, (4) pagans, (5) radicals

be anxious to portray our noblest. But then all human conceptions are idealizations of half truths, vague longings, blank prejudices, blind fancy, are component parts of all our thinking and feeling. We shall never gain the ears of this group, the willing or the foe, by putting ourselves for their inaspicability attitude or by displaying the irrationalness of justification that lies beneath it. If we wish to win back their allegiance it will be by a persistent and frank appreciation of those very gifts of idealism and character which have been thrown away. And we shall make a grave mistake if we suppose that in any age of the world least of all our own that spirit have is on alert to any expression of the higher life.

My general attitude must be far from the foregoing questions. The attitude of college students toward organized religion is very far from what we should like it to be, but the trouble is not so much with these young men as with our own organizations. Able and sensitive youth are naturally religious. They are also naturally scrupulous; that whatever of religion they have themselves loyally observe shall be candid in spirit, beautiful in content, beautiful and dignified in expression. If there is to be again a warm and confident alliance between academic and ecclesiastical life and if the ablest youths are again to enter the ministry, the churches will have to change more than the colleges. In so far as religious institutions adapt their interpretations of religious experience to the world-view of to-day, presenting as they presumably propose to present, not formed in and the problems of a furnished and simpler order of society but adapted to the new and urgent problems of an urban and industrial civilization, and in so far as they can symbolize that the beautiful has as much place in life as the holy and the good, they will interest and attract such recruits. There is an intimate pathos in the wistfulness with which many idealistic boys regard the church to-day, as an organization hostile to mental irritant, indifferent to beauty and insistent on a presumption morality; there is something deeper than a careless indifference and almost contempt which exists between so many youth in the most generous generation and that American church. If their creed of beliefs those boys would like to worship, to believe, to prove, regarding the holy and a sanctified life. If this be true, what is the reason the church can do so little with them.

RACIAL PROBLEMS

Introd. {
The Problem (unsolable)
Difference in Self Suff.
Causes of or R— Problem not Prov

Economic Causes of R— Prej—

RACIAL MINORITIES [1]

Geroid Tanquary Robinson

[Geroid Tanquary Robinson (1892-   ) studied at Stanford, the University of California, and Columbia. He was a member of the editorial board of the *Dial*, and is now a lecturer in Modern European History at Columbia University and a member of the editorial staff of the *Freeman*. He served for sixteen months during the War as a First Lieutenant (Adjutant) in the American Air Service. Residence in Virginia, North Carolina, Colorado, Arizona, and California has given him the opportunity to observe at first hand some of the modes and manners of race-prejudice.
Racial Minorities appeared as an essay in *Civilization in the United States*, edited by Harold Stearns.]

". . . not to laugh at the actions of men, nor yet to deplore or detest them, but simply to understand them."—*Spinoza*.

In America, the race-problem is not only without answer; thus far it is even without formulation. In the face of ordinary economic, political, and religious difficulties, people habitually formulate creeds which give a kind of rhyme and reason to their actions; but where inter-racial relations are concerned, the leaders go pussy-footing all around the fundamental question, while the emotions of the masses translate themselves into action, and action back again into emotion, with less consideration of means and ends than one expects of the maddest bomb-thrower. Everybody has some notion of the millennial aims of the Communist Party, the National Association of Manufacturers, the W. C. T. U., the Holy Rollers; but what are the Southerners getting at, when they educate the Negro, and refuse him the ballot; what ultimate result does the North expect from the granting of the franchise and the denial of social equality? Do both the North and the South hope to maintain a permanent racial division of the country's population? If so, are the Indians, the Jews and the Asiatics to be classed with the Negroes, as unassimilable minorities? How is the

---

[1] Reprinted by permission of, and by special arrangement with, Harcourt, Brace and Co., from *Civilization in the United States*, edited by Harold Stearns.
Questions and topics for the discussion of this essay, and of other phases of the general subject with which it deals, will be found on pages 287 and 527.

conduct of the American majority suited to this aim, if it is an aim? How can permanent division be maintained, except by permanent prejudice? What do the racial liberators, ameliorators, uplifters, and general optimists think about it; or do they think about it at all?

From the moment of initial contact between the mass of the American population and the country's most important racial minorities—the Indian, the Jew, the Oriental, and the Negro—the self-congratulatory feelings of the majority have always found a partial or complete counterpart everywhere except among the slaves and the children of the slaves. The long delay in the inception of All-Africanism in America, and the groping uncertainty which still characterizes its manifestations, are due in large part to the cultural youthfulness of the American Negro. Biologically, the black race was matured in Africa; culturally it had made considerable advances there, before the days of the slave-trade. The process of enslavement could not strip away the physical characteristics of the race, but in all that has to do with cultural life and social inheritance, the Negro was re-born naked in the new world.

When one compares the condition of the Negro with that of the other three racial minorities at the moment of contact with the miscellaneous white population, the Indian seems closer to the Jew and the Oriental than to the slave. In a general way, the condition of the Indian tribes resembled that of the Negroes in Africa, but the Indians were left in possession of most of the elements of savage culture and were never entirely deprived of the means of maintaining themselves in this stage of development. Needless to say, the Jews and the Orientals were in still better case than the Indians, for their imported cultural equipment was far more elaborate and substantial, and their economic position much better.

The four racial minorities thus varied widely in the degree of their self-sufficiency, and likewise, inversely, in the degree of their need for absorption into the current of American life. Quite obviously the Negro was least independent and most in need of assimilation. However, the necessity of the alien group has not been the only factor of importance in this matter of assimilation. Each of the minorities has been from the beginning subjected to the prejudice of the majority, and that group which first lost all life of its own through contact with the whites has been signalled out for the maximum amount of persecution.

The standard explanation or excuse for race-prejudice is the theory of the inequality of racial stocks. However, for all their eagerness to bolster up a foregone conclusion, the race-patriots have not been able to prove by any sort of evidence, historical, biological, or psychological, that racial differences are not simply indications of unlikeness, rather than of inherent superiority or inferiority. The anthropologists are pretty well agreed that physical differences divide mankind into three major groups, European (including the Jews), Mongoloid (including the American Indians), and Negroid; but science has set no definite limit to the respective potentialities of these groups. In other words, it has remained for race-prejudice to assume an unproved inferiority, and to devise all possible measures for making the life of the objectionable races exactly what it would be, in the absence of interference, if the assumed inferiority were real.

To accept the term "race-prejudice" as accurately descriptive of the feelings to which it is usually applied, is to assume that these feelings originate in race-differences, if not in the inequality of races. This, however, is still to be proved. Race-differences are a factor of the situation wherever two races are in contact, but it is a matter of common knowledge that the members of two or more racial groups sometimes intermingle on terms of greatest friendliness. To attribute "race-prejudice" to race-difference, and to leave race-friendliness entirely unexplained, is to blind oneself deliberately to the existence of variable causes which alone can account for the variable results that appear in the presence of racial constants. Racial inequality of intelligence, if it actually exists, is simply one of a number of ever-present race-differences, and in all these differences taken together one can find no adequate explanation of the variable phenomenon commonly called "race-prejudice," but so designated here only for the sake of convenience.

Any serious attempt to get at the non-racial causes of "race-prejudice" in America would necessarily involve the comparison, point by point, of economic, social, political, and intellectual conditions in various localities in the United States with corresponding local conditions in other countries where the races here in conflict are more nearly at peace. In the present state of knowledge, the racial theory of race-prejudice is demonstrably inadequate, while the non-racial theory is an hypothesis which can neither be proved nor disproved. Such being the case, the haphazard speculations which follow are not offered as a proof of this hypothesis, or as an explanation of the existence of race-prejudice in America, but simply as a stimulus to inquiry.

Beginning with these speculations, it may be said that the goods and opportunities of the material life, unlike those of the intellectual life, are frequently incapable of division without loss to the original possessor.   On this account, competition is likely to be particularly keen and vindictive where material interests are given the foremost place.   It is also perhaps safe to say that the long preoccupation of the American majority with the development of its material inheritance has brought to the majority a heavy heritage of materialism.   One may hazard the statement that the prejudice of America's native white majority against the Negroes, the Indians, the Jews, and the Asiatics, is now and has always been in some sense attributable and proportional to the majority's fear of some action on the part of the minority which might injure the material interests of the majority; while the only race-differences which have had any real importance are those superficial ones which serve to make the members of the minorities recognizable at sight.   At any rate, an examination of some of the facts that come most easily to hand shows an interesting coincidence between the prejudice of the majority and the power of the minority.

Before the Civil War, the structure of Southern society was bottomed on slavery, and the fear of any humanization of the Negro which would make him appear worthy of emancipation was strong enough to arouse any degree of prejudice, and any amount of repression.   The prejudice of the Southern white populace as a whole reached its maximum intensity when emancipation threatened to place the blacks in permanent political and economic control of certain portions of the South.   Even to-day, fear of the political power of the Negroes, and perhaps also the over-emphasized fear of black "outrages," still acts upon the white population as a unifying force; but in spite of this fact, class-interests have become plainly visible.   When Black Republicanism had once been driven to cover, the masters set about rebuilding their privileges upon the foundation of Negro labour which is still their chief support.   Only a few Negroes have been able to compete directly for a share in these privileges, and accordingly most of the fears of the well-to-do people of the South are anticipatory rather than immediate.

With the "poor whites," the case is altogether different.   Here there is no question of keeping the Negro in his place, for ever since the Emancipation the place of the Negro has been very much that of the poor white himself, at least in so far as economic status is concerned. In the view of the white labourer, the Negro rises too high the moment he becomes a competitor for a job, and every Negro is potentially just that. Accordingly, the prejudice of the poorer whites is bitter and indiscriminate, and is certainly not tending to decrease with the cityward drift of the Negro population.

With the appearance of Negro workers in large numbers in Northern industrial centres, race-prejudice has begun to manifest itself strongly among the white workers. The Northern masters have, however, shown little tendency to reproduce the sentiments of their Southern peers, for in the North there is no fear of political dominance by the blacks, and a supply of cheap labour is as much appreciated as it is south of the Line.

In spite of the fact that the proportion of Negroes in the total population of the United States has declined steadily from 15.7 per cent. in 1850 to 9.9 per cent. in 1920, the attitude of both Northerners and Southerners is somewhat coloured by the fear that the blacks will eventually overrun the country. If prejudice had no other basis than this, there would perhaps be no great difficulty in effecting its cure. As a matter of course, immigration accounts in part for the increasing predominance of the white population; but this hardly disposes of the fact that throughout the South, during the years 1890-1910, the percentage of native whites of native parentage advanced in both urban and rural communities. Discussion of comparative birth-rates also gives rise to numerous alarums and excursions, but the figures scarcely justify the fears expressed. Statistics show that, in spite of the best efforts of the people who attempt to hold the black man down, and then fear him all the more because he breeds too generously, the improvement in the material condition of the Negro is operating inevitably to check the process of multiplication.

If the case of the Negro is complicated in the extreme, that of the Indian is comparatively simple. Here race-prejudice has always followed the frontier. As long as the Indian interfered with the exploitation of the country, the pioneers feared him, and disliked him cordially. Their feelings worked themselves out in all manner of personal cruelty, as well as in a process of wholesale expropriation, but as soon as the tribes had been cooped up on reservations, the white man's dislike for the Indian began to cool off perceptibly. From the beginning, the Indian interfered with expansion, not as an economic competitor, but as a military enemy; when the dread of him as a fighter disappeared, there was no new fear to take its place. During the years 1910 to 1920 the Indian population actually decreased 8.6 per cent.

If the Indian has neither shared the privileges nor paid the price of a generous participation in American life, the Jew has certainly done both. In every important field of activity, the members of this minority have proved themselves quite able to compete with the native majority, and accordingly the prejudice against them is not confined to any one social class, but is concentrated rather in those regions where the presence of Jews in considerable numbers predicates their competitive contact with individuals of all classes. Although as a member of one branch of the European racial family, the Jew is by no means so definitely distinguished by physical characteristics as are the members of the other minorities here under discussion, it is nevertheless true that when the Jew has been identified by his appearance, or has chosen to identify himself, the anti-Semite takes on most of the airs of superiority which characterize the manifestations of prejudice towards the other minorities. Nevertheless, the ordinary run of anti-Semitic talk contains frequent admissions of jealousy and fear, and it is safe to say that one must look chiefly to such emotions, as intensified by the rapid increase of the Jewish population from 1,500,000 in 1906 to 3,300,000 in 1918, rather than to the heritage of European prejudice, for an explanation of the growth of anti-Semitism in America. The inclusion of anti-Semitism with the other types of race-prejudice here under discussion follows naturally enough from the fact that the Jew is thought of as primarily a Jew, whatever the country of his origin may have been, while the Slav, for instance, is popularly regarded as a Russian, a Pole, a Serb—a *national* rather than a *racial* alien.

Like the Jew, the Oriental has come into the United States as a "foreigner," as well as a member of an alien race. The absence of this special disqualification has not particularly benefited the Negro and the Indian, but its presence in the case of the Japanese has been of considerable service to the agitators. The prevalent dislike and fear of the new Japan as a world-power has naturally coloured the attitude of the American majority toward the Japaese settlers in this country; but this in itself hardly explains why the Californians, who were burning Chinamen out of house and home in the 'seventies, are now centering their prejudice upon the Japanese agriculturist. The fact is that since the passage of the Exclusion Laws the Chinese population of the United States has fallen off more than 40 per cent., and the importance of Chinese competition has decreased accordingly, while on the other hand the number of Japanese increased 53.9 per cent. between 1910 and 1920, and the new competitors are showing themselves more than a match for the white farmers. With a frankness that neither Negrophobia nor anti-Semitism has made us familiar with, many of the Californians have rested their case against the Japanese on an economic foundation, and have confessed that they are unable to compete with the Japanese on even terms. As a matter of course, there is the usual flow of talk about the inferiority of the alien race, but the fear of competition, here so frankly admitted, would be enough in itself to account for this new outbreak of "race-prejudice."

When one considers thus the course that prejudice has taken in the case of the Negro, the Indian, the Jew, and the Oriental, it begins to appear that this sentiment may wax and wane and change about astonishingly in the presence of racial factors that remain always the same. Such being the case, one is led to wonder what the attitude of the native majority would be, if the minorities were recognizable simply as groups, but *not* as *racial* groups. In other words, what would be the result if the racial factor were reduced simply to recognizability? The question has a more than speculative interest.

If the causes of race-prejudice lie quite beyond the reach of any simple explanation, the manifestations of this prejudice on the part of the American majority are perhaps capable of an analysis which will render the whole situation somewhat more comprehensible. By and large, and with all due allowance for exceptions, it may be said that, in its more familiar manifestations, race prejudice takes a direction exactly opposite to that taken by prejudice against the ordinary immigrant of European stock; in the former case, a conscious effort is made to magnify the differences between the majority and the minority, while in the latter, a vast amount of energy is expended in the obliteration of these differences. Thus race-prejudice aspires to preserve and even to increase that degree of unlikeness which is its excuse for being, while alien-prejudice works itself out of a job, by "Americanizing" the immigrant and making him over into an unrecognizable member of the majority. On one hand, enforced diversity remains as a source of friction, while on the other, enforced uniformity is demanded as the price of peace.

Although no purpose can be served by cataloguing here all the means employed in the South to keep the black man in his place, a few examples may be cited, in order to show the scope of these measures of repression. In the economic field, there is a pronounced tendency to restrict Negro workers to the humblest occupations, and in the agricultural areas the system of peonage or debt-slavery is widely employed for the purpose of attaching Negro families to the soil. Residence-districts are regularly segregated, Jim Crow regulations are everywhere in force, and inter-racial marriages are prohibited by law in all the States of the South. The administration of justice is in the hands of white judges and white juries, and the Negro's chances in such company are notoriously small. In nearly one-fourth of the counties of the South, the population is half, or more than half black, but the denial of the ballot excludes the Negroes from local, State, and national political activities. In religious organizations, segregation is the invariable rule. Theatres and even public libraries are regularly closed to the Negro, and in every State in the South segregation in schools is prescribed by law. Some idea of the significance of the latter provision may be drawn from O. G. Ferguson's study of white and Negro schools in Virginia. In this comparatively progressive State, the general rating of the white school is 40.8, as against 22.3 for the coloured schools, the latter figure being seven points lower than the lowest general rating for any State in the Union.

Such are some of the legal, extra-legal, and illegal manifestations of that prejudice which finds its supreme expression in the activities of the lynching-mob and the Ku Klux Klan. There is still a considerable annual output of lynchings in this country (in 1920 the victims numbered sixty-five, of whom fifty were Negroes done to death in the South), but the casualty-list for the South and for the country as a whole has decreased steadily and markedly since 1889, and the proportion of Negro victims who were accused of rape or attacks on women has also decreased, from 31.8 per cent. in 1889-1893 to 19.8 per cent. in 1914-1918.

On the other hand, the Ku Klux Klan has now re-commenced its ghost-walking activities, under the command of an "Imperial

Wizard" who claims that he has already enlisted 100,000 followers in the fight to maintain the "God-ordained" preëminence
of the Anglo-Saxon race in America. Other statements from the
lips of the Wizard seem to indicate that his organization is not only
anti-African, but anti-Semitic, anti-Catholic, and anti-Bolshevik as
well. Indeed, the bearers of the fiery cross seem bent upon organizing an all-American hate society, and the expansion of the Klan
in the North is already under way.

However, the Klansmen might have succeeded in carrying the
war into the enemy's country even without adding new prejudices
to their platform. There has always been some feeling against the
Negro in the North, and the war-time migration of the blacks to
Northern industrial centres certainly has not resulted in any diminution of existing prejudice. The National Urban League estimates
that the recent exodus from Dixie has produced a net increase of a
quarter of a million in the coloured population of twelve cities above
the Line. This movement has brought black and white workers
into competition in many industries where Negroes have hitherto
been entirely unknown, and frequently the relations between the
two groups have been anything but friendly. Since about half the
"internationals" affiliated with the American Federation of Labour
still refuse to accept Negro members, the unions themselves are in
no small part to blame for the use that employers have made of
Negro workers as strike-breakers.

In twelve Northern and Western States there are laws on the
statute-books prohibiting marriage between whites and blacks. Jim
Crow regulations are not in force north of Maryland, but in most
of the cities there has been a continuous effort to maintain resi-
dential segregation, and the practice of discrimination in hotels
and restaurants is the rule rather than the exception. Lynchings
are infrequent, but the great riots of Washington and Chicago
were not exactly indicative of good feeling between the races. One
situation which revealed a remarkable similarity of temper between the North and the South was that which arose in the army
during the war. It is notorious that Northerners in uniform fell
in easily with the Southern spirit, and gave all possible assistance
in an energetic Jim-Crowing of the Negroes of Michigan and the
Negroes of Mississippi, from the first day of their service right
through to the last.

The treatment of the Negro in literature and on the stage also
reveals an unconscious but all the more important unanimity of

opinion. It is true the North has produced no Thomas Dixons, but it is also true that the gentle and unassuming Uncle Tom of Northern song and story is none other than the Uncle Remus whom the South loves so much. In Boston, as in Baton Rouge, the Negro who is best liked is the loyal, humble, and not too able mammie or uncle of the good old days before the war. If an exception be made in the case of Eugene O'Neill's "Emperor Jones," it may be said that American literature has not yet cast a strong, upstanding black man for any other rôle than that of beast and villain.

And yet all these forms of discrimination and repression are not fully expressive of the attitude of the white population. The people of the South are fully sensible of the necessity of keeping the Negro in his place; still they do not keep him from attending school. Educational facilities, of a sort, are provided, however reluctantly, and in half the States of the South school attendance is even made compulsory by laws (which may or may not be enforced). The schooling is not of a kind that will fit the Negroes for the permanent and contented occupancy of a servile position. Generally speaking, the coloured children do not receive a vocational education that will keep them in their place, but an old-style three-R training that prepares for nothing but unrest. If unrest leads to urbanization, the half-hearted education of the Negro perhaps serves the interests of the new industrialists; but these industrial employers are so few in number that their influence cannot outweigh that of the planters who lose their peons, and the poor whites who find the Negro with one grain of knowledge a somewhat more dangerous competitor than the Negro with none. Hence there is every reason to believe that if the white South had rationalized this situation, the Negro would be as ruthlessly excluded from the school as he now is from the ballot-box. In fact, the education of the Negro seems quite inconsistent with race-prejudice as it is generally preached and practised in the South.

In the North there is no discrimination in the schools, and black children and white are put through the same mill. In the industrial field, prejudice cannot effectually close to the Negroes all those openings which are created by general economic conditions, and in politics the Northern Negro also finds some outlet for his energies.

While it would be quite impossible to show that the existence of these miscellaneous educational, industrial, and political opportunities is due to any general desire upon the part of the members of the white majority to minimize the differences between themselves and the Negroes, it is certainly true that this desire exists in a limited section of the white population. At the present time, white friends of the Negro are actively engaged in efforts to eliminate certain legal and illegal forms of discrimination and persecution, and are giving financial support to much of the religious work and most of the private educational institutions among the blacks. The Inter-racial Committee of the War Work Council of the Y. M. C. A. has listed thirty-three social and economic agencies, and twenty-three religious agencies, in which members of both races are working co-operatively. It must be admitted, however, that many, if not most, of the white participants in work of this sort are affected by race-prejudice to the extent that they desire simply to ameliorate the lowly condition of the Negro, without altogether doing away with a certain wholesome degree of racial segregation. For the complete elimination of the flavour of condescension, one must usually seek out those extreme socialist and syndicalist agitators who preach political or non-political class-organization, as a substitute for the familiar national and racial groupings.

In the case of the American Indian, the prejudice and self-interest of the white majority have placed the emphasis on geographic rather than social segregation. Here the demand of the whites has been for land rather than for labour, and by consequence servility has never been regarded as a prime virtue of Indian character.

If the early white settlers had so desired, they of course could have enslaved a considerable portion of the Indian population, just as the Spaniards did, in regions farther to the southward. However, the Americans chose to drive the Indians inland, and to replace them in certain regions with African tribesmen who in their native state had been perhaps as war-like as the Indians themselves. Thus in the natural course of events the African warrior was lost in the slave, while the Indian chief continued to be the military opponent rather than the economic servant of exploitation, and eventually gained romantic interest by virtue of this fact. The nature of this operation of debasement on one hand, and ennoblement on the other, is plainly revealed in American literature. The latter phase of the work is carried forward to-day with great enthusiasm by the Camp Fire Girls and the Boy Scouts, whose devotion to the romantic ideal of Indian life is nowhere paralleled by a similar interest in African tribal lore.

If the Indian has been glorified by remote admirers, he has also been cordially disliked by some of his nearest neighbours, and indeed the treatment he has received at the hands of the Government seems to reflect the latter attitude rather than the former. In theory most of the Indian reservations are still regarded as subject principalities, and the Indians confined within their boundaries are almost entirely cut off from the economic, social, and political life of the neighbouring white communities. Many of the tribes still receive yearly governmental grants of food, clothing, arms, and ammunition, but these allowances only serve to maintain them in a condition of dependence, without providing any means of exit from it. In justice it should be said, however, that the Government has declared an intention to make the Indian self-supporting, and accordingly it restricts the grants, in principle, to the old and the destitute. Several States have shown their complete sympathy with the system of segregation by enacting laws prohibiting the inter-marriage of Indians and whites.

On the other hand, the mental and moral Americanization of the red man has been undertaken by Protestant and Catholic missions, and more recently by Government schools. The agencies of the latter sort are especially systematic in their work of depriving the Indian of most of the qualities for which he has been glorified in romance, as well as those for which he has been disliked by his neighbours. Many a Western town enjoys several times each year the spectacle of Indian school-boys in blue uniforms and Indian school-girls in pigtails and pinafores, marching in military formation through its streets. As long as these marchers are destined for a return to the reservation the townsmen can afford to look upon them with mild curiosity. The time for a new adjustment of inter-racial relations will not come until the procession turns towards the white man's job on the farm and in the factory—if it ever does turn that way.

Attention has already been called to the fact that the Jewish immigrant normally marches from the dock directly to the arena of economic competition. Accordingly his progress is not likely to be at any time the object of mere curiosity. On the other hand, the manifestations of prejudice against the Jew have been less aggressive and much less systematic than those repressive activities which affect the other minorities. Where anti-Semitism is present in America, it seems to express itself almost entirely in social discrimination, in the narrow sense. On the other hand, economic, political, and educational opportunities are opened to the Jews with a certain amount of reluctance. A major exception to this rule of discrimination must be made in the case of those socialists, syndicalists and trade-unionists who have diligently sought the support of the Jewish workers.

The Chinaman has also some friends now among the people who once regarded him as the blackest of villains. Indeed, the Californian's attitude toward the Orientals has in it an element of unconscious irony which somewhat illuminates the character of the race-problem. The average Easterner will perhaps be surprised to learn that in Western eyes the Chinaman is an inferior, of course, but nevertheless an honest man, noted for square dealing and the prompt payment of his debts, while the Jap is a tricky person whom one should never trust on any account.

In California the baiting of the Japanese is now almost as much a part of political electioneering as is the abuse of the Negro in the South. The Native Sons of the Golden West and the American Legion have gone on record in determined opposition to any expansion of Japanese interests in California, while the Japanese Exclusion League is particularly active in trouble-making propaganda. Economic discrimination has taken statutory form in the Alien Land Laws of 1913 and 1920; discriminatory legislation of the same general type has been proposed in Texas and Oregon; a bill providing for educational segregation has been presented for a second time at Sacramento; Congress has been urged to replace the "gentlemen's agreement" with an absolute prohibition of Japanese immigration; and there is even a demand for a constitutional amendment which will deny citizenship to the American-born children of aliens who are themselves ineligible for naturalization. The method of legislation is perhaps preferable to the method of force and violence, but if the previous history of race-prejudice means anything, it means that force will be resorted to if legislation fails. At bottom, the spirit of the California Land Laws is more than a little like that of a Georgia lynching; in the one case as in the other, the dominant race attempts to maintain its position, not by a man-to-man contest, with fair chances all around, but by depositing itself bodily and *en masse* on top of the subject people and crushing them.

If in the realm of individual conduct this sort of behavior

works injury to the oppressor, as well as to the oppressed, it is not otherwise where masses of men are concerned. Stephen Graham, in his recent book, *The Soul of John Brown,* says that "in America to-day and especially in the South, there is a hereditary taint left by slavery, and it is to be observed in the descendants of the masters as much as in the descendants of the slaves. It would be a mistake to think of this American problem as exclusively a Negro problem." Indeed, it is true that in every case the race-problem is the problem of the majority as well as of the minority, for the former can no more escape the reaction of prejudice than the latter can escape its direct effects.

To-day the white South is still under the influence of a system of life and thought that is far more enduring than the one institution which gave it most complete expression. The Emancipation abolished slavery, but it did not rid the master of the idea that it is his right to live by the labour of the slave. The black man is not yet relieved of the duty of supporting a certain proportion of the white population in leisure; nor does it appear that the leisured Southerner of to-day makes a better use of his time than his ancestors did before him. Indeed, an historian who judged the peoples chiefly by their contribution to science and the arts would still be obliged to condemn the white South, not for enslaving the Negro, but for dissipating in the practices of a barren gentility the leisure that Negro labour created, and still creates, so abundantly. It is notorious also that in the South the airs of gentility have been more widely broadcast among the white population than the leisure necessary for their practice, with the result that much honest work which could not be imposed upon the black man has been passed on to posterity, and still remains undone.

Any one who seeks to discover the cause of the mental lethargy that has converted the leisure of the South so largely into mere laziness must take some account of a factor that is always present where race-prejudice exists. The race which pretends to superiority may not always succeed in superimposing itself economically upon the inferior group; and yet the pride and self-satisfaction of the members of the "superior" race will pretty surely make for indolence and the deadening of the creative spirit. This will almost inevitably be true where the superiority of the one race is acknowledged by the other, and where no contest of wits is necessary for the maintenance of the *status quo.* This is the condition that has always obtained and still obtains in most of the old slave territory.

In Dixie it is a career simply to go through life inside of a white skin. However ignorant and worthless the white man may be, it is still his privilege to proclaim on any street corner that he is in all respects a finer creature than any one of several million human beings whom he classes all together as "good-for-nothin' niggers." If the mere statement of this fact is not enough to bring warm applause from all the blacks in the neighbourhood, the white man is often more than willing to use fire and sword to demonstate a superiority which he seldom stoops to prove in any other fashion. Naturally this feeling of God-given primacy tends to make its possessors indolent, immune to new ideas of every sort, and quite willing to apply "the short way with the nigger" to any one who threatens the established order of the universe.

It would be foolish indeed to suppose that the general intolerance, bigotry, and backwardness which grow out of race-prejudice have affected the South alone. The North and the West have their prejudices too, their consciousness of a full-blooded American superiority that does not have to be proved, their lazy-mindedness, their righteous anger, their own short way with what is new and strange. No sane man will attribute the origin of all these evils to race-prejudice alone, but no honest man will deny that the practice of discrimination against the racial minorities has helped to infect the whole life and thought of the country with a cocky and stupefying provincialism.

Perhaps the most interesting phase of the whole racial situation in America is the attitude which the minorities themselves have maintained in the presence of a dominant prejudice which has constantly emphasized and magnified the differences between the minorities and majority, and has even maintained the spirit of condescension, and the principle of segregation in such assimilative activities as education and Christian mission work. One would naturally expect that such an attitude on the part of the majority would stimulate a counter race-prejudice in each of the minorities, which would render them also intent upon the maintenance of differentiation.

Although such a counter prejudice has existed from the beginning among the Indians, the Jews, and the Asiatics, it is only now beginning to take form among the Negroes. The conditions of the contact between the black minority and the white majority have thus been substantially different from those which existed in the other cases, and the results of this contact seem to justify the state-

ment that, so long as it remains *one-sided,* the strongest race-prejudice cannot prevent the cultural and even the biological assimilation of one race to another. In other words, prejudice defeats
itself, in a measure, just so long as one of the parties accepts an
inferior position; in fact, it becomes fully effective only when the
despised group denies its own inferiority, and throws the reproach
back upon those with whom it originated. Thus the new racial
self-consciousness of a small section of the Negro population gives
the prejudiced whites a full measure of the differentiation they
desire, coupled with an absolute denial of the inferiority which is
supposed to justify segregation. .

It has already been pointed out that the enslavement of the
Negroes deprived them of practically everything to which racial
pride might attach itself, and left them with no foundation of
their own on which to build. Thus they could make no advances
of any sort except in so far as they were permitted to assimilate
the culture of the white man. In the natural course of events,
the adoption of the English language came first, and then shortly
the Negro was granted such a share in the white man's heaven as
he has never yet received of the white man's earth. As the only
available means of self-expression, religion took a tremendous hold
upon the slaves, and from that day to this, the black South has
wailed its heart out in appeals to the white man's God for deliverance from the white man's burden. The Negro "spirituals" are
not the songs of African tribesmen, the chants of free warriors.
Indeed, the white man may claim full credit for the sadness that
darkens the Negro's music, and put such words as these into the
mouth of the Lord:

> Go down, Moses,
>   Way down in Egyp' lan'
>   Tell ole Pharaoh
>   Le' ma people go!
> Israel was in Egyp' lan'
>   Oppres' so hard dey could not stan',
>   Le' ma people go!

When casual observers say that the black man is naturally
more religious than the white, they lose sight of the fact that the
number of church-members per thousand individuals in the Negro
population is about the same as the average for the United States
as a whole; and they forget also the more important fact that the

Negro has never had all he wanted of anything except religion—
and in segregated churches at that. It is more true of the black
man than of Engel's proletarians, that they have been put off for
a very long time with checks on the bank of Heaven.

Emancipation and the Fourteenth Amendment seemed to open
the path to an earthly paradise; but this vision was soon eclipsed
by a second Civil War that resulted in a substantial victory for
the white South. Economic repression could not be made entirely
effective, however, and in the fifty-three years from 1866 to 1919
the number of American Negro home-owners increased from 12,-
000 to 600,000 and the number of Negroes operating farms from
20,000 to 1,000,000. In 1910 the Negro population still remained
72.6 per cent. rural, but the cityward movement of the blacks
during the years 1890 to 1910 was more rapid than that of the
whites. Education has directly facilitated economic progress, and
has resulted in an increase of literacy among the Negroes from
ten per cent. in 1866 to eighty per cent. in 1919. During the
period 1900 to 1910, the *rate* of increase of literacy among the
blacks was much more rapid than that among the whites. Thus
from the day he was cut off from his own inheritance the American
Negro has reached out eagerly for an alien substitute, until to-day,
in practically everything that has to do with culture, he is not
black but white—and artificially retarded.

Since America has deprived the Negro of the opportunity to
grow up as an African, and at the same time has denied him the
right to grow up as a white man, it is not surprising that a few
daring spirits among the Negroes have been driven at last to the
conclusion that there is no hope for their race except in an exodus
from the white man's culture and the white man's continent. The
war did a great deal to prepare the way for this new movement;
the Negroes of America heard much talk of democracy not meant
for their ears; their list of wrongs was lengthened, but at the same
time their economic power increased; and many of them learned
for the first time what it meant to fight back. Some of them armed
themselves, and began to talk of taking two lives for one when the
lynching-mob came. Then trouble broke in Chicago and Washington—and the casualties were not all of one sort. Out of this
welter of unrest and rebellion new voices arose, some of them calling upon the Negro workers to join forces with their white brothers; some fierce and vengeful, as bitterly denunciatory of socialism
and syndicalism as of everything else that had felt the touch of

the white man's hand; some intoxicated, ecstatic with a new religion, preaching the glory of the black race and the hope of the black exodus.

With much travail, there finally came forth, as an embodiment of the extreme of race-consciousness, an organization called the Universal Negro Improvement Association and African Communities League. This clan lays claim to a million members in the United States, the West Indies, South America and South Africa, and announcees as its final object the establishment of a black empire in Africa. Connected with the U. N. I. A. are the Black Star Line, capitalized at $10,000,000, and the Negro Factories Corporation, capitalized at $2,000,000. Just what these astonishing figures mean in actual cash it is impossible to say, but this much is certain: the Black Star Line already owns three of the many vessels which—say the prophets of the movement—will some day ply among the Negro lands of the world.

To cap the climax, the U. N. I. A. held in New York City during the month of August, 1920, "the first International Negro Convention," which drew up a Negro Declaration of Independence, adopted a national flag and a national anthem, and elected "a Provisional President of Africa, a leader for the American Negroes, and two leaders for the Negroes of the West Indies, Central and South America."

The best testimony of the nature of this new movement is to be found in an astonishing pamphlet called the "Universal Negro Catechism," and issued "by authority of the High Executive Council of the Universal Negro Improvement Association." In this catechism one discovers such items as the following, under the head of "Religious Knowledge":

Q. Did God make any group or race of men superior to another?
A. No; He created all races equal, and of one blood, to dwell on all the face of the earth.

Q. What is the colour of God?
A. A spirit has neither colour, nor other natural parts, nor qualities.

Q. If . . . you had to think or speak of the colour of God, how would you describe it?
A. As black; since we are created in His image and likeness.

Q. What did Jesus Christ teach as the essential principle of true religion?
A. The universal brotherhood of man growing out of the universal Fatherhood of God.

Q. Who is responsible for the colour of the Ethiopians?

A. The Creator; and what He has done cannot be changed. Read Jeremiah 13:23.

Q. What prediction made in the 68th Psalm and the 31st Verse is now being fulfilled?

A. "Princes shall come out of Egypt, Ethiopia shall soon stretch out her hands unto God."

Q. What does this verse prove?

A. That Negroes will set up their own government in Africa with rulers of their own race.

Q. Will Negroes ever be given equal opportunity and treatment in countries ruled by white men?

A. No; they will enjoy the full rights of manhood and liberty only when they establish their own nation and government in Africa.

Perhaps enough has already been said to make it clear that there exists in America no distinctive black culture which could spontaneously give rise to such a movement as this. Culturally the black man is American; biologically he is African. It is solely and entirely the prejudice of the American majority that has forced this group of Negroes to attempt to reconstruct a cultural and sentimental connection that was destroyed long ago. The task which faces the leaders of the new movement is one of almost insurmountable difficulty, for in spite of every sort of persecution, the general life and thought of America are still far more easily accessible to the Negro than is anything distinctively his own.

The cultural shipwreck of the Negro on the American shore has thus placed him more completely at the mercy of the majority than the other minorities have ever been. In the case of the Indians, the Jews, and the Orientals, the race-name has not stood simply for an incomplete Americanism, but for a positive cultural quality which has persisted in the face of all misfortune. These races were provisioned, so to speak, for a long siege, while the Negro had no choice but to eat out of the white man's hand, or starve.

The reservation-system has reduced many of the Indian tribes to a state of economic dependence, but it has also helped to preserve their cultural autonomy. In most cases the isolated communities on the reservations are distinctly Indian communities. The non-material inheritance of the past has come down to the present generation in a fairly complete form, with the result that the Indian of to-day may usually take his choice between Indian culture and white. Under these conditions the labours of missionaries and educators have not been phenomenally successful, as is witnessed by the fact that the number of Protestant Christians per thousand Indians is still only about one-seventh as large as that for the Negroes, while the percentage of illiterates is much larger among the Indians. However, school attendance is increasing at a more rapid rate than among the whites, and the prospect is that the Government schools will eventually deprive the country of all that is attractive in Indian life.

Toward the close of the 19th century, the Indian's resentment of the white man's overbearing actions found expression in a religious movement which originated in Nevada and spread eastward till it numbered among its adherents nearly all the natives between the Rocky Mountains and the Missouri River. This messianic faith bore the name of a ceremonial connected with it, the Ghost Dance, and was based upon a divine revelation which promised the complete restoration of the Indian's inheritance. Such doctrines have, of course, been preached in many forms and in many lands, but it is no great compliment to the amiability of American civilization that the gospel of deliverance has found so many followers among the Negroes, the Indians, and the Jews who dwell within the borders of the country.

It does not seem likely that the Zionist version of this gospel will produce any general exodus of the last-named minority from this country, for in spite of prejudice, the Jews have been able to make a large place for themselves in the United States. Since the movements of the Jews have not been systematically restricted, as those of the Negroes and the Indians have been, the great concentration of the Jewish population in the cities of the East would seem to be due in large measure to the choice of the Jews themselves. At the present time they dominate the clothing industry, the management of the theatre, and the production of motion-pictures. Approximately one-tenth of the trade-unionists in the United States are Jews, and the adherence of a considerable number of Jews to the doctrines of socialism and syndicalism has unquestionably been one of the causes of prejudice against the race.

In matters that pertain more directly to the intellectual life, the Jews have exhibited every degree of eagerness for and opposition to, assimilation. There are among them many schools for the teaching of the Hebrew language, and some other schools—private and expensive ones—in which only non-Jewish, "all-American" teachers are employed. Of the seventy-eight Jewish periodicals published in the United States, forty-eight are printed in English. In every Jewish centre, Yiddish theatres have been established for the amusement of the people; but Jewish managers, producers, actors, and playwrights have also had a large part in the general dramatic activities of the country. Finally, in the matter of religion, the response of the Jews to Christian missionary work has been very slight indeed, while, on the other hand, the number of synagogue-members per thousand Jews is only about one-fourth the general average of religious affiliation for the United States as a whole. When one considers the fact that in some fields the Jews have thus made advances in spite of opposition, while in others they have refused opportunities offered to them, it seems at least probable that the incompleteness of their cultural assimilation is due as much to their own racial pride as to the prejudice of the majority.

Similarly in the case of the Orientals, the pride and self- sufficiency of the minority has helped to preserve for it a measure of cultural autonomy. In the absence of such a disposition on the part of the Chinese, it would be difficult to account for the fact that their native costume has not disappeared during the thirty-nine years since the stoppage of immigration. San Francisco's Chinatown still remains very markedly Chinese in dress largely because the Chinese themselves have chosen to keep it so. The Japanese have taken much more kindly to the conventional American costume, but one is hardly justified in inferring from this that they are more desirous for general assimilation. Indeed, one would expect the opposite to be the case, for most of the Japanese in America had felt the impress of the nationalistic revival in Japan before their departure from that country. In a measure this accounts for the fact that Japanese settlers have established a number of Buddhist temples and Japanese-language schools in the United States. However, figures furnished by the "Joint Committee on Foreign Language Publications," which represents a number of Evangelical denominations, seem to indicate that the Japanese in the United States are much more easily Christianized than the Chinese, and are even less attached to Buddhism than are the Jews to their native faith. In the nature of things, the domestic practice of Shinto-worship among the Japanese is incapable of statistical treatment.

Thus the combination of all the internal and external forces that affect the racial minorities in America has produced a partial, but by no means a complete, remodelling of minority-life in accordance with standards set by the majority. Prejudice and counter-prejudice have not prevented this change and there is no accounting for the condition of the American minorities to-day without due attention to the positive factor of cultural assimilation, as well as to the negative factor of prejudice.

Since it has already been implied that a greater or less assimilation by the minorities of the culture of the majority is inevitable, it is apparent that the relation of this assimilative change to the biological fusion of the groups is a matter of ultimate and absolute importance. Wherever friction exists between racial groups, the mere mention of biological fusion is likely to stir up so much fire and smoke that all facts are completely lost to sight; and yet it is quite obvious that the forces of attraction and repulsion which play upon the several races in America have produced biological as well as cultural results.

The mulatto population of the United States is the physical embodiment of a one-sided race-prejudice. By law, by custom, even by the visitation of sudden and violent death, the master-class of the South expresses a disapproval of relations between white women and coloured men, which does not apply in any forcible way to similar relations between white men and coloured women. The white male is in fact the go-between for the races. The Negroes have not the power, and sometimes not even the will, to protect themselves against his advances, and the result is that illegitimate mulatto children in great numbers are born of Negro mothers and left to share the lot of the coloured race.

If the infusion of white blood were stopped entirely, the proportion of mulattoes in the Negro race would nevertheless go on increasing, since the children of a mulatto are usually mulattoes, whether the other parent be mulatto or black. There is, however, no reason for supposing that under such conditions the proportion of mulattoes to blacks would increase *more* rapidly in one geographic area than in another. The fact is that during the period 1890 to 1910 the number of mulattoes per 1,000 blacks *decreased* in the North from 390 to 363, and *increased* in the South from 159 to 252; the inference as to white parenthood is obvious. During the same period the black population of the entire United States increased 22.7 per cent, while the mulatto population increased 81.1 per cent. The mulatto group is thus growing far more rapidly than either the black or the white, and the male white population of the South is largely responsible for the present expansion of this class, as well as for its historical origin.

Thus the South couples a maximum of repression with a maximum of racial intermixture; indeed, the one is naturally and intimately associated with the other. The white population as a whole employs all manner of devices to keep the Negro in the social and economic status most favorable to sexual promiscuity, and aggressive white males take full advantage of the situation thus created.

While it is not generally admitted in the South that the progressive whitening of the black race is a natural result of the maintenance of a system of slavery and subjection, the converse of this proposition is stated and defended with all possible ardor. That is to say, it is argued that any general improvement in the condition of the Negro will increase the likelihood of racial intermixture on a higher level, through inter-marriage. The Southerners who put forth this argument know very well that inter-marriage is not likely to take place in the presence of strong race-prejudice, and they know, too, that the negro who most arouses their animosity is the "improved" Negro who will not keep his place. They are unwilling to admit that this increase in prejudice is due largely, if not wholly, to the greater competitive strength of the improved Negro; and likewise they prefer to disregard the fact that such a Negro resents white prejudice keenly, and tends to exhibit on his own part a counter prejudice which in itself acts as an additional obstacle to inter-marriage.

In the absence of such factors as Negro self-consciousness and inter-racial competition, it would be difficult to account for the extreme rarity of marriages between blacks and whites in the Northern States. No comprehensive study of this subject has been made, but an investigation conducted by Julius Drachsler has shown that of all the marriages contracted by Negroes in New York City during the years 1908 to 1912, only 0.93 per cent. were mixed. The same investigation revealed the fact that Negro men contracted mixed marriages about four times as frequently as Negro women.

Marriages betwen whites and Indians have not been so vigorously condemned by the American majority as those between whites and Negroes, and the presumption is that the former have been much more frequent. However, it appears that no systematic investigation of Indian mixed marriages has been made, and certainly no census previous to that of 1910 gives any data of value on the subject of mixed blood among the Indians. The enumeration of 1910 showed that 56.5 per cent. of the Indians were full-blooded, 35.2 per cent. were of mixed blood, and 8.4 per cent. were unclassified. Although it is impossible to fix the responsibility as definitely here as in the case of the Negro, it is obvious that an infusion of white blood half again as great as that among the Negroes cannot be accounted for in any large part by racial inter-marriages. Without question, it is chiefly due to the same sort of promiscuity that has been so common in the South, and the present and potential checks upon the process of infusion are similar to those already discussed.

In the case of the Jews and the Asiatics, it seems that the only figures available are those gathered by Drachsler. He found that only 1.17 per cent. of the marriages contracted by Jews in New York City during the years 1908 to 1912 were classifiable as "mixed," while the corresponding percentage for the Chinese and the Japanese were 55.56 and 72.41 respectively. The largeness of the figures in the case of Orientals is accounted for in part by the fact that there are comparatively few women of Mongolian race in New York City. Besides this, it must be remembered that, whatever the degree of their cultural assimilation, the Chinese and Japanese residents of the metropolis are not sufficiently numerous to form important competitive groups, while the Jews constitute one-quarter of the entire population of the city. Does any one doubt that the situation in regard to mixed marriages would be partially reversed in San Francisco?

When due allowance is made for special conditions, Drachsler's figures do not seem to run contrary to the general proposition that an improvement in the economic and social condition of one of the minorities, and a partial or complete adoption by the minority of the culture of the majority, does not necessarily prepare the way for racial fusion, but seems to produce exactly the opposite effect by increasing the competitive power of the minority, the majority's fear of its rivals, and the prejudice of each against the other.

In spite of all that prejudice can do to prevent it, the economic, social, and intellectual condition of the minorities is becoming increasingly like that of the majority; and yet it is not to be expected that as long as the minorities remain physically recognizable this change will result in the elimination of prejudice, nor is it likely that the cultural assimilation which checks the process of racial intermixture through promiscuous intercourse will result automatically in intermixture on a higher level, and the consequent disappearance of the recognizability of the minorities. Prejudice does not altogether prevent cultural assimilation; cultural assimilation increases competitive strength without eliminating recognizability; competitive strength *plus* recognizability produces more prejudice; and so on . . . and so on. . . . Thus it seems probable that race-prejudice will persist in America as long as the general economic, social, political, and intellectual system which has nurtured it endures. No direct attack upon the race-problem, as such, can alter this system in any essential way.

Is this conception sound, or not? It stands very high upon a slim scaffolding of facts, put together in pure contrariness after it had been stated that no adequate foundation for such a structure could be found anywhere. But, after all, it is no great matter what happens to the notion that race-prejudice can be remedied only incidentally. If the conditions which surround race-prejudice are only studied comparatively, this notion and others like it will get all the attention they deserve.

RACE PROBLEMS

(The answers are merely by way of suggestion, but the questions may prove to be worthy of serious attention.)

Q. Has the inherent inferiority of any human race been established by historical, biological or psychological evidence?
A. No.

Q. Does the theory of the inequality of human races offer a satisfactory explanation of the existence of race-prejudice?
A. No.

Q. Do physical characteristics make the members of the several races recognizable?
A. Yes.

Q. Is race-prejudice inherent and inevitable, in the sense that it always exists where two recognizably different races are in contact?
A. No.

Q. How does it happen that in the presence of *racial* factors which remain constant, race-prejudice exists in some localities, and is absent in others?
A. No satisfactory explanation of these local variations in inter-racial feeling has yet been given; however, the existence of the varia-

tions themselves would seem to indicate that the primary causes of race-prejudice are *not racial* but *regional.*

Q. What study will lead most directly to an understanding of race-prejudice—that of universal racial differences, or that of regional environmental differences which are associated with the existence and non-existence of racial prejudice?
A. The latter.

Q. Does the systematic study of regional environmental differences in the United States, in their relation to race-prejudice, yield any results of importance?
A. No such systematic study has ever been made; a casual glance seems to reveal an interesting coincidence between race-prejudice and the fear of competition.

Q. Is competition more likely to produce race-prejudice in the United States than elsewhere?
A. Because of the general preoccupation of the American people with material affairs, *economic* competition is likely to produce unusually sharp antagonisms.

Q. Does the coincidence between race-prejudice and the fear of competition offer a complete explanation of the existence and strength of race-prejudice in the United States?
A. No; no such claim has been advanced.

Q. Is the assimilation by the minorities of the culture of the majority taking place continuously, in spite of the prejudice of the majority and the counter-prejudice of three of the minorities?
A. Yes.

Q. Does this cultural assimilation make for better inter-racial feeling?
A. Probably not, because as long as physical race-differences remain, cultural assimilation increases the strength of the minority as a *recognizable* competitive group, and hence it also increases the keenness of the rivalry between the minorities and the majority.

Q. How can the recognizability of the minorities be eliminated?
A. By blood-fusion with the majority.

Q. How can blood-fusion come about if cultural assimilation increases rivalry and prejudice?
A. ....

Q. Is it then true that, as things stand, the future of inter-racial relations in the United States depends upon the ratio between cultural assimilation, which seems inevitable, and biological assimilation, which seems unlikely?
A. It so appears.

Q. Does the race-problem in the United States then seem practically insoluble as a separate problem?
A. It does.

Q. Has the race-problem ever been solved anywhere by direct attack upon it as a *race* problem?

A. Probably not.

Q. Does not this conclusion involve a return to the assumption that race-prejudice is inevitable wherever race-differences exist; and has this not been emphatically denied?

A. On the contrary, the implication is that race-prejudice is inevitable where *race-prejudice* exists. The conclusion in regard to the United States is based on the single assumption that the *non-racial* conditions under which race-prejudice has arisen will remain practically unchanged.

Q. Is it then conceivable that a complete alteration of non-racial conditions—as, for instance, an economic revolution which would change the whole meaning of the word "competition"—might entirely revise the terms of the problem?

A. It is barely conceivable—but this paper is not an accepted channel for divine revelation.

Altho there are no ebeio-historical, biological or historical evidence that racial differences indicate inferiority, yet it seems probable that race prejudice will persist in America as long as the general economic, social, political, system which has brought it about it endures.

Altho our race problems are unsolved the following statements may be made about it, racial prejudice is largely caused by economic competition, it attempts to increase and preserve the racial differences, it has not prevented cultural assimilation but has prevented blood fusion.

Seh steltifis the majority

ADDRESS AT THE OPENING OF THE ATLANTA
EXPOSITION [1]

Booker T. Washington

[Booker T. Washington (1858?-1915) was generally regarded as the leader of his race. The story of his life is best recounted in his autobiography, *Up from Slavery;* observations upon the experiences of his maturity are interestingly set forth in his later volume, *My Larger Education.*

Mr. Washington's influence as a national character was largely due to the general recognition accorded him as a symbolic figure, representative of the efforts of his race. Tuskegee Normal and Industrial Institute, to which his life was devoted, could not of itself have given Mr. Washington more than local prominence; but with skill and sincerity he pleaded its cause, and with it the cause of his people, before the entire nation. Considerable emphasis should be placed upon the development of his power of public address as a factor in his career. His own attitude toward it is significant:

"In my efforts on the public platform I have never been able to understand why people come to hear me speak. This question I can never rid myself of. Time and again, as I have stood in front of a building and have seen men and women passing in large numbers into the audience-room where I was to speak, I have felt ashamed that I should be the cause of people—as it seemed to me—wasting a valuable hour of time. People often ask me if I feel nervous before speaking, or else they suggest that, since I speak so often, they suppose I get used to it. In answer to this question I have to say that I always suffer intensely from nervousness before speaking. More than once, just before I was to make an important address, this nervous strain has been so great that I have resolved never again to speak in public. I not only feel nervous before speaking, but after I have finished I usually feel a sense of regret, because it seems to me as if I had left out of my address the main thing and the best thing I had to say.

There is a great compensation, though, for this preliminary nervous suffering, that comes to me after I have been speaking about ten minutes, and have come to feel that I have really mastered my audience, and that we have gotten into full and complete sympathy with each other. It seems to me that there is rarely such a combination of mental and physical delight in any effort as that which comes to a public speaker when he feels that he has a great audience completely within his control. There is a thread of sympathy and oneness that connects a public speaker with his audience, that is just as strong as though it was something tangible and visible.

---

[1] Reprinted from *Up from Slavery,* by permission of Doubleday, Page and Co. Questions and topics for the discussion of this address, and of other phases of the general subject with which it deals, will be found on pages 524 and 527.

I believe that one always does himself and his audience an injustice when he speaks merely for the sake of speaking. When one feels, from the bottom of his feet to the top of his head, that he has something to say that is going to help some individual or some cause, then let him say it; and in delivering his message I do not believe that many of the artificial rules of elocution can, under such circumstances, help him very much. Although there are certain things, such as pauses, breathing, and pitch of voice, that are very important, none of these can take the place of *soul* in an address. When I have an address to deliver, I like to forget all about the rules for the proper use of the English language, and all about rhetoric and that sort of thing, and I like to make the audience forget all about these things, too.''

Although Mr. Washington properly regarded the technical problems of speaking as subordinate, he was not ignorant of them. He was skilful as well as sincere. Of his early training in speaking at Hampton Institute he says:

''Whatever ability I may have as a public speaker, I owe in a measure to Miss Lord (a teacher at Hampton Institute). When she found out that I had some inclination in this direction she gave me private lessons in the matter of breathing, emphasis and articulation. The debating societies at Hampton were a constant source of delight to me. These were held on Saturday evening; and during my whole life at Hampton I do not recall that I missed a single meeting.''

In 1878 West Virginia discussed the removal of its capital from Wheeling. Charleston, one of the competing cities, was only five miles from Malden, Washington's home at the time. The white people of Charleston invited him to canvass the state in the interests of the city.

''I accepted, and spent nearly three months in speaking in various parts of the state. The reputation that I made as a speaker during this campaign induced a number of persons to make an earnest effort to get me to enter political life, but I refused, still believing that I could find other service which would prove of more permanent value to my race.''

Mr. Washington early saw his problems at Tuskegee in their relation to the large social and educational questions of the day, and formulated a policy for dealing with public opinion on the race question.

''There was a temptation to say to the white man the thing that the white man wanted to hear; to say to the colored man the thing the colored man wanted to hear; to say one thing in the North and another in the South. Perhaps I should have yielded to this temptation if I had not perceived that in the long run I should be found out, and that if I hoped to do anything of lasting value for my own people or for the South I must first get down to bedrock.''

As a result of one of Mr. Washington's northern speeches in behalf of Tuskegee, he was asked to address the National Educational Association at Milwaukee. Here he had an audience of about four thousand; and this occasion, he says, was the real beginning of his career as a public speaker. After this, invitations to address various northern meetings were more numerous than he could accept. His desire to address a southern white audience, and its fulfilment, are recorded in a chapter entitled, ''Two Thousand Miles for a Five Minute Speech.'' It was in 1893, and he was invited to address the international meeting of Christian Workers at Atlanta.

"When this invitation came to me, I had engagements in Boston that seemed to make it impossible for me to speak in Atlanta. Still, after looking over my list of dates and places carefully, I found I could take a train from Boston that would get me into Atlanta about thirty minutes before my address was to be delivered, and that I could remain in that city about sixty minutes before taking another train back to Boston. My invitation stipulated that I was to confine my address to five minutes. The question, then, was whether or not I could put enough into a five-minute address to make it worth while for me to make such a trip. . . . . I spoke for five minutes to an audience of two thousand people, composed mostly of Northern and Southern whites. What I said seemed to be received with favour and enthusiasm. I felt I had in some degree accomplished my object—that of getting a hearing from the dominant class of the South.''

This speech, Mr. Washington says, was possibly the prime cause of the opportunity to deliver the address at the opening of the Atlanta Exposition. It was this latter speech which gave him his national reputation. The circumstances are recounted in some detail in the autobiography, from which excerpts are quoted.

"The papers, North and South, had taken up the discussion of my coming speech, and as the time for it drew near this discussion became more widespread. Not a few Southern papers were unfriendly to the idea of my speaking. From my own race I received many suggestions as to what I ought to say. I prepared myself as best I could for the address, but as the 18th of September drew nearer, the heavier my heart became, and the more I feared that my effort would prove a failure and a disappointment . . . I felt a good deal as I suppose a man feels when he is on the way to the gallows. In passing through the town of Tuskegee I met a white farmer who lived some distance out in the country. In a jesting manner he said, 'Washington, you have spoken before the Northern white people, the Negroes in the South, and to us country white people in the South: but in Atlanta, tomorrow, you will have before you the Northern whites, the Southern whites and the Negroes all together. I am afraid you have got yourself in a tight place.' ''

After the speech, James Creelman telegraphed an account to the New York *World*, from which the following is quoted:

"When Professor Booker T. Washington, Principal of an industrial school for coloured people in Tuskegee, Ala., stood on the platform of the Auditorium, with the sun shining over the heads of the auditors into his eyes, and with his whole face lit up with the fire of prophecy, Clark Howell, the successor of Henry Grady, said to me, 'That man's speech is the beginning of a moral revolution in America.'

It is the first time that a Negro has made a speech in the South on any important occasion before an audience composed of white men and women. It electrified the audience, and the response was as if it had come from the throat of a whirlwind.

Mrs. Thompson had hardly taken her seat when all eyes were turned on a tawny Negro sitting in the front row of the platform. It was Professor Booker T. Washington, President of the Tuskegee Normal and Industrial Institute, who must rank from this time forth as the foremost man of his race in America. Gilmore's band played the 'Star-Spangled Banner,' and the audience cheered. The tune changed to 'Dixie' and the audience roared with shrill 'hi-yis.' Again the music changed, this time to 'Yankee Doodle,' and the clamor lessened.

All this time the eyes of the thousands present looked straight at the Negro orator. A strange thing was to happen. A black man was to speak for his people, with none to interrupt him. As Professor Washington strode to the edge of the stage, the low, descending sun shot fiery rays through the windows into his face. A great shout greeted him. He turned his head to avoid the blinding light, and moved about the platform for relief. Then he turned his wonderful countenance to the sun without a blink of the eyelids and began to talk.

There was a remarkable figure; tall, bony, straight as a Sioux chief, high forehead, straight nose, heavy jaws, and a strong, determined mouth, with big white teeth, piercing eyes, and a commanding manner. The sinews stood out on his bronzed neck, and his muscular right arm swung high in the air, with a lead-pencil grasped in the clinched brown fist. His big feet were planted squarely, with the heels together and the toes turned out. His voice rang out clear and true, and he paused impressively as he made each point. Within ten minutes the multitude was in an uproar of enthusiasm—handkerchiefs were waved, canes were flourished, hats were tossed in the air. The fairest women of Georgia stood up and cheered. It was as if the orator had bewitched them.

And when he held his dusky hand high above his head, with the fingers stretched wide apart, and said to the white people of the South on behalf of his race, 'In all things that are purely social we can be as separate as the fingers, yet one as the hand in all things essential to mutual progress,' the great wave of sound dashed against the walls, and the whole audience was on its feet in a delirium of applause, and I thought at that moment of the night when Henry Grady stood among the curling wreaths of tobacco smoke in Delmonico's banquet-hall and said, 'I am a Cavalier among Roundheads.'

I have heard the great orators of many countries, but not even Gladstone himself could have pleaded a cause with more consummate power than did this angular Negro, standing in a nimbus of sunshine, surrounded by the men who once fought to keep his race in bondage. The roar might swell ever so high, but the expression of his earnest face never changed.

A ragged, ebony giant, squatted on the floor in one of the aisles, watched the orator with burning eyes and tremulous face until the supreme burst of applause came, and then the tears ran down his face. Most of the Negroes in the audience were crying, perhaps without knowing just why.

At the close of the speech Governor Bullock rushed across the stage and seized the orator's hand. Another shout greeted this demonstration, and for a few minutes the two men stood facing each other, hand in hand.''

President Cleveland wrote to Mr. Washington concerning the address, ''I thank you with much enthusiasm for making the address. I have read it with intense interest, and I think the Exposition would be fully justified if it did not do more than furnish the opportuty for its delivery.''

The address was generally regarded as a platform upon which blacks and whites could stand with full justice to each other. It was praised as a model of tact and persuasiveness. But while the address is remarkable for its adaptation to audience and occasion, it is also true that its sincerity cannot be questioned. The principles set forth in it governed Mr. Washington's whole life; and he had scant sympathy with the "intellectuals" of his race who felt that he was accepting a position of permanent inferiority for the Negro.

Frederick Douglass, the negro orator and recognized leader of his race, had died only a few months before the Atlanta Address was delivered. Immediately after the address, letters, telegrams and editorials poured in upon Mr. Washington, demanding that he take the place of "leader of the Negro people," left vacant by the death of Frederick Douglass. "Until these suggestions began to pour in upon me," says Mr. Washington, "I had never had the remotest idea that I should be selected or looked upon in any such sense as Frederick Douglass had been, as a leader of the Negro people. I was at that time merely a Negro school teacher in a rather obscure industrial school." From the time of this address, however, Mr. Washington's position as a leader of his race could not be seriously questioned, even by those who disagreed with his policies.]

Mr. President and Gentlemen of the Board of Directors and Citizens.

One-third of the population of the South is of the Negro race. No enterprise seeking the material, civil, or moral welfare of this section can disregard this element of our population and reach the highest success. I but convey to you, Mr. President and Directors, the sentiment of the masses of my race when I say that in no way have the value and manhood of the American Negro been more fittingly and generously recognized than by the managers of this magnificent Exposition at every stage of its progress. It is a recognition that will do more to cement the friendship of the two races than any occurrence since the dawn of our freedom.

Not only this, but the opportunity here afforded will awaken among us a new era of industrial progress. Ignorant and inexperienced, it is not strange that in the first years of our new life we began at the top instead of at the bottom; that a seat in Congress or the State legislature was more sought than real estate or industrial skill; that the political convention or stump speaking had more attractions than starting a dairy farm or truck garden.

A ship lost at sea for many days suddenly sighted a friendly vessel. From the mast of the unfortunate vessel was seen a signal, "Water, water; we die of thirst!" The answer from the friendly vessel at once came back, "Cast down your bucket where you are." A second time the signal, "Water, water; send us water!" ran up from the distressed vessel, and was answered, "Cast down you bucket where you are." And a third and fourth signal for water was answered, "Cast down your bucket where you are." The captain of the distressed vessel, at last heeding the injunction, cast down his bucket, and it came up full of fresh sparkling water from the mouth of the Amazon River. To those of my race who depend on bettering their condition in a foreign land or who underestimate the importance of cultivating friendly relations with the Southern white man, who is their next-door neighbor, I would say: "Cast down your bucket where you are"—cast it down in making friends in every manly way of the people of all races by whom we are surrounded.

Cast it down in agriculture, in mechanics, in commerce, in domestic service, and in the professions. And in this connection it is well to bear in mind that whatever other sins the South may be called to bear, when it comes to business, pure and simple, it is in the South that the Negro is given a man's chance in the commercial world, and in nothing is this Exposition more eloquent than in emphasizing this chance. Our greatest danger is that in the great leap from slavery to freedom we may overlook the fact that the masses of us are to live by the productions of our hands, and fail to keep in mind that we shall prosper in proportion as we learn to dignify and glorify common labor and put brains and skill into the common occupations of life; shall prosper in proportion as we learn to draw the line between the superficial and the substantial, the ornamental gewgaws of life and the useful. No race can prosper till it learns that there is as much dignity in tilling a field as in writing a poem. It is at the bottom of life we must begin, and not at the top. Nor should we permit our grievances to overshadow our opportunities.

To those of the white race who look to the incoming of those of foreign birth and strange tongue and habits for the prosperity of the South, were I permitted I would repeat what I say to my own race, "Cast down your bucket where you are." Cast it down among the eight millions of Negroes whose habits you know, whose fidelity and love you have tested in days when to have proved treacherous meant the ruin of your firesides. Cast down your bucket among these people who have, without strikes and labor wars, tilled your fields, cleared your forests, builded your railroads and cities, and brought forth treasures from the bowels of the earth and helped make possible this magnificent representation of the progress of the South. Casting down your bucket among my people, helping and encouraging them as you are doing on these grounds, and to education of head, hand, and heart, you will find that they will buy your surplus land, make blossom the waste places in your fields and run your factories. While doing this, you can be sure in the future, as in the past, that you and your families will be surrounded by the most patient, faithful, law-abiding, and unresentful people that the world has seen. As we have proved our loyalty to you in the past, in nursing your children, watching by the sick-bed of your mothers and fathers, and often following them with tear-dimmed eyes to their graves, so in the future, in our humble way, we shall stand by you with a devotion that no foreigner can approach, ready to lay down our lives, if need be, in defence of yours, interlacing our industrial, commercial, civil, and religious life with yours in a way that shall make the interests of both races one. In all things that are purely social we can be as separate as the fingers, yet one as the hands in all things essential to mutual progress.

There is no defence or security for any of us except in the highest intelligence and development of all. If anywhere there are efforts tending to curtail the fullest growth of the Negro, let these efforts be turned into stimulating, encouraging, and making him the most useful and intelligent citizen. Effort or means so invested will pay a thousand per cent. interest. These efforts will be twice blessed, "blessing him that gives and him that takes."

There is no escape through law of man or God from the inevitable:—

> The laws of changeless justice bind
> Oppressor with oppressed;
> And close as sin and suffering joined
> We march to fate abreast.

Nearly sixteen millions of hands will aid you in pulling the load upward, or they will pull against you the load downward. We shall constitute one-third and more of the ignorance and crime of the South, or one-third its intelligence and progress; we shall contribute one-third to the business and industrial prosperity of the South, or we shall prove a veritable body of death, stagnating, depressing, retarding every effort to advance the body politic.

Gentlemen of the Exposition, as we present to you our humble effort at an exhibition of our progress, you must not expect overmuch. Starting thirty years ago with ownership here and there in a few quilts and pumpkins and chickens (gathered from miscellaneous sources), remember the path that has led from these to the inventions and production of agricultural implements, buggies, steam-engines, newspapers, books, statuary, carving, paintings, the management of drug stores and banks, has not been trodden without contact with thorns and thistles. While we take pride in what we exhibit as a result of our independent efforts, we do not for a moment forget that our part in this exhibition would fall far short of your expectations but for the constant help that has come to our educational life, not only from the Southern States, but especially from Northern philanthropists, who have made their gifts a constant stream of blessing and encouragement.

The wisest among my race understand that the agitation of questions of social equality is the extremest folly, and that progress in the enjoyment of all the privileges that will come to us must be the result of severe and constant struggle rather than of artificial forcing. No race that has anything to contribute to the markets of the world is long in any degree ostracized. It is important and right that all privileges of the law be ours, but it is vastly more important that we be prepared for the exercise of these privileges. The opportunity to earn a dollar in a factory just now is worth infinitely more than the opportunity to spend a dollar in an opera-house.

In conclusion, may I repeat that nothing in thirty years has given more hope and encouragement, and drawn us so near to you of the white race, as this opportunity offered by the Exposition; and here bending, as it were, over the altar that represents the struggles of your race and mine, both starting practically empty-handed three decades ago, I pledge that in your effort to work out the great and intricate problem which God has laid at the doors of the South, you shall have at all times the patient, sympathetic help of my race; only let this be constantly in mind, that, while from representations in these buildings of the product of field, of forest, of mine, of factory, letters, and art, much good will come, yet far above and beyond material benefits will be that higher good, that, let us pray God, will come, in a blotting out of sectional differences and racial animosities and suspicions, in a determination to administer absolute justice, in a willing obedience among all classes to the mandates of the law. This, coupled with our material prosperity, will bring into our beloved South a new heaven and a new earth.

THE NEGRO PROBLEM [1]

W. E. B. DuBois

[W. E. Burghardt DuBois (1868-   ), editor of the *Crisis,* and President of the National Association for the Advancement of Colored People, says he was "born with a flood of Negro blood, a strain of French, a bit of Dutch, but, thank God! no 'Anglo-Saxon.'" His early years were spent in New Bedford, Massachusetts, where he was graduated from high school. He was graduated from Fisk University in 1888 with a scholarship that enabled him to enter Harvard, where he received the bachelor's degree two years later. In 1895 he gained the doctoral degree also, and left Harvard for the University of Berlin. From 1896 to 1910 he was Professor of Economics and History in Atlanta University. He left this position to found the *Crisis* and to direct the work of the National Association for the Advancement of Colored People.

Dr. DuBois has never accepted Mr. Washington's position that industrial education is the first need of their people. "The Negro race, like all races," he writes in his vigorous essay, *The Talented Tenth* "is going to be saved by its exceptional men. The problem of education, then, among Negroes must first of all deal with the Talented Tenth; it is the problem of developing the Best of this race that they may guide the Mass away from the contamination and death of the worst, in their own and other races."

As a speaker, Dr. DuBois is "a gentleman conversing." He writes with distinction. His general position on race problems is set forth in his volumes, *Souls of Black Folk,* and *Darkwater.* The address here printed was delivered at the International Congress on Racial Relations held in London in 1911.]

The American Negro problem is the question of the future status of the ten million Americans of Negro descent. It must be remembered that these persons are Americans by birth and descent. They represent, for the most part, four or five American born generations, being in that respect one of the most American groups in the land. Moreover, the Negroes are not barbarians. They are, as a mass, poor and ignorant; but they are growing rapidly in both wealth and intelligence, and larger and larger numbers of them demand the rights and privileges of American citizens as a matter of undoubted desert.

To-day these rights are largely denied. In order to realize the disabilities under which Negroes suffer regardless of education,

[1] Reprinted by permission of the author from *Universal Races Congress: Papers on Inter-racial Problems,* edited by G. Spiller.

Questions and topics for the discussion of this address, and of other phases of the general subject with which it deals, will be found on pages 525 and 527.

wealth, or degree of white blood, we may divide the United States into three districts.

(a) The Southern South, containing 75 per cent. of the Negroes.
(b) The border States, containing 15 per cent. of the Negroes.
(c) The North and West, containing 10 per cent. of the Negroes.

In the Southern South by law or custom Negroes—

1. Cannot vote, or their votes are neutralized by fraud.
2. Must usually live in the least desirable districts.
3. Receive very low wages.
4. Are, in the main, restricted to menial occupations or the lower grades of skilled labour and cannot expect preferment or promotion.
5. Cannot by law inter-marry with whites.
6. Cannot join white churches or attend white colleges or join white cultural organizations.
7. Cannot be accommodated at hotels and restaurants or in any place of public entertainment.
8. Receive a distinct standard of justice in the courts and are especially liable to mob violence.
9. Are segregated as far as possible in every walk of life— in railway stations, railway trains, street-cars, lifts, &c., and usually made to pay equal prices for inferior accommodations.
10. Are often unable to protect their homes from invasion, their women from insult, and their savings from exploitation.
11. Are taxed for public facilities like parks and libraries, which they may not enter.
12. Are given meagre educational facilities and sometimes none at all.
13. Are liable to personal insults unless they appear as servants or menials or show deference to white folks by yielding the road, &c.

To many of these disabilities there are personal and local exceptions. In cities, for instance, the chance to defend the home, get an education, and somewhat better wages is greater, and mob violence less frequent. Then there are always some personal exceptions—cases of help and courtesy, of justice in the courts, and of good schools. These are, however, exceptions, and, as a rule, all Negroes, no matter what their training, possessions, or desert, are subjected to the above disabilities. Within the limits of these caste restrictions there is much goodwill and kindliness between the races, and especially much personal charity and help.

The 15 per cent. of the Negro population living on the border States suffer a little less restriction. They have some right of voting, are better able to defend their homes, and are less discriminated against in the expenditure of public funds. In the cities their schools are much better and public insult is less noticeable.

In the North the remaining 10 per cent. of the Negro population is legally undiscriminated against and may attend schools and churches and vote without restriction. As a matter of fact, however, they are made in most communities to feel that they are undesirable. They are either refused accommodation at hotels, restaurants, and theatres, or received reluctantly. Their treatment in churches and general cultural organizations is such that few join. Inter-marriage with whites brings ostracism and public disfavor, and in courts Negroes often suffer undeservedly. Common labour and menial work is open to them, but avenues above this in skilled labour or the professions (save as they serve their own race), are extremely difficult to enter, and there is much discrimination in wages. Mob violence has become not infrequent in later years.

There are here also many exceptional cases; instances of preferment in the industrial and political world; and there is always some little social intercourse. On the whole, however, the Negro in the North is an ostracized person who finds it difficult to make a good living or spend his earnings with pleasure.

Under these circumstances there has grown up a Negro world in America which has its own economic and social life, its churches, schools, and newspapers; its literature, public opinion, and ideals. This life is largely unnoticed and unknown even in America, and travellers miss it almost entirely.

The average American in the past made at least pretence of excusing the discrimination against Negroes, on the ground of their ignorance and poverty and their tendencies to crime and disease. While the mass is still poor and unlettered, it is admitted by all to-day that the Negro is rapidly developing a larger and larger class of intelligent property-holding men of Negro descent; notwithstanding this more and more race lines are being drawn which involve the treatment of civilized men in an uncivilized manner. Moreover, the crux of the question to-day is not merely a matter of social eligibility. For many generations the American Negro will lack the breeding and culture which the most satisfactory human intercourse requires. But in America the discrimination against

Negroes goes beyond this, to the point of public discourtesy, civic disability, injustice in the courts, and economic restriction.

The argument of those who uphold this discrimination is based primarily on race. They claim that the inherent characteristics of the Negro race show its essential inferiority and the impossibility of incorporating its descendants into the American nation. They admit that there are exceptions to the rule of inferiority, but claim that these but prove the rule. They say that amalgamation of the races would be fatal to civilization and they advocate therefore a strict caste system for Negroes, segregating them by occupations and privileges, and to some extent by dwelling-place, to the end that they (a) submit permanently to an inferior position, or (b) die out, or (c) migrate.

This philosophy the thinking Negroes and a large number of white friends vigorously combat. They claim that the racial differences between white and black in the United States offer no essential barrier to the races living together on terms of mutual respect and helpfulness. They deny, on the one hand, that the large amalgamation of the races already accomplished has produced degenerates, in spite of the unhappy character of these unions; on the other hand, they deny any desire to lose the identity of either race through inter-marriage. They claim that it should be possible for a civilized black man to be treated as an American citizen without harm to the republic, and that the modern world must learn to treat coloured races as equals if it expects to advance.

They claim that the Negro race in America has more than vindicated its ability to assimilate modern culture. Negro blood has furnished thousands of soldiers to defend the flag in every war in which the United States has been engaged. They are a most important part of the economic strength of the nation, and they have furnished a number of men of ability in politics, literature, and art, as, for instance, Banneker, the mathematician; Phillis Wheatley, the poet; Lemuel Haynes, the theologian; Ira Aldridge, the actor; Frederick Douglass, the orator; H. O. Tanner, the artist; B. T. Washington, the educator; Granville Woods, the inventor; Kelly Miller, the writer; Rosamond Johnson and Will Cook, the musical composers; Dunbar, the poet; and Chestnut, the novelist. Many other Americans, whose Negro blood has not been openly acknowledged, have reached high distinction. The Negroes claim, therefore, that a discrimination which was originally based on certain social conditions is rapidly becoming a persecution based simply on race prejudice, and that no republic built on caste can survive.

At the meeting of two such diametrically opposed arguments it was natural that councils of compromise should appear, and it was also natural that a nation, whose economic triumphs have been so noticeable as those of the United States, should seek an economic solution to the race question. More and more in the last twenty years the business men's solution of the race problem has been the development of the resources of the South. Coincident with the rise of this policy came the prominence of Mr. B. T. Washington. Mr. Washington was convinced that race prejudice in America was so strong and the economic position of the freedmen's sons so weak that the Negro must give up or postpone his ambitions for full citizenship and bend all his energies to industrial efficiency and the accumulation of wealth. Mr. Washington's idea was that eventually when the dark man was thoroughly established in the industries and had accumulated wealth, he could demand further rights and privileges. This philosophy has become very popular in the United States, both among whites and blacks.

The white South hastened to welcome this philosophy. They thought it would take the Negro out of politics, tend to stop agitation, make the Negro a satisfied labourer, and eventually convince him that he could never be recognized as the equal of the white man. The North began to give large sums for industrial training, and hoped in this way to get rid of a serious social problem.

From the beginning of this campaign, however, a large class of Negroes and many whites feared this program. They not only regarded it as a program which was a dangerous compromise, but they insisted that to stop fighting the essential wrong of race prejudice just at the time, was to encourage it.

This was precisely what happened. Mr. Washington's program was announced at the Atlanta Exposition in 1896. Since that time four states have disfranchised Negroes, dozens of cities and towns have separated the races on street cars, 1,250 Negroes have been publicly lynched without trial, and serious race riots have taken place in nearly every Southern State and several Northern States, Negro public school education has suffered a set-back, and many private schools have been forced to retrench severely or to close. On the whole, race prejudice has, during the last fifteen years, enormously increased.

This has been coincident with the rapid and substantial advance of Negroes in wealth, education, and morality, and the two movements of race prejudice and Negro advance have led to an anomalous and unfortunate situation. Some, white and black, seek to minimize and ignore the flaming prejudice in the land, and emphasize many acts of friendliness on the part of the white South, and the advance of the Negro. Others, on the other hand, point out that silence and sweet temper are not going to settle this dangerous social problem, and that manly protest and the publication of the whole truth is alone adequate to arouse the nation to its great danger.

Moreover, many careful thinkers insist that, under the circumstances, the "business men's" solution of the race problem is bound to make trouble; if the Negroes become good cheap labourers, warranted not to strike or complain, they will arouse all the latent prejudice of the white working men whose wages they bring down. If, on the other hand, they are to be really educated as men, and not as "hands," then they need, as a race, not only industrial training, but also a supply of well-educated, intellectual leaders and professional men for a group so largely deprived of contact with the cultural leaders of the whites. Moreover, the best thought of the nation is slowly recognizing the fact that to try to educate a working man, and not to educate the man, is impossible. If the United States wants intelligent Negro labourers, it must be prepared to treat them as intelligent men.

This counter movement of intelligent men, white and black, against the purely economic solution of the race probem, has been opposed by powerful influences both North and South. The South represents it as malicious sectionalism, and the North misunderstands it as personal dislike and envy of Mr. Washington. Political pressure has been brought to bear, and this insured a body of coloured political leaders who do not agitate for Negro rights. At the same time, a chain of Negro newspapers was established to advocate the dominant philosophy.

Despite the well-intentioned effort to keep down the agitation of the Negro question and mollify the coloured people, the problem has increased in gravity. The result is the present widespread unrest and dissatisfaction. Honest Americans know that present conditions are wrong and cannot last; but they face, on the one hand, the seemingly implacable prejudice of the South, and, on the other hand, the undoubted rise of the Negro challenging that prejudice. The attempt to reconcile these two forces is becoming increasingly futile, and the nation simply faces the question: Are we willing to do justice to a dark race despite our prejudices? Radical suggestions of wholesale segregation or deportation of the race have now and then been suggested; but the cost in time, effort, money, and economic disturbance is too staggering to allow serious consideration. The South, with all its race prejudice, would rather fight than lose its great black labouring force, and in every walk of life throughout the nation the Negro is slowly forcing his way. There are some signs that the prejudice in the South is not immovable, and now and then voices of protest and signs of liberal thought appear there. Whether at last the Negro will gain full recognition as a man, or be utterly crushed by prejudice and superior numbers, is the present Negro problem of America.

WAR AND PEACE

THE MORAL EQUIVALENT OF WAR[1]

William James

[William James (1842-1910) is frequently called the most eminent American philosopher. His early education was somewhat irregular. A residence of three years in Europe gave him an early familiarity with European languages and culture. At eighteen he spent a year in the study of painting. Abandoning this, he studied chemistry and anatomy for two years at the Lawrence Scientific School at Harvard. In 1863 he began the study of medicine. This work was interrupted by an expedition to Brazil with Louis Agassiz, and by study in the University of Berlin. In 1869 he took his doctorate in medicine at Harvard, and in 1872 began his academic career as an instructor in psychology. In 1880 he became Assistant Professor of Philosophy. In 1885 he was made Professor of Philosophy, and in 1889 he took the Chair of Psychology. In 1897 he reassumed his title of Professor of Philosophy.

The student of persuasive public address may well give some days and nights to James. The psychological principles involved in persuasion have been set forth with unequaled clarity in his *Principles of Psychology*. But it is not theory only that is to be found in James. Few public addresses have had a greater influence on American thought than his lectures in popular philosophy. His *Talks to Teachers on Psychology and to Students on Some of Life's Ideals, Is Life Worth Living, The Will to Believe, The Social Value of the College Bred, On a Certain Blindness in People*, all delivered before more or less popular audiences, not only possessed a fascination for the immediate hearers, but they have been widely read and have greatly increased the general interest in philosophical thinking. James seized upon problems of interest to all men as men, and he treated them in such a fashion that many of his contributions to philosophy and psychology have also a place in polite literature. Nor was his writing and speaking for general audiences entirely a matter of "popularizing." His thought was illumined by the imagination of the literary man; and as with the poet, it is difficult to recall his ideas without remembering his words. Ralph Barton Perry, a student of James's at Harvard, and later a colleague, says,

"It is easy to say that he owed much to his style; but it is plain that his style owed everything to him. He was, it is true, a lover of form, endowed with the finest sensibilities, and stirred by the creative impulse; but his style was always his instrument. He found it above all a means of communication; for nothing was more notable about him than the social quality of his thought. He wrote for his readers, his vivid imagination of their presence guiding him infallibly to the centre of

[1] Reprinted by permission of the American Association for International Conciliation, and of Longmans, Green and Co., publishers of *Memories and Studies*, by William James.
Questions and topics for the discussion of this essay, and of other phases of the general subject with which it deals, will be found on pages 529 and 533.

their minds. And his style was also the means of faithfully representing his experience. It was figurative and pictorial, because the
world he saw was a procession of concrete happenings, abounding in
novelty and uniqueness.''

The Moral Equivalent of War was James's last public utterance. Although written in 1910 for the American Society for International Conciliation, the substance of the essay had previously been set forth in an address
before the Peace Banquet of 1904.]

The war against war is going to be no holiday excursion or
camping party. The military feelings are too deeply grounded to
abdicate their place among our ideals until better substitutes are
offered than the glory and shame that come to nations as well as to
individuals from the ups and downs of politics and the vicissitudes
of trade. There is something highly paradoxical in the modern
man's relation to war. Ask all our millions, north and south,
whether they would vote now (were such a thing possible) to have
our war for the Union expunged from history, and the record of a
peaceful transition to the present time substituted for that of its
marches and battles, and probably hardly a handful of eccentrics
would say yes. Those ancestors, those efforts, those memories and
legends, are the most ideal part of what we now own together, a
sacred spiritual possession worth more than all the blood poured
out. Yet ask those same people whether they would be willing in
cold blood to start another civil war now to gain another similar
possession, and not one man or woman would vote for the proposition. In modern eyes, precious though wars may be, they must
not be waged solely for the sake of the ideal harvest. Only when
forced upon one, only when an enemy's injustice leaves us no
alternative, is a war now thought permissible.

It was not thus in ancient times. The earlier men were hunting
men, and to hunt a neighboring tribe, kill the males, loot the village and possess the females, was the most profitable, as well as the
most exciting, way of living. Thus were the more martial tribes
selected, and in chiefs and peoples a pure pugnacity and love of
glory came to mingle with the more fundamental appetite for
plunder.

Modern war is so expensive that we feel trade to be a better
avenue to plunder; but modern man inherits all the innate pugnacity and all the love of glory of his ancestors. Showing war's
irrationality and horror is of no effect upon him. The horrors
make the fascination. War is the *strong* life; it is life *in extremis;*

war taxes are the only ones men never hesitate to pay, as the budgets of all nations show us.

History of a bath of blood. The Iliad is one long recital of how Diomedes and Ajax, Sarpedon and Hector, *killed.* No detail of the wounds they made is spared us, and the Greek mind fed upon the story. Greek history is a panorama of jingoism and imperialism—war for war's sake, all the citizens being warriors. It is horrible reading, because of the irrationality of it all—save for the purpose of making "history"—and the history is that of the utter ruin of a civilization in intellectual respects perhaps the highest the earth has ever seen.

Those wars were purely piratical. Pride, gold, women, slaves, excitement, were their only motives. In the Peloponnesian war, for example, the Athenians asked the inhabitants of Melos (the island where the "Venus of Milo" was found), hitherto neutral, to own their lordship. The envoys meet, and hold a debate which Thucydides gives in full, and which, for sweet reasonableness of form, would have satisfied Matthew Arnold. "The powerful exact what they can," said the Athenians, "and the weak grant what they must." When the Meleans say that sooner than be slaves they will appeal to the gods, the Athenians reply: "Of the gods we believe and of men we know that, by a law of their nature, wherever they can rule they will. This law was not made by us, and we are not the first to have acted upon it; we did but inherit it, and we know that you and all mankind, if you were as strong as we are, would do as we do. So much for the gods; we have told you why we expect to stand as high in their good opinion as you." Well, the Meleans still refused, and their town was taken. "The Athenians," Thucydides quietly says, "thereupon put to death all who were of military age and made slaves of the women and children. They then colonized the island, sending thither five hundred settlers of their own."

Alexander's career was piracy pure and simple, nothing but an orgy of power and plunder, made romantic by the character of the hero. There was no rational principle in it, and the moment he died his generals and governors attacked one another. The cruelty of those times is incredible. When Rome finally conquered Greece, Paulus Æmilius was told by the Roman Senate to reward his, soldiers for their toil by "giving" them the old kingdom of Epirus. They sacked seventy cities and carried off a hundred and fifty thousand inhabitants as slaves. How many they killed I know not; but in Etolia they killed all the senators, five hundred and fifty in number. Brutus was "the noblest Roman of them all," but to reanimate his soldiers on the eve of Philippi he similarly promises to give them the cities of Sparta and Thessalonica to ravage, if they win the fight.

Such was the gory nurse that trained societies to cohesiveness. We inherit the warlike type; and for most of the capacities of heroism that the human race is full of we have to thank this cruel history. Dead men tell no tales, and if there were any tribes of other type than this they have left no survivors. Our ancestors have bred pugnacity into our bone and marrow, and thousands of years of peace won't breed it out of us. The popular imagination fairly fattens on the thought of wars. Let public opinion once reach a certain fighting pitch, and no ruler can withstand it. In the Boer war both governments began with bluff, but couldn't stay there, the military tension was too much for them. In 1898 our people had read the word WAR in letters three inches high for three months in every newspaper. The pliant politician McKinley was swept away by their eagerness, and our squalid war with Spain became a necessity.

At the present day, civilized opinion is a curious mental mixture. The military instincts and ideals are as strong as ever, but are confronted by reflective criticisms which sorely curb their ancient freedom. Innumerable writers are showing up the bestial side of military service. Pure loot and mastery seem no longer morally avowable motives, and pretexts must be found for attributing them solely to the enemy. England and we, our army and navy authorities repeat without ceasing, arm solely for "peace," Germany and Japan it is who are bent on loot and glory. "Peace" in military mouths to-day is a synonym for "war expected." The word has become a pure provocative, and no government wishing peace sincerely should allow it ever to be printed in a newspaper. Every up-to-date dictionary should say that "peace" and "war" mean the same thing, now *in posse,* now *in actu.* It may even reasonably be said that the intensely sharp competitive *preparation* for war by the nations *is the real war,* permanent, unceasing; and that the battles are only a sort of public verification of the mastery gained during the "peace" interval.

It is plain that on this subject civilized man has developed a sort of double personality. If we take European nations, no legitimate interests of any one of them would seem to justify the tremendous destructions which a war to compass it would necessarily entail. It would seem as though common sense and reason ought to find a way to reach agreement in every conflict of honest interests. I myself think it our bounden duty to believe in such international rationality as possible. But, as things stand, I see how desperately hard it is to bring the peace party and the war party together, and I believe that the difficulty is due to certain deficiencies in the program of pacificism which set the militarist imagination strongly, and to a certain extent justifiably, against it. In the whole discussion both sides are on imaginative and sentimental ground. It is but one utopia against another, and everything one says must be abstract and hypothetical. Subject to this criticism and caution, I will try to characterize in abstract strokes the opposite imaginative forces, and point out what to my own very fallible mind seems the best utopian hypothesis, the most promising line of conciliation.

In my remarks, pacificist though I am, I will refuse to speak of the bestial side of the war régime (already done justice to by many writers) and consider only the higher aspects of militaristic sentiment. Patriotism no one thinks discreditable; nor does any one deny that war is the romance of history. But inordinate ambitions are the soul of every patriotism, and the possibility of violent death the soul of all romance. The militarily patriotic and romantic-minded everywhere, and especially the professional military class, refuse to admit for a moment that war may be a transitory phenomenon in social evolution. The notion of a sheep's paradise like that revolts, they say, our higher imagination. Where then would be the steeps of life? If war had ever stopped, we should have to reinvent it, on this view, to redeem life from flat degeneration.

Reflective apologists for war at the present day all take it religiously. It is a sort of sacrament. Its profits are to the vanquished as well as to the victor; and quite apart from any question of profit, it is an absolute good, we are told, for it is human nature at its highest dynamic. Its "horrors" are a cheap price to pay for rescue from the only alternative supposed, of a world of clerks and teachers, of coeducation and zoöphily, of "consumer's leagues" and "associated charities," of industrialism unlimited and feminism unabashed. No scorn, no hardness, no valor any more! Fie upon such a cattleyard of a planet!

So far as the central essence of this feeling goes, no healthy-minded person, it seems to me, can help to some degree partaking of it. Militarism is the great preserver of our ideals of hardihood, and human life with no use for hardihood would be contemptible. Without risks or prizes for the darer, history would be insipid indeed; and there is a type of military character which every one feels that the race should never cease to breed, for every one is sensitive to its superiority. The duty is incumbent on mankind, of keeping military characters in stock—of keeping them, if not for use, then as ends in themselves and as pure pieces of perfection,—so that Roosevelt's weaklings and mollycoddles may not end by making everything else disappear from the face of nature.

This natural sort of feeling forms, I think, the innermost soul of army writings. Without any exception known to me, militarist authors take a highly mystical view of their subject, and regard war as a biological or sociological necessity, uncontrolled by ordinary psychological checks and motives. When the time of development is ripe the war must come, reason or no reason, for the justifications pleaded are invariably fictitious. War is, in short, a permanent human *obligation*. General Homer Lea, in his recent book, *The Valor of Ignorance*, plants himself squarely on this ground. Readiness for war is for him the essence of nationality, and ability in it the supreme measure of the health of nations. Nations, General Lea says, are never stationary—they must necessarily expand or shrink, according to their vitality or decrepitude. Japan now is culminating; and by the fatal law in question it is impossible that her statesmen should not long since have entered, with extraordinary foresight, upon a vast policy of conquest—the game in which the first moves were her wars with China and Russia and her treaty with England, and of which the final objective is the capture of the Philippines, the Hawaiian Islands, Alaska, and the whole of our coast west of the Sierra Passes. This will give Japan what her ineluctable vocation as a state absolutely forces her to claim, the possession of the entire Pacific Ocean; and to oppose these deep designs we Americans have, according to our author, nothing but our conceit, our ignorance, our commercialism, our corruption, and our feminism. General Lea makes a minute technical comparison of the military strength which we at present could oppose to the strength of Japan, and concludes that the islands, Alaska, Oregon, and Southern California, would fall almost without resistance, that San Francisco must surrender in a fortnight to a Japanese investment, that in three or four months the war would be over, and our Republic, unable to regain what it had heedlessly neglected to protect sufficiently, would then "disintegrate," until perhaps some Cæsar should arise to weld us again into a nation.

A dismal forecast indeed! Yet not unplausible, if the mentality of Japan's statesmen be of the Cæsarian type of which history shows so many examples, and which is all that General Lea seems able to imagine. But there is no reason to think that women can no longer be the mothers of Napoleonic or Alexandrian characters; and if these come in Japan and find their opportunity, just such surprises as *The Valor of Ignorance* paints may lurk in ambush for us. Ignorant as we still are of the innermost recesses of Japanese mentality, we may be foolhardy to disregard such possibilities.

Other militarists are more complex and more moral in their considerations. The *Philosophie des Krieges,* by S. R. Steinmetz, is a good example. War, according to this author, is an ordeal instituted by God, who weighs the nations in its balance. It is the essential form of the state, and the only function in which peoples can employ all their powers at once and convergently. No victory is possible save as the resultant of a totality of virtues, no defeat for which some vice or weakness is not responsible. Fidelity, cohesiveness, tenacity, heroism, conscience, education, inventiveness, economy, wealth, physical health and vigor—there isn't a moral or intellectual point of superiority that doesn't tell, when God holds his assizes and hurls the peoples upon one another. *Die Weltgeschichte ist das Weltgericht;*[1] and Dr. Steinmetz does not believe that in the long run chance and luck play any part in apportioning the issues.

The virtues that prevail, it must be noted, are virtues anyhow, superiorities that count in peaceful as well as in military competition; but the strain on them, being infinitely intenser in the latter case, makes war infinitely more searching as a trial. No ordeal is comparable to its winnowings. Its dread hammer is the welder of men into cohesive states, and nowhere but in such states can human nature adequately develop its capacity. The only alternative is "degeneration."

Dr. Steinmetz is a conscientious thinker, and his book, short as it is, takes much into account. Its upshot can, it seems to me, be summed up in Simon Patten's word, that mankind was nursed in

[1] The history of the world is the judgment of the world.

pain and fear, and that the transition to a "pleasure economy" may be fatal to a being wielding no powers of defense against its disintegrative influences. If we speak of the *fear of emancipation from the fear régime*, we put the whole situation into a single phrase; fear regarding ourselves now taking the place of the ancient fear of the enemy.

Turn the fear over as I will in my mind, it all seems to lead back to two unwillingnesses of the imagination, one æsthetic, and the other moral: unwillingness, first to envisage a future in which army life, with its many elements of charm, shall be forever impossible, and in which the destinies of peoples shall nevermore be decided quickly, thrillingly, and tragically, by force, but only gradually and insipidly by "evolution," and, secondly unwillingness to see the supreme theater of human strenuousness closed, and the splendid military aptitudes of men doomed to keep always in a state of latency and never show themselves in action. These insistent unwillingnesses, no less than other æsthetic and ethical insistencies, have, it seems to me, to be listened to and respected. One cannot meet them effectively by mere counter-insistency on war's expensiveness and horror. The horror makes the thrill; and when the question is of getting the extremest and supremest out of human nature, talk of expense sounds ignominious. The weakness of so much merely negative criticism is evident—pacificism makes no converts from the military party. The military party denies neither the bestiality nor the horror, nor the expense; it only says that these things tell but half the story. It only says that war is *worth* them; that, taking human nature as a whole, its wars are its best protection against its weaker and more cowardly self, and that mankind cannot *afford* to adopt a peace economy.

Pacifists ought to enter more deeply into the æsthetical and ethical point of view of their opponents. Do that first in any controversy, says J. J. Chapman; *then move the point*, and your opponent will follow. So long as anti-militarists propose no substitute for war's disciplinary function, no *moral equivalent* of war, analogous, as one might say, to the mechanical equivalent of heat, so long they fail to realize the full inwardness of the situation. And as a rule they do fail. The duties, penalties, and sanctions pictured in the utopias they paint are all too weak and tame to touch the military minded. Tolstoi's pacificism is the only exception to this rule, for it is profoundly pessimistic as regards all this world's values, and makes the fear of the Lord furnish the moral spur provided elsewhere by the fear of the enemy. But our socialistic peace advocates all believe absolutely in this world's values; and instead of fear of the Lord and the fear of the enemy, the only fear they reckon with is the fear of poverty if one be lazy. This weakness pervades all the socialistic literature with which I am acquainted. Even in Lowes Dickinson's exquisite dialogue,[1] high wages and short hours are the only forces invoked for overcoming man's distaste for repulsive kinds of labor. Meanwhile men at large still live as they always have lived, under a pain-and-fear economy—for those of us who live in an ease economy are but an island in the stormy ocean—and the whole atmosphere of present-day utopian literature tastes mawkish and dishwatery to people who still keep a sense for life's more bitter flavors. It suggests, in truth, ubiquitous inferiority.

Inferiority is always with us, and merciless scorn of it is the keynote of the military temper. "Dogs, would you live forever?" shouted Frederick the Great. "Yes," say our utopians, "let us live forever, and raise our level gradually." The best thing about our "inferiors" to-day is that they are as tough as nails, and physically and morally almost as insensitive. Utopianism would see them soft and squeamish, while militarism would keep their callousness, but transfigure it into a meritorious characteristic needed by "the service" and redeemed by that from the suspicion of inferiority. All the qualities of a man acquire dignity when he knows that the service of the collectivity that owns him needs them. If proud of the collectivity, his own pride rises in proportion. No collectivity is like an army for nourishing such pride; but it has to be confessed that the only sentiment which the image of pacific cosmopolitan industrialism is capable of arousing in countless worthy breasts is shame at the idea of belonging to such a collectivity. It is obvious that the United States of America as they exist to-day impress a mind like General Lea's as so much human blubber. Where is the sharpness and precipitousness, the contempt for life, whether one's own, or another's? Where is the savage "yes" and "no," the unconditional duty? Where is the conscription? Where is the blood tax? Where is anything that one feels honored by belonging to?

Having said thus much in preparation, I will now confess my own utopia. I devoutly believe in the reign of peace and in the gradual advent of some sort of a socialistic equilibrium. The fatal-

[1] *Justice and Liberty.* New York, 1909.

istic view of the war function is to me nonsense, for I know that war-making is due to definite motives and subject to prudential checks and reasonable criticisms, just like any other form of enterprise. And when whole nations are the armies, and the science of destruction vies in intellectual refinement with the sciences of production, I see that war becomes absurd and impossible from its own monstrosity. Extravagant ambitions will have to be replaced by reasonable claims, and nations must make common cause against them. I see no reason why all this should not apply to yellow as well as to white countries, and I look forward to a future when acts of war shall be formally outlawed as between civilized peoples.

All these beliefs of mine put me squarely into the anti-militarist party. But I do not believe that peace either ought to be or will be permanent on this globe, unless the states pacifically organized preserve some of the old elements of army discipline. A permanently successful peace economy cannot be a simple pleasure economy. In the more or less socialistic future towards which mankind seems drifting we must still subject ourselves collectively to these severities which answer to our real position upon this only partly hospitable globe. We must make new energies and hardihoods continue the manliness to which the military mind so faithfully clings. Martial virtues must be the enduring cement; intrepidity, contempt of softness, surrender of private interest, obedience to command, must still remain the rock upon which states are built—unless, indeed, we wish for dangerous reactions against commonwealths fit only for contempt, and liable to invite attack whenever a center of crystallization for military-minded enterprise gets formed anywhere in their neighborhood.

The war party is assuredly right in affirming and reaffirming that the martial virtues, although originally gained by the race through war, are absolute and permanent human goods. Patriotic pride and ambition in their military form are, after all, only specifications of a more general competitive passion. They are its first form, but that is no reason for supposing them to be its last form. Men now are proud of belonging to a conquering nation, and without a murmur they lay down their persons and their wealth, if by so doing they may fend off subjection. But who can be sure that *other aspects of one's country* may not, with time and education and suggestion enough, come to be regarded with similarly effective feelings of pride and shame? Why should men not some

day feel that it is worth a blood tax to belong to a collectivity
superior in *any* ideal respect? Why should they not blush with
indignant shame if the community that owns them is vile in any
way whatsoever? Individuals, daily more numerous, now feel this
civic passion. It is only a question of blowing on the spark till the
whole population gets incandescent, and on the ruins of the old
morals of military honor, a stable system of morals of civic honor
builds itself up. What the whole community comes to believe in
grasps the individual as in a vise. The war function has grasped
us so far; but constructive interests may some day seem no
less imperative, and impose on the individual a hardly lighter
burden.

Let me illustrate my idea more concretely. There is nothing
to make one indignant in the mere fact that life is hard, that men
should toil and suffer pain. The planetary conditions once for all
are such, and we can stand it. But that so many men, by mere
accidents of birth and opportunity, should have a life of *nothing
else* but toil and pain and hardness and inferiority imposed upon
them, should have *no* vacation while others natively no more deserving never get any taste of this campaigning life at all,—*this*
is capable of arousing indignation in reflective minds. It may
end by seeming shameful to all of us that some of us have nothing
but campaigning, and others nothing but unmanly ease. If now—
and this is my idea—there were, instead of military conscription a
conscription of the whole youthful population to form for a certain
number of years a part of the army enlisted against *Nature*, the
injustice would tend to be evened out, and numerous other goods
to the commonwealth would follow. The military ideals of hardihood and discipine would be wrought into the growing fiber of the
people; no one would remain blind as the luxurious classes now are
blind, to man's real relations to the globe he lives on, and to the
permanently sour and hard foundations of his higher life. To coal
and iron mines, to freight trains, to fishing fleets in December,
to dishwashing, clothes washing, and window washing, to road
building and tunnel making, to foundries and stokeholes, and to
the frames of skyscrapers, would our gilded youths be drafted off,
according to their choice, to get the childishness knocked out of
them, and to come back into society with healthier sympathies and
soberer ideas. They would have paid their blood tax, done their
own part in the immemorial human warfare against nature, they

would tread the earth more proudly, the women would value them more highly, they would be better fathers and teachers of the following generation.

Such a conscription, with the state of public opinion that would have required it, and the many moral fruits it would bear, would preserve in the midst of a pacific civilization the manly virtues which the military party is so afraid of seeing disappear in peace. We should get toughness without callousness, authority with as little criminal cruelty as possible, and painful work done cheerily because the duty is temporary, and threatens not, as now, to degrade the whole remainder of one's life. I spoke of the ''moral equivalent'' of war. So far, war has been the only force that can discipline a whole community, and until an equivalent discipline is organized, I believe that war must have its way. But I have no serious doubt that the ordinary prides and shames of social man, once developed to a certain intensity, are capable of organizing such a moral equivalent as I have sketched, or some other just as effective for preserving manliness of type. It is but a question of time, of skilful propagandism, and of opinion-making men seizing historic opportunities.

The martial type of character can be bred without war. Strenuous honor and disinterestedness abound elsewhere. Priests and medical men are in a fashion educated to it, and we should all feel some degree of it imperative if we were conscious of our work as an obligatory service to the state. We should be *owned,* as soldiers are by the army, and our pride would rise accordingly. We could be poor, then, without humiliation, as army officers now are. The only thing needed henceforward is to inflame the civic temper as past history has inflamed the military temper. H. G. Wells, as usual, sees the center of the situation. ''In many ways,'' he says, ''military organization is the most peaceful of activities. When the contemporary man steps from the street of clamorous insincere advertisement, push, adulteration, underselling and intermittent employment, into the barrack yard, he steps on to a higher social plane, into an atmosphere of service and coöperation and of infinitely more honorable emulations. Here at least men are not flung out of employment to degenerate because there is no immediate work for them to do. They are fed and drilled and trained for better services. Here at least a man is supposed to win promotion by self-forgetfulness and not by self-seeking. And beside the feeble and irregular endowment of research by commercialism, its little short-sighted snatches at profit by innovation and scientific economy, see how remarkable is the steady and rapid development of method and appliances in naval and military affairs! Nothing is more striking than to compare the progress of civil conveniences which has been left almost entirely to the trader, to the progress in military apparatus during the last few decades. The house appliances of to-day, for example, are little better than they were fifty years ago. A house of to-day is still almost as ill-ventilated, badly heated by wasteful fires, clumsily arranged and furnished as the house of 1858. Houses a couple of hundred years old are still satisfactory places of residence, so little have our standards risen. But the rifle or battleship of fifty years ago was beyond all comparison inferior to those we possess; in power, in speed, in convenience alike. No one has a use now for such superannuated things.'' [1]

Wells adds [2] that he thinks that the conceptions of order and discipline, the tradition of service and devotion, of physical fitness, unstinted exertion, and universal responsibility, which universal military duty is now teaching European nations, will remain a permanent acquisition, when the last ammunition has been used in the fireworks that celebrate the final peace. I believe as he does. It would be simply preposterous if the only force that could work ideals of honor and standards of efficiency into English or American natures should be the fear of being killed by the Germans or the Japanese. Great indeed is Fear; but it is not, as our military enthusiasts believe and try to make us believe, the only stimulus known for awakening the higher ranges of men's spiritual energy. The amount of alteration in public opinion which my utopia postulates is vastly less than the difference between the mentality of those black warriors who pursued Stanley's party on the Congo with their cannibal war cry of ''Meat! Meat!'' and that of the ''general staff'' of any civilized nation. History has seen the latter interval bridged over: the former one can be bridged over much more easily.

[1] *First and Last Things*, 1908, p. 215.
[2] *Ibid.*, p. 226.

THE FUTURE OF MILITARISM[1]

G. Lowes Dickinson

[Goldsworthy Lowes Dickinson, essayist and philosopher, is Fellow and Lecturer at King's College, Cambridge, and Lecturer at the London School of Economics and Political Science. In 1912-13 he traveled in India, China, and Japan on the Otto Kahn Fellowship. He has also traveled and lectured in America. The fundamental purpose of his writings is a critical examination of the social, political, and philosophical ideas of modern civilization. As a lover of the contemplative life he has been appreciative of the virtues of a less active civilization than ours, and his *Letters from a Chinese Official,* published in 1903, present eloquently the Chinese desire to protect oriental ideals from western commercialism. As a classicist Dickinson also draws upon Greek literature and philosophy in his criticism of modern life. He has used the literary form of the Platonic dialogue in his *Justice and Liberty, The Meaning of Good,* and *A Modern Symposium.* In *The Greek View of Life* he has given us an idealized paganism. His volume of traveler's notes, *Appearances,* contains a critical section concerning the United States. His earlier writings belong to history and philosophy by subject matter, but their classic beauty of style gives them a place in literature. Of late, he has turned to more immediate public problems, especially to war and peace, and he has exercised a wide-reaching influence upon public opinion. *The Future of Militarism* is the first chapter of *The Choice Before Us,* published in 1917. The volume is a notable contribution to thought on militarism and internationalism.]

The political relations of the European States have consisted for centuries past of war and preparation for war. In the present war, this practice has culminated in a catastrophe which, it might seem, must lead to a reaction. Perhaps it may. But it certainly will not do so, unless it be by a deliberate and conscious change in the ideas and the wills of men. Meantime people already talk of the "next war." It is therefore important to make some forecast of what kind of a war that is likely to be, and, more generally, what kind of a future the continuation and extension of militarism would prepare for mankind.

A Russian general, Skugarewski, has recently attempted a forecast of the next war,[1] which he anticipates in ten or twenty years,

---

[1] Reprinted by permission of Dodd, Mead and Co., from *The Choice Before Us.* Questions and topics for the discussions of this essay, and of other phases of the general subject with which it deals, will be found on pages 530 and 533.

[2] See the Russian Supplement to *The Times* of July 29, 1916, which reproduces the general's contribution to the *Russkoe Slovo.*

if Germany is not "conclusively conquered." He starts by remarking that every war he can remember, beginning from the
Crimean War, was an "unprecedented" war; and his moral is
that "humanity must at last learn how to prepare for war." "In
the future struggle of nations all men capable of bearing arms
will be taken into the ranks of the nations' armies, and for them
everything will be ready in peace-time." This will mean that
Russia will have an army of forty millions and Germany of twenty
millions. For an army of forty million men three hundred thousand officers will be required. To secure them "it will be necessary
to introduce conscription for officers: all young men who have received not even complete middle-school education will be obliged
to serve as officers." Further, it will be necessary to replace, so
far as possible, by women the men who under existing arrangements are kept in the rear by non-combatant duties. Perhaps
therefore "it will be necessary to introduce conscription for girls
and childless widows, so that more men can be sent to the front."
As to armaments, "there will be required for such an army one
hundred thousand guns, a million maxims, tens of thousands of
motorcars, armoured, freight, and light cars. By the beginning
of the war at least fifty million gun-projectiles must be prepared,
and five thousand million rifle cartridges. Besides machine-gun
detachments, each company of a regiment will have its portable
machine guns on light stands." Aviation, of course, "will receive
special development." "It is clear that in ten to twenty years
every State will reckon the numbers of its dirigibles in thousands
and the number of its aeroplanes in tens, if not hundreds of thousands. The dropping of shells from above on to large stretches of
country will be extensively practised. And if the laws of war permit the application of inflammable materials and substances for
the development of poisonous gases, then the raids of aerial flotillas
will instantly convert large districts of several square versts [1] into
complete deserts where every vestige of animal and vegetable life
will be slain and where large units of armies will be annihilated
to a single man." The range of guns will be enormously increased
and "perhaps Dover will be shelled from Calais." The general
proceeds to estimate the cost of such a war at twenty millions a
day. The peace establishment of Russia will cost a hundred
millions a year.

"Besides the existing material conscriptions, it may perhaps be

[1] Such as London or Berlin—Author.

necessary to introduce conscription for grain, meat, and fodder. All industrial establishments—mills, factories, workshops, even handicraftsmen—on declaration of war will have to work for the army in accordance with a special plan of mobilization." In short, "expedients for the extermination of humanity will be of such a nature that everything of which we hear nowadays will pale in comparison. The number of killed will be reckoned by millions, of wounded by tens of millions."

This is not a romance by Mr. Wells. It is a very sober description, certainly not overdrawn, of what is likely to occur in that "next war" to which so many people are already looking forward.[1] Let us carry the description a little further.

And, first, as to methods of war. It is as probable as anything can be that these will be of a kind which will make the worst that has been done in this war seem by comparison like humanity and kindness. Not only will every weapon that has been used in this war be employed in the next, except those that have been rendered obsolete by the invention of worse ones, but science will have discovered new and far more destructive means of murder. We have long applied chemistry to war; but we have not begun to apply bacteriology. In the future, the deliberate spread of lethal diseases among the enemy is likely to be a principal and recognized method of destruction. Further the war will be waged, without any restriction, on non-combatants. Already a German professor[2] has written a book to show that this is permitted by the "new" law of nations, created by the experiences of this war. And, of course, the logic of war is in favour of it. For a munition-worker, or a producer of any kind, is just as much helping the enemy to win the war as a soldier at the front.

We must therefore expect that in any future war any and every weapon of extermination will be used freely against non-combatants as well as combatants. Rules of war may be drawn up to prevent this. But the issues of a modern war are so tremendous, that such rules are likely to break at the first tension put upon

---

[1] "I believe it to be a fact that there are some people going about even now saying, and trying to induce other people to believe, that we should never have another war. All I can say is that in my humble opinion the people who say it either wittingly or unwittingly are nothing more or less than traitors to their country" (Lord Lilford, at Thrapston. Quoted in *Labour Leader*, August 12, 1915).

[2] Dr. Paul Eltzbacher, formerly rector of the Hochschule at Berlin, in his book *Totes und Lebendiges Völkerrecht*. München and Leipzig: Duncker u. Humbolt. See *Blätter für Zwischenstaatliche Organisation*. July 1916, p. 210.

them. One combatant succumbs to one temptation, another to another. Each breach of the law by one is followed by breaches by the others, under guise of reprisals. Neither religion, morals, nor humanity have availed to arrest this process in the present war. Why should we suppose they will be more potent in the future?

But destruction by war does not end with the lives of the immediate sufferers. Every man of sound stock who is killed childless extinguishes with himself whole generations. But it is the sound that are killed in war, and the unsound preserved, for it is the sound that are selected to go to the front. Further, among those that survive, men and women, the conditions of war tend to disseminate over wider and wider areas venereal and other diseases, and this again reacts upon the stock. So that, whoever wins or loses the war, winners and losers alike have impaired irremediably the strength of their nation. War may preserve liberty for posterity, but it is a posterity weakened and enfeebled that will enjoy it.

War, then, means not merely the destruction of the best among the living, but an irreparable impoverishment of the race; and that on a scale proportional to the scale of the war. But the scale of modern wars is world-wide. So, therefore, is the impoverishment. War is a way of racial suicide. Soldiers and statesmen do not think of such remote effects; but they do not cease to happen because they are not thought of. And in comparison with them victory or defeat, and the other results of war, are negligible in the balance.

Let us turn now from the biological to the social effects of war. War implies preparation for war. And if the international anarchy is to continue, so that States are compelled to arm against one another, each driving on each to ever more tremendous efforts, there can be no pause in the process and no limit to it. We have no right to dismiss as improbable, still less as impossible, any extremity that lies in the logic of the movement. Let us therefore without shrinking develop that logic to the full.

First, universal service will be introduced as a permanent institution into the countries that have hitherto escaped it; and it is probable that it will be organized on the complete Prussian model. There are, I am aware, some who look forward to what they call a "popular" army, such as is maintained in Switzerland and was proposed for France by Jaurès. Their idea is, first, that an army may be organized for defence only, and not for offence. Secondly, that it may be so organized that it cannot become the instrument of a military caste. A full discussion of these points is not possible here; but there are one or two obvious considerations which must be borne in mind. In the first place, there is not, and cannot be, any clear and universally accepted distinction between offence and defence, until there is an international agreement as to what shall constitute offence. Every nation in every war that I have ever heard of has claimed to be on the defensive. The mere act of declaring war, or of taking the first step in war, cannot be accepted as proof of aggression, for it may be merely a reasonable precaution of defence. It may be urged that the act of invasion should be the test of offence, and that an army of defence must never cross the frontier. But would any military authority accept that view? And, in particular, is it applicable to this country, where in any future war the transport of an army to the Continent will be the first necessity, if any of our continental allies are also involved? The Territorials were enlisted for home defence; and we see what has come of that, under the first pressure of war. The distinction, then, between an army for offence and an army for defence is unreal and must remain unreal, unless and until we have a system of international agreements and guarantees which would transform the whole situation out of which wars arise.

Secondly, whatever organization be adopted for an army, however short the period to be spent in barracks, however democratic the method of recruiting and promotion, it does not seem possible that a force on the modern scale of numbers and efficiency could be maintained without the aid of a very large class of professional officers, and without giving to these a large measure of social prestige and political influence. The British tradition, whereby the officer rarely appears in uniform, and is not felt in time of peace as an element in society or in politics, must disappear, it would seem, with the permanent adoption of universal service. The more numerous, highly-trained, and intelligent the officer caste, the more influential they will become. And as they will be trained exclusively for war, and will regard war both as their own sole business and as the sole business of the nation, they are not likely to abstain from bringing their influence to bear upon foreign policy. But such political influence of an officer caste is precisely one of the most important elements in militarism. And the moment officers begin to wear their uniforms in time of peace will be the moment when militarism starts to run its course in England.

In any case, whatever form of military organization be adopted, we shall have everywhere universal service; and that, as General Skugarewski foresees, on a scale hitherto unknown in history. Every man between the ages, let us say, of 17 and 50, will be liable to military service. Boys under 17 will have compulsory "preliminary training" as boy scouts, in officers' training corps, and the like. Women and girls will be enrolled for the various noncombatant services—unless indeed, which is quite possible, it be decided to raise combatant corps of amazons. In any case, the question of the fitness of people for military service, in character or temperament or conviction, will not enter into consideration. In the past, in pagan societies—ancient India, for example, or Japan —men were selected as soldiers by their own choice or by hereditary aptitude. In the twentieth century of Him who came to bring peace among mankind, we do not hesitate to compel all men into the army without reference to their aptitude or choice, and in defiance of their moral, religious, or political scruples. Thus, as conscription extends, so does the necessity of persecution. And if international war is to continue, persecution will be established as an institution in all countries.

Having forced the men (and the women it may be) into the army, the next thing will be to train them. What the object of military training is was once summed up as follows by a military officer. "The one object," he said, "of a military system is to overcome a man's natural reluctance to kill and to be killed. To accomplish this we have three devices. The first is to make the soldier more afraid of his own officers than he is of the enemy. The second is to convert him into an automaton by perpetual drill, so that he obeys instinctively every order given without any intervention of his own choice or will. The third device is a just cause." This last device is rather the business of the politicians than the soldiers, and it is one they very well understand. As to the others there seems to be some question, in modern warfare, as to the extent to which it is necessary to destroy the soldier's individuality. But it can hardly be doubtful that the more it is possible to overcome beforehand, not only his reluctance to kill and to be killed, but his squeamishness as to methods of killing, the better soldier he will be. And we may expect developments in this direction which would surprise and shock our present susceptibilities, formed, as they have been, in and for peace.

But to make a nation efficient for war it will not be enough to conscript the whole population, to train them in the use of any and every weapon, and to counteract their humane instincts. Much more important will be the religious and moral training. The soul as well as the body of a good soldier must be militarized; and for this purpose a new direction must be given to the State religion. Exactly how revolutionary the change must be it is not easy to say. The attitude of the clergy in the present war has shown that the apparent teaching of the Gospels need not interfere with an enthusiastic support of war by ministers of a Christian Church; and that, in the view of many, the dispensation of Jesus left standing in full authority that of the God of the Jews. The Sermon on the Mount, we have been told in effect, was merely a string of amiable metaphors. The real Jesus Whom we are to treat as our Master was the one Who used the scourge of small cords in the Temple, not the one who bade us turn the other cheek. When He said, "Greater love hath no man than this, that he give his life for his friend," what He meant was that we are to kill our enemies. And when He said, "Render unto Cæsar the things that are Cæsar's," He already by anticipation condemned those who, in the future, in His name, might refuse military service. This adaptability of Christianity, as professed by the Churches, suggests that its forms might still be preserved even in an era of universal militarism. Nor need we be troubled by the fact that Christianity is a universal religion, and that all Christians are supposed to worship the same God. For we have seen also, in this war, that each nation can claim, with the full support of its Church, that its national god is really the universal god; so that Christian nations may not only fight against one another with a good conscience, but each may be sure, in so doing, that it is fighting for the true God, Who is being denied by its enemies.

There seems, then, on the whole, good reason to think that the forms of Christianity may still continue to direct the militaristic societies of the future. At the same time we must make no mistake about the reality. The real religion of the future, if war is to continue, will be the religion of the God-State; for the essential requirement will be an unquestioning submission to the will of the State. It is this that has given such moral strength to the Germans in the present war, and the fact will be noted and its lesson applied by other nations.

The essence of this religion, stated without compromise or qualification, is as follows: The State is the purpose and end for which individuals come into existence. It is a god; and, like other gods, it is mysterious. Its nature is unknowable and undefinable. This does not prevent the existence of whole libraries of "Statology" about It or Him. But these volumes do not really serve, and are not intended to serve, to dispel the darkness. The State is something supernatural. It is not the sum of its members. It is not their trend, their purpose, or their impulse. It works through governmental agents, who may be called its priests. But it is not they. It works upon the people, but it is not they. Neither their happiness nor their well-being, nor even the well-being of the Government, is its purpose. Its purpose is Its own Being and Power. It has, in fact, only one point of contact with its worshippers: it demands their sacrifice to itself. A sacrifice complete, unreserved, unquestioning; a sacrifice not only of their lives (that is little) but of their most profound instincts, their most passionate feelings, their deepest convictions. They must have no conscience but its, no belief but its, no cause but its. They must be its slaves, not body only, but mind and soul. They are nothing; It is all.

I am aware that this expression of the militarist theory of the State will be repudiated, even by Germans. Of course they do not so express it. But they imply all that has been here expressed, though no doubt they may be unaware of the implications. Not only so, but much that is said and thought in other countries, not excluding England, really involves the same presuppositions. I shall have occasion later to return to this point, when I consider the theory of foreign policy. At present, what interests me is the connexion of the theory with war. The unquestioning and uncritical sacrifice demanded in the name of the State is for the purpose of extending its power by war. The State is a god of war, as once the God of the Jews was. And that is why the religion of the State will more and more drive out every other, if the process of militarizing the world continues. Other countries, in this respect, will follow the lead of Germany. And the philosophy we have been repudiating as devilish because Germany was our enemy, we shall end by adopting ourselves in order to be the better prepared to fight her. We may expect that, in a militarist future, this doctrine of the God-State, in essence if not in set terms, will be taught in every school, college, university, and pulpit. Thus, both before and after the period of actual military training, the citizen will be prepared and confirmed for his main business in life by every form of spiritual exhortation. Education will mean training for war. The effort to teach men to think and judge for themselves will be eliminated. For nothing could be more directly opposed than this to the cult of the State and of war. That cult requires what is rather a discipline than an education. The student must be taught dogmatically.what the purposes of life are; not permitted, still less encouraged, to examine the question for himself. He must be taught from infancy up, that he came into the world to sacrifice himself in war; that the reason of this is a mystery; and that into that mystery it is blasphemy and pride for the human reason to pry.

We have spoken so far of that part of education (the most important part) which is concerned with the purposes of life and which (as we shall doubtless be told) in all well-organized States has always rested on revelation. Upon this depends all the rest. The teaching of morals must of course conform to that of religion; and the religion of the God-State will require a different code to that which has hitherto been professed by Christians. The old profession must now be brought into accord with the new practice required by the age of war. Pity, gentleness, charity, must not merely not be practised, they must be branded as crimes against the social order; the practical lessons in brutality which will form the main part of military training must be reinforced by preaching, teaching, and example at every stage of life; and for the cult of humanity which has increasingly prevailed in democratic societies we must substitute the Nietzschean formula "Be hard."

The new religion and the new ethics will be accompanied by a new development of scientific teaching. For science will be more necessary than ever in the strenuous competition that lies before us. It will be necessary for industry. On that I need not dwell. But above all it will be necessary for war. The nation, we shall be told, that is most successful in inventing new methods of destruction will be the nation that will "survive"; and we shall be urged no longer to hamper our efforts by the scruples and limitations of a romantic tradition and a system of pseudo-law. What this may imply in the actual invention of lethal weapons it would be idle to try to forecast. But to one thing we must make up our minds. Whenever there emerges, in any generous young soul, the passion for truth and the genius for discovery, he will be seized upon by society and urged, nay compelled, to devote his idealism not to the perfecting but to the destruction of human life. The perversion of the intellect will follow from the perversion of the soul. And reason, distorted from its trend to comprehend truth and serve mankind, will become more devilish than ever mere bestiality could be, and make of man something as infinitely lower than the brutes as he had it in him to be infinitely higher. Germany boasts that she has introduced into the world the new gospel of "organization." Perhaps she has. But if war is to continue, and to govern all the effort of men, the gospel of organization is the gospel of Satanism.

The development of religion and education which I have thus sketched is likely to be accompanied by a transformation of political institutions. Democracy is a bad medium for war. For democracy, in the first place, is hard to discipline. That goes without saying. And for that reason alone lovers of discipline look upon it with mistrust. In the second place, democracy is averse from, and perhaps incapable of, policies looking far ahead. Its essence is responsiveness to the movements of public opinion; and public opinion, in a free democracy, is always in movement. But war, and the policies war subserves, require long views. It is not without reason that, even in democratic countries, foreign policy, and the military and naval policy which is its handmaid, has been withdrawn as far as possible from popular control. But that withdrawal has not been sufficient. The democracies have not been able to prepare with the deliberation and thoroughness of the autocracies. This is true both of England and of France. As to England, it would be superfluous to repeat here the condemnation that has been dealt out to our government, both from militarists and from pacifists. As to France, we have the interesting record of M. Sembat's book: "Faites un roi. Sinon faites la paix." M. Sembat is (or was) a democrat and a socialist. But he deliberately affirmed, before the war, and it is hardly likely that he has changed his view since, that a Republic was incompetent to prepare adequately for war against an autocracy, and that either France must make up her quarrel with Germany, or she must convert herself into a monarchy. By dint of an unexampled coalition of forces, the inadequacy of preparation in the two democracies has been counterbalanced by the greater resources. But how near a thing it has been! How immense has been and is the technical superiority of the autocracy! The "militarism" we condemn in Germany is a condition of efficiency for war. And if war is to continue, other nations must adopt it, in its political as well as its other manifestations. The franker organs of our militarists at home, like the *Morning Post,* have recognized that from the beginning of the war. And even before the war the same view was set forth in militarist publications with a candor and a force which opponents of militarism should be the first to recognize.

I may refer, in this connexion, to a remarkable book by Captain Ross, entitled *Representative Government and War,* published in 1903, and based in part upon the experience acquired in the Boer War. This book, had it had the good fortune to become known in Germany, would doubtless have aroused as much attention there as the book of General Bernhardi did in England. Its philosophy is the same, its frankness is as complete, its brutality as uncompromising. It justifies beforehand, in principle if not in set terms, everything the Germans have done; their declaration of war, their invasion of Belgium, their methods of conducting war. It is not, however, on that aspect of the matter that I desire now to dwell. It is the political views of the author to which I could call attention. The form of government which he admires is that of Germany; and he desires, by a *coup d'état* or otherwise, to convert the government of England into that form. He points out that the preparation for war is not only military but political; that the publicity, or comparative publicity, of parliamentary government not only makes more difficult the appropriation of enormous funds to armaments and secret service, but also hampers that preparation for war by diplomacy which is essential if war is to be made at the right moment against the right enemy. For the only business of diplomacy is to make war; not defensive, but aggressive war. The gallant captain perceives that such objects cannot be avowed by governments and would hardly be tolerated by peoples. His remedy for this disastrous state of things is to remove from even the shadow of popular control not only the administration of the armed forces and the conduct of war, but the whole of foreign policy. He would make the King commander-in-chief, and allow him to govern through three military chiefs, who should direct not only the forces but the diplomacy of the country. He sees no hope of achieving this purpose (short of a *coup d'état*) until the country has accepted conscription. For only a conscript people will tolerate military

rule. Thus he definitely desires universal service, not only for
military but also, and mainly, for political purposes; he desires
it as a means to destroy free government and put the country
under the heel of a military dictatorship. For his grudging
admission—"it is too much to expect of the British race that
it shall make matters of internal administration in any way subject to the will of an autocrat, and it is unnecessary"—still leaves
the people without any say in what is most important to their
welfare, crushed under an ever increasing burden of armaments,
and subject, at least once in a generation, to wars becoming
ever more destructive not only of life but of humanity itself.

Some readers may be inclined to set aside a book of this kind
as the raving of a madman. But to do so would be to do injustice
to the author and to his position. Granted certain assumptions—
the struggle for existence between States, the consequent necessity of war, the subordination of home to foreign policy, the
conception that the main aim of the latter is to prepare aggressive war—granted, in fact, the philosophy of militarism, and all
the contentions of the author follow. And unless we root militarism out of our minds and souls (its real dwelling-place) and
in consequence out of our institutions, national and international,
we have no defense against that logic and therefore none against
the policies it engenders. Let the international anarchy and
international war continue, and there is an end of political liberty. What those who hate this prospect have most to fear is
that they should be dupes of their own optimism. The connexion
between war and autocracy is essential. We see it immediately
when we are actually at war. Thus, during the last two years
we have abandoned to the Executive liberty of person and of
speech. We have sat still and watched while a Government department abolished the Habeas Corpus Act. We have reintro-
duced religious persecution, and condemned young men to death
and sent them to penal servitude for obeying their consciences;
and we have permitted the military authorities to take charge
not only of the policing of the country, but of the expression
and formation of opinion. Democrats no doubt flatter themselves that they will recover their liberties and their constitution
after the war. But whether they will or no depends on whether
or no the international anarchy is to continue. If it is, the
nation will be cajoled and bullied to sacrifice its political liberty to the need of national defence. By that kind of imperceptible

process by which our constitution develops, the military authority will thrust aside the civilian; and we shall find ourselves living under a Prussian system, without having ever taken a clear decision in the matter or at any moment definitely surrendered our liberties and rights. Meantime the discipline and training which I have described will be operating on the younger generation. So that it will not be long before they have lost even the remembrance of liberty, and become as proud of their passive abnegation before an officer caste as any German can be. Political liberty has been the capital achievement of the British race. But it, above all things, is threatened by the rising flood of militarism. And while it thinks it stands, it may well take heed lest it falls.

The militarism of which I have thus outlined the possible development is primarily a European phenonemon. The Far East (with the very notable exception of Japan) and the Far West are as yet hardly touched by it. For that reason, those parts of the world are the hope of the world. But then, their development is strictly conditioned by that of Europe. For the world is now one, for evil as well as for good. Every contagion spreads, and every cause produces effects round the whole girdle of the globe. Turning first to the United States of America, we find that that great country—the greatest potential force, material, moral, and spiritual, in the world—has realized, with a shock of dismay, that it is no longer isolated from the European madness. It is part of the system, or rather the anarchy, of States. Americans can on longer disconnect themselves from the chain of international policy. Their future is bound up with the future of Europe. Either they must arm for self-defence, and by so doing join and exasperate the international anarchy; or they must combine with the European Powers to end it. That is what President Wilson has realized, and what he has been saying to a skeptical and uncomprehending Europe. This question of the American attitude is the crucial one for civilization as a whole, and for that of Europe in particular. For once let the United States arm on the European scale, once let the Far East do the same, and where will Europe be? If the West and the East do not combine with Europe to stay this madness they will be driven to participate in it, to the ruin of Europe as well as of themselves. To reject the overtures of President Wilson at this crisis is to reject what is perhaps the last hope of civilization. Let me, then, cite his words, for they are too little known in this country :—

We are not mere disconnected lookers on. The longer the war lasts, the more deeply do we become concerned. . . . When it comes to an end we shall be as much concerned as the nations at war to see peace assume an aspect of permanence that will give promise of days from which anxiety and uncertainty shall be lifted and bring some assurance that peace and war shall hereafter be reckoned as part of the common interest of mankind. We are participants, whether we would or not, in the life of the world. The interests of all the nations are our own also. We are partners with the rest. What affects mankind is inevitably our affair as well as the affair of the nations of Asia and Europe.

The repeated utterances of the leading statesmen of most of the great nations now engaged in war have made it plain that their thought has come to this—that the principle of public right must henceforth take precedence over the individual interests of particular nations, and that the nations of the world must in some way band themselves together to see that right prevails as against any sort of selfish aggression; that henceforth Alliance must not be set up against Alliance, Understanding against Understanding, but that there must be a common agreement for a common object, and that at the heart of that common object must lie the inviolable rights of people and of mankind. . . . This is undoubtedly the thought of America, this is what we ourselves will say when there comes the proper occasion to say it. In the dealings of nations with one another arbitrary force must be rejected, and we must move forward to the thought of the modern world, the thought of which peace is the very atmosphere. That thought constitutes the chief part of the passionate conviction of America. We believe these fundamental things:—

Firstly: That every people has the right to choose the sovereignty under which they shall live.

Like other nations, we have ourselves, no doubt, once and again offended against that principle when for a little while controlled by selfish passion, as our franker historians have been honourable enough to admit, but it has become more and more our rule of life and action.

Secondly: That the small States of the world have the right to enjoy the same respect for their sovereignty and for their territorial integrity that the great and powerful nations expect and insist upon.

Thirdly: That the world has the right to be free from every disturbance to its peace that has its origin in aggression and the disregard of the rights of peoples and nations.

So sincerely do we believe in these things, that I am sure I speak the mind and wish of the people of America when I say that the United States is willing to become a partner in any feasible association of nations formed in order to realize these objects and to make them secure against violation.[1]

[1] Since this speech was made the President has reaffirmed the position then taken up, most notably in his speech to the Senate of January 22, 1917, and

So speaks America to Europe.　How will Europe respond? Accept, and America comes in to save civilization.　Refuse, and she arms, whether she will or no, to destroy it.

And now look East.　It is the same alternative.　China, next to, perhaps even beyond, the United States, is a storehouse of potential energy with which all Europe would contend in vain once it were developed.　But Europe is compelling its development; compelling it not only in the economic but in, the military sense.　For centuries China has preached and acted on the gospel of peace.　Europe, taking advantage of her weakness, mocks at the philosophy which has led to it.　Europe is as anxious to instruct her in war as to instruct her in industry.　Well, in both, Europe is prevailing.　Listen to the words of a Chinese Confucian, and see what thoughts European policies have forced upon these men who once believed in reason:—

The contact of China with Europe in the last two decades has revived the martial spirit of the people, which died out in the middle of the Manchu reign.　The rise of Japan as a military Power has set them an admirable and practical example.　This European conflict has again brought home to them the absolute necessity of an adequate efficient army and navy for the security of their national independence and existence. To the intelligent Chinese of the present generation no person appears to deserve a more appropriate worship than the Krupp engineer who produces a 75-cm. gun, and no nation can give a better lead than the one that raises a voluntary army of three millions in a short period of six months. To cite an instance, I might be permitted to give an extract of a letter I received from a Chinese schoolboy who was expecting to go to America. The letter says: "Having finished my secondary education, I am not entering any university in China.　I solemnly hope that in the future I shall be a Hindenburg or a Pétain.　Germany and France being now at war, I am going to be trained as a soldier in the land of Generals Jackson and Lee."

To fight is the nature of man!　To urge man to fight is the nature of woman!　To this the Chinese are no exception.　Courage, patience, and endurance, which form their physical and moral character, are the basis of the good soldier.　Lord Wolseley, speaking with his personal experience of the China War, says that the Chinese soldier is a mighty and worthy foe.　Lord Curzon, criticizing the Sino-Japanese War, admits that, man for man, the Chinese are superior to their opponents.　It only needs training to utilize these soldierly qualities and to create a gallant army and a mighty navy for the defence of the country and for its war of liberation.

In the last five years Bill after Bill has been considered by the Govern-

again in the speech in which he announced the entry of the United States into the war.

ment for universal conscription; proposal after proposal has been submitted to President Yuan Shih-Kai for the extension of arsenals and the establishment of shipbuilding yards. The War Office is busily engaged in training army officers and the Admiralty in training naval cadets. Flying schools have been opened, flying corps have been formed; cavalry, artillery, infantry, commissariat, Boy Scouts, Red Cross nurses, and even Woman Volunteer Corps—all have come into being, and all will grow to full strength in time. It is certain that once the foundation has been laid, the structure will be firm; and that once the seeds have been sown the fruits will be wholesome. It may take them fifty years or more before they can be tested in the field, but the day will come when their sinews of war have been provided through the opening up of their resources, when their strategic railways have been extensively built, and when their national education has been speeded up—the day will come when China, possessing one-fourth of the world's population, and occupying an area twenty times as great as Great Britain, will adequately defend her vast Empire and claim the voice and place to which she is entitled in the family of nations.[1]

We see, then, that the prospect I have been opening out extends far beyond Europe. There is no part or corner of the world which is not threatened. Militarism spreads like an epidemic. And either we must cut it off, root and branch, here in Europe, or we must look forward to its extension East and West, to return thence against ourselves and consummate by destruction from without our own internecine strife. Europe is not only committing *harikari;* she is at the same time arming the hand that is to strike off her head, after she has made the fatal cut.[2]

[1] *Clare Market Review*, "The Action and Reaction of the War in China," by S. G. Cheng.

[2] Since this chapter was written a book has been published by a M. Alphonse Séché entitled *Les Guerres d'Enfer* (Deuxième Édition. E. Sansot, Paris, 1915), which develops at length the positions of this chapter. It is to be noted that, by a fatalism too common among French intellectuals, the author regards the whole process as "inevitable." This war is only the prelude to centuries of wars on a scale and of an intensity of destructiveness of which this is only the foretaste.

Page 322.—Methods of Warfare

1. *Submarining.*

The fact that the British in this war have not found it necessary to imitate German methods of warfare at sea cannot pru-
dently be taken as prophetic of the conduct of such warfare in
the future. Holding the command of the seas, we have been able
to carry on our blockade without too violent a breach with the
traditional sea-law. But the submarine has none the less altered
the whole position. And already before this war a distinguished
British authority both foresaw and justified the policy which the
Germans have adopted. Writing in *The Times* a fortnight before
the war broke out, Sir Percy Scott said that a declaration of
blockade accompanied by the threat to sink by submarines and
mines ships attempting to break the blockade "would in my
opinion be perfectly in order; and once it had been made, if
any British or neutral ships disregarded it and attempted to run
the blockade they would not be held to be engaged in peaceable
occupations and avocations, and if they were sunk in the attempt
it would not be describable as a relapse into savagery or piracy
in the blackest form" (*The Times,* July 16, 1914).

2. *Air Raids.*

After long hesitation the British have now (1917) sanctioned
reprisals in kind for the German air raids. The French suc-
cumbed earlier to the temptation, as the following official German
account of the Karlsruhe raid may illustrate:—

"It was obviously no mere coincidence that the French chose
Corpus Christi Day for their raid. They knew that on this great
Catholic festival, under the bright sunshine, crowds of people,
athirst for light and air, would be sure to stream through the
streets and squares. That it was people's lives they aimed at is
proved by the sort of bombs they threw. Incendiary bombs were
only used in small number. Nearly all the bombs were small,

but filled with very strong explosives. They thus broke into very small splinters and destroyed the maximum of human lives, their effect being increased by poisonous gases. Their preparations and intentions had only too great a success. On the Karlsruhe Festplatz, where Hagenbeck's zoo had erected tents, there moved a joyous crowd. Happy children's laughter mingled with the sounds of music. . . . Before there was time to bring the people into safety the first shots fell. . . . The enemy's worst destruction was . . . achieved around the Festplatz amongst the innocent children, who a few minutes before had been so happy. When the French airmen disappeared a quarter of an hour later they could boast of having killed 117 people . . . of whom 82 were children, . . . and wounded 140 people . . . of whom 72 were children. . . ."

On this the *New York Evening Post* comments (June 27, 1915): "Such is the latest record of legitimate warfare under the recognized form of 'reprisals'! Does the human conscience find any justification for such savagery in the fact that Karlsruhe has only been punished for what the Germans have done in France and England? Even in colonial warfare, against tribes who tortured their prisoners and maimed the dead, the nations of Europe have not resorted to reprisals on women and children. . . . It is an outbreak of primitive brutality which fitly marks the status of European 'civilization' after two years of war."

It must be remembered that even the existing international law sanctions the bombardment from the air of "defended" places, and that every great capital is in this sense "defended." Thus London, in the German view, is a "fortress." So, of course, is Antwerp; and in reference to the first Zeppelin raid on that city *The Times* wrote:—

"It marks the beginning of a new epoch in the conflicts of mankind. . . . Much indignation was expended yesterday, much of it was misdirected. Antwerp is a formidable fortress, protecting a strong army, and its bombardment is permissible. Bombs dropped from aircraft are not more destructive than great shells fired from siege howitzers. In all bombardments of defended places the civil population is not exempt, and even the British *Official Manual* declares that in operations against such places 'the town and forts form an indivisible whole.' . . . How is the commander of a hostile airship to give notice of bombardment?" (*The Times*, August 27, 1914.)

We are not, therefore, surprised to read in the Press of September 29, 1916, the following notice (German Wireless):—

"During a British bombing attack on Brussels 15 houses were destroyed and 13 Belgians killed, while 28 were wounded."

On April 6, 1916, we find the *Daily News* complacently remarking of a British aeroplane raid upon the airship shed of Hoboken (Antwerp), which killed 42 German working men and wounded 62 others, that this particular raid "is far and away the most effective air bombardment during the war."

3. *Starvation of the Civilian Population.*

The object of the British blockade of Germany and of the German blockade of England is, of course, to reduce by famine the civilian population; and no one will contend that either party would relax their measures because they found that they were succeeding and that little children were actually dying by hundreds and thousands. Each would say that the enemy ought to give in, and that if they did not the consequences were on their own head. Thus, in a leading article of one of the principal "Liberal" newspapers I read: "We shall be sustained, no doubt, by the belief, which all available information endorses as valid, that Germany and Austria have not merely less than they want, but less, far less, than they need."

In Poland, it would seem, the death by starvation or disease of women, children, and old people is already an accomplished fact. In an appeal for funds for Polish relief signed by Paderewski and Ex-President Taft, the following description of conditions in Poland is given:—

"The latest reports from Poland have been of such a nature that unless we obtain more assistance from you the whole Polish nation will be wiped out of existence. Over 20,500 villages have been levelled to the ground. More than 200 towns have completely disappeared. Sixteen hundred churches are in ruins. Loss in property destroyed over 2 billions (500 million pounds). More than 100,000 young girls of Poland have had their lives shattered by the greatest tragedy that can come to a woman. Victims of the conquering and the retiring armies that have incessantly swept over Poland since the beginning of the war, these unfortunate young mothers, whose babies have died for want of food, clothing and shelter, find themselves outcasts—helpless, alone, having known of maternity nothing but the sorrows. Fourteen million [1] Poles, including all

---

[1] *Sic.* (?) 4,000,000 or 1,400,000 (?). The figure clearly is wrongly reproduced.

the children under seven years of age, have actually been wiped out of existence. A prominent American, who has just returned from Poland, where he had been investigating conditions on behalf of a well-known American war relief organization, reports as follows: 'Having had occasion to travel on the main road from Warsaw and Pinsk, about 150 miles long, I noticed that the ground was simply littered with civilian garments and cradles. Four hundred thousand human beings must have dropped dead along that road. The retreating army had burned their homes and compelled them to evacuate the land. There had been no time to bury those who fell. The birds of prey, as well as the wild animals, had cleaned the bones, and the invader, after gathering these bones and grinding them, had used them for fertilizing the fields in his own home land.' And now winter is coming again with all its horrors. It will bring untold misery to the homeless, shelterless, foodless Polish sufferers. Thousands more must die. They are doomed. Help cannot reach them in time. However, out of a population of 34,000,000 (?) Poles still quite a number remain whom you can help us to save, for food can still be obtained in Poland, but only at extremely high prices" (from the *New York Tribune*, November 1916).

Those who still speak of the ennobling and regenerating effects of war are invited to contemplate these facts.

Page 325—Conscription Breeding Persecution

It is hardly necessary to illustrate this point by the case of the "conscientious objectors." The objection of these men, who number in England many thousands, is either religious or political, and in both cases conscientious. Yet the effort of the Government to give them security against being forced into the army has been defeated by the Tribunals with the full support of public opinion. Hundreds of men, as I write, are undergoing sentences of imprisonment for obeying their conscience, and few voices are raised in their behalf, though those few are pertinacious and courageous. It is clear that the English public does not disapprove this kind of persecution. It is also clear, to any one who knows the English, that there will always be, in every generation, people who will face persecution on this issue. Resistance will breed resistance. The public will become more exasperated as the victims become more obstinate. And it may not be long, if conscription is continued after the war, before these men will be shot, with the full approval of the Press, the Universities, and the Churches.

Page 324—Military Training and Its Effects

This is a large subject, on which I profess no expert knowledge. If the reader wants confirmation of the statements in the text, I advise him to make inquiry among officers and soldiers who have been through the war and are willing to tell the truth. I mention only what has come before my own notice. Thus, for example, in the training for bayonet charges the men are taught to kick the enemy in the genital organs at the same time that they make their thrust. They are trained to charge at sacks or dummy men on which the vital parts are marked. I have heard of men fainting with physical horror under this discipline. More commonly, I am told, it has no effect at all on their imagination. But if the training does not actively promote brutality, it must at least passively hinder the motions of humanity. Suggest to men, by a matter-of-fact teaching, that any course you like to think of is normal and approved, and you will get them to adopt it. For they will not either think or imagine for themselves. If these good-natured boys in all the armies saw or conceived the remote consequence of every bomb they throw in the spirit of cricket, or every gun they fire in the spirit of sport, is it to be supposed that they could do what they do? It is essential both to war and to preparation for war that men should not be allowed, or allow themselves, to realize what they are doing.

That training for war, whether or no it actually encourages brutality, gives opportunity for it is clear from the well attested records of outrages by non-commissioned officers in conscript armies abroad. To convince the reader that those possibilities lie quite near to us at home, I will ask him to consider the following case of the treatment of a recalcitrant conscientious objector, not by Germans but by Englishmen.

"G. B. appeared before the —— Local Tribunal on July 10th to claim exemption as a conscientious objector on moral grounds. Immediately he had made his statement, the military representatives read a case from a circular sent out for the guidance of tribunals, in which an applicant had been turned down on the ground that the objection was a political one, and not moral, and the military representative held that B.'s case was analogous, B. contended that his objection was not analogous, and that his objection, based on his conception of war as murder, was moral. The tribunal upheld the contention of the military representative, and he was turned down. The appeal was heard at —— on August 8th, and before B. had finished his case or called his witnesses the chairman announced that the tribunal were unanimously of opinion that his case was analogous, and the appeal would be dismissed. B. tried to elicit from the chairman whether in his opinion a moral objection apart from religious belief could be sustained. No answer was given to this question. Feeling that this point was of the most vital importance to objectors on moral grounds, B. asked for leave to go before the Central Tribunal, but this was refused. He was left, therefore, without remedy.

"On the morning of August 29th he reported, in answer to a notice, at the —— Town Hall, and was sent the same day to ——. From the start he refused to be medically examined, to sign papers, or to obey military orders. On the attempt forcibly to dress him in khaki he consented to dress himself, but refused to wear puttees. He was handcuffed while the puttees were put on, but he pulled them off when the handcuffs were removed. He was placed in the guardroom, and spent Tuesday night there.

"On Wednesday he was allocated to the 3rd —— and sent back to ——. The escort tied his kit-bag round his neck, nearly choking him, but a soldier from the camp, seeing his condition, cut the string, and placed the kit-bag in a cart from the camp. On arrival here the military policeman threw the kit-bag at him, striking him on the forehead and making it bleed.

"Thursday morning saw the attempt in earnest to tame the conscientious objector. For an hour and a half before breakfast several men told off for the purpose tried to force him to obey orders, and on his refusal he was pummelled until he was bruised from head to foot. In this state he was dragged out to parade after breakfast, and dragged by main force round the field. When he refused to march or mark time his ankles were kicked until they were swollen and a source of torture, fresh relays of men keeping up the fusillade of blows and kicks and arm and wrist twisting. It should be remembered that B. had taken no food after Wednesday noon, and this was Thursday morning. His physical condition with hunger *plus* brutality can be dimly imagined. The major was riding about the field on horseback, and sent for B. to interrogate him as to the reason of his attitude. B. pointed out that he had already stated his attitude, and under proper conditions he would be willing to restate it. He was then handed over to the Gym squad for a further course of 'discipline.'

"The exhibition of the next hour took place in a public park before a large number of men, women and children. At 11 a. m. the wife and sister of B. arrived in the park and were eye-witnesses. He was first taken to the water-jump. The men take a run, vault over a rail, and then leap over the pool of water. B. resisted. He was dragged to the rail, roughly bundled over, and as he refused to leap he was pushed time after time into the water. No time was allowed him to recover his breath. As he scrambled out of the water he was seized and harried round the field by fresh men as fast as they could force him, only to be brought back with the object of making him leap. After he had been doused about a dozen times the attempt was abandoned, and he was taken to a palisade 7 feet high. Men clamber up one side and drop down the other. Five men seized B. and threw him bodily towards the top, but being a fairly big man, instead of landing him clear they caught him on the top, and as he fell over the other side they caught him. This was not 'efficient' enough for the officer. He was dragged back, hurled bodily over the top, and as the men ran to catch him this officer shouted, 'Stand clear!' and he was allowed to fall on the ground like a log. This was repeated a third time, and he was hurried to a frame platform reached by an inclined plank. In a state of physical exhaustion B. was seized on every side and forced at full length up the sloping plank. At the top he was turned head over heels time after time, and finally dumped on the ground helpless and bleeding. . . ." [1]

This treatment was accorded by English soldiers to an English-man under the supervision and direction of an English officer, presumably a gentleman. It would, I believe, be repugnant to the natural feeling of most Englishmen thus to treat a defence-less man. But military discipline makes it possible, even though it be illegal. For no natural kindness or sense of fair play can preserve the soldier from obeying such orders once they are given.

To complete the story I will cite the following authentic letter from a corporal who had been compelled to do the bullying (not in the case quoted above, but in another) :—

[1] See *Manchester Guardian* of September 20, 1916. Since this date other cases of brutality have occurred amounting even to torture. Several conscientious objectors have committed suicide.

"Excuse me writing this, but I cannot help it, because of such an act of injustice nobody every heard. When I was at ⸻ as corporal, I was stripped of my stripes because of obeying orders. Anyway, you know what I did. I did the dirty work, after which I was stripped of stripes so as somebody else could get the credit of doing it, although there was no credit in the human eye for what I did; there was no credit for the men having signed articles after the force was used against them. . . . The sooner I am dead the better. I recognize, now it is too late, that I was to do this thing and make a brute of myself by so doing. . . . I will either get my discharge from the Service, for which I am totally unfit, or take my own life."

At present, conscription being new to us, public opinion is against such treatment and the higher military command discourages it. It is in a comparatively few cases that these scenes have occurred. But if conscription becomes a permanent institution in England, how long will it be before such occurrences are regarded as a matter of course? It must be remembered that there is a powerful strain of the bully in many Englishmen. I may illustrate by the following episode, to which attention was called by a letter in the *Daily News* on November 4, 1916:—

"Sir,—In a corner of your issue to-day I find an item of news which ought surely to be rescued from obscurity:
"At an inquest at Surbiton on Private R. G. Eley, of the Royal Fusiliers, who was knocked down by a train near New Malden, the father said his son complained of being bullied by sergeants and could not face going back after his leave.
The Coroner: 'Well, I can tell you I served in the ranks as a young fellow, and I know a lot about that bullying. It is the way to smarten a soldier up.'
An open verdict was returned."
Will the authorities allow to pass unrebuked an utterance which cannot but gravely impair our military efficiency by bringing the army into disrepute and odium. I know nothing of 'crowner's quest law,' but was it not the official's plain duty to call for evidence as to the treatment to which the young man had been subjected?"

The connexion between military training and the militaristic ideal is well stated by one of the German writers who is opposed to the latter:—

"Sometimes when I watch boys enthusiastically drilling, I cannot escape from the impression that this one-sided physical training must have a bad effect on the nobler development of spirit and heart. As a natural consequence, the young people must come to the conclusion that there is nothing nobler and more ideal on earth than to carry rifles, march in line, and enthuse in the trenches. In my judgment the vision of a higher goal and a religious ideal must perish utterly among men brought up in this one-sided cult of nationalism " (*Vorwärts*, December, 3, 1915).

Page 326—Christianity and the War

According to Mr. Outhwaite, speaking in the House of Commons:—

"The Venerable Archdeacon Wilberforce, who read the prayers in the House, preaching in St. Margaret's Church at the beginning of the war, said: 'To kill Germans is a divine service in the fullest acceptation of the term.' . . . A leading minister in his division had said that if Christ came to the world to-day he would expect to see Him using a bayonet." (See *Hansard* of January 20, 1916.)

Extract from a letter from a conscientious objector (1916) :—

"We had the priest in just before dinner and he told us the tale. Of course he was in uniform. He said the Catholic Church upheld this war, and that we as Catholics were bound to fight under pain of sin. He said we were not Catholics, as no Catholic could have a conscientious objection to warfare, and that he could not give us absolution if we went to confession."

With regard to the possibility of the fusion of Christianity, as professed by the Churches, with the religion of the God-State, the following passage is worth citing from a translation of an article by Professor Ernst Troeltsch which appeared in the New York *Sun*. The professor is dealing with the ideas fermenting in Germany in war-time, and he speaks of "the German Imperialists, to whom belong the majority of the German historians, a large number of national economists, the industrial magnates and many officers. They saw all their previous teaching confirmed, and celebrated the great moment of the final breaking-through of the Germans to be the world-race. Races and States must grow or go under. The goal of every great and noble people, to become a world-Power, seemed to have approached very near. . . . To be sure, in this teaching there plays no religious tone; Christianity is not denied, but is warned against every humanitarian and sentimental understanding."

The last sentence gives the key to a position which the Churches of all countries may feel it easy and perhaps imperative to adopt.

It is perhaps worth while to append the following example of militant Christianity from the *Morning Post*, January 2, 1915:—

"The war opens out a vast field of usefulness for the Christian Church; as it reminds people of death, so it reminds them of faith; as it destroys their wealth, so it suggests to them spiritual consolations; as it teaches them the folly of sloth and self-indulgence, so it instructs them in the deeper purposes and meanings of life. Therefore war and faith go commonly hand in hand; and war teaches mankind what child-birth teaches women. The spiritual field is plowed and harrowed by such terrible events, and the seed which the Church sows should fall upon prepared ground. And if the Church uses the opportunity well, and scorns all comfortable doctrine, not confusing safety with virtue or war with evil, it should reap a great spiritual harvest."

As a pendant to this, I cite the following letter from a German evangelical divine:—

"The peaceable settlement of future international disputes by way of conciliation or juridical decision is a dream which can never be realized. Think of the Hague Palace with its portraits of the Czar and of Edward. As a clergyman you should know that so long as men live on earth, sin reigns, and so long as that is the case, the Government must wield the sword lent it by God" (*Blätter für Zwischenstaatliche Organisation*, October 1916, p. 302).

And this:—

"The whimpering and howling over the misery and havoc of the war I can no longer endure. The war is not Germany's misfortune, it is Germany's good fortune. Thank God that the war has come! I say it even now in the third year of the war. And thank God that we have no peace yet; I say it still, in spite of all the victims. . . . Therefore I say it again and again, Thank God that we have the war! It alone can save our people, if they be yet capable of salvation. It is the great operator's knife with which the great Physician of the nations cuts out the most terrible of cancers. Thank God that we have yet no peace! The wounds would close too quickly and the evil become worse than ever" (Herr Pastor Philips, President of the Christian Socialist Party. Cited in *Die Welt am Montag*, October 9, 1916. As the editor remarks, it is a pity that this gentleman—and many others one could think of—should not pass twenty-four hours on the Somme).

In quoting these passages I do not intend to imply that there is no other attitude to war than this to be found among the clergy. I note, for instance, with satisfaction, that a body of Congregational ministers have issued a letter in which they state that "any compromise between Christianity and militarism involves ultimately betrayal of Christ," and that the principles of Christianity and war cannot be reconciled.

Page 327—Preconceptions of Militarism

As an example of the way people imply in their thought a doctrine they nevertheless deny in words, I may refer to an article which appeared in the *Deutsche Tageszeitung* dealing with the contrast between German and American political ideas. The author cites an American writer as taking the view (which of course is the one generally taken outside Germany) that the German philosophy of the State rests on two preconceptions: one, that Might is Right; the other that the individual exists for the State, not vice versa. Repudiating this interpretation of the German view, he says, as to the first point:—

"The rule 'might is right,' at any rate in the sense that every Power ought to be allowed to stretch and contract Right according to its good pleasure, has never been defended by any reputable German. Only the enthusiastic perversion that Might ought to be nothing but a servant of Right has been rejected, and rightly, as an ideological soap-bubble."

The latter part of this passage, of course, admits the whole case the writer supposes himself to be refuting.

On the second point he has nothing to say, except that the individual, according to German philosophers, ought to submit himself to the moral law. The charge made against the German view is that it supposes the State to be the ultimate judge of the moral law. And the author does not seem even to perceive this point, so deeply engrained in him is the belief that the State is in fact the judge. (See *Deutsche Tageszeitung*, August 11, 1915.)

Here is another example of the sophistries of the "Might is Right" theory. Dr. Zacher, a "Geheimer Regierungsrath," writes to the *Müncher-Augsburger Zeitung* of September 14, 1916:—

"Seldom has so much confusion been produced by a misunderstood foreign word as has been created by the word 'annexations' in the conflict of opinion about the aims of the war. According to common usage the word to 'annex' carries with it the connotation of seizure contrary to Right, while the meaning of the word really is 'to bind one thing with another,' in the sense of 'joining on.' In the case of territory occupied and held in war, there can be no question of wrongful seizure. In such a case one speaks logically of the 'Right' of the conqueror, who creates a new 'Right' adapted to the new relations of Might."

This citation is given in the *Blätter für Zwischenstaatliche Organisation* for September 1916 (p. 306). And the editor appropriately comments: "This new 'Right,' with the creation of which German professors are now trying to throw dust in the eyes of the German people, is unfortunately the ancient right of savagery, whereby the order of social relations was measured by nothing but brute force. To reintroduce this old 'Right' into the modern world is to annihilate our civilization and to reduce ourselves to cannibals."

The views and sophistries here illustrated are not peculiar to Germany. They are those of the militarists of all countries. And they follow from accepting the position that the State, not the individual conscience, is the ultimate depository of moral truth, and that the power of the State is the highest aim of life.

Page 328—Militarism and Morals

It is well known that German writers, with that sense of logical consequence which makes them the *enfants terribles* of the world, have stated definitely that what the Teutonic race most needs is a new religion freed from the humanitarianism and universalism of professed Christianity. If English militarists were as clear-sighted or as frank, they would adopt the same position. Captain Ross, in his book, *Representative Government and War*, to which I refer in the text, is as contemptuous of morality or honesty or honour as any German could be. He regards the liberation of the slaves of South Africa as simply bad strategy. "What mattered it that black men were slaves? . . . What mattered it even that that country were denuded of these black men, provided that white men grew up in love and reverence for the Mother Country?" The support by the British Government of the interests of the natives against those of white settlers was an "indelible disgrace to the British nation." And this, observe, is all quite in the logic of the worship of the God-State. For in the captain's view those procedures of the British Government (based upon Christian principle) were inimical to the interests of the Empire. "Justice!—injustice!" he cries elsewhere. "What are such things when the national existence is at stake?" And again: "Morality!—immorality! What are such things to great nations when their fate is at stake?"

The reader should seriously consider that the sentiments here frankly stated are practically endorsed, in sheer muddleheadedness, by many people who are shocked by the statement of them.

Page 328—Militarism and Education

A correspondent of the *Manchester Guardian,* writing of the new educational movement in Germany, says:—

"As with us, the experiences of the war are making the Germans overhaul the principles and practices of their educational system and forecast the best developments for the future. As with us, unfortunately, the German writers on education all of them presuppose that there will be war in the future, and education must prepare for it. They take war for granted, and instead of shaping education in such a way as to make war impossible, their sole idea is, by means of education, to produce the best possible men for fighting purposes.

Speaking generally, educational writers are sublimely satisfied with the way in which the aims and methods of their education have approved themselves again in this war as they did in the war of 1870-1. Writing at the end of the first year of war, when German arms were in the ascendant, they claim that the German soldier has proved himself superior to the Russian and the Italian on two grounds: first, because the national system of education has imbued the youth of Germany with a stronger sense of discipline; and, secondly, because an educated population lends itself more readily to organization and concerted effort on the largest scale. Special stress is laid on discipline and subordination of self. These results are accredited to the elementary school, but the part which the universities and the secondary schools have played comes in also for special commendation, and the 'volunteers' (i.e. the privileged soldiers of one year's service) are contrasted with 'the educated shirkers of France.' The writer quotes a Turkish newspaper and the King of Bavaria in confirmation of his views. The Ministry of Education has not been slow to avail itself of the tide of patriotic feeling. A new syllabus for the teaching of history has been promulgated which came into force last Easter— Easter marks the close of the educational year throughout Germany. The new syllabus is avowedly experimental, and headmasters are to report on its success in 1918. Briefly, the aim is to concentrate study upon the last half-century, and more especially upon the achievement of national unity under Prussia and the rise of united Germany to the position of a great world-Power. Hohenzollern Day opened the floodgates of panegyric. The reigning dynasty was extolled as having given to Prussia the schools which had made it mighty in the world of learning and of military power. The reigning Emperor was extolled as the direct inspirer of all educational reforms which followed as the result of the great Conference of 1890. The qualities which have made Prussia are analysed, and emphasis is laid upon the sense of social obligation and the habitude of obedience. The authority of the State must increase, the individualism which was threatening the country must be repressed. The State must be more and more; the individual must be less and less. The teaching of Socialism is held up as having been in reality individualistic in its tendency, because it disposes the individual 'to make greater claims upon life for personal pleasure and self-indulgence.' Extremists are not wanting. Some writers would exclude all teaching of English and French from the schools, and admit Russian and Spanish only because of their commercial importance. In view of the all-transcending greatness of German education, all disposition to study foreign systems, Swedish, English, or American, is sternly reprimanded."

In the same spirit, one understands, German is being dropped in English schools.

The following passage is taken from an article by Professor Wilhelm von Blume in the *Europäische Staats- und Wirthschaft Zeitung*, p. 951:—

"Internal policy must be determined by external policy in a State whose existence is perpetually threatened. It is from this point of view that the Constitution, the Law, and the Administration must be treated. We must fashion the State with a view to war in order to preserve peace, and save our skin, if we can do it in no other way. We must—I do not shrink from saying it—cultivate our militarism even more consciously than before.

War is an act of the whole nation, not only of the army. Therefore the whole nation must be made ready for war, its intellectual (*geistige*) force, its moral force, its economic force. War is above all an act of the 'common man' however important may be the services of leaders. It follows that every individual must be educated for the State and trained for service in the State. War is a product of technique. We must therefore develop the technical production of our people to the greatest possible perfection. There remains for us therefore no other way than this: we must 'statify' (*verstaatlichen*) the life of the nation in a much higher degree than before."

A member of the German Reichstag, Müller-Meiningen, has proposed compulsory physical training for all boys from the age of six to sixteen, and military training from sixteen upwards. It has then been further proposed that this training be entrusted to military officers, and even to any non-commissioned officer. A Dr. Adolf Matthias, after saying that "There must be made of your youth a giant in military force before which, even in peacetime, our foes will shrink in terror," adds: "The State orders and regulates *not only the acts but the thoughts of its citizens.*" This latter sentence gives the full logic of the God-State.

It should, however, be added that, as a counter to these sentiments, there is a movement among German students for greater freedom from State dictation and leave to shape their own ideals. Which of these tendencies will triumph depends upon the way

Europe is shaped after the war; and that depends upon the kind of peace that is made.[1]

Similar ideas are found in France. Thus: "Three members of the French Chamber have tabled the proposal that after the war all French boys shall be subject to a Spartan military training from the age of twelve onwards."

The English are likely at first to go slowly in this matter. They will begin by teaching "patriotism" in the schools; that is, a falsification of history (which is what State-instructed patriotism is bound to mean) and a hatred and mistrust of all other nations except those which at the moment are allied with them. The teaching of "religion" will be fused with this, and the pupil will get a general idea that the mission of Jesus Christ is fulfilled, and can only be fulfilled, in the British Empire. The movement will ascend from the elementary to the secondary schools, and from these to the universities. All the time, of course, the official religion will continue to preach an academic preference for peace—in short, the pulpit variety of the song, "We don't want to fight, but, by jingo, if we do," and we shall point with horror to the wicked "foreigners" who positively glorify war.

[1] The above remarks are based on an article in the *Friedenswarte* of August-September 1916, "Richtlinien innerhalb der deutschen Studentenschaft," by Dr. Cornelius Bergmann.

INTERNATIONAL RELATIONS

IDEALISM AND REALITIES [1]

The Earl of Birkenhead

[Frederick Edwin Smith, Earl of Birkenhead (1872-   ), was Lord High Chancellor of England from 1919 to 1922. David Lloyd-George characterized him as the most brilliant of recent Lord Chancellors. As an undergraduate, he was President of the Oxford Union. He was later Fellow and Lecturer of Merton College, Oxford. In 1896 he entered Parliament. As one of Sir Edward Carson's lieutenants in Ulster during Irish difficulties, he was known as "Galloper Smith of Park Down." He served in France with the Indian Corps, and was Captain in the King's Own Oxfordshire Hussars. He is a recognized authority on international law. Among his books are, *International Law, International Law in the Far East, My American Visit,* and *The Indian Corps in France.*

In the summer of 1923, Lord Birkenhead was one of the speakers at the Williamstown Institute of Politics, and his address raised a storm of controversy. He urged the United States to abandon her policy of isolation, and to intervene in the European situation; but he deprecated the altruistic point of view in international affairs. America, he thought, should intervene only if intervention would "advance the fortunes of the American people." The evils of idealism were exemplified in the career of President Wilson, who "became, paradoxically enough, the agent of all those post-war developments from which his altruistic mind would most specially have recoiled." Both English and American papers attacked what they regarded as the cynical tone of the speech; they also questioned the propriety of the reference to President Wilson.

On November 7, 1923, Lord Birkenhead was installed as Lord Rector of Glasgow University, and he took occasion to present in his rectorial address (here printed) a considered statement of the views which he had previously expressed at Williamstown. The speech was keenly resented, although some Tory papers praised his courage. The *Morning Post* said, "He is the plain-spoken and sharp-tongued champion of men of sense and logic, disillusioned of any hopes they may once have entertained of the regeneration of a wicked world, and stoically resigned to make the best of it." The speech was roundly denounced at a demonstration against war, immediately after the address had been delivered. At a meeting of the League of Nations Union, the Bishop of Kingston condemned the article as "blasphemy to the memory of the men who gave their lives, not for self-interest, but for the ideals of honor, right, and truth." The *Spectator* considered the generally hostile reception of the speech as one of "the few cheerful signs in a gloomy world." The address has been criticized for its cynicism, but it contains a vigor of conviction and a sincerity of utterance that lifts it above the merely smart sayings of the disillusioned.]

[1] Reprinted from the London *Daily Telegraph*, November 8, 1923. This address was also printed in the *Living Age*, December 22, 1923.
Questions and topics for the discussion of this address, and of other phases of the general subject with which it deals, will be found on pages 535 and 543.

Idealism may be defined, as well as in another way, by calling it the spirit which impels an individual, or group of individuals, to a loftier standard of conduct than that which ordinarily prevails around him or them. This definition does not, of course, impinge upon the philosophical conception that in external conceptions the objects immediately known are ideas; that, in other words, all reality is in its nature psychical. With such abstractions—though they are of great interest—we are not practically at this moment concerned. Idealism in the international field is the spirit which would carry into the relations of States the kind of ethical progress generally indicated above. Now, it is evident that every sane and reasonable citizen must desire that the relationship between States shall be increasingly regulated in accordance with the highest attainable standards of conscientious conduct. Conflict, therefore, is little likely to arise so long as attention is confined to the larger generalizations which the term suggests. The subject, however, of this observation is naturally neither an attempt to examine or appraise the value, either in national or international affairs, of a loftier standpoint or of a more austere ethical outlook. Such abstract discussion would be unprofitable; nor would it lend itself to any profitable disputation. It is when attention is directed to the sharply contrasted views of those who are distinguished in political matters as "Idealists" or "Realists" that the subject matter of this examination becomes apparent. The use of these discordant terms makes it plain that the word idealism is employed in current phraseology to indicate a point of view in relation to life which may be challenged without either absurdity or cynicism. No one, for instance, imagines that the school of political thought which is conveniently described as Realistic, would impeach the conception or definition of Idealism with which this address began. The term, therefore, is used in a narrower or more specialized sense, which must be somewhat more carefully analyzed. In current language, an idealist is one who places before himself in private or public affairs as attainable a goal which other citizens, perhaps equally moral, do not believe to be so attainable. Provided that the idealist be a sound judge of moral valuations, nothing but good can proceed from his admonitions. If he wrenches in his individual exertions even a tiny fragment from the area of a grosser world he will not perish without the glory of achievement. It has, of course, naturally happened that the greatest of idealists have been teachers or preachers.

Of all these Jesus Christ was evidently the most preëminent. But it would be unreasonable to suppose that when He admonished him who was assaulted to turn the other cheek to the smiter, or him who was rich to sell all his possessions and give them to the poor, He was laying down standards of conduct which He either expected or desired to see generally adopted. He was, on the contrary, diffusing, in the language of metaphor, a sweet and beautiful moral atmosphere for the purification of imperfect manhood. Were an autocrat to issue a ukase within his own dominions ordering all rich men to divest themselves of their possessions in favor of the poor, he would be, assuming morality of purpose, an idealist in the narrower sense, but he would also be an idealist in a more aggressive and dangerous connotation with which we shall in this discussion be principally concerned. An analysis of the subject derives some guidance from the use of the term in private as opposed to public policy. For such an examination makes it plain how small has been the conquest of idealist thought, even over the comparatively easy domain of individual conduct.

The school of idealism is the very antithesis of the school of self-interest. And yet nothing is more apparent than that, politically, economically, and philosophically, the motive of self-interest not only is, but must be, and ought to be, the mainspring of human action. Bentham long since pointed out in his *Theory of Legislation* how inconvenient, and even mischievous, the conseqences would be if every individual were to regulate his conduct, not in relation to his own interests, which he is likely to understand, but in relation to the interests of others, concerning which he is very likely to be imperfectly informed.

Economically the matter is not less plain. Mankind subsists precariously upon this globe on the terms of constant and contributory toil. The experience of thousands, perhaps hundreds of thousands, of years has shown that the desire of self-advancement is the only adequate incentive for that standard of labor and achievement which each individual may be required in the common scheme to afford. The only legitimate sphere, therefore, of the idealist, within the field of private morality, is to elevate, if he can, the standards by reference to which conduct is, in the existing scheme of things, adjusted, without attempting to impair motives which are fundamental in human nature and vital to social economy.

If we turn to the relationship of States we shall find it necessary to draw similar distinctions even more clearly; for many causes combine in this field to contract the area within which altruism is likely to win adherence. The man who cries, 'My country, right or wrong,' may or may not be a patriot; he is certainly not an idealist. The latter, in this connection, must again be conceived of not merely as one who desires to see the substitution in international practice of law for war, the complete purification of international morality, and perhaps 'the Parliament of man, the Federation of the world.' For in this vague sentiment of benevolence many admirable citizens of many countries would concur.

But the idealist, in the sense which concerns us, is he who believes that these things are in fact attainable; that we ought to take steps and make exertions, and even sacrifices, in order to attain them. And he would indeed, in most cases, actually shape the policy of his country, and even compromise its interests, because he believes in the prospects which he indicates, and in the sanctity and infallibility of international compacts.

Twenty-four years ago a Tsar of Russia issued to the world a very sonorous and idealist message. It announced the hope that war might be forever ended. It made specific proposals in that sense. And thus there came into existence a Hague Conference, with the history of which most of us are familiar. It would be foolish to deny that this conference did some useful work in its secondary tasks; namely the consideration of international disputes and the alleviation of avoidable cruelty in the prosecution of war, which, of course, is itself in its very essence cruel. But it has achieved absolutely nothing in the direction of its major and more imposing purpose. In a book upon international law, which I wrote immediately after the appearance of the Tsar's communication, I observed:—

No sensible person with the slightest knowledge of history will believe that human nature has so profoundly altered as to afford the most remote prospect that this dream will ever be realized.

This conclusion was much assailed at the time by our sentimentalists. But a few years later that same Russia was hurling men in millions in the attempt to destroy Japan. And continuously thereafter the junta of evil and ambitious men, of whom the Kaiser was the mouthpiece and the figurehead, was projecting the stupendous tragedy which has almost destroyed the civilization of Europe. Untaught by previous experience, undeterred by the shattering refutation of their beliefs which the Great War brought with it, the idealists immediately had the temerity to exploit its outbreak for their own controversial purposes. It was indeed unfortunate, they admitted, that the war should have occurred at all, and especially war so savagely conducted and flung over so enormous an area. But, after all, it had its bright side. For it was to be a war to end war. This time at least, when once the plowshare, according to the correct tradition, had ousted weapons, there was to be no further relapse into primeval savagery. And so we were to have a League of Nations consisting in time of all nations, great and small, equipped with military and naval force; and, therefore, able to make good its decisions against a recalcitrant member.

While I thought and think that there was and still is a modest area within which the League of Nations may make useful contribution to the harmony of the world, the larger claims made on its behalf always seemed to me to be fantastic. They forgot human nature as absurdly as they neglected history. What in the history of the world had ever happened which afforded foothold for expectations so megalomaniac? Divide the history of the world into two broad epochs, with the birth of Jesus Christ as the dividing line. An examination in terms, however general, of these two periods equips a scientific observer with some material for forming a true decision.

Of the earlier period first: I do not pause to deal here with the countless minor struggles which everywhere marked the infancy of the world. I mention, only to note it, the evidence collected by Darwin and his followers showing at work in every department of life the survival of the fittest. But I must bestow a moment upon the lessons, if indeed in this connection they are lessons, to be derived from the Old Testament.

According to Holy Writ, the chosen people were set in motion in order that they might forcibly possess themselves of a land flowing with milk and honey. They are "utterly to destroy their enemies." And thereafter we find them over a long period of time, protracted no doubt by their own peccadillos, engaged in violent and bloody strife with various antagonists. It may, of course, be said, in view of their desperate struggles with the Philistines, that the latter were very wicked men. Unfortunately, however, there always have existed in the world very wicked men. Perhaps, therefore, it is necessary to import the qualification that all wars are to cease, except against very wicked men. But even here a difficulty presents itself, for every war that I know of has recurrently presented the same phenomenon that each protagonist believed, or pretended to believe, in the moral vileness of the other. In 1914, for instance, the French affirmed the Germans to be wicked aggressors, whereas the German people loudly proclaimed the criminal aggression of Russia. It must, therefore, be admitted that the history of the chosen people and, indeed, the Old Testament, taken as a whole, afford little ground for optimism in this regard.

A similar but more extended observation would apply to all the great empires of the ancient world. Indeed, in this connection, somber images throng the mind. Egyptians, Medes, Persians, Assyrians—all these achieved empire at the point of the sword. Of how many dead empires does the silent and immobile East contain the record? In what graves reposed the millions of their unprotesting slain? A happier and humaner experience might have been looked for from that exquisite intellectual efflorescence which we associate with the greatest of the Greek States. Yet their records tell of almost continuous strife. So bitterly, indeed, and amid such jealousies, did they wage war with one another that they could not combine even against the fierce Macedonian, and so one more rare and beautiful civilization perished utterly from the earth. To Greece succeeded Rome, teaching the entire world through the whole of its stern, dominating, and imperial sway that might was right, and that a sharp sword in the hand of a disciplined soldier was the most persuasive argument in world diplomacy.

And there came, too, the message of Jesus Christ, tender in its simplicity, superhuman in its humanity. The creed of Him who was crucified was to spread with incredible swiftness over a large part of the world's surface. Mighty Powers and great princes have rendered homage to the message of mercy and peace which came from those divine and persuasive lips. And yet, while we take note of the spread of the Christian religion, we must none the less ask what has been its reaction upon international conduct. What was its influence over the recent world-convulsion? What was its spiritual or intellectual contribution to the poignant problem—why an omnipotent Deity so suddenly doomed so many innocent victims to bestial destruction? Did the greatest Priest in the world, enthroned in his Roman palace, ever pronounce a clear and intelligible conclusion upon the moral responsibility for the outbreak of war or upon the methods by which that war was conducted? Was he prevented by the fact that his flock diverged beneath different standards? If so, he ceased to be the divinely appointed mouthpiece of the higher morality and descended to a place, such as it was, among the politicians.

After Rome, the barbarians; after the barbarians, countless decades of anarchical chaos. And then throughout the centuries a long succession of almost uninterrupted wars—wars dynastic, wars territorial, wars on points of honor, and wars of naked aggression. England and France, England and Spain, England and Holland, England and France again, France and Germany, and thereafter the violent emergence of the Hohenzollern dynasty, more cynically based on blood and iron, more determined *debellare superbos*, than any power since mighty Rome.

Are we really to learn nothing from all that has happened over this immense period of time? Does any warrant exist for the belief that human nature has altered its whole character? And if so, what is that warrant? And when did that alteration take place? And, more particularly, what evidence of this great reformation do we find in what has happened in Europe since the Armistice? There have been wars and rumors of wars. I do not myself know of a moment in the last four years in which there has appeared to be less prospect of permanent peace in Europe than at the present moment. Nor is it an answer to say, as some do, that the infirmities of the Treaty of Versailles were responsible for the unrest and the violence which distract Europe to-day. If there were infirmities in that treaty, these again were infirmities in human nature which cannot be corrected. For the statesmen who put their names to that treaty, to the territorial readjustments of that treaty, were themselves the mouthpieces of imperious and victorious democracies; and the views under discussion here are largely founded upon the expectation that the human nature of democracies will not undergo much modification. And if it does not they will have the statesmen they deserve.

So we are bound to conclude that from the very dawn of the world man has been a combative animal. To begin with, he fought violently for his own elemental needs; later, perhaps in tribal or communal quarrel; later still, with the growth of greater communities, upon a larger and more sophisticated scale. And it is to be specially noticed that there have nevertheless almost always existed men who sincerely, but very foolishly, believed, firstly, that no war would arise in their own day, and, secondly, when that war did arise, that for some reason or other it would be the last.

At this point the idealist degenerates into the pacifist; and it is at this point consequently that he becomes a danger to the community of which he is a citizen. Athens in her decline had no lack of such advisers, and, unhappily for the City of the Violet Crown, she preferred their sloppy folly to the ardent eloquence of Demosthenes. In the days of Napoleon—who had a very just contempt for these idealogues—Charles Fox harnessed his eloquence to the chariot of sentimentalism. But he switched rather abruptly as soon as he became Prime Minister. And in our own day we have been afforded convincing evidence of the real peril to national security which arises when idealists secure control over a powerful political party. This is what happened in 1906. Every sensible person now realizes that even in that year the German scheme was being nebulously conceived; and its deadly menace increased with every year which passed. I myself, in a book called *Unionist Policy,* published in 1910, devoted a long article to demonstrating the soundness of Lord Roberts's warnings.

But the immense increase in the German army, the construction of strategic railways upon the Belgian boundary, the creation of a mighty fleet, left our idealists unconvinced. And accordingly every year the annual meeting of a great party's federation, with fatuous and recurrent imbecility, passed resolutions in favor of reducing our military and naval expenditure.

It was indeed in these years that idealism became rampant with those in power. Notorious and most vital facts were everywhere ignored. German editors were entertained by English editors in London, and dilated with fluent eloquence upon the pacific intentions of the Fatherland. English editors in their turn visited

Berlin, to enjoy in that martial capital the same agreeable re-
assurances. And all the time the armies grew. All the time a
mighty instrument was being fashioned in the German fleet. All
the time Heligoland frowned more impregnably upon the North
Sea. All the time those great military railways, unneeded for
peaceful traffic, were debouching upon the defenseless Belgian
frontier.

In the welter of sentimentality, amid which Great Britain might
easily have mouldered into ruin, Lord Haldane presented a figure
alike interesting, individual, and arresting. In speech fluent,
and even infinite, he yielded to no living idealist in the easy
coinage of sentimental phraseology. Herein, indeed, he was a
match for those who distributed the chloroform of Berlin. Do
we not remember, for instance, that Germany was his spiritual
home? But he none the less prepared himself and the Empire
to speak, when the time came, to his spiritual friends in language not in the least spiritual. He devised the Territorial Army,
which was capable of becoming the nucleus of national conscription. He created the Imperial General Staff. He founded the
Officers Training Corps. And two other names require special
and honorable mention in an age of sloppy folly. Lord Roberts
devoted the evening of an illustrious life to warnings of marvelous
prescience, which passed almost unheeded. General Baden-Powell
used the laurels which he had gained at Mafeking to inspire and
sustain the noblest and most promising movement which has taken
place in our lifetime. The foundation of the Boy Scouts established for this gifted and imaginative soldier a monument more
lasting than bronze.

It has been thought worth while to retrace the events of these
fateful years with some particularity in order to show that
idealism in national affairs is not merely impracticable, but may
easily degenerate into a deadly source of national peril. Still a
further illustration may be drawn from recent events. The signing of the Armistice immediately released all the sentimentalists.
Not only was the Great War ended, but there was never to be
another. The League of Nations was to be equipped with functions and resources which would in effect enthrone it in super-
sovereignty over the contributory nations. But herein the statesman, who of all others should most completely have understood
the American people, demonstrated that in fact he understood
them least of all. That people is the most generous people in

the world in the field of international charity. The United States have lavished countless millions of dollars upon the starving population of Russia. They were first in the field with bountiful relief to stricken Japan. But they draw—and rightly draw—a sharp and logical distinction between idealism in their capacity as private citizens for private charities and idealism in their corporate or national character. And, accordingly, they exercise their undoubted right in repudiating at the first opportunity an idealist conception which they believed to be at once impracticable, strange to their traditions, and incompatible with their national interests.

A broader consideration must now in its turn be examined. We are told that the object to be aimed at is the abolition of war. Everybody recognizes that war is both cruel and hateful. But is it even conceivable that it can ever be abolished? Is the ownership of the world to be stereotyped by perpetual tenure in the hands of those who possess its different territories to-day? If it is, very strange and undesirable consequences will one day follow. For nations wax and wane, so that a power competent in one age to govern an empire, perhaps remote, in the general interest of the world, will in another abuse a dominion for which it no longer possesses the necessary degree of vigor.

The history of Spain supplies familiar illustrations. Her chivalry was second to none in Europe. Her high standard of gallant conduct was disfigured only by the cruelties of the Inquisition. Her stately galleons brought a quiver of apprehension even to the stout bosom of Queen Elizabeth, and were never discredited until the rout of her superb Armada. And in exuberant colonial enterprise she was the mistress and pioneer of Europe. She flung her civilization and her language into the remote parts of the world, deriving incredible titles from successive Papal Bulls. And coincidently, or almost so, with this immense maritime enterprise, she hurled the martial Moor from Spain. But her decline was as rapid as her ascension. She proved no adequate custodian of her overseas possessions.

Had a League of Nations existed, when she began to lose them, would it have assisted Spain or the insurgents of Spain, or, in another case, the despoilers of Spain? The general extrusion of savage races from the American continent and certain of the South Sea Islands, to which they had some legal right, shows that, rightly or wrongly, nations of stronger fiber, confronted by indigenous weaklings, have asserted the right of forcible expropriation. No one, indeed, who has studied the history of the world has ever defended the view that the supreme interest of evolutionary humanity can support a definitive delimitation of the surface of the globe.

But if such a final distribution is impracticable, and even undesirable, by what agency are modifications to be made? Voluntary cessions of territory have not been frequent in the past; and there seems little reason to suppose that they will become more fashionable in the future. For many thousands of years the emergence of a new and martial nation has been gradually marked by violent readjustments of national boundaries. It may, of course, be the case that human nature has so completely altered that some new method is discoverable. I confess, however, that none has up to the present occurred to my own mind.

It may perhaps be charged against those who sincerely hold the views which I have attempted to make plain that we carry in our veins the virus which colored the somber and unmoral genius of Treitschke, and which found popular expression in the mosquito propaganda of Von Bernhardi. But such a change, if made, would be patently unjust. We neither hold nor have we preached these doctrines. We diagnose certain diseases. We did not create them. A distinction must surely be drawn between him who calls attention to the risk of conflagration and that other who puts his torch to inflammable material.

The purport and the moral of these general observations may be summarized in a few concluding observations. For as long a time as the records of history have been preserved mankind has passed through a ceaseless process of evolution. This process has been sometimes pacific, but very often it has been attended by warlike disturbances. The strength of different nations, measured in terms of arms, varies from century to century. The world continues to offer glittering prizes to those who have stout hearts and sharp swords; it is therefore extremely improbable that the experience of future ages will differ in any material respect from that which has happened since the twilight of the human race. It is for us, therefore, who in our history have proved ourselves a martial rather than a military people, to abstain, as has been our habit, from provocation; but to maintain in our own hand the adequate means for our own protection, and, so equipped, to march with heads erect and bright eyes along the road of our Imperial destiny.

AMERICA AND THE INTERNATIONAL PROBLEM [1]

[*America and the International Problem* first appeared in *The Round Table*, a quarterly review of the politics of the British Commonwealth, which aims "to publish once a quarter a comprehensive review of Imperial politics, free from the bias of local party issues." Its articles are unsigned. This essay has been selected for its breadth of view and its keen analysis of significant factors in present-day international relationships. In direct opposition to Lord Birkenhead's gospel of national self-interest, it presents "the recognition of the Golden Rule as the standard in international affairs" as "the only real road to lasting prosperity as well as lasting peace."]

Every day it is becoming clearer that neither the European nor the world problem can be solved without some form of American coöperation. The reparations question, which lies at the heart of the European complex, is inseparably bound up with the question of interallied indebtedness, in which the United States is vitally concerned, like the rest of us. The United States is also equally interested in the solution of the Russian question, whatever it may be. And in the growing scandal of the Near East the United States is the one great Power left with a sufficiently disinterested position to call effectively upon the nations concerned to make a fresh start.

Yet, so far as surface indications go, the United States to-day is more set upon its policy of isolation than ever before. President Harding, during the 1920 election campaign, declared himself vaguely as being in favor of an Association of Nations in place of the League of Nations. But the Washington Conference, which successfully dealt with certain aspects of the problems of naval disarmament and the Pacific, seems to have exhausted the zeal of the present Republican Administration for association with other Powers. There has been no discussion of the basis of an Association of Nations, and to every request of the European Powers that the United States should take part in joint deliberations about Russia, reparations, interallied debts,

[1] Reprinted by permission from *The Round Table*, September 1922. This essay has also been reprinted in the pamphlets of the American Association for International Conciliation, No. 183, February 1923.

Questions and topics for the discussion of this essay, and of other phases of the general subject with which it deals, will be found on pages 537 and 543.

or economic reconstruction, the Washington Administration has returned a courteous but firmly negative reply. It was only on second thoughts and with evident reluctance that it agreed to share in a very limited inquiry into the Kemalist atrocities in Asia Minor.

None the less, though surface signs are unpropitious, there are strong indications of an impending change. Wilsonism and the League of Nations are undoubtedly growing again in popular favor. There is a strong body of opinion, especially among the churches, which feels deeply about the continued refusal of the United States to take any part in trying to clean up the aftermath of the war. There is also a growing sense among the larger business men that the future prosperity of the country is bound up with the prosperity of the outside world to a far greater extent than before the war, and that the present depression will not fully disappear until international trade becomes normal again all over the earth. Finally, there is always the swing of the political pendulum. The Democrats are strengthening their position, and they still stand steadfastly by the League.

But, if the undercurrent is setting once more in the direction of international coöperation, it is not likely to carry the United States back to the program of 1919. America has reacted from the war, has rejected the League of Nations, is disillusioned about the possibilities of regenerating Europe in a hurry, and is determined not to become mixed up in what she regards as properly Europe's own internal concerns. If she is to embark upon a deliberate policy of international coöperation it will probably be because the problem has been thought out *de novo*, and because she has become convinced that there is a method of coöperation which is both consistent with her own political faith and ideals, and has a better chance of achieving practical results, than the abortive idealism of the period of the Paris Conference.

It is the purpose of this article to attempt to estimate what America's fundamental ideas about international coöperation are likely to be, and consider how far they are likely to be compatible with the views and necessities of Europe.

I. The American Standpoint

In estimating the probable attitude of any country to external problems it is seldom a good thing to take too much account of the ephemeral currents of opinion at the moment. It is the duty of the diplomat and practical politician to do this; the philosophic writer is entitled to take a longer view. It is his business to estimate the fundamental ideas upon which the political life of the country is based, and the traditions and geographical and other conditions which have shaped the national policy over a long period of time. It is these, in America as elsewhere, which determine action in the long run, and which it is most important to appraise rightly.

There is one great difference between the outlook of Europe and America which should be noted from the outset, for it colors nearly everything else. Every European tends to look backwards. He is born into a nationality which has a strongly marked racial individuality, which has a long history, usually of conquest or repression, and which seems destined to an apparently eternal struggle for existence or for supremacy with hostile neighbors. He has no sense of being a European except in a purely geographical way, until he goes abroad. He is a Frenchman, a German, a Russian, etc., and his outlook on international affairs is primarily concerned with the future freedom and success of the national entity to which he belongs in the eternal struggle of the European States for place and power.

The American is entirely different. He will recognize some Americans with pride, some Americans with indifference, or even dislike, that his ancestors came from England, or Ireland, or Scandinavia, or Germany, or Russia, or Italy. But that makes little practical difference. To-day he is an American, and to be an American is not something racial or national as it is understood in Europe, but is to live in a new and better world than Europe and to have a certain kind of forward-looking outlook on life. Somebody has described the people of the United States as a nation of international orphans. By this he meant that America, as an entity, has no historical past reaching back into the mists of antiquity, as have most European peoples. America came into being in 1776. She is, as a nation, utterly unconcerned with anything that happened before that date. She was born to repudiate certain political dogmas and all organic connection with the old world, and to demonstrate and maintain the ideas of freedom and government embodied in the Declaration of Independence and the Constitution of the United States, and she has been almost wholly concerned ever since with the application of these ideas to the needs of the rapidly expanding area of the United States, and its rapidly growing population.

Further, throughout its history the United States has had no foreign problems to embarrass it. Its only neighbor was the British Empire, which, after 1783, entirely accepted American independence and, after 1823, was an active supporter of the Monroe Doctrine that there should be no more European intervention on the two American continents. America, therefore, has never had to consider her own future in terms of rivalry with, or fear of, other nations. Having made a fresh start in a new world, she has been able to pursue her way according to her own ideas regardless of what the rest of the peoples of the globe were doing.

This orphanhood of America may have had certain cultural disadvantages, in so far as it tended to cut her off mentally from the great literary and artistic heritages of Greece and Rome and Europe. But it had three supreme advantages. It freed America from the ancient and deep-rooted hates and grudges which estrange and embitter and paralyze the peoples of Europe. It started America without the class and social distinctions which have been so long a hindrance to England, and without the military and diplomatic traditions which are the bane of the Continent. And it left Christianity without a rival as the dominant moral and spiritual appeal in her life. Modern Europe is the child of the Renaissance, modern America of the Reformation.

The spirit of America, in consequence, is different from that of any European people. It can best be judged, perhaps, by considering what thinking Americans mean when they talk of Americanism as the gospel which has somehow to be instilled into the immigrant if he is to be worthy of his citizenship. Americanism means that you accept absolutely the view that all men are by nature equal; that everybody should have free opportunity and should be judged by the use he makes of that opportunity, and not by any social, economic, racial, official or hereditary privilege; that it is the American people and not the abstract entity called "America" that matters; that government should be democratic in the sense that it must be conducted with the consent of all the governed; and that the future depends upon the vigor and initiative and ability with which the individual citizens "make good" in their chosen sphere of life, and are "good citizens" in their social and political activities. To the European America often seems to permit outrages on personal liberty which would not be tolerated in other lands. This is true, but on examination it will be found that it is the defect of a quality. Europeans resent state interference largely because the state, for historical or class reasons, seems something apart from themselves. In America the prevailing sentiment is that the will of the people must govern, even where it is intolerant and unreasonable, and that no claims of individual liberty can be allowed to stand in its way.

This spirit, born in the fresh air of the new world, strengthened in the struggle for independence from British control, and developed by the Civil War, has been intensified by the fact that during the past fifty years America has again become a nation of pioneers, pioneers from the eastern states, starting off to colonize and build up the vast undeveloped West, pioneers from Europe who left all to make a fresh start in a new land. This spirit is to-day the great energizing, creative and assimilating force in America. It has made America what she is. And when it really begins to turn outwards, it will be, perhaps, America's greatest contribution to the solution of the world problem. Its buoyancy, its energy, its self-reliance, its absolute faith in the possibility of the progressive improvement and upbuilding of mankind, its rejection of authority and privilege and the enervating and cloying traditions of the past, and its profound belief in the gradual healing efficacy of equality and education and democracy, and its confidence that no problem, national or international, however difficult, is insoluble to reason and energy and common sense, are just what the tired and disheartened old world needs to-day.

It is easy, of course, to point to countless lapses in modern America from these ideals. The cynic would find it easy to tear these statements to shreds and tatters. Nobody can fail to be impressed with the violence and intolerance of public opinion, and the way in which it is swept by waves of mass feeling unchecked by serious individual thinking. But when all is said and done about the degeneracy of much in the United States to-day, it is none the less true that in America has been brought into being a spirit which previously had existed nowhere else, and which, if it can be translated into international terms, is the principal hope of the future. Without America the probability of Europe pulling itself straight, or of Asia or Africa lifting themselves on to a law-abiding, self-governing and peace-loving basis would be small indeed. The fact that she has been able to absorb tens of millions of Europeans, free them from race hatred, from subservience, from social limitation, and turn them into good American citizens, devoted to American ideas, hard-working, prosperous, self-respecting, is some indication of what this same spirit will be able to do when it gets abroad in the world.

II. The Basis for American Coöperation

If American coöperation in international affairs is to be secured it will only be because the ideal set up is such as will commend itself to this fundamental American point of view. Most nations are involved in international problems whether they want it or not. They are surrounded by contiguous neighbors, more or less like themselves, and their vital interests are inseparably bound up with the policy and actions of those neighbors. America is not so placed. To all intents and purposes she has no neighbors. Whatever may be the position in the future, she is to-day nearly self-supporting. The only reasons which will drive her to take part in international affairs will be that she thinks that it will be to her own advantage, or that she ought to do so.

Up to the present America has had no world policy. The nearest thing to such a policy was formulated by ex-President Wilson in his addresses between the date when the United States entered the war, April 2, 1917, and the signing of the Covenant of the League of Nations on June 30, 1919. But these, while containing general ideals to which American public opinion gave hearty assent at the time, were too closely associated with the European issues at stake in the world war, and early became too inter-twined with the internal party politics which led to the rejection of the League of Nations, to serve as the text for American policy. Washington's warning against entangling alliances and the Monroe Doctrine— the broad idea that it is America's business to build up a better civilization than Europe's, as a model to mankind, rather than to exhaust herself in trying to put the old world straight—these still hold the field as the primary elements in America's external outlook.

Judging, however, from the fundamental American point of view, it is not difficult to see the kind of ideal for which America would stand. To the American spirit the future of the world can only lie in the progressive realization of equality, higher civilization and democracy among all peoples. The idea of the government of one people by another is deeply repugnant to the American mind. Patent necessity alone can justify it, and even so it is viewed with suspicion and dislike as being contrary to the instinct that every man ought to be master of his own fate, and that it is usually better for him to get into and out of trouble for himself than to be guided and kept out of it by another. If America is ever to throw herself into the task of international coöperation, it will be because she sees that there is a practicable way of equalizing nations, pacifying their quarrels, ending imperialism, uplifting backward races to the level of independent civilized self-government, and so of producing a peaceful, prosperous, progressive world of peoples united in friendly relations, in which law reigns and war has no longer a place. America had some such vision when she entered the war. But the spectacle of the apparently ineradicable hatreds and intrigues of Europe, coupled with a largely partisan political appeal to narrow self-interest, especially directed to her less enlightened citizens, has clouded that vision, so that to-day idealism is blindfold and selfishness is in the saddle. But the idealism is latent. It has only to be focused in a practical direction to begin to operate once more.

But America will always dislike active intervention in other nations' affairs as a means of bringing into being a new and better world. Her whole tradition of independence is against allowing any outside authority to interfere with her own complete freedom of choice. She is inveterately anti-militarist. She will recoil vehemently from any proposal that looks like the creation of a superstate. She will rely primarily on influence, argument and example to bring wisdom and order into international affairs. There is already a school of opinion that thinks that the United States is too unwieldy, that despite modern means of communication, it is almost impossible for public opinion to be effectively reached or to make itself felt, except on a very few of the most obvious issues of the time. Moreover, it is clear that the present machinery of democracy has been stretched to the limit in the greater states. A parliament of man on present parliamentary lines is a manifest impossibility. The population of the globe is about 2,000,000,000, and a world assembly would consist of some 20,000 delegates if there was only one member for every 100,000 voters. Whatever the far future may bring forth, progress for the moment, at any rate so far as America is concerned, must be by way of the increasing association of the leading Powers in maintaining conditions under which it is possible for every nation and people to work out their own salvation in their own way, subject to their respecting the right of all their neighbors to do the same.

But if the United States has within itself a spirit and many of the ideas which are vital to international reconstruction and peace, it has one supreme defect. It is extraordinarily self-centered, as a nation. America has very little sense of the brotherhood of nations. Her people have a strong humanitarian sense, which finds expression in the constant and generous works of relief and missionary enterprise, which they finance. She has a strong instinct for social reform, which is not only manifest within her own borders, but which extends to many subjects, such as the opium traffic in the international field. But she does not understand that in a world of nations it is her action, as a nation, which matters, and is vital to the promotion of that world progress and world peace which she really has at heart. America does not feel herself consciously a member of the great family of nations. Her instinct is to lay stress on the importance of independence and self-government and to pay little attention to the necessary complement, the means of maintaining peace and coöperation between these separate entities. A perusal of the debates in the Senate on such matters as the tariff, the Panama Tolls Bill, the Shipping Subsidies Bill, or interallied debts, all matters which affect other nations very closely, shows that the idea that the United States has to take into account the effect of its actions on other nations hardly ever emerges. America may decide on a generous or a selfish policy, but that is purely her own concern. She is clearly entitled to do exactly as she likes without consulting anybody else, or trying to meet their views. In the international sense she is not a good neighbor, or a good citizen. President Wilson's action in starting to negotiate the terms of an armistice with the Germans without any consultation with the Allies who were principally concerned was doubtless typical of the ex-President himself, but it was also typical of the general attitude of America in her relation to the outside world.

America, in fact, has got, in a much less malignant but still in a very definite form, the same disease of national selfishness which, as we shall see, is the principal cause of Europe's troubles, the greatest breeder of wars, and the chief impediment along the road of world liberty and world peace. It is this concentration on itself which explains why it took the United States so long to realize that the great war was a world question, and not merely a European question. And it explains why, after the United States had reversed its traditions, and entered effectively into the war, it suddenly turned round, within a year, and blasted the best hopes of European reconstruction and world peace by deserting the councils of the Allies, where its moderating and inspiring presence was of priceless value, and retired once more within its own shell. It could not have done this if it had understood or thought at all about what its action was going to cost its neighbors. It must have been thinking about itself alone.

It is not difficult to see the causes of this attitude. There is first of all the great historical tradition in favor of isolation. It began with Washington, who warned his countrymen against the perils of entangling alliances. At the time Washington was perfectly right. The United States would never have become what it is if during the formative period it had exhausted itself and probably strained its constitution by becoming involved in foreign wars. But the doctrine is absurd now that the United States has become the richest and most powerful state in the world. The tendency to isolation, however, has another historical foundation. The whole early history of the United States stressed the ideas of independence and state rights as opposed to the ideas of unity and coöperation. It was this feeling for separateness, originating in the Puritan settlements, and in itself common in new lands, which presented the greatest obstacle to the formation of the Union itself, and which, when combined with the slavery issue, cost the people a five years' war and a million lives to preserve the Union. It is this same feeling to-day which blinds them to the fact that wars can be prevented and liberty assured only by the active coöperation of the United States with other progressive Powers.

The second great bulwark of the isolation policy is the immense mass of only partially assimilated foreign-born immigrants. These immigrants, for the most part enthusiastic Americans, have absorbed far more of the letter than of the spirit of the founders of America and of its constitution. They do not yet understand the underlying ideas which are commonplaces to the true American. Yet they have votes, and the politician knows how to appeal to get them. Their presence operates in two ways. It increases the hesitation of the better-class American to get mixed up with European questions lest divisions might be caused inside the United States if its Government began to take sides as between the various nationalities of Europe. And it adds enormously to the numbers of those who want America to live unto herself alone. The immigrants feel that they have left the old bad Europe, and they can see no reason why their new free motherland should get mixed up with the evils they themselves have escaped. The greatest obstacle to the internal progress of America to-day is the power of the low-class politician to organize votes in racial *blocs* or by narrow and unworthy appeals. And the greatest obstacle to America's taking an effective part in the world's affairs is the power of that same politician to appeal to narrow and short-sighted American self-interest or anti-foreign prejudice.

Two other influences must be mentioned. One is the gigantic size of America. It is 3,000 miles across, and the majority of the 110,000,000 people who dwell within it live between the Alleghenies and the Rocky Mountains, absorbed in the business of raising crops or manufacturing for their own needs and without any direct contact with the outside world. To those people the rest of the world is extraordinarily remote, and it is very difficult for them to realize that they belong to it or have any concern with its affairs. The other influence is the feeling, already noticed, that it is rather America's business to show the rest of the world a progressively improving example of how a people can live happily and prosperously rather than to go crusading to help other nations in distress. And this feeling has been intensified by the spectacle of Europe since the war. If many Americans have felt acutely that the United States should take a hand in the work of reconstruction, they have also felt that the greatest necessity of all is that the nations of Europe should themselves begin to show some sense of European community, and not try to make America take sides in their own internal quarrels.

III. THE EUROPEAN IMPASSE

But if there are difficulties from the side of America in developing international coöperation for permanent peace, what are we to say when we turn to Europe? Europe to-day, despite its preoccupation with international affairs, is a far more formidable obstacle to progress than the United States with its indifference to international affairs. The United States understands the ideas necessary to establish peace and order on earth, but is reluctant to do much to help to spread them. Europe hardly yet knows of them, and is indeed committed to a doctrine which is incompatible with their realization. That doctrine, or rather religion, for it has all the sanctity of religion, is nationalism in its most virulent form.

Europe to-day is mad with nationalism, a nationalism which largely takes the form of hatred and suspicion of other nations. The war freed her from the three great military despotisms of Russia, Austria-Hungary, and Germany, and extended democracy right up to the Russian frontier; but in doing so it stirred to the very bottom the racial and national animosities which lie at the root of European history. Every nation on the Continent of Europe to-day, mesmerized by the traditions of the past, maddened by the propaganda of national hate and national ambition, is thinking of the future almost exclusively in terms of its own self and of jealous rivalry of its neighbors. Here and there a sane voice which tells of the need for European concord and a long view may be heard. But as Genoa showed, they receive little attention amidst the babel of nationalist cries. It is the freedom, the riches, the glory and power of France, or Germany, or Italy, or any of the new States of Eastern Europe that matter, and when one comes to analyze what these mean, somehow or other they involve the suppression or the weakening of their neighbors. The only obvious rival to nationalism to-day is, not the low quiet voice of reason and goodwill, but the blatant preaching of another hatred, the class hatred of Karl Marx.

The results of these intense national fears, rivalries and jealousies have been shown forth in history, time and time again. Every nation, regarding itself as being surrounded by dangerous and designing foes, has to rely upon its own armaments or on military alliances with others for its own safety. Every change in relative armament is jealously watched, for it may alter the balance of power. Competition in armaments inevitably sets in, the tension from suspicion rises, until finally an incident occurs, mobilization is ordered, and before anybody can prevent it, the nations are at one another's throats in an agony of hatred and fear, and killing and destruction continue until exhaustion or victory calls a halt, when the whole process of building up the conditions of a new war begins again. And every century or so some powerful state or despot tries to end the strain by establishing a military autocracy over all Europe, which produces a conflict for national freedom that embraces the world.

There can never be any end to war, there can be no progress towards international liberty, law and peace in Europe, so long as nationalism in its extreme form holds the European field. Nationalism, in the sense of the desire of a community united by history, language, or race, for independence and freedom of individual expression, is a fine thing. France as a nation has made tremendous contributions to democracy, to thought, to the arts. Germany, Italy, Spain, Russia have all added to the sum of human achievement. Yet all the work they have accomplished, all that together they might do for their common European motherland, is endangered, and millions of lives are sacrificed on the altar of a savage and egotistical worship of the national self, a worship which not only does not protect the object of its devotion, but ruins and enfeebles it by continual wars. There is only one way in which the European peoples can secure what they are really seeking, peace, freedom and opportunity for individuality, and that is not by aggressive self-assertion, but by being ready to concede to their neighbors what they claim for themselves, and by establishing some common institution for the adjustment of European affairs, as England and Scotland did in 1707 and the thirteen American colonies did in 1789.

How fundamentally shallow are the foundations of the national fears and suspicions which keep the European peoples apart can be seen by contemplating what happens to these same races when they go to America. The United States is built up of precisely the same racial ingredients as Europe, though in somewhat different proportions. It contains English, Scots, Irish, French, Germans, Italians, Jews, Magyars, Russians, Czecho-Slovaks, Yugo-Slavs, Greeks, etc. The only different stocks are the Red Indian and the Negro. These 100,000,000 people of European stock inhabit a country of about the same size as Europe. The natural resources of the two are not dissimilar. Each has coal, iron, agricultural products, forests, water-power, minerals in abundance. The climates are much the same. They profess the same Christian religion in varying forms and draw their culture from common roots. Yet the very races which combine in America, losing all sense of fear and hatred and distrust of one another and coöperating perfectly well together, in Europe are divided into groups which hate and fear and distrust one another with terrible intensity, believing that no good can come out of the other and in consequence trusting to armaments and the diplomacy of force with which to obtain what everybody within America or the British Commonwealth of Nations has under the protection of law. The only reason for the difference is that in Europe humanity is grouped by nationalities and is being continually soaked by tradition, by politicians, by propaganda and the press in the wrongs of the past and in fears for the future, while in America or the British Commonwealth they are intermingled under the influence of Anglo-Saxon ideas embodied in the common law and in membership of a single constitutional union. It would serve no purpose to underrate the strength and tenacity of racial feelings. They will not yield in a day or a month or in many years. But this contrast serves to show that the trouble lies, not in the nature of the humanity of Europe, but in the beliefs and ideals into which it has been born and educated. If the natural unity of Europe has been destroyed by education in an egotistical nationalism and mistrust, it can be restored by education of a wiser and better kind.

But if the outlook at the moment seems black, the underlying signs in Europe are not unpropitious. Nationalism as a disease is clearly coming to its crisis. All Europe must soon see what many Europeans already see, that Europe must master self-centered nationalism or nationalism will destroy European civilization. The war has removed the despotism which throve on national jealousies and fears. It can only be a question of time for those issues to be solved which now exacerbate the relations of the European Powers and keep alive the passions of the war, and especially the reparations question, the insolvency of the national finances, and the Bolshevik propaganda of suspicion and unrest. If the British Commonwealth and the United States play their part there is good hope that the European peoples will then begin to come together and recognize that they must live harmoniously together if they are to live at all.

IV. The British Commonwealth

What of the British Commonwealth? Where does it stand? It occupies a very peculiar position, for it is not possible to speak of it as a single entity. From the international point of view it has three aspects—Great Britain, the Dominions, and India and the peoples which are not yet self-governing. Great Britain, owing to the existence of the Channel, stands midway between Europe and America. Great Britain is an old and experienced Power, and has been intimately associated with all the chief aspects of the world's political history for centuries. Perhaps for that reason she has nothing like the same forward-looking outlook as the United States. Nor has she ever had the revolution of social equality, though the old class distinctions are rapidly passing away. In consequence the atmosphere of hereditary privilege and of imperialism, though greatly weakened since 1900, has clung about her council chambers, and has strengthened the idea that the British Government ought to make itself responsible for other and more backward peoples, rather than encourage them to work out their own salvation just as quickly as is practically possible, which has lain at the root of half the discontent in India and Egypt. Great Britain, too, despite the fact that she gave birth to *Magna Charta,* to the common law, and to the Mother of Parliaments, has nothing like the same abounding faith in democracy or in the infinite capacity of man for progress and regeneration under a self-governing system as is characteristic of the United States and which is necessary to move the mountains of doubt and scepticism and ignorance which stand in the way of world unity.

On the other hand, she is not drugged by the ancient race hatreds and nationalist fears of Europe. She was the first of the great Powers to overcome the bane of nationalism in the union of England and Scotland and Wales, and these three strongly marked and previously hostile racial individualities now combine happily in one parliament. With Ireland alone has she failed. She has, too, overcome the evils of nationalism still more successfully by keeping voluntarily together in one Commonwealth the great number of peoples and nations which go to make up the British Empire to-day. Moreover, if Great Britain is less idealist and less progressive as regards the future than America, there is no nation in the world which is so tolerant and considerate in its handling of international problems or which recognizes more fully that no nation can dictate to others the way they should go, and that international peace and progress can only be won by the slow and patient process of inducing nations to come along of their own accord. Great Britain, perhaps because of her experience in handling the national problem of the British Empire, is essentially a good neighbor in the international sense. Though for centuries she has been mixed up with the problems of the whole earth, there is no people which has so consistent a record for the sane and steadfast support of reason, fair play and liberality in the conduct of international affairs.

The second element in the British Commonwealth is the Dominions. In fundamental outlook they stand on much the same ground as America. They are new countries looking to the future rather than to the past. They are intense believers in democracy, social equality, in the doctrine that every man must have opportunity and be judged by the use he makes of it. Their influence in the counsels of the Commonwealth will be steadily cast for the progressive view, but it will be tempered by a much more tolerant and responsible view of international affairs than in the case of the United States by reason of their membership in the Imperial Conference and their consequent understanding of the realities of world politics. The contrast between their attitude and performance in the world war and that of the United States is an instance of their broader international outlook.

The third element in the British Commonwealth is symbolized by India. In the relations between the white nations and the peoples who are still not able to take full charge of their own affairs, the British Commonwealth has to deal with what in the long run is going to be a greater problem even than the relations between the great civilized Powers. For the relations between the backward and the advanced peoples are necessarily complicated by differences of color, religion and civilization. The attempt which is already being made, not merely to introduce democracy among the 325,000,000 people of India, but to bridge the gulf between East and West by making India a member of the Imperial Conference, is an example of exactly that process of direct and personal consultation which must be followed in all international problems, if misunderstanding, prejudice and suspicion are to be dispelled and international questions are to be adjusted in friendliness, justice and peace.

The British Commonwealth, therefore, may be less idealistic, less democratic, less confident of the future than the United States, when taken as a whole. But it is less tainted by nationalism, the great international evil of the day, than either Europe or America, for it is itself an association of nations. It is also a standing attempt to disprove the doctrine that East and West cannot understand one another and coöperate together, though the issue of this experiment is still in doubt. It has, too, of all states the widest range of international experience. It is clear, therefore, that it has a great contribution to bring to the solution of the international problem. Moreover, it is daily becoming clearer that the British Commonwealth can only solve its own problems in proportion as

it helps to solve the world's problems. For the British Commonwealth is a microcosm of the world, and it is manifest that peoples
divided by race and language and color, to say nothing of civilization, religion and the seven seas, will never integrate into a single
organic whole separate from, and perhaps in opposition to, their
fellow men. Its own internal questions are inseparably bound up
at every point with those of the rest of the world. The problems
of the future relations of the various self-governing members to
one another, and of the Asiatic and African peoples to the British
and to the Dominions, will only be solved as they are seen to be
part of the larger question of the mutual relations between all the
civilized Powers, and between civilization as a whole and the backward peoples.

V. Conclusion

One conclusion seems to stand out from the considerations advanced in the foregoing pages with transparent clearness. Whatever the other difficulties in the world may be, difficulties from
color, from varying degrees of civilization in Europe, and from
the peace settlement, the paramount evil from which the world is
suffering to-day is the worship of the false god of selfish nationalism. So long as that religion is in the ascendant every other problem is insoluble. It makes every people look at the problems of
the world from their own narrow point of view. It makes for
suspicion and fear and blind folly where trust and long views
are essential. It leads inevitably to reliance on armaments and
diplomacy instead of on fair play, open deliberation and the growth
of law. And every few years it drives nations to try to settle their
disputes and rivalries with the sword, with results which not only
exhaust the combatants themselves, but damage the prosperity of
the whole earth and leave behind fresh fountains of enmity and
hate. The biggest single reason for the failure to deal with the
post-war problem has been the inability of the nations, especially
since the withdrawal of the United States from the deliberations of
the world, to rise in the consideration of the reparations issue, the
debts problem, the Near Eastern problem, above their own national
standpoints. How comparatively easy of solution these questions
are when they are really looked at from the standpoint of what
will most promote the general good can be seen by anybody who
will begin to consider how they should be dealt with from that
point of view.

There is no people that is free from belief in this false religion. With some it takes the form of fear and jealousy of their neighbors. With others it takes the form of indifference to others and of thinking only of themselves. Even in the case of the British Commonwealth, which, by reason of its composition, has the disease less intensely than most, the sense of loyalty and brotherhood is more or less confined to those who dwell beneath the Union Jack.

The religion of national selfishness has at regular intervals produced wars in the past. Unless it is overcome it will infallibly produce them in the future. One has only to look at the attitude of the United States—certainly one of the most advanced and progressive communities in the world—towards Japan, to see what is bound to happen again unless this evil is grappled with. The attitude of American public opinion before the Washington Conference, in its suspicion and intolerance and reckless assertion of its own point of view, was exactly like the attitude of the European states towards one another before the war. People continually spoke evil of Japan and openly spoke of impending war. Fortunately the Washington Conference was summoned. It dealt with the issues of the moment in a fair and friendly spirit, and the war cloud which a few weeks before had threatened to break vanished into thin air. The Pacific problem is not permanently solved. It will reappear. But the Washington Conference showed the way in which all international questions can be dealt with when something larger than a purely national standpoint is kept in view. It is only necessary that the spirit of the Washington Conference should become universal, should be embodied in some permanent machinery embracing all nations, which will enable all international problems to be handled in the same way, for the danger of another world war to disappear from the earth.

What is needed above all else now is the growth of the world standpoint. Nothing less wide will meet the case. It will be extraordinarily difficult to get America to feel that she ought to take a very active part in helping to set Europe alone straight. But present the problem to her as one of making the whole world a place of liberty and peace and she will respond. It is the same with Europe itself. The purely European divisions are so old and, so deep-rooted that they are difficult to forget. It would be easier in many ways to lift Europe out of nationalism and armaments as part of a world movement than to make it forget its animosities by itself. And obviously the problem of dealing properly with such questions as the Turks, or the color problem, or the treatment of backward peoples, can only in the long run be handled uniformly and well from a world standpoint.

Further, is not the recognition of the Golden Rule as the standard in international affairs the only real road to lasting prosperity as well as lasting peace? It is a commonplace that civilization and enterprise grow in every country in proportion as law and order take the place of anarchy and the rule of the strongest. It will be exactly the same in the international sphere. Can anyone doubt, if to-morrow every nation were to abandon its aggressive armaments and to abolish that other great example of international fear and suspicion, its high exclusive tariffs, that a wave of prosperity and enterprise would go round the world, which is absolutely impossible so long as every people tries to make itself a watertight compartment, bristling with armaments and impediments to trade. For the moment such an idea seems to be preposterous and absurd. Yet, on a dispassionate consideration, is there any other way in the long run in which mankind can gain the peace, the prosperity and the mutual understanding which are necessary to its future?

One other conclusion also seems to stand out. The road of progress lies in unity gradually increasing through education, example, and free conference of free peoples. It will never come through control imposed from above. The creation of a world state has been attempted several times from without. Napoleon, who saw clearly the evils of competitive nationalism in Europe, tried it and failed against the stronger instinct for self-government. Some of the more far-sighted Germans thought it was the mission of Germany to do for Europe by force what Bismarck had done for Germany by force fifty years before. The Roman Empire actually succeeded in giving law, unity and peace to the whole known civilized world, but it decayed because the larger it grew the more centralized and autocratic it became, until all spontaneous and democratic life disappeared. If the unity of the world is to come about under the reign of law it must be by voluntary growth from within and not by imposition from without. Christianity transformed Europe in its earlier days. By no political control, but by the spirit which it breathed, it abolished pagan idolatry, it humanized and made more merciful the law, it mitigated and finally abolished the rigors of slavery, it conquered the barbarian and gave once more unity to the civilized world. But in the process ecclesiasticism and organization had overlaid the more creative and powerful working of its spirit. The attempts of the Holy Roman Emperors and of the Papacy under Hildebrand broke down because they sought to do by force from without what could only be done voluntarily from within. But in breaking down they gave place to the Renaissance, which restored something of the freedom of thought and spirit which had been lost, though it let loose again the racial and national passions which previously Christianity had stilled. It is the Christian method which is fundamentally needed again to-day, though it will find expression in external institutions.

What the future organization of the world will be, whether it will be a revived League of Nations or a new Association of Nations, none can say. But that it will be a gradual growth towards world peace, world law, world freedom, by a process of voluntary international conferences, at which the humanity point of view steadily defeats and destroys the selfishly nationalist point of view seems certain. There is no chance and there would be no permanence and no vitality or freedom in unity reached by any other road. America, too, is right in one thing. She is convinced that it is of more value to the world that she herself and all other nations should show a progressively improving standard of democratic government than that they should imperil their own standards by unnecessary interference with others. Had the governing classes in England during the last fifty years spent more time in improving conditions at home, in dealing with slums and poverty and in perfecting democracy, and less in giving to eastern countries under a benevolent despotism an extraordinarily high standard of governmental integrity and efficiency, at the price of excluding their peoples from real responsibility, it would probably have been better for both. On the other hand, Great Britain is right about another thing. No nation can live unto itself alone. If so, it will lose "that which it hath." Peace and international liberty will not just "grow." They will grow if the nations mean them to grow, and if the peoples which have the highest standards set to work patiently and without discouragement to help others to see what can be done. Without their help in constant conference and patient deliberation about all the world's affairs, and occasionally, where necessary, by intervention, to maintain the conditions in which liberty and progress can develop, how can the ideals for which they stand get a chance? If the Washington Conference was an example of what can be done in propitious circumstances, the Genoa Conference was an example of what must be attempted again and again in unfavorable conditions, until fear and prejudice and selfishness yield to the larger view, national selfishness is swallowed up in the world view, and armaments and wars disappear from the earth. It will not be easy to rebuild the broken temple of the world's peace, shattered first by the war, and later by the break-up in the unity of the Allies. But if these failures mean that a new attempt is to be made, from the only standpoint which can ultimately succeed, a standpoint which embraces all mankind, the sufferings and failures of the last few years will not have been in vain.

PUBLIC DUTY

THE SCHOLAR IN A REPUBLIC [1]

Wendell Phillips

[Wendell Phillips (1811-1884), orator and reformer, was graduated from the Harvard law school in 1834. In college he was known for his skill in debate. While waiting in Boston for clients that did not come, he interested himself in the anti-slavery movement. When in 1835, a mob dragged William Lloyd Garrison, editor of the *Liberator*, through the streets, Phillips became an avowed abolitionist. Two years later he became famous overnight as a result of his speech upon the murder of Lovejoy. Lovejoy, who edited an anti-slavery paper in Alton, Illinois, was killed while defending his press from a mob. The abolitionists of Boston called a meeting in Fanueil Hall to express their indignation at the outrage. The more conservative Bostonians felt that Lovejoy had by his utterances invited his fate, and the Attorney-General of Massachusetts said as much from the platform. Phillips, who was then twenty-six years of age, was in the audience. Making his way to the platform, he rebuked the Attorney-General in a speech which has become a classic in American oratory. He was immediately recognized as a leader of the abolitionists, and he spoke constantly from their platforms in various parts of the country. As a result of his activities, his friends among the old families of Boston deserted him, and at Harvard he was regarded as fanatical and intolerant.

After the Proclamation of Emancipation, Phillips espoused various causes. He spoke upon the rights of the newly-freed negroes, upon temperance, women's rights, Indian rights, and the Irish question. In 1881 he was invited to deliver the Phi Beta Kappa oration at Harvard. The occasion offered an opportunity for him to rebuke college men for their apathy, and to present his own conception of the duty of a scholar in a republic. The address was delivered with such spontaneity that no one suspected Phillips of having previously sent it to the printer. Although Phillips had been accustomed to popular audiences, he so delighted the conservative scholars before him that they applauded the expression of sentiments which they could never approve. "It was marvelous and delightful," said Longfellow, "but preposterous from beginning to end." Charles Eliot Norton wrote to James Russell Lowell that "It was a great and memorable performance. It will be one of the historic Phi Beta orations. Charles Eliot made a forcible and eloquent five-minute speech at the dinner, vigorously rejecting Phillips's doctrine and exposing the essential fallacy of his discourse."]

Mr. President and Brothers of the P. B. K.: A hundred years ago our society was planted—a slip from the older root in Virginia. The parent seed, tradition says, was French,—part of that

[1] Reprinted by permission of Lee and Shepard from *Speeches, Lectures and Letters*, Wendell Phillips.
Questions and topics for the discussion of this address, and of other phases of the general subject with which it deals, will be found on pages 545 and 549.

conspiracy for free speech whose leaders prated democracy in the *salons*, while they carefully held on to the flesh-pots of society by crouching low to kings and their mistresses, and whose final object of assault was Christianity itself. Voltaire gave the watchword,—

> "Crush the wretch."
> *"Écrasez l'infame."*

No matter how much or how little truth there may be in the tradition: no matter what was the origin or what was the object of our society, if it had any special one, both are long since forgotten. We stand now simply a representative of free, brave, American scholarship. I emphasize *American* scholarship.

In one of those glowing, and as yet unequalled pictures which Everett drew for us, here and elsewhere, of Revolutionary scenes, I remember his saying, that the independence we then won, if taken in its literal and narrow sense, was of no interest and little value; but, construed in the fulness of its real meaning, it bound us to a distinctive American character and purpose, to a keen sense of large responsibility, and to a generous self-devotion. It is under the shadow of such unquestioned authority that I used the term "American scholarship."

Our society was, no doubt, to some extent, a protest against the sombre theology of New England, where a hundred years ago, the atmosphere was black with sermons, and where religious speculation beat uselessly against the narrowest limits.

The first generation of Puritans—though Lowell does let Cromwell call them "a small colony of pinched fanatics"—included some men, indeed not a few, worthy to walk close to Roger Williams and Sir Harry Vane, the two men deepest in thought and bravest in speech of all who spoke English in their day, and equal to any in practical statesmanship. Sir Harry Vane—in my judgment the noblest human being who ever walked the streets of yonder city— I do not forget Franklin or Sam Adams, Washington or Fayette, Garrison or John Brown. But Vane dwells an arrow's flight above them all, and his touch consecrated the continent to measureless toleration of opinion and entire equality of rights. We are told we can find in Plato "all the intellectual life of Europe for two thousand years:" so you can find in Vane the pure gold of two hundred and fifty years of American civilization, with no particle of its dross. Plato would have welcomed him to the Academy, and Fénelon kneeled with him at the altar. He made Somers and John

Marshall possible; like Carnot, he organized victory; and Milton pales before him in the stainlessness of his record. He stands among English statesman preëminently the representative, in practice and in theory, of serene faith in the safety of trusting truth wholly to her own defence. For other men we walk backward, and throw over their memories the mantle of charity and excuse, saying reverently, "Remember the temptation and the age." But Vane's ermine has no stain; no act of his needs explanation or apology; and in thought he stands abreast of our age,—like pure intellect, belongs to all time.

Carlyle said, in years when his words were worth heeding, "Young men, close your Byron, and open your Goethe." If my counsel had weight in these halls, I should say, "Young men, close your John Winthrop and Washington, your Jefferson and Webster, and open Sir Harry Vane." The generation that knew Vane gave to our Alma Mater for a seal the simple pledge,—*Veritas*.

But the narrowness and poverty of colonial life soon starved out this element. Harvard was re-dedicated *Christo et Ecclesiæ;* and, up to the middle of the last century, free thought in religion meant Charles Chauncy and the Brattlestreet Church protest, while free thought hardly existed anywhere else. But a single generation changed all this. A hundred years ago there were pulpits that led the popular movement; while outside of religion and of what called itself literature, industry and a jealous sense of personal freedom obeyed, in their rapid growth, the law of their natures. English common sense and those municipal institutions born of the common law, and which had saved and sheltered it, grew inevitably too large for the eggshell of English dependence, and allowed it to drop off as naturally as the chick does when she is ready. There was no change of law,—nothing that could properly be called revolution,—only noiseless growth, the seed bursting into flower, infancy becoming manhood. It was life, in its omnipotence, rending whatever dead matter confined it. So have I seen the tiny weeds of a luxuriant Italian spring upheave the colossal foundation of the Cæsars' palace, and leave it a mass of ruins.

But when the veil was withdrawn, what stood revealed astonished the world. It showed the undreamt power, the serene strength, of simple manhood, free from the burden and restraint of absurd institutions in church and state. The grandeur of this new Western constellation gave courage to Europe, resulting in the French Revolution, the greatest, the most unmixed, the most unstained and wholly perfect blessing Europe has had in modern times, unless we may possibly except the Reformation, and the invention of Printing.

What precise effect that giant wave had when it struck our shore we can only guess. History is, for the most part, an idle amusement, the day-dream of pedants and triflers. The details of events, the actors' motives, and their relation to each other, are buried with them. How impossible to learn the exact truth of what took place yesterday under your next neighbor's roof! Yet we complacently argue and speculate about matters a thousand miles off, and a thousand years ago, as if we knew them. When I was a student here, my favorite study was history. The world and affairs have shown me that one-half of history is loose conjecture, and much of the rest is the writer's opinion. But most men see facts, not with their eyes, but with their prejudices. Any one familiar with courts will testify how rare it is for an honest man to give a perfectly correct account of a transaction. We are tempted to see facts as we think they ought to be, or wish they were. And yet journals are the favorite original sources of history. Tremble, my good friend, if your sixpenny neighbor keeps a journal. "It adds a new terror to death." You shall go down to your children not in your fair lineaments and proportions, but with the smirks, elbows, and angles he sees you with. Journals are excellent to record the depth of the last snow and the date when the May-flower opens; but when you come to men's motives and characters, journals are the magnets that get near the chronometer of history and make all its records worthless. You can count on the fingers of your two hands all the robust minds that ever kept journals. Only milksops and fribbles indulge in that amusement, except now and then a respectable mediocrity. One such journal nightmares New-England annals, emptied into history by respectable middle-aged gentlemen, who fancy that narrowness and spleen, like poor wine, mellow into truth when they get to be a century old. But you might as well cite "The Daily Advertiser" of 1850 as authority on one of Garrison's actions.

And, after all, of what value are these minutiæ? Whether Luther's zeal was partly kindled by lack of gain from the sale of indulgences, whether Boston rebels were half smugglers and half patriots, what matters it now? Enough that he meant to wrench the gag from Europe's lips, and that they were content to suffer keenly, that we might have an untrammelled career. We can only hope to discover the great currents and massive forces which have shaped our lives: all else is trying to solve a problem of whose elements we know nothing. As the poet historian of the last generation says so plaintively, "History comes like a beggarly gleaner in the field, after Death, the great lord of the domain, has gathered the harvest, and lodged it in his garner, which no man may open." But we may safely infer that French debate and experience broadened and encouraged our fathers. To that we undoubtedly owe, in some degree, the theoretical perfection, ingrafted on English practical sense and old forms, which marks the foundation of our republic. English civil life, up to that time, grew largely out of custom, rested almost wholly on precedent. For our model there was no authority in the record, no precedent on the file; unless you find it, perhaps, partially, in that Long Parliament bill with which Sir Harry Vane would have outgeneralled Cromwell, if the shameless soldier had not crushed it with his muskets.

Standing on Saxon foundations, and inspired, perhaps, in some degree, by Latin example, we have done what no race, no nation, no age, had before dared even to try. We have founded a republic on the unlimited suffrage of the millions. We have actually worked out the problem that man, as God created him, may be trusted with self-government. We have shown the world that a church without a bishop, and a state without a king, is an actual, real, everyday possibility. Look back over the history of the race: where will you find a chapter that precedes us in that achievement? Greece had her republics, but they were the republics of a few freemen and subjects and many slaves; and "the battle of Marathon was fought by slaves, unchained from the doorposts of their masters' houses." Italy had her republics: they were the republics of wealth and skill and family, limited and aristocratic. The Swiss republics were groups of cousins. Holland had her republic,—a republic of guilds and landholders, trusting the helm of state to property and education. And all these, which at their best, held but a million or two within their narrow limits, have gone down in the ocean of time.

A hundred years ago our fathers announced this sublime, and, as it seemed then, foolhardy declaration, that God intended all men to be free and equal,—all men, without restriction, without qualification, without limit. A hundred years have rolled away since that venturous declaration; and to-day, with a territory that joins ocean to ocean, with fifty millions of people, with two wars behind her, with the grand achievement of having grappled with the fearful disease that threatened her central life, and broken four millions of fetters, the great republic, stronger than ever, launches into the second century of her existence. The history of the world has no such chapter in its breadth, its depth, its significance, or its bearing on future history.

What Wycliffe did for religion, Jefferson and Sam Adams did for the State,—they trusted it to the people. He gave the masses the Bible, the right to think. Jefferson and Sam Adams gave them the ballot, the right to rule. His intrepid advance contemplated theirs as its natural, inevitable result. Their serene faith completed the gift which the Anglo-Saxon race makes to humanity. We have not only established a new measure of the possibilities of the race: we have laid on strength, wisdom, and skill a new responsibility. Grant that each man's relations to God and his neighbor are exclusively his own concern, and that he is entitled to all the aid that will make him the best judge of these relations; that the people are the source of all power, and their measureless capacity the lever of all progress; their sense of right the court of final appeal in civil affairs; the institutions they create the only ones any power has a right to impose; that the attempt of one class to prescribe the law, the religion, the morals, or the trade of another is both unjust and harmful,—and the Wycliffe and Jefferson of history mean this if they mean anything,—then, when, in 1867, Parliament doubled the English franchise, Robert Lowe was right in affirming, amid the cheers of the House, "Now the first interest and duty of every Englishman is to educate the masses—our masters." Then, whoever sees farther than his neighbor is that neighbor's servant to lift him to such higher level. Then, power, ability, influence, character, virtue, are only trusts with which to serve our time.

We all agree in the duty of scholars to help those less favored in life, and that this duty of scholars to educate the mass is still more imperative in a republic, since a republic trusts the state wholly to the intelligence and moral sense of the people. The experience of the last forty years shows every man that law has no atom of strength, either in Boston or New Orleans, unless, and only so far as, public opinion indorses it, and that your life, goods, and good name rest on the moral sense, self-respect, and law-abiding mood of the men that walk the streets, and hardly a whit on the provisions of the statute-book. Come, any one of you, outside of the ranks of popular men, and you will not fail to find it so. Easy men dream that we live under government of law. Absurd mistake! we live under a government of men and newspapers. Your first attempt to stem dominant and keenly-cherished opinions will reveal this to you.

But what is education? Of course it - is not book-learning. Book-learning does not make five per cent of that mass of common sense that "runs" the world, transacts its business, secures its progress, trebles its power over nature, works out in the long run a rough average justice, wears away the world's restraints, and lifts off its burdens. The ideal Yankee, who "has more brains in his hand than others have in their skulls," is not a scholar; and two-thirds of the inventions that enable France to double the world's sunshine, and make Old and New England the work shops of the world, did not come from colleges or from minds trained in the schools of science, but struggled up, forcing their way against giant obstacles, from the irrepressible instinct of untrained natural power. Her workshops, not her colleges, made England, for a while, the mistress of the world; and the hardest job her workman had was to make Oxford willing he should work his wonders.

So of moral gains. As shrewd an observer as Governor Marcy of New York often said he cared nothing for the whole press of the seaboard, representing wealth and education (he meant book-learning), if it set itself against the instincts of the people. Lord Brougham, in a remarkable comment on the life of Romilly, enlarges on the fact that the great reformer of the penal law found all the legislative and all the judicial power of England, its colleges and its bar, marshalled against him, and owed his success, as all such reforms do, says his lordship, to public meetings and popular instinct. It would be no exaggeration to say that government itself began in usurpation, in the feudalism of the soldier and the bigotry of the priest; that liberty and civilization are only fragments of rights wrung from the strong hands of wealth and book-learning. Almost all the great truths relating to society were not the result of scholarly meditation, "hiving up wisdom with each curious year," but have been first heard in the solemn protests of martyred patriotism and the loud cries of crushed and starving labor. When common sense and the common people have stereotyped a principle into a statute, then book-men come to explain how it was discovered and on what ground it rests. The world makes history, and scholars write it, one half truly, and the other half as their prejudices blur and distort it.

New England learned more of the principles of toleration from a lyceum committee doubting the dicta of editors and bishops when they forbade it to put Theodore Parker on its platform; more from a debate whether the anti-slavery cause should be so far countenanced as to invite one of its advocates to lecture; from Sumner and Emerson, George William Curtis, and Edwin Whipple, refusing to speak unless a negro could buy his way into their halls as freely as any other,—New England has learned more from these lessons than she has or could have done from all the treatises on free printing from Milton and Roger Williams, through Locke, down to Stuart Mill.

Selden, the profoundest scholar of his day, affirmed, "No man is wiser for his learning"; and that was only an echo of the Saxon proverb, "No fool is a perfect fool until he learns Latin." Bancroft says of our fathers, that "the wildest theories of the human reason were reduced to practice by a community so humble that no statesman condescended to notice it, and a legislation without precedent was produced off-hand by the instincts of the people." And Wordsworth testifies, that, while German schools might well blush for their subserviency,—

> "A few strong instincts and a few plain rules,
> Among the herdsmen of the Alps, have wrought
> More for mankind at this unhappy day
> Than all the pride of intellect and thought."

Wycliffe was, no doubt, a learned man. But the learning of his day would have burned him, had it dared, as it did burn his dead body afterwards. Luther and Melanchthon were scholars, but were repudiated by the scholarship of their time, which followed Erasmus, trying "all his life to tread on eggs without breaking them;" he who proclaimed that "peaceful error was better than tempestuous truth." What would college-graduate Seward weigh, in any scale, against Lincoln bred in affairs?

Hence I do not think the greatest things have been done for the world by its book-men. Education is not the chips of arithmetic and grammar,—nouns, verbs, and the multiplication table; neither is it that last year's almanac of dates, or series of lies agreed upon, which we so often mistake for history. Education is not Greek and Latin and the air-pump. Still, I rate at its full value the training we get in these walls. Though what we actually carry away is little enough, we do get some training of our powers, as the gymnast or the fencer does of his muscles: we go hence also with such general knowledge of what mankind has agreed to consider proved and settled, that we know where to reach for the weapon when we need it.

I have often thought the motto prefixed to his college library catalogue by the father of the late Professor Peirce,—Professor Peirce, the largest natural genius, the man of the deepest reach and firmest grasp and widest sympathy, that God has given to Harvard in our day,—whose presence made you the loftiest peak and farthest outpost of more than mere scientific thought,—the magnet who, with his twin Agassiz, made Harvard for forty years the intellectual Mecca of forty States,—his father's catalogue bore for a motto, *"Scire ubi aliquid invenias magna pars eruditionis est;"* and that always seemed to me a gage very nearly all we acquired at college, except facility in the use of our powers. Our influence in the community does not really spring from superior attainments, but from this thorough training of faculties, and more even, perhaps, from the deference men accord to us.

Gibbon says we have two educations, one from teachers, and the other we give ourselves. This last is the real and only education of the masses,—one gotten from life, from affairs, from earning one's bread; necessity, the mother of invention; responsibility, that teaches prudence, and inspires respect for right. Mark the critic out of office: how reckless in assertion, how careless of consequences; and then the caution, forethought, and fair play of the same man charged with administration. See that young, thoughtless wife suddenly widowed; how wary and skilful! what ingenuity in guarding her child and saving his rights! Any one who studied Europe forty or fifty years ago could not but have marked the level of talk there, far below that of our masses. It was of crops and rents, markets and marriages, scandal and fun. Watch men here, and how often you listen to the keenest discussions of right and wrong, this leader's honesty, that party's justice, the fairness of this law, the impolicy of that measure;—lofty, broad topics, training morals, widening views. Niebuhr said of Italy, sixty years ago, "No one feels himself a citizen. Not only are the people destitute of hope, but they have not even wishes touching the world's affairs; and hence all the springs of great and noble thoughts are choked up."

In this sense the Fremont campaign of 1856 taught Americans more than a hundred colleges; and John Brown's pulpit at Harper's Ferry was equal to any ten thousand ordinary chairs. God lifted a million of hearts to his gibbet, as the Roman cross lifted a world to itself in that divine sacrifice of two thousand years ago. As much as statesmanship had taught in our previous eighty years, that one week of intellectual watching and weighing and dividing truth taught twenty millions of people. Yet how little, brothers, can we claim for book-men in that uprising and growth of 1856! And while the first of American scholars could hardly find, in the rich vocabulary of Saxon scorn, words enough to express, amid the plaudits of his class, his loathing and contempt for John Brown, Europe thrilled to him as proof that our institutions had not lost all their native and distinctive life. She had grown tired of our parrot note and cold moonlight reflection of older civilizations. Lansdowne and Brougham could confess to Sumner that they had never read a page of their cotemporary, Daniel Webster; and you spoke to vacant eyes when you named Prescott, fifty years ago, to average Europeans; while Vienna asked, with careless indifference, "Seward, who is he?" But long before our ranks marched up State Street to the John Brown song, the banks of the Seine and of the Danube hailed the new life which had given us another and nobler Washington. Lowell foresaw him when forty years ago he sang of,—

> "Truth forever on the scaffold,
>   Wrong forever on the throne;
> Yet that scaffold sways the future:
>   And behind the dim unknown
> Standeth God, within the shadow,
>   Keeping watch above his own."

And yet the book-men, as a class, have not yet acknowledged him.

It is here that letters betray their lack of distinctive American character. Fifty million of men God gives us to mold; burning questions, keen debate, great interests trying to vindicate their right to be, sad wrongs brought to the bar of public judgment, —these are the people's schools. Timid scholarship either shrinks from sharing in these agitations, or denounces them as vulgar and dangerous interference by incompetent hands with matters above them. A chronic distrust of the people pervades the book-educated class of the North; they shrink from that free speech which is God's normal school for educating men, throwing upon them the grave responsibility of deciding great questions, and so lifting them to a higher level of intellectual and moral life. Trust the people—the wise and the ignorant, the good and the bad—with the gravest questions, and in the end you educate the race. At the same time you secure, not perfect institutions, not necessarily good ones, but the best institutions possible while human nature is the basis and the only material to build with. Men are educated and the state uplifted by allowing all—every one—to broach all their mistakes and advocate all their errors. The community that will not protect its most ignorant and unpopular member in the free utterance of his opinions, no matter how false or hateful, is only a gang of slaves!

Anacharsis went into the Archon's court of Athens, heard a case argued by the great men of that city, and saw the vote by five hundred men. Walking in the streets, some one asked him, "What do you think of Athenian liberty?" "I think," said he, "wise men argue cases, and fools decide them." Just what that timid scholar, two thousand years ago, said in the streets of Athens, that which calls itself scholarship here says to-day of popular agitation,— that it lets wise men argue questions and fools decide them. But that Athens where fools decided the gravest questions of policy and of right and wrong, where property you had gathered wearily to-day might be wrung from you by the caprice of the mob to-mor-row,—that very Athens probably secured, for its era, the greatest amount of human happiness and nobleness; invented art, and sounded for us the depths of philosophy. God lent to it the largest intellects, and it flashes to-day the torch that gilds yet the mountain peaks of the Old World: while Egypt, the hunker conservative of antiquity, where nobody dared to differ from the priest or to be wiser than his grandfather; where men pretended to be alive, though swaddled in the grave-clothes of creed and custom as close as their mummies were in linen,—that Egypt is hid in the tomb it inhabited, and the intellect Athens has trained for us digs to-day those ashes to find out how buried and forgotten hunkerism lived and acted.

I knew a signal instance of this disease of scholar's distrust, and the cure was as remarkable. In boyhood and early life I was honored with the friendship of Lothrop Motley. He grew up in the thin air of Boston provincialism, and pined on such weak diet. I remember sitting with him once in the State House when he was a member of our Legislature. With biting words and a keen crayon he sketched the ludicrous points in the minds and persons of his fellow-members, and, tearing up the pictures, said scornfully, "What can become of a country with such fellows as these making its laws? No safe investments; your good name lied away any hour, and little worth keeping if it were not." In vain I combated the folly. He went to Europe,—spent four or five years. I met him the day he landed, on his return. As if our laughing talk in the State House had that moment ended, he took my hand with the sudden exclamation, "You were all right: I was all wrong! It *is* a country worth dying for; better still, worth living and working for, to make it all it can be!" Europe made him one of the most American of all Americans. Some five years later, when he sounded that bugle-note in his letter to "The London Times," some critics who knew his early mood, but not its change, suspected there might be a taint of ambition in what they thought so sudden a conversion. I could testify that the mood was five years old: years before the slightest shadow of political expectation had dusked the clear mirror of his scholar life.

This distrust shows itself in the growing dislike of universal suffrage, and the efforts to destroy it made of late by all our easy classes. The white South hates universal suffrage; the so-called cultivated North distrusts it. Journal and college, social-science convention and the pulpit, discuss the propriety of restraining it. Timid scholars tell their dread of it. Carlyle, that bundle of sour prejudices, flouts universal suffrage with a blasphemy that almost equals its ignorance. See his words: "Democracy will prevail when men believe the vote of Judas as good as that of Jesus Christ." No democracy ever claimed that the vote of ignorance and crime was as good in any sense as that of wisdom and virtue. It only asserts that crime and ignorance have the same right to vote that virtue has. Only by allowing that right, and so appealing to their sense of justice, and throwing upon them the burden of their full responsibility, can we hope ever to raise crime and ignorance to the level of self-respect. The right to choose your governor rests on precisely the same foundation as the right to choose your religion; and no more arrogant or ignorant araignment of all that is noble in the civil and religious Europe of the last five hundred years ever came from the triple crown on the Seven Hills than this sneer of the bigot Scotsman. Protestantism holds up its hands in holy horror, and tells us that the Pope scoops out the brains of his churchmen, saying, "I'll think for you: you need only obey." But the danger is, you meet such popes far away from the Seven Hills; and it is sometimes difficult at first to recognize them, for they do not by any means always wear the triple crown.

Evarts and his committee, appointed to inquire why the New York City government is a failure, were not wise enough or did not dare, to point out the real cause, the tyranny of that tool of the demagogue, the corner grog-shop; but they advised taking away the ballot from the poor citizen. But this provision would not reach the evil. Corruption does not so much rot the masses: it poisons Congress. Credit-Mobilier and money rings are not housed under thatched roofs: they flaunt at the Capitol. As usual in chemistry, the scum floats uppermost. The railway king disdained canvassing for voters: "It is cheaper," he said, "to buy legislatures."

It is not the masses who have most disgraced our political annals. I have seen many mobs between the seaboard and the Mississippi. I never saw or heard of any but well-dressed mobs, assembled and countenanced, if not always led in person, by respectability and what called itself education. That unrivaled scholar, the first and greatest New England ever lent to Congress, signalled his advent by quoting the original Greek of the New Testament in support of slavery, and offering to shoulder his musket in its defence; and forty years later the last professor who went to quicken and lift the moral mood of those halls is found advising a plain, blunt, honest witness to forge and lie, that this scholarly reputation might be saved from wreck. Singular comment on Landor's sneer, that there is a spice of the scoundrel in most of our literary men. But no exacting level of property qualifications for a vote would have saved those stains. In those cases Judas did not come from the unlearned class.

Grown gray over history, Macaulay prophesied twenty years ago that soon in these States the poor, worse than another inroad of Goths and Vandals, would begin a general plunder of the rich. It is enough to say that our national funds sell as well in Europe as English consols; and the universal-suffrage Union can borrow money as cheaply as great Britain, ruled, one half by Tories, and the other half by men not certain that they dare call themselves Whigs. Some men affected to scoff at democracy as no sound basis for national debt, doubting the payment of ours. Europe not only wonders at its rapid payment, but the only taint of fraud that touches even the hem of our garment is the fraud of the capitalist cunningly adding to its burdens, and increasing unfairly the value of his bonds; not the first hint from the people of repudiating an iota even of its unjust additions.

Yet the poor and the unlearned class is the one they propose to punish by disfranchisement.

No wonder the humbler class looks on the whole scene with alarm. They see their dearest right in peril. When the easy class conspires to steal, what wonder the humbler class draws together to defend itself? True, universal suffrage is a terrible power; and, with all the great cities brought into subjection to the dangerous classes by grog, and Congress sitting to register the decrees of capital, both sides may well dread the next move. Experience proves that popular governments are the best protectors of life and property. But suppose they were not, Bancroft allows that "the fears of one class are no measure of the rights of another."

Suppose that universal suffrage endangered peace and threatened property. There is something more valuable than wealth, there is something more sacred than peace. As Humboldt says, "The finest fruit earth holds up to its Maker is a man." To ripen, lift, and educate a man is the first duty. Trade, law, learning, science, and religion are only the scaffolding wherewith to build a man. Despotism looks down into the poor man's cradle, and knows it can crush resistance and curb ill-will. Democracy sees the ballot in that baby-hand; and selfishness bids her put integrity on one side of those baby footsteps and intelligence on the other, lest her own hearth be in peril. Thank God for his method of taking bonds of wealth and culture to share all their blessings with the humblest soul he gives to their keeping! The American should cherish as serene a faith as his fathers had. Instead of seeking a coward safety by battening down the hatches and putting men back into chains, he should recognize that God places him in this peril that he may work out a noble security by concentrating all moral forces to lift this weak, rotting, and dangerous mass into sunlight and health. The fathers touched their highest level when, with stout-hearted and serene faith, they trusted God that it was safe to leave men with all the rights he gave them. Let us be worthy of their blood, and save this sheet-anchor of the race,—universal suffrage,— God's church, God's school, God's method of gently binding men into commonwealths in order that they may at last melt into brothers.

I urge on college-bred men, that, as a class, they fail in republican duty when they allow others to lead in the agitation of the great social questions which stir and educate the age. Agitation is an old word with a new meaning. Sir Robert Peel, the first English leader who felt himself its tool, defined it to be "marshalling the conscience of a nation to mold its laws." Its means are reason and argument,—no appeal to arms. Wait patiently for the growth of public opinion. That secured, then every step taken is taken forever. An abuse once removed never re-appears in history. The freer a nation becomes, the more utterly democratic in its form, the more need of this outside agitation. Parties and sects laden with the burden of securing their own success cannot afford to risk new ideas. "Predominant opinions," said Disraeli, "are the opinions of a class that is vanishing." The agitator must stand outside of organizations, with no bread to earn, no candidate to elect, no party to save, no object but truth,—to tear a question open and riddle it with light.

In all modern constitutional governments, agitation is the only peaceful method of progress. Wilberforce and Clarkson, Rowland Hill and Romilly, Cobden and John Bright, Garrison and O'Connell, have been the master spirits in this new form of crusade. Rarely in this country have scholarly men joined, as a class, in these great popular schools, in these social movements which make the great interests of society "crash and jostle against each other like frigates in a storm."

It is not so much that the people need us, or will feel any lack from our absence. They can do without us. By sovereign and superabundant strength they can crush their way through all obstacles.

"They will march prospering,—not through our presence;
    Songs will inspirit them,—not from our lyre;
    Deeds will be done—while we boast our quiescence;
    Still bidding crouch whom the rest bid aspire."

The misfortune is, we lose a God-given opportunity of making the change an unmixed good, or with the slightest possible share of evil, and are recreant beside to a special duty. These "agitations" are the opportunities and the means God offers us to refine the taste, mold the character, lift the purpose, and educate the moral sense of the masses, on whose intelligence and self-respect rests the state. God furnishes these texts. He gathers for us this audience, and only asks of our coward lips to preach the sermons.

There have been four or five of these great opportunities. The crusade against slavery—that grand hypocrisy which poisoned the national life of two generations—was one,—a conflict between two civilizations which threatened to rend the Union. Almost every element among us was stirred to take a part in the battle. Every great issue, civil and moral, was involved,—toleration of opinion, limits of authority, relation of citizen to law, place of the Bible, priest and layman, sphere of woman, question of race, state rights and nationality; and Channing testified that free speech and free printing owed their preservation to the struggle. But the pulpit flung the Bible at the reformer; law visited him with its penalties; society spewed him out of its mouth; bishops expurgated the pictures of their Common Prayer books; and editors omitted pages in republishing English history; even Pierpont emasculated his Class-book; Bancroft remodelled his chapters; and Everett carried Washington though thirty States, remembering to forget the brave words the wise Virginian had left on record warning his countrymen of this evil. Amid this battle of the giants, scholarship sat dumb for thirty years until imminent deadly peril convulsed it into action, and colleges, in their despair, gave to the army that help they had refused to the market-place and the rostrum.

There was here and there an exception. That earthquake scholar at Concord, whose serene word, like a whisper among the avalanches, topples down superstitions and prejudices, was at his post, and, with half a score of others, made the exception that proved the rule. Pulpits, just so far as they could not boast of culture, and nestled closest down among the masses, were infinitely braver than the "spires and antique towers" of stately collegiate institutions.

Then came reform of penal legislation,—the effort to make law mean justice, and substitute for its barbarism Christianity and civilization. In Massachusetts Rantoul represents Beccaria and Livingston, Mackintosh and Romilly. I doubt if he ever had one word of encouragement from Massachusetts letters; and, with a single exception, I have never seen, till within a dozen years, one that could be called a scholar active in moving the Legislature to reform its code.

"The London Times" proclaimed, twenty years ago, that intemperance produced more idleness, crime, disease, want, and misery than all other causes put together; and "The Westminster Review" calls it a "curse that far eclipses every other calamity under which we suffer." Gladstone, speaking as Prime Minister, admitted that "greater calamities are inflicted on mankind by intemperance than by the three great historical scourges,—war, pestilence, and famine." De Quincey says, "The most remarkable instance of a combined movement in society which history, perhaps, will be summoned to notice, is that which, in our day, has applied itself to the abatement of intemperance. Two vast movements are hurrying into action by velocities continually accelerated,—the great revolutionary movement from *political* causes concurring with the great *physical* movement in locomotion and social intercourse from the gigantic power of steam. At the opening of such a crisis, had no *third movement arisen of resistance to intemperate habits,* there would have been ground of despondency as to the melioration of the human race." These are English testimonies, where the state rests more than half on bayonets. Here we are trying to rest the ballot-box on a drunken people. "We can rule a great city," said Sir Robert Peel, "America cannot;" and he cited the mobs of New York as sufficient proof of his assertion.

Thoughtful men see that up to this hour the government of great cities has been with us a failure; that worse than the dry-rot of legislative corruption, than the rancor of party spirit, than Southern barbarism, than even the tyranny of incorporated wealth, is the giant burden of intemperance, making universal suffrage a failure and a curse in every great city. Scholars who play statesmen, and editors who masquerade as scholars, can waste much excellent anxiety that clerks shall get no office until they know the exact date of Cæsar's assassination, as well as the latitude of Pekin, and the Rule of Three. But while this crusade—the temperance movement—has been, for sixty years, gathering its facts and marshalling its arguments, rallying parties, besieging legislatures and putting great States on the witness-stand as evidence of the soundness of its methods, scholars have given it nothing but a sneer. But if universal suffrage ever fails here for a time,—permanently it cannot fail,—it would not be incapable civil service, nor an ambitious soldier, nor Southern vandals, nor venal legislatures, nor the greed of wealth, nor boy statesmen rotten before they are ripe, that will put universal suffrage into eclipse: it will be rum intrenched in great cities and commanding every vantage ground.

Social science affirms that woman's place in society marks the level of civilization. From its twilight in Greece, through the Italian worship of the Virgin, the dreams of chivalry, the justice of the civil law, and the equality of French society, we trace her gradual recognition; while our common law, as Lord Brougham confessed, was, with relation to women, the opprobrium of the age and of Christianity. For forty years, plain men and women, working noiselessly, have washed away that opprobrium; the statute-books of thirty States have been remodelled, and woman stands to-day almost face to face with her last claim,—the ballot. It has been a weary and thankless, though successful, struggle. But if there be any refuge from that ghastly curse, the vice of great cities, —before which social science stands palsied and dumb,—it is in this more equal recognition of woman. If, in this critical battle for universal suffrage,—our fathers' noblest legacy to us, and the greatest trust God leaves in our hands,—there be any weapon, which, once taken from the armory, will make victory certain, it will be, as it has been in art, literature, and society, summoning woman into the political arena.

But, at any rate, up to this point, putting suffrage aside, there can be no difference of opinion: everything born of Christianity, or allied to Grecian culture or Saxon law, must rejoice in the gain. The literary class, until half a dozen years, has taken note of this great uprising only to fling every obstacle in its way. The first glimpse we get of Saxon blood in history is that line of Tacitus in his "Germany," which reads, "In all grave matters they consult their women." Years hence, when robust Saxon sense has flung away Jewish superstition and Eastern prejudice, and put under its foot fastidious scholarship and squeamish fashion, some second Tacitus, from the valley of the Mississippi, will answer to him of the Seven Hills, "In all grave questions we consult our women."

I used to think that then we could say to letters as Henry of Navarre wrote to the Sir Philip Sidney of his realm, Crillon, "the bravest of the brave," "We have conquered at Arques, *et tu n'y étais pas, Crillon,*"—"You were not there, my Crillon." But a second thought reminds me that what claims to be literature has been always present in that battle-field, and always in the ranks of the foe.

Ireland is another touchstone which reveals to us how absurdly we masquerade in democratic trappings while we have gone to seed in tory distrust of the people; false to every duty, which, as eldest-born of democratic institutions, we owe to the oppressed, and careless of the lesson every such movement may be made in keeping public thought clear, keen, and fresh as to principles which are the essence of our civilization, the groundwork of all education in republics.

Sydney Smith said, "The moment Ireland is mentioned the English seem to bid adieu to common sense, and to act with the barbarity of tyrants and the fatuity of idiots." "As long as the patient will suffer, the cruel will kick. . . . If the Irish go on withholding and forbearing, and hesitating whether this is the time for discussion or that is the time, they will be laughed at another century as fools, and kicked for another century as slaves." Byron called England's union with Ireland "the union of the shark with his prey." Bentham's conclusion, from a survey of five hundred years of European history, was, "Only by making the ruling few uneasy can the oppressed many obtain a particle of relief." Edmund Burke—Burke, the noblest figure in the Parliamentary history of the last hundred years, greater than Cicero in the senate and almost Plato in the academy—Burke affirmed, a century ago, "Ireland has learnt at last that justice is to be had from England, only when demanded at the sword's point." And a century later, only last year, Gladstone himself proclaimed in a public address in Scotland, "England never concedes anything to Ireland except when moved to do so by fear."

When we remember these admissions, we ought to clap our hands at every fresh Irish "outrage," as a parrot-press styles it; aware that it is only a far-off echo of the musket-shots that rattled against the Old State House on the 5th of March, 1770, and of the war-whoop that made the tiny spire of the Old South tremble when Boston rioters emptied the three India tea-ships into the sea,—welcome evidence of living force and rare intelligence in the victim, and a sign that the day of deliverance draws each hour nearer. Cease ringing endless changes of eulogy on the men who made North's Boston port-bill a failure while every leading journal sends daily over the water wishes for the success of Gladstone's copy of the bill for Ireland. If all rightful government rests on consent,—if, as the French say, you "can do almost anything with a bayonet except sit on it,"—be at least consistent, and denounce the man who covers Ireland with regiments to hold up a despotism, which, within twenty months, he has confessed rests wholly upon fear.

Then note the scorn and disgust with which we gather up our garments about us and disown the Sam Adams and William Prescott, the George Washington and John Brown, of St. Petersburg, the spiritual descendants, the living representatives, of those who make our history worth anything in the world's annals, the Nihilists.

Nihilism is the righteous and honorable resistance of a people crushed under an iron rule. Nihilism is evidence of life. When "order reigns in Warsaw," it is spiritual death. Nihilism is the last weapon of victims choked and manacled beyond all other resistance. It is crushed humanity's only means of making the oppressor tremble. God means that unjust power shall be insecure; and every move of the giant, prostrate in chains, whether it be to lift a single dagger or stir a city's revolt, is a lesson in justice. One might well tremble for the future of the race if such a despotism could exist without provoking the bloodiest resistance. I honor Nihilism; since it redeems human nature from the suspicion of being utterly vile, made up only of heartless oppressors and contented slaves. Every line in our history, every interest of civilization, bids us rejoice when the tyrant grows pale and the slave rebellious. We cannot but pity the suffering of any human being, however richly deserved; but such pity must not confuse our moral sense. Humanity gains. Chatham rejoiced when our fathers rebelled. For every single reason they alleged, Russia counts a hundred, each one ten times bitterer than any Hancock or Adams could give. Sam Johnson's standing toast in Oxford port was "Success to the first insurrection of slaves in Jamaica," a sentiment Southey echoed. "Eschew cant," said that old moralist. But of all the cants that are canted in this canting world, though the cant of piety may be the worst, the cant of Americans bewailing Russian Nihilism is the most disgusting.

I know what reform needs, and all it needs, in a land where discussion is free, the press untrammeled, and where public halls protect debate. There, as Emerson says, "What the tender and poetic youth dreams to-day, and conjures up with inarticulate speech, is to-morrow the vociferated result of public opinion, and the day after is the charter of nations." Lieber said, in 1870, "Bismarck proclaims to-day in the Diet the very principles for which we were hunted and exiled fifty years ago." Submit to risk your daily bread, expect social ostracism, count on a mob now and then, "be in earnest, don't equivocate, don't excuse, don't retreat a single inch," and you will finally be heard. No matter how long and weary the waiting, at last,—

"Ever the truth comes uppermost,
  And ever is justice done.
For Humanity sweeps onward:
  Where to-day the martyr stands,
On the morrow crouches Judas
  With the silver in his hands;

Far in front the cross stands ready,
  And the crackling fagots burn,
While the hooting mob of yesterday
  In silent awe return
To glean up the scattered ashes
  Into History's golden urn."

In such a land he is doubly and trebly guilty, who, except in
some most extreme case, disturbs the sober rule of law and order.

But such is not Russia. In Russia there is no press, no debate,
no explanation of what government does, no remonstrance allowed,
no agitation of public issues. Dead silence, like that which reigns
at the summit of Mont Blanc, freezes the whole empire, long ago
described as "a despotism tempered by assassination." Meanwhile, such despotism has unsettled the brains of the ruling family, as unbridled power doubtless made some of the twelve Cæsars
insane: a madman, sporting with the lives and comfort of a hundred million of men. The young girl whispers in her mother's ear,
under a ceiled roof, her pity for a brother knouted and dragged
half dead into exile for his opinions. The next week she is stripped
naked, and flogged to death in the public square. No inquiry, no
explanation, no trial, no protest, one dead uniform silence, the
law of the tyrant. Where is there ground for any hope of peaceful change? Where the fulcrum upon which you can plant any
possible lever?

Macchiavelli's sorry picture of poor human nature would be
fulsome flattery if men could keep still under such oppression.
No, no! in such a land dynamite and the dagger are the necessary
and proper substitutes for Faneuil Hall and "The Daily Advertiser." Anything that will make the madman quake in his bed-
chamber, and rouse his victims into reckless and desperate resistance. This is the only view an American, the child of 1620 and
1776, can take of Nihilism. Any other unsettles and perplexes
the ethics of our civilization.

Born within sight of Bunker Hill, in a commonwealth which

adopts the motto of Algernon Sidney, *sub libertate quietem* ("accept no peace without liberty"),—son of Harvard, whose first pledge was "Truth," citizen of a republic based on the claim that no government is rightful unless resting on the consent of the people, and which assumes to lead in asserting the rights of humanity,—I at least can say nothing else and nothing less,—no, not if every tile on Cambridge roofs were a devil hooting my words!

I shall bow to any rebuke from those who hold Christianity to command entire non-resistance. But criticism from any other quarter is only that nauseous hypocrisy, which, stung by three-penny tea-tax, piles Bunker Hill with granite and statues, prating all the time of patriotism and broadswords, while, like another Pecksniff, it recommends a century of dumb submission and entire non-resistance to the Russians, who, for a hundred years, have seen their sons by thousands dragged to death or exile, no one knows which, in this worse than Venetian mystery of police, and their maidens flogged to death in the market-place, and who share the same fate if they presume to ask the reason why.

"It is unfortunate," says Jefferson, "that the efforts of mankind to secure the freedom of which they have been deprived should be accompanied with violence and even with crime. But while we weep over the means, we must pray for the end." Pray fearlessly for such ends: there is no risk! "Men are all tories by nature," says Arnold, "when tolerably well off: only monstrous injustice and atrocious cruelty can rouse them." Some talk of the rashness of the uneducated classes. Alas! ignorance is far oftener obstinate than rash. Against one French Revolution—that scarecrow of the ages—weigh Asia, "carved in stone," and a thousand years of Europe, with her half-dozen nations meted out and trodden down to be the dull and contented footstools of priest and kings. The customs of a thousand years ago are the sheet-anchor of the passing generation, so deeply buried, so fixed, that the most violent efforts of the maddest fanatic can drag it but a hand's-breadth.

Before the war Americans were like the crowd in that terrible hall of Eblis which Beckford painted for us,—each man with his hand pressed on the incurable sore in his bosom, and pledged not to speak of it: compared with other lands, we were intellectually and morally a nation of cowards.

When I first entered the Roman States, a custom-house official seized all my French books. In vain I held up to him a treatise by

Fénelon, and explained that it was by a Catholic archbishop of Cambray. Gruffly he answered, "It makes no difference: *it is French.*" As I surrendered the volume to his remorseless grasp, I could not but honor the nation which had made its revolutionary purpose so definite that despotism feared its very language. I only wished that injustice and despotism everywhere might one day have as good cause to hate and to fear everything American.

At last that disgraceful seal of slave complicity is broken. Let us inaugurate a new departure, recognize that we are afloat on the current of Niagara,—eternal vigilance the condition of our safety,—that we are irrevocably pledged to the world not to go back to bolts and bars,—could not if we would, and would not if we could. Never again be ours the fastidious scholarship that shrinks from rude contact with the masses. Very pleasant it is to sit high up in the world's theatre and criticise the ungraceful struggles of the gladiators, shrug one's shoulders at the actors' harsh cries, and let every one know that but for "this villainous saltpeter you would yourself have been a soldier." But Bacon says, "In the theatre of man's life, God and his angels only should be lookers-on." "Sin is not taken out of man as Eve was out of Adam, by putting him to sleep." "Very beautiful," says Richter, "is the eagle when he floats with outstretched wings aloft in the clear blue; but sublime when he plunges down through the tempest to his eyry on the cliff, where his unfledged young ones dwell and are starving." Accept proudly the analysis of Fisher Ames: "A monarchy is a man-of-war, stanch, iron-ribbed, and resistless when under full sail; yet a single hidden rock sends her to the bottom. Our republic is a raft, hard to steer, and your feet always wet; but nothing can sink her." If the Alps, piled in cold and silence, be the emblem of despotism, we joyfully take the ever-restless ocean for ours,—only pure because never still.

Journalism must have more self-respect. Now it praises good and bad men so indiscriminately that a good word from nine-tenths of our journals is worthless. In burying our Aaron Burrs, both political parties—in order to get the credit of magnanimity —exhaust the vocabulary of eulogy so thoroughly that there is nothing left with which to distinguish our John Jays. The love of a good name in life and a fair reputation to survive us—that strong bond to well-doing—is lost where every career, however stained, is covered with the same fulsome flattery, and where what men say in the streets is the exact opposite of what they say to each other. *De mortuis nil nisi bonum* most men translate, ''Speak only good of the dead.'' I prefer to construe it, ''Of the dead say nothing unless you can tell something good.'' And if the sin and the recreancy have been marked and far-reaching in their evil, even the charity of silence is not permissible.

To be as good as our fathers we must be better. They silenced their fears and subdued their prejudices, inaugurating free speech and equality with no precedent on the file. Europe shouted ''Madmen!'' and gave us forty years for the shipwreck. With serene faith they persevered. Let us rise to their level. Crush appetite and prohibit temptation if it rots great cities. Intrench labor in sufficient bulwarks against that wealth, which, without the tenfold strength of modern incorporation, wrecked the Grecian and Roman States; and, with a sterner effort still, summon women into civil life as re-enforcement to our laboring ranks in the effort to make our civilization a success.

Sit not, like the figure on our silver coin, looking ever backward.

> "New occasions teach new duties;
> Time makes ancient good uncouth;
> They must upward still, and onward,
> Who would keep abreast of Truth.
> Lo! before us gleam her camp-fires!
> We ourselves must Pilgrims be,
> Launch our Mayflower, and steer boldly
> Through the desperate winter sea,
> Nor attempt the Future's portal
> With the Past's blood-rusted key."

THE LEADERSHIP OF EDUCATED MEN [1]

George William Curtis

[George William Curtis (1824-1892), widely known as an orator, was also a man of letters. In his early youth he was greatly influenced by Emerson, and by a residence of two years at Brook Farm. Of this latter experience he wrote, ''There never were such witty potato patches, and such sparkling corn-fields before or since. The weeds were scratched out of the ground to the music of Tennyson and Browning, and the nooning was an hour as gay and bright as any brilliant night at Ambrose's.''

From his twenty-second to his twenty-ninth year he traveled in Europe. He wrote letters to New York papers upon public men and affairs in the countries he visited. Shortly after returning to America, he published his first work, *Nile Notes of a Howadji.* There followed a period of lecturing and journalism. In addition to his articles upon current politics he wrote musical and dramatic criticism and book reviews. *The Potiphar Papers* and *Prue and I*, enhanced his literary reputation. As editor of *Harper's Weekly*, he became actively interested in New York politics, and was associated with Thomas Nast, the cartoonist, in bringing to an end the rule of the Tweed ring. The one cause which he served most continuously was that of civil service reform.

William Winter, in a eulogy pronounced shortly after the death of Curtis, said,

''The art in which Curtis excelled all his contemporaries of the last thirty years was the art of oratory. Many other authors wrote better in verse, and some others wrote as well in prose. But in felicity of speech Curtis was supreme above all other men of his generation. He could make an extemporaneous speech, but as a rule his speeches were carefully prepared. They had not always been written, but they had always been composed and considered. . . . He created the absolute illusion of spontaneity. You never felt that you had been beguiled by art: you only felt that you had been entranced by nature.''

Perhaps Curtis's most notable oratorical triumph was his after-dinner speech, *The Puritan Principle: Liberty under Law,* delivered at the banquet of the Forefathers' Society of the City of New York, in 1876. Of the speech and the occasion Edward Everett Hale wrote:

''It was at the moment when the Hayes-Tilden difficulty was at its very worst. Intelligent men and even decent newspapers spoke freely of the possibility of civil war. . . . It would have been easy for a timid man to avoid the great subject of the hour. But Mr. Curtis was not a timid man. He was much more than a man of delicate taste, well trained and elegant. And therefore he plunged right into the terrible subject. . . . He carried with him every man in the assembly. Those

[1] Reprinted, by permission, from the *Orations and Addresses of George William Curtis:* Copyright, 1893, by Messrs. Harper and Brothers.
Questions and topics for the discussion of this address, and of other phases of the general subject with which it deals, will be found on pages 547 and 549.

three hundred men of mark went home that night, and went to their business the next day, to say that a court of arbitration must be established to settle that controversy. In that moment of Mr. Curtis's triumph, as I believe, it was settled.

Because I remember Mr. Curtis in a scene like this, where he showed the courage of his convictions, I am a little sensitive when I hear people speak of his 'elegance' and 'eloquence', and of his being the 'last of the orators,' as. if he were only or chiefly a dainty man, who valued especially the arts of expression. Undoubtedly he did value them, for he was not a fool. But he valued them for the use which he could make of them for the welfare of the state, not for themselves or for his own immediate reputation.''

The Leadership of Educated Men was delivered before the alumni of Brown University in 1882. It is, in a way, a reply to Wendell Phillips, whose *Scholar in a Republic* Curtis had heard at Harvard a year before.]

There is a modern English picture which the genius of Hawthorne might have inspired. The painter calls it, ''How they met themselves.'' A man and a woman, haggard and weary, wandering lost in a somber wood, suddenly met the shadowy figures of a youth and a maid. Some mysterious fascination fixes the gaze and stills the hearts of the wanderers, and their amazement deepens into awe as they gradually recognize themselves as once they were; the soft bloom of youth upon their rounded cheeks, the dewy light of hope in their trusting eyes, exulting confidence in their springing step, themselves blithe and radiant with the glory of the dawn. To-day, and here, we meet ourselves. Not to these familiar scenes alone—yonder college-green with its reverend traditions; the halcyon cove of the Seekonk, upon which the memory of Roger Williams broods like a bird of calm; the historic bay, beating forever with the muffled oars of Barton and of Abraham Whipple; here, the humming city of the living; there, the peaceful city of the dead;—not to these only or chiefly do we return, but to ourselves as we once were. It is not the smiling freshmen of the year, it is your own beardless and unwrinkled faces, that are looking from the windows of University Hall and of Hope College. Under the trees upon the hill it is yourselves whom you see walking, full of hopes and dreams, glowing with conscious power, and ''nourishing a youth sublime;'' and in this familiar temple, which surely has never echoed with eloquence so fervid and inspiring as that of your commencement orations, it is not yonder youths in the galleries who, as they fondly believe, are whispering to yonder maids; it is your younger selves who, in the days that are no more, are murmuring to the fairest mothers and grandmothers of those maids.

Happy the worn and weary man and woman in the picture could they have felt their older eyes still glistening with that earlier light, and their hearts yet beating with undiminished sympathy and aspiration. Happy we, brethren, whatever may have been achieved, whatever left undone, if, returning to the home of our earlier years, we bring with us the illimitable hope, the unchilled resolution, the inextinguishable faith of youth.

It was as scholars that you were here; it is to the feeling and life of scholars that you return. I mean the scholar not as a specialist or deeply proficient student, not like Darwin, a conqueror greater than Alexander, who extended the empire of human knowledge; nor like Emerson, whose serene wisdom, a planet in the cloudless heaven, lighted the path of his age to larger spiritual liberty; nor like Longfellow, sweet singer of our national spring-time, whose scholarship decorated his pure and limpid song as flowers are mirrored in a placid stream—not as scholars like these, but as educated men, to whom the dignity and honor and renown of the educated class are precious, however remote from study your lives may have been, you return to the annual festival of letters. "Neither years nor books," says Emerson, speaking of his own college days, "have yet availed to extirpate a prejudice then rooted in me that a scholar is the favorite of heaven and earth, the excellency of his country, the happiest of men."

But every educated man is aware of a profound popular distrust of the courage and sagacity of the educated class. Franklin and Lincoln are good enough for us, exclaims this jealous skepticism; as if Franklin and Lincoln did not laboriously repair by vigorous study the want of early opportunity. The scholar appealing to experience is proudly told to close his books, for what has America to do with experience? as if books were not the ever-burning lamps of accumulated wisdom. When Voltaire was insulted by the London mob, he turned at his door and complimented them upon the nobleness of their national character, their glorious constitution, and their love of liberty. The London mob did not feel the sarcasm. But when I hear that America may scorn experience because she is a law to herself, I remember that a few years ago a foreign observer came to the city of Washington, and said: "I did not fully comprehend your greatness until I saw your Congress. Then I felt that if you could stand that you could stand anything, and I understood the saying that God takes care of children, drunken men, and the United States."

The scholar is denounced as a coward. Humanity falls among thieves, we are told, and the college Levite, the educated Pharisee, pass by on the other side. Slavery undermines the Republic, but the clergy in America are the educated class, and the Church makes itself the bulwark of slavery. Strong drink slays its tens of thousands, but the educated class leaves the gospel of temperance to be preached by the ignorant and the enthusiast, as the English Establishment left the preaching of regeneration to Methodist itinerants in fields and barns. Vast questions cast their shadows upon the future: the just relations of capital and labor; the distribution of land; the towering power of corporate wealth; reform in administrative methods; but the educated class, says the critic, instead of advancing to deal with them promptly, wisely, and courageously, and settling them as morning dissipates the night, without a shock, leaves them to be kindled to fury by demagogues, lifts a panic cry of communism, and sinks paralyzed with terror. It is the old accusation. Erasmus was the great pioneer of modern scholarship. But in the fierce contest of the Reformation Luther denounced him as a time-server and a coward. With the same feeling, Theodore Parker, the spiritual child of Luther, asked of Goethe, "Tell me, what did he ever do for the cause of man?" and when nothing remained for his country but the dread alternative of slavery or civil war, Parker exclaimed sadly of the class to which he belonged, "If our educated men had done their duty, we should not now be in the ghastly condition we bewail."

Gentlemen, we belong to the accused class. Its honor and dignity are very precious to us. Is this humiliating arraignment true? Does the educated class of America especially deserve this condemnation of political recreancy and moral cowardice? Faithless scholars, laggard colleges, bigoted pulpits, there may be; signal instances you may find of feebleness and pusillanimity. This has been always true. Leigh Hunt said, "I thought that my Horace and Demosthenes gave me a right to sit at table with any man, and I think so still." But when De Quincey met Dr. Parr, who knew Horace and Demosthenes better than any man of his time, he described him as a lisping scandal-monger, retailing gossip fit only for washerwomen to hear. During the earthquake of the great civil war in England, Sir Thomas Browne sat tranquilly in scholarly seclusion, polishing the conceits of the "Urn Burial," and modulating the long-drawn music of the "Religio Medici." Looking at Browne and Parr, at Erasmus and Goethe, is it strange that scholars are impatiently derided as useless pedants or literary voluptuaries, and that the whole educated class is denounced as feeble and impracticable?

But remember what Coleridge said to Washington Alston, "Never judge a work of art by its defects." The proper comment to make upon recreant scholars is that of Brummell's valet upon the tumbled cambric in his hands, "These are our failures." Luther, impatient of the milder spirit of Erasmus and Colet and Sir Thomas More, might well have called them our failures, because he was of their class, and while they counseled moderation, his fiery and impetuous soul sought to seize triple-crowned error and drag it from its throne. But Luther was no less a scholar, and stands equally with them for the scholarly class and the heroism of educated men. Even Erasmus said of him with friendly wit, "He has hit the Pope on the crown and the monks on the belly." If the cowled scholars of the Church rejected him, and universities under their control renounced and condemned him, yet Luther is justified in saying, as he sweeps his hand across them and speaks for himself and for the scholars who stood with him, "These are not our representatives; these are our failures."

So on our side of the sea the educated body of Puritan Massachusetts Bay, the clergy and the magistrates, drove Roger Williams from their borders—Roger Williams, also a scholar and a clergyman, and, with John Milton, the bright consummate flower of Puritanism. But shall not he stand for the scholar rather than Cotton Mather, torturing terrified old women to death as witches! I appeal from Philip drunk to Philip sober—from the scholarship that silenced Mrs. Hutchinson and hung Mary Dyer and pressed Giles Corey to death, to the scholarship that argued with George Fox and founded a political commonwealth upon soul liberty. A year ago I sat with my brethren of the Phi Beta Kappa at Cambridge, and seemed to catch echoes of Edmund Burke's resounding impeachment of Warren Hastings in the sparkling denunciation of the timidity of American scholarship. Under the spell of Burke's burning words Hastings half believed himself to be the villain he heard described. But the scholarly audience of the scholarly orator of the Phi Beta Kappa, with an exquisite sense of relief, felt every count of his stinging indictment recoil upon himself. He was the glowing refutation of his own argument. Gentleman, scholar, orator—his is the courage that never quailed; his the white plume of Navarre that flashed meteor-like in the front

of battle; his the Amphion music of an eloquence that leveled the
more than Theban walls of American slavery. At once judge, cul-
prit, and accuser, in the noble record of his own life he and his
class are triumphantly acquitted.

Must we count such illustrations as exceptions? But how can
we do so when we see that the Reformation, the mental and moral
new birth of Christendom, was the work of the educated class?
Follow the movement of liberty in detail, and still the story is
the same. The great political contest in England, inspired by the
Reformation, was directed by University men. John Pym in the
Commons, John Hampden in the field, John Milton in the Cabinet
—three Johns, and all of them well-beloved disciples of liberty—
with the grim Oliver himself, purging England of royal despotism,
and avenging the slaughtered saints on Alpine mountains cold,
were all of them children of Oxford and Cambridge. In the next
century, like a dawn lurid but bright, the French Revolution
broke upon the world. But the only hope of a wise direction of
the elemental forces that upheaved France vanished when 'the educated leadership lost control, and Marat became the genius and
the type of the Revolution. Ireland also bears witness. As its
apostle and tutelary saint was a scholar, so its long despair of
justice has found its voice and its hand among educated Irishmen.
Swift and Molyneux, and Flood and Grattan and O'Connell,
Duffy, and the young enthusiasts around Thomas Davis who sang
of an Erin that never was and dreamed of an Ireland that cannot
be, were men of the colleges and the schools, whose long persistence of tongue and pen fostered the life of their country and
gained for her all that she has won. For modern Italy, let Silvio
Pellico and Foresti and Maroncelli answer. It was Italian education which Austria sought to smother, and it was not less Cavour
than Garibaldi who gave constitutional liberty to Italy. When
Germany sank at Jena under the heel of Napoleon, and Stein—
whom Napoleon hated, but could not appall—asked if national
life survived, the answer rang from the universities, and from them
modern Germany came forth. With prophetic impulse Theodore
Koerner called his poems ''The Lyre and the Sword,'' for, like
the love which changed the sea-nymph into the harp, the fervent
patriotism of the educated youth of Germany turned the poet's
lyre into the soldier's victorious sword. In the splendor of our
American day let us remember and honor our brethren, first in
every council, dead upon every field of freedom from the Volga to

the Rhine, from John O'Groat's to the Adriatic, who have steadily drawn Europe from out the night of despotism, and have vindicated for the educated class the leadership of modern civilization.

Here in America, where as yet there are no ruins save those of ancient wrongs, undoubtedly New England has inspired and molded our national life. But if New England has led the Union, what has led New England? Her scholarly class. Her educated men. And our Roger Williams gave the key-note. "He has broached and divulged new and dangerous opinions against the authority of magistrates," said Massachusetts as she banished him. A century later his dangerous opinions had captured Massachusetts. Young Sam Adams, taking his Master's degree at Cambridge, argued that it was lawful to resist the supreme magistrate if the State could not otherwise be preserved. He was a college stripling. But seven years afterward, in 1750, the chief pulpit orator in New England, Jonathan Mayhew, preached in Boston the famous sermon which Thornton called the morning gun of the Revolution, applying to the political situation the principles of Roger Williams. The New England pulpit echoed and re-echoed that morning gun, arousing the country, and twenty-five years later its warning broke into the rattle of musketry at Lexington and Concord and the glorious thunder of Bunker Hill.

It was a son of Harvard, James Otis, who proposed the assembly of an American congress without asking the king's leave. It was a son of Yale, John Morin Scott, who declared that if taxation without representation were to be enforced, the colonies ought to separate from England. It was a group of New York scholars, John Jay and Scott and the Livingstones, which spoke for the colony in response to the Boston Port Bill and proposed the Continental Congress. It was a New England scholar in that Congress, whom Rufus Choate declared to be the distinctive and comprehensive orator of the Revolution, John Adams, who, urging every argument, touching every stop of passion, pride, tenderness, interest, conscience, and lofty indignation, swept up his country as into a chariot of fire and soared to independence.

I do not forget that Virginian tongue of flame, Patrick Henry, nor that patriotism of the field and fireside which recruited the Sons of Liberty. The inspiring statue of the Minute Man at Concord—and a nobler memorial figure does not stand upon our soil—commemorates the spirit that left the plow standing in the furrow, that drew Nathaniel Greene from his anvil and Esek Hopkins from his farm; the spirit that long before had sent the poor parishioners of Scrooby to Holland, and filled the victorious ranks of the Commonwealth at Naseby and at Marston Moor. But in America as in England they were educated men who in the pulpit, on the platform and through the press, conducted the mighty preliminary argument of the Revolution, defended the ancient traditions of English liberty against reactionary England, aroused the colonists to maintain the cause of human nature, and led them from the Gaspee and Bunker Hill across the plains of Saratoga, the snows of Valley Forge, the sands of Monmouth, the hills of Carolina, until at Yorktown once more the king surrendered to the people, and educated America had saved constitutional liberty.

In the next brief and critical period, when through the travail of a half-anarchical confederation the independent States, always instinctively tending to union, rose into a rural constitutional republic, the good genius of America was still the educated mind of the country. Of the fifty-five members of the Convention, which Bancroft, changing the poet's line, calls "the goodliest fellowship of law-givers whereof this world holds record," thirty-three were college graduates, and the eight leaders of the great debate were all college men. The Convention adjourned, and while from out the strong hand of George Clinton, Hamilton, the son of Columbia, drew New York into the Union, that placid son of Princeton, James Madison, withstanding the fiery energy of Patrick Henry, placed Virginia by her side. Then Columbia and Princeton uniting in Hamilton, Jay, and Madison, interpreted the Constitution in that greatest of commentaries, which, as the dome crowns the Capitol, completed the majestic argument which long before the sons of Harvard had begun. Take away the scholarly class from the discussion that opened the Revolution, from the deliberations that guided it, from the debates of the Constitutional Convention that ended it—would the advance of America have been more triumphant? Would the guarantees of individual liberty, of national union, of a common prosperity, have been more surely established? The critics laughed at the pictured grapes as unnatural. But the painter was satisfied when the birds came and pecked at them. Daily the educated class is denounced as impracticable and visionary. But the Constitution of the United States is the work of American scholars.

Doubtless the leaders expressed a sentiment which was shared by the men and women around them. But it was they who had formed and fostered that sentiment. They were not the puppets of the crowd, light weathercocks which merely showed the shifting gusts of popular feeling. They did not follow what they could not resist, and make their voices the tardy echo of a thought they did not share. They were not dainty and feeble hermits because they were educated men. They were equal citizens with the rest; men of strong convictions and persuasive speech, who showed their brethren what they ought to think and do. That is the secret of leadership. It is not servility to the mob, it is not giving vehement voice to popular frenzy, that makes a leader. That makes a demagogue; Cleon, not Pericles; Catiline, not Cicero. Leadership is the power of kindling a sympathy and trust which all will eagerly follow. It is the genius that molds the lips of the stony Memnon to such sensitive life that the first sunbeam of opportunity strikes them into music. In a great crisis it is thinking so as to make others think, feeling so as to make others feel, which tips the orator's tongue with fire that lights as well as burns. So when Lord Chatham stood at the head of England organizing her victories by land and sea, and told in parliament their splendid story, his glowing form was Britain's self, and the roar of British guns and the proud acclamation of British hearts all around the globe flashed and thundered in his eloquence. "This is a glorious morning," said the scholar Samuel Adams, with a price set on his head, as he heard the guns at Lexington. "Decus et decorum est," said the young scholar Joseph Warren gayly, as he passed to his death on Bunker Hill. They spoke for the lofty enthusiasm of patriotism which they had kindled. It was not a mob, an ignorant multitude swayed by a mysterious impulse; it was a body of educated men, wise and heroic because they were educated, who lifted this country to independence and laid deep and strong the foundations of the Republic.

Is this less true of the maintenance and development of the government? Thirty years ago, walking on the Cliff at Newport with Mr. Bancroft, I asked him to what point he proposed to continue his history. He answered: "If I were an artist painting a picture of this ocean my work would stop at the horizon. I can see no further. My history will end with the adoption of the Constitution. All beyond that is experiment." This was long ago. But the Republic is an experiment no longer. It has been strained to the utmost along the very vital fiber of its frame, and it has emerged from the ordeal recreated. Happy venerable historian, who has survived both to witness the triumph of the experiment, and to complete his stately story to the very point which he contemplated thirty years ago! He has reached what was then the horizon, and may a gracious Providence permit him yet to depict the new and further and radiant prospect which he and all his countrymen behold!

In achieving this great result has educated America been sluggish or skeptical or cowardly? The Constitution was but ten years old when the author of the Declaration of Independence, speaking with great authority and for a great party, announced that the Constitution was a compact of which every State must judge for itself both the fact of violation and the mode of redress. Jefferson sowed dragon's teeth in the fresh soil of the young Union. He died, but the armed men appeared. The whole course of our politics for nearly a century was essentially revolutionary. Beneath all specific measures and party policies lay the supreme question of the nature of the government which Jefferson had raised. Is the Union a league or a nation? Are we built upon the solid earth or unstably encamped, like Sinbad's company, upon the back of a sea-monster which may dive at any moment? Until this doubt was settled there could be no peace. Yet the question lay in our politics only like the far black cloud along the horizon, flashing and muttering scarce heard thunders until the slavery agitation began. That was a debate which devoured every other, until the slave-power, foiled in the hope of continental empire, pleaded Jefferson's theory of the Constitution as an argument for national dissolution. This was the third great crisis of the country, and in the tremendous contention, as·in the war that followed, was the American scholar recreant and dumb?

I do not ask, for it is not necessary, whether in the ranks of the powerful host that resisted agitation there were not scholars and educated men. I do not ask whether the educated or any other class alone maintained the fight, nor whether there were not unquailing leaders who were not educated men, nor whether all were first, or all approved the same methods, or all were equally wise or equally zealous. Of course, I make no exclusive claim. I do not now speak of men like Garrison, whose name is that of a great patriot and a great human benefactor, and whose sturdy leadership was that of an old Hebrew prophet. But was the great battle fought and won while we and our guild stood passive and hostile by?

The slavery agitation began with the moral appeal, and as in the dawn of the Revolution educated America spoke in the bugle note of James Otis, so in the moral onset of the antislavery agitation rings out the clear voice of a son of Otis' college, himself the Otis of the later contest, Wendell Phillips. By his side, in the stormy dawn of the movement, stands a grandson of Quincy of the Revolution, and among the earliest antislavery leaders is more than a proportionate part of liberally educated men. In Congress the commanding voice for freedom was that of the most learned, experienced, and courageous of American statesmen, the voice of a scholar and an old college professor, John Quincy Adams. Whittier's burning words scattered the sacred fire, Longfellow and Lowell mingled their songs with his, and Emerson gave to the cause the loftiest scholarly heart in the Union. And while Parker's and Beecher's pulpits echoed Jonathan Mayhew's morning gun and fired words like cannon-balls, in the highest pulpit of America, foremost among the champions of liberty stood the slight and radiant figure of the scholarly son of Rhode Island, upon whom more than upon any of her children the mantle of Roger Williams had worthily fallen, William Ellery Channing.

When the national debate was angriest, it was the scholar of the Senate of the United States who held highest in his undaunted hands the flag of humanity and his country. While others bowed and bent and broke around him, the form of Charles Sumner towered erect. Commerce and trade, the mob of the clubs and of the street, hissed and sneered at him as a pedantic dreamer and fanatic. No kind of insult and defiance was spared. But the unbending scholar revealed to the haughty foe an antagonist as proud and resolute as itself. He supplied what the hour demanded, a sublime faith in liberty, the uncompromising spirit which interpreted the Constitution and the statutes for freedom and not for slavery. The fiery agitation became bloody battle. Still he strode on before. "I am only six weeks behind you," said Abraham Lincoln, the Western frontiersman, to the New England scholar; and along the path that the scholar blazed in the wild wilderness of civil war, the path of emancipation, and the constitutional equality of all citizens, his country followed fast to union, peace, and prosperity. The public service of this scholar was not less than that of any of his predecessors or any of his contemporaries. Criticize him as you will, mark every shadow you can find.

"Though round his base the rolling clouds are spread,
Eternal sunshine settles on his head."

It would indeed be a sorrowful confession for this day and this assembly, to own that experience proves the air of the college to be suffocating to generous thought and heroic action. Here it would be especially unjust, for what son of this college does not proudly remember that when, in the Revolution, Rhode Island was the seat of war, the college boys left the recitation-room for the field, and the college became a soldiers' barrack and hospital? And what son of any college in the land, what educated American, does not recall with grateful pride that legion of college youth in our own day—"Integer vitæ scelerisque purus"—who were not cowards or sybarites because they were scholars, but whose consecration to the cause of country and man vindicated the words of John Milton, "A complete and generous education is that which fits a man to perform justly, skillfully, and magnanimously all the offices, both private and public, of peace and war"? That is the praise of the American scholar. The glory of this day and of this Commencement season is that the pioneers, the courageous and independent leaders in public affairs, the great apostles of religious and civil liberty, have been, in large part, educated men, sustained by the sympathy of the educated class.

But this is not true of the past alone. As educated America was the constructive power, so it is still the true conservative force of the Republic. It is decried as priggish and theoretical. But so Richard Henry Lee condemned the Constitution as the work of visionaries. They are always called visionaries who hold that morality is stronger than a majority. Goldwin Smith says that Cobden felt that at heart England was a gentleman and not a bully. So thinks the educated American of his own country. He has faith enough in the people to appeal to them against themselves, for he knows that the cardinal condition of popular government is the ability of the people to see and correct their own errors. In a Republic, as the majority must control action, the majority tends constantly to usurp control of opinion. Its decree is accepted as the standard of right and wrong. To differ is grotesque and eccentric. To protest is preposterous. To defy is incendiary and revolutionary. But just here interposes educated intelligence, and asserts the worth of self-reliance and the power of the individual. Gathering the wisdom of ages as into a sheaf of sunbeams, it shows

that progress springs from the minority, and that if it will but
stand fast time will give it victory.

It is the educated voice of the country which teaches patience in
politics and strengthens the conscience of the individual citizen
by showing that servility to a majority is as degrading as servility
to a Sultan or a Grand Lama. Emerson said that of all his friends
he honored none more than a quiet old Quaker lady who, if she
said yea and the whole world said nay, still said yea. One of the
pleasantest stories of Garfield is that of his speech to his constitu-
ents in which he quaintly vindicated his own independence. "I
would do anything to win your regard," he said, "but there is one
man whose good opinion I must have above all, and without whose
approval I can do nothing. That is the man with whom I get up
every morning and go to bed every night, whose thoughts are my
thoughts, whose prayers are my prayers; I cannot buy your confidence at the cost of his respect." Never was the scholarly Garfield so truly a man, so patriotically an American, and his constit-
uents were prouder than ever of their representative who complimented them by asserting his own manhood.

It is the same voice which exposes the sophists who mislead the
mob and pitilessly scourges the demagogues who flatter it. "All
men know more than any man," haughtily shout the larger and
lesser Talleyrands. That is a French epigram, replies the scholar,
but not a general truth. A crowd is not wiser than the wisest man
in it. For the purpose of the voyage the crew does not know
more than the master of the ship. The Boston town-meeting was
not more sagacious than Sam Adams. "Vox populi vox Dei,"
screams the foaming rhetoric of the stump; the voice of the people
is the voice of God. The voice of the people in London, says history, declared against street-lamps and denounced inoculation as
wanton wickedness. The voice of the people in Paris demanded the
head of Charlotte Corday. The voice of the people in Jerusalem
cried, "Away with Him! crucify Him! crucify Him!" "God is
on the side of the strongest battalions," sneers the party swindler
who buys a majority with money or place. On the contrary, answers the cool critic, reading history and interpreting its lessons,
God was with Leonidas, and not with Xerxes. He was with the
exile John Robinson at Leyden, not with Laud and the hierarchy
at Westminster.

Despite Napoleon even battles are not sums in arithmetic.
Strange that a general, half of whose success was due to a senti-

ment, the glory of France, which welded his army into a thunder-
bolt, and still burns for us in the fervid song of Béranger, should
have supposed that it is numbers and not conviction and enthusiasm which win the final victory. The career of no man in our
time illustrates this truth more signally than Garibaldi's. He was
the symbol of the sentiment which the wise Cavour molded into a
nation, and he will be always canonized more universally than any
other Italian patriot, because no other represents so purely and
simply to the national imagination the Italian ideal of patriotic
devotion. His enthusiasm of conviction made no calculation of
defeat, because while he could be baffled he could not be beaten. It
was a stream flowing from a mountain height, which might be delayed or diverted, but knew instinctively that it must reach the
sea. *"Italia farà da se."* Garibaldi was that faith incarnate, and
the prophecy is fulfilled. Italy, more proud than stricken, bears
his bust to the Capitol, and there the eloquent marble will say,
while Rome endures, that one man with God, with country, with
duty and conscience, is at last the majority.

But still further, it is educated citizenship which, while defining
the rightful limitation of the power of the majority, is most loyal
to its legitimate authority, and foremost always in rescuing it from
the treachery of political peddlers and parasites. The rural statesmen who founded the Republic saw in vision a homogeneous and
intelligent community, the peace and prosperity and intelligence
of the State reflected in the virtue and wisdom of the government.
But is this our actual America or a glimpse of Arcadia? Is this
the United States or Plato's Republic or Harrington's Oceana or
Sir Thomas More's Utopia? What are the political maxims of the
hour? In Rome, do as the Romans do. Fight fire with fire. Beat
the devil with his own weapons. Take men as they are, and don't
affect superior goodness. Beware of the politics of the moon and
of Sunday-school statesmanship. This is our current political wisdom and the results are familiar. "This is a nasty State," cries
the eager partisan, "and I hope we have done nasty work enough
to carry it." "The conduct of the opposition," says another, "was
infamous. They resorted to every kind of base and contemptible
means, and, thank God, we have beaten them at their own game."
The majority is overthrown by the political machinery intended
to secure its will. The machinery is oiled by corruption and grinds
the honest majority to powder. And it is educated citizenship,
the wisdom and energy of men who are classed as prigs, pedants

and impracticables, which is first and most efficient in breaking the machinery and releasing the majority. It was this which rescued New York from Tweed, and which everywhere challenges and demolishes a Tweed tyranny by whatever name it may be known.

Every year at the college Commencement the American scholar is exhorted to do his duty. But every newspaper proves that he is doing it. For he is the most practical politician who shows his fellow-citizens, as the wise old sailor told his shipmates, that "God has somehow so fixed the world that a man can afford to do about right." Take from the country at this moment the educated power, which is contemned as romantic and sentimental, and you would take from the army its general, from the ship its compass, from national action its moral mainspring. It is not the demagogue and the shouting rabble; it is the people heeding the word of the thinker and the lesson of experience, which secures the welfare of the American republic and enlarges human liberty. If American scholarship is not in place, it is in power. If it does not carry the election to-day, it determines the policy of to-morrow. Calm, patient, confident, heroic, in our busy and material life it perpetually vindicates the truth that the things which are unseen are eternal. So in the cloudless midsummer sky serenely shines the moon, while the tumultuous ocean rolls and murmurs beneath, the type of illimitable and unbridled power; but, resistlessly marshalled by celestial laws, all the wild waters, heaving from pole to pole, rise and recede, obedient to the mild queen of heaven.

Brethren of Brown, we have come hither as our fathers came, as our children will come, to renew our observation of that celestial law; and here, upon the old altar of fervid faith and boundless anticipation, let us pledge ourselves once more that, as the courage and energy of educated men fired the morning gun and led the contest of the Revolution, founded and framed the Union and, purifying it as with fire, have maintained the national life to this hour, so day by day, we will do our part to lift America above the slough of mercenary politics and the cunning snares of trade, steadily forward toward the shining heights which the hopes of its nativity foretold.

PUBLIC DISCUSSION

STUMP-ORATOR [1]

Thomas Carlyle

[Thomas Carlyle (1795-1881) published the *Latter-Day Pamphlets,* of which *Stump-Orator* is number five, in 1850. The events of 1848 in Europe were still fresh in his mind, and his essays were tirades at large against Democracy. The papers were journalistic in style, and did considerable damage to his reputation for political wisdom. In attacks upon Democracy the demagogue never escapes denunciation, and Carlyle gives full vent to his feelings in *Stump-Orator.* The latter part of the essay is omitted.]

It lies deep in our habits, confirmed by all manner of educational and other arrangements for several centuries back, to consider human talent as best of all evincing itself by the faculty of eloquent speech. Our earliest schoolmasters teach us, as the one gift of culture they have, the art of spelling and pronouncing, the rules of correct speech; rhetorics, logics follow, sublime mysteries of grammar, whereby we may not only speak but write. And onward to the last of our schoolmasters in the highest university, it is still intrinsically grammar, under various figures grammar. To speak in various languages, on various things, but on all of them to speak, and appropriately deliver ourselves by tongue or pen,—this is the sublime goal towards which all manner of beneficent preceptors and learned professors, from the lowest hornbook upwards, are continually urging and guiding us. Preceptor or Professor, looking over his miraculous seedplot, seminary as he well calls it, or crop of young human souls, watches with attentive view one organ of his delightful little seedlings growing to be men,—the tongue. He hopes we shall all get to speak yet, if it please Heaven. "Some of you shall be book writers, eloquent review writers, and astonish mankind, my young friends: others in white neck-cloths shall do sermons by Blair and Lindley Murray, nay, by Jeremy Taylor and judicious Hooker, and be priests to guide men heavenward by skilfully brandished handkerchief and the torch of rhetoric. For others there is Parliament and the election beerbarrel, and

---

[1] Reprinted from *Latter-Day Pamphlets.*
Questions and topics for the discussion of this essay, and of other phases of the general subject with which it deals, will be found on pages 550 and 555.

a course that leads men very high indeed; these shall shake the senate-house, the morning newspapers, shake the very spheres, and by dextrous wagging of the tongue disenthral mankind, and lead our afflicted country and us on the way we are to go. The way if not where noble deeds are done, yet where noble words are spoken, —leading us, if not to the real Home of the Gods, at least to something which shall more or less deceptively resemble it!''

So fares it with the son of Adam, in these bewildered epochs; so, from the first opening of his eyes in this world, to his last closing of them, and departure hence. Speak, speak, O speak;—if thou have any faculty, speak it, or thou diest and it is no faculty! So in universities, and all manner of dames' and other schools, of the very highest class as of the very lowest; and society at large, when we enter there, confirms with all its brilliant review-articles, successful publications, intellectual tea-circles, literary gazettes, parliamentary eloquences, the grand lesson we had. Other lesson in fact we have none, in these times. If there be a human talent, let it get into the tongue, and make melody with that organ. The talent that can say nothing for itself, what is it? Nothing; or a thing that can do mere drudgeries, and at best make money by railways.

All this is deep rooted in our habits, in our social, educational and other arrangements; and all this, when we look at it impartially, is astonishing. Directly in the teeth of all this it may be asserted that speaking is by no means the chief faculty a human being can attain to; that his excellence therein is by no means the best test of his general human excellence, or availability in this world; nay, that, unless we look well, it is liable to become the very worst test ever devised for said availability. The matter extends very far, down to the very roots of the world, whither the British reader cannot conveniently follow me just now; but I will venture to assert the three following things, and invite him to consider well what truth he can gradually find in them:

First, that excellent speech, even speech *really* excellent, is not, and never was, the chief test of human faculty, or the measure of a man's ability, for any true function whatsoever; on the contrary, that excellent *silence* needed always to accompany excellent speech, and was and is a much rarer and more difficult gift.

Secondly, that really excellent speech,—which I, being possessed of the Hebrew Bible or Book, as well as of other books in my own and foreign languages, and having occasionally heard a wise man's word among the crowd of unwise, do almost unspeakably esteem, as a human gift,—is terribly apt to get confounded with its counterfeit, sham-excellent speech! And furthermore, that if really excellent human speech is among the best of human things, then sham-excellent ditto deserves to be ranked with the very worst. False speech,—capable of becoming, as some one has said, the falsest and basest of all human things:—put the case, one were listening to *that* as to the truest and noblest! Which, little as we are conscious of it, I take to be the sad lot of many. excellent souls among us just now. So many as admire parliamentary eloquence, divine popular literature, and suchlike, are dreadfully liable to it just now: and whole nations and generations seem as if getting themselves asphyxiaed, constitutionally, into their last sleep, by means of it just now!

For alas, much as we worship speech on all hands, here is a *third* assertion, which a man may venture to make, and invite considerate men to reflect upon: That in these times, and for several generations back, there has been, strictly considered, no really excellent speech at all, but sham-excellent merely; that is to say, false or quasi-false speech getting itself admired and worshiped instead of detested and suppressed. A truly alarming predicament; and not the less so if we find it a quite pleasant one for the time being, and welcome the advent of *asphyxia,* as we would that of comfortable natural sleep;—as, in so many senses, we are doing! Surly judges there have been who did not much admire the "Bible of Modern Literature," or anything you could distil from it, in contrast with the ancient Bibles; and found that in the matter of speaking, our far best excellence, where that could be obtained, was excellent silence, which means endurance and exertion, and good *work* with lips closed; and that our tolerablest speech was of the nature of honest commonplace introduced where indispensable, which only set-up for being brief and true, and could not be mistaken for excellent.

These are hard sayings for many a British reader, unconscious of any damage, nay, joyfully conscious to himself of much profit, from that side of his possessions. Surely on this side, if on no other, matters stood not ill with him? The ingenuous arts had softened his manners; the parliamentary eloquences supplied him with a succedaneum for government, the popular literatures with the finer sensibilities of the heart: surely on this *wind*ward side of things the British reader was not ill off?—Unhappy British reader!

In fact, the spiritual detriment we unconsciously suffer, in every province of our affairs, from this our prostrate respect to power of speech is incalculable. For indeed it is the natural consummation of an epoch such as ours. Given a general insincerity of mind for several generations, you will certainly find the Talker established in the place of honor; and the Doer, hidden in the obscure crowd, with activity lamed, or working sorrowfully forward on paths unworthy of him. All men are devoutly prostrate, worshipping the eloquent talker; and no man knows what a scandalous idol he is. Out of whom in the mildest manner, like comfortable natural rest, comes mere asphyxia and death everlasting! Probably there is not in Nature a more distracted phantasm than your commonplace eloquent speaker, as he is found on platforms, in parliaments, on Kentucky stumps, at tavern-dinners, in windy, empty, insincere times like ours. The 'excellent Stump-Orator,' as our admiring Yankee friends define him, he who in any occurrent set of circumstances can start forth, mount upon his 'stump,' his rostrum, tribune, place in parliament, or other ready elevation, and pour forth from him his appropriate 'excellent speech,' his interpretation of the said circumstances, in such manner as poor windy mortals round him shall cry bravo to,—he is not an artist I can much admire, as matters go! Alas, he is in general merely the windiest mortal of them all; and is admired for being so, into the bargain. Not a windy blockhead there who kept silent but is better off than this excellent stump-orator. Better off, for a great many reasons; for this reason, were there no other: the silent one is *not* admired; the silent suspects, perhaps partly admits, that he is a kind of blockhead, from which salutary self-knowledge the excellent stump-orator is debarred. A mouthpiece of Chaos to poor benighted mortals that lend ear to him as to a voice from Cosmos, this excellent stump-orator fills me with amazement. Not empty these musical wind-utterances of his; they are big with prophecy; they announce, too audibly to me, that the end of many things is drawing nigh!

Let the British reader consider it a little; he too is not a little interested in it. Nay, he, and the European reader in general, but he chiefly in these days, will require to consider it a great deal, —and to take important steps in consequence by and by, if I mistake not. And in the meanwhile, sunk as he himself is in that bad element, and like a jaundiced man struggling to discriminate yellow colors,—he will have to meditate long before he in any measure get the immense meanings of the thing brought home to him; and discern, with astonishment, alarm, and almost terror and despair, towards what fatal issues, in our Collective Wisdom and elsewhere, this notion of talent meaning eloquent speech, so obstinately entertained this long while, has been leading us! Whosoever shall look well into origins and issues, will find this of eloquence and the part it now plays in our affairs, to be one of the gravest phenomena; and the excellent stump-orator of these days to be not only a ridiculous but still more a highly tragical personage. While the many listen to him, the few are used to pass rapidly, with some gust of scornful laughter, some growl of impatient malediction; but he deserves from this latter class a much more serious attention.

In the old Ages, when Universities and Schools were first instituted, this function of the schoolmaster, to teach mere speaking, was the natural one. In those healthy times, guided by silent instincts, and the monition of Nature, men had from of old been used to teach themselves what it was essential to learn, by the one sure method of learning anything, practical apprenticeship to it. This was the rule for all classes; as it now is the rule, unluckily, for only one class. The Working Man as yet sought only to know his craft; and educated himself sufficiently by plowing and hammering, under the conditions given, and in fit relation to the persons given: a course of education, then as now and ever, really opulent in manful culture and instruction to him; teaching him many solid virtues, and most indubitably useful knowledges; developing in him valuable faculties not a few both to do and to endure,—among which the faculty of elaborate grammatical utterance, seeing he had so little of extraordinary to utter, or to learn from spoken or written utterances, was not bargained for; the grammar of Nature, which he learned from his mother, being still amply sufficient for him. This was, as it still is, the grand education of the Working Man.

As for the Priest, though his trade was clearly of a reading and speaking nature, he knew also in those veracious times that grammar, if needful, was by no means the one thing needful, or the chief thing. By far the chief thing needful, and indeed the one thing then as now, was, that there should be in him the feeling and the practice of reverence to God and to men; that in his life's core there should dwell, spoken or silent, a ray of pious wisdom fit for illuminating dark human destinies;—not so much that he should possess the art of speech, as that he should have something to speak! And for that latter requisite the Priest also trained himself by apprenticeship, by actual attempt to practice, by manifold long-continued trial, of a devout and painful nature, such as his superiors prescribed to him. This, when once judged satisfactory, procured him ordination; and his grammar learning, in the good times of priesthood, was very much of a parergon with him, as indeed in all times it is intrinsically quite insignificant in comparison.

The young Noble again, for whom grammar schoolmasters were first hired and high seminaries founded, he too without these, or over and above these, had from immemorial time been used to learn his business by apprenticeship. The young Noble, before the schoolmaster as after him, went apprentice to some elder noble; entered himself as page with some distinguished earl or duke; and here, serving upwards from step to step, under wise monition, learned his chivalries, his practice of arms and of courtesies, his baronial duties and manners, and what it would beseem him to do and to be in the world,—by practical attempt of his own, and example of one whose life was a daily concrete pattern for him. To such a one, already filled with intellectual substance, and possessing what we may call the practical gold-bullion of human culture, it was an obvious improvement that he should be taught to speak it out of him on occasion; that he should carry a spiritual banknote producible on demand for what of "gold-bullion" he had, not so negotiable otherwise, stored in the cellars of his mind. A man, with wisdom, insight and heroic worth already acquired for him, naturally demanded of the schoolmaster this one new faculty, the faculty of uttering in fit words what he had. A valuable super-addition of faculty:—and yet we are to remember it was scarcely a new faculty; it was but the tangible sign of what other faculties the man had in the silent state: and many a rugged inarticulate chief of men, I can believe, was most enviably "educated," who had not a Book on his premises; whose signature, a true sign-manual, was the stamp of his iron hand duly inked and clapt upon the parchment; and whose speech in Parliament, like the growl of lions, did indeed convey his meaning, but would have torn Lindley

Murray's nerves to pieces! To such a one the schoolmaster adjusted himself very naturally in that manner; as a man wanted for teaching grammatical utterance; the thing to utter being already there. The thing to utter, here was the grand point. And perhaps this is the reason why among earnest nations, as among the Romans for example, the craft of the schoolmaster was held in little regard; for indeed as mere teacher of grammar, of ciphering on the abacus and suchlike, how did he differ much from the dancing-master or fencing-master, or deserve much regard?—Such was the rule in the ancient healthy times.

Can it be doubtful that this is still the rule of human education; that the human creature needs first of all to be educated not that he may speak, but that he may have something weighty and valuable to say! If speech is the banknote for an inward capital of culture, of insight and noble human worth, then speech is precious, and the art of speech shall be honored. But if there *is* no inward capital; if speech represent no real culture of the mind, but an imaginary culture; no bullion, but the fatal and now almost hopeless deficit of such? Alas, alas, said banknote is then a *forged* one; passing freely current in the market; but bringing damages to the receiver, to the payer, and to all the world, which are in sad truth infallible, and of amount incalculable. Few think of it at present; but the truth remains forever so. In parliaments and other loud assemblages, your eloquent talk, *dis*-united from Nature and her facts, is taken as wisdom and the correct image of said facts: but Nature well knows what it is, Nature will not have it as such, and will reject your forged note one day, with huge costs. The foolish traders in the market pass it freely, nothing doubting, and rejoice in the dextrous execution of the piece: and so it circulates from hand to hand, and from class to class; gravitating ever downwards towards the *practical* class; till at last it reaches some poor *working* hand, who can pass it no farther, but must take it to the bank to get bread with it, and there the answer is, "Unhappy caitiff, this note is forged. It does not mean performance and reality, in parliaments and elsewhere, for thy behoof; it means fallacious semblance of performance, and thou, poor dupe, art thrown into the stocks on offering it here!"

Alas, alas, looking abroad over Irish difficulties, Mosaic sweating-establishments, French barricades, and an anarchic Europe is it not as if all the populations of the world were rising or had risen into incendiary madness; unable longer to endure such an avalanche of forgeries, and of penalties in consequence, as had accumulated upon them? The speaker is "excellent," the notes he does are beautiful? Beautifully fit for the market, yes; *he* is an excellent artist in his business;—and the more excellent he is, the more is my desire to lay him by the heels, and fling *him* into the treadmill, that I might save the poor sweating tailors, French Sansculottes, and Irish Sanspotatoes from bearing the smart!

For the smart must be borne; some one must bear it, as sure as God lives. Every word of man is either a note or a forged-note; have these eternal skies forgotten to be in earnest, think you because men go grinning like enchanted apes? Foolish souls, this now as of old is the unalterable law of your existence. If you know the truth and do it, the Universe itself seconds you, bears you on to sure victory everywhere:—and, observe, to sure defeat everywhere if you do *not* do the truth. And alas, if you *know* only the eloquent fallacious semblance of the truth, what chance is there of your ever doing it? You will do something very different from *it*, I think!—He who well considers, will find this same "art of speech" as we moderns have it, to be a truly astonishing product of the Ages; and the longer he considers it, the more astonishing and alarming. I reckon it the saddest of all the curses that now lie heavy on us. With horror and amazement, one perceives that this much-celebrated "art" so diligently practised in all corners of the world just now, is the chief destroyer of whatever good is born to us (softly, swiftly shutting-up all nascent good as if under exhausted glass-receivers, there to choke and die); and the grand parent-manufactory of evil to us,—as it were, the last finishing and varnishing workshop of all the Devil's ware that circulates under the sun. No Devil's sham is fit for the market till it have been polished and enameled here; this is the general assaying-house for such, where the artists examine and answer, "Fit for the market; not fit!" Word will not express what mischiefs the misuse of words has done, and is doing, in these heavy-laden generations.

Do you want a man *not* to practise what he believes, then encourage him to keep often speaking it in words. Every time he speaks it, the tendency to do it will grow less. His empty speech of what he believes, will be a weariness and an affliction to the wise man. But do you wish his empty speech of what he believes to become farther an insincere speech of what he does not believe? Celebrate to him his gift of speech; assure him that he shall rise in Parliament by means of it, and achieve great things without any performance; that eloquent speech, whether performed or not, is admirable. My friends, eloquent unperformed speech, in Parliament or elsewhere, is horrible! The eloquent man that delivers, in Parliament or elsewhere, a beautiful speech, and will perform nothing of it, but leaves it as if already performed,—what can you make of that man? He has enrolled himself among the *Ignes Fatui* and Children of the Wind; means to serve, as beautifully illuminated Chinese Lantern, in that corps henceforth. I think, the serviceable thing you could do to that man, if permissible, would be a severe one: To *clip-off* a bit of his eloquent tongue by way of penance and warning; another bit, if he again spoke without performing; and so again, till you had clipt the whole tongue away from him,—and were delivered, you and he, from at least one miserable mockery: "There, eloquent friend, see now in silence if there be any redeeming deed in thee; of blasphemous wind-eloquence, at least, we shall have no more!" How many pretty men have gone this road, escorted by the beautifulest marching music from all the "public organs"; and have found at last that it ended —where? It is the *broad* road, that leads direct to Limbo and the Kingdom of the Inane. Gifted men, and once valiant nations, and as it were the whole world with one accord, are marching thither, in melodious triumph, all the drums and hautboys giving out their cheerfulest *Ça-ira*. It is the universal humor of the world just now. My friends, I am very sure you will *arrive,* unless you halt!

Considered as the last finish of education, or of human culture, worth and acquirement, the art of speech is noble, and even divine; it is like the kindling of a Heaven's light to *show* us what a glorious world exists, and has perfected itself, in a man. But if no world exist in the man; if nothing but continents of empty vapor, of greedy self-conceits, commonplace hearsays, and indistinct loomings of a sordid *chaos* exist in him, what will be the use of "light" to show us that? Better a thousand times that such a man do not speak, but keep his empty vapor and his sordid chaos to himself, hidden to the utmost from all beholders. To look on that, can be good for no human beholder; to look away from that, must be good. And if, by delusive semblances of rhetoric, logic, first-class degrees, and the aid of elocution-masters and parliamentary reporters, the poor proprietor of said chaos should be led to persuade himself, and get others persuaded,—which it is the nature of his sad task to do, and which, in certain eras of the world, it is fatally possible to do,—that this is a *cosmos* which he owns; that *he*, being so perfect in tongue-exercise and full of college-honors, is an "educated" man, and pearl of great price in his generation; that round him, and his parliament emulously listening to him, as round some divine apple of gold set in a picture of silver, all the world should gather to adore: what is likely to become of him and the gathering world? An apple of Sodom set in the clusters of Gomorrah; that, little as he suspects it, is the definition of the poor chaotically eloquent man, with his emulous parliament and miserable adoring world!—Considered as the whole of education, or human culture, which it now is in our modern manners; all apprenticeship except to mere handicraft having fallen obsolete, and the "educated" man being with us emphatically and exclusively the man that can speak well with tongue or pen, and astonish men by the quantities of speech he has *heard* ("tremendous *reader*," "walking encyclopedia," and suchlike),—the Art of Speech is probably definable in that case as the short summary of all the Black Arts put together.

But the Schoolmaster is secondary, an effect rather than a cause in this matter: what the Schoolmaster with his universities shall manage or attempt to teach will be ruled by what the Society with its practical industries is continually demanding that men should learn. We spoke once of vital *lungs* for Society: and in fact this question always rises as the alpha and omega of social questions. What methods the Society has of summoning aloft into the high places, for its help and governance, the wisdom that is born to it in all places and of course is born chiefly in the more populous or lower places? For this, if you will consider it, expresses the ultimate available result, and net sum-total, of all the efforts, struggles, and confused activities that go on in the Society; and determines whether they are true and wise efforts, certain to be victorious, or false and foolish, certain to be futile, and to fall captive and caitiff. How do men rise in your Society? In all Societies, Turkey included, and I suppose Dahomey included, men do rise: but the question of questions always is, What kind of men? Men of noble gifts, or men of ignoble? It is the one or the other; and a life-and-death inquiry which! For in all places and all times, little as you may heed it, Nature most silently but most inexorably demands that it be the one and *not* the other. And you need not try to palm an ignoble sham upon her, and call it noble; for she is a judge. And her penalties, as quiet as she looks, are terrible; amounting to world-earthquakes, to anarchy and death everlasting; and admit of no appeal!—

Surely England still flatters herself that she has *lungs;* that she can still breathe a little? Or is it that the poor creature, driven into mere blind industrialisms; and as it were, gone pearl-diving this long while many fathoms deep, and tearing-up the oyster-beds so as never creature did before, hardly knows,—so busy in the belly of the oyster-chaos, where is no thought of "breathing"— whether she has lungs or not? Nations of a robust habit, and fine deep chest, can sometimes take-in a deal of breath *before* diving; and live long, in the muddy deeps, without new breath: but they too come to need it at last, and will die if they cannot get it!

To the gifted soul that is born in England, what is the career, then, that will carry him, amid noble Olympic dust, up to the immortal gods? For his country's sake, that it may not lose the service he was born capable of doing it; for his own sake, that his life be not choked and perverted, and his light from Heaven be not changed into lightning from the Other Place,—it is essential that there be such a career. The country that can offer no career in that case, is a doomed country; nay it is already a dead country; it has secured the ban of Heaven upon it; will not have Heaven's light, will have the Other Place's lightning; and may consider itself as appointed to expire, in frightful coughings of street musketry or otherwise, on a set day, and to be in the eye of law dead. In no country is there not some career, inviting to it either the noble Hero, or the tough Greek of the Lower Empire: which of the two do your careers invite? There is no question more important. The kind of careers you offer in countries still living, determines with perfect exactness the kind of the life that is in them,—whether it is natural blessed life, or galvanic accursed ditto, and likewise what degree of strength is in the same.

Our English careers to born genius are twofold. There is the silent or unlearned career of the Industrialisms, which are very many among us; and there is the articulate or learned career of the three professions, Medicine, Law, (under which we may include Politics), and the Church. Your born genius, therefore, will first have to ask himself, Whether he can hold his tongue or cannot? True, all human talent, especially all deep talent, is a talent to *do,*

and is intrinsically of silent nature; inaudible, like the Sphere
Harmonies and Eternal Melodies, of which it is an incarnated
fraction. All real talent, I fancy, would much rather, if it listened
only to Nature's monitions, express itself in rhythmic facts than
in melodious words, which latter at best, where they are good
for anything, are only a feeble echo and shadow or foreshadow of
the former. But talents differ much in this of power to be silent;
and circumstances, of position, opportunity and suchlike, modify
them still more;—and Nature's monitions, oftenest quite drowned
in foreign hearsays, are by no means the only ones listened to in
deciding!—The Industrialisms are all of silent nature; and some
of them are heroic and eminently human; others, again, we may
call unheroic, not eminently human: *beaverish* rather, but still
honest; some are even *vulpine*, altogether inhuman and dishonest.
Your born genius must make his choice.

If a soul is born with divine intelligence, and has its lips touched
with hallowed fire, in consecration for high enterprises under the
sun, this young soul will find the question asked of him by England
every hour and moment: "Canst thou turn thy human intelligence
into the beaver sort, and make honest contrivance, and accumulation of capital by it? If so, do it; and avoid the vulpine kind,
which I don't recommend. Honest triumphs in engineering and
machinery await thee; scrip awaits thee, commercial successes, kingship in the counting room, on the stock-exchange;—thou shalt be
the envy of surrounding flunkies, and collect into a heap more gold
than a dray-horse can draw."—"God, so much gold?" answers
the ingenious soul, with visions of the envy of surrounding flunkies
dawning upon him; and in very many cases decides that he will
contract himself into beaverism, and with such a horse-draught of
gold, emblem of a never-imagined success in beaver heroism, strike
the surrounding flunkies yellow.

This is our common course; this is in some sort open to every
creature, what we call the beaver career; perhaps more open in,
England, taking in America too, than it ever was in any country
before. And, truly, good consequences follow out of it: who can
be blind to them? Half of a most excellent and opulent result is
realized to us in this way; baleful only when it sets-up (as too
often now) for being the whole result. A half-result which will
be blessed and heavenly so soon as the other half is had,—namely
wisdom to guide the first half. Let us honor all honest human
power of contrivance in its degree. The beaver intellect, so long

as it steadfastly refuses to be vulpine, and answers the tempter pointing out short routes to it with an honest "No, no," is truly respectable to me; and many a highflying speaker and singer whom I have known, has appeared to me much less of a developed man than certain of my mill-owning, agricultural, commercial, mechanical, or otherwise industrial friends, who have held their peace all their days and gone on in the silent state. If a man *can* keep his intellect silent, and make it even into honest beaverism, several very manful moralities, in danger of wreck on other courses, may comport well with that, and give it a genuine and partly human character; and I will tell him, in these days he may do far worse with himself and his intellect than change it into beaverism, and make honest money with it. If indeed he could become a *heroic* industrial, and have a life "eminently human"! But that is not easy at present. Probably some ninety-nine out of every hundred of our gifted souls, who have to seek a career for themselves, go this beaver road. Whereby the first half-result, national wealth namely, is plentifully realized; and only the second half, or wisdom to guide it, is dreadfully behindhand.

But now if the gifted soul be not of the taciturn nature, be of vivid, impatient, rapidly-productive nature and aspire much to give itself sensible utterance,—I find that, in this case, the field it has in England is narrow to an extreme; is perhaps narrower than ever offered itself, for the like object, in this world before. Parliament, Church, Law: let the young vivid soul turn whither he will for a career, he finds among variable conditions one condition invariable, and extremely surprising, That the proof of excellence is to be done by the tongue. For heroism that will not speak, but only act, there is no account kept:—The English Nation does not need that silent kind, then, but only the talking kind? Most astonishing. Of all the organs a man has, there is none held in account, it would appear, but the tongue he uses for talking. Premiership, woolsack, mitre, and quasicrown; all is attainable if you can talk with due ability. Everywhere your proof-shot is to be a well-fired volley of talk. Contrive to talk well, you will get to Heaven, the modern Heaven of the English. Do not talk well, only work well, and heroically hold your peace, you have no chance whatever to get thither; with your utmost industry you may get to Threadneedle Street, and accumulate more gold than a drayhorse can draw. Is not this a very wonderful arrangement? I have heard of races done by mortals tied in sacks; of human competitors, high aspirants, climbing heavenward on the soaped pole; seizing the soaped pig; and clutching with deft fist, at full gallop, the fatted goose tied aloft by its foot;—which feats do prove agility, toughness and other useful faculties in man; but this of dextrous talk is probably as strange a competition as any. And the question rises, Whether certain of these other feats, or perhaps an alternation of all of them, relieved now and then by a bout of grinning through the collar, might not be profitably substituted for the solitary proof-feat of talk, now getting rather monotonous by its long continuance? Alas, Mr. Bull, I do find it is all little other than a proof of toughness, which is a quality I respect, with more or less expenditure of falsity and astucity superadded, which I entirely condemn. Toughness *plus* astucity: —perhaps a simple wooden mast set up in Palace-Yard, well soaped and duly presided over, might be the honester method? Such a method as this by trial of talk, for filling your chief offices in Church and State, was perhaps never heard of in the solar system before. You are quite used to it, my poor friend; and nearly dead by the consequences of it; but in the other Planets, as in other epochs of your own Planet it would have done had you proposed it, the thing awakens incredulous amazement, world-wide Olympic laughter, which ends in tempestuous hootings, in tears and horror! My friend, if you can, as heretofore this good while, find nobody to take care of your affairs but the expertest talker, it is all over with your affairs and you. Talk never yet could guide any man's or nation's affairs; nor will it yours, except towards the *Limbus Patrum*, where all talk, except a very select kind of it, lodges at last.

Medicine, guarded too by preliminary impediments, and frightful medusa-heads of quackery, which deter many generous souls from entering, is of the *half*-articulate professions, and does not much invite the ardent kinds of ambition. The intellect required for medicine might be wholly human, and indeed should by all rules be,—the profession of the Human Healer being radically a sacred one and connected with the highest priesthoods, or rather being itself the outcome and acme of all priesthoods, and divinest conquests of intellect here below. As will appear one day, when men take off their old monastic and ecclesiastic spectacles, and look with eyes again! In essence the Physician's task is always heroic, eminently human: but in practice most unluckily at present we find it too become in good part *beaverish;* yielding a money-result alone. And what of it is not beaverish,—does not that too go mainly to ingenious talking, publishing of yourself, ingratiating of yourself; a partly human exercise or waste of intellect, and alas a partly vulpine ditto;—making the once sacred 'Ιατρὸς, or Human Healer more impossible for us than ever!

Angry basilisks watch at the gates of Law and Church just now; and strike a sad damp into the nobler of the young aspirants. Hard bonds are offered you to sign; as it were, a solemn engagement to constitute yourself an imposter, before ever entering; to declare your belief in incredibilities,—your determination, in short, to take Chaos for Cosmos, and Satan for the Lord of things, if he come with money in his pockets, and horsehair and bombazeen decently wrapped about him. Fatal preliminaries, which deter many an ingenuous young soul, and send him back from the threshold, and I hope will deter ever more. But if you do enter, the condition is well known: "Talk; who can talk best here? His shall be the mouth of gold, and the purse of gold; and with my μίτρα (once the head-dress of unfortunate-females, I am told) shall his sacred temples be begirt."

Ingenuous souls, unless forced to it, do now much shudder at the threshold of both these careers, and not a few desperately turn back into the wilderness rather, to front a very rude fortune, and be devoured by wild-beasts as is likeliest. But as to Parliament, again, and its eligibility if attainable, there is yet no question anywhere; the ingenuous soul, if possessed of money-capital enough, is predestined by the parental and all manner of monitors to that career of talk; and accepts it with alacrity and clearness of heart, doubtful only whether he shall be *able* to make a speech. Courage, my brave young fellow. If you can climb a soaped pole of any kind, you will certainly be able to make a speech. All mortals have a tongue; and carry on some jumble, if not of thought, yet of stuff which they could talk. The weakest of animals has got a cry in it, and can give voice before dying. If you are tough enough, bent upon it desperately enough, I engage you shall make a speech;—but whether that will be the way to Heaven for you, I do not engage.

These, then, are our two careers for genius: mute Industrialism, which can seldom become very human, but remains beaverish mainly: and the three Professions named learned,—that is to say, able to talk. For the heroic or higher kinds of human intellect, in the silent state, there is not the smallest inquiry anywhere; apparently a thing not wanted in this country at present. What the supply may be, I cannot inform M'Croudy; but the market-demand, he may himself see, is *nil*. These are our three professions that require human intellect in part or whole, not able to do with mere beaverish; and such a part does the gift of talk play in one and all of them. Whatsoever is not beaverish seems to go forth in the shape of talk. To such length is human intellect wasted or suppressed in this world!

If the young aspirant is not rich enough for Parliament, and is deterred by the basilisks or otherwise from entering on Law or Church, and cannot altogether reduce his human intellect to the beaverish condition, or satisfy himself with the prospect of making money,—what becomes of him in such case, which is naturally the case of very many, and ever of more? In such case there remains but one outlet for him, and notably enough that too is a talking one: the outlet of Literature, of trying to write Books. Since, owing to preliminary basilisks, want of cash, or superiority to cash, he cannot mount aloft by eloquent talking, let him try it by dexterous eloquent writing. Here happily, having three figures, and capital to buy a quire of paper, he can try it to all lengths, and in spite of all mortals: in this career there is happily no public impediment that can turn him back; nothing but private starvation,—which is itself a *finis* or kind of goal,—can pretend to hinder a British man from prosecuting Literature to the very utmost, and wringing the final secret from her: "A talent is in thee; No talent is in thee." To the British subject who fancies genius may be lodged in him, this liberty remains; and truly it is, if well computed, almost the only one he has.

A crowded portal, this of Literature, accordingly! The haven of expatriated spiritualisms, and, alas, also of expatriated vanities and prurient imbecilities: here do the windy aspirations, foiled activities, foolish ambitions, and frustrate human energies reduced to the vocable condition, fly as to the one refuge left; and the Republic of Letters increases in population at a faster rate than even the Republic of America. The strangest regiment in her Majesty's service, this of the Soldier of Literature:—would your Lordship much like to march through Coventry with them? The immortal gods are there (quite irrecognizable under these disguises), and also the lowest broken valets;—an extremely miscellaneous regiment. In fact the regiment, superficially viewed, looks like an immeasurable motley flood of discharged playactors, funambulists, false prophets, drunken ballad-singers; and marches not as a regiment, but as a boundless canaille,—without drill, uniform, captaincy or billet: with huge *over*-proportion of drummers; you would say, a regiment gone wholly to the drum, with hardly a good musket to be seen in it,—more a canaille than a regiment. Canaille of all the loud-sounding levities, and general winnowings of Chaos, marching through the world in a most ominous manner; proclaiming, audibly if you have ears: "Twelfth hour of the Night; ancient graves yawning; pale clammy Puseyisms screeching in their winding-sheets; owls busy in the City regions; many goblins abroad! Awake, ye living; dream no more; arise to judgment! Chaos and Gehenna are broken loose; the Devil with his Bedlams must be flung in chains again, and the Last of the Days is about to dawn!" Such is Literature to the reflective soul at this moment.

But what now concerns us most is the circumstance that here too the demand is, Vocables, still vocables. In all appointed courses of activity and paved careers for human genius, and in this unpaved, unappointed, broadest career of Literature, broad way that leadeth to destruction for so many, the one duty laid upon you is still, Talk, talk. Talk well with pen or tongue, and it shall be well with you; do not talk well, it shall be ill with you. To wag the tongue with dexterous acceptability, there is for human worth and faculty, in our England of the Nineteenth Century, that one method of emergence, and no other. Silence, you would say, means annihilation for the Englishman of the Nineteenth Century. The worth that has not spoken itself, is not; or is potentially only, and as if it were not; Vox is the God of this Universe. If you have human intellect, it avails nothing unless you either make it into beaverism, or talk with it. Make it into beaverism, and gather money; or else make talk with it, and gather what you can. Such is everywhere the demand for talk among us; to which, of course, the supply is proportionate.

From dinners up to woolsacks and divine mitres, here in England much may be gathered by talk; without talk, of the human sort nothing. Is Society become wholly a bag of wind, then, ballasted by guineas? Are our interests in it as sounding brass and a tinkling cymbal?—In Army or Navy, when unhappily we have war on hand, there is, almost against our will, some kind of demand for certain of the silent talents. But in peace, that too passes into mere demand of the ostentations, of the pipeclays and the blank cartridges; and,—except that Naval men are occasionally, on long voyages, forced to hold their tongue, and converse with the dumb elements, and illimitable oceans, that moan and rave there without you and within you, which is a great advantage to the Naval man,—our poor United Services have to make conversational wind-bags and ostentational paper-lanterns of themselves, or do worse, even as the others.

My friends, must I assert, then, what surely all men know, though all men seem to have forgotten it, That in the learned professions as in the unlearned, and in human things throughout, in every place and in every time, the true function of intellect is *not* that of talking, but of understanding and discerning with a view to performing! An intellect may easily talk too much, and perform too little. Gradually, if it get into the noxious habit of talk, there will less and less performance come of it, talk being so delightfully handy in comparison with work; and at last there will no work, or thought of work, be got from it at all. Talk, except as the preparation for work, is worth almost nothing;—sometimes it is worth infinitely less than nothing; and becomes, little conscious of playing such a fatal part, the general summary of pretentious nothingnesses, and the chief of all the curses the Posterity of Adam are liable to in this sublunary world! Would you discover the Atropos of Human Virtue; the sure Destroyer, "by painless extinction," of Human Veracities, Performances, and Capabilities to perform or to be veracious,—it is this, you have it here.

Unwise talk is matchless in unwisdom. Unwise work, if it but persist, is everywhere struggling towards correction, and restoration to health; for it is still in contact with Nature, and all Nature incessantly contradicts it, and will heal it or annihilate it: not so with unwise talk, which addresses itself, regardless of veridical Nature, to the universal suffrages; and can, if it be dextrous, find harbor there till all the suffrages are bankrupt and gone to Houndsditch, Nature not interfering with her protest till then. False speech, definable as the acme of unwise speech, is capable, as we already said, of becoming the falsest of all things. Falsest of all things:—and whither will the general deluge of that, in Parliament and Synagogue, in Book and Broadside, carry you and your affairs, my friend, when once they are embarked on it as now?

ELOQUENCE [1]

Ralph Waldo Emerson

[Ralph Waldo Emerson (1803-1882) gave his lecture on *Eloquence* in Boston in 1847. Twenty years later he delivered another lecture upon the same subject in Chicago. In repeating the lectures he frequently introduced several examples of eloquence, which he was fond of reading to his audience. He once said that there was no time in his life when the offer of a professorship of rhetoric and oratory, even from the smallest country college, would not have been tempting to him. Edward Waldo Emerson says of his father:

> Eloquence in boyhood and youth had been his idol. He had used every opportunity to hear the finished speakers of that day, when rhetoric and oratory were more prized than now. In those days apparently the great body of the students at Cambridge voluntarily went to hear the Seniors declaim. The florid and fervid oratory of the young Southerners had a great charm for the Northern boys. The young Emerson himself took the Boylston prize for speaking.

In his Journal for the year 1850, Emerson expressed his dissent from Carlyle's view of oratory:

> At the Concord celebration I was struck with the talent of Everett and Choate and the delight of the people in listening to their eloquence. . . . It is of great worth, this stump-oratory (though much decried by Carlyle and others), and very rare. There have been millions and millions of men, and a good stump-orator only once in an age. There have been but few since history began; Demosthenes and Chatham and Daniel Webster and Cobden,—and yet all the human race are competitors in the art. Of course the writers prefer their own art. Stump-oratory requires presence of mind, heat, spunk, continuity, humanity.

In his essay, *Emerson the Lecturer*, James Russell Lowell says:

> It is a singular fact, that Mr. Emerson is the most steadily attractive lecturer in America. Into that somewhat cold-waterish region adventurers of the sensational kind come down now and then with a splash, to become disregarded King Logs before the next season. But Mr. Emerson always draws. A lecturer now for something like a third of a century, one of the pioneers of the lecturing system, the charm of his voice, his manner, and his matter has never lost its power over his earlier hearers, and continually winds new ones in its enchanting meshes. What they do not fully understand they take on trust, and listen, saying to themselves, as the old poet of Sir Philip Sidney,—

[1] Reprinted by permission of Houghton Mifflin Company from *Society and Solitude*.
Questions and topics for the discussion of this address, and of other phases of the general subject with which it deals, will be found on pages 551 and 555.

"A sweet, attractive, kind of grace,
  A full assurance given by looks,
Continual comfort in a face,
  The lineaments of gospel books."

We call it a singular fact, because we Yankees are thought to be fond of the spread-eagle style, and nothing can be more remote from that than his. We are reckoned a practical folk, who would rather hear about a new air-tight stove than about Plato; yet our favorite teacher's practicality is not in the least of the Poor Richard variety. . . . We do not go to hear what Emerson says so much as to hear Emerson. . . .

I have heard some great speakers and some accomplished orators, but never any that so moved and persuaded men as he. There is a kind of undertow in that rich baritone of his that sweeps our minds from their foothold into deeper waters with a drift we cannot and would not resist. And how artfully (for Emerson is a long-studied artist in these things) does the deliberate utterance, that seems waiting for the fit word, appear to admit us partners in the labor of thought and make us feel as if the glance of humor were a sudden suggestion, as if the perfect phrase lying written there on the desk were as unexpected to him as to us. In that closely-filed speech of his at the Burns centenary dinner, every word seemed to have just dropped down to him from the clouds. He looked far away over the heads of his hearers, with a vague kind of expectation, as into some private heaven of invention, and the winged period came at last obedient to his spell. "My dainty Ariel!" he seemed murmuring to himself as he cast down his eyes as if in deprecation of the frenzy of approval and caught another sentence from the Sibylline leaves that lay before him, ambushed behind a dish of fruit and seen only by nearest neighbors. Every sentence brought down the house, as I never saw one brought down before,—and it is not so easy to hit Scotsmen with a sentiment that has no hint of native brogue in it. I watched, for it was an interesting study, how the quick sympathy ran flashing from face to face down the long tables, like an electric spark thrilling as it went, and then exploded in a thunder of plaudits. I watched till tables and faces vanished, for I, too, found myself caught up in the common enthusiasm, and my excited fancy set me under the *bema* listening to him who fulmined over Greece.]

For whom the Muses smile upon,
And touch with soft persuasion,
His words, like a storm-wind, can bring
Terror and beauty on their wing;
In his every syllable
Lurketh nature veritable;
And though he speak in midnight dark,—
In heaven no star, on earth no spark,—
Yet before the listener's eye
Swims the world in ecstasy,
The forest waves, the morning breaks,
The pastures sleep, ripple the lakes,

Leaves twinkle, flowers like persons be
And life pulsates in rock or tree.

It is the doctrine of the popular music-masters that whoever can speak can sing. So probably every man is eloquent once in his life. Our temperaments differ in capacity of heat, or, we boil at different degrees. One man is brought to the boiling-point by the excitement of conversation in the parlor. The waters, of course, are not very deep. He has a two-inch enthusiasm, a patty-pan ebullition. Another requires the additional caloric of a multitude and a public debate; a third needs an antagonist, or a hot indignation; a fourth needs a revolution; and a fifth, nothing less than the grandeur of absolute ideas, the splendors and shades of Heaven and Hell.

But because every man is an orator, how long soever he may have been a mute, an assembly of men is so much more susceptible. The eloquence of one stimulates all the rest, some up to the speaking-point, and all others to a degree that makes them good receivers and conductors, and they avenge themselves for their enforced silence by increased loquacity on their return to the fireside.

The plight of these phlegmatic brains is better than that of those who prematurely boil, and who impatiently break silence before their time. Our county conventions often exhibit a small-pot-soon-hot style of eloquence. We are too much reminded of a medical experiment where a series of patients are taking nitrous-oxide gas. Each patient in turn exhibits similar symptoms,— redness in the face, volubility, violent gesticulation, delirious attitudes, occasional stamping, an alarming loss of perception of the passage of time, a selfish enjoyment of his sensations, and loss of perception of the sufferings of the audience.

Plato says that the punishment which the wise suffer who refuse to take part in the government, is, to live under the government of worse men; and the like regret is suggested to all the auditors, as the penalty of abstaining to speak,—that they shall hear worse orators than themselves.

But this lust to speak marks the universal feeling of the energy of the engine, and the curiosity men feel to touch the springs. Of all the musical instruments on which men play, a popular assembly is that which has the largest compass and variety, and out of which, by genius and study, the most wonderful effects can be drawn. An audience is not a simple addition of the individuals that compose it. Their sympathy gives them a certain social organism, which fills each member, in his own degree, and most of all the orator, as a jar in a battery is charged with the whole electricity of the battery. No one can survey the face of an excited assembly, without being apprised of new opportunity for painting in fire human thought, and being agitated to agitate. How many orators sit mute there below! They come to get justice done to that ear and intuition which no Chatham and no Demosthenes has begun to satisfy.

. The Welsh Triads say, "Many are the friends of the golden tongue." Who can wonder at the attractiveness of Parliament, or of Congress, or the bar, for our ambitious young men, when the highest bribes of society are at the feet of the successful orator? He has his audience at his devotion. All other fames must hush before his. He is the true potentate; for they are not kings who sit on thrones, but they who know how to govern. The definitions of eloquence describe its attraction for young men. Antiphon the Rhamnusian, one of Plutarch's ten orators, advertised in Athens "that he would cure distempers of the mind with words." No man has a prosperity so high or firm but two or three words can dishearten it. There is no calamity which right words will not begin to redress. Isocrates describes his art as "the power of magnifying what was small and diminishing what was great"—an acute but partial definition. Among the Spartans, the art assumed a Spartan shape, namely, of the sharpest weapon. Socrates says: "If any one wishes to converse with the meanest of the Lacedæmonians, he will at first find him despicable in conversation, but when a proper opportunity offers, this same person, like a skilful jaculator, will hurl a sentence worthy of attention, short and contorted, so that he who converses with him will appear to be in no respect superior to a boy." Plato's definition of rhetoric is, "the art of ruling the minds of men." The Koran says, "A mountain may change its place, but a man will not change his disposition"; yet the end of eloquence is—is it not?—to alter in a pair of hours, perhaps in a half-hour's discourse, the convictions and habits of years. Young men, too, are eager to enjoy this sense of added power and enlarged sympathetic existence. The orator sees himself the organ of a multitude, and concentrating their valors and powers:—

> "But now the blood of twenty thousand men
> Blushed in my face."

That which he wishes, that which eloquence ought to reach, is not a particular skill in telling a story, or neatly summing up evidence, or arguing logically, or dexterously addressing the prejudice of the company,—no, but a taking sovereign possession of the audience. Him we call an artist who shall play on an assembly of men as a master on the keys of the piano,—who, seeing the people furious, shall soften and compose them, shall draw them, when he will, to laughter and to tears. Bring him to his audience, and, be they who they may,—coarse or refined, pleased or displeased, sulky or savage, with their opinions in the keeping of a confessor, or with their opinions in their bank-safes,—he will have them pleased and humored as he chooses; and they shall carry and execute that which he bids them.

This is that despotism which poets have celebrated in the Pied Piper of Hamelin, whose music drew like the power of gravitation, —drew soldiers and priests, traders and feasters, women and boys, rats and mice; or that of the minstrel of Meudon, who made the pall-bearers dance around the bier. This is a power of many degrees and requiring in the orator a great range of faculty and experience, requiring a large composite man, such as Nature rarely organizes; so that in our experience we are forced to gather up the figure in fragments, here one talent and there another.

The audience is a constant meter of the orator. There are many audiences in every public assembly, each one of which rules in turn. If anything comic and coarse is spoken, you shall see the emergence of the boys and rowdies, so loud and vivacious that you might think the house was filled with them. If new topics are started, graver and higher, these roisters recede; a more chaste and wise attention takes place. You would think the boys slept, and that the men have any degree of profoundness. If the speaker utter a noble sentiment, the attention deepens, a new and highest audience now listens, and the audiences of the fun and of facts and of the understanding are all silenced and awed. There is also something excellent in every audience,—the capacity of virtue. They are ready to be beatified. They know so much more than the orator,—and are so just! There is a tablet there for every line he can inscribe, though he should mount to the highest levels. Humble persons are conscious of new illumination; narrow brows expand with enlarged affections—delicate spirits, long unknown to themselves, masked and muffled in coarsest fortunes, who now hear their own native language for the first time, and leap to hear it.

But all these several audiences, each above each, which successively appear to greet the variety of style and topic, are really composed out of the same persons; nay, sometimes the same individual will take active part in them all, in turn.

This range of many powers in the consummate speaker, and of many audiences in one assembly, leads us to consider the successive stages of oratory.

Perhaps it is the lowest of the qualities of an orator, but it is, on so many occasions, of chief importance,—a certain robust and radiant physical health; or,—shall I say?—great volumes of animal heat. When each auditor feels himself to make too large a part of the assembly, and shudders with cold at the thinness of the morning audience, and with fear lest all will heavily fail through one bad speech, mere energy and mellowness are then inestimable. Wisdom and learning would be harsh and unwelcome, compared with a substantial cordial man, made of milk as we say, who is a house-warmer, with his obvious honesty and good meaning, and a hue-and-cry style of harangue, which inundates the assembly with a flood of animal spirits, and makes all safe and secure, so that any and every sort of good speaking becomes at once practicable. I do not rate this animal eloquence very highly; and yet, as we must be fed and warmed before we can do any work well,—even the best,—so is this semi-animal exuberance, like a good stove, of the first necessity in a cold house.

Climate has much to do with it,—climate and race. Set a New Englander to describe any accident which happened in his presence. What hesitation and reserve in his narrative! He tells with difficulty some particulars, and gets as fast as he can to the result, and, though he cannot describe, hopes to suggest the whole scene. Now listen to a poor Irishwoman recounting some experience of hers. Her speech flows like a river,—so unconsidered, so humorous, so pathetic, such justice done to all the parts! It is a true transubstantiation,—the fact converted into speech, all warm and colored and alive, as it fell out. Our Southern people are almost all speakers, and have every advantage over the New England people, whose climate is so cold that 'tis said we do not like to open our mouths very wide. But neither can the Southerner in the United States, nor the Irish, compare with the lively inhabitant of the south of Europe. The traveler in Sicily needs no gayer melodramatic exhibition than the *table d'hôte* of his inn will afford him in the conversation of the joyous guests.

They mimic the voice and manner of the person they describe; they crow, squeal, hiss, cackle, bark, and scream like mad, and, were it only by the physical strength exerted in telling the story, keep the table in unbounded excitement. But in every constitution some large degree of animal vigor is necessary as material foundation for the higher qualities of the art.

But eloquence must be attractive, or it is none. The virtue of books is to be readable, and of orators to be interesting; and this is a gift of Nature; as Demosthenes, the most laborious student in that kind, signified his sense of this necessity when he wrote, "Good Fortune," as his motto on his shield. As we know, the power of discourse of certain individuals amounts to fascination, though it may have no lasting effect. Some portion of this sugar must intermingle. The right eloquence needs no bell to call the people together, and no constable to keep them. It draws the children from their play, the old from their arm-chairs, the invalid from his warm chamber: it holds the hearer fast; steals away his feet, that he shall not depart; his memory, that he shall not remember the most pressing affairs; his belief, that he shall not admit any opposing considerations. The pictures we have of it in semi-barbarous ages; when it has some advantages in the simpler habit of the people, show what it aims at. It is said that the Khans or story-tellers in Ispahan and other cities of the East, attain a controlling power over their audience, keeping them for many hours attentive to the most fanciful and ertravagant adventures. The whole world knows pretty well the style of these improvisators, and how fascinating they are, in our translations of the Arabian Nights. Scheherezade tells these stories to save her life, and the delight of young Europe and young America in them proves that she fairly earned it. And who does not remember in childhood some white or black or yellow Scheherezade, who, by that talent of telling endless feats of fairies and magicians and kings and queens, was more dear and wonderful to a circle of children than any orator in England or America is now?

The more indolent and imaginative complexion of the Eastern nations makes them much more impressible by these appeals to the fancy.

These legends are only exaggerations of real occurrences, and every literature contains these high compliments to the art of the orator and the bard, from the Hebrew and the Greek down to the Scottish Glenkindie, who

"harpit a fish out o' saut-water,
    Or water out of a stone,
Or milk out of a maiden's breast
    Who bairn had never none."

Homer specially delighted in drawing the same figure. For what is the Odyssey but a history of the orator, in the largest style, carried through a series of adventures furnishing brilliant opportunities to his talent? See with what care and pleasure the poet brings him on the stage. Helen is pointing out to Priam, from a tower, the different Grecian chiefs. "The old man asked: 'Tell me, dear child, who is that man, shorter by a head than Agamemnon, yet he looks broader in his shoulders and breast. His arms lie on the ground, but he, like a leader, walks about the bands of the men. He seems to me like a stately ram, who goes as a master of the flock.' Him answered Helen, daughter of Jove, 'This is the wise Ulysses, son of Laertes, who was reared in the state of craggy Ithaca, knowing all wiles and wise counsels.' To her the prudent Antenor replied again: 'O woman, you have spoken truly. For once the wise Ulysses came hither on an embassy, with Menelaus, beloved by Mars. I received them and entertained them at my house. I became acquainted with the genius and the prudent judgments of both. When they mixed with the assembled Trojans, and stood, the broad shoulders of Menelaus rose above the other; but, both sitting, Ulysses was more majestic. When they conversed, and interweaved stories and opinions with all, Menelaus spoke succinctly,—few but very sweet words, since he was not talkative nor superfluous in speech, and was the younger. But when the wise Ulysses arose and stood and looked down, fixing his eyes on the ground, and neither moved his scepter backward nor forward, but held it still, like an awkward person, you would say it was some angry or foolish man; but when he sent his great voice forth out of his breast, and his words fell like the winter snows, not then would any mortal contend with Ulysses; and we, beholding, wondered not afterwards so much at his aspect.' " Thus he does not fail to arm Ulysses at first with this power of overcoming all opposition by the blandishments of the speech. Plutarch tells us that Thucydides, when Archidamus, King of Sparta, asked him which was the best wrestler, Pericles or he, replied, "When I throw him, he says he was never down, and he persuades the very spectators to believe him." Philip of Macedon said of Demosthenes, on hearing the report of one of his orations, "Had

I been there, he would have persuaded me to take up arms against myself"; and Warren Hastings said of Burke's speech on his impeachment, "As I listened to the orator, I felt for more than half an hour as if I were the most culpable being on earth."

In these examples, higher qualities have already entered, but the power of detaining the ear by pleasing speech, and addressing the fancy and imagination, often exists without higher merits. Thus separated, as this fascination of discourse aims only at amusement, though it be decisive in its momentary effect, it is yet a juggle, and no lasting power. It is heard like a band of music passing through the streets, which converts all the passengers into poets, but is forgotten as soon as it has turned the next corner; and unless this oiled tongue could, in Oriental phrase, lick the sun and moon away, it must take its place with opium and brandy. I know no remedy against it, but cotton-wool, or the wax which Ulysses stuffed into the ears of his sailors to pass the Sirens safely.

There are all degrees of power, and the least are interesting, but they must not be confounded. There is the glib tongue and cool self-possession of the salesman in a large shop, which, as is well known, overpower the prudence and resolution of housekeepers of both sexes. There is a pretty lawyer's fluency, which is sufficiently impressive to him who is devoid of that talent, though it be, in so many cases, nothing more than a facility of expressing with accuracy and speed what everybody thinks and says more slowly; without new information; or precision of thought, but the same thing, neither less nor more. It requires no special insight to edit one of our country newspapers. Yet whoever can say off currently, sentence by sentence, matter neither better nor worse than what is there printed, will be very impressive to our easily pleased population. These talkers are of that class who prosper, like the celebrated schoolmaster, by being only one lesson ahead of the pupil. Add a little sarcasm and prompt allusion to passing occurrences and you have the mischievous member of Congress. A spice of malice, a ruffian touch in his rhetoric, will do him no harm with his audience. These accomplishments are of the same kind, and only a degree higher than the coaxing of the auctioneer, or the vituperative style well described in the street-word "jawing." These kinds of public and private speaking have their use and convenience to the practitioners; but we may say of such collectively that the habit of oratory is apt to disqualify them for eloquence.

One of our statesmen said, "The curse of this country is eloquent men." And one cannot wonder at the uneasiness sometimes manifested by trained statesmen, with large experience of public affairs, when they observe the disproportionate advantage suddenly given to oratory over the most solid and accumulated public service. In a Senate or other business committee, the solid result depends on a few men with working talent. They know how to deal with the facts before them, to put things into a practical shape, and they value men only as they can forward the work. But a new man comes there who has no capacity for helping them at all, is insignificant and nobody in the committee, but has a talent for speaking. In the debate with open doors, this precious person makes a speech which is printed and read all over the Union, and he at once becomes famous, and takes the lead in the public mind over all these executive men, who, of course, are full of indignation to find one who has no tact or skill and knows he has none, put over them by means of this talking-power which they despise.

Leaving behind us these pretensions, better or worse, to come a little nearer to the verity,—eloquence is attractive as an example of the magic of personal ascendency,—a total and resultant power, rare, because it requires a rich coincidence of powers, intellect, will, sympathy, organs and, over all, good fortune in the cause. We have a half belief that the person is possible who can counterpoise all other persons. We believe that there may be a man who is a match for events, one who never found his match, against whom other men being dashed are broken,—one of inexhaustible personal resources, who can give you any odds and beat you. What we really wish for is a mind equal to any exigency. You are safe in your rural district, or in the city, in broad daylight, amidst the police, and under the eyes of a hundred thousand people. But how is it on the Atlantic, in a storm,—do you understand how to infuse your reason into men disabled by terror, and to bring yourself off safe then?—how among thieves, or among an infuriated populace, or among cannibals? Face to face with a highwayman who has every temptation and opportunity for violence and plunder, can you bring yourself off safe by your wit exercised through speech?—a problem easy enough to Cæsar or Napoleon. Whenever a man of that stamp arrives, the highwayman has found a master. What a difference between men in power of face! A man succeeds because he has more power of eye than another, and so coaxes or confounds him. The newspapers, every week, report the adventures of some impudent swindler who, by steadiness of carriage, duped those who should have known better. Yet any swindlers we have known are novices and bunglers, as is attested by their ill name. A greater power of face would accomplish anything, and, with the rest of their takings, take away the bad name. A greater power of carrying the thing loftily and with perfect assurance, would confound merchant, banker, judge, men of influence and power, poet and president, and might head any party, unseat any sovereign, and abrogate any constitution in Europe and America. It was said that a man has at one step attained vast power, who has renounced his moral sentiment, and settled it with himself that he will no longer stick at anything. It was said of Sir William Pepperell, one of the worthies of New England, that, "put him where you might, he commanded, and saw what he willed come to pass." Julius Cæsar said to Metellus, when that tribune interfered to hinder him from entering the Roman treasury, "Young man, it is easier for me to put you to death than to say that I will"; and the youth yielded. In earlier days, he was taken by pirates. What then? He threw himself into their ship, established the most extraordinary intimacies, told them stories, declaimed them; if they did not applaud his speeches, he threatened them with hanging,—which he performed afterwards,—and, in a short time, was master of all on board. A man this is who cannot be disconcerted, and so can never play his last card, but has a reserve of power when he has hit his mark. With a serene face, he subverts a kingdom. What is told of him is miraculous; it affects men so. The confidence of men in him is lavish, and he changes the face of the world, and histories, poems and new philosophies arise to account for him. A supreme commander over all his passions and affections; but the secret of his ruling is higher than that. It is the power of Nature running without impediment from the brain and will into the hands. Men and women are his game. Where they are, he cannot be without resource. "Whoso can speak well," said Luther, "is a man." It was men of this stamp that the Grecian States used to ask of Sparta for generals. They did not send to Lacedæmon for troops, but they said, "Send us a commander"; and Pausanias, or Gylippus, or Brasidas, or Agis, was despatched by the Ephors.

It is easy to illustrate this overpowering personality by these examples of soldiers and kings; but there are men of the most peaceful way of life and peaceful principle, who are felt wherever they go, as sensibly as a July sun or a December frost,—men who, if they speak, are heard, though they speak in a whisper,—who, when they act, act effectually, and what they do is imitated; and these examples may be found on very humble platforms as well as on high ones.

In old countries a high money value is set on the services of men who have achieved a personal distinction. He who has points to carry must hire, not a skilful attorney, but a commanding person. A barrister in England is reported to have made thirty or forty thousand pounds per annum in representing the claims of railroad companies before committees of the House of Commons. His clients pay not so much for legal as for manly accomplishments,—for courage, conduct and a commanding social position, which enable him to make their claims heard and respected.

I know very well that among our cool and calculating people, where every man mounts guard over himself, where heats and panics and abandonment are quite out of the system, there is a good deal of skepticism as to extraordinary influence. To talk of an overpowering mind rouses the same jealousy and defiance which one may observe round a table where anybody is recounting the marvelous anecdotes of mesmerism. Each auditor puts a final stroke to the discourse by exclaiming, "Can he mesmerize *me?*" So each man inquires if any orator can change *his* convictions.

But does any one suppose himself to be quite impregnable? Does he think that not possibly a man may come to him who shall persuade him out of his most settled determination?—for example, good sedate citizen as he is, to make a fanatic of him,—or, if he is penurious, to squander money for some purpose he now least thinks of,—or, if he is a prudent, industrious person, to forsake his work, and give days and weeks to a new interest? No, he defies any one, every one. Ah! he is thinking of resistance, and of a different turn from his own. But what if one should come of the same turn of mind as his own, and who sees much farther on his own way than he? A man who has tastes like mine, but in greater power, will rule me any day, and make me love my ruler.

Thus it is not powers of speech that we primarily consider under this word *eloquence*, but the power that being present, gives them their perfection, and being absent, leaves them a merely superficial value. Eloquence is the appropriate organ of the highest personal energy. Personal ascendency may exist with or without adequate talent for its expression. It is assuredly felt as a mountain or a planet; but when it is weaponed with a power of speech, it seems first to become truly human, works actively in all directions, and supplies the imagination with fine materials.

This circumstance enters into every consideration of the power of orators, and is the key to all their effects. In the assembly, you shall find the orator and the audience in perpetual balance; and the predominance of either is indicated by the choice of topic. If the talents for speaking exist, but not the strong personality, then there are good speakers who perfectly receive and express the will of the audience, and the commonest populace is flattered by hearing its low mind returned to it with every ornament which happy talent can add. But if there be personality in the orator, the face of things changes. The audience is thrown into the attitude of pupil, follows like a child its preceptor, and hears what he has to say. It is as if, amidst the king's council at Madrid, Ximenes urged that an advantage might be gained of France, and Mendoza that Flanders might be kept down, and Columbus, being introduced, was interrogated whether his geographical knowledge could aid the cabinet; and he can say nothing to one party or to the other, but he can show how all Europe can be diminished and reduced under the King, by annexing to Spain a continent as large as six or seven Europes.

This balance between the orator and the audience is expressed in what is called the pertinence of the speaker. There is always a rivalry between the orator and the occasion, between the demand of the hour and the prepossession of the individual. The emergency which has convened the meeting is usually of more importance than anything the debaters have in their minds, and therefore becomes imperative to them. But if one of them have anything of commanding necessity in his heart, how speedily he will find vent for it, and with the applause of the assembly! This balance is observed in the privatest intercourse. Poor Tom never knew the time when the present occurrence was so trivial that he could tell what was passing in his mind without being checked for unreasonable speech; but let Bacon speak and wise men would rather listen though the revolution of kingdoms was on foot. I have heard it reported of an eloquent preacher, whose voice is not yet forgotten in this city, that, on occasions of death or tragic disaster which overspread the congregation with gloom, he ascended the pulpit with more than his usual alacrity, and turning to his favorite lessons of devout and jubilant thankfulness,—"Let us praise the Lord,"—carried audience, mourners and mourning along with him, and swept away all the impertinence of private sorrow with his hosannas and songs of praise. Pepys says of Lord Clarendon (with whom "he is mad in love") on his return from a conference, "I did never observe how much easier a man do speak when he knows all the company to be below him, than in him, for though he spoke indeed excellent well, yet his manner and freedom of doing it, as if he played with it, and was informing only all the rest of the company, was mighty pretty."

This rivalry between the orator and the occasion is inevitable, and the occasion always yields to the eminence of the speaker; for a great man is the greatest of occasions. Of course the interest of the audience and of the orator conspire. It is well with them only when his influence is complete; then only they are well pleased. Especially he consults his power by making instead of taking his theme. If he should attempt to instruct the people in that which they already know, he would fail; but by making them wise in that which he knows he has the advantage of the assembly every moment. Napoleon's tactics of marching on the angle of an army, and always presenting a superiority of numbers, is the orator's secret also.

The several talents which the orator employs, the splendid weapons which, went to the equipment of Demosthenes, of Æschines, of Demades the natural orator, of Fox, of Pitt, of Patrick Henry, of Adams, of Mirabeau, deserve a special enumeration. We must not quite omit to name the principal pieces.

The orator, as we have seen, must be a substantial personality. Then, first, he must have power of statement,—must have the fact, and know how to tell it. In any knot of men conversing on any subject, the person who knows most about it will have the ear of the company if he wishes it, and lead the conversation, no matter what genius or distinction other men there present may have; and in any public assembly, him who has the facts and can and will state them, people will listen to, though he is otherwise ignorant, though he is hoarse and ungraceful, though he stutters and screams.

In a court of justice the audience are impartial; they really wish to sift the statements and know what the truth is. And in the examination of witnesses there usually leap out, quite unexpectedly, three or four stubborn words or phrases which are the pith and fate of the business, which sink into the ear of all parties, and stick there, and determine the cause. All the rest is repetition and qualifying; and the court and the county have really come together to arrive at these three or four memorable expressions which betrayed the mind and meaning of somebody.

In every company the man with the fact is like the guide you hire to lead your party up a mountain, or through a difficult country. He may not compare with any of the party in mind or breeding or courage or possessions, but he is much more important to the present need than any of them. That is what we go to the courthouse for,—the statement of the fact, and of a general fact, the real relation of all the parties; and it is the certainty with which, indifferently in any affair that is well handled, the truth stares us in the face through all the disguises that are put upon it,—a piece of the well known human life,—that makes the interest of a court-room to the intelligent spectator.

I remember long ago being attracted, by the distinction of the counsel and the local importance of the cause, into the court-room. The prisoner's counsel were the strongest and cunningest lawyers in the commonwealth. They drove the attorney for the state from corner to corner, taking his reasons from under him, and reducing him to silence, but not to submission. When hard pressed, he revenged himself, in his turn, on the judge, by requiring the court to define what *salvage* was. The court, thus pushed, tried words, and said everything it could think of to fill the time, supposing cases, and describing duties of insurers, captains, pilots and miscellaneous sea-officers that are or might be,—like a schoolmaster puzzled by a hard sum, who reads the context with emphasis. But all this flood not serving the cuttle-fish to get away in, the horrible shark of the district attorney being still there, grimly awaiting with his "The court must define,"—the poor court pleaded its inferiority. The superior court must establish the law for this, and it read away piteously the decisions of the Supreme Court, but read to those who had no pity. The judge was forced at last to rule something, and the lawyers saved their rogue under the fog of a definition. The parts were so well cast and discriminated that it was an interesting game to watch. The government was well enough represented. It was stupid, but it had a strong will and possession, and stood on that to the last. The judge had a task beyond his preparation, yet his position remained real: he was there to represent a great reality,—the justice of states, which we could well enough see beetling over his head, and which his trifling talk nowise affected, and did not impede, since he was entirely well meaning.

The statement of the fact, however, sinks before the statement of the law, which requires immeasurably higher powers, and is a rarest gift, being in all great masters one and the same thing,—in lawyers nothing technical, but always some piece of common sense, alike interesting to laymen as to clerks. Lord Mansfield's merit is the merit of common sense. It is the same quality we admire in Aristotle, Montaigne, Cervantes, or in Samuel Johnson or Franklin. Its application to law seems quite accidental. Each of Mansfield's famous decisions contains a level sentence or two which hit the mark. His sentences are not always finished to the eye, but are finished to the mind. The sentences are involved, but a solid proposition is set forth, a true distinction is drawn. They come from and they go to the sound human understanding; and I read without surprise that the black-letter lawyers of the day sneered at his "equitable decisions," as if they were not also learned. This, indeed, is what speech is for,—to make the statement; and all that is called eloquence seems to me of little use for the most part to those who have it, but inestimable to such as have something to say.

Next to the knowledge of the fact and its law is method, which constitutes the genius and efficiency of all remarkable men. A crowd of men go up to Faneuil Hall; they are all pretty well acquainted with the object of the meeting; they have all read the facts in the same newspapers. The orator possesses no information which his hearers have not, yet he teaches them to see the thing with his eyes. By the new placing, the circumstances acquire new solidity and worth. Every fact gains consequence by his naming it, and trifles become important. His expressions fix themselves in men's memories, and fly from mouth to mouth. His mind has some new principle of order. Where he looks, all things fly into their places. What will he say next? Let this man speak, and this man only. By applying the habits of a higher style of thought to the common affairs of this world, he introduces beauty and magnificence wherever he goes. Such a power was Burke's, and of this genius we have had some brilliant examples in our own political and legal men.

Imagery. The orator must be, to a certain extent, a poet. We are such imaginative creatures that nothing so works on the human mind, barbarous or civil, as a trope. Condense some daily experience into a glowing symbol, and an audience is electrified. They feel as if they already possessed some new right and power over a fact which they can detach, and so completely master in thought. It is a wonderful aid to the memory, which carries away the image and never loses it. A popular assembly, like the House of Commons, or the French Chamber, or the American Congress, is commanded by these two powers,—first by a fact, then by skill of statement. Put the argument into a concrete shape, into an image, —some hard phrase, round and solid as a ball, which they can see and handle and carry home with them,—and the cause is half won.

Statement, method, imagery, selection, tenacity of memory, power of dealing with facts, of illuminating them, of sinking them by ridicule or by diversion of the mind, rapid generalization, humor, pathos, are keys which the orator holds; and yet these fine gifts are not eloquence, and do often hinder a man's attainment of it. And if we come to the heart of the mystery, perhaps we should say that the truly eloquent man is a sane man with power to communicate his sanity. If you arm the man with the extraordinary weapons of this art, give him a grasp of facts, learning, quick fancy, sarcasm, splendid allusion, interminable illustration,—all these talents, so potent and charming, have an equal power to ensnare and mislead the audience and the orator. His talents are too much for him, his horses run away with him; and people always perceive whether you drive or whether the horses take the bits in their teeth and run. But these talents are quite something else when they are subordinated and serve him; and we go to Washington, or to Westminster Hall, or might well go round the world, to see a man who drives, and is not run away with,—a man who, in prosecuting great designs, has an absolute command of the means of representing his ideas, and uses them only to express these; placing facts, placing men; amid the inconceivable levity of human beings, never for an instant warped from his erectness. There is for every man a statement possible of that truth which he is most unwilling to receive,—a statement possible, so broad and so pungent that he cannot get away from it, but must either bend to it or die of it. Else there would be no such word as eloquence, which means this. The listener cannot hide from himself that something has been shown him and the whole world which he did not wish to see; and as he cannot dispose of it, it disposes of him. The history of public men and affairs in America will readily furnish tragic examples of this fatal force.

For the triumphs of the art somewhat more must still be required, namely a reinforcing of man from events, so as to give the double force of reason and destiny. In transcendent eloquence, there was ever some crisis in affairs, such as could deeply engage the man to the cause he pleads, and draw all this wide power to a point. For the explosions and eruptions, there must be accumulations of heat somewhere, beds of ignited anthracite at the center. And in cases where profound conviction has been wrought, the eloquent man is he who is no beautiful speaker, but who is inwardly drunk with a certain belief. It agitates and tears him, and perhaps almost bereaves him of the power of articulation. Then it rushes from him as in short, abrupt screams, in torrents of meaning. The possession the subject has of his mind is so entire that it insures an order of expression which is the order of Nature itself, and so the order of greatest force, and inimitable by any art. And the main distinction between him and other well-graced actors is the conviction, communicated by every word, that his mind is contemplating a whole, and inflamed by the contemplation of the whole, and that the words and sentences uttered by him, however admirable, fall from him as unregarded parts of that terrible whole which he sees and means that you shall see. Add to this concentration a certain regnant calmness, which, in all the tumult, never utters a premature syllable, but keeps the secret of its means and method; and the orator stands before the people as a demoniacal power to whose miracles they have no key. This terrible earnestness makes good the ancient superstition of the hunter, that the bullet will hit its mark, which is first dipped in the marksman's blood.

Eloquence must be grounded on the plainest narrative. Afterwards, it may warm itself until it exhales symbols of every kind and color, speaks only through the most poetic forms; but, first and last, it must still be at bottom a biblical statement of fact. The orator is thereby an orator, that he keeps his feet ever on a fact. Thus only is he invincible. No gifts, no graces, no power of wit or learning or illustration will make any amends for want of this. All audiences are just to this point. Fame of voice or of rhetoric will carry people a few times to hear a speaker; but they soon begin to ask, "What is he driving at?" and if this man does not stand for anything, he will be deserted. A good upholder of anything which they believe, a fact-speaker of any kind, they will long follow; but a pause in the speaker's own character is very properly a loss of attraction. The preacher enumerates his classes of men and I do not find my place therein; I suspect then that no man does. Everything is my cousin; and whilst he speaks things, I feel that he is touching some of my relations, and I am uneasy; but whilst he deals in words we are released from attention. If you would lift me you must be on higher ground. If you would liberate me you must be free. If you would correct my false view of facts,—hold up to me the same facts in the true order of thought, and I cannot go back from the new conviction.

The power of Chatham, of Pericles, of Luther, rested on this strength of character, which, because it did not and could not fear anybody, made nothing of their antagonists, and became sometimes exquisitely provoking and sometimes terrific to these. We are slenderly furnished with anecdotes of these men, nor can we help ourselves by those heavy books in which their discourses are reported. Some of them are writers, like Burke; but most of them were not, and no records at all adequate to their fame remains. Besides, what is best is lost,—the fiery life of the moment. But the conditions for eloquence always exist. It is always dying out of famous places and appearing in corners. Wherever the polarities meet, wherever the fresh moral sentiment, the instinct of freedom and duty, come in direct opposition to fossil conservatism and the thirst of gain, the spark will pass. The resistance to slavery in this country has been a fruitful nursery of orators. The natural connection by which it drew to itself a train of moral reforms, and the slight yet sufficient party organization it offered, reinforced the city with new blood from the woods and mountains. Wild men, John Baptists, Hermit Peters, John Knoxes, utter the savage sentiment of Nature in the heart of commercial capitals. They send us every year some piece of aboriginal strength, some tough oak-stick of a man who is not to be silenced or insulted or intimidated by a mob, because he is more mob than they,—one who mobs the mob,—some sturdy countryman, on whom neither money, nor politeness, nor hard words, nor eggs, nor blows, nor brickbats make any impression. He is fit to meet the barroom wits and bullies; he is a wit and a bully himself, and something more: he is a graduate of the plow, and the stub-hoe, and the bushwhacker; knows all the secrets of swamp and snow-bank, and has nothing to learn of labor or poverty or the rough of farming. His hard head went through, in childhood, the drill of Calvinism, with text and mortification, so that he stands in the New England assembly a purer bit of New England than any, and flings his sarcasms right and left. He has not only the documents in his pocket to answer all cavils and to prove all his positions, but he has the eternal reason in his head. This man scornfully renounces your civil organizations,—county or city, or governor, or army;—is his own navy and artillery, judge and jury, legislature and executive. He has learned his lesson in a bitter school. Yet, if the pupil be of a texture to bear it, the best university that can be recommended to a man of ideas is the gauntlet of the mobs.

He who will train himself to mastery in this science of persuasion must lay the emphasis of education, not on popular arts, but on character and insight. Let him see that his speech is not differenced from action; that when he has spoken he has not done nothing, nor done wrong, but has cleared his own skirts, has engaged himself to wholesome exertion. Let him look on opposition as opportunity. He cannot be defeated or put down. There is a principle of resurrection in him, an immortality of purpose. Men are averse and hostile, to give value to their suffrages. It is not the people that are in fault for not being convinced, but he that cannot convince them. He should mold them, armed as he is with the reason and love which are also the core of their nature. He is not to neutralize their opposition, but he is to convert them into fiery apostles and publishers of the same wisdom.

The highest platform of eloquence is the moral sentiment. It is what is called affirmative truth, and has the property of invigorating the hearer; and it conveys a hint of our eternity, when he feels himself addressed on grounds which will remain when everything else is taken, and which have no trace of time or place or party. Everything hostile is stricken down in the presence of the sentiments; their majesty is felt by the most obdurate. It is observable that as soon as one acts for large masses, the moral element will and must be allowed for, will and must work; and the men least accustomed to appeal to these sentiments invariably recall them when they address nations. Napoleon, even, must accept and use it as he can.

It is only to these simple strokes that the highest power belongs,—when a weak human hand touches, point by point, the eternal beams and rafters on which the whole structure of Nature and society is laid. In this tossing sea of delusion we feel with our feet the adamant; in this dominion of chance we find a principle of permanence. For I do not accept that definition of Isocrates, that the office of his art is to make the great small and the small great; but I esteem this to be its perfection,—when the orator sees through all masks to the eternal scale of truth, in such sort that he can hold up before the eyes of men the fact of to-day steadily to that standard, thereby making the great great, and the small small, which is the true way to astonish and to reform mankind.

All the chief orators of the world have been grave men, relying on this reality. One thought the philosophers of Demosthenes's own time found running through all his orations,—this namely, that "virture secures its own success." "To stand on one's own feet" Hceren finds the key-note to the discourses of Demosthenes, as of Chatham.

Eloquence, like every other art, rests on laws the most exact and determinate. It is the best speech of the best soul. It may well stand as the exponent of all that is grand and immortal in the mind. If it do not so become an instrument, but aspire to be somewhat of itself, and to glitter for show, it is false and weak. In its right exercise, it is an elastic, unexhausted power,—who has sounded, who has estimated it?—expanding with the expansion of our interests and affections. Its great masters, whilst they valued every help to its attainment, and thought no pains too great which contributed in any manner to further it,—resembling the Arabian warrior of fame, who wore seventeen weapons in his belt, and in personal combat used them all occasionally,—yet subordinated all means; never permitted any talent—neither voice, rhythm, poetic power, anecdote, sarcasm—to appear for show; but were grave men, who preferred their integrity to their talent, and esteemed that object for which they toiled, whether the prosperity of their country, or the laws, or a reformation, or liberty of speech or of the press, or letters, or morals, as above the whole world, and themselves also.

DISCUSSION AND PUBLIC OPINION.[1]

Edward Alsworth Ross

[Edward Alsworth Ross (1866-   ) was graduated from Coe College in 1886, and received the doctoral degree from Johns Hopkins University in 1891. He has been professor of economics, and of sociology, at Leland Stanford University, the University of Nebraska, and the University of Wisconsin. He is a prolific writer in his field, and his works are notable for their wealth of illustration and vigor of style. He has traveled widely, and has recorded his observations in many articles and books. Among the latter are *The Changing Chinese, Changing America,* and *Russia in Upheaval.* His sociological thought is most systematically presented in his *Principles of Sociology.* The two books which are perhaps of the greatest significance to the student of public discussion and persuasion, are *Social Control* and *Social Psychology.* While the conclusions of the social psychologists are yet largely tentative, the phenomena they investigate must be taken into account by all who are interested in the formation of opinion. The essays here printed form two chapters in the *Social Psychology.*]

DISCUSSION

Sometimes a struggle can be summarily closed by invoking some authority acknowledged by both sides; for example, the Pope on dogma, Tyndall on spontaneous generation, the Prince of Wales on some point of etiquette. Oftener, however, it is discussion that settles a struggle when it reaches an acute stage. For discussion *hurries conflicts to a conclusion.* Sixty years ago the silent struggle between man and woman became vocal, and the result has been a hasty removal of many barriers that hemmed in woman, and a rapid improvement in her social position. In the United States, African slavery would, no doubt, have died out in time by the silent operation of economic and moral forces, but discussion greatly hastened its end. Since, about a generation ago, a few bold spirits began to ask "Why?" in public, the religious *tabu* on theatre, dancing, card-playing, secular literature and art, has loosened more than in all the previous interval since the Puritan Commonwealth. So, the disapproval of drinking has developed more in the seventy years since Father Mathew began the temperance agitation, than in the two centuries before. Hence, *all losing sides dread discus-*

[1] Reprinted by permission of the Macmillan Co. from *Social Psychology.*
    Questions and topics for the discussion of this essay, and of other phases of the general subject with which it deals, will be found on pages 552 and 555.

sion, for it shortens their lease of life. Silence is for them a kind of reprieve. Their instinct, then, is to choke off discussion at all hazards. The geocentrists got the Papal Index for nearly two hundred years to forbid the faithful from reading "all books which affirm the motion of the earth." The Index of the books absolutism forbids to be printed or circulated in Russia reads like a list of the monumental works of modern research and thought. The tottering Old Régime in France persecuted and hounded the Encyclopedists. The German monarchists long sought to withstand the rising tide of social democracy with a "law of associations and meetings." The French militarists endeavored to gag discussion of the Dreyfus case. In the lower South after 1835 all open criticism of slavery was prohibited, and on the border desperate means were taken to silence the abolitionists.[1] In the state of Delaware and in the city of Detroit frantic attempts have been made by rich tax-dodgers to throttle single-tax speakers.

Conversely, the side that feels sure of its case does not persecute. Therefore it is safe to infer that the cause which courts publicity and discussion has time on its side, whereas the cause that ducks, slinks, or applies the gag, ought to rest under suspicion. Seeing that no great wrong can long survive open discussion, we may characterize free speech, free assemblage, and free press as *the rights preservative of all rights*. Safeguard these fundamentals, and the rest must come. This is why free government, although it is by no means the same thing as popular government, is usually the vestibule to it. When discussion is free, all use of violence to change the *personnel* or the form of government is criminal, seeing that a peaceful way lies open to the reformer. When, on the other hand, brute force is employed to prevent an unhappy people from organizing their minds into that spiritual structure we call public opinion, they have as much right

[1] The result is stated by Hart: "Nothing could have been more favorable to the abolitionists than this succession of outbreaks, which flashed public attention upon Garrison, Birney, and Lovejoy, and placed their personal character in the strongest contrast to the means employed to silence them. Mob violence emphasized the fact that the abolitionists were not acting contrary to law, and it aroused the fighting spirit of thousands of people who knew very little about the controversy except that the abolitionists had something to say so important that it must be prevented by violence and murder."— *Slavery and Abolition*, 249.

"To assure the world that slavery was God-given, hallowed by the experience of mankind, enjoined by Scripture, the foundation of republican government, the source of all Southern blessings—and then to insist that it could be overthrown by the mere wind of doctrine—was a confession that it was really unstable and iniquitous. No great institution contributing to human enlightenment has ever needed to be protected by silence."—*Ibid.*, 312. See also 234-237.

to strike out destructively as the householder who wakes to find the fingers of a burglar closing on his throat.

Discussion presupposes mental contact, hence is favored by modern facilities for communication,—press, telegraph, cheap travel, cheap books, free libraries, etc. These substitute discussion of principles and policies for petty gossip, and attention to general concerns for attention to private, family, or neighborhood concerns. There is to-day a far greater amount of fructifying discussion than ever before, and it touches more topics, plays over more of life. That "nowadays no subject is sacred" means that every belief, practice, and institution is called upon to justify itself. Male sexual license, the indissoluble marriage, the marriage bond itself, are required to furnish reasons. It is coming to be recognized that there is nothing of concern to human beings which may not profitably be discussed in the right spirit, by the right persons, at the right time. This is why the downfall of an effete dogma, the abandonment of an unwise policy, a harmful practice, a vicious custom, or a wasteful process, is prompter now than ever before. This explains the miracles of transformation we witness in human relations and arrangements. It is because that great radical, Discussion, invades every department of life and hurries to a close long-smoldering conflicts, that ours is such a revolutionary epoch. "Age of endless talk," sneers the cynic, forgetting that, but for the copious talk and print, it could not be an age of reason and redress. Well has it been said:—

"It is safe to suppose that one-half of the talk of the world on subjects of general interest is waste. But the other half certainly tells. We know this from the change in ideas from generation to generation. We see that opinions which at one time everybody held became absurd in the course of half a century,—opinions about religion and morals and manners and government. Nearly every man of my age can recall old opinions of his own, on subjects of general interest, which he once thought highly respectable, and which he is now almost ashamed of having ever held. He does not remember when he changed them, or why, but somehow they have passed away from him. In communities these changes are often very striking. The transformation, for instance, of the England of Cromwell into the England of Queen Anne, or of the New England of Cotton Mather into the New England of Theodore Parker and Emerson, was very extrordinary, but it would be very difficult to say in detail what brought it about, or when it began. Lecky has some curious observations, in his 'History of Rationalism,' on these silent changes in new beliefs apropos of the disappearance of the belief in witchcraft. Nobody could say what had swept it away, but it appeared that in a certain year people were ready to burn old women as witches, and a few years later were ready to laugh at or pity any one who thought old women could be witches. 'At one period,' says he, 'we find every one disposed to believe in witches; at a later period we find this predisposition has silently passed away.' The belief in witchcraft may perhaps be considered a somewhat violent illustration, like the change in public opinion about slavery in this country. But there can be no doubt that it is talk—somebody's, anybody's, everybody's talk—by which these changes are wrought, by which each generation comes to feel and think differently from its predecessor. No one ever talks freely about anything without contributing something, let it be ever so little, to the unseen forces which carry the race on to its final destiny. Even if he does not make a positive impression, he counteracts or modifies some other impression, or sets in motion some train of ideas in some one else, which helps to change the face of the world. So I shall, in disregard of the great laudation of silence which filled the earth in the days of Carlyle, say that one of the functions of an educated man is to talk, and, of course, he should try to talk wisely." [1]

In areas where, after all, *feeling* or *instinct*, not *reason*, decides, discussion can do little to accelerate the issue. *De gustibus non est disputandum.* Barren are discussions of Italian opera, and German opera, æstheticism, Whitman's poetry, Whistler's "arrangements," race amalgamation. For here the matter is one of taste, and a common basis is lacking. The best type of discussion is that between parties who agree as to ends and differ only as to means, because we have feelings about ends but are cold-blooded in choosing means. "Shall we by law prohibit child labor?" Compare two friends of children discussing this, one a believer in state action, the other a believer in trade union action, with the discussion of it between a philanthropist and a factory owner. "Shall we retain the Philippines?" Compare discussion of this between two men whose aim is the welfare of the natives, with the discussion between one of these men and an exploiter whose maxim is, "the Philippines for the Americans!" "Shall we announce from the pulpit the results of the Higher Criticism?" yields a

[1] Godkin, *Problems of Modern Democracy*, 221-224.

very different discussion between two lovers of truth than between one who cares only for truth, and one who cares only for dogma. "Shall we adopt the direct primary?" is a much more fertile topic if discussed by two friends of good government than if discussed by a friend of good government and a corrupt boss. When means or methods are in question, we appeal to the judgment; when ends are in question, we aim at the feelings. Thus, the prohibitionist tries to inspire disgust for the saloon. His opponent endeavors to arouse resentment against "interference with personal liberty."

Without a common basis discussion becomes wrangling, the effort not to win over opponents, but to win neutrals. Hence, ridicule and vilification, coining of epithets, catch phrases and slogans. Hence, appeals to passion and prejudice, such as "Do you want your daughter to marry a nigger?" "Vote as you shot —against the South!" "Vote for the Liberal and you vote for the Boer!" "Who will haul down the flag?" "Godless" public schools! "Freedom of contract." "Dreyfusards." "Little Englanders." An inventory of the stock appeals of a political campaign shows how inapt is the phrase "campaign of education." The really profitable discussion of political questions is that which occurs before the subsidized newspapers and the hired spell-binders have filled the air with dust.

The reason why theological controversy so fatally descends into polemic is that *all discussion of things supernal contains the seeds of degeneration.* It is owing to this that we hear of an *odium theologicum,* but not of an *odium scientificum.* Theologians are certainly as just and kindly men as scientists, but after they have marshalled in vain their texts and their reasonings, they have nothing else to appeal to. When the scientist has exhausted his ammunition without effect, he can go after fresh evidence. It is not easy to settle by observation the question of the open Polar Sea, the sources of the Nile, or the canals on Mars; but it is child's play compared with getting decisive facts on the question of the nature of the Godhead, or the future state of unbaptized infants. Compare the battle between trans-substantiationists and con-substantiationists, *homo-ousians* and *homoi-ousians,* with the debate between the Neo-Lamarckians and the Neo-Darwinians. When the naturalists found they could not decide the question without more facts, they declared a truce and went to cutting off the tails of successive generations of mice!

Sometimes, as in the struggle between two prejudices, tastes, or prestiges, both disputants wrangle; but, when a merit is pitted against a prestige or a sentiment, one side argues while the other vituperates. This is plainly seen in the debates on the social recognition of negroes, the recognition of the labor unions, the regulation of corporations, the taxation of site values, and woman suffrage. In the discussing of vivisection, compulsory vaccination, the segregation of vice, the legal control of prostitution, the census-taking of disease, etc., one side appeals to reason, the other to sentiment. Beyond wrangling lie the appeals that rally the partisans of either side, and the passing of the struggle from the realm of social psychology into that of pugilistics.[1]

The efficacy of discussion in abbreviating conflicts depends on the access of people to its influence. When folks are matted together into impermeable strata, classes, or communities, the ferment of discussion operates only on the exterior of the mass. Chinatown, French Canada, Liberia, the Ghetto, the slums, the Black Belt in the South, the Hungarian district in Pennsylvania,

---

[1] The fatal trend is shown in "Truthful James's" account of the row "That broke up our Society upon the Stanislow."

> "Now nothing could be finer or more beautiful to see
> Than the first six months' proceedings of that same Society,
> Till Brown of Calaveras brought a lot of fossil bones
> That he found within a tunnel near the tenement of Jones.
>
> Then Brown he read a paper, and he reconstructed there,
> From those same bones, an animal that was extremely rare;
> And Jones then asked the Chair for a suspension of the rules,
> Till he could prove that those same bones was one of his lost mules.
>
> Then Brown he smiled a bitter smile, and said he was at fault,
> It seemed he had been trespassing on Jones's family vault;
> He was a most sarcastic man, this quiet Mr. Brown,
> And on several occasions he had cleaned out the town.
>
> Now I hold it is not decent for a scientific gent
> To say another is an ass,—at least, to all intent;
> Nor should the individual who happens to be meant
> Reply by heaving rocks at him, to any great extent.
>
> Then Abner Dean of Angel's raised a point of order, when
> A chunk of old red sandstone took him in the abdomen,
> And he smiled a kind of sickly smile, and curled up on the floor,
> And the subsequent proceedings interested him no more.
>
> For, in less time than I write it, every member did engage
> In a warfare with the remnants of the palæozoic age;
> And the way they heaved those fossils in their anger was a sin,
> Till the skull of an old mammoth caved the head of Thompson in."

—BRET HARTE, "Poems."

the Mennonite villages in North Dakota,—these reveal what happens when social islands are formed. As pulverizing a lump of lime hastens its slaking, as comminuting food aids digestion, as splintering wood accelerates its combustion, so there is a speedier termination of the conflict between the peculiar and the general when social lumps are broken up. Such has been the effect of stirring a Gentile leaven through the Mormon communities. Outside the cotton belt, slavery brought the white and black races into close personal contact and hastened the civilizing of the blacks. Since emancipation, there has been a marked tendency to segregate,[1] resulting in spots in conditions almost Liberian. The French Canadian is inaccessible to modern ideas at home, but he succumbs in the Massachusetts factory town where discussion and example have a fair chance at him. The effects of a trade union in detaching the immigrant from his clan organizations and exposing him to the play of Americanizing influences is thus set forth by Colonel Wright:[2] "In every trade union, however conservative, there are members who will occasionally get the floor and advise their hearers to vote high wages and shorter hours at the ballot box. As the groups of Slovaks gather around after the business is over to have these things explained to them, many get their first real idea of what the ballot and election day mean, and the relation of these to the Government itself. In their own home countries the two essential, if not only, elements of the peasant and agricultural laborer's mind is to believe and obey, or follow. Advantage is taken of this fact here by clan politicians, as well as the clan leader in every department. Once the leader can make these people believe in him, he thinks for the entire group, and insists that their duty consists in following his lead implicitly. Necessarily, the trade union, in order to get them to break away from the leader that opposed the union on industrial lines, would be compelled to urge them to consider their own personal and group interests as wage workers; to think and act for themselves along lines where they know the real conditions better than any one else, and certainly better than their leader in a child insurance society, or something else as remote. Here, too, are the first germs of what may be called departmental thinking implanted in their minds—that is, that while a leader may be worthy of their con-

[1] See "America's Race Problems," 115, 123-124, 128, 136-137.
[2] U. S. Bulletin of Labor, January, 1905, "The Influence of Trade Unions on Immigrants," 6.

fidence in one thing, it does not necessarily follow that he is so in some other class of interests.

"It is doubtful if any organization other than a trade union could accomplish these things, for only the bread-and-butter necessity would be potent enough as an influence to bring these people out of the fixed forms and crystallizations of life into which they have been compressed. Certain it is that no other organization is attempting to do this work, at least not by amalgamation, which is the only way assimilation can be secured among these various foreign elements. The drawing of these people away from their petty clique leaders and getting them to think for themselves upon one line of topics, namely, the industrial conditions and the importance of trade organization, result in a mental uplift. The only way they can pull a Slovak away from his leader is to pull him up until he has gotten above his leader along the lines of thought they are working on."

In discussion three phases of conflict may be observed, corresponding to the possible relations between two incompatible beliefs or desires.[1]

1. *A denies or opposes B, but B does not deny or oppose A.*— This is seen when A is an established dogma or institution, B an innovation. The book that gave the world the heliocentric theory crept forth with a grovelling preface to the effect that Copernicus had propounded the doctrine of the earth's movement not as a fact, but as a hypothesis! Galileo sought to reconcile the discoveries of his telescope with the Scriptures, and when he brought out his *Dialogo* signed a stultifying preface in which the Copernican theory was virtually exhibited as a play of the imagination. Boscovich, obedient Jesuit that he was, said: "I regard the earth as immovable; nevertheless for simplicity in explanation I will argue as if the earth moves; for it is proved that of the two hypotheses the appearances favor this idea." The theologians, on the other hand, exaggerated the incompatibility of heliocentrism with their system. They declared the former "vitiates the whole Christian plan of salvation," "casts suspicion on the doctrine of the incarnation," "tends toward infidelity," "is of all heresies the most abominable, the most pernicious, the most scandalous. Argument against the immortality of the soul, the existence of God, and the incarnation, should be tolerated sooner than an argument to prove that the earth moves." The author was denounced as "heretic,"

[1] See Tarde, "La logique sociale," 138-141.

"infidel," and "atheist." In the same spirit the theologian de-nounces early geology as "infidel," while geology professes no antagonism whatever to the Church. The mass of belief behind infant science is so little that priests, eager to crush science while it is yet weak, accentuate the contradiction between them; while science, conscious of its weakness, avoids conflict and pleads only to be let alone. The same attitude is seen in certain of the early Fathers who sought to propitiate their Pagan neighbors by em-phasizing the agreements between Greek Philosophy and the Chris-tian belief. So the "rights of man" professed nothing subversive at first; while the privileged orders instantly declared war on them. So new tastes timidly introduce themselves alongside the older needs; but conservatives promptly oppose "the new-fangled for-eign luxuries" as Cato denounced Greek works of art and Asiatic refinements.

2. *A and B mutually deny and oppose one another.*—This is the phase of fiercest contention, when the new feels strong enough to throw off the mask and declare its downright incompatibility with the old. Then Luther succeeds Erasmus; La Place, Galileo; Vol-taire, Descartes; Strauss, Reimarus; Huxley, Darwin; and Danton, Mirabeau. Astronomy, finding a current in its favor, no longer pretends to furnish confirmation for dogmas which respond only with anathemas. Science declares war on the traditional cos-mogony and boldly admits that theology and science cannot be reconciled. So democracy takes the field against privilege, and labor avows that it aims at nothing less than securing for the laborer "the whole produce."

3. *A does not deny or oppose B, but B denies or opposes A.*— The confidence in the methods of science at last becomes so great that theology no longer dares accentuate its contradiction. It strives to compromise with science, clutches eagerly at "scientific" proofs,[1] and seeks to rebuild its shattered dogmas in the region as yet unsubdued by advancing science. Divines eagerly "recon-cile" Genesis and Geology, but geologists go on with their work careless whether the two are reconciled or not. Theology forms all sorts of amalgam with science; but science declines even to

---

[1] Speaking of Hoffmann's "scientific" theory of the action of the devil in causing Job's boils, White says: "This effort at a *quasi*-scientific explanation which should satisfy the theological spirit, comical as it at first seems, is really worthy of serious notice, because it must be considered as the beginning of that inevitable effort at compromise which we see in the history of every science when it begins to appear triumphant."—*Op. cit.* II, 62.

discuss, and passes by in silent scorn the horde of bastard theories. So, nowadays, selfish privilege no longer openly opposes democracy, but champions "imperialism." Capitalism no longer flouts the demand for legislation to protect labor, but pleads "constitutional limitations." Men no longer denounce woman as "strongminded" and "unwomanly" when she asks for equal opportunities, but profess that the hampering restrictions upon her are in the interest of woman herself!

Such are the phases to be noticed in a particular logical duel. But the product of one of these duels becomes the starting-point of the next, so that there is a certain *evolution of discussion* to be discerned in the history of a civilization. The cause and course of this evolution cannot be better stated than in the words of Tarde:[1]—

"It is only after the mental discussion between contradictory ideas within the same mind has ended, that any verbal discussion is possible between two men who have solved the question differently. Similarly, if verbal, written, or printed discussions between groups of men, and groups that are ever widening, take the place of verbal discussion between two men, it is because the more limited discussion has been brought to an end by some relative and temporary agreement, or some sort of unanimity. These groups are first split up into an endless multitude of little coteries, clans, churches, forums, and schools, which combat one another; but at length, after many polemics, they are welded into a very small number of great parties, religions, parliamentary groups, schools of philosophy, and schools of art, which engage one another in mortal combat. Was it not thus that the Catholic faith became gradually established? In the first two or three centuries of the Church's history, countless discussions, always intense and often bloody, were waged among the members of each local church, ending in their agreeing upon a creed; but this creed, disagreeing in certain particulars with those of neighboring churches, gave rise to conferences and provincial councils, which solved the difficulties, excepting that they occasionally disagreed with one another, and were forced to carry their disputes higher up, to national or œcumenical councils. . . . The unity of legal codes has long since been accomplished in an analogous manner: countless local customs have arisen, settling thousands of individual discussions concerning rights (though not all, as the court records prove); these

[1] "Social Laws," 125-132 *passim.*

customs, coming into conflict with one another, have been reconciled by certain sectional customs, which have finally been replaced by uniform legislation. The unity of science, operating slowly over a wide field, through a succession of discussions, alternately settled and reopened, among scientists and scientific schools, would give rise to similar reflections. . . .

"The objection may possibly be raised that as races become more civilized they tend more and more to discussion, and that, far from taking the place of private discussion, our public discussions, polemics of the press, and parliamentary debates only add fuel to them. But such an objection would be without force. For if savages and barbarians discuss little (which is fortunate, since most of their discussions degenerate into quarrels and combats), it is because they scarcely speak or think at all. When we consider the very small number of their ideas, we ought to be surprised that they clash so often, relatively speaking; and we should marvel to find men with so few different interests so quarrelsome. On the other hand, a thing which we ought to wonder at, but which we scarcely notice, as a matter of fact, is this: that in our own civilized cities, despite the great current of ideas sweeping over us in conversation and reading, there are, on the whole, so few discussions, and these so lacking in warmth. We should be amazed to find that men who think and talk so much contradict one another so seldom, to see that they accomplish so much and clash so little; just as we should wonder at seeing so few carriage accidents in our streets, which are so animated and crowded, or at seeing so few wars break out in this era of complex and far-reaching international relations. What is it, then, that has brought us into agreement on so many points? It is the three great productions that have been gradually wrought out by centuries of discussion; namely, Religion, Jurisprudence, and Science. . . .

"To sum up. The strife of opposition in human society, in its three principal forms—war, competition, and discussion—proves obedient to one and the same law of development through ever widening areas of temporary pacification, alternating with renewals of discord more centrally organized and on a larger scale, and leading up to a final, at least partial, agreement."

PUBLIC OPINION

A discussion that attracts general attention finds its natural issue in a state of *public* (or *social*) *opinion*.[1] The formation of this may best be observed during a discussion that must close at a certain date, *i.e.*, a campaign. A campaign is a social deliberation. This does not necessarily mean general individual irresolution. If nobody had made up his mind, there could be no conflict whatever in the social mind. Says Tarde:[2]—

"Let us suppose, although it is an hypothesis that could never be realized, that all the members of the nation were simultaneously and indefinitely in a state of indecision. Then war would be at an end, for an ultimatum or a declaration of war presupposes the making of individual decisions by cabinet officers. For war to exist, the clearest type of logical duel in society, peace must first have been established in the minds of the ministers or rulers who before that hesitated to formulate the thesis and antithesis embodied in the two opposing armies. For the same reason there would be no more election contests. There would be an end to religious quarrels and to scientific schisms and disputes, because this division of society into separate churches or theories presupposes that some single doctrine has finally prevailed in the previously divided thought or conscience of each of their respective followers. Parliamentary discussions would cease. There would be an end to litigation. . . . There would be an end to the struggles and encroachments of different kinds of law, such as those between the customary law and the Roman law of mediæval France, for such national perplexity means that individuals have chosen one or the other of the two bodies of law."

All these instances of social struggle imply that over a part of society irresolution has ceased. The effort of each party is to destroy the irresolution still remaining, or to create doubt in the

---

[1] The reader should distinguish *preponderant opinion* from *public opinion*. There is a preponderant opinion as to coeducation, or the legitimacy of the tontine life insurance policy, or the moral effects of religious revivals, but not a public opinion. The latter implies the direction of social attention usually, though not necessarily, in view of some collective decision or action.

[2] "Laws of Imitations," 165.

minds of those who have gone with the other side. In a campaign the public is like a more or less inert substance placed between two chambers containing different active acids. The acid that eats into and assimilates this substance the more rapidly is the propaganda of the winning party. Sometimes there is a simple acid acting on a homogeneous substance—the communion cup agitation in a certain church, or the policy of withdrawal from the state militia mooted in a labor organization. Usually, however, the substance is heterogeneous, and each acid has a number of ingredients,—arguments, appeals, proposals, planks,—each of which is presumed to be effective with some section of the public. The acid must be complex when, as in a political campaign, the entire public is being acted upon.

The affinities individuals develop are by no means determined simply by the rational balancing of opposing considerations. There is first the factor of prepossession and prejudice. Says Bryce:[1] "Every one is, of course, predisposed to see things in some one particular light by his previous education, habits of mind, accepted dogmas, religious or social affinities, notions of his own personal interest. No event, no speech or article ever falls upon a perfectly virgin soil; the reader or listener is always more or less biassed already. When some important event happens, which calls for the formation of a view, these preëxisting habits, dogmas, affinities, help to determine the impression which each man experiences, and so are factors in the view he forms."

This original impression is soon overlaid by a variety of influences of social origin. Nearly every man looks for guidance to certain quarters, bows to the example of trusted leaders, of persons of influence or authority. Every editor, politician, banker, capitalist, railroad president, employer, clergyman, or judge has a following with whom his opinion has weight. He, in turn, is likely to have *his* authorities. The anatomy of collective opinion shows it to be organized from centres and subcentres, forming a kind of intellectual feudal system. The average man responds to several such centres of influence, and when they are in accord on a particular question he is almost sure to acquiesce. But when his authorities disagree, there results either confusion or else independence of judgment.

We might compare the individual to a cell in the social brain knit to other cells by *afferent* and *efferent* filaments of influence.

[1] "The American Commonwealth," II, ch. LXXVI.

When he influences more people than have the power to influence him, the *efferent* filaments predominate; but when he is chiefly a recipient of influences, the *afferent* predominate.

Why, in the course of forming a public opinion, the primary impression, or the element of pure personal conviction arising out of individual thinking, nearly disappears in the process is brought out by Mark Twain:[1]—

"There are seventy-five million men and women among us who do not know how to cut out and make a dress suit, and they would not think of trying; yet they all think they can competently think out a political or religious scheme without any apprenticeship to the business, and many of them believe they have actually worked that miracle. But, indeed, the truth is, almost all the men and women of our nation or of any other get their religion and their politics where they get their astronomy—entirely at second hand. Being untrained, they are no more able to intelligently examine a dogma or a policy than they are to calculate an eclipse.

"Men are usually competent thinkers along the lines of their specialized training only. Within these limits alone are their opinions and judgments valuable; outside of these limits they grope and are lost—usually without knowing it. In a church assemblage of five hundred persons, there will be a man or two whose trained mind can seize upon each detail of a great manufacturing scheme and recognize its value or its lack of value promptly; and can pass the details in intelligent review, section by section, and finally as a whole, and then deliver a verdict upon the scheme which cannot be flippantly set aside nor easily answered. And there will be one or two other men there who can do the same thing with a great and complicated educational project; and one or two others who can do the like with a large scheme for applying electricity in a new and unheard-of way; and one or two others who can do it with a showy scheme for revolutionizing the scientific world's accepted notions regarding geology. And so on, and so on. But the manufacturing experts will not be competent to examine the educational scheme intelligently, and their opinion about it would not be valuable; neither of these two groups will be able to understand and pass upon the electrical scheme; none of these three batches of experts will be able to understand and pass upon the geological revolution; and probably not one man in the entire lot would be competent to examine,

[1] *North American Review,* 176, pp. 174-175.

capably, the intricacies of a political or religious scheme, new or old, and deliver a judgment upon it which any one need regard as precious. . . . Not ten among the five hundred—let their minds be ever so good and bright—will be competent, by grace of the requisite specialized mental training, to take hold of a complex abstraction of any kind and make head or tail of it.

"The whole five hundred are thinkers, and they are all capable thinkers—but only within the narrow limits of their specialized trainings. Four hundred and ninety of them cannot competently examine either a religious plan or a political one. A scattering few of them do examine both—that is, they think they do. With the results as precious as when I examine the nebular theory and explain it to myself."

The disposition of individual minds to fall gradually into a kind of spiritual organization, in which one may balance ten thousand, explains the importance of the time element in the making of a social decision. The polling of people on a question when first it comes up brings to light much prejudice, passion, and stupidity. The polling of the same persons after there has been time for free discussion and the maturing of a public opinion, reveals an intelligence and foresight far above that of the average man. It is, therefore, a slander to declare that manhood suffrage equalizes Socrates and Sambo. At its best estate a popular election merely records the outcome of a vast social deliberation in which the philosopher has a million times the influence of the field hand. This collective rumination corrects the ballot-box falsehood that one man is as good as another, and brings it to pass that the decisions of a political democracy may be quite as intelligent as those of an aristocratic society, and at the same time free from the odious class selfishness of the latter.

Although public opinion at its final stage always exhibits the hierarchical structure, this hierarchy of influence need not be identical with the political or social hierarchy, else there could be no popular movements, no peasant revolts, no branching off of humble sects (Dunkers, Doukhobors), no confrontation of classes and masses. A democratic society is characterized by the depreciation of mere social position and the exaltation of the wisdom and competency of the average man. Ultra-democracy presumes the independency of each citizen's opinions, just as ultra-Protestantism assumes that every good Christian will from his prayerful study of the Scriptures have worked out for himself a system of theology. The encouragement of the common man in his own conceit profoundly alters the relation of leaders and led. Contrast the "habitual deference" towards certain classes, which in England has prevented universal suffrage from working out its normal effects, with the powerlessness of any one class continuously to dominate Australasian or American opinion. Nevertheless, during the decade 1895-1905, a widespread infatuation with the commercial-financial magnates, the so-called "captains of industry," came near to giving this class the control of American public opinion.

An organ of public opinion is at once an expression of existing views and a factor in further moulding the common judgment. Men like to be on the prevailing side—to go with the view that seems likely to win. Hence, the utterance of an organ of public opinion is at once a disclosure of an existing force and a further force in influencing others. This fact multiplies the organs of expression but confuses their utterances, because every voice seeks to represent itself as that of the greater or at least of a growing number. Newspapers are conventionally organs of public opinion, but too many become advocates and thus cease to be indexes or mirrors. On political questions we can follow the drift of opinion in independent or semi-independent journals—the mugwump newspapers, the non-political press, the religious or literary sheets. In general, an advocate is worthless as an index of public opinion on its own hobby, but on related topics it may be valuable. For example, the utterances of the great anti-saloon organ may be significant and representative on everything save "prohibition."

Published letters, interviews, pulpit and platform utterances, the resolutions of mass-meetings, the views of bodies and associations,—all these are straws indicating the set of the current of public opinion. But, again, the attitude of associations is not significant on questions connected with their main purpose. The attitude of the women of the Woman's Christian Temperance Union on temperance, or of the American Federation of Labor on an eight-hours bill has no revelatory significance. The sphere of competency of such associations is a group of questions whereon they are not committed, but which they are fit to judge. A resolution of a temperance organization on child labor, of a bankers' association on the Torrens system, of a scientific society on rain-making experiments, is at once index and shaper of public opinion.

After an overwhelming public opinion has been reached in consequence of adequate discussion, the subject is dismissed from the attention of society and the conclusion, entering the current of tradition, passes quietly down from generation to generation along with other transmitted beliefs and standards. The settled aversion of our own society to gladiatorial combats, polygamy, chattel slavery, the judicial use of torture, the press gang, the use of flogging in the navy, or the official tampering with private correspondence can be traced in every case to a more or less general discussion, that issued in a principle or maxim or canon that, since then, has been accepted without question.

APPENDIX

A LIST OF SIMILAR BOOKS

The books listed below might prove valuable auxiliaries to *Persistent Questions in Public Discussion.* The text-books mentioned approach the problems of composition through selected essays dealing with ideas which seem to their respective editors significant and timely for the particular level of students for which the various texts are planned. The prefaces and introductions of these volumes should be studied by teachers of writing and speaking. The books written for the general reader are perhaps more useful for classes in extemporaneous speaking than the texts. A shelf of these and similar volumes might be especially convenient for teacher and student.

Harold E. Stearns, *Civilization in the United States,* New York, Harcourt, Brace and Co., 1922; Charles F. Horne, *The Meaning of Modern Life,* New York, The National Alumni, 1907; F. S. Marvin, *The Unity of Western Civilization,* New York, Oxford University Press, 1915; Walter Lippmann, *A Preface to Politics,* New York, Mitchell Kennedy, 1913; Julia E. Johnsen, *The Negro Problem,* New York, H. W. Wilson Co., 1921, see also other volumes in the Wilson Handbook Series; Northup, Lane, and Schwab, *Representative Phi Beta Kappa Orations,* Boston, Houghton Mifflin, 1915.

Frank Aydelotte, *College English,* New York, Oxford University Press, 1913; Maurice Garland Fulton, *College Life,* New York, Macmillan, 1915; *National Ideals and Problems,* New York, Macmillan, 1918; *Bryce on American Democracy,* New York, Macmillan, 1920; Foerster and Pierson, *American Ideals,* Boston, Houghton Mifflin, 1917; Bruce and Montgomery, *The New World,* New York, Macmillan, 1921; Lionel D. Edie, *Current Social and Industrial Forces,* New York, Boni and Liveright, 1920; Richard Rice, Jr., *College and the Future,* New York, Scribner's Sons, 1915; Scott and Zeitlin, *College Readings in English Prose,* New York, Macmillan, 1914; James H. Tufts, *The Real Business of Living,* New York, Henry Holt, 1918; Berdan, Schultz, and Joyce, *Modern Essays,* New York, Macmillan, 1921; Lester W. Boardman, *Modern American Speeches,* New York, Longmans, Green and Co., 1923.

The editors wish particularly to acknowledge their early indebtedness to George Pierce Baker's *Forms of Public Address,* New York, Henry Holt and Co., 1904; and to Steeves and Ristine's *Representative Essays in Modern Thought,* New York, American Book Co., 1913.

A WORD TO TEACHERS

The addresses and essays included in *Persistent Questions in Public Discussion* present, as an effective adjunct to other methods of training in speaking and writing, opinions which are constant subjects of public discussion. The editors have sought stimulating and provocative readings which adequately state conflicting views on a series of selected public questions. Many teachers will already have emphasized the importance of these problems. Experience shows that the majority of thoughtful students choose subjects in the general fields of discussion here tentatively marked out. There are obvious advantages to such a limitation of the problems discussed that the teacher may reasonably hope to have more than a superficial knowledge of some of the subjects of student themes and speeches. The readings themselves furnish source material for many speeches and articles. But they are primarily intended to arouse interest in further investigation and discussion of ideas which are central in our political and social thinking.

Besides forming a general background for public discussion and a spur to further special investigations, the readings illustrate a variety of rhetorical methods and styles. As they range from the simplest lucid expositions to the richest eloquence (even to perfervid "rhetoric") the student will find excellent models for study or for imitation.

The study of models becomes barren unless the subject-matter holds attention by a reasonably immediate appeal to the interest and information of the student. So perfectly adapted to its audience and occasion is good public discourse, that the discovery of its sources of effectiveness is often difficult unless its substance is of either universal or current interest. When "models" unite interesting and readily intelligible thought with excellence of form, they quicken the perception of the inseparability of form and substance. An early recognition of this unity is essential to work in conscious conformity with the rules of any art. "No man's style is better than his matter." Study and discussion of material which has been carefully thought out and vividly expressed affords a training in expression more fundamental than any based entirely on the technical rules of rhetoric and composition.[1]

This collection also furnishes materials for the study of persuasion.

---

[1] See, for example, *Literary Taste, How to Form It*, by Arnold Bennett, Doran, Chapter VI, on *The Question of Style*.

The conflicting ideals, opinions, interpretations of events, motives and temperaments presented are striking evidence of the diverse natures of men and of the necessity of harmonizing presented thought with the color of other minds. Some acquaintance with these ideas and opinions will form no mean addition to the mental equipment of any one who proposes to address the public as speaker, editor, publicist or citizen.

In practice, as already tested in courses in public speaking, eight groups or pairs of readings are assigned for a year's course.

Approximately three-fourths of the impromptu speaking and discussion of the course centres around topics suggested by the readings. Definite class hours are given to discussion led by the instructor. The twelve "prepared" speeches of the year, naturally require much additional reading and investigation, to which the lists of collateral readings serve as an introduction. The student is expected to make from two-thirds to three-fourths of his "prepared" speeches with some reference to the readings, but is, of course, permitted freedom of choice when his information and personal interest make a good case for selecting a subject outside the very wide range of topics correlated in the readings. As the content of the volume is rather surprisingly unified, students may be interested in viewing a topic suggested by one reading from the varying angles of a number of others. The relation of principles set forth in the various readings to many subjects of undergraduate and campus interest will readily be seen.[1]

Some of the methods which have proved satisfactory for classes in public speaking are as follows: a single idea suggested by the reading may be refuted or amplified; the address or article may be summarized and its conclusions enforced or disputed; general principles set forth may be applied to some problem of immediate and practical interest to the speaker or his audience; the clash of opinions may be formally debated or discussed in open forum; the arguments advanced may be briefed; the brief may be expanded into an article or a speech with fresh illustrations and material; unified selections or adaptations may be declaimed; portions may be used for reading aloud; summaries of an address may be given with extended quotations from the original interpolated; memorized passages may be used for drill in delivery.

The thoughtful student will not be dependent on the suggestions in the appendix. The teacher will naturally perfect methods adapted to his particular needs and objectives. The lists of questions, topics and collateral readings—they combine the suggestions of instructors and students—are included in the volume for ready reference when invention flags.

Texts which satisfactorily present the principles of writing and speaking will, of course, be used in conjunction with *Persistent Questions in Public Discussion*.

[1] See page 557.

AMERICAN CHARACTER AND IDEALS

QUESTIONS ON
FIVE AMERICAN CONTRIBUTIONS TO CIVILIZATION

By Charles W. Eliot

1. "This pernicious influence [the "crushing power of military society"] Americans have escaped, and they show other nations how to escape it." If this escape has been largely due to natural conditions here, how can Europe profit by it? [*Page* 5.]
2. Why have American wars been fought at small loss to liberty? What loss of liberty did we suffer in the War of 1812? The Civil War? The Spanish War? The European War? Does the loss of liberty vary with the magnitude of the war? [*Page* 6.]
3. How account for the unfortified boundary between the United States and Canada? [*Page* 8.]
4. What national evils other than a belief in paper money, and pensions, had their origin in the Civil War? [*Page* 9.]
5. Has "the violence of strikers made the 'scab' a creditable type of the nineteenth century hero"? [*Page* 11.]
6. Does the present state of the nation lead to the belief that the late war increased national unity? Did the Spanish-American War do this? [*Page* 12.]
7. Have we had more religious liberty in the United States because of the number of religious denominations? [*Page* 15.]
8. "The church as a whole, in the United States, has not been an effective opponent of any form of human rights." Why? [*Page* 15.]
9. "No splendid architectural exhibitions of church power have interested or overawed the population." Is this usually counted to our credit? What cathedrals have "overawed the population" of Europe? Should the building of cathedrals in America be opposed? [*Page* 15.]
10. Does Eliot's second-named contribution [religious toleration] seem a product of purpose or circumstance? [*Pages* 14-16.]
11. Is universal suffrage "the ultimate goal of successful democracy"? If so, when should it be employed among so-called "backward peoples"? [*Page* 16.]

12. Who are most educated by universal suffrage, the leaders or those who are led? [*Page* 18.]

13. Is the submission of grave and delicate questions to the mass of voters an expensive way of educating them? Is it worth the cost? [*Page* 18.]

14. "There is no better mental exercise for the most highly trained man than the effort to expound a difficult subject in so clear a way that the untrained man can understand it." Is this the art of the demagogue? [*Page* 18.]

15. "Native good judgment and good feeling are not proportional to education." Is our faith in education greater than the results seem to warrant? [*Page* 18.]

16. "In a Democracy, it is important to discriminate influence from authority." How may this be done? What persons have wielded large influence in American democracy without possessing authority? What of Charles W. Eliot? [*Page* 19.]

17. Does it constitute a serious charge against our form of government to say with Eliot that "political leaders are seldom leaders of thought"? Why is this so? [*Page* 19.]

18. Does university education seem to furnish "better powers of argument and persuasion"? [*Page* 19.]

19. Is democracy in Europe likely to relieve us of serving as a political haven? [*Page* 22.]

20. "The ultimate effect of these inventions is quite as much intellectual as physical." Is it? See Arthur Pound, *The Iron Man in Industry*. Boston. The Atlantic Monthly Press. 1922. [*Page* 24.]

21. Has Eliot ignored intellectual and æsthetic aspects of American Democracy? Would emphasis upon them help or hurt the case?

QUESTIONS ON *AMERICAN CHARACTER* BY BRANDER MATTHEWS

1. What does Matthews mean when he says "the assertion that foreign nations are a contemporaneous posterity is not quite true"? [*Page* 26.]

2. Concerning the charge that Americans care most for making money, offer some explanation for this besides national depravity. How has this idea of Americans gained currency? [*Page* 27.]

3. What motives might lead Europeans to emphasize this charge of materialism? [*Page* 27.]

4. "The warlike temper, the aggressiveness, the imperialistic sentiment, are no new developments of unexpected ambition." Explain the origin of these qualities. See Turner, *The Frontier in American History*. New York. Henry Holt. 1920. [*Page* 28.]

5. Is the American delight in making money for the fun of it a peculiar

characteristic of the people, or is it largely the result of abundant opportunities? [*Page* 28.]

6. Could the philanthropies of America be made to support the assertion that we are more generous than Europeans? Has this seemed to be true in the case of funds raised for the relief of sufferers from famines, earthquakes and wars? [*Page* 29.]

7. What reply other than Matthews's assertion that America is not entirely devoid of artists can you suggest for the charge that we ignore the arts and despise beauty? [*Page* 31.]

8. If it be true that America "has given birth to very few indeed of the foremost poets, dramatists, novelists, painters, sculptors, architects, or scientific discoverers of the last hundred years," are we to be reproached for it? What can we do about it? [*Page* 33.]

9. What of Matthews's defense against the charge of lack of idealism? What examples have given rise to the European opinion? What added defense can you make? See Bliss Perry, "American Idealism," *The American Mind*. Boston. Houghton Mifflin. 1912. [*Page* 35.]

10. Offer some reasons for the difference in the treatment of the Tories after the Revolution and the Confederates after the Civil War. See Charles Kendall Adams, "Some Neglected Aspects of the Revolutionary War." *Atlantic Monthly*. August, 1898; Vol. 82, p. 174. See also Carl Schurz, "General Amnesty." *Speeches, Correspondence and Political Papers of Carl Schurz*. New York. Putnam's. 1913. Vol. 2, p. 320. Reprinted, Baker, *Forms of Public Address*. New York. Henry Holt. 1904. p. 353. [*Page* 38.]

11. "This distrust of those who dwell elsewhere than we do is common all over Europe today. Here in America it has yielded to friendly neighborliness." Is this due to different human qualities in Americans? What has produced such a state of affairs in Europe? Does such a distrust have any bearing on the doctrine of self-determination for small nations? [*Page* 39.]

12. "Excessive optimism may be as corrupting to the fiber of the people as the 'Sabbathless pursuit of fortune.'" Is the "Sabbathless pursuit of fortune" peculiarly American? How account for American optimism? Is it tending to disappear? [*Page* 39.]

13. Has the spread of the psychological test increased our faith in the rightness of the majority? Granting the scientific accuracy of these tests, do they warrant conclusions hostile to democracy? [*Page* 40.]

14. "Each party tried to demonstrate that it was more peaceable, more equitable, more sincerely devoted to lawful and righteous behavior than the other." What is the value of the large amount of lip service paid to ideals in a democracy? [*Page* 40.]

SUGGESTIONS FOR FURTHER READING ON AMERICAN CHARACTER AND IDEALS

ALEXANDER, HARTLEY BURR. "Americanism." *New Republic.* (January, 1918, Vol. 13, p. 270.)

"Americanization." *Nation.* (September, 1919, Vol. 109, p. 367.)

ARNOLD, MATTHEW. *Civilization in the United States.* Boston. Cupples and Hurd. 1888.

BAGGER, E. S. "Intellectual America." *Atlantic Monthly.* (February, 1921, Vol. 127, p. 200.)

BENNETT, ARNOLD. *Your United States.* New York and London. Harper and Bros. 1912.

BOURNE, RANDOLPH. "Our Cultural Humility." *Atlantic Monthly.* (October, 1914, Vol. 114, p. 503.)

BROOKS, JOHN GRAHAM. *As Others See Us.* New York. Macmillan. 1908. (Has bibliography of works of foreign observers of the United States.)

BRYCE, JAMES. *The American Commonwealth.* New York and London. Macmillan. 1896. (Especially Vol. 2, chapters 74, 111, 114, 115, 116.)

BUTLER, NICHOLAS MURRAY. *The American As He Is.* New York. Macmillan. 1908.

BECKER, CARL. "Kansas." *Essays in History Dedicated to F. J. Turner.* New York. Henry Holt. 1910.

DICKINSON, G. LOWES. *Appearances.* Garden City. Doubleday, Page and Co. 1914. (Part 4.)

EMERSON, RALPH WALDO. "The American Scholar." *Miscellanies.* Boston. J. R. Osgood. 1877.

GRUENING, E. H. *These United States: A Symposium.* New York. Boni and Liveright. 1923.

HIGGINSON, T. W. "Americanism in Literature." *Atlantic Monthly.* (January, 1870, Vol. 25, p. 56.)

KALLEN, HORACE M. *Culture and Democracy in the United States.* New York. Boni and Liveright. 1924.

KULAMER, JOHN. "Americanization: the Other Side of the Case." *Atlantic Monthly.* (March, 1920, Vol. 125, p. 416.)

MATTHEWS, BRANDER. *The American of the Future and Other Essays.* New York. C. Scribner's Sons. 1909.

PERRY, BLISS. *The American Mind.* Boston. Houghton Mifflin. 1912.

REID, L. R. "The Small Town." *Civilization in the United States.* Edited by Harold Stearns. New York. Harcourt, Brace & Co. 1922.

ROOSEVELT, THEODORE. *American Ideals and Other Essays.* New York and London. G. P. Putnam's Sons. 1897.

"Nationalism in Literature and Art." *Proceedings American Academy of Arts and Letters.* No. 10. New York. 1917. (Copies may be obtained from the Secretary of the American Academy of Arts and Letters, 70 Fifth Ave., New York City.)

SANTAYANA, GEORGE. *Character and Opinion in the United States.* New York. Scribner's. 1921.

STUART, HENRY L. "American Civilization as an Englishman Sees It." *Civilization in the United States.*

TOCQUEVILLE, ALEXIS DE. *Democracy in America.* New York. D. Appleton and Co. 1904.

TURNER, F. J. "The Significance of the Frontier in American History." *The Frontier in American History.* New York. Henry Holt. 1920.

WILSON, WOODROW. "The Making of the Nation." *Atlantic Monthly.* (July, 1897, Vol. 80, p. 1.)

"A Calendar of Great Americans." "The Course of American History." *Mere Literature and Other Essays.* Boston. Houghton Mifflin. 1896.

SOME TOPICS FOR THE DISCUSSION OF AMERICAN CHARACTER AND IDEALS

America and her immigrants. National unity. American foreign policy. American view of church and state. America and caste. American art. American literature. American love of organization. Efficiency in America. American prestige abroad. Why foreign critics deal harshly with us. New England and Americanism. Americanism in the Middle West. America and mediocrity. Equality of opportunity in America. Americans who prefer to live abroad. American and European universities. Effect of frontier life in America. The spirit of the West in America. American and European conservation of resources. Contribution of immigrants to America. American provincialism. American diplomacy. American public men. Ideal Americans: Washington, Jackson, Webster, Lee, Lincoln, Emerson, Mark Twain, Franklin. American science. American philanthropy. Effect of climate on Americans. American municipal government. American traditions. American versatility. American conceit. The American abroad. American manners. American haste. American nervousness. American optimism. American exaggeration. American love of taking chances. American oratorical temperament. American irreverence. American lawlessness. American conservatism. American individualism. American practicality. American influence in the European War. American fighting qualities. Americanism in the schools. American history as propaganda. American liberty.

DEMOCRACY

QUESTIONS ON
DEMOCRACY

By J. S. Blackie

1. "There has always been a class of persons of hasty wit and superficial conclusions who have been of the opinion, etc., . . . The maintainers of this opinion are known in history as democrats." What can you say of this as an introductory statement of an opponent's position? Discuss such argumentative introductions in general. [*Page* 47.]

2. "Not in the style of a political declamation from the hustings. . . ." Has Blackie been free from this style in his introduction? [*Page* 48.]

3. Is a man who starts from the conception that democracy is the "idol worship of the multitude" likely to come to a fair conclusion? [*Page* 48.]

4. "A House of Representatives, therefore, is only a committee of the people, and exists only for the sake of carrying their decisions into execution." Has this theory of representation been generally held in America? [*Page* 50.]

5. "It is the greatest of all delusions to suppose that profound study is necessary for the first steps of political action." What examples could be cited of good citizenship among relatively uneducated peoples? [*Page* 50.]

6. "These . . . are the leading propositions which express the principles and the purposes of the democratic party." Do these statements about freedom, equality, self-government, representation and majority rule, seem to be the cardinal doctrines in American political faith? Has Blackie stated them fairly? [*Page* 50.]

7. "Mere liberty is the first and lowest and smallest condition of human society." Then why do we eulogize it? [*Page* 51.]

8. What is there in Blackie's paragraph on equality that is contrary to democratic doctrine? [*Page* 53.]

9. "But of this healthy feeling of respect and reverence for what is superior, democracy knows nothing." Is there no respect for superiority in America? [*Page* 54.]

10. In what way do modern governments suffer from the crowd characteristics here mentioned? Do modern methods of communication increase the dangers of the mob mind? [*Page* 55.]

11. ". . . those occasional captains of popular movements whom their admirers call friends of the people, but whom I prefer to call demagogues." Who is the demagogue? Tell of some notable ones. [*Page* 57.]

12. "The man who does this [appeals to the people], however unselfish he may be in his purpose, and pure in his intent, is the declared enemy to the constitution of his country." Discuss, giving instances when this has been done by American statesmen. [*Page* 59.]

13. ". . . if he, the representative of the people, on any occasion, should take a fancy to have an independent opinion, they will soon let him know that he does not understand his duty, and must be dismissed." Has this generalization been borne out by American history? [*Page* 59.]

14. "What people ought to desire is, to be governed by the wisest and best of the community." Compare with Wendell Phillips's statement that to put absolute power into the hands of even the wisest man would be to stereotype monstrous error upon a people. [*Page* 59.]

15. "An appeal to the decision of the majority is always the resource of despair." Is it? [*Page* 60.]

16. "As for Christianity, I have yet to learn that it has ever leavened the public morality to such an extent as to have any appreciable effect on political affairs." Does the "church vote" exercise any influence in America? [*Page* 63.]

17. "What we want [in an elector] is wisdom, clear-headedness, discretion, moderation, coolness, independence, moral courage, experience of life, and position in society. Of these qualities a property qualification may afford a certain rough guarantee; a knowledge qualification will afford none." Is a property qualification a better guarantee of the above qualities than a knowledge qualification? [*Page* 64.]

18. "No young man, however well educated, should have anything to do with politics." Why? [*Page* 64.]

19. "It cannot be, it never will be, that a majority can be composed of superior men." Does this constitute a final argument against government by the majority? [*Page* 65.]

20. "The long political history of Athens . . . is only a lecture on the vanity of all attempts at self-government on the part of unchecked multitudes." Do historians agree upon this? [*Page* 70.]

21. "When people are fighting for their existence, it is a great man that is necessary more than a good constitution." Discuss in the light of the European War, the Civil War. [*Page* 71.]

22. "If it should have pleased God to create a superior race of reasonable beings beyond the Atlantic, capable of solving easily social problems which have puzzled all the rest of the world, it will be our business to look on with admiration and gratitude." Does such a statement offer any hope that the speaker will present an unprejudiced examination of the evidence in America? [*Page* 74.]

23. Explain how it is that Bright would direct Blackie to De Tocqueville for evidence favorable to democracy, and that Blackie should find there "chiefly the most damning evidence" against it. [*Page* 75.]

24. Is Blackie consistent in dismissing material prosperity so easily after he has (page 64) asked for a property qualification as a rough guarantee of wisdom in the voter? [*Page* 75.]

25. Does Blackie's refusal to be impressed by our educational system seem to indicate a determination to disregard our merits, or is he justified in regarding wealth and education as non-essentials? [*Page* 75.]

26. Would a fair-minded observer readily accept such an indictment of a whole nation as is here quoted from James Spence? What motives were back of Spence's *The American Union?* [*Page* 76.]

27. From what is here cited by Blackie, what would he probably say of prohibition? [*Page* 76.]

28. What recent parallels to the incident of 1812 might be cited? [*Page* 77.]

29. The quotations concerning corruption here quoted by Blackie are cited as an indictment of Democracy. Is it the form of government or certain individuals that should be held accountable? [*Pages* 79-86.]

30. "The only way to escape the taint is to retire from the contagious atmosphere altogether." Discuss. What did George William Curtis and Theodore Roosevelt have to say on this? [*Page* 81.]

31. Has the progress in American municipal government since the time of this speech involved a departure from democracy? [*Pages* 83-84.]

32. What democratic advance was made by the Reform Bill of 1832? [*Page* 88.]

33. Could it be said that Blackie's fears for English aristocracy are being realized? [*Page* 94.]

34. Discuss Blackie's opinion of the House of Lords. [*Page* 94.]

QUESTIONS ON *DEMOCRACY VINDICATED* BY ERNEST JONES

1. Does democracy "temper one class with another"? Does the largest class numerically have any limits upon its power? [*Page* 96.]

2. "There may be a democracy under a king as well as under a president." What grounds are there for the statement that England is more democratic than the United States? [*Page* 96.]

3. What differences between "heathen Athens or pagan Rome, and Christian Britain in the nineteenth century," are favorable to the development of democracy? [*Page* 96.]

4. What has the religious belief of a country to do with democracy? See Bryce, *Modern Democracies*. New York. Macmillan. 1921. (Vol. 1, Chap. 9.) [*Page* 97.]

5. Who was George Grote, and why should advocates of democracy quote him? [*Page* 98.]

6. Read the "Funeral Oration" of Pericles here referred to and discuss it as an exposition of democracy. *Thucydides*, Book II, Chaps. 35-46. Jowett translation, Oxford. Clarendon Press. 1881. For commentary see Graham Wallas, *Our Social Heritage*. New Haven. Yale University Press. 1921. Chap. 7. [*Page* 100.]

7. Is it a proof of the merit of democracy that under it Rome's power increased until "she rapidly became more than a match for Carthage and Macedon"? [*Page* 101.]

8. What was Garibaldi's contribution to democracy? Is the government of the *Fascisti* in Italy a democratic government? [*Page* 102.]

9. Did the French Revolution have an influence upon democracy in America? What was its effect in England and in Europe? Compare Jones's opinion of it with that of Phillips in *The Scholar in a Republic*. [*Page* 102.]

10. What effect did the Civil War have upon European opinion of democracy? What world-wide significance was attached to the peaceful disbanding of the Union Army, and the payment of our war debts? [*Page* 104.]

11. Is it true that in the United States "education stands higher than in any other country in the world"? [*Page* 104.]

12. Has American municipal government been to the credit of democracy? [*Page* 104.]

13. "But New York does not represent democracy." Why not? Who was responsible for conditions in New York when Jones spoke? [*Page* 105.]

14. Do we now regard the New England mills with democratic pride? Compare American democracy today in any one particular with Jones's picture of it. [*Page* 106.]

15. Is it true that "wherever democracy has reigned, there has society reached its highest development, moral, social and intellectual"? What of the Elizabethan age? [*Page* 107.]

16. Have trades unions benefited democracy? [*Page* 108.]

17. Does Jones's statement of reforms favored by the people seem to bear out Phillips's statement that educated men have been on the wrong side of most public questions? [*Pages* 108-109.]

18. What progress was made by democracy through the English Reform Bills of 1832, 1867, 1884? [*Page* 109.]

19. "Instead of wanting education to fit them for the franchise, they need the franchise to enable them to obtain education." How far can this be applied to "backward peoples"? [*Page* 110.]

20. Is it true that in America "manhood suffrage has created the best educated people in the world"? How could this be determined? [*Page* 110.]

21. Is Jones's *reductio ad absurdum* on the property qualification for voting, a sound argument? [*Page* 110.]

22. "Here, too, the earth is monopolized by a few families." What changes in land ownership in England have occurred since this debate? See Harold Cox, "Changes in Land Ownership in England." *Atlantic Monthly.* (April, 1922; Vol. 129, pp. 556-562.) [*Page* 113.]

23. In what ways do the speeches of this debate differ from those which would be delivered before an audience of workingmen today? Is Jones's oratory "old-fashioned"?

24. What elements of oratorical style are particularly noticeable in Jones?

25. Discuss the use of historical analogies by Jones and Blackie; in public discussion generally.

26. How have the issues changed since the Blackie-Jones debate? Do we now compare democracy and monarchy? Is there any incompatibility between democracy and Bolshevism?

27. Compare Jones and Blackie as to, (a) the persuasiveness of their introductions, (b) their facility in the use of historical illustrations, (c) apparent fair-mindedness, (d) the significance of their speeches fifty years later.

SUGGESTIONS FOR FURTHER READING ON DEMOCRACY

ADAMS, BROOKS. "The American Democratic Ideal." *Yale Review.* (January, 1916, Vol. 5, pp. 225-33.)

ARNOLD, MATTHEW. "Democracy." "Equality." *Mixed Essays.* New York. Macmillan. 1883.

BARKER, J. ELLIS. "Democracy and War's Iron Broom." *Nineteenth Century.* (February, 1916, Vol. 79, pp. 289-323.)

BECKER, CARL. *The United States: An Experiment in Democracy.* New York. Harper and Bros. 1920.

BROWN, P. M. "Democracy and Diplomacy." *North American Review.* (November, 1916, Vol. 204, p. 691.)

BRYCE, JAMES. *Modern Democracies.* New York. Macmillan. 1921. *The American Commonwealth.* New York. Macmillan. 1910.

BULLARD, A. "Democracy and Diplomacy." *Atlantic Monthly.* (April, 1917, Vol. 119, p. 491.)

BUTLER, NICHOLAS MURRAY. *True and False Democracy.* New York, London. Macmillan. 1907.

CANNON, CORNELIA. "American Misgivings." *Atlantic Monthly.* (February, 1922, Vol. 129, pp. 145-57.)

CARLYLE, THOMAS. "Democracy." *Past and Present.* London. Chapman and Hall. 1843.

CONKLIN, E. G. "Biology and Democracy." Scribner's Magazine. (April, 1919, Vol. 65, pp. 405-12.)

COX, HAROLD. "Changes in Land Ownership in England." *Atlantic Monthly.* (April, 1922, Vol. 129, pp. 556-62.)

CUTTEN, GEORGE B. "The Reconstruction of Democracy." *School and Society.* (October 28, 1922, Vol. 16, p. 477-89.)

DEMING, SEYMOUR. "This Distrust of Democracy." *Century Magazine.* (March, 1917, Vol. 93, pp. 785-90.)

DICKINSON, G. LOWES. "Democratic Control of Foreign Policy." *Atlantic Monthly.* (August, 1916, Vol. 118, p. 145.)

ELIOT, CHARLES W. "The Working of the American Democracy." "Family Stocks in a Democracy." "Some Reasons Why the American Republic May Endure." *American Contributions to Civilization.* New York. Century Co. 1898.

FRANKLIN, FABIAN. "Democracy and Liberty." *Unpopular Review.* (October, 1918, Vol. 10, p. 343.)

GODKIN, E. L. "An American View of Popular Government." *Nineteenth Century.* (February, 1886, Vol. 19, p. 177.) (Reply to Maine, *Popular Government.*)

"The Real Problems of Democracy." *Atlantic Monthly.* (July, 1896, Vol. 78, p. 1.)

GRAHAM, E. K. "Culture and Commercialism." *Education and Citizenship and Other Papers.* New York and London. G. P. Putnam's Sons. 1919.

HART, ALBERT BUSHNELL. "The Hope of Democracy." *Representative Phi Beta Kappa Orations.* Boston. Houghton Mifflin. 1915.

HARPER, W. R. "The University and Democracy." *The Trend in Higher Education.* Chicago. The University of Chicago Press. 1905.

HENDERSON, HANFORD. "The Aristocratic Spirit." *North American Review.* (March, 1920, Vol. 211, pp. 387-401.)

HOBHOUSE, L. T. *Democracy and Reaction.* London. Fisher Unwin. 1904.

INGE, W. R. "Democracy and the Future." *Atlantic Monthly.* (March, 1922, Vol. 129, pp. 289-98.)

LAUGHLIN, J. LAURENCE. "Business and Democracy." *Atlantic Monthly.* (July, 1915, Vol. 116, p. 89.)

LECKY, W. E. H. *Democracy and Liberty.* Two vols. London. Longmans, Green and Co. 1896.

LEE, JOSEPH. "Democracy and the Expert." *Atlantic Monthly.* (November, 1908, Vol. 102, pp. 611-20.)

LOWELL, JAMES RUSSELL. "Democracy." *Democracy and Other Papers.* Boston. Houghton Mifflin. 1898.

MAINE, HENRY SUMNER. "The Prospects of Popular Government." *Popular Government.* London. J. Murray. 1897.

"The Prospects of Popular Government" is reprinted in Steeves and Ristine, *Representative Essays in Modern Thought.* New York. American Book Company. 1913.

"Mr. Godkin on Popular Government." *Nineteenth Century.* (March, 1886, Vol. 19, p. 366.)

MILL, JOHN STUART. "True and False Democracy." *Representative Government.* New York. E. P. Dutton and Co. 1905.

MORLEY, JOHN. "Maine on Popular Government." *Studies in Literature.* London and New York. Macmillan. 1891.

"Lecky on Democracy." "Democracy and Reaction." *Critical Miscellanies.* New York. Macmillan. 1898.

MURRAY, S. L. "Aristocracy and Democracy." *Nineteenth Century.* (March, 1921, Vol. 89, p. 521.)

PERRY, R. B. "What Do We Mean by Democracy?" *International Journal of Ethics.* (July, 1918, Vol. 28, p. 449.)

ROOT, ELIHU. "The Effect of Democracy on International Law." *Proceedings American Society of International Law.* 1917. Vol. 2, p. 11. Reprinted, American Association for International Conciliation. Paper No. 117, August, 1917.

ROSS, E. A. "The Middle West: A Reassertion of Democracy." *Century Magazine.* (March, 1912, Vol. 83, pp. 686-92.) Reprinted, *Changing America.* New York. Century Co. 1912.

SHARP, DALLAS LORE. "Patrons of Democracy." *Atlantic Monthly.* (November, 1919, Vol. 124, pp. 649-60.)

SHOWERMAN, GRANT. "The Making of a Democrat." *Yale Review.* (January, 1912, Vol. 1, pp. 221-34.)

SICHEL, WALTER. "Monarchy and Democracy." *Nineteenth Century.* (June, 1917, Vol. 81, pp. 1225-32.)

TOCQUEVILLE, ALEXIS DE. *Democracy in America.* New York. D. Appleton and Co. 1904.

TURNER, F. J. "Western Contributions to Democracy." *Atlantic Monthly.* (January, 1903, Vol. 91, p. 83.) Reprinted, *The Frontier in American History.* New York. Henry Holt. 1920.

SOME TOPICS FOR THE DISCUSSION OF DEMOCRACY

Are fraternities democratic? Democracy on the campus. Why do colleges seem to grow less democratic as they grow older? The effect of college traditions upon college democracy. What effect does the location of a college have upon its democracy? Should student self-support receive special consideration from instructors as an encouragement of democracy? Why are so many heroes of democracy men who were born poor? Democracy and efficiency. The failure of democracy in cities. Commission government or city-manager plan as an aid to democracy. Effects of the party system upon democracy. Effects of democracy upon literature and art. The meaning of the democratic doctrine of equality. Democracy and mediocrity. The political boss in a democracy. The function of the expert in a democracy. Democracy and war. Democracy in the control of foreign relations. Democracy and free land. Democracy and liberty. Do scholars as a class distrust democracy? Our constitution and democracy. What did the framers of our government think of democracy? Is popular government likely to endure? Democracy in Switzerland. Democracy in England. Democracy and Bolshevism. The democratic contempt for excellence. Contributions of an aristocracy to the public taste. How much independence may be exercised by the representatives of the people in a democracy? Is a property qualification for voting undemocratic? Is an educational qualification for voting undemocratic? Majority rule. Democracy in the city-states. Some differences between ancient and modern democracies. How have decisions upon great public issues been reached in America? Have decisions upon public questions in America warranted a faith in democracy? Are the political ideas dominant in America the ideas of the average man? The psychological attack upon democracy. The services of corporations to democracy. Effect of inheritance laws upon democracy. Effect of democracy upon manners. Family stocks in a democracy. Are we a democracy? Democracy and child labor. Democracy and education. Leadership in a democracy. Germanic statecraft and democracy. Monarchy and democracy. The New England town meeting. Public opinion in a democracy. Influence of the West on democracy. Proportional representation.

LIBERTY OF THOUGHT AND DISCUSSION

QUESTIONS ON
THE BASIS OF TOLERATION

By Walter Bagehot

1. Illustrate our dislike for strange beliefs or manners. [*Page* 123.]
2. Show that persecution which silences alleged error does not create positive belief. Take the case of the attempt to suppress the teaching of evolution, for example. [*Page* 124.]
3. Would Bagehot's argument that the State power should not be used to arrest discussion hold against suppressions in war time? [*Page* 125.]
4. Illustrate by reference to a change of public opinion on some question, Bagehot's statement of the process by which truth wins in a discussion. See Ross, *Discussion*, p. 471 of this volume. [*Page* 125.]
5. Make a statement of some benefits of persecution. [*Page* 126.]
6. "Early ages need a coercive despotism more than they need anything else." Would this justify the careers of Frederick the Great, or Bismarck? [*Page* 126.]
7. "Every parent wisely teaches his child his own creed." Why compel familiarity with a creed which will probably be outgrown? [*Page* 126.]
8. "No man is on all points so wise as the mass of men after a good discussion." Why? Compare this with the statement of George William Curtis that "A crowd is not wiser than the wisest man in it." [*Page* 127.]
9. Is the perpetual flux of opinion a valid argument against making any opinion the basis of coercion? [*Page* 127.]
10. Bagehot commends the tolerance of the British government in India. Do the natives agree? [*Page* 128.]
11. Would you permit a mass meeting of Filipinos to discuss their independence, or of striking miners to consider their grievances? Are they "able to bear discussion"? Could Bagehot's theory be made a defense of intolerance? [*Page* 128.]
12. What of Bagehot's second reservation as to tolerance, that "no government is bound to permit a controversy which will annihilate itself"? What suppressions might be justified by it? [*Page* 128.]

13. Do you have any ideas which are "not the result of an investigation consciously pursued, but the effect of a multiplicity of facts involuntarily presented"? Are such ideas especially liable to become the basis of persecution? [*Page* 131.]

14. What contributions to society are made by the men with "attractive voice but limited mind"? [*Page* 134.]

15. Why does Bagehot illustrate his theories about moral and religious persecution with "parables" concerning "æsthetical persecution"? [*Page* 135.]

16. Cite some specific case where you think the good life of a man whose beliefs were thought bad should have produced greater toleration. In such a case what distinction would you make between a man and his teaching? [*Page* 137.]

QUESTIONS ON *WHAT MODERN LIBERTY MEANS*
BY WALTER LIPPMANN

1. "From our recent experience it is clear that the traditional liberties of speech and opinion rest on no solid foundation." Illustrate with specific cases. See Chaffee, *Freedom of Speech*. New York. Harcourt, Brace and Co. 1920. [*Page* 138.]

2. "The goal is never liberty, but liberty for something or other." How real is the anti-prohibitionist's concern for liberty as an absolute ideal? [*Page* 139.]

3. "Liberty is to be permitted where differences are of no great moment." Is our "modern religious toleration," really toleration or indifference? [*Page* 142.]

4. "In times when men feel themselves secure, heresy is cultivated as the spice of life." Illustrate. Does this explain "parlor Bolshevism?" [*Page* 142.]

5. "Nine tenths of the effort to live and let live consists in proving that the thing we wish to have tolerated is really a matter of indifference." How is this statement illustrated in the controversies between "modernists" and "fundamentalists"? [*Page* 142.]

6. "The arguments of this staunch apostle of liberty can be used honestly, and in fact are used, to justify the bulk of the suppressions which have recently occurred." How is it that ideas of liberty entertained by judges result in decisions and injunctions that are attacked as acts of suppression? [*Page* 143.]

7. For fuller understanding of the reference to Bertrand Russell, see the last chapter of *Why Men Fight,* especially p. 356. New York. Century Co. 1917. Does it seem to be true that Mr. Russell, "like every authoritarian who has preceded him, is interested in the unfettered development of only that which seems good to him"? [*Page* 144.]

8. "The public, when it is dependent upon testimony and is protected by no rules of evidence, can act only upon the excitement of its pugnacities and its hopes." Was this illustrated at the time of our declaration of war with Spain? Why is trained judgment in the use of evidence necessary for the preservation of liberty? See Dickinson Miller, "Democracy and Our Intellectual Plight." *New Republic.* (June 21, 1922, Vol. 31, p. 93.) [*Pages* 144-145.]

9. Why is "the task of selecting and ordering news one of the truly sacred and priestly offices in a democracy"? [*Page* 148.]

10. The attempt to draw fine distinctions between 'liberty' and 'license' . . . consists in trying to make opinion responsible to prevailing social standards, whereas the really important thing is to try and make opinion increasingly responsible to the facts." Make this distinction clear by applying it to some question at issue in the public mind; for example, Bolshevism in Russia. [*Page* 153.]

11. "In this view liberty is the name we give to measures by which we protect and increase the veracity of the information upon which we act." To what extent is the problem of liberty of opinion independent of the problem of "veracity of information"? [*Page* 155.]

12. Discuss the practical remedies offered by Mr. Lippmann in "Liberty and the News." *Atlantic Monthly.* (December, 1919, Vol. 124, p. 779.) Also in volume entitled *Liberty and the News.* New York. Harcourt and Brace. 1920.

SUGGESTIONS FOR FURTHER READING ON LIBERTY OF THOUGHT AND DISCUSSION

ANGELL, NORMAN. "Freedom of Discussion in War Time." *Annals of the American Academy.* (July, 1918, Vol. 78, p. 194.)

BAGEHOT, WALTER. "The Age of Discussion." *Physics and Politics.* New York. D. Appleton and Co. 1873.

BARROWS, DAVID P. "Academic Freedom." *School and Society.* (April 17, 1920, Vol. 11, p. 451.)

BELL, B. I. "The Danger of Tolerance in Religion." *Atlantic Monthly.* (July, 1914, Vol. 114, p. 92.)

BEVERIDGE, A. J. "The Assault upon American Fundamentals." *Reports of the American Bar Association.* 1920. Baltimore. The Lord Baltimore Press. 1920.

BOURNE, RANDOLPH. "Dodging the Pressures." *Youth and Life.* Boston. Houghton Mifflin. 1913.

BRYCE, JAMES. "The Tyranny of the Majority." *American Commonwealth.* (Vol. 2, p. 85.) New York. Macmillan. 1896.

CHAFFEE, Z. *Freedom of Speech.* New York. Harcourt, Brace and Co. 1920.

CREEL, GEORGE. "Public Opinion in War Time." *Annals of the American Academy.* (July, 1918, Vol. 78, p. 185.)

ELIOT, CHARLES W. "Academic Freedom." *Representative Phi Beta Kappa Orations.* Boston. Houghton Mifflin. 1915.

FRANKLIN, FABIAN. "Some Free Speech Delusions." *Unpopular Review.* (October, 1914, Vol. 2, p. 223.)

HACKETT, FRANCIS. "The Invisible Censor." *New Republic.* (December 3, 1919, Vol. 21, p. 11.)

HALL, JAMES P. "Free Speech in War Time." *University of Chicago Record.* April, 1921. New Series. (Vol. 7, p. 75.)

JAMES, WILLIAM. "The True Harvard." *Memories and Studies.* New York. Longmans, Green and Co. 1911.

JOHNSON, ALVIN. "The Soul of Capitalism." *Unpopular Review.* (June, 1914, Vol. 1, p. 227.)

LIPPMANN, WALTER. "Liberty and the News." *Atlantic Monthly.* (December, 1919, Vol. 124, p. 779. Reprinted in *Liberty and the News.* New York. Harcourt, Brace and Co. 1920.)

MACY, JOHN. "Journalism." *Civilization in the United States.* Edited by Harold Stearns. New York. Harcourt, Brace and Co. 1922.

MCCRACKEN, J. H. "Liberty and Co-operation." *College and Commonwealth.* New York. Century Co. 1920.

MILL, JOHN STUART. *On Liberty.* London. Longmans, Green and Co. 1865.

MILTON, JOHN. *Areopagitica.* Cambridge. Cambridge University Press. 1918.

PERRY, RALPH BARTON. "The University and the Individual." *The Free Man and the Soldier.* New York. C. Scribner's Sons. 1916.

POLLOCK, FREDERICK. "The Theory of Persecution." *Essays in Ethics and Jurisprudence.* London. Macmillan. 1882.

ROSS, E. A. "Discussion." *Social Psychology.* New York. Macmillan. 1908. (Chap. 18.)

ROOT, R. K. "The Virtue of Intolerance." *Atlantic Monthly.* (March, 1920, Vol. 125, p. 385.)

RUSSELL, BERTRAND. *Free Thought and Official Propaganda.* New York. Huebsch. 1922.

SCHROEDER, THEODORE. *Constitutional Free Speech.* New York. Free Speech League. 1919.

STEPHEN, JAMES FITZ JAMES. *Liberty, Equality and Fraternity.* London. Smith, Elder and Co. 1873. (See especially chapter 2 for reply to Mill, *On Liberty.*)

THOMAS, NORMAN. *The Conscientious Objector in America.* New York. Huebsch. 1924.

TOCQUEVILLE, ALEXIS DE. *Democracy in America.* New York. D. Appleton and Co. 1904. (See especially Vol. 1, chaps. 11, 12, 15, 16. Vol. 2, chaps. 5, 6, 7.)

WALLAS, GRAHAM. "The Price of Intolerance." *Atlantic Monthly.* (January, 1920, Vol. 125, p. 116.)

Our Social Heritage. New Haven. Yale University Press. 1921. (Chap. 7.)

SOME TOPICS FOR THE DISCUSSION OF LIBERTY OF THOUGHT AND DISCUSSION

Should any books recognized as literature be suppressed? Should school histories which are lacking in patriotism be suppressed? Conscientious objectors. Should expressions of sympathy with strikers or agitators be allowed? President Lincoln's attitude toward freedom of discussion in war time. President Wilson's attitude toward freedom of discussion in war time. The Debs case. Toleration and indifference. Education for intolerance. Education for tolerance. Toleration in war time. Deportation of radicals. Alien and Sedition laws. The tyranny of the majority. Censorship of the press. Censorship of amusements. Academic freedom. Specific cases of violation of academic freedom. Amnesty for political prisoners. The work of George Creel in the war. The work of Senator Lusk. The work of Anthony Comstock. The intolerance of reformers. The intolerance of vested interests. The scientific spirit and the growth of tolerance. Services of violent and faulty minds in public discussion. Liberty and co-operation. Loyalty and liberty. The legal profession as a guardian of liberty. Trial by jury as a guaranty of liberty. Local self-government and liberty. Government ownership of mines and railways and its effect on liberty. Liberty and equality. Justifiable coercion in morals and religion. Capitalism as an agent of moral and religious toleration. Effects of organizations and societies on liberty. Student traditions as organized intolerance. Radicalism and social standing in universities. American and European university students as free thinkers. The censorship of convention. The revolt of the younger generation. Self-determination of small nations in relation to liberty. Influence of liberty on taste. Why a conservative should welcome freedom of discussion. Freedom of discussion as a preventive of violence. Intolerance in the last war compared with previous times. Labor legislation and personal liberty. The eighteenth amendment and personal liberty. Changing conception of liberty. The Supreme Court as a guardian of liberty. Elective system of studies and personal liberty. Freedom and responsibility. Freedom and free land.

ECONOMIC SOCIETY

QUESTIONS ON
THE SOCIAL PLAINT

By Elisha Benjamin Andrews

1. Is it true that "Individuals are only in the rarest instances to blame. for any ills from which society may suffer"? [*Page* 159.]
2. If suffering on account of laziness is a social good, what of minimum wage laws, old age pensions, and governmental remedies for unemployment? [*Page* 160.]
3. Does our moral sense object to "accidental or artificial advantages" when they are used for public welfare, as for instance, large gifts for libraries, museums, universities, and hospitals? [*Page* 160.]
4. "Conveyance of one's thought across this continent in an hour, and of one's body in a week, was formerly deemed impossible. Poverty may yet disappear." Does this analogy strengthen the hope? [*Page* 160.]
5. (a) "Many men are rich, either altogether without economic merit, or wholly out of proportion to their economic merit." (b) "A great many men are poor without the slightest economic demerit." Are these two propositions causally related? [*Pages* 161 *and* 164.]
6. What are the social benefits of speculation? [*Page* 162.]
7. Are poets, musicians, novelists, lawyers, preachers, actors, historians, creators of social wealth? [*Page* 162.]
8. Describe the process of "freezing out" small stockholders; forming sub-corporations to secure all the profits of main corporations under forms of law; creating artificial "corners." [*Page* 162.]
9. How do monopolies arise in a "natural way"? [*Page* 162.]
10. How does it hurt society to have the unearned increment of land values go to private individuals? [*Page* 164.]
11. Why is it that "in a vast majority of cases the taker of pure economic rent earns nothing"? [*Page* 164.]
12. What are some of the remedies proposed for the fluctuations in the purchasing power of money? [*Page* 164.]
13. What "curses" as well as "blessings" have been wrought by "the extreme division of labor"? [*Page* 165.]

14. The statistics cited in this essay are old. What effect upon the con-
    clusions of the speaker will it have if more recent figures are sub-
    stituted? [*Pages* 165-166.]
15. "In many respects, indeed, the toiling masses are no whit better off
    today than in England four centuries ago." In what respects?
    [*Page* 168.]
16. "From this point of view, the wages-system itself, inevitable as it
    after all seems to be, is yet an evil, at least in comparison with the
    older one of masters, associates, and apprentices." Does guild
    socialism offer a remedy for the evils of the wage system? [*Page*
    170.]
17. "If you are verdant enough still to speak of the 'dignity of labor,'
    people smile at you. That old aphorism has gone to the rubbish
    pile." Is it possible to have a stable society without a belief in
    the dignity of labor? [*Page* 170.]
18. "Trade-unions often operate against one another, and they continually
    keep down instead of elevating the unskilled masses." Should
    trade-unions therefore be abolished? [*Page* 171.]
19. What is the *laissez faire* theory of society? [*Page* 171.]
20. Should "needlessly large houses and grounds" be condemned? [*Page*
    171.]
21. "The best men in a trade do not fix its maxims and practices, but the
    worst." Why? [*Page* 173.]

QUESTIONS ON *EDUCATION AND THE SOCIALIST MOVEMENT*
By JOHN BATES CLARK

1. Is Cleveland's hope that universities would bar the progress of revolutionary doctrines being realized in your institution? [*Page* 175.]
2. What signs are there of an alliance between intelligence and discontented labor? [*Page* 175.]
3. Does Clark's admission of the attractiveness of the socialistic ideal
   seem to be a genuine concession or merely a tactful introduction?
   [*Page* 176.]
4. Would the great increase in interest in political contests predicted by
   Clark in the socialist state be an unmixed evil? [*Page* 179.]
5. Is there any way out of the differences in the desirability of labor?
   What bearing did the Brook Farm experiment have on this? Is
   there any hope in machine industry? [*Page* 179.]
6. "The pursuit of wealth now furnishes the outlet for the overmastering
   ambition of many persons." How is the pursuit of wealth a source
   of public tranquillity? [*Page* 179.]
7. Give examples of the effect of bureaucracy on "technical progress."
   Does capitalism offer no checks to such progress? [*Page* 181.]

8. "Easily, naturally, painlessly, the great accretions of capital come; mainly by advances in technical operations in production." Who should benefit most by accretions of capital due to advances in technical operation and production? [*Page* 183.]
9. "One may not affirm with positiveness that the worst form of Malthusianism would actually operate under socialism; but there would be danger of this." How do dangers of Malthusianism threaten socialistic reforms? [*Page* 184.]
10. Does Clark seem to be overly hopeful about the progress of society as at present organized? [*Page* 188.]

Suggestions for Further Reading on Economic Society

CARVER, T. N. "Four Labor Programs." *Quarterly Journal of Economics*. (February, 1919, Vol. 33, pp. 334-67.)
"How Wealth Ought to be Distributed." "The Question of Inheritance." "The Responsibility of the Rich for the Condition of the Poor." *Essays in Social Justice*. Cambridge. Harvard University Press. 1915.

CATCHINGS, W. "Our Common Enterprise." *Atlantic Monthly*. (February, 1922, Vol. 129, pp. 218-29.)

CLARK, J. M. "The Empire of Machines." *Yale Review*. (October, 1922, Vol. 12, pp. 132-44.)

ELIOT, C. W. "Present Disadvantages of Rich Men." *American Contributions to Civilization*. New York. Century Co. 1898.

FAIRCHILD, H. P. "Can the Wage System Last?" *Unpartizan Review*. (July, 1920, Vol. 14, pp. 14-34.)

FRANKLIN, FABIAN. "Social Untruth and Social Unrest." *Unpopular Review*. (April, 1914, Vol. 1, pp. 252-71.)

FREY, J. P. "The Ideals in the American Labor Movement." *International Journal of Ethics*. (July, 1918, Vol. 28, pp. 485-98.)

GEORGE, HENRY. *Progress and Poverty*. Garden City, New York. Doubleday, Page and Co. 1915.

HADLEY, A. T. "The Ethics of Corporate Management." *Standards of Public Morality*. New York. Macmillan. 1912. Reprinted, Steeves and Ristine. *Representative Essays in Modern Thought*. American Book Co., New York. 1913.
Economic Problems of Democracy. New York. Macmillan. 1923.

HAMILTON, W. H. *Current Economic Problems*. Chicago. The University of Chicago Press. 1919.

HOLT, HENRY. "The New Irrepressible Conflict." *Unpopular Review*. (January, 1914, Vol. 1, p. 1.)
"Labor, Law and Order." *Unpopular Review*. (October, 1915, Vol. 4, pp. 374-97.)

JOHNSON, ALVIN. "Endowment for the State." *Atlantic Monthly*. (January, 1915, Vol. 115, pp. 25-35.)

"The Soul of Capitalism." *Unpopular Review*. (April, 1914, Vol. 1, p. 227.)

"The War—By an Economist." *Unpopular Review*. (October, 1914, Vol. 2, pp. 420-8.)

"Unsocial Investments." *Unpopular Review*. (July, 1914, Vol. 2, p. 1.)

KNOLLENBERG, B. "Reflections on the Income Tax." *Atlantic Monthly*. (July, 1920, Vol. 126, p. 112.)

MALLOCK, W. H. *Property and Progress*. New York. G. P. Putnam's Sons. 1884. (Reply to Henry George.)

MATHER, F. J. "Minor Uses of the Middling Rich." *Unpopular Review*. (July, 1914, Vol. 2, pp. 104-15.)

MERRIT, W. G. "Thoughts on Industrial Peace." *Unpopular Review*. (April, 1919, Vol. 11, pp. 364-78.)

"Social Control of Industrial Strife." *Unpartizan Review*. (January, 1921, Vol. 15, p. 1.)

"Organized Labor and Democracy." *Unpopular Review*. (April, 1916, Vol. 5, pp. 254-75.)

MORRIS, WM. *True and False Society*. Collected Works of William Morris. New York and London. Longmans, Green and Co. 1915. Vol. 23, pp. 215-237. Originally published under the title of *The Labour Question from the Socialist Standpoint*. Claims of Labour Lectures, No. 5. Edinburgh. Co-operative Printing Co. 1886. Reprinted under original title, Steeves and Ristine. *Representative Essays in Modern Thought*. New York. American Book Co. 1913.

MOULTON, H. G. "The Rising Tide of Social Unrest." *Yale Review*. (October, 1919, Vol. 9, pp. 1-16.)

ORTH, S. P. "Germany, a Model or a Warning." *World's Work*. (July, 1913, Vol. 26, p. 315.)

POUND, ARTHUR. *The Iron Man in Industry*. Boston. The Atlantic Monthly Press. 1922.

ROSS, E. A. *Sin and Society*. Boston. Houghton Mifflin. 1907.

RUSSELL, BERTRAND. "Industry in Undeveloped Countries." *Atlantic Monthly*. (July, 1920, Vol. 126, p. 112.)

SLICHTER, S. H. "Industrial Morale." *Quarterly Journal of Economics*. (November, 1920, Vol. 35, pp. 36-60.)

SLOSSON, P. "Is Socialism Coming?" *Unpopular Review*. (October, 1914, Vol. 2, pp. 236-47.)

SPARGO, JOHN. *Socialism*. New York. Macmillan. 1906.

VEBLEN, T. *The Engineers and the Price System*. New York. Huebsch. 1921.

The Theory of the Leisure Class. New York. Macmillan. 1899.

Some Topics for the Discussion of Economic Society

Competition. Unemployment. Trade unions. Minimum wage. Old age pensions. Mothers' pensions. Collective bargaining. Open and closed shop. Compulsory arbitration. Strikes in basic industries. Child labor. Women in industry. Employer's liability laws. Co-operative marketing. A merchant marine. Protective tariffs. Free trade. Inheritance taxes. Specialization. Machine industry. The business cycle. Speculation. Occupational diseases. Fatigue. The living wage. Large scale production. Freedom of contract. Injunctions in labor disputes. Profit-sharing. Class legislation. Imperialism. The distribution of wealth. Vocational education. The British Labor Party. The American Federation of Labor. The I. W. W. The growth of cities. The single tax. Unearned increments. Poverty. Corporations. Government regulation or ownership. Interlocking directorates. Panics. The Federal Reserve System. The balance of trade. Sabotage. The income tax. The passing of the frontier. Scientific management.

EDUCATION

QUESTIONS ON
EDUCATION FOR EFFICIENCY

By Eugene Davenport

1. Why must universal education contain a large element of the vocational? [*Page* 193.]
2. "Within the limits of needful activities one occupation is as important as another, and a system of universal education must enrich them all." Why then should it be supposed that some studies have more value or dignity than others? [*Page* 193.]
3. Why should poetry and sculpture be included among the useful activities? [*Page* 194.]
4. If we cannot tell "whether food or religion is the more essential to human life; or whether art or industry contributes most to its fullest development," what basis is there for a distinction between the liberal and the vocational? [*Page* 194.]
5. "Such plans and policies [of education] must be observed as shall prevent social cleavage along vocational lines." Does this involve a leveling downward? [*Page* 195.]
6. "The best results will always follow when as many subjects as possible and as many vocations as may be are taught together in the same school." Does this mean that the university is more effective for all educational purposes than the small college? Is it true that a college of liberal arts in a university gains from having among its students many who are primarily interested in the professional schools? [*Page* 195.]
7. Davenport is arguing for "a single system of schools adapted to the education of all classes." Should privately endowed colleges regard themselves as a part of this system? Should college entrance requirements dominate public education, or vice versa; or is some third course possible? [*Page* 195.]
8. "The truth is, there is no such thing as a 'general education,' except one that fits for nothing in particular. . . . In so far as this type of general education exists among us, the quicker we abolish it the better." What is to be done with the large mass of students who do not know what they want to be fitted for? [*Page* 195.]

9. Does the fact (if it be a fact) that most students in the college of arts and sciences are taking their courses for professional purposes, prove that the courses in arts and sciences are not by nature general and non-technical? [*Page* 196.]

10. "The old-line courses were as distinctly vocational to the learned professions as are the newer courses to the industrial occupations." Does this justify the abolition of all distinction between the "old-line courses" and the "newer courses"? [*Page* 197.]

11. What would be gained by breaking down the tradition of "set courses of study four years long"? [*Page* 198.]

12. What is the difference between studying *subjects* and studying *courses?* [*Page* 198.]

13. "Either the high schools will expand and teach the vocational, or other schools will be established that will do it." Which is to be preferred? [*Page* 199.]

14. "In a very large sense the land-grant university is the model for the public high school." What should distinguish the university from the high school? Is there sufficient distinction at present? [*Page* 200.]

15. Is it true that the school should be "a true picture of life outside in all its essential activities"? [*Page* 200.]

16. Is it "dangerous to attempt to educate a live boy with no reference to the vocational"? [*Page* 201.]

17. Is it an evil that college courses should be "planned and conducted almost solely in the interest of the few who graduate"? [*Page* 202.]

18. Is the analogy between education and "a trunk line railroad without side switches or way stations, but with splendid terminal facilities," a sound one? Would you "reconstruct the policy of the system by making all trains local, both to take on and leave off passengers"? [*Page* 203.]

19. Is it true that "the common man with an opportunity is a common man no longer"? [*Page* 206.]

20. What are the difficulties in attempting "to teach all subjects to all men in the same school"? [*Page* 207.]

21. Would you "have it so that the occupation of an American citizen may not be known by his dress, his manner, his speech, or his prejudices"? [*Page* 207.]

22. "The State universities were established primarily to teach the branches of knowledge related especially to the industries of life." What effect has this had upon them? [*Page* 208.]

23. Is it true that "the enduring things will always be the useful things"? [*Page* 208.]

QUESTIONS ON *THE THEORY OF THE LIBERAL COLLEGE*
BY ALEXANDER MEIKLEJOHN

1. Does the teacher "stand before his pupils and before the community at large as the intellectual leader of his time"? [*Page* 209.]
2. Is the college "first of all, a place of the mind"? [*Page* 210.]
3. Should the liberal college leave special and technical training to other schools, or should the liberal and the vocational be combined in every educational institution? [*Page* 211.]
4. What does Meiklejohn mean when he says the technical school furnishes training which is not intellectual but practical? [*Page* 211.]
5. Why should college teachers be unwilling to cut up their sciences into segments and to allow students to select those segments which may be of service in the practice of an art or a profession? [*Page* 212.]
6. Why is a liberal college not a practical institution? [*Page* 212.]
7. Is there any reason why a liberal college, as Meiklejohn conceives it, should be supported by public taxation?
8. Why have state universities had more of the vocational in their courses than privately endowed institutions?
9. Do you agree that the making of friends, the improvement of manners, and the development of character are not the chief concern of the liberal college? [*Page* 212.]
10. What is meant by the ignorant pursuit of knowledge? [*Page* 213.]
11. Why are knowledge and thinking good in themselves? [*Page* 213.]
12. Is it true that those who have no time for the joys of the mind are relatively dull and stupid? [*Page* 214.]
13. To what extent is it true that "actions become more successful as they pass from the sphere of feeling to that of understanding"? [*Page* 216.]
14. What are the distinguishing characteristics of technical, professional, and liberal training? [*Page* 216.]
15. Discuss the belief that it makes no difference in what department of knowledge a student studies? [*Page* 219.]
16. What are the principal arguments for and against the elective system? [*Page* 219.]
17. Why is it that "when a man minds his own business because he does not know any other business," he does not really understand his own affairs? [*Page* 222.]
18. What ranges of information "have virtually no significance for the purposes of a liberal education"? [*Page* 223.]

Suggestions for Further Reading on Education

ADAMS, CHARLES FRANCIS. *Three Phi Beta Kappa Addresses.* Boston. Houghton Mifflin. 1907.

ADAMS, CHARLES KENDALL. "The Relations of Higher Education to National Prosperity." *Representative Phi Beta Kappa Orations.* Boston. Houghton Mifflin. 1915.

ARNOLD, MATTHEW. "Sweetness and Light." *Culture and Anarchy.* New York. Macmillan. 1902.

BALFOUR, A. J. "The Pleasures of Reading." *Essays and Addresses.* Edinburgh. D. Douglas. 1893. Reprinted, *Rectorial Addresses of the University of St. Andrews.* London. A. and C. Black. 1894. Reprinted, *Modern Eloquence.* New York. University Society. 1900. Vol. 7. (A reply to Frederic Harrison's "The Choice of Books.")

BIRGE, E. A. "A Change of Educational Emphasis." *Atlantic Monthly.* (February, 1909, Vol. 103, pp. 189-200.)

BOURNE, RANDOLPH. "The College: An Undergraduate View." *Atlantic Monthly.* (November, 1911, Vol. 108, pp. 667-74.)

BUTLER, NICHOLAS MURRAY. *Scholarship and Service.* New York. C. Scribner's Sons. 1921.

CAIRD, JOHN. *University Addresses.* Glasgow. James MacLehose and Sons. 1899.

COOPER, LANE. *Two Views of Education.* New Haven. Yale University Press. 1922.

DAVENPORT, EUGENE. *Education for Efficiency.* Boston. D. C. Heath. 1909.

DRAPER, A. S. *American Education.* Boston. Houghton Mifflin. 1909.

ELIOT, CHARLES W. "The New Definition of the Cultivated Man." *Education for Efficiency.* Boston. Houghton Mifflin. 1909.
Educational Reform. New York. Century Co. 1898.

FULTON, M. G. *College Life, Its Conditions and Problems.* New York. Macmillan. 1915.

GILMAN, D. C. "Characteristics of a University." *University Problems in the United States.* New York. Century Co. 1898.

HADLEY, A. T. "The Relation Between Higher Education and the Public Welfare. *The Education of the American Citizen.* New York. C. Scribner's Sons. 1902.
"What is Education?" *Harper's Monthly.* (December, 1922, Vol. 146, pp. 13-22.)

HARPER, WILLIAM R. "Coeducation." "The Situation of the Small College." *The Trend in Higher Education.* Chicago. University of Chicago Press. 1905.

HARRISON, FREDERICK. "The Choice of Books." *The Choice of Books and Other Literary Pieces*. London. Macmillan. 1886. Reprinted, *Modern Eloquence*, Vol. 5.

HUDSON, J. W. *The College and New America*. New York and London. D. Appleton. 1920.

HUXLEY, T. H. "Science and Culture." "A Liberal Education." *Collected Essays*. Vol. 3. New York and London. D. Appleton. 1896.

HYDE, W. D. *The College Man and the College Woman*. Boston. Houghton Mifflin. 1906.

LOWELL, A. L. "Competition in College." *Atlantic Monthly*. (June, 1909, Vol. 103, pp. 822-31.)

MEIKLEJOHN, A. "The College in the Next Hundred Years." *Amherst Graduates' Quarterly*. (August, 1921.)
The Liberal College. Boston. Marshall Jones. 1920.
Freedom and the College. New York. Century Co. 1923.

NEWMAN, JOHN HENRY. "Knowledge Viewed in Relation to Learning." *The Idea of a University*. New York and London. Longmans, Green and Co. 1902.

OSBORN, HENRY F. *Huxley and Education*. New York. C. Scribner's Sons. 1910.

PAGE, WALTER HINES. "The Cultivated Man in an Industrial Era." *University of Chicago Record*. (June, 1904, Vol. 9, pp. 48-55.) Reprinted, *World's Work*. (July, 1904, Vol. 8, pp. 4980-4985.)

PALMER, GEORGE HERBERT. "Doubts About University Extension." "Erroneous Limitations of the Elective System." "Necessary Limits of the Elective System." "Specialization." *The Teacher*. Boston. Houghton Mifflin. 1908.

RUSSELL, BERTRAND. "The Place of Science in a Liberal Education." *Mysticism and Logic*. New York. Longmans, Green and Co. 1918.

SCHELLING, FELIX. "Humanities, Gone and To Come." *Representative Phi Beta Kappa Orations*. Boston. Houghton Mifflin. 1915.

SHARP, DALLAS LORE. "Education for Authority." *Atlantic Monthly*. (July, 1921, Vol. 128, pp. 13-21.)

WEST, A. F. "The Tutorial System in College." *American Liberal Education*. New York. C. Scribner's Sons. 1907.

WILSON, WOODROW. "What is a College For?" *Scribner's Magazine*. (November, 1909, Vol. 46, p. 570.) Reprinted, Rice, Richard. *College and the Future*. New York. C. Scribner's Sons. 1915. Reprinted, Fulton, M. G., *College Life*. New York. Macmillan. 1915.
"The Spirit of Learning." *Representative Phi Beta Kappa Orations*. Boston. Houghton Mifflin. 1915.

SOME TOPICS FOR THE DISCUSSION OF EDUCATION

The educational function of student activities. Is there too much or too little freedom in choice of studies in this institution? Is there too much or too little contact with instructors here? Are too many people in college? Should the federal government aid the public schools? What is a liberal education? What are the differences between a college and a university? General and professional education. Teaching as a profession. The junior college movement. Examinations. The lecture method. Required attendance upon classes. The honor system. The honors system. Differences between state and privately endowed universities. Effect of self-support upon a college course. The function of the scholar. The place of science in a liberal education. The classics. Vocational education. Intelligence tests. Fraternity life. Athletics as an educational agency. The elimination of unsatisfactory students. Phi Beta Kappa—or other honorary societies. Competition in college. The elective system. The alumni. American and English universities. American and German universities. French universities. What is pedantry? The social life of the campus. Coeducation. College spirit. Does the student of arts and sciences study less than the professional student? Agricultural education. Architectural education. Legal education. Engineering education. Medical education. Graduate study. When should specialization begin? A federal department of education with a secretary in the cabinet. Rural schools. Negro education in the South. Illiteracy in America. University extension. Exchange of scholars with foreign universities. German education. Prussianizing American education. Educative influence of books and nature. Self-education.

RELIGION

QUESTIONS ON
THE RELIGION OF THE FUTURE

By Charles W. Eliot

1. What have been the sources of religious authority? Attempt an estimate of some elements that will disappear from our lives as a result of the decline of authority. [*Page* 231.]

2. What do you understand by the term "Biblical criticism"? [*Page* 231.]

3. What does literature owe to "personification of the primitive forces of nature"? [*Page* 231.]

4. ". . . no identification of any human being, however majestic in character, with the Eternal Deity." Has this been a common feature of all religions? Can a religion be powerful without it? [*Page* 231.]

5. "Heretofore the great religions of the world have held out hopes of direct intervention of the deity in favor of his faithful worshippers." To what extent was this the case in the European War? [*Page* 232.]

6. What part has the personal welfare and safety of the individual played in the theological doctrines of the past? [*Page* 232.]

7. "The new religion will not teach that character is likely to be suddenly changed." Are the phenomena of conversion to be disregarded? See James, *Varieties of Religious Experience*. New York. Longmans, Green and Co. 1902. [*Page* 233.]

8. "It will teach that repentance wipes out nothing of the past and is only the first step toward reformation and a sign of a better future." Is this essentially a new doctrine? Relate it to the doctrine of purgatory? [*Page* 233.]

9. "It will not deal chiefly with sorrow and death, but with joy and life." Can such a religion satisfy? Does the growth of Christian Science seem to support Eliot? Can a religion which assigns a secondary place to consolation spread except among people who are relatively fortunate and happy? [*Page* 233.]

10. "He may not speculate on the origin of evil in general, but will surely try to discover the best way to eradicate the particular evil or

517

wrong he has recognized." Should a man's speculation about the origin of evil be satisfied by serving on a vice commission or a wage board? [*Page* 234.]

11. Can Eliot's "new thought of God" be made vital to uneducated people? Is that a consideration? [*Page* 234.]

12. Does it seem to be scientific reasoning to reject the conception that man tends downward by nature, because it is inconsistent with "a humane, civilized, or worthy idea of God"? [*Page* 235.]

13. "It will be an all-saints religion." Have religions of the past failed to "treasure up all tales of human excellence and virtue"? [*Page* 236.]

14. "In this simple and natural faith there will be no place for metaphysical complexities." Does this seem too simple? [*Page* 236.]

15. Can a religion without future compensation for the ills of this world exert any appreciable influence upon moral conduct? [*Pages* 236-237.]

16. "Its priests will be men especially interested in religious thought, possessing unusual gifts of speech on devotional subjects, and trained in the best methods of improving the social and industrial conditions of human life." Compare this with an older conception of the "call to the ministry." [*Page* 237.]

17. "Such promises of future blessedness have done infinite mischief in the world." Illustrate. [*Page* 238.]

18. "That surgeon is one of the ministers of the new religion." How if he have only a scientific interest in the problem before him? [*Page* 238.]

19. For human ills the new religion will offer "the consolation of being one's self wiser and tenderer than before." Can this suffice for more than the few exceptional natures? [*Page* 240.]

20. "Self-sacrifice is not a good or a merit in itself." Why has self-sacrifice been enjoined by religious teachers? [*Page* 241.]

21. ". . . a virtue which is comparatively new in the world—the love of truth and the passion for seeking it." Have we any evidence that this virtue is becoming more common? Is it chiefly fostered by science? [*Page* 242.]

22. "But it will doubtless have symbols." What part has symbolism played in religion? [*Page* 243.]

QUESTIONS ON *WHAT IS THE ATTITUDE OF COLLEGE STUDENTS TOWARDS ORGANIZED RELIGION* BY ALBERT PARKER FITCH

1. Do you believe that "it is not so much the intrinsic worth of organized religion as it is its by-product of stability, comfort, and professional security which endears it to its defenders"? [*Page* 248.]

2. Does age seem to demand more of youth in the way of intellectual and moral docility than it, itself, is prepared to give? [*Page* 248.]

3. "A community of young people strives on the whole toward higher standards of thought and conduct than does the armored and respectable middle age around it." See Aristotle's *Rhetoric*, Book 2, Chapter 12, on youth and age. Jebb translation. Cambridge University Press. 1919. Why should age be troubled about the morality of youth? [*Page* 248.]

4. Do most of the undergraduates who are connected with organized religion fall under the classification into natural conformists, institutionalists, humanitarians? [*Pages* 249-252.]

5. "They take refuge from the difficulties of thought in the opportunities of action." Explain. [*Page* 253.]

6. What does it mean to be at least capable of religious experience? [*Page* 253.]

7. "They are more vulgar than vicious." Explain the distinction. [*Page* 253.]

8. What percentage of students whom you know would come under Fitch's classification of "modern pagans"? What is paganism? [*Page* 253.]

9. "There are speculative, mystical, and æsthetic values in religious truth which do not enter into scientific observation of fact." What relation have these truths to poetry? [*Page* 255.]

10. "Able youth are sent to college believing that the truth of religion stands or falls with historical accuracy of the gospel narrative." Explain how it may be possible to separate the two. Is the historical accuracy of the gospel narrative as important as the history of the institution founded on it? [*Page* 255.]

11. "They are aware how far contemporary psychological and social science has advanced beyond the consciousness of most preachers." Why is the "consciousness of preachers" in arrears, if it is? Does the scientist see more, or less, of life than the religionist? [*Page* 256.]

12. If "both the theory and the practice of our imperialistic and ruthlessly competitive society" are "inconsistent with the ethics of Jesus," how is it that "the laity support the churches quite as much for social and economic as for religious reasons"? [*Page* 256.]

13. "They give themselves to philosophy or economic or political science; they are still devoted men, but their devotion is to wisdom, they worship truth, not the God of truth." What difference does it make? [*Page* 257.]

14. "Religious and moral leadership of this generation offers a herculean task." Specifically what tasks are meant? [*Page* 258.]

15. "The churches will have to change more than the colleges." How? [*Page* 259.]

Suggestions for Further Reading on Religion

Ames, E. S. *The Psychology of Religious Experience*. Boston. Houghton Mifflin. 1910.

Arnold, Matthew. "The True Greatness of Christianity." *Literature and Dogma*. New York. Macmillan. 1902.

"The God of Miracles." *God and the Bible*. New York. Macmillan. 1901.

"Hebraism and Hellenism." *Culture and Anarchy*. New York. Macmillan. 1883.

Bell, B. I. "Social Service and the Churches." *Atlantic Monthly*. (February, 1915, Vol. 115, p. 161.)

Brooks, Phillips. "Authority and Conscience." "The Healthy Conditions of a Change of Faith." *Essays and Addresses*. New York. E. P. Dutton and Co. 1894.

Toleration: Two Lectures. New York. E. P. Dutton and Co. 1887.

Bryan, W. J. "The Fundamentals." *Forum*. (July, 1923, Vol. 70, p. 1665.) Debate with Newell Dwight Hillis.

Bryce, James. "Democracy and Religion." *Modern Democracies*. New York. Macmillan. 1921.

Chesterton, G. K. "Paganism and Mr. Lowes Dickinson." *Heretics*. New York. J. Lane Co. 1905. Reprinted, Lane Cooper; *The Greek Genius and its Influence*. New Haven. Yale University Press. 1917.

Clark, Francis E. "The Menace of the Sermon." *Yale Review*. (October, 1922, Vol. 12, pp. 87-96.)

Clarke, James Freeman. *Ten Great Religions*. Boston. Houghton Mifflin. 1883.

Clifford, W. K. "The Ethics of Belief." "The Ethics of Religion." *Lectures and Essays*. New York and London. Macmillan. 1901. "The Ethics of Belief" is reprinted in Steeves and Ristine, *Representative Essays in Modern Thought*. New York. American Book Co. 1913.

Dole, C. F. "Truth and Immortality." *Harvard Theological Review*. (April, 1909, Vol. 11, p. 202.) Reprinted, Steeves and Ristine, *Representative Essays in Modern Thought*. New York. American Book Co. 1913.

Drake, Durant. *Problems of Religion*. Boston. Houghton Mifflin. 1916.

Ellis, Havelock. "The Art of Religion." *The Dance of Life*. Boston. Houghton Mifflin. 1923.

Emerson, Ralph Waldo. "Spiritual Laws." "The Over-Soul." *Essays*. First Series. Boston. J. Munroe and Co. 1841.

FISKE, JOHN. *The Unseen World, and Other Essays.* Boston. Houghton Mifflin. 1902.

The Destiny of Man. Boston. Houghton Mifflin. 1893.

The Idea of God. Boston. Houghton Mifflin. 1886.

Through Nature to God. Boston. Houghton Mifflin. 1909.

GEROULD, KATHERINE F. "Reflections of a Grundy Cousin." *Atlantic Monthly.* (August, 1920, Vol. 126, p. 157.)

HARPER, W. R. "The University and Religious Education." *The Trend in Higher Education.* Chicago. The University of Chicago Press. 1905.

HARRIS, GEORGE. "The Ethics of College Students." *Harvard Theological Review.* (April, 1916, Vol. 9, p. 190.)

HILLIS, NEWELL DWIGHT. "Religion or Dogma." *Forum.* (July, 1923, Vol. 70, p. 1681.) Reply to Bryan.

HOBHOUSE, WALTER. *The Church and the World in Idea and in History.* Bampton Lectures. London. Macmillan. 1910.

HUXLEY, T. H. "Agnosticism and Christianity." *Science and Christian Tradition.* New York. D. Appleton & Co. 1894.

"The Lights of the Church and the Light of Science." *Science and Hebrew Tradition.* New York. D. Appleton and Co. 1894.

HYDE, WM. D. *Five Great Philosophies of Life.* New York. Macmillan. 1911.

INGE, W. R. *Truth and Falsehood in Religion;* six lectures delivered at Cambridge to undergraduates in the Lent term, 1906. New York. Dutton. 1907.

Christian Mysticism. New York. C. Scribner's Sons. 1899.

"The Indictment Against Christianity." *Outspoken Essays.* New York and London. Longmans, Green and Co. 1921.

JAMES, WILLIAM. "The Will to Believe." *The Will to Believe and Other Essays in Popular Philosophy.* New York. Longmans, Green and Co. 1897.

Varieties of Religious Experience. New York. Longmans, Green and Co. 1917.

LEWIS, EDWARD. "The Failure of the Church." *Atlantic Monthly.* (December, 1914, Vol. 114, p. 729.)

LODGE, OLIVER. *Science and Immortality.* New York. Moffat, Yard and Co. 1908.

MALLOCK, W. H. "The Scientific Bases of Optimism." *Fortnightly Review.* (January, 1889, Vol. 51, pp. 80-106.) Reprinted, Steeves and Ristine, *Representative Essays in Modern Thought.* New York. American Book Co. 1913. *The Reconstruction of Religious Belief.* New York and London. Harper. 1905.

MELISH, JOHN HOWARD. "The Social Mission of the Church." *Atlantic Monthly.* (February, 1915, Vol. 115, p. 165.)

MODE, PETER G. "Revivalism as a Phase of Frontier Life." *The Journal of Religion.* (July, 1921, Vol. 1, p. 337.)

MORE, PAUL ELMER. "The Religious Ground of Humanitarianism." *Shelburne Essays,* First Series. New York. G. P. Putnam's Sons. 1907.

MORISON, J. C. *The Service of Man;* An Essay towards the Religion of the Future. London. K. Paul, Trench, Trübner and Co. 1892.

MORLEY, JOHN. "Of the Possible Utility of Error." "Religious Conformity." *On Compromise.* London. Chapman and Hall. 1874. "Of the Possible Utility of Error" is reprinted in Steeves and Ristine, *Representative Essays in Modern Thought.* New York. American Book Co. 1913.

NICHOLSON, MEREDITH. "Should Smith Go to Church?" *Atlantic Monthly.* (June, 1912, Vol. 109, p. 721.)

OSBORN, HENRY FAIRFIELD. *Evolution and Religion.* New York. C. Scribner's Sons. 1923.

PRATT, JAMES B. "Religion and the Younger Generation." *Yale Review.* (April, 1923, Vol. 12, pp. 394-416.)

PRITCHETT, HENRY. *What is Religion?* Boston. Houghton Mifflin. 1906.

RUSSELL, BERTRAND. "The Free Man's Worship." *Mysticism and Logic.* New York. Longmans, Green and Co. 1918.

SANTAYANA, GEORGE. "Little Essays on Religion." *Little Essays,* Drawn from the Writings of George Santayana by Logan Pearsall Smith. New York. C. Scribner's Sons. 1920.

SHOTWELL, JAMES T. *The Religious Revolution of Today.* Boston. Houghton Mifflin. 1913. The William Brewster Clark Memorial Lectures at Amherst College.

SMITH, GOLDWIN. *Guesses at the Riddle of Existence.* New York and London. Macmillan. 1897.

STEPHEN, LESLIE. "Religion as a Fine Art." *Essays on Free Thinking and Plain Speaking.* New York and London. G. P. Putnam's Sons. 1905. "The Scepticism of Believers." "Toleration." *An Agnostic's Apology.* New York. Putnam's. 1903.

TOCQUEVILLE, ALEXIS DE. "Religion Considered as a Political Institution." *Democracy in America.* New York. D. Appleton and Co. 1904. Chapter 17.

TUFTS, J. H. "Religion's Place in Securing a Better World Order." *The Journal of Religion.* (March, 1922, Vol. 2, p. 113.)

TYNDALL, JOHN. "Belfast Address." *Fragments of Science.* New York. D. Appleton and Co. 1900. Reprinted, Steeves and Ristine, *Representative Essays in Modern Thought.* New York. American Book Co. 1913.

WALSH, J. J. "The Supposed Opposition of Science and Religion."
Catholic Churchmen in Science. Philadelphia. American Ecclesiastical Review. 1906.
The Popes and Science. New York. Fordham University Press. 1908.
WHITE, ANDREW D. *A History of the Warfare of Science with Theology in Christendom.* New York. D. Appleton and Co. 1910.
WOOD, H. G. "Religion as a Unifying Influence in Western Civilization." *The Unity of Western Civilization,* edited by F. S. Marvin. London, New York. H. Milford. 1915.

SOME TOPICS FOR THE DISCUSSION OF RELIGION

Influence of universities upon religion. Influence of religion upon universities. The debt of education to religion in America. Church and state. The function of the church college. The Y. M. C. A. The college chapel service. Religion in the public schools. Religious foundations in universities. Mr. Bryan's attack upon the scepticism of colleges and universities. Missions as religious propaganda. The revival meeting. The place of miracles in religious faith. Church-going. The place of the sermon in a religious service. The place of ritual in religious service. Æsthetic elements in worship. Religion of priest and prophet. Effects of institutionalizing religion. Causes for the decreasing number of men entering the ministry. Effects of religion upon the fine arts. Effects of a decline in religion upon national life. The social mission of the church. The community church. Church federation. Religious symbolism. The phenomena of conversion. The place of the Bible in religious faith. Religion as a unifying influence. Holy wars. Religion as poetry. Other-worldliness in religion. Religion and superstition. Religion and morality. Religious faith of the Puritans. Could America have been settled by a generation of sceptics? Puritanism. Class distinctions in the churches. Conflict of Christianity with Mohammedanism in Africa. The country church. Religious toleration in America. Toleration and indifference. Consolations of religion. Hymns and hymn-singing. Darwinism and Christianity. Religion as a fine art. The comparative study of religions. The significance of origins in religions. Fact and truth in religion. Religion of the future. Present-day ignorance of the Bible. Mystics and mysticism. Cathedrals and national culture. Religious elements in prohibition and censorship. Some great preachers and their work. The missionary spirit. The church as a political institution. Revivals and mob psychology. Religion and emotion. The utility of prayer.

RACIAL PROBLEMS [1]

QUESTIONS ON
THE ATLANTA ADDRESS

By Booker T. Washington

1. What appeals to the fundamental interests are found in this address?
   (a) What fundamental interests does the speaker touch in appealing to the blacks in the audience?
   (b) What fundamental interests are touched in appealing to the whites present? [*Pages* 294-297.]
2. What use does the speaker make of the "familiar"?
3. Is the "novel" found in this speech?
4. How does the speaker relate and connect the lower motives of property, power, self-interest, etc., to the higher motives of justice, affections, reputation, religion, etc.?
5. How far does the imagination affect persuasion in this address?
6. In view of the audience and occasion, what particular significance is attached to the words, "cast down your buckets where you are"? [*Page* 295.]
7. What do you think of the wisdom of the above advice? [*Page* 295.]
8. Read Russell Conwell's lecture, "Acres of Diamonds" (*Modern Eloquence,* Vol. 4, p. 307), and tell how he makes use of the idea, "Cast down your buckets where you are."
9. In the first paragraph of the address, how does Mr. Washington get on common ground with his audience? [*Page* 294.]
10. Would you say that the speaker had (a) unity of thought, (b) unity of feeling, (c) unity of purpose with his audience? Discuss this question, giving your reasons pro and con.
11. What is meant by "unity in variety"? Is this exemplified in the address?
12. What is the speaker's central idea?
13. Brief the speech. Give suitable sentences for (1) Introduction, (2) Discussion, with subheads, and (3) Conclusion.

[1] *Questions on Racial Minorities,* by G. T. Robinson, are appended to his essay. See p. 287.

14. Note these words: "In all things that are purely social we can be as separate as the fingers, yet one as the hand in all things essential to mutual progress." Rewrite the sentence, making it specific and concrete. What reactions would this produce in the minds of the audience? [*Page* 296.]

15. Note the restatement in the closing paragraph. Point out several ways in which a consideration of this can be of value to the student of public speaking. In answering the question, present a careful analysis of the paragraph. [*Page* 297.]

QUESTIONS ON *THE NEGRO PROBLEM* BY W. E. B. DUBOIS

1. Which of the limitations upon negroes here mentioned are the least defensible? Are any of them defensible? What would be the effect of abolishing them? [*Page* 229.]

2. Is there reason for expecting the negro race to (a) submit permanently to an inferior position, or (b) die out, or (c) migrate? [*Page* 301.]

3. Examine the work of any of the eminent negroes here mentioned. [*Page* 301.]

4. Mr. Washington's idea was that when the dark man was thoroughly established in the industries and had accumulated wealth, he could demand further rights and privileges. Discuss the idea. [*Page* 302.]

5. "To educate a working man, and not to educate the man is impossible." Does vocational education do this? [*Page* 303.]

6. Compare and contrast the program for the negro race laid down by Booker Washington and Dr. Dubois.

SUGGESTIONS FOR FURTHER READING ON RACIAL PROBLEMS

ADLER, F. "The Fundamental Principle of Inter-Racial Ethics." *Inter-Racial Problems*. Edited by G. Spiller. London. P. S. King. 1911.

BERKSON, I. B. *Theories of Americanization*. (A critical study with special reference to the Jewish group.) Teachers College. Columbia University. Columbia University Press. 1920.

BERNHEIMER, C. S. *The Russian Jew in the United States*. Philadelphia. The J. C. Winston Co. 1905.

BOAS, FRANZ. "Instability of Human Types." *Inter-Racial Problems*, p. 99.

"Problems of the American Negro." *Yale Review*. (Vol. 19, pp. 385-99.)

BOAS, RALPH P. "Jew-Baiting in America." *Atlantic Monthly.* (May, 1921, Vol. 127, p. 658.)

BRAWLEY, BENJAMIN. *The Negro in Literature and Art in the United States.* New York. Duffield and Co. 1921.

BRUCE, P. A. "Evolution of the Negro Problem." *Sewanee Review.* (October, 1911, Vol. 19, pp. 385-99.)

BRYCE, JAMES. *Relations of the Advanced and Backward Races of Mankind.* (Romanes Lecture.) Oxford. Clarendon Press. 1902.

BUELL, R. L. "Development of the Anti-Japanese Agitation in the United States." *Political Science Quarterly.* (December, 1922, and March, 1923.)

CHICAGO COMMISSION ON RACE RELATIONS. *The Negro in Chicago.* University of Chicago Press. 1923.

COLLIER, JOHN. "America's Treatment of Her Indians." *Current History.* (August, 1923, Vol. 18, p. 771.)

DICKINSON, G. LOWES. *Letters from a Chinese Official.* Garden City, N. Y. Doubleday, Page and Co. 1910.

DRACHSLER, J. *Democracy and Assimilation—the Blending of Immigrant Heritages in America.* New York. Macmillan. 1920.

DUBOIS, W. E. B. *The Souls of Black Folk.* Chicago. A. C. McClurg and Co. 1903. (See especially the chapter on Booker T. Washington.)

Darkwater. New York. Harcourt, Brace and Howe. 1920.

FINCH, EARL. "The Effects of Social Miscegenation." *Inter-Racial Problems.*

HENDRICK, BURTON J. "The Jews in America." *World's Work.* (December, 1922, to February, 1923.)

HODGE, F. W. *Handbook of American Indians North of Mexico.* Washington. Government Printing Office, 1907, 1910, 1912.

JACKSON, HELEN HUNT. *A Century of Dishonor.* Boston. Roberts Brothers. 1885.

JOHNSEN, JULIA. *The Negro Problem.* New York. H. W. Wilson Co. 1922. (Handbook. Classified bibliography and selected articles.)

KINNEY, H. W. "Light on the Japanese Question." *Atlantic Monthly.* (December, 1920, Vol. 126, p. 832.)

LEUPP, FRANCIS E. *The Indian and His Problem.* New York. C. Scribner's Sons. 1910.

LUSCHEN, FELIX VON. "Anthropological View of Race." *Inter-Racial Problems.*

MILLER, KELLY. *Race Adjustment.* New York and Washington. The Neale Publishing Company. 1908.

MOOREHEAD, W. K. *The American Indian in the United States.* Andover, Massachusetts. Andover Press. 1917.

MYERS, CHARLES S. "On the Permanence of Racial Mental Differences." *Inter-Racial Problems.*

PHELAN, J. D. "The False Pride of Japan." *Atlantic Monthly.* (March, 1921, Vol. 127, p. 395.)

PHILLIPS, WENDELL. *Toussaint L'Ouverture.* New York. Levy & Voytits. 1869. Reprinted in *Modern Eloquence.* New York. The University Society. 1900. Vol. 6, p. 846.

RUSSELL, BERTRAND. "Chinese Civilization and the West." *Dial.* (Vol. 72, p. 356.)
"Some Traits in Chinese Character." *Atlantic Monthly.* (Vol. 128, p. 771.)

SPARGO, JOHN. *The Jew and American Ideals.* New York and London. Harper and Brothers. 1921.

SPILLER, G. "The Problem of Racial Equality." *Inter-Racial Problems.*

STEPHENSON, G. T. *Race Distinctions in American Law.* New York and London. D. Appleton and Company. 1910.

STODDARD, LOTHROP. *The Rising Tide of Color.* New York. C. Scribner's Sons. 1920.

TREAT, PAYSON J. "California and the Japanese." *Atlantic Monthly.* (April, 1921, Vol. 127, p. 536.)

WASHINGTON, BOOKER T. *Up from Slavery.* Garden City, New York. Doubleday, Page & Company. 1915.
The Story of the Negro. New York. Doubleday, Page & Company. 1909.

ZANGWILL, ISRAEL. "The Jewish Race." *Inter-Racial Problems.*

SOME TOPICS FOR THE DISCUSSION OF RACIAL PROBLEMS

The northward movement of negroes. Anti-Semitism in the United States. Race discrimination in colleges and universities. The Ku Klux Klan. The higher education of negroes. Nordic supremacy. The disfranchisement of negroes. Segregation of negroes. Negro education in the south. The negro in literature and art. Effect upon any race of a belief in its own superiority. The negro in industry. Attempts at deportation of negroes. Southern people during reconstruction. Lincoln on slavery and emancipation. The Japanese in California. The Japanese in Hawaii. The Japanese in the Philippines. The population question in Japan. Growth of Japan since the Russo-Japanese war. The Jew in the theaters. Jews in the clothing industry. Jews as financiers. Jews in literature and art. Indian education in the U. S. The Indian in literature and art. Is there a "white man's burden"? British government in India. Hindu philosophy, literature or art. Effect of civilization upon primitive peoples. Why send missionaries to other races? What discriminations may justly be included in our immigration laws? Japanese expansion in Australia. Booker T. Washington. Toussaint L'Ouverture. Joseph Brant. Indian civilization in the southwestern states. Indian civilization in South and Central America. Indian religion. Relations of advanced and backward peoples. Capitalistic exploitation of backward peoples. The industrialization of backward races. Ethical ideals of the Chinese. Mental differences in races. Treatment of the Indians by frontier settlers. Treatment of the Indians by the U. S. government. Race distinctions in American law. Racial equality.

WAR AND PEACE

QUESTIONS ON
THE MORAL EQUIVALENT OF WAR
By William James

1. Why is it a reproach to say that a country is "a nation of shop-keepers"? [*Page* 308.]
2. Apropos of James's statement that we glory in wars which we would not care to fight again, what would have been the effect upon national tradition if our wars had been settled by a series of compromises? See Andrew D. White, "Evolution versus Revolution in Politics." *Representative Phi Beta Kappa Orations.* Boston. Houghton Mifflin. 1915. [*Page* 308.]
3. Is it true that "Greek history is horrible reading"? What of the Old Testament? [*Page* 309.]
4. If "our squalid war with Spain became a necessity," who was to blame? See H. E. Flack, *Spanish-American Diplomatic Relations Preceding the War of 1898.* Baltimore. Johns Hopkins Historical Studies. 1906. Series 24, Nos. 1 and 2. [*Page* 310.]
5. "Innumerable writers are showing up the bestial side of military service." Does the literature growing out of the European War seem on the whole to glorify it? [*Page* 310.]
6. "Pure loot and mastery seem no longer morally avowable motives, and pretexts must be found for attributing them solely to the enemy." Does this mark a moral advance? [*Page* 310.]
7. "In the whole discussion both sides are on imaginative and sentimental ground." Does the militarist think of himself as a romanticist or as an intensely practical person? See Lowes Dickinson on militarist and pacifist ideals. *The Choice Before Us.* New York. Dodd, Mead and Co. 1917. Chapter 2. [*Page* 311.]
8. "Human life with no use for hardihood would be contemptible." Does this suggest a defense for public athletic exhibitions? Is the man in the bleachers given a spirit of hardihood? [*Page* 312.]
9. In connection with the citation from General Lea, read W. H. Gardiner, "A Naval View of the Conference." *Atlantic Monthly.* (April, 1922, Vol. 129, p. 521.) Does General Lea's view seem justifiable? [*Page* 312.]

10. Is there another parallel with intercollegiate athletics in the citation from Steinmetz? Is an athletic victory often taken as "the resultant of a totality of virtues" in a college? Should it be? [*Page* 313.]

11. Explain the phrase, "the fear of emancipation from the fear régime." Is it applicable to other realms than war? Religion and morals, for instance. [*Page* 314.]

12. Would it be unfortunate if "the splendid military aptitudes of men" were "doomed to keep always in a state of latency and never show themselves in action"? What are some of the marked changes in the relative positions of men in war time? Do they make life more interesting? [*Page* 314.]

13. "High wages and short hours are the only forces invoked for overcoming man's distaste for repulsive kinds of labor." For some reasons why workers welcome war, see Albert Jay Nock, "Peace the Aristocrat." *Atlantic Monthly.* (May, 1915, Vol. 115, p. 593.)' [*Page* 315.]

14. "Having said thus much in preparation." What does James gain by giving most of his space to an admission of the force of the arguments for war? [*Page* 315.]

15. Support the statement that "the martial virtues are absolute and permanent human goods." [*Page* 316.]

16. Why is it probably impossible to create a public opinion that would countenance "a military conscription of the whole youthful population to form for a number of years a part of the army enlisted against Nature?" [*Page* 317.]

QUESTIONS ON *THE FUTURE OF MILITARISM*
BY G. LOWES DICKINSON

1. There will be no reaction against war "unless by a deliberate and conscious change in the ideas and the wills of men." Relate this to James's statement, "Our ancestors have bred pugnacity into our bone and marrow, and thousands of years won't breed it out of us." [*Page* 320.]

2. "It is therefore important to make some forecast of what kind of war that is likely to be." Relate this to James's statement, "One cannot meet them [militarist arguments] effectively by mere counter-insistence on war's expensiveness or horror." What does it matter what kind of war the next one will be? [*Page* 320.]

3. "And if the laws of war permit the application of inflammable materials and substances for the development of poisonous gases. . . ." Discuss the statement made about this by Admiral Sims, *Nation.* (June 28, 1922, Vol. 114, p. 761.) Is any faith to be put in what "the laws of war permit"? [*Page* 321.]

4. "Neither religion, morals nor humanity have availed to arrest this process in the present war." Is there any hope in a wider acceptance of Christian doctrines? [*Page* 323.]

5. "War, then means . . . an irreparable impoverishment of the race." How? See David Starr Jordan, *War and the Breed*. Boston. The Beacon Press. 1915. [*Page* 323.]

6. What is to be said in favor of universal military service? See Ralph Barton Perry, *The Free Man and the Soldier*. New York. C. Scribner's Sons. 1916. [*Page* 323.]

7. What are some of the effects of a military caste, feared by Dickinson? What does German experience show? [*Page* 324.]

8. "Thus, as conscription extends, so does the necessity of persecution." Why? See John W. Graham, *Conscription and Conscience*. London. Allen and Unwin. 1922. Also Norman Thomas, *The Conscientious Objector in America*. New York. Huebsch. 1924. [*Page* 325.]

9. The second device for overcoming "a man's natural reluctance to kill and be killed," is to "convert him into an automaton." Illustrate. See Norman Angell, "The Real Implications of Conscription." *New Republic*. (April 8, 1916, Vol. 6, p. 266.) [*Page* 325.]

10. "The third device is a just cause." What are some of the means of creating a belief that the cause is just? [*Page* 325.]

11. "The soul as well as the body of the good soldier must be militarized; and for this purpose a new direction must be given to the state religion." How was religion a support for war in all countries throughout the recent struggle? See F. W. Farrar, "Christianity and Imperialism." *North American Review*. (September, 1900, Vol. 171, p. 289.) And the reply by Goldwin Smith, "War as a Moral Medicine." *Atlantic Monthly*. (December, 1900, Vol. 86, p. 735.) Also W. A. Smith, "Some False Consolations of War." *Atlantic Monthly*. (December, 1915, Vol. 116, p. 843.) [*Page* 326.]

12. Make a statement of the German state religion. See John Dewey, *German Philosophy and Politics*. New York. Henry Holt. 1915. [*Pages* 326-327.]

13. "We may expect that, in a militarist future, this doctrine of the God-state, in essence if not in set terms, will be taught in every school, college, university and pulpit." For illustration of this in the South before the Civil War, see Dodd, *The Cotton Kingdom*. New Haven. Yale University Press. 1920. Chapters 3 and 5. [*Page* 327.]

14. Make a statement of the teachings of Bernhardi or Treitschke. See Bernhardi, *Germany and the Next War*. New York. Longmans, Green and Co. 1914. Translated by A. H. Powles. Treitschke,

Lectures on Politics. New York. F. A. Stokes Co. 1914. Translated by A. L. Gowans. [*Page* 327.]

15. Why is "democracy a bad medium for war"? [*Page* 329.]

16. "Even in democratic countries, foreign policy . . . has been withdrawn as far as possible from popular control." What are the necessary limitations of open diplomacy? See Brown, "Democracy and Diplomacy." *North American Review.* (November, 1916, Vol. 204, p. 491.) [*Page* 329.]

17. Which material would be more effective before an audience, Dickinson's essay, or his illustrative notes? Does Dickinson generalize from too few particulars? What evidence should be required to justify the assertion that war brutalizes a nation?

SUGGESTIONS FOR FURTHER READING ON WAR AND PEACE

ALLEN, JAMES LANE. "War and Literature." *Bookman.* (February, 1915, Vol. 40, p. 648.)

ANGELL, NORMAN. "The Real Implications of Conscription." *New Republic.* (April 8, 1916, Vol. 6, p. 266.)

The Great Illusion. New York. G. P. Putnam's Sons. 1913.

ARCHER, WILLIAM. "Fighting a Philosophy." *North American Review.* (January, 1915, Vol. 201, p. 30.)

BERNHARDI, F. VON. *Germany and the Next War.* New York. Longmans, Green and Co. 1914. Translated by A. H. Powles. (Especially Chapters 1 and 2, "The Right to Make War," "The Duty to Make War.")

BOURNE, RANDOLPH. "War and the Intellectuals." *Seven Arts.* (June, 1917, Vol. 2, p. 133.)

Towards an Enduring Peace. New York. American Association for International Conciliation. 1917. (A symposium of peace proposals and programs, 1914-16.)

BRYCE, JAMES. "War and Human Progress." *Atlantic Monthly.* (September, 1916, Vol. 118, p. 301.) Reprinted, Publications of the American Association for International Conciliation, No. 108, November, 1916.

Reprinted, *Essays and Addresses in War Time.* New York. Macmillan. 1918.

DICKINSON, G. LOWES. *The Choice Before Us.* New York. Dodd, Mead and Co. 1917.

FARRAR, F. W. "Imperialism and Christianity." *North American Review.* (September, 1900, Vol. 171, p. 289.)

JORDAN, DAVID STARR. *War and the Breed.* Boston. The Beacon Press. 1915.

LEA, HOMER. *The Valor of Ignorance.* New York and London. Harper and Brothers. 1909.

MALLOCK, W. H. "The State as a Fighting Savage: Treitschke vs. Spencer." *Living Age.* (August 21, 1915, Vol. 286, p. 451.)

"General Bernhardi on the Moral Logic of War." *Nineteenth Century.* (December, 1914, Vol. 76, p. 1360.)

NOCK, ALBERT JAY. "Peace the Aristocrat." *Atlantic Monthly.* (May, 1915, Vol. 115, p. 593.)

PERRY, RALPH BARTON. *The Free Man and the Soldier.* New York. C. Scribner's Sons. 1916.

"What Is Worth Fighting For." *Atlantic Monthly.* (December, 1915, Vol. 116, p. 822.) (A reply to Russell's *War and Non-Resistance.*)

PUGH, E. "The Cowardice of Warfare." *Fortnightly.* (April, 1916, Vol. 105, p. 727.)

RUSSELL, BERTRAND. "War as an Institution." *Why Men Fight.* New York. Century Co. 1917.

"War and Non-Resistance." *Atlantic Monthly.* (August, 1915, Vol. 116, p. 266.)

SMITH, GOLDWIN. "War as a Moral Medicine." *Atlantic Monthly.* (December, 1900, Vol. 86, p. 735.) (Reply to Farrar's "Imperialism and Christianity.")

SMITH, WILLIAM A. "Some False Consolations of War." *Atlantic Monthly.* (December, 1915, Vol. 116, p. 834.)

SUMNER, WILLIAM GRAHAM. "War." *War and Other Essays.* New Haven. Yale University Press. 1911.

VAN RIPER, B. W. "War and Religion." *Unpopular Review.* (October, 1917, Vol. 8, p. 235.)

SOME TOPICS FOR THE DISCUSSION OF WAR AND PEACE

Nature of the next war. Does war retard civilization? Passive resistance is war (late Indian movement). Use of barbarian troops by civilized nations. Romance of war. Courts martial and justice. Our war with Mexico. Roosevelt's theory of controlling backward nations. Was peace between North and South peace without victory? Lincoln and war. Grant and war. Democracy and war. Effects of a military caste. War and literature. A moral equivalent of war. Conscientious objectors. Conscription. Non-resistance. Propaganda in war time. War songs. War and national unity. Spiritual benefits of war. The R. O. T. C. The Swiss military system. Use of gas in war. Use of submarines. Attempts to regulate war. Reprisals in war. Atrocities, actual and rumored. Religion and war. Cowardice of warfare. The military virtues. War as a revealer of men. War and the population

question. Universal military training. Morals of army life. The army
or navy as an opportunity for a career. Life at West Point or Annapolis.
Biological arguments for or against war. War and liberty. Economic
competition and war. Imperialism and war. Armaments as a cause of
war. Small nations as a cause of war. Secret diplomacy and war.
National honor and war. What is worth fighting for? The war record
of American colleges. A league to enforce peace. Nietzsche and war.
Treitschke and war. Bernhardi and war. Carlyle and war. Morale in
war. Public opinion in war time. War powers of the President.

INTERNATIONAL RELATIONS

QUESTIONS ON
IDEALISM AND REALITIES

By the Earl of Birkenhead

1. Why would an enforcement of ideals be dangerous? [*Page* 355.]
2. Why should individual conduct be regarded as a "comparatively easy domain"? [*Page* 355.]
3. Is it possible to agree with Birkenhead that self-interest "is and ought to be the mainspring of human action," without accepting all of his conclusions? [*Page* 355.]
4. Do all idealistic schemes for the elevation of morals involve a weakening of the motive of self-advancement? What if they do? [*Page* 355.]
5. Is it true that efforts to eliminate war and to purify international morality rest upon a belief in the possibility of attaining such aims? Can any effort be made without this belief? Does such a belief render a man unfit to face facts as they are? [*Page* 356.]
6. What are the practical consequences of guiding the policy of a country by a belief or disbelief in the possibility of peace and the infallibility of international compacts? [*Page* 356.]
7. Is it true that the Hague Conference "has achieved absolutely nothing in its major purpose"? [*Page* 356.]
8. What is proved by the citation of the attempt of Russia to destroy Japan, shortly after the Tsar had "issued to the world a very sonorous and idealist message?" [*Page* 356.]
9. Do you condemn the idealists for attempting to exploit the Great War "for their own controversial purposes"? Have all controversialists done this? [*Page* 357.]
10. Do you regard the larger claims made on behalf of the League of Nations as "fantastic"? [*Page* 357.]
11. Do you hold with Birkenhead that "the work in every department of life of the survival of the fittest," confirms the belief in the permanence of war? [*Page* 357.]
12. Is it consistent with an evolutionary view to regard Old Testament history as an indication of the permanence of war? [*Page* 357.]

13. Is it still true that "a sharp sword in the hand of a disciplined soldier" is "the most persuasive argument in world diplomacy"? [*Page* 358.]

14. Has the Christian religion appreciably affected international conduct? [*Pages* 358-359.]

15. Did the Pope "descend to a place, such as it was, among the politicians," in the War? [*Page* 359.]

16. Does the belief in the possibility of permanent peace rest upon the assumption that a change will be wrought in human nature? [*Page* 359.]

17. Are we to regard "what has happened in Europe since the Armistice" as an evidence of the futility of organized efforts for peace? [*Page* 359.]

18. Is the pacifist to be regarded as "a danger to the community of which he is a citizen"? [*Page* 360.]

19. What were the warnings of Lord Roberts? [*Page* 360.]

20. Was England's policy of reducing military and naval expenditure, before the War, a policy of "fatuous imbecility"? [*Page* 360.]

21. Should England regret that "idealism became rampant with those in power" before the War? [*Page* 360.]

22. Was the foundation of the Boy Scouts a militaristic move? [*Page* 361.]

23. Did Woodrow Wilson demonstrate that he did not understand the American people? [*Page* 361.]

24. Do the people of the United States "draw a sharp and logical distinction between idealism in their capacity as private citizens for private charities, and idealism in their corporate or national character"? Should they? [*Page* 362.]

25. Does the League of Nations mean that "the ownership of the world" is "to be stereotyped by perpetual tenure in the hands of those who possess its different territories today"? [*Page* 362.]

26. Does Birkenhead seem to defend the stronger nations who "have asserted the right of forcible expropriation"? Why should he object to *Deutschland über alles?* [*Page* 363.]

27. Is Birkenhead's disavowal of the doctrines of Bernhardi and Treitschke convincing? [*Page* 363.]

28. Is it "improbable that the experience of future ages will differ in any material respect from that which has happened since the twilight of the human race"? [*Page* 363.]

29. What is the distinction between a martial and a military people? [*Page* 363.]

30. What is an "Imperial destiny"? What use has been made in our history of the doctrine of "manifest destiny"? [*Page* 363.]

QUESTIONS ON *AMERICA AND THE INTERNATIONAL PROBLEM*

1. Is it true that "the United States today is more set upon its policy of isolation than ever before"? [*Page* 364.]
2. What is meant by "Wilsonism"? See W. E. Dodd, "Wilsonism." *Political Science Quarterly.* (March, 1923, Vol. 38, pp. 115-132.) [*Page* 365.]
3. "To be an American is not something racial or national as it is understood in Europe, but it is to live in a new and better world than Europe and to have a certain kind of forward-looking outlook on life." Is this due to the wisdom or virtue of Americans? Have we reason to believe that this difference between America and Europe is a permanent one? [*Page* 366.]
4. Do the moral and political advantages of America's isolation outweigh the cultural disadvantages? Do critics or eulogists of American life usually weigh all the factors? [*Page* 367.]
5. What is the significance of the statement that "modern Europe is the child of the Renaissance, modern America of the Reformation"? [*Page* 367.]
6. Does the author's statement of the meaning of Americanism seem satisfactory? [*Page* 367.]
7. How is it that more governmental interferences with personal liberty will be tolerated in a democracy than in other forms of government? [*Page* 368.]
8. Is it likely that America can long continue to contribute a pioneer spirit "to the solution of world problems"? [*Page* 368.]
9. Is it true that America has been able to free tens of millions of Europeans from race hatred? [*Pages* 368-369.]
10. Is it "American Spirit" that has freed immigrants from social limitations, or American natural resources? If economic opportunity plays a large part in the elevation of the immigrant, is it worth while to preach "American Spirit" in countries which have not our economic possibilities? [*Page* 369.]
11. Would it seem a convincing statement of the isolationist's point of view that "it is America's business to build up a better civilization than Europe's, as a model to mankind, rather than to exhaust herself in trying to put the old world straight"? [*Page* 369.]
12. "The idea of the government of one people by another is deeply repugnant to the American mind." Does this seem to be supported by our policy in the island possessions? [*Page* 370.]
13. "Today idealism is blindfold and selfishness is in the saddle." Would Birkenhead regard this as the cause of the international situation? [*Page* 370.]

14. What actions of the United States seem to justify the assertion that America "is not a good neighbor or a good citizen"? [*Page* 371.]

15. Is there a necessary conflict between the opinion of the author of this article that national selfishness is a malignant disease, and the opinion of Birkenhead that "idealism in national affairs is not merely impracticable, but may easily degenerate into a source of national peril"? [*Page* 371.]

16. Does the power of the United States make the fear of entangling alliances "absurd"? [*Page* 372.]

17. What controversies illustrate the statement that "the whole early history of the United States stressed the ideas of independence and state rights as opposed to the ideas of unity and coöperation"? [*Page* 372.]

18. Is it a part of America's international duty to keep her own population homogeneous? What can be done about it? [*Page* 373.]

19. How is the doctrine of class hatred a rival to nationalism? [*Page* 374.]

20. Why would the establishment of the United States of Europe be more difficult than was the establishment of the United States of America? [*Page* 375.]

21. Does the coöperation of peoples in America who are hostile in Europe prove that national fears and suspicions are fundamentally shallow? [*Page* 375.]

22. How is English imperialism connected with hereditary privilege? [*Page* 377.]

23. Does the history of the British Commonwealth encourage the belief that the way to peace lies in the spread of empire? [*Pages* 376-379.]

24. How did the Washington Conference improve the relations between Japan and the United States? [*Page* 380.]

25. Why do "high exclusive tariffs" constitute "a great example of international fear and suspicion"? [*Page* 381.]

26. As a criticism of American foreign policy, is this article persuasive?

SUGGESTIONS FOR FURTHER READING ON INTERNATIONAL RELATIONS

ABBOT, WILBUR C. "After Napoleon and after Wilhelm II." *Unpopular Review.* (April, 1919, Vol. 11, pp. 233-245.)

AMERICAN SOCIETY OF INTERNATIONAL LAW. *Proceedings.* 1914. Norwood, Mass. Plimpton Press. (Papers of the session devoted to the Monroe Doctrine.)

ANGELL, NORMAN. *The Great Illusion.* New York. Putnam's. 1910.
"The Great Illusion." *North American Review.* (June, 1912, Vol. 195, pp. 754-772. Reply to Rear-Admiral A. T. Mahan.)

ARRAGON, R. F. "Some Latin-American Experience." *Unpopular Review.* (April, 1919, Vol. 11, pp. 246-261.)

BECK, JAMES M. "The League of Nations and Anglo-American Unity." *Fortnightly.* (January, 1920, Vol. 113, pp. 41-52.) (See also a reply by D. H. Rees, "America's Attitude toward the Peace Treaty." *Fortnightly.* (April, 1920, Vol. 113, pp. 511-521.)

BERNHARDI, F. VON. *Germany and the Next War.* New York. Longmans, Green and Co. 1914. Translated by A. H. Powles.

BEVERIDGE, ALBERT J. "The March of the Flag." *Modern Eloquence.* Philadelphia. John D. Morris and Co. 1903. (Vol. XI, p. 224.)

BINGHAM, HIRAM. *The Monroe Doctrine, An Obsolete Shibboleth.* New Haven. Yale University Press. 1915.

BISMARCK, OTTO VON. "War and Armaments in Europe." *Modern Eloquence.* (Vol. XI, p. 244.)

BORCHARD, E. M. "The Permanent Court of International Justice." *North American Review.* (July, 1923, Vol. 218, pp. 1-16.)

BRAILSFORD, H. N. *A League of Nations.* New York. Macmillan. 1917.

BROWN, P. M. *International Realities.* New York. C. Scribner's Sons. 1917.

BRYAN, W. J., and TAFT, W. H. *The Proposal for a League to Enforce Peace.* New York. American Association for International Conciliation. Paper No. 106. September, 1916.

BUTLER, NICHOLAS MURRAY. *The International Mind.* New York. C. Scribner's Sons. 1912. Also printed by the American Association for International Conciliation. Paper No. 55. June, 1912.

CHAMBERLAIN, JOSEPH. "The True Conception of Empire." *Modern Eloquence.* (Vol. 12, p. 536.)

CLARK, CHAMP. "On the Annexation of Hawaii." *Modern Eloquence.* (Vol. 12, p. 615.)

CORWIN, THOMAS. "Against War with Mexico." *Modern Eloquence.* (Vol. 12, p. 724.)

DODD, WILLIAM E. "Wilsonism." *Political Science Quarterly.* (March, 1923, Vol. 38, pp. 115-132.)

DOLLIVER, J. P. "The American Occupation of the Philippines." *Modern Eloquence.* (Vol. 13, p. 919.)

DUGGAN, S. P. *The League of Nations: the Principle and the Practice.* Boston. Atlantic Monthly Press. 1919. (This book is edited by S. P. Duggan. Each chapter is by a different author. There are especially valuable bibliographical notes by Lindsay Rogers. The appendix contains the Covenant of the League of Nations. The chapters and authors are as follows: Chap. I, "Introduction," S. P. Duggan. Chap. II, "The Historical Background of the League of Nations," C. J. H. Hayes. Chap. III, "The Making of International Coöperation During the Great War," J. P. Cotton

and Dwight W. Morrow. Chap. IV, "Some Essentials of a League
for Peace," John Bassett Moore. Chap. V, "The League of
Nations and the National State," Lindsay Rogers. Chap. VI,
"The League of Nations: Its Organization and Operation," A.
Lawrence Lowell. Chap. VII, "International Sanctions and the
Limitation of Armaments," Frederic Austin Ogg. Chap. VIII,
"International Administration," Francis Bowes Sayre. Chap. IX,
"National Self-Determination and the Problems of Small Nations,"
Harry E. Barnes. Chap. X, "The League of Nations and Eco-
nomic Internationalism," Glenn Frank. Chap. XI, "The Problem
of Backward Areas and of Colonies," Edwin M. Borchard. Chap.
XII, "International Control of International Waterways, Railways
and Highways," Joseph P. Chamberlain. Chap. XIII, "Labor
in the Peace Treaty," John B. Andrews. Chap. XIV, "The Free-
dom of the Seas," Raymond Garfield Gettell. Chap. XV, "The
United States and the Policy of Isolation," Henry F. Munro.
Chap. XVI, "The Monroe Doctrine and the League of Nations,"
Everett Kimball.)

DUNNING, W. A. *The British Empire and the United States.* New York.
C. Scribner's Sons. 1914. (Historic Review of the One Hundred
Years of Peace since the signing of the Treaty of Ghent, prepared
by authority and under the direction of the Committee on Historic
Review of the American Peace Centenary Committee.)

FLACK, H. G. *Spanish-American Diplomatic Relations Preceding the
War of 1898.* Baltimore. Johns Hopkins Press. 1906. Johns
Hopkins Historical Studies. Series 24, Nos. 1 and 2.

FOSDICK, RAYMOND B. "The League of Nations as an Instrument of
Liberalism." *Atlantic Monthly.* (October, 1920, Vol. 126, pp.
553-63.) "The League of Nations after Two Years." *Atlantic
Monthly.* (August, 1922, Vol. 130, pp. 256-68.)

FOSTER, JOHN W. *A Century of American Diplomacy.* Boston. Houghton Mifflin. 1900.

FULLER, B., and REES, J. D. "Is a League of Nations Practicable?"
Nineteenth Century. (April, 1921, Vol. 89, pp. 700-20.)

GARDINER, WILLIAM H. "A Naval View of the Conference." *Atlantic
Monthly.* (April, 1922, Vol. 129, pp. 521-539.)

GIDDINGS, FRANKLIN H. *The Bases of an Enduring Peace.* New York.
American Association for International Conciliation. (Paper No.
113, April, 1917.)

Democracy and Empire. New York. Macmillan. 1900. (Especially
chapter 17, "Imperialism.")

GRANT, A. J., GREENWOOD, A., HUGHES, J. D., KERR, P. H., URQUHART,
F. F. *An Introduction to the Study of Foreign Relations.* London.
Macmillan. 1916.

HART, ALBERT BUSHNELL. *Foundations of American Foreign Policy.* New York and London. Macmillan. 1901. "School Books and International Prejudices." American Association for International Conciliation. (Paper No. 38, January, 1911.)

HILL, DAVID JAYNE. *Present Problems in Foreign Policy.* New York. D. Appleton & Co. 1919. (Appendix contains President Wilson's Fourteen Points, the Covenant as originally agreed upon, the Senate "Round Robin," amendments proposed, the Covenant as revised.)

"Betrayal of the Monroe Doctrine: President Wilson's Foreign Policies." *North American Review.* (November, 1920, Vol. 212, pp. 577-93.)

HOAR, GEO. F. "The Subjugation of the Philippines." *Modern Eloquence.* (Vol. 13, p. 1194.)

HOLT, HENRY. "The Scheme Proposed." *Unpopular Review.* (April, 1919, Vol. 11, pp. 262-274.)

"The Mark of the Beast." *Unpartizan Review.* (October, 1920, Vol. 14, pp. 223-35.)

HUDSON, M. O. "Shall America Support the New World Court?" *Atlantic Monthly.* (January, 1923, Vol. 131, pp. 129-36.)

JACKS, L. P. "The Degradation of Policy." *Atlantic Monthly.* (September, 1919, Vol. 124, pp. 298-309.)

"The International Mind." *Atlantic Monthly.* (March, 1920, Vol. 125, pp. 299-311.)

"A League of Nations or a League of Governments." *Atlantic Monthly.* (February, 1923, Vol. 131, pp. 161-171.)

JOHNSON, WILLIS F. *America's Foreign Relations.* Two volumes. New York. Century Co. 1916.

KEEN, F. N. *Towards International Justice.* London. Allen and Unwin. 1923. (Essays in support of the League of Nations.)

KEYNES, J. M. *The Economic Consequences of the Peace.* New York. Harcourt, Brace and Howe. 1920.

LATANE, J. H. *From Isolation to Leadership.* Garden City, New York. Doubleday, Page and Co. 1922.

LEAGUE TO ENFORCE PEACE. *Enforced Peace.* Proceedings of the First Annual National Assemblage of the League to Enforce Peace. Washington. 1916.

LIPPMANN, WALTER. *The Stakes of Diplomacy.* New York. Henry Holt. 1915.

MACHIAVELLI, NICOLA. *The Prince.* Translated by W. K. Marriot. London. J. M. Dent. New York. E. P. Dutton. 1908. Everyman's Library.

MAHAN, A. T. *Armaments and Arbitration.* New York. Harper's. 1912. "The Great Illusion." *North American Review.* (March, 1912, Vol. 195; pp. 319-332. Attack upon Norman Angell's *Great Illusion.*)

MUIR, RAMSAY. *Nationalism and Internationalism.* Boston. Houghton Mifflin. 1917.

  The Expansion of Europe. Boston. Houghton Mifflin. 1917. (Especially chapter 1. "The Meaning and Motives of Imperialism.")

NEARING, SCOTT. *The American Empire.* New York. The Rand School of Social Science. 1921.

ORTH, S. P. *The Imperial Impulse.* New York. Century Co. 1916.

PAGE, WALTER HINES. *The United States and Great Britain.* American Association for International Conciliation. (Paper No. 120. November, 1917.)

PAUL, HAROLD S. "Why a League?" *Unpopular Review.* (April, 1919, Vol. 11, pp. 223-32.)

  "American Tradition and the League of Nations." *Unpartizan Review.* (January, 1920, pp. 170-176.)

PHELPS, E. M. *Selected Articles on a League of Nations.* New York. H. W. Wilson Co. 1918.

POLLOCK, FREDERICK. *The League of Nations.* London. Stevens and Son. 1920. (Contains exposition of the Covenant of the League.)

POUND, A. "The Iron Man in International Politics." *Atlantic Monthly.* (November, 1921, Vol. 128, pp. 611-618.) Reprinted, *The Iron Man in Industry.* Boston. Atlantic Monthly Press. 1922.

ROOSEVELT, THEODORE. "Sound Nationalism and Sound Internationalism." *The Great Adventure.* New York. C. Scribner's Sons. 1919.

ROSEBERY, EARL OF. "Questions of Empire." *Modern Eloquence.* (Vol. 15, p. 1785.)

ROOT, ELIHU. *The Effect of Democracy on International Law.* New York. American Association for International Conciliation. (Paper No. 117, August, 1917.)

  Addresses on International Subjects. Collected and edited by Robert Bacon and James Brown Scott. Cambridge. Harvard University Press. 1916.

ROSE, J. H. *Nationality in Modern History.* New York. Macmillan. 1916.

RUSSELL, BERTRAND. "Is Nationalism Moribund?" *Seven Arts.* (October, 1917.)

SEYMOUR, CHARLES. "The League of Nations." *Yale Review.* (October, 1919, Vol. 9, pp. 28-43.)

SMUTS, J. C. *The British Commonwealth of Nations.* American Association for International Conciliation. (Paper No. 120, November, 1917.)

SPARGO, JOHN. "Socialism and Internationalism." *Atlantic Monthly.* (September, 1917, Vol. 120, pp. 300-312.)

STEPHENS, H. "A League of Dreams." *Nineteenth Century.* (January, 1919, Vol. 85, pp. 11-24. For reply, see Mallet, Walston and

Bland. "League of Dreams or League of Realities." *Nineteenth Century.* February, 1919, Vol. 85, pp. 258-86.)

TAFT, W. H. "The League of Nations: What it Means and Why it Must Be." *National Geographic Magazine.* (January, 1919, Vol. 35, pp. 43-66.)

THAYER, W. R. "Specious Internationalism." *Harper's Magazine.* (February, 1920, Vol. 140, pp. 298-308.)

TREITSCHKE, HEINRICH. *Selections from Treitschke's Lectures on Politics.* Translated by A. L. Gowans. New York. F. A. Stokes Co. 1914.

USHER, ROLAND G. *Pan-Americanism.* London. Constable and Co. 1915.

VEBLEN, THORSTEIN. *The Nature of Peace.* New York. Macmillan. 1917. (Especially Chapter 4, "Peace Without Honour.")

WEYL, WALTER E. *American World Policies.* New York. Macmillan. 1917.

WILSON, WOODROW. *President Wilson's Foreign Policy: Messages, Addresses, Papers.* Edited with introduction and notes by James Brown Scott. New York and London. Oxford University Press. 1918.

SOME TOPICS FOR THE DISCUSSION OF INTERNATIONAL RELATIONS

The United States and the League of Nations. Accomplishments of the Hague Conference. Theory of arbitration and the Monroe Doctrine. The Drago Doctrine. Independence and empire in the Caribbean. International policy and the Panama Canal. Was our war with Mexico justifiable? (Read Corwin's speech against the war. *Modern Eloquence,* Vol. 12, p. 724.) A comparison of the views of Beveridge and Hoar on the Philippines. (See Beveridge, "The March of the Flag," *Modern Eloquence,* Vol. 11, p. 224, and Hoar, "The Subjugation of the Philippines," *Modern Eloquence,* Vol. 13, p. 1194.) Pan-Americanism. The solution of the Philippine problem. Territorial conquests by the United States. Foreign policy of the "Cotton Kingdom." Our policy towards Mexico. Bryan's arbitration treaties. Arbitration of the Monroe Doctrine. The control of the Pacific. Protecting foreign investments by arms. A British-American alliance. Should we have guaranteed France protection against German aggression? Unfriendly Latin America. Significance of our unprotected Canadian border. International industrial organizations. International labor organizations. International scientific organizations. International implications of the Japanese problem in California. Trade follows the flag. Control of weak nations by the stronger. Our "squalid war with Spain." American imperialism. Making the Mexicans behave. Our motives in opening up Japan in 1856. Our theory of the freedom of the seas. Why meddle in Europe? Should the United States accept mandates under the treaty of Versailles? American business and South

American revolutions. Reasons for American unpreparedness. New imperial alignments. Competition for control of undeveloped countries. Our subject peoples. Exploiting foreign resources. Causes of American expansion. Capitalism and empire. The recognition of Soviet Russia. Indian tribes as independent nations within our borders. Wars of steel, gold, and oil. The white man's burden. Article X of the Treaty of Versailles. The German theory of the state in relation to international affairs. Is democratic diplomacy possible? Democracies and republics as empires. The *Pax Romana*. Civilizing by conquest. Conquest of the Boer Republic. The international mind. Surplus populations. War as an instrument of progress. Washington's doctrine of American isolation. Causes of American wars. Woodrow Wilson, idealist. Theodore Roosevelt, realist. An international police force. The League to Enforce Peace. Creating markets by educating barbarians. The culture of Latin America. French Canada, an orphan nation. Effect of modern ease of communication on international relations. The spirit of nationalism. What constitutes nationality? The age of nationalism. Is an international state possible? The place of backward nations in international organization. Has socialism affected international relations? Enlighted self-interest in international affairs. The effect of American prosperity upon our international outlook. Oil fields and national defense. Questions which cannot be arbitrated. National honor. International democracy of learning. The attitude of scholars in Germany, in England, in France, or in America, during the Great War. Does propaganda for a league of nations weaken our national strength? Bismarck, the realist. Is peace the most important object of international organization? Are trained diplomats needed? Perils of self-determination. The Permanent Court of International Justice.

PUBLIC DUTY

QUESTIONS ON
THE SCHOLAR IN A REPUBLIC

By Wendell Phillips

1. What is the significance of changing a college seal from *Veritas* to *Christo et Ecclesiae?* [*Page* 389.]
2. Do you agree to the statement that the French Revolution was "the greatest, the most unmixed, the most unstained and wholly perfect blessing Europe has had in modern times"? [*Pages* 389-390.]
3. Is it true that "one half of history is loose conjecture, and much of the rest is the writer's opinion"? Are modern historians increasing the trustworthiness of history? Is a historical judgment about the Civil War likely to contain more of truth than one about the European War? [*Page* 390.]
4. Does it matter whether we think of Boston rebels as smugglers or patriots? Should school histories be written primarily to increase the influence of patriotic traditions? [*Page* 390.]
5. Is it true that "we have actually worked out the problem that man, as God created him, may be trusted with self-government"? What assurance is there that our own government will not go "down in the ocean of time"? (See Charles W. Eliot, "Some Reasons Why the American Republic May Endure." *American Contributions to Civilization.* New York. Century Co. 1898.) [*Page* 391.]
6. Do we still believe that little industrial progress comes from the schools? [*Page* 393.]
7. Is is true that "no man is wiser for his learning"? [*Page* 394.]
8. Why was "John Brown's pulpit at Harper's Ferry equal to any ten thousand ordinary chairs" in the colleges? Is the martyr always a greater instrument of education and progress than the scholar? What has martyrdom contributed in the struggle for political and religious rights? [*Page* 396.]
9. Is democracy a government under which wise men argue cases and fools decide them? [*Page* 397.]
10. Is the "thin air of Boston provincialism" any different from the provincialism of other cities? [*Page* 397.]

11. Does democracy assert that "crime and ignorance have the same right to vote that virtue has"? [*Page* 398.]

12. Compare the report of Evarts and his committee with the opinion of George William Curtis, in *The Public Duty of Educated Men.* See selection from this speech in Winans, *Public Speaking,* p. 462. New York. Century Co. 1920. [*Page* 399.]

13. Discuss agitation as a means of progress. What part did it play in the abolition of slavery, in civil service reform, prohibition, woman suffrage? [*Page* 401.]

14. Was the refusal of colleges to join in the anti-slavery agitation consistent with their readiness to send soldiers to the Civil War? [*Page* 402.]

15. Is it always true that pulpits, "just so far as they cannot boast of culture, and nestle closest among the masses," are "infinitely braver than the 'spires and towers' of stately collegiate institutions"? [*Page* 402.]

16. Do scholars today "sneer" at prohibition? Should they? [*Page* 403.]

17. Are we today so hopeful of women's influence in public affairs? (See George Madden Martin, "Women and Public Affairs." *Atlantic Monthly.* (February, 1924, Vol. 133, p. 169.) [*Page* 404.]

18. Would Phillips have cause to regard contemporary novelists, poets, historians, and biographers as reactionary? [*Page* 404.]

19. Have subsequent events supported Phillips in his charges against the English in Ireland? [*Pages* 404-405.]

20. Was Phillips justified in speaking of the nihilists as the spiritual descendants of Adams and Washington? Would he praise Lenine and Trotsky? [*Page* 406.]

21. How is Phillips's defense of nihilism an argument for free speech? [*Page* 406.]

22. Is it true that the customs of a thousand years ago are so fixed that no conservative need fear "the most violent efforts of the maddest fanatic"? [*Page* 408.]

23. Is there still need for an exhortation to entrench labor against capital? [*Page* 410.]

24. Does Phillips's speech possess unity of purpose, thought, and feeling?

25. Does this speech show the oratorical temperament, or the zeal of the reformer?

26. Discuss the persuasive qualities of the speech as a whole, giving examples of sentiments that would conciliate or irritate (a) the audience to which the speech was originally addressed, (b) yourself as reader, (c) your associates as an audience.

27. Select illustrations which Phillips seems to use for (a) making his meaning clear, (b) giving vividness, (c) establishing his own authority.

28. What causes might Phillips commend to the attention of scholars today?

QUESTIONS ON *THE LEADERSHIP OF EDUCATED MEN*
By GEORGE WILLIAM CURTIS

1. Show how both Phillips and Curtis take their introduction from the occasion. Contrast the two. [*Page* 412.]
2. Read Curtis's introduction aloud. Note the rhythm. Is this conversational in style? [*Page* 412.]
3. To what extent is Curtis's statement of the charges against scholars a summary of Phillips's speech? [*Page* 414.]
4. Discuss the reference to Phillips. [*Page* 415.]
5. What difference between Phillips and Curtis concerning the French Revolution? [*Page* 416.]
6. What contributions to revolt in Ireland have scholars made since Curtis spoke? [*Page* 416.]
7. What would we now say of defending scholars by citing modern Germany as a product of the universities? [*Page* 416.]
8. What do Curtis and Phillips prove by their examples? Is logical proof their object?
9. Discuss Curtis's treatment of the revolution and the adoption of the constitution as an oratorical presentation of history. [*Pages* 417-420.]
10. "But the Republic is an experiment no longer." What factors determine when a government is beyond the experimental stage? [*Page* 419.]
11. Compare with Curtis's estimate of Charles Sumner, Gamaliel Bradford's sketch in his *Union Portraits*. Boston. Houghton Mifflin. 1916. [*Page* 421.]
12. Compare with Curtis's estimate of Phillips's part in the anti-slavery agitation, the characterization of Phillips in Barrett Wendell's *Literary History of America*. New York. C. Scribner's Sons. 1900. Pp. 348-50. [*Page* 421.]
13. Does Curtis's case improve when he presents the scholar as conservative rather than as reformer? Compare this part of the speech with Grover Cleveland, "The Influence of Universities." *Modern Eloquence*. New York. University Society. (1900, Vol. 7, p. 249.) Also reprinted in Baker, *Forms of Public Address*. New York. Henry Holt. (1904, p. 187.) [*Page* 422.]
14. Is it true that "a crowd is not wiser than the wisest man in it"? [*Page* 423.]
15. Is Curtis less vigorous than Phillips in denouncing corruption? What constitutes the difference in emphasis? [*Pages* 424-425.]

16. Does Curtis in his presentation of the scholar as conservative seem to bear witness to the statement of Phillips that "a chronic distrust of the people seems to pervade the book educated class of the North"? [*Pages* 422-425.]
17. Is there any substantial difference between the perorations of Phillips and Curtis? Which appeal, taking the speeches as a whole, is more effective? Why? [*Page* 425.]

Suggestions for Further Reading on Public Duty

Adams, Charles Francis. "An Undeveloped Function." *American Historical Review*. (January, 1902, Vol. 7, pp. 201-237.)

Angell, James B. "The Influence of the Lawyer Outside His Profession." *Selected Addresses*. New York. Longmans, Green and Co. 1912.

Beyer, O. S. "Engineering." *Civilization in the United States*. Edited by Harold Stearns. New York. Harcourt, Brace and Co. 1922.

Burton, Theodore. "Prevalent Misconceptions Concerning Our Political Life." *Columbia University Quarterly*. (September, 1911, Vol. 13, pp. 410-422.)

Cleveland, Grover. "The Influence of Universities." *Forms of Public Address*. Edited by G. P. Baker. New York. Henry Holt. 1904. *Modern Eloquence*. Edited by T. B. Reed. New York. (1901, Vol. 7, p. 249.)

Curtis, George William. "The Public Duty of Educated Men." *Orations and Addresses of George William Curtis*. Edited by C. E. Norton. New York. Harper and Brothers. 1894.

Hadley, A. T. "Political Duties of the Citizen." *Standards of Public Morality*. New York. Macmillan. 1912. Reprinted in Fulton, M. G., *College Life, Its Conditions and Problems*. New York. Macmillan. 1914.

James, William. "The Social Value of the College Bred." *McClure's Magazine*. (February, 1908, Vol. 30, p. 419.) Reprinted in Fulton, M. G., *National Ideals and Problems*. New York. Macmillan. 1918. Also in Rice, Richard, *College and the Future*. New York. C. Scribner's Sons. 1915.

Lewis, E. "The Professional Ministry." *Atlantic Monthly*. (November, 1915, Vol. 116, p. 678.)

Lodge, Henry Cabot. "Good Citizenship." *A Frontier Town and Other Essays*. New York. C. Scribner's Sons. 1906. Reprinted in Fulton, M. G., *National Ideals and Problems*. New York. Macmillan. 1914.

Matthews, Brander. "Reform and Reformers." *American of the Future and Other Essays*. New York. C. Scribner's Sons. 1909.

MERRIAM, CHARLES E. "Citizenship." *University of Chicago Magazine.* (July, 1911, Vol. 3, p. 275.)

PERRY, BLISS. "The College Professor and the Public." *Atlantic Monthly.* (February, 1902, Vol. 89, p. 282.) Reprinted in *The Amateur Spirit.* Boston. Houghton Mifflin. 1904.

ROOSEVELT, THEODORE. "The Manly Virtues and Practical Politics." "The College Graduate and Public Life." *American Ideals and Other Essays.* New York and London. G. P. Putnam's Sons. 1897.

TUCKER, WILLIAM JEWETT. "What Has Patriotism the Right to Demand of Education?" *Public-Mindedness.* Concord. The Rumford Press. 1910.

WADDELL, J. A. L. *Addresses to Engineering Students.* Kansas City, Mo. Waddell and Harrington. 1911.

WILSON, WOODROW. *The Minister and the Community.* New York. Association Press. 1912.

SOME TOPICS FOR THE DISCUSSION OF PUBLIC DUTY

Why the best men do not enter politics. The party man and the independent voter. The support of third-party movements. An educational qualification for voting. Effect of universal suffrage on political leadership. Should a lawyer enter politics immediately after being admitted to the bar? Should a man seek the office, or the office the man? Public office a public trust. The spoils system. English and American public men. Should a man without independent means enter politics? At what age should a man enter politics? The consular service. Diplomacy as a career. Why has the South produced more public men than the North? Why does "invisible government" flourish? Should a representative always follow the will of his constituency? Citizenship as the ideal of the liberal college. Industrial leadership of engineers. The minister as a community leader. Public services of doctors, lawyers, journalists,— or of any profession or occupation. The professor and the public. Public services of Benjamin Franklin, Walt Whitman, Mark Twain, Augustus St. Gaudens, Susan B. Anthony, Carl Schurz, Wendell Phillips, James Russell Lowell, Woodrow Wilson, Abraham Lincoln. The relation of privately endowed schools to the public. "Drives": a public service, or a nuisance. Some advantages of public indifference to public questions. Reform and reformers. Milton's conception of the educated man. The professional and the amateur in public affairs. College spirit and public spirit.

PUBLIC DISCUSSION

QUESTIONS ON
STUMP-ORATOR

By Thomas Carlyle

1. Is the faculty of speech popularly taken as the best single criterion of cultivation? If so, is it a mistake? [*Page* 429.]
2. Is Carlyle using rhetoric to make book-reviewing, preaching, political oratory and journalism appear as necessarily contemptible pursuits? Are these pursuits less condemned today? [*Pages* 429-430.]
3. "All this [the idea that talent is expressed in speech] is deep-rooted in our habits, in our social, educational and other arrangements." How did so great a fallacy take root? [*Page* 430.]
4. ". . . excellent silence, which means endurance and exertion, and good work with lips closed." What sort of experiences probably gave rise to the proverb "Silence is golden"? [*Page* 431.]
5. Carlyle's third assertion about speech is: "That in these times and for several generations back, there has been, strictly considered, no really excellent speech at all, but sham-excellent merely." Have men always felt thus about their own times? [*Page* 431.]
6. What evils arise from "this our prostrate respect to the power of speech"? [*Page* 432.]
7. "The 'excellent stump-orator,' as our Yankee friends define him." Characterize American stump-oratory. See E. L. Godkin, "An American View of Popular Government." *Nineteenth Century.* (February, 1886, Vol. 19, p. 177.) [*Page* 432.]
8. "In those healthy times, guided by silent instincts and the monition of Nature." When were those times? [*Page* 433.]
9. "This was [self-education by ploughing and hammering] as it still is, the grand education of the Working Man." Relate this to Carlyle's notion of democracy; also to present tendencies in American vocational education. [*Page* 433.]
10. If education should first concern itself "not so much that he should possess the art of speech, as that he should have something to speak," when should speaking and writing be studied? [*Page* 435.]
11. "And perhaps this is the reason why among earnest nations, as among the Romans for example, the craft of schoolmaster was held in

little regard." How did the Romans regard oratory and teachers of oratory? Does the position of pedagogue change much from age to age? [*Page* 435.]

12. Does Carlyle seem to regard the "art of speech" as peculiarly a product of his own degenerate days? What reason had he for feeling it to be worse in his own time? [*Page* 436.]

13. "Every time he speaks it, the tendency to do it will grow less." Does this account for the general opinion of professional talkers? [*Page* 436.]

14. "Considered as the whole of education, or human culture, which it now is in our modern manners, the Art of Speech is probably definable in that case as a short summary of all the Black Arts put together." Point out present-day attempts to make the art of speech appear as the whole of education. Is this evil more flagrant in one period than another? Has Democracy any bearing upon it? [*Page* 438.]

15. In America, what has the art of speech to do with public leadership?

16. "The kind of careers you offer in countries still living, determines with perfect exactness the kind of life that is in them." How may the working of this principle be observed in America? What do American public careers indicate about American life? [*Page* 439.]

17. "There is the silent or unlearned career of the Industrialisms, which are very many among us; and there is the articulate or learned career of the three professions, Medicine, Law (under which we may include Politics) and the Church." Is this a fairly complete statement of the possibilities open to the present-day university graduate? [*Page* 439.]

18. "All human talent, especially all deep talent, is a talent to *do*." Is action the only test of talent? [*Page* 439.]

19. "The Industrialisms are all of silent nature." Why? [*Page* 440.]

20. Attempt to make concrete Carlyle's conception of Beaverism. [*Page* 440.]

21. "Premiership, woolsack, mitre, and quasi-crown: all is attainable if you can talk with due ability." To what extent was this true during the war? Were the national leaders talkers? [*Page* 441.]

22. "Talk never yet could guide any man's or nation's affairs." What does? Compare those periods of government by a Frederick the Great, a Napoleon, a Cæsar, with popular government by discussion. [*Page* 442.]

QUESTIONS ON *ELOQUENCE* BY RALPH WALDO EMERSON

1. "The highest bribes of society are at the feet of the successful orator." Compare Emerson's attitude toward this with Carlyle's. [*Page* 450.]

2. "That which eloquence ought to reach, is not a particular skill in telling a story, or neatly summing up evidence, or arguing logically, or dexterously addressing the prejudice of the company,—no, but a taking sovereign possession of the audience." Discuss the difference between the "good speaker" and the orator. [*Pages* 450-451.]

3. ". . . requiring a large composite man, such as nature rarely organizes." What men have been so organized? [*Page* 451.]

4. What speakers have succeeded because of animal vigor, or in spite of lack of it? [*Page* 452.]

5. Why is the habit of oratory apt to disqualify speakers for eloquence? [*Page* 456.]

6. Describe the oratory of Napoleon or Cæsar. For incident here related of Cæsar, see Plutarch's account of his life. What part did military oratory play in the last war? [*Page* 457.]

7. "Personal ascendancy may exist with or without adequate talent for its expression." See Ross, E. A., *Social Control*. New York. Macmillan. 1901. Cooley, C. H., *Human Nature and the Social Order*. New York. C. Scribner's Sons. 1902. What qualities make for personal leadership? [*Page* 459.]

8. "By applying the habits of a higher style of thought to the common affairs of this world, he introduces beauty and magnificence wherever he goes." Relate this to the notion that the press now fulfills the function of the orator. [*Page* 462.]

9. "The truly eloquent man is the sane man with power to communicate his sanity." In what sense might it be replied that there is something of insanity about the orator? [*Page* 463.]

10. "There is for every man a statement possible of that truth which he is most unwilling to receive,—a statement possible, so broad and so pungent that he cannot get away from it, but must either bend to it or die of it." Should the orator endeavor to adapt all truth to all men? [*Page* 463.]

11. "Eloquence must be grounded on the plainest narrative." Explain. [*Page* 463.]

12. "If the pupil be of a texture to bear it, the best university that can be recommended to a man of ideas is the gauntlet of the mobs." What men have been educated by the "gauntlet of the mobs"? [*Page* 466.]

QUESTIONS ON *DISCUSSION AND PUBLIC OPINION*
BY EDWARD ALSWORTH ROSS

(These questions are in part taken from the exercises appended to the chapters on "Discussion" and "Public Opinion," in *Social Psychology*, by E. A. Ross.)

1. "Sixty years ago the silent struggle between man and woman became vocal." For an admirable introduction to what at the time seemed a radical position, see John Stuart Mill, *The Subjection of Women*. New York. F. A. Stokes Co. 1911. With foreword by Carrie Chapman Catt. The first chapter of this is reprinted in Steeves and Ristine, *Representative Essays in Modern Thought*. New York. American Book Co. 1913. Show how Mill's introduction is applicable to many reform movements. [*Page* 468.]

2. If "African slavery would, no doubt, have died out in time by the silent operation of economic and moral forces," do the abolition agitators deserve the gratitude of the country? [*Page* 468.]

3. Is the relaxation of religious *tabus* as largely due to public discussion as the other reforms mentioned by Ross? [*Page* 468.]

4. Do the prohibitionists, having won their victory, now stand to lose by public discussion? [*Page* 169.]

5. "The side that feels sure of its case does not persecute." Is this true in war time? [*Page* 469.]

6. Ross speaks of Discussion as "that great radical." Is it ever a great conservative? [*Page* 470.]

7. If discussions concerning tastes are fruitless, should they be abandoned? [*Page* 471.]

8. What are the rules to be observed if discussion is to be enlightening and fruitful? [*Pages* 471-472.]

9. Show that the battle of new truth is sometimes against organized dogmatism's desire to limit knowledge, sometimes against organized conservatism's desire to limit action.

10. Compare scientific and theological discussion. [*Page* 472.]

11. Compare the methods of these foes of new truth:
    (a) The bigotry of the ignorant, (b) The impatience of temperamental conservatives, (c) The alarmed self-interest of crafts, professions, or classes "in danger to be set at naught."

12. To what extent should the untrained man take his religious or political opinions from experts?

13. Does universal suffrage imply the rule of the average man? [*Page* 480.]

14. Why is it that the single-idea party becomes the many-idea party when it approaches success?

15. In what respects is the rule of public opinion unlike the rule of the mob? [*Pages* 479-484.]

16. Why is the attitude of associations not significant about public opinion "on questions connected with their main purpose"? [*Page* 483.]

17. What are the good and bad points in the guidance of public opinion by, (a) the "better classes," (b) the moral and intellectual élite, (c) experts?

Suggestions for Further Reading on Public Discussion

ADAMS, JOHN QUINCY. "Intellectual and Moral Qualities of an Orator." *Lectures on Rhetoric and Oratory*. Cambridge. Hilliard and Metcalf. 1810. (Lecture 15.)

BAGEHOT, WALTER. "The Age of Discussion." *Physics and Politics*. (Chapter V.) New York. D. Appleton and Co. 1873.

BALFOUR, A. J. "Public Speaking." *Arthur James Balfour as Philosopher and Thinker*. Edited by W. Short. London and New York. Longmans, Green and Co. 1912.

BERNAYS, EDWARD L. *Crystallizing Public Opinion*. New York. Boni and Liveright. 1924.

BRYCE, JAMES. "Hints on Public Speaking." *University and Historical Addresses*. New York. Macmillan. 1913.

"American Oratory." *American Commonwealth*. New York and London. Macmillan. 1906.

CABOT, R. C. "Belligerent Discussion and Truth Seeking." *International Journal of Ethics*. (October, 1898, Vol. 9, p. 29.)

CHESTERFIELD, EARL OF. Letters of advice to his son on public speaking. Letters III, XVI, CXVIII, CXX, CXXI, CLIX, CCV, CCXXI. *The Letters of Philip Dormer Stanhope, Earl of Chesterfield*. Edited by J. Bradshaw. London. S. Sonnenschein and Co. 1892.

CLARK, CHAMP. "Is Congressional Oratory a Lost Art?" *Century Magazine*. (December, 1910, Vol. 81, pp. 307-10.)

CRILLY, C. "After-Dinner Oratory of America." *Nineteenth Century*. (May, 1905, Vol. 57, pp. 853-68.) Reprinted, *Living Age*. (June 17, 1905, Vol. 245, pp. 716-28.)

CURZON, GEORGE N., EARL OF KEDLESTON. *Modern Parliamentary Eloquence*. New York and London. Macmillan. 1913.

EMERSON, RALPH WALDO. "Eloquence." *Letters and Social Aims*. Boston. Houghton Mifflin. 1904.

FOLLET, MARY P. *The New State: Group Organization the Solution of Popular Government*. New York. Longmans, Green and Co. (Especially the first six chapters.)

FRANK, GLENN. "The Parliament of the People." *Century Magazine*. (July, 1919, Vol. 98, pp. 401-16.)

HAZLITT, WILLIAM. "On the Difference between Speaking and Writing." *The Plain Speaker*. (Essay 24.) *Collected Works of William Hazlitt*. Edited by A. R. Walker and Arnold Glover. London. J. M. Dent and Co. 1906. (Vol. 7.)

HOLLAND, J. G. "The Popular Lecture." *Atlantic Monthly*. (March, 1865, Vol. 15, p. 362.)

JACKS, L. P. "Government by Talk." *Hibbert Journal.* October, 1923, Vol. 22, pp. 5-19.)

"An Alternative to Government by Talk." *Hibbert Journal.* (January, 1924, Vol. 22, pp. 209-229.)

LLOYD-GEORGE, DAVID. "Politics as a Profession." (Inaugural address as Rector of Edinburgh University. *World's Work.* June, 1923, Vol. 46, pp. 140-147.)

MACDONAGH, MICHAEL. "Is the Orator Born or Made?" *Living Age.* (October 1, 1904, Vol. 242, pp. 25-33.)

"The Tradition of Oratory." *Living Age.* (July 16, 1904, Vol. 242, pp. 163-74.)

"Maiden Speeches." *Living Age.* (August 24, 1901, Vol. 230, pp. 470-482.)

MATTHEWS, BRANDER. "Persuasion and Controversy." *The American of the Future and Other Essays.* New York. C. Scribner's Sons. 1909.

MILL, JOHN STUART. "Liberty of Thought and Discussion." *On Liberty.* London. Longmans, Green and Co. 1865.

MURPHY, ELMER. "The Decline of Oratory." *Bookman.* (April, 1923, Vol. 57, pp. 129-32.)

OVERSTREET, HARRY. "Reason and the Fight Image." *New Republic.* (December 20, 1922, Vol. 33, p. 94.)

SHEFFIELD, A. D. "What Discussion Aims to Do." *Joining in Public Discussion.* New York. Doran. 1922. (Preface.)

STEVENSON, ROBERT LOUIS. "Talk and Talkers." *Memories and Portraits.* New York. C. Scribner's Sons. 1915.

THURBER, E. A. "Eloquence." *North American Review.* (June, 1921, Vol. 213, pp. 833-43.)

WALLAS, GRAHAM. "The Organization of Thought." *The Great Society.* New York. Macmillan. 1917. (Chapter XI.)

Periodical articles, anonymous.

"The Dangers of Public Speaking." *Nation.* (June 22, 1911, Vol. 92, p. 618.)

"Concerning Orators." *Nation.* (August 6, 1908, Vol. 87, p. 109.)

"New Style of Public Speaking." *Nation.* (November 21, 1907, Vol. 85, p. 463.)

SOME TOPICS FOR THE DISCUSSION OF PUBLIC DISCUSSION

The press and the platform. The "decline of oratory." American stump oratory. The anti-slavery agitation. The woman's rights agitation. The prohibition agitation. The anti-prohibition agitation. Propaganda. The four-minute speakers. Propaganda in the Great War. Propaganda in the Civil War. Henry Ward Beecher's English mission. The Lincoln-

Douglas debates. The Webster-Hayne debate. Belligerent discussion and truth-seeking. Cross-examination. Public speaking as a test of liberal education. Some evils of judging a man by his speaking. The publicist. The class-room lecture as a public speech. Should university professors lecture frequently before the general public? Is the orator born or made? The orator and the "good speaker." The training of American statesmen in public address. The work of any particular orator. The place of oratory in American literature. The place of oratory in English literature. The demagogue. The success of the ignorant man as a speaker. Is oratory a fine art? Public discussion and democracy. The chautauqua system. The popular lecture. The lyceum before the Civil War. The influence of international organizations as "mere debating societies." The training of the English parliamentary orators. Greek oratory. Roman oratory. The college and university president as a wielder of public opinion. After-dinner speaking. The art of persuasion. Academic oratory. The distrust of oratory. The open-forum movement. The effect of the radio on public discussion. Differences between speaking and writing. Qualifications of the orator, of the journalist.

SOME CAMPUS TOPICS

Should "Americanism" be "taught" in colleges? Should departments of history accept special responsibility for patriotism? Some differences between American and English or European university life. Are fraternities democratic? Democracy on the campus. Do colleges grow less democratic as they grow older? The democracy of college traditions. Democracy and student self-support. Democratic principles in the choice of teams which are to represent the school. Is it democratic to regard "liberal" subjects as superior to the "vocational"? Is one subject as good as another? Is it the duty of a state university to prepare men for war? If so, is it right to discuss the benefits of pacifism in college? Is it wise so to organize the curriculum as to combine college study with industrial employment? Should a student receive academic credit for other than academic or scholarly work? Should academic credit be given to editors of the college paper, or to members of the debating teams? Should courses sympathetically expounding the doctrines of socialism be permitted? Should agitators be allowed to speak on the college campus? Scott Nearing? William Z. Foster? Eugene Debs? Margaret Sanger? Should religious agitators be allowed to speak on the college campus? Billy Sunday? A Mormon missionary? Should smoking be allowed on the college campus? Should chapel attendance be compulsory? Should student committees have a right to expel students from college? Is a college wise in attempting to exclude students of foreign birth or alien race, in order that its student body may be a representative cross-section of the population of the country? Should a college try to "serve its own community," or try to have its student body as representative as possible of the whole nation? If a college limits its registration, should a student from its own state be excluded to permit the entrance of one from a distant state? Compare college patriotism with nationalism. Would Wendell Phillips censure the best educated students of the American colleges of today for refusing to mingle in college politics? Should racial discrimination be shown in choosing members of college organizations—glee clubs, dramatic clubs, debating teams—which "represent" the college socially away from home? If a teacher should be dismissed for radical utterances, should students expressing similar views be expelled? Should evolution or "Darwinism" be taught as scientifically established truth? Has a college a right to demand physical training or athletics of students who do not wish to participate? Individuality and college education. Should the state support higher education? Should the state support vocational education? Should religion be discussed in college courses? Should religious organizations—churches, the Y. W. C. A., Y. M. C. A., etc.— be allowed to locate on the college campus? Should colleges require courses in Biblical literature as literature? Should colleges attempt to train its students as scholars or as citizens? Are the ablest men in college leaders in college politics? The educational function of student activities. Examinations. The lecture method. Intelligence tests. Segregation of students in sections on the basis of ability and scholarship. The social life of the campus. Competition in college. The honor system. Should greater effort be made to distinguish the student of exceptional ability? Should courses be planned for the best, or for the average, student? The prestige of honorary societies. Following the crowd in college. Should students vote in their college town? Is it worth while to "play at business" in college? A liberal education for the business man. For the professional man. What is a trained mind? Spencer's view of education. When should specialization begin? Is compulsory military drill in a university a good thing? Should a university be advertised? How? The upper-classman's right to rule. Faculty responsibility for student conduct, and its limits. Are there differences in this in the small college and in the university? Should a freshman be compelled to wear a freshman cap? Should the faculty censor student publications? Should student publications be free to criticize the President, the Trustees, the Faculty, or the Commons management? Does the faculty govern too much? Should a college levy a compulsory athletic tax on all students. Should athletic coaches be professors? Should students be dragooned into buying athletic or other tickets, or into subscribing to college publications? Should college patriotism be invoked to support undergraduate activities? Is there a defense for the "grind"? Public speaking on the campus. The class-room lecture as a public speech. Some differences in addressing the class and other student organizations. Is debating primarily a game? Should inter-collegiate debating teams be coached? The Oxford system of debating. Why is not debating popular? Debating as a preparation for participation in public affairs. The college oratorical contest.